Old Parish Life

A guide

for the curious

Old Parish Life

A guide
for the curious

Parish Life in England,
broadly from medieval to Victorian times,
particularly from *c.* 1500 to *c.* 1700,
as revealed in churchwardens' accounts
and other records

Edited by

Justin Lovill

The Bunbury Press

2022

First published in 2022
by the Bunbury Press

Selection, material in this form, and
new material © Justin Lovill 2022

ISBN 978-0-9562046-2-2

A CIP catalogue record for this book is available
from the British Library

Printed by T J Books Ltd, Padstow, Cornwall

Frontispiece
Principalities (the first order of the inferior hierarchy of angels),
from a 15th-century rood screen panel at Barton Turf, Norfolk

CONTENTS

Decorated initial letters from the churchwardens' accounts of two London parishes.
UPPER St Martin in the Fields, 1569. LOWER St Michael, Cornhill, 1557.

Introduction

From medieval to Victorian times the parish, embodied in its church, dominated every local community in England and was the most significant institution in most people's lives. It presented them with a Christian vision and sought to guide their steps through life. It marked their individual progress, from baptism with holy water to burial in consecrated earth. It bound them together with their neighbours in worship, celebration and mourning. It provided correction when they erred, solace when they grieved, succour if they grew sick, and alms should they be poor. Being based on firm religious belief it was at odds with many modern priorities, and even on its own terms was often flawed in practice, but it was undoubtedly central to English life.

Today, in contrast, and despite valiant efforts, many a parish church has an abandoned air, apparently bereft of purpose and of life, like a once mighty sailing ship left stranded upon a sandbank as the sea of faith has withdrawn. Having once filled it with people and paraphernalia and treasures, history's tides and intellectual fashions have long since taken them away. The hulk rests quietly now for much of the time, bothered only by the occasional curious visitor, a silent reminder of a world that once was.

Like any apparent relic it is liable to provoke questions. What happened here? Why did they do those things? What was that about?

This book seeks to provide some answers by way of an informal guide. It draws heavily on original records relating to every part of the country, from Cornwall to Northumberland, the aim being to build up a picture of old parish life from many fragments. It extends from medieval to Victorian times but is largely concerned with the 16th and 17th centuries, when the parish endured the upheavals of religious reformation and civil war.

The guide arose from an (admittedly odd) enthusiasm for churchwardens' accounts. These have long been mined and debated over by historians but are largely unknown to the general reader, not least because, like most financial records, they tend to be impersonal, repetitive and dull. They contain gold nonetheless: a thousand and more glimpses of what went on when each parish church was the hub and heart of its village or town.

1457   For drink given to the ringers when it thundered ... 1d (Yeovil, Somerset)

1522   For a coat made when the Resurrection was played, for him that in playing represented the part of Almighty God ... 1s (Rye, Sussex)

1619   Paid Rafe Coney for whippinge dogges out of church & overseeinge wicked & unruly children in church ... 12d (Holy Trinity, Chester)

1713   Paid George Gregory his years salary for driving the pigs out of the churchyard ... 10s (South Molton, Devon)[1]

From costuming God to managing hogs: that gives a sense of the churchwardens' broad remit, and the records they left see the mundane and the holy, the secular and the sacred, jostling cheek by jowl at many a turn.

The initial plan was to string together chronologically a selection of such entries – augmented by others from parish registers (recording baptisms, marriages and burials), vestry minute books (recording parish meetings), presentments (reporting wrongdoing to the Church authorities), and wills (recording bequests and burial requests) – so as to create a kind of 'great parish book' for the whole of England. However, it quickly became apparent that the main text would end up swamped by all the footnotes required to explain the stream of now unfamiliar details. An introductory guide would limit the need for notes, but then such a guide would be improved if some of the original entries were incorporated to exemplify each point … The result is the present book, which is in a sense a very long introduction to a chronicle that does not exist.

Some limitations should be acknowledged.

i.   Despite its length the guide is not comprehensive, largely because it concentrates on matters covered extensively in the records used, particularly churchwardens' accounts. Subjects skimped or omitted include church building styles and their development; church monuments; confession; confirmation; the content of church services; the historical development of the parish as an institution; liturgical colours; nonconformism; tithes; and social conditions of any kind.

ii. The approach is anecdotal rather than analytical. No attempt is made to assess underlying historical forces, nor is any view offered as to the claims of Christianity. If God exists and Christ was and is his son then the activity recorded in these pages matters for obvious reasons; if not, the same activity becomes all the more poignant while also serving as a reminder of the capacity of humans to erect elaborate structures upon air and of illusion to shape and enrich a civilisation.

iii. For all their richness as a resource, churchwardens' accounts have their own limitations which are worth bearing in mind. They more or less never give a sense of the attitudes of those involved. They cannot be relied upon to provide a full picture of a parish's expenditure and activity. Their patchy survival means that generalisations based upon them need to be approached with care. As a result the reader will notice words such as 'often', 'commonly' and 'typically' doing quite a lot of work. A general caveat might be: this is how it was in this place at this time, at least as far as it was recorded, and it was probably more or less like this in many other parishes as well, but the further you move away in terms of time and/or place the more likely it is that practice varied to some degree.

iv. The inclusion of many extracts means that the text is in parts rather note-like, so that 'scrapbook cum guide' might be a more accurate description.

On the positive side the reliance on first hand material allows the past to speak for itself as much as possible, which seems a good idea.

In addition the book offers a fairly full account of the nuts and bolts (or more often nails and hinges) of parish activity. The reader will find plenty of information here about bells and burial, dog-whipping and dung clearance, foundlings and funeral hearses, pews and perambulations, along with how to deal with birds in churches and other relatively out-of-the-way matters. In the process we gain fleeting glimpses of parish characters otherwise lost to history: Bummer the beadle, watching houses suspected of plague; Dame Lofthouse, holding up the parish umbrella to protect the minister as he reads the burial service in rainy weather; and unruly parish clerk Thomas Milborne, singing with a 'jesticulous tone' and 'squeaking like a gelded pig'.

Also emerging from the shadows a little are the supporting cast who have looked after and maintained churches over the centuries. Their names alone conjure a world reminiscent of Shakespeare's 'mechanicals' in *A Midsummer Night's Dream*. At Bishop's Stortford 'little Robin the carpenter' mends a canopy. At St Edmund, Salisbury, Batten the joiner provides new bell wheels while Cowslipe the smith forges a clapper and Kettle the plumber repairs the roof. At Kilmington, Devon, George Puddinge thatches and Thomas Tredwyne tends to the bells. At St Bartholomew Exchange, in the City of London, John Mould, an aptly named chandler, supplies the candles and Mr Fox the scavenger takes away the rubbish. Not to mention Willi Crampe, found working iron at St Mary, Leicester.[2]

The guide's final section, charting the intrusion of history, is included in its own right, for the light it sheds on old parish life, but parallels with recent times are hard to ignore. The Reformation, which saw England leaving a continental superstructure in controversial circumstances, bears obvious comparison with the United Kingdom's exit from the European Union. The plagues which visited parishes in the 16th and 17th centuries prompted reactions and restrictions which naturally call to mind the Covid pandemic. Above all, the iconoclastic 'cleansings' of the Reformation and Civil War periods, and the associated purgings of people who refused to adhere to newly 'correct' beliefs and views, may strike the modern reader as familiar. In each case, however, we may consider ourselves fortunate and scantly tested in comparison with previous generations.

More generally it is hoped that the guide provides the reader with an enhanced sense of the varied activity found in and around parish churches in their heyday. Such churches may or may not provide a connection to God, but they certainly provide a connection to our ancestors. Here they walked and talked and prayed and misbehaved. Here the stages of their lives were marked, and here their bones lie still. It is the world most of us come from and a world we have largely lost.

Glossary &c.

.... Indicates that the amount paid is lacking in the source accounts as printed.

| Within quotations indicates a new item or line or a paragraph break in the original.

&c. Et cetera.

archdeacon. Originally the leading deacon attendant on a bishop. Over time the role grows and the bishop delegates to him authority for a fixed area within the diocese known as an archdeaconry.

beadsman, bedesman. Originally a poor person employed to pray for the soul or spiritual welfare of another, and later used more generally of those receiving alms. Literally it means one who prays, from Old English *biddan*, to pray, the use of small spherical bodies in counting prayers giving rise to the familiar modern sense of 'bead'.

bren, brent. Burn, burnt.

canon. A rule, law or decree of the Church. A notable set of such rules, the Canons of 1604, is often referred to in the text.

chrism. Oil mingled with balm and consecrated for use in administering certain sacraments, including baptism and anointing the sick.

church house. Building usually situated near the church and used for parish activities such as brewing and serving church ales, storing grain and holding meetings.

consistory court. A bishop's court, usually conducted by a deputy.

di., dim. Abbreviations of Latin *dimidium*, half.

dirige, dirge. A traditional name for matins in the Office for the Dead.

find. Provide, provide funds for, support.

Goodman, Goodwife. Titles usually indicating respectable but modest social status, and sometimes used to indicate one who is the head of a household.

hearse. 1. A frame set about a corpse while it rests in a church before burial. 2. A triangular candlestick used in the services known as Tenebrae in Holy Week.

l.s.d. l from Latin *libra*, pound (and the origin of the £ sign). **s** from Latin *solidus*, used for shillings. **d** from Latin *denarius*, used for pence. There were 12 pennies in a shilling and 20 shillings in a pound.

latten. A mixed metal of yellow colour, identical with or closely resembling brass.

li. *Libra*, pound (weight).

ob. Obolus. A halfpenny, or more generally any small coin or sum of money.

obit. Service commemorating a dead individual, usually on the anniversary of death.

ordinary. A person who has jurisdiction in ecclesiastical cases, such as the archbishop in a province or the bishop or bishop's deputy in a diocese.

pontifical. Book or manuscript containing the ceremonies performed by a bishop.

Powles, Polles, etc. St Paul's (cathedral or churchyard).

presentment. A formal complaint or report of an offence or fault to the Church authorities, usually made by a churchwarden.

purgatory. In pre-Reformation doctrine, an intermediate place or state in which the soul of a dead person is purged of its sins before admission into heaven.

quer, quere, etc. Choir, indicating either a church's singers or the part of the building in which they sing.

rubric. Direction in a liturgical book as to how a service should be conducted, traditionally written or printed in red. From Latin *rubrica*, red ochre.

Sarum use, rite, etc. Based on the Roman rite, the form of services used at Salisbury Cathedral and adopted very widely across England up to the Reformation.

Sir. In relation to priests, a courtesy title, mainly in use before the Reformation and given to those who are not graduates.

thorow. Through.

vestry. 1. The part of a church where vestments etc are kept. 2. A group of parishioners who take decisions on parish business, or a meeting of the same, so named from the fact that they often gather in the vestry.

visitation. A **parochial visitation** is an inspection of a church, churchyard, etc by the bishop or archdeacon or those acting on their behalf. A **general visitation** is a sitting of the bishop's or archdeacon's court at which representatives of a number of parishes report on and answer for the state of their churches, the morals of parishioners, etc.

Editorial approach

For details of the editorial handling of source material please see the **Note on the text** (p536). While it is hoped that the extracts as presented are relatively easy to read, it may occasionally help to bear in mind how the words sound: the original writers of parish accounts were often unlettered and as a result wrote phonetically.

Parish information

Parishes in London are identified simply by the name of the church (e.g. St Michael, Cornhill), so if a parish name appears without any indication of town, city or county it is in Westminster or the City of London. In other places with more than one old church (typically cities and larger towns) the particular parish is usually identified by dedication and place name but with the county omitted. In places with only one old church (typically villages and smaller towns) the parish is usually identified simply by place name and county.[3]

Some exceptions have been made to the above general rules, mainly to save space and in relation to parishes which occur often, so if expected dedication or county information is lacking the parish probably falls into that category. Details can be found in the **Note on the text**. In case of any uncertainty please see the **Parish index**.

Some recurring sources

Guillaume Durand, also known as William Durandus (*c.* 1230-1296). Bishop of Mende, France, from 1286 but best known to posterity for his *Rationale divinorum officiorum*, a detailed account of medieval church customs thought to have been written in the 1280s.

John Mirk. Author of influential handbooks for priests written between *c.* 1380 and *c.* 1410.

Thomas Becon (*c.* 1512-1567). Clergyman and writer of colloquial reforming works sharply critical of the old Church.

The Popish Kingdome or reigne of Antichrist. Written in Latin verse by Thomas Kirchmeyer, first published in 1553, translated into English by Barnabe Googe in 1570. Kirchmeyer is describing the Catholic Church on the continent and some of the extravagances he describes are not recorded in England. However, he does provide a lively, sarcastic, and generally useful picture of pre-Reformation practice.

ABOVE Lich-gate, Ditcheat, Somerset. The apt inscription reads *Mors janua vitae* (Death, the door of life). BELOW A versatile alternative to a lich stone, Down St Mary, Devon.

TOUR

Churchyard

1. Entrance, cross, orientation, consecration

The churchyard is bounded all around, usually by a wall, although fences, hedges, ditches and ponds may play a part. Before entering you may notice, outside the wall and near the main entrance, a small platform or horse-block, usually of stone but sometimes of wood, for mounting and dismounting, the one at Reydon, Suffolk, being used by farmers' wives when they ride pillion. There may also be shackles to secure horses' feet while their riders are at church.[1]

> 1530 For a horse locke to ye cherche gate ... 8d (Yatton, Somerset)

> 1712 Paid Christofer Burley for mending the staiers to the horse block nere the church ... 1s 6d (Redenhall, Norfolk)[2]

The entrance to the churchyard is sometimes in the roofed form of a lich-gate (from Anglo-Saxon *lic*, corpse), or gate of the dead, designed to provide shelter for the body and its bearers while they wait for the priest to arrive to conduct the funeral. Some of these gates have a raised slab or lich stone in the middle on which to rest the corpse or coffin.

In addition to the main gate there may be a stile or two giving less formal access.

> 1597 To John Scot for ... makinge and settinge two stiles for the churchyard wall ... 10d (Pittington, co. Durham)[3]

The churchyard cross is often near the gate, usually standing between it and the church porch, perhaps up a few steps on a stone platform.

> 1540 To Fischepond for mending ye crosse that stond in the churcheyard, himself & his 2 lads a day & half ... 12d (St Mary, Bungay, Suffolk)[4]

Prior to the Reformation such crosses play an important part in processions, particularly those occurring on Palm Sunday, but during the religious upheavals of the 16th and 17th centuries most are destroyed or dismantled.

> 1573 To Richard Bowdon for defacing the crosse in the church yard ... 4d (Woodbury, Devon)

> 1578 They have a stumpe of a crosse in their churchyard, the head beinge smitten off. (Warburton, Cheshire)[5]

Looking ahead we see the church itself aligned west-east, at least as far as the site allows, with the most important parts, the chancel and altar, at the east end. This orientation is thought to have originated in imitation of the pagan practice of praying to the rising sun, but there are also a number of Christian explanations.

i.   The east is the location of Paradise to which we seek to return. St Basil, writing in the mid 4th century, notes that 'we all look to the east in our prayers, but few of us know that in doing so we seek our native land Paradise, which the lord planted in Eden, toward the sun rising' (Genesis 2:8, 'God planted a garden eastward in Eden'). This explanation is also among those given by St Thomas Aquinas in his *Summa Theologiae*, written *circa* 1270.[6]

ii. Christ is identified symbolically with light and the breaking of day. 'The day-spring from on high hath visited us, to give light to them that sit in darkness' (Luke 1:78-79). 'Then spake Jesus again unto them, saying, I am the light of the world' (John 8:12).

iii. His birth, crucifixion and resurrection occurred in the east, and on the cross he looked to the west. According to St John of Damascus, writing in the early 8th century, 'Christ, when he hung on the cross, had his face turned towards the west, and so we worship, striving after Him'. Lancelot Andrewes, writing in the 17th century, favours this explanation: 'the Christians in Europe ... at their praiers looking into the east, behold the countrey where Christ was conversant on earth, and in so beholding may behold the face of Christ upon the crosse looking upon them'.[7]

iv. He is expected to come from the east at the Day of Judgement. This is the final reason given by Aquinas. 'For behold the day cometh, that shall burn as an oven, and all the proud, yea, and all that do wickedly, shall be stubble ... | But unto you that fear my name shall the Sun of righteousness arise with healing in his wings' (Malachi 4:1-2). 'As the lightning cometh out of the east, and shineth even unto the west, so shall also the coming of the Son of Man be' (Matthew 24:27).[8]

Few churchyard crosses survive today in their original form, but the shafts of others now serve as sundials, as at Tong, Shropshire, above

Consecration

In medieval times churchyards are consecrated in a service designed to drive out evil spirits. Four or five wooden crosses are planted, one at each point of the compass (or corner of the churchyard) and usually one at the centre. The bishop walks the circuit, sprinkling holy water as he goes. At each cross in turn he prays for the churchyard to be purified, blessed and sanctified, and places three candles, one on the top of the cross and one on each of its arms. Afterwards solemn mass is celebrated in the church.

After the Reformation the form of service varies but is simpler and typically omits the crosses and candles.

In all periods, should the ground subsequently be defiled – for example by the spilling of blood in a fight – it will need to be reconciled or reconsecrated before it can be used again.[9]

Parts of the ceremony, from a pontifical, 1520

2. Place of burial

The churchyard is of course pre-eminently a cemetery (from Latin *coemeterium*, and in turn from the Greek for dormitory) or sleeping place of the dead. In the words of a 17th-century bishop, they wait 'lyinge in their graves ... to be raised againe at the last day, by the voice of the archangel, as those which lie in their beddes are raised in the dawninge of the day by the cockes crowinge'. The bodies are laid on their backs parallel with the church, their feet to the east. The reasons for this mirror those relating to the orientation of the church, but with particular emphasis on being ready for the Last Judgement. According to Guillaume Durand, writing in the later 13th century,

> A man ought so to be buried that while his head lies to the west his feet are turned to the east, for thus he prays as it were by his very position and suggests that he is ready to hasten from the west to the east.

He adds that the corpse should be clothed and shod so as to be ready to meet its judge.[1]

In similar vein, writing a century later, John Mirk observes that the body is buried as it is 'to be the more redy to see Christ that cometh out of the east to the doom [Last Judgement], and so rise against [towards] him'.[2]

Before about 1600 there are few gravestones in churchyards, not least because there is generally still space for those who can afford such memorials to be buried inside the church, but there are some. In 1527 William Swetesyre of North Cray, Kent, leaves 26s 8d for a brick tomb over his grave in the churchyard, 'to be three foote of hight, and over that a marble stone' with his name and that of his wife engraved upon it. Seven years later William Forstall of East Langdon in the same county asks to be buried 'on the right hand of the west side of the porch ... and my grave to be made up 2 ft high, and thereupon a marble slab laid that the people may rest upon it'.[3]

Generally, however, early memorials are of wood. For example, in 1502 John Coote asks to be buried in the churchyard of St Mary, Bury St Edmunds, and 'to have 2 crosses goodly of timber, one at my hede the tother at my feete, with my armes thereupon, and also a writing to pray the peopell of ther charitye to pray for my soule'. Over time such markers naturally decay with the result that, just as the flesh of the corpse decomposes and becomes one with the earth, so the identities of buried individuals are subsumed into the community of the parish dead.[4]

The early churchyard is therefore a relatively open space, but from the 17th century onwards stone memorials proliferate. This annoys some bishops, who seek to have them removed. In 1662 Bishop Wren of Ely enquires of his clergy, 'Is your church yard pestered and cloyed with frames of wood, piles of brick, or stones laid over the graves? Do any take upon them (as they please) to set up, or lay great stones there at the head and foot of any grave, without the incumbents leave and the licence of the ordinary?' The incoming tide of individualism is nonetheless too strong and during the 18th century such memorials tend to become more numerous and more elaborate, with urns, table tombs and long inscriptions.[5]

Another result of centuries of burying is that the ground level of the yard may be raised, sometimes giving rise to dampness inside the church. At St Mary Magdalen, Taunton, in the 1840s they address the problem by removing some 500 cartloads of soil and selling it to farms as manure. According to the sexton, 'Such was the spectacle presented by the bones scattered over the fields, that ... they had to be gathered together and put into a hole.'[6]

A SOUTH VIEW OF Chesterfield CHURCH.
Printed and Sold by J. Ford, Chesterfield

Proliferating gravestones at Chesterfield, Derbyshire, a church noted for its twisted spire. FACING PAGE The dead arise, from a book of prayers, 1578.

The ground is particularly likely to be raised on the south side of the churchyard, which is almost always the preferred resting place, not only because it enjoys more sunlight but also because the path from gate to porch is usually here, so that the graves are passed by the living as they make their way to and from church. In addition, in some places north sides of churchyards are associated with the devil and other evil spirits, and they may be used for the burial of excommunicants, suicides and other outcasts.

> 1643 Nov. 17th. John Edwards the hangman buried in north church yard
>   in the west towards Boyds garden nooke. (St Mary on the Hill, Chester)[7]

At Selborne in the 1780s Gilbert White notes that 'all wish to be buried on the south side, which is become such a mass of mortality that no person can be there interred without disturbing or displacing the bones of his ancestors. ... At the east end are a few graves; yet none till very lately on the north side'.[8]

In busy graveyards bodies often end up stacked several deep. Old bones disturbed in digging new graves may be placed in large communal pits dug for the purpose, or in charnel or bone houses, which themselves need periodic tidying and clearance.[9]

> 1547 For digging a hole in the churchyard, to bury all the bones that lay in
>   the charnel-house, and for making clean the house and the churchyard
>   ... 5s (Rye, Sussex)

> 1683 To John Glendall and his boyes for pileing up the bones in the bone
>   house ... 1s (St Mary, Warwick)[10]

Well-stacked bones in the crypt at Hythe, Kent, *c.* 1890, and a skull there

3. Animals

Having one's bones stowed in a charnel may seem undignified, but at least there they should be safe from the animals which roam many churchyards. At Mersham, Kent, 'hogges digg up the graves' (1511); at Alne, Yorkshire, 'ten or twelve swine of the Ladie Bethells' do the same (1633) ; and at Tydd St Giles, Cambridgeshire, 'there is a dore opening into the churchyard from Wm. Watkinson's house, whereby his pigges come into the churchyard and the graves are rooted up' (1638). In the last named year the Bishop of Norwich asks his parishes to confirm that their graves are 'preserved from violation' and in particular that they are 'kept from scraping of dogs' and 'rooting up of hogs'.[1]

Efforts are made to address such problems

1617 To George Stanton for stoppinge swine out of the churcheyarde ... 2d (Worfield, Shropshire)

1713 Paid George Gregory his years salary for driving the pigs out of the churchyard ... 10s (South Molton, Devon)[2]

but it is a losing battle.

While parishioners view churchyards as common ground, and often use them to graze their animals, legally they are part of the rector's freehold and he is entitled not only to graze his animals but also to enjoy any profit arising from the ground, except that structural timber is reserved for repairing the church (see below). This does not stop the parishioners of Whitstable complaining that their parson's cattle and sheep 'do much annoy and foul the churchyard with their dung' (1600), while at Ardeley, Hertfordshire, they complain that the yard is 'in decay' because the vicar lets it out 'to them that useth it with vile beastes' (1542).[3]

Whether the animals involved belong to parishioners or clergy, the natural result is a good deal of dung and the occasional cadaver.

1547 To Thomas Gibbes for the caryage out of a horse out of ye church-yarde & for digging a hole to put the said horse in ... 8d (St Martin in the Fields)

1577 To Wright for throwing away the dong from the churche yard ... 6d (Kingston upon Thames, Surrey)

1804 Puling in the pig dying in the churchyard ... 1s (St Mary Bourne, Hants)[4]

Domestic animals may also need to be removed.

1601 For ... carrying 2 dead dogs out of the church yard [etc] ... 4d | 1605 For carrying away seven cattes at two several times ... 6d (St Bartholomew Exchange)[5]

4. Yews and other trees

The churchyard is nonetheless a generally peaceful place and you may find an inviting bench to sit on.

> 1597 For 3 crooked planks, to make a seate aboute the tree in the church yarde ... 2s 8d (Wandsworth, Surrey)
>
> 1646 Received of Thomas Hill towards the setinge up of a bench about the youth-tree ... 12d (Chedder, Somerset)
>
> 1762 For old ship-plank for seats in the church-yard ... 12s 3d (Littleham, near Exmouth, Devon)[1]

The promising-sounding tree at Chedder is one of the kind most associated with churchyards.

> 1620 For two yew trees fetching from Sainte Margrets and for setting them and for dunge for them and for bushinge of the said yew trees ... 11d (Strood, Kent)[2]

A traditional assumption that yews were planted in churchyards to provide wood for archers' bows is now considered mistaken, not least because bowyers preferred 'outlandish' yew from Spain and Italy. Churchyard yew is sometimes used for such a purpose: in 1558-60 the wardens of Ashburton, Devon, receive 3s 4d 'for lopping the yew tree' and pay 12s 'to the bowyer for making of bowes'.

Archers, from panels in Ugborough church, Devon, depicting the martyrdom of St Sebastian

However, its main use is as a substitute for palm for decking the church and carrying in procession. Indeed, in many places yew trees are referred to as palm trees: at Lydd, Kent, a carpenter is paid for mending 'the stile by the palme tree' in 1528, while at Woodbury, Devon, the accounts mention 'a yew or palm tree' being planted south of the church in the 1770s, 'in ye same place where was one blown down by ye wind a few years ago'.[3]

Sussex yews, standing proud at Clayton and heavily propped at Wilmington. The Wilmington tree is believed to be 1,600 years old.

Other trees may also be in evidence.

1589 Unto Grimsbye for one crotche setting under the apple tree [etc] ...
      2s (Cratfield, Suffolk)

1611 For five vines and one apricock tree and for the planting of them
      before the vestry window ... 10s (St Margaret, Westminster)[4]

The vexed question of who owns trees in churchyards is addressed by Edward I
circa 1307, echoing an order of the Synod of Exeter twenty years earlier.

> Because we do understand that controversies do oft-times grow between
> parsons of churches and their parishioners, touching trees growing in the
> churchyard, both of them pretending that they do belong unto themselves,
> we have thought it good, rather to decide this controversie by writing than
> by statute. Forasmuch as a churchyard ... is the soil of a church, and what-
> soever is planted belongeth to the soil, it must needs follow that those trees
> which be growing in the churchyard, are to be reckoned amongst the goods
> of the church, the which lay-men have no authority to dispose ...
>
> And yet seeing those trees be often planted to defend [prevent] the force
> of the wind from hurting of the church, we do prohibit the parsons of the
> church, that they do not presume to fell them down unadvisedly, but when
> the chancel of the church doth want necessary reparations. Neither shall
> they be converted to any other use, except the body of the church doth need
> like repair, in which case the parsons of their charity shall do well to relieve
> the parishioners with bestowing upon them the same trees, which we will
> not command to be done, but we will commend it when it is done.[5]

The distinction made between different parts of the building is explained by
the fact that in Church law the incumbent is responsible for the upkeep of the
chancel and the parishioners for that of the rest of the church.

Despite the king's statement difficulties continue down the years. For example,
in 1343 Archbishop Stratford of Canterbury complains that some parishioners
'fell, pull up, or mow, the trees and grass' in churchyards in his province, 'without
and against the consent of the rectors and vicars ... and apply them to the use of
themselves, or of the churches, or of other men'. He condemns such 'rash scorners'
to excommunication. Some fifty years later a churchwarden at East Shefford,
Berkshire, fells churchyard trees without permission and is sentenced to be beaten
twice round the church in procession while carrying a branch.[6]

Ministers, too, may be found wanting. In 1624 the vicar of Lancing in Sussex
is presented to the authorities by his parishioners because he 'hath caused to be felled
all the principal trees in the churchyard, which were the lengthe and defence of the
church'. It doesn't help that 'by reason of the great spoiles and felling the trees ...
the walls are beaten downe and the churchyard filled with sawpits, logs and trees,
so as it lieth more like a wood yard than the churchyard — most unseemly'.[7]

5. Processions

Before the Reformation churchyards feature prominently in processions at major festivals, although the route may not always be clear. At Ruckinge, Kent, it is complained that use of the yard by animals means that 'the curate and the parishoners may no go in procession for dunging of beasts', while at Barham in the same county 'the trees in the churcheyard are an impediment for them that bere the crosse in processione insomuche it cannot be borne uprighte for the bows [boughs]'.[1]

Sometimes (as at East Shefford above) procession is used for administering exemplary punishment. In 1469, having spilt a minister's blood in Grantham churchyard, Thomas Wortley is sentenced to walk humbly at the head of the procession at Candlemas then kneel at the yard's four corners and be disciplined with a rod by the curate in charge.[2]

The illustration, from a Book of Hours *c.* 1500, probably shows the procession at another festival, Corpus Christi.

6. Churchyard games

The common ground provided by the churchyard is often resorted to by those looking to pass the time, children in particular.

> 1771 Paid crier to discharge the boys playin in church yard ... 6d (St Peter, Northampton)[1]

Before the proliferation of gravestones both children and adults use the invitingly open spaces for a variety of games including bowling, cricket and football. Cock-fighting is also popular, cockpits being found in several churchyards.[2]

If the church is amply buttressed it may serve for fives, which is played in a number of churchyards, particularly in the west country. Shutters are sometimes installed to protect the windows, but sometimes not. At Kilmington, Devon, the glazier is paid 3s for mending windows damaged by the players (1625). At Wrington, Somerset, a man is paid 'to hinder the fives playing', which takes place against the church tower (1648). At Somerton, in the same county, prisoners confined at the church after the battle of Sedgemoor in 1685 pass the time by playing the game, breaking windows in the process and sending a large number of balls onto the roof, where they are discovered during later repairs. Nor are members of the clergy always averse. On 22nd June 1764 the young James Woodforde, in his first post as a curate in Somerset, notes in his diary that his guests 'plaid at fives in Babcary churchyard this evening, and I lost there with Mr Lewis Bower at betting with him 0 1 6'.[3]

7. The jangle of commerce

A law of 1285 orders 'that from henceforth neither fairs nor markets be kept in church-yards, for the honour of the church'. The Canons of 1604 go further, forbidding any 'profane usage' in either church or churchyard, proscribing in particular 'plays, feasts, banquets, suppers, church-ales, drinkings'.[1]

Many parishes nonetheless look to augment their income by letting out church ground to traders, particularly at the time of markets and fairs.

> 1457 Received of Margaret the fruterer for standinge at the church dore ... 6d (St Andrew Hubbard)

> 1490 Of divers men chese sellers which stode at the church walle ... 18d | 1499 Of divers tanners & other craftesmen having & occupieng stalls & stacions within the walls of churcheyerd & without at Seint Edmundes feyer this yere ... 2s 4d (St Edmund, Salisbury)[2]

The holding of such events nearby may bring incidental problems.

> 1660 For keeping cattell from the church walls three fair daies ... 2s (St Mary, Beverley, Yorks)[3]

Space in the churchyard may also be rented out at festival times to those putting on entertainments of various kinds.

> 1565 Received of Hugh Grimes, for licens geven to certen players, to playe their enterludes in the churche-yard, from [Easter until Michaelmas], every holy daye, to the use of the parishe ... 27s 8d | Of Richard Dickinson, for licens geven to him to make scaffoldes in the churche-yard, and the parishe to have the thirde penny, bearinge no charge, for that he doth receive of the persons that doth stande upon the scaffolde for 3 holy dayes in the Easter week ... 6s 8d (St Katharine Cree, Leadenhall Street)[4]

At St Margaret, Westminster, they take advantage of being able to offer a prime view of the Abbey next door.

> 1661 Of Francis Daye and Thomas Chandler, for eighty foot of ground in the old church yard, to build scaffolds on against the king's coronation, at 1s 8d the foot ... £6 13s[5]

ABOVE Less room for playing: the churchyard at Bushey, Hertfordshire, by William Henry Hunt, *c.* 1822.

BELOW St Margaret, Westminster, from the west, in the mid 18th century.

ABOVE Shingled spire, Piddinghoe, Sussex, topped by a salmon.
BELOW. LEFT A closer view of shingles at nearby Southease.
RIGHT Weathercock, Ripe, Sussex.

Church

1. Roof

Before going inside it is worth looking at the roof. The various materials used include thatch, the earliest type.

> 1634 To the thatcher for rushes and bindings and broaches, which he used to roove the church withall, & for his wages ... 15s (Stockton, Norfolk)[1]

Also tiles of various kinds, including shingles, small ones formed from thin pieces of oak.

> 1594 To the shinglers for hewinge of shingle ... 50s | For their work about the steple ... £6 10s (Lindfield, Sussex)[2]

And slate, which in some areas is used in conjunction with moss.

> 1560 To Thomas Sherlocke and his servantes for working at the churche in slating and mossing it ... 31s 4d | For the karyage of the slates from Rainforth to the churche ... 4s 9d | For mosse to the churche to serve Thomas Sherlocke with ... 4s 8d (Prescot, Lancs)

> 1664 Paid two poor women for 17 burthens of mosse ... for the ruff [roof] of the church ... 5s 8d (St James, Bristol)[3]

According to a 19th-century inhabitant of Eskdale, Cumberland, 'the old, imperfect way of slating the roof made it necessary to stuff the slates with moss (as a ship is caulked) to make the roof weather tight when there was wind and driving rain and snow.'[4]

In later centuries strips and sheets of lead are widely used.

> 1585 For making a pitte to melt leade in ... 4d | For boords for the roofe of the churche and to make a molde to caste the sheets of leade in ... 2s 6d (Stanford, Berks)

> 1624 For the turning the leades of the church ... 4s 4d (Redenhall, Norfolk)[5]

Often the top of the steeple or tower is crowned by a weather vane. These take a variety of forms – St Bartholomew Exchange in Threadneedle Street has a ship, St Mary le Bow in Cheapside a dragon, and Piddinghoe in Sussex a fish – but much the most common is that of a cockerel.

Weathercocks have the practical advantage that their tails catch the wind, but their widespread use on churches is thought to derive from early popes: Gregory I (590-604) describes the cock as an apt emblem for Christianity as it is the sign of St Peter, who denied Christ three times before the cock crowed; Leo IV (847-855) has one placed on the old St Peter's in Rome; and Nicholas I (858-867) is said to have ordered one to be placed on every church steeple. In the 13th century Guillaume Durand sees the cock as an emblem of preachers, or of the clergy more generally: 'He arouseth the sleepers; he foretelleth the approach of day'.[6]

Care and attention are often lavished upon them.

1602 To John Reve the trumpeter for his workmanship and brasse done
about the wether cocke upon the steple ... 3s 4d (St Peter Mancroft,
Norwich)

1605 For fitting the spindle to the wethercocke, and for making the flower
de luce [fleur-de-lis] on the toppe ... 3s 4d | For fastening the tale of the
cocke ... 3s | For gilding the cocke ... 28s (Holy Trinity, Coventry)

1699 To the man that put up the cock, for beer ... 6d (St Andrew, Plymouth)[7]

Like other parts of the church, weathercocks are sometimes hallowed, as at
Louth in 1515.

Memorandum the 15 Sonday after Holy Trenete this yer the wedercoke
was set upon the broch ... ther being Will Ayleby parish prest with many of
his breder [brother] prests ther present haloing the said wedercoke and the
stone that it stands upon, and so conveyed upon the said broch, and then
the said prests singing *Te deum laudamus* [You, God, we praise] with organs,
and then the kirke wardens garte [caused to] ringe all the bels and caused
all the pepull ther being to have brede & ale. And all to the loving of God,
our lady and all saints.[8]

As with other roof work, the raising of cocks can be dangerous. John Stow
records that at St Paul's Cathedral the 'steeple was repaired in the yeare 1462 and
the weather-cocke againe erected. Robert Godwin winding it up, the rope brake,
and he was destroyed on the pinacles and the cocke was sore brused'.[9]

In later centuries churches often raise a flag on the steeple or tower to mark
notable occasions.

1727 For a flag to hoist on ye kings birth day with staples and lines to it ...
£1 4s (Holy Cross Westgate, Canterbury)

1787 For a flag for the church ... £5 10s | Paid Robert Buckland for going
to Wapping Wall to order the flag and bringing it home when ready ...
2s | For a bag to keep the flag in ... 5s 6d (Fulham, Middlesex)[10]

2. Porch

We enter the church via the porch, usually found on the south side. In the Middle
Ages porches are used for various purposes including the first part of the marriage
ceremony, Chaucer's Wife of Bath famously noting that 'housbondes at chirche
dore have I had five'. Some porches have an upper chamber, well placed for the
keeping of an eye on comings and goings and occasionally provided as lodging
for a sexton or junior cleric.[1]

1540 [Agreed that] Richard Hampson, being a servante, or under-sexton,
in the churche of Yarmouth, should have the chamber over the church

porche, freely to his owne use, for his chamber to lodge in ... (Great Yarmouth, Norfolk)

1594 For timber for the roofe of the deacons chamber over the churche porche ... 3s (Ludlow, Shropshire)[2]

Like the surrounding churchyard, porches are liable to suffer from the presence of animals. At Netheravon, Wiltshire, the vicar keeps his horse in the churchyard and uses the porch as a stable (1405). At St Edmund, Salisbury, 'beastes and ... cattell ... come into the church porch, and sometimes into the church' (1630). At Wenhaston, Suffolk, the wardens report that they have 'a door to ye church porch to keep cattell out, at present not well hung' (1686).[3]

Double storey porch, Aylsham, Norfolk, 1488

You may notice one or more animal heads hung upon the church door or at some other prominent spot. This is part of the campaign against 'noyfull fowells and vermin' which the parish is responsible for waging from Tudor times onwards.*

1661 Naileing a fox head on the church dore .... (Gateshead, co. Durham)

1665 Payed unto William Throughegood and William Ravensden of Warden for foure foxes heades and for one badgers heade set up in the churcheyard upon Whitsunday ... 5s (Northill, Beds)

1705 Paid Adam Craggs for a fox head placed [at or on the] church dore ... 1s (All Saints, Newcastle)[4]

At Hope, Derbyshire, the bodies of foxes are hung up over the entrance to the porch in a canopied niche formerly occupied by a figure of St Peter, while at St Andrew, Plymouth, they are hung upon the branches of churchyard trees. At Cartmel and Hawkshead in Lancashire fox heads are fixed to the churchyard gates.[5]

Porches also serve as places of human refuge, women with nowhere else to go sometimes giving birth here. Others leave newborn infants, confident that the parish will arrange for their care, although there is always the risk that the child will die before or soon after it is discovered.

1592 Annis Parker, the daughter supposed of Thomas Parker, of Mordoun, beinge lefte in the churche portch by that harlot her mother, buried Dec. 18. (Mitcham, Surrey)

1593 Two children, twins, were baptised. Anne Knoxson (the mother) being delivered of them two children in the streete, came and laide her-self with her two children in oure churche porche. (St Peter, Cheapside)

1605 Rebekah daughter of John & Mary Emity, vagrants, baptised 7 Feb. She was born in the church porch Feb. 3. (Aston Abbots, Bucks)[6]

Others too seek shelter here and eventually are forced to leave.

1613 To Goodie Meakins for makeing cleane the church porch when Nan Robinson was removed thence ... 3d (Wandsworth)

1650 For removeing of a poore man out of the church porch ... 4d (St Peter Mancroft, Norwich)[7]

According to John Aubrey, the porch is resorted to on Midsummer eve by those 'more curious than ordinary', the belief being that if they 'sit all night in the church porch ... they should see the apparitions of those that should die in the parish that yeare come and knock at the dore'.[8]

The bones of those already dead are often here beneath our feet, some wills requesting such a resting place and leaving bequests designed to secure it.

---

* Brief details of the relevant legislation are on pp146, 148.

1531 To be buried in the churche porche ... and 6s 8d to the paving of the same porche, and if it will not do it I will 40d more to have it well done. (Robert Luddesdon, High Halstow, Kent)

1549 To the church wardens ... towards the reparacon of the churche 3s 4d so that they suffer me to lie in the church porche. (William Lendall *alias* Levindall, Chislehurst, Kent)[9]

Those who have served the church may also be buried here.

1596 September ... The 23th was buried Nicholas Bedworth who beinge parishe clarke was laide in the churche porche. (St Martin in the Fields)[10]

Before passing over such bones to enter the church you may wish to pause at the holy water stoup near the doorway, perhaps in a niche in the wall on our right. The water is mixed with salt and blessed, and on entering the devout dip their fingers in it before making the sign of the cross on their bodies as an act of self-purification. Belief in the demonifugal efficacy of such water is evident at St Mary Northgate, Canterbury, in the 1540s when it is reported that 'against tempests of thunder and lightning many run to the church for holy water to cast about their houses to drive away ill spirits and devils'.[11]

Niches for holy water stoups in south porches.
UPPER Wenhaston, Suffolk, with stoup surviving. LOWER Arlington, Sussex.

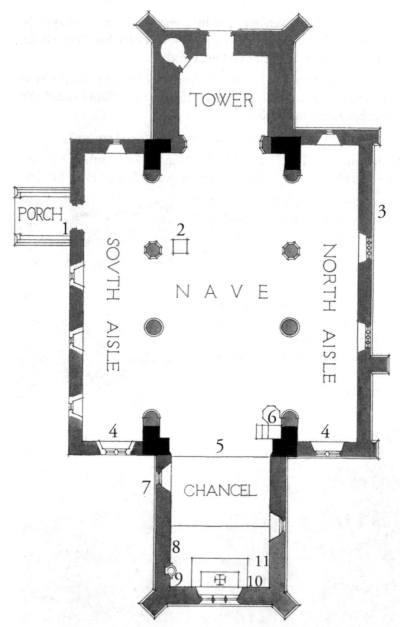

Some typical church features

Italic indicates casualties of the Reformation,
whether through removal or disuse.
1 *Holy water stoup*.   2 Font.   3 *North door*.
4 *Side altars*.   5 Rood/Chancel screen with *rood* and *rood loft* above.   6 Pulpit.
7 *Low side window*.   8 *Sedilia*.   9 *Piscina*.
10 *Image of patron saint*.   11 *Easter sepulchre*.

3. Alms box, flooring, font

As we enter the church, near the door there may be an alms box for donations for the poor, usually secured by three locks. Royal injunctions of 1547 require each parish to provide

> a strong chest with a hole in the upper part thereof ... having three keys, whereof one shall remain in the custody of the parson, vicar or curate, and the other two in the custody of the churchwardens ... Which chest you shall set and fasten near unto the high altar, to the intent the parishioners should put into it their oblation and alms for their poor neighbours. And the parson, vicar or curate shall diligently from time to time ... call upon, exhort and move their neighbours to confer and give, as they may well spare, to the said chest ...

However, the Canons of 1604 simply instruct the churchwardens to 'set and fasten' a chest 'in the most convenient place, to the intent the parishioners may put into it their alms'. As a result it is often placed near the main door so as to be noticed by everyone entering and leaving the church.[1]

> 1552 For making a cheste bounde with iron and 3 locks for the poore mens awsmes according to the kings injunctions ... 15s (Paglesham, Essex)
>
> 1633 Paid the smith for mending the 3 lockes for the poores box at the church doore and making 3 new keyes ... 2s 6d | Paid the painter for painting the poores box and for making the table wretten *Remembring the poore* over it ... 4s (St Bartholomew Exchange)[2]

This is a common inscription. At St Mary, Reading, the box is inscribed encouragingly, 'Remember the poore and God will bles thee and thy store.'[3]

Norfolk alms boxes: Watton; St Peter, Walpole; Great Walsingham

Looking down, the nature of the floor beneath our feet depends on where we are and when. Large town and city churches are paved early, but many rural churches only begin to replace their original flooring of stamped earth in the 17th century.

Whether of earth, brick, tile or flagstone, the floor may well be covered with straw or rushes, laid for their pleasant smell (to begin with at least), for insulation, to absorb dirt, and to provide a softer surface, particularly for kneeling.[4]

1476-78 For rushes for the pewes ... 1d (St Andrew Hubbard)

1520 For brede and ale at the bringing of the gras at midsomer to strewe withall the chirche ... 2d (Bishop's Stortford, Herts)[5]

The font (from Latin *fons*, fountain or spring of water) is usually ahead of us and near the main door. This has practical advantages as in early times the baptism ceremony, largely performed at the font, begins at the door, but it can also be seen as symbolising the fact that it is through that rite that individuals enter the Church.

Norman font, with carvings of Adam and Eve and a later wooden cover, Hook Norton, Oxfordshire.

FACING PAGE. LEFT Finial forming the top of a spire-shaped 15th-century font cover at Ewelme, Oxfordshire, perhaps depicting St Michael the Archangel.

RIGHT 14th-century font and cover, East Winch, Norfolk.

The water for the font is ceremonially blessed each Easter and is sought after for superstitious purposes, including the encouragement of growth in crops. As a result in the 13th century various orders require that fonts are secured against theft: for example, in 1236 Archbishop Edmund directs that they be 'kept locked and covered on account of sorcery'. He also orders that the water within be renewed within seven days after any baptism.[6]

Early font covers are flat and of wood and are fastened on each side by staples which often survive to the present day.

> 1492 For the reparacions for the font, for 56 li. of lede ... 2s 4d | For a stapell of iron & a bar ... 3d | For a mason to make a hole in the font ... 2d | For a pade loke to loke it ... 2d (St Andrew Hubbard)[7]

Over time covers tend to become large and elaborate, often spire-shaped and requiring a pulley.

> 1634 For the font cover ... 10s | For a cord to draw it up ... 8d (Hawkhurst, Kent)[8]

4. Nave, rood, rood loft

Proceeding north we enter the nave (from Latin *navis*, ship), the main body of the church and intended for the use of the congregation. The name probably derives from early symbolism which sees the church as a ship or ark in which the faithful can find salvation, while in physical terms the nave with its roof timbers exposed can be seen as resembling an upturned ship.[1]

If we are here before the Reformation, looking east we see a rood screen, separating the nave from the chancel beyond. It is often finely carved and its lower sections may feature painted panels.

Hammerbeam nave roof, Cawston, Norfolk, looking east

15th-century rood screen at Barton Turf, Norfolk, and closer views of the first two panels on the right-hand side depicting two orders of angels, Cherubim (*left*) and Principalities. The feathers of the former are studded with eyes, emblematic of omniscience.

Above the screen, and dominating the central space of the church, is the rood (from Old English *rod*, cross), a representation of Christ crucified. Just as the font (signifying baptism) marks the passing from the world into the church/Church, so the rood (signifying Christ's giving of his life to secure immortality for mankind) marks the transition from the nave to the chancel beyond, or in symbolic terms from earth to heaven.

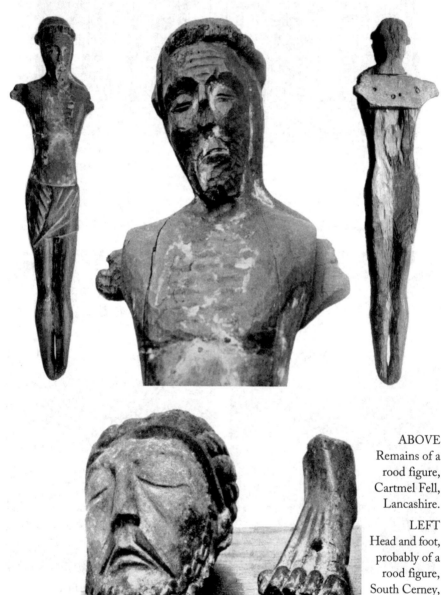

ABOVE
Remains of a
rood figure,
Cartmel Fell,
Lancashire.

LEFT
Head and foot,
probably of a
rood figure,
South Cerney,
Gloucester-
shire.

The means by which the rood is supported varies from place to place. It may be attached to the top of the screen or to a separate rood beam high up above the screen. Often there is a rood loft resting above the screen, and a front horizontal timber of the loft may serve to support the rood. Alternatively it may be suspended from the roof.

> 1497 For the long bolt of iron coming down from the roofe, & for stapilles & spikinges [spike-nails] to fasten it to the roode ... 5s 6d | To Hew Materson, smith, for clampes, nailles & hokes that the roode hangith by ... 8d (St Mary at Hill)[2]

It may form the centrepiece of a 'doom' or depiction of the Last Judgement painted either onto the wall above the chancel arch or onto a wooden tympanum fitted within the arch, as at Wenhaston, Suffolk (see overleaf below).*

The rood is accompanied by two figures present at the crucifixion, the Virgin Mary to Christ's right (i.e. to the north) and St John the Evangelist to his left.

> 1475 For 2 barres of iron with stapulles and nailes to them to staye with owre lady and Sainte John in the rodelofte ... 3s 5d ob. | To a carpenter to make holes in the said 2 images and to make them fast with the said 2 barres of iron ... 8d (St Michael, Cornhill)[3]

There may also be additional saints and angels in attendance.

> 1502 [Received] of Agnes Haselwood for ye painting of the angel before the rood ... 1d | [Paid] for painting of ye angel ... 2s (Worfield, Shropshire)

> 1526 To the gilding or peanting of the 12 apostoles in the rode lofte, 6s 8d. (will of W. Manton, Blatherwycke, Northants)[4]

The various figures are usually gilded or painted in this way, and in some places the central ones are clothed and shod. At St Olave, Silver Street, the figure of Christ is adorned with 'a shewe of silver' and 'a cote of crimson velvet', while at St Andrew, Canterbury, there are '2 shoue of silver fixed to the fete of the rode'. At St Clement, Sandwich, Thomas Toller leaves a substantial sum in his will for gilding the rood along with a piece of silver 'for to make him a crown, and another broken silver as well, to make him a pair of gloves'.[5]

At Thame in Oxfordshire there is a crown of lights, perhaps suspended above Christ's head in place of a crown of thorns.

> 1448 For 2 li. of wyrde [white] kandel that served ye crowne befor ye rode ... 2d ob. | For making ye poleys for ye crowne with ye lampis ... 1d[6]

---

* In some dooms - such as the one at St Thomas, Salisbury - Christ appears only once, on high as the bringer of the Last Judgement. In others - including those at Wenhaston and in the Trinity Chapel at Stratford upon Avon - the rood group is incorporated within the composition so that he also appears (or appeared) lower down and upon the cross.

ABOVE & RIGHT The Wenhaston Doom, now placed against a side wall. The blank spaces show the positions originally occupied by the rood and the Virgin Mary (left) and St John the Evangelist (right). As usual in such scenes those judged worthy of admission to heaven are shown on the left while those drawn by the devil into the jaws of hell are on the right.

BELOW The former positions of the three figures evident above the chancel arch at Raunds, Northants.

Rood loft, St Margaret's, Herefordshire

As noted above, any beam supporting the rood may also form part of the front or west side of a rood loft, either at parapet level or as the supporting timber, with the loft's east side usually being supported by the top of the rood screen.[7]

A detailed record of the erection and decoration of one loft occurs in the accounts of Yatton, Somerset, for 1454-55.

> For bords from Sowtheampton ... 6s 8d
> For caryage of the same borde betwene [South] Hampton and Chew ...
>   6s 8d | [And] betwene Chew and home ... 10d
> To Crosse [the carpenter] for his labor in the lofte ... 11s
> For ale given to Crosse in certein tymis in his worke to make him wel
>   wellede [well-willed] ... 2d ob.
> For erneste peny* to the image maker ... 1d
> For the images to the rodelofte, in number 69 ... £3 10s 4d
> To setting up of the images ... 4d
> For colers late boffte at Bristow [bought at Bristol] ... 2s 1d
> For a quarte of painting oile ... 10d | For golde to painte the angel ... 6s
> For the painter his hire a weke ... 20d | [And for] his bedde ... 2d
> For fetching of a stone from Chelvey to grinde colers therwith ... 1d
> For vernaysche [varnish], a pound and a quarter ... 10d
> For the chandler† ... 13s 4d[8]

* *Earnest penny.* A small sum, usually but not always a penny, paid in confirmation of an agreement for work to be done.

† *Chandler.* One who makes or sells candles.

Such lofts are usually about 6 foot deep with a carved wooden parapet along the nave-facing front. A contract dated 1520 for one at St Mary the Great, Cambridge, stipulates that it should be 'in depnesse 8 foots ... with suche yomags [images] as schal be advised and appointed by the parochiners'. All the timber is to be 'full seasoned' and certain fittings are to be 'of good and hable oke withoute sappe, rifte, wyndeshakk,* or other deformatiff hurtefull'.[9]

Many lofts are served by a winding stone staircase, usually on the north side, sometimes within an aisle wall or a pier of the chancel arch, sometimes in a turret external to the main building. Alternatively they may be reached by way of wooden steps of various kinds.[10]

> 1540 For making a ladder unto the rode lofte ... 5d (St Mary on the Hill, Chester)[11]

Whatever the means of access, given the loft's height there is a risk of accidents.

> 1551 The thirde day of Maye paid for sendinge for ye crowner [coroner] to sit upon Habgrow that fell out of the rood loft and died ... 8d (Thame)

The unfortunate Habgrow had recently been paid for ringing curfew so was perhaps the sexton or parish clerk.[12]

The loft is likely to be where the church's small and relatively portable organ is set up.

> *c.* 1481 In the ... rode lofte is a peire orgons ... Also, a stonding lecterne for to ley on a boke to pleye by. Also, a stole to sit on whan he pleythe on the orgons. (St Stephen, Walbrook, inventory)

> 1524 Paid for 4 porters for removinge of the organs into the roode lofte ... 12d (St Peter, Cheapside)[13]

Early accounts often refer as above to 'a pair of organs' but the term seems to have been used of any instrument with several pipes.[14]

Some lofts also serve as a gallery for singers and readers on festival days.

> 1526 For wine on Passion Sonday spent on the quier in the rode loft ... 6d (Lydd, Kent)[15]

In recalling the church of Long Melford, Suffolk, as it was before the Reformation one parishioner notes that 'there was a fair rood loft with the rood ... which loft extended all the breadth of the church, and on Good Friday a priest then standing by the rood sang the Passion'. However, widespread and frequent use of lofts by vestmented clergy seems unlikely given the narrowness and steepness of most rood stairways and the fact that they are usually accessed from the nave rather than the chancel.[16]

---

* *Hable.* Suitable, fit. *Wind-shake.* A flaw or crack in wood, supposed to be due to strain caused by wind.

Rood loft stairway,
Denton, Sussex,
inside and out

Helpfully for anyone who is performing in the loft, its eastern parapet may be open or have apertures, allowing a view of the service as it progresses in the chancel so that cues can be taken accordingly, as at Llanelieu, Breconshire, Wales, below.

The loft also serves to hold and display an array of lamps, candles and tapers.

1465 For oile for ye lompes in ye rode loft & for a pot ... 3d (Thame)

1556 For 9 taper dishes for the rode loft ... 9s (St Martin, Leicester)[17]

Typically these include a central rood light to illuminate the figure of Christ, although this may be otherwise affixed.

1491 For 3 li. wire to hold up the tapers of the roode light ... 12d (St Margaret, Westminster)

1521 Received of a man that will not be named for finding of a candell brenning before the rode in the rode loft every Sunday in the yere at the sakering* of hye masse ... 16d (Thame)[18]

At St Mary Abchurch, London, they have '29 candelstickes of latten standinge in the roode lofte', and when at the Reformation they sell 'all the latten' in the loft

* *Sacring*. Consecration of the eucharistic elements, bread and wine.

the weight amounts to 93 pounds. The wax also adds up. At St Edmund, Lombard Street, they sell '45 lb. of wax that was in the candilstickes in the roode lofte', and at St Thomas the Apostle 'fifty pounde weight of wax' from the lights there.[19]

The loft may also be used to display banners.

1532 For nailes to make fast the irons in the rode lofte to set in the baners ... 1d (St Mary at Hill)[20]

Some larger lofts even have their own altars.

1447 1 stened cloth to hang befor the auter in the rode lofte. (Bridgwater, Somerset, inventory)[21]

On a more practical level, lofts often serve as relatively secure places to stow chests and coffers containing church goods.

c. 1481 In the rode lofte ... a litel peintid cheste with many smale imagis set abowt it made like a shrine, and there bene therein many relikes and [papal] bulles of pardon. (St Stephen, Walbrook, inventory)[22]

At St Mary Woolnoth the loft is home to 'an old ship chest', two other chests, and miscellaneous clobber including 'a painted cloth of St George', '8 stremers of silk stained', '16 banner staves long and short', 'an old pair organs', 'a desk of wood with a falcon', 'an old settill', and 'a lader with 14 staves'.[23]

LEFT Niche for a piscina at loft level indicating the presence of an altar, Eastbourne, Sussex. RIGHT Loft level doorway, Harlaxton, Lincolnshire.

5. Other images
with a digression on purgatory, side altars, chantries and guilds

i. Types and subject matter

The rood and its attendant figures, along with any chancel arch doom above and rood screen panels below, are only the most prominent among a host of images to be found in pre-Reformation churches. Indeed, images may be found more or less everywhere – from fonts, pews and choir stalls to windows, walls and roof spaces – and are created using a range of crafts and materials – whether carving in stone and wood, staining of glass, or painting on panels and walls.

The subjects depicted also range widely but can be divided into five categories.[1]

i. Christ and scenes from his life

ii. Saints and scenes from their lives (see overleaf below)

iii. 'Moralities' including depictions of the seven deadly sins and Last Judgement

iv. Angels and other religious figures which do not form part of a scene or story

v. Miscellaneous other figures and decorative schemes

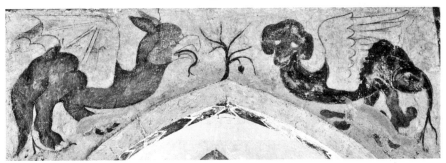

i. Mural: entombment, Easby, Yorkshire.

iii. Stained glass: to hell in a handcart, Ticehurst, Sussex.

iv. Wood carving: misericord, Wintringham, Yorkshire.

v. Murals: mythical beasts, Hailes, Gloucestershire; man holding up chancel arch, Coombes, Sussex.

Apart from the Virgin Mary, the most commonly depicted saints include St George, often shown vanquishing a dragon; St Michael the Archangel, also often fighting a dragon but distinguished by having angel wings; and St Catherine of Alexandria, shown with a spiked wheel from the tradition that, having protested against the persecution of Christians, she was punished by being tied to a wheel, tortured and beheaded. Also popular is St Christopher, patron saint of travellers, who is shown crossing a stream with the child Jesus on his back or shoulder (Christopher meaning 'bearer of Christ' in Greek). He is often depicted on the north wall, facing the south door, so as to be seen by all those entering the church, it being believed that sight of him provides protection from accident and death for the rest of the day.[2]

St Christopher, by the Master of Sir John Fastolf, from a Book of Hours, *circa* 1430. While more finely detailed than the images typically found in parish churches, it gives an idea of what some of the more accomplished ones may have looked like before the deterioration arising from occasional vandalism and centuries of damp.

FACING PAGE. UPPER St George on a misericord, St Mary, Beverley, Yorkshire. LOWER St Catherine, stained glass, Kingerby, Lincolnshire.

ii. At side altars and in chapels

Many images of saints are found at side altars or in chapels dedicated to them.

Such settings for supplementary worship proliferate in the later Middle Ages as the idea of purgatory comes to dominate western Christianity.* The belief is that after death the soul has to pass through an intermediate state or place where its venial or forgivable sins can be purged so as to render it ready for admission into heaven. The Church has some good news, however: the saying of masses for the soul in question will reduce the time it spends in purgatory and the pains it endures there. This naturally leads to a huge rise in demand for the saying of masses as people make provision, usually in their wills, to ease the process for their own souls and for those of their loved ones. In consequence, in many churches the main altar is unable to accommodate all the desired observances and further altars are added, often with additional priests to serve them.[3]

Such additional altars are usually dedicated to one or more of the saints, or to an element of Christian belief such as the Trinity, and are provided with an image accordingly. Generally the image is carved in wood and painted and is placed on or above the altar, perhaps in a tabernacle, perhaps in a niche or upon a corbel, and with a lamp or candles set before it.

Most pre-Reformation churches have at least one such altar, and some have half a dozen or more. St Edmund, Salisbury, for example, has separate ones dedicated to at least seven saints as well as to the Holy Cross. At their most modest such altars are pressed up against a pillar in the nave, and at their grandest they occupy their own richly furnished chapels. Whatever their location they are usually separated from the rest of the church by parcloses or other screens and they are almost always placed against an easterly wall or other surface so that prayers and masses said at them are directed eastward. Indeed, the demand for such walls is one cause of the expansion of churches in the period, new chapels sprouting on one or both sides of the chancel (as at Burford, Oxfordshire) or from the east sides of any transepts (as at Chesterfield: see p5). The commonest form of expansion is the addition of north and south aisles to the nave, and the eastern ends of these are the most popular location for side altars. In large churches the aisles may each be home to several chapels, screens providing easterly surfaces against which altars can be set. At Ludlow, for example, there are three chapels in the north aisle and four in the south.[4]

While such secondary altars and their images may be supported by general parish funds many are established and maintained by chantries or guilds.

> *c.* 1380 For an image bought ... £1 6s | For a throne with instruments and
> 6 angels each bearing in his hand a wax taper burning before the image
> ... £2 14s 4d | For a marble stone for the altar ... £2 13s 4d | For making
> a parclose ... £33 6s 8d | For a vestment, and certain necessaries for the

---

* While the process is gradual, one milestone is the Council of Lyons of 1274 at which the doctrine of purgatory is formally defined.

chapel ... £29 7s | For a chest for the vestments ... 16s (Guild of the Holy Trinity, Wisbech, Cambs)[5]

c. 1389 For making, painting and gilding an image of St John the Baptist ... £6 6s | For painting a crucifix in St John's chapel ... 15s | For an iron beam for the lamp there ... £1 | For 4 brass candlesticks ... £1 3s | For the repair and dedication of the altar ... £1 10s | For the repair of the vestments belonging to it ... £1 10s | For keeping up the lights in the chapel, and for vermilion, rosin and white lead in painting the torches ... £24 | For painting the inclosure of the said chapel ... 8s | For the priest's salary during the whole term ... £23 6s 8d (Guild of St John the Baptist, Wisbech)[6]

Chantries are endowments for a priest or priests to celebrate masses for the soul of one or more individuals, usually the founder and his or her close relatives, and the word comes also to be used for any altar or chapel endowed for such a purpose. Typically a chantry involves mass being said every day at a specified altar by a particular priest who receives a salary.

Because of the cost, chantries are largely the preserve of the rich, but to secure similar benefits those of more modest means often club together in a religious fraternity or **guild**. While guilds have various other functions they almost always provide for masses to be said for members' souls after death. To this end they may employ one or more priests and establish and maintain altars, rather as individuals do through chantry bequests.

Parclose in north aisle, Winthorpe, Lincolnshire. To its right are rood loft doorways.

iii. Creation, repair, decoration, lights

Early accounts tend to use the word 'image' in referring to all likenesses and it is therefore sometimes hard to know what type of work is being paid for. The following entries relating to the Virgin Mary appear to refer to three-dimensional figures.

> 1464 Paid John Dawes for a large tree for making an image of the blessed Mary ... 4s (Saffron Walden, Essex)
>
> 1480-82 To the kerver at London Walle for making of our lady ... 12d | 1497 For the setting in of the image of our lady in her tabernakell, to a joiner ... 5d (St Andrew Hubbard)
>
> 1521 To the peinter for gilding of a crowne for our lady ... 2s 4d (Bishop's Stortford)[7]

The following are more varied.

> 1503 To Miles painter for painting of Seint Christofer ... 8s 4d | For new pargeting [plastering] of the wall where St Christofer is painted ... 6d (St Lawrence, Reading)
>
> 1556 For the image of Saint Michell ... 20s | For carreing home the same image ... 4d | For my chargs & my horse goinge to Assheforth [Ashford] to fett home the said image ... 6d (Smarden, Kent)
>
> 1557 To Lewes the copper smith in Gutter lane for the image of Sainte Peter ... 50s (St Peter, Cheapside)[8]

Some images are life-size and larger. At St Lawrence, Reading, a notable three-dimensional George with its own loft is created in the 1530s.

> For makeing the loft that Saint George standeth apon ... 6d
> For 2 plonks for the same loft ... 8d
> For makeing the iron that the horse resteth apon ... 6d
> For 4 caffes [calves] skines & 2 horse skines [for the horse's coat] ... 4s 6d
> For makeing of Saint George's cote ... 8d
> For roses, bells, girdle, sword, & dager ... 3s 4d[9]

He is not alone in being made to appear more lifelike by the addition of clothes.

> 1492 To Isbell Passchelew for making of the klothes to Sent John ... 20d (Walberswick, Suffolk)
>
> 1499 For a clue of worsted* to make an apron for St Cuthberga ... 4s 6d (Wimborne Minster, Dorset)[10]

---

* *Clue*. Ball of yarn or thread. The familiar modern sense of 'clue' arises from the use of the same as a guide in entering or exiting a labyrinth. *Worsted*. Named after the Norfolk parish of Worstead, notable from at least the 12th century for the manufacture of woollen cloth.

At Long Melford there are three 'coats belonging to our lady', one of crimson velvet, one of white damask,* and one 'for the good days, of cloth tissue', while at St Stephen, Coleman Street, they have four.[11]

Lights are placed before images not only to illuminate them but also as an offering and in simple veneration.

> 1506 For scowering of the lampe before Seint John Baptist ... 6d | For a rope for to hang up the light before Seint Margett ... 4d (St John the Baptist, Peterborough)

> 1519 For finding of ye light before All Seints ... 3s (Guild of All Saints, Wymondham, Norfolk)[12]

iv. Images and the parishioner

Secondary altars and their images offer the parishioner a literally more approachable alternative to the main altar and the rood's lofty representation of the crucified Christ. Prayers are said and offerings made in these less intimidating settings in the hope that the chosen saint will reward the devotion shown by providing protection while you are alive and interceding for you when you die, with the result that your path from purgatory to heaven will be eased – rather as, in an earthly context, you might ask a courtier to intercede on your behalf with a remote and all-powerful king.

The best placed figure of all in the court of heaven is of course the Virgin Mary. As a result, in places the devotion shown towards her altar and image threatens to eclipse that shown at the main altar, as a satirical account of the unreformed Church pointedly records.

> Her image do they bravely decke with sumptuous show to sight,
> Her altar set about with bowes, and lampes, and candels bright.
> Eche man his candle present hath, that burneth thorow the yeare,
> And franckensense in every place doth smoke, and singinge cleare
> With organs in the church resoundes; the people brings in pence,
> And on the altar offer all with wondrous reverence.
> Such honors are not here bestowed on Christ in any place,
> He is not thought to do so much, nor of so great a grace ...
> *The Popish Kingdome*[13]

Such devotions dismay Protestants. Thomas Cranmer notes critically that before the Reformation 'images were kneeled unto, offered unto, prayed unto, sought unto, incensed, and pilgrimages done unto them', while a later writer considers it 'not meete that a Christian should be occupied by the eyes' when they should be occupied 'by the meditation of the minde'.[14]

---

* Originally a rich silk fabric from Damascus woven with elaborate designs and figures. Later used of any rich figured fabric.

The attachment felt by individual parishioners to images, and to the saints they represent, is nonetheless attested by the many gifts and bequests made to establish and support them.

> 1512 My executors to sell my beste gown of tawney and my harness ... and my crosbowe and with the money to buy a image of Saint George to be set in the churche. (Peter Horney, Cobham, Kent)

> 1525 [For] a bason and 5 tapers of virgin wex to be set afore oure lady in the litell chauncell, 20s. (William Both, Bromley, Kent)

> 1529 Christina Timewell bequeved her beste gowne to helpe to bye a new image of our lady for ye wiche gowne was resseved ... 4s (Morebath, Devon)[15]

Particularly useful are gifts of hives of bees, providing a direct source of wax.

> 1537 I beqweth to maintene ye light afor All Hallows in ye church of Bromley, one hive of beene, and another hive to ye light afor ye sepulcur, and another hive to ye light of Senct Antony. (Margaret White, Bramley, Hants)

The parish may sell any surplus along with the honey: four years later Bramley parish receives 8d 'for wax and huny of an hive for ye church', perhaps one of those left by Margaret White.[16]

In rural areas it is also common to leave livestock to the parish, to be rented out or sold so as to produce the necessary funds.

> 1501 I will 8 lambes be solde to the painting of the image of Seint Margaret. (Thomas Dalam, High Halstow, Kent)

> 1524 To Saint Nicholas light 8 schepe and they to laste for evermore. (William Foreste, Allhallows, Hoo, Kent)

> 1535 To our lady chapel my best cowe. To our lady alter my best tablecoth. (Alice Saunders, Long Buckby, Northants)[17]

The intention in the last case is probably that the tablecloth be placed upon the altar. Similarly, in the following the gifts are probably to be placed on or about the image.

> 1521 To our lady of piety a pair of jete beds with a ring of them. (Isabella Longeman, Allhallows, Hoo)

> 1535 To our ladie 2 wedding rings, a tache,* a pair hoks and my wifes beades. (John Hickenson, Beckenham, Kent)[18]

---

* A clasp, buckle, hook and eye, or other contrivance for attaching or fastening two parts together.

The sense of familiarity suggested by such bequests is also found in church accounts, which often seem to be referring to images as if they are the saints themselves. In part of course this is just a convenient shorthand to save time and ink, but the medieval mind tended to be less rigid than ours in separating representation from reality, and it is hard not to sense a certain familiar tenderness in some entries.[19]

1482 For repairing St Dorothy ... 12d | For a hook for St Christopher ... 1½d (St Petrock, Exeter)

1483-85 For an hoke to hold up Seint Katherine ... 4d (St Andrew Hubbard)

1530 [For] carting home of our lady ... 2d | For bred and drink to them that helped her in to the carte ... 1d (Sutterton, Lincs)[20]

6. Texts, royal arms, banners, funeral garlands

This cast of mind is dealt a profound blow by the Reformation when each church's panoply of images is swept away. As a result of this change, if we are visiting after about 1560 we will see texts rather than images on the walls, with the Ten Commandments and Lord's prayer in prominent positions, painted directly onto plaster, or onto hanging boards or cloths.*[1]

1567 Mr Raynard for setting up the Skripptwer in the hie chauncell ... 6s 8d | For coals to dry his work ... 6d (Kingston upon Thames, Surrey)

1571 To Charnocke ye peinter for peinting the 10 Commandements, the Lord's Prayer, and the articles of ye faith ... 12s | More for his meate and drinke for 4 days and a half ... 2s 3d (Stoke Charity, Hants)

1584 For ye iron work and nailes to hange ye table of ye commandments of God over ye chaunsell doore ... 4d (Chelmsford, Essex)

1635 For writing the sentences upon the church walls, being fourteen yards and a half, at two shillings a yard ... 29s (Weybread, Suffolk)

1638 For 6 yards of canvice to write the ten Commandments on ... 6s | For souing the aforesaid canvis together fit to work ... 2d (Saffron Walden, Essex)

1720 To Samuel Basford for stoping ye cracks in ye commandments ... 6d (Towcester, Northants)[2]

* In a letter of 22nd January 1560-61 to the commissioners for causes ecclesiastical, Queen Elizabeth orders that 'the tables of the commandments may be comlye set or hung up in the east end of the chauncell, to be read not only for edification, but also to give some comlye ornament and demonstration that the same is a place of religion and prayer'. This is reiterated in the Canons of 1604, canon 82 ordering that 'the Ten Commandments be set up on the east end of every church and chapel, where the people may best see and read the same, and other chosen sentences written upon the walls ... in places convenient'. The 'chosen sentences' are usually the creed and Lord's prayer.

Other rules may also be in evidence, including 'tables' or boards warning against marriage with anyone too closely related.

1588 For the table of Consanguinitie and for a frame to it ... 6d (Ludlow)

1647 For a table against prophane swearinge set up neere the church doore ... 1s (St Bartholomew Exchange)[3]

There may also be a board commemorating those who have given to good causes.

1671 To Mr Moore ... for recording the names of the benefactors to the church and poor of this parish, in two tables, with gold letters at the west end of the church ... £10 (St Margaret, Westminster)[4]

If visiting after the Reformation it is likely we will also find royal arms, similarly painted either directly onto the wall, on wooden panels, or on canvas. They are always in a prominent position, often above the chancel arch in place of the rood, as if to assert that it has indeed become the church of England.

1547 To the goodman Child for the refressing of the kings armes standing in the rode lofte ... 3s (St Matthew, Friday Street)

1573 For a boord to set over the churche dore to painte the queens armes theron ... 3s 4d (St Andrew, Canterbury)

1606 For 16 yards of arisste* and half a hundred of oaken boards to make the king's armes in the church ... 4s 8d | For eyes and hookes for the king's armes ... 12d (Thatcham, Berks)

1773 To Jas. Puddington, J. Roberts & Wm. Hardy for puting up ye kings armes which fell down ... 2s (Peakirk, Northants)[5]

A visitation in Kent in 1557 notes that at Boughton Monchelsea 'the kinges armes is over the alter'.[6]

Before the Reformation there may be religious banners on poles hanging from the church walls, although they may be in the rood loft or tucked away in the vestry and only brought out for processions.

1431 1 baner with 1 swan of silver. | 1 baner with 3 lions of golde. | 1 penon with Sante George armes and the kinges. | 1 baner of grey tartaryn with popygeys.† (St Peter, Cheapside, inventory)[7]

An inventory of 1541 for St Mary Abchurch lists eighteen banners including one 'of red silke with lions of golde' and five featuring the church's patron saint.[8]

After the Reformation any banners typically bear the royal arms or those of notable organisations, families or individuals associated with the church.

---

* *Arras.* A rich tapestry fabric, originally made in the French town of that name.
† *Tartarin.* A rich stuff, apparently of silk, imported from the East, probably through Tartary, hence the name. *Popinjay.* Parrot.

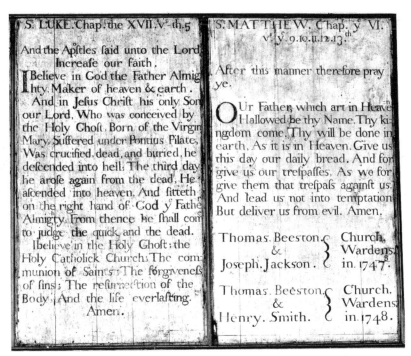

Creed and Lord's prayer on boards, Burnham Overy, Norfolk

Tympanum in chancel arch, Ellingham, Hampshire. Above, from left to right, the Lord's prayer, Commandments and creed. Below, flanked by biblical quotations, the royal arms.

ABOVE Arms of Queen Elizabeth, with lion and dragon supporters, painted on panel, Preston, Suffolk.

BELOW Carved arms from the reign of James I, with lion and unicorn supporters, crowning the chancel screen, Croscombe, Somerset.

The church's walls and beams may also be hung with sadder mementoes in the form of the funeral garlands of female parishioners who have died unmarried. Made of real or imitation flowers, they are carried in the funeral procession and then suspended in the church, usually over the seat formerly occupied by the dead girl or young woman.

Not everyone is sympathetic to such offerings. In 1662 Bishop Wren of Ely enquires of his parish clergy,

> Are any ... mean toyes and childish gew-gawes (such as the fonder sort of people prepare at some burials) suffered to be fastened up in your church at any ones pleasure? Or any garlands and other ordinary funeral ensigns to hang, where they hinder the prospect, or until they grow foul and dusty, withered and rotten?[9]

The custom remains popular nonetheless. In the 1780s Gilbert White notes of Selborne that

> in the middle aisle there is nothing remarkable, but I remember when its beams were hung with garlands in honour of young women of the parish, reputed to have died virgins; and recollect to have seen the clerk's wife cutting, in white paper, the resemblances of gloves, and ribbons to be twisted into knots and roses, to decorate these memorials of chastity. In the church of Faringdon, which is the next parish, many garlands of this sort still remain.[10]

'A garland fresh and faire, | Of lilies there was made, | In signe of her virginity, | And on her coffin laid.' Woodcut from *The Bride's Buriall*, a ballad printed in 1635.

In 1860 Llewellynn Jewitt finds five garlands still hanging in the church of Ashford-in-the-Water near Bakewell, Derbyshire.

Each garland contains a single glove, and a kerchief or collar ... [They] are formed of hoops and bands of wood ... covered with paper 'frilled' or 'fulled' on like the border of a cap, and tied round with ribband. ... On the collar or kerchief of each has been written a verse of poetry, and the name, age, and date of death of the virgin in whose honour they were prepared.

He finds most to be indecipherable because of the decay of the paper, the fading of the ink, and the difficulty of examining in situ, but on one he makes out the following verse.

Be always ready, no time delay,
I in my youth was called away,
Great grief to those that's left behind.
But I hope I'm great joy to find.
Ann Swindel,
Aged 22 years,
Dec. 9th, 1798.[11]

Garlands hanging
LEFT At Matlock, Derbyshire, drawn by Llewellynn Jewitt, one of six found there by him.
RIGHT At Abbotts Ann, Hampshire, photographed in the 1940s.

7. Consecration crosses
with a digression on the consecration ceremony

In looking up you may also see crosses a little above head height on the walls, perhaps with candle brackets below. These were made at the church's consecration, an elaborate ceremony described by Thomas Becon in his *Reliques of Rome* (1563).

> First all the people muste depart out of the church, and the deacon must remain there only, having all the doors shut fast unto him. The bishop with the clergy shall stand without before the church door, and make holy water mingled with salt. In the mean season within the church there must be set up 12 candles brenning before 12 crosses, that are appointed upon the church walls.
>
> Afterward the bishop, accompanied with the clergy and people, shall go thrice about the church without, and the bishop having in his hand a staff with a bunch of hyssop on the end, shall with the same cast holy water upon ye church walls: and at every time the bishop shall come unto ye church door and strike ye threshold therof with his crossier staff and say, *Tollite portas* [etc], that is, 'Lift up your gates, O ye princes ... & the king of glory shall enter in.' Then shall the deacon or minister that is within say, *Quis est iste rex gloriae?* That is, 'Who is this king of glory?' To whom the bishop shall answer, and say, *Dominus fortis et potens ...* That is, 'It is the Lord strong and mightie ...' At ye third time the deacon shall open the church door, and the bishop shall enter into the church accompanied with a few ministers, the clergy and the people abiding still without. Entering into the church, the bishop shall say, *Pax huic domui.* That is, 'Peace be unto this house.' And afterward the bishop with them that are in the church shall say the litany.
>
> These things done, there must be made in the pavement of the church a cross of ashes and sand, wherein ye whole alphabet or Christs crosse shall be written in Greek and Latin letters. After these things the bishop must hallow another water with salt, and ashes, and wine, and consecrate ye altar.
>
> Afterward the twelve crosses that are painted upon the church walls, the bishop must anoint them with chrism, commonly called cream. These things once done, the clergy and the people may freely come into the church, ring the bells for joy, &c.[1]

Various explanations are given for the abecedarium or alphabet part of the ceremony, including that the Greek and Latin languages represent the Jews and the Gentiles respectively, that the meeting of the two languages in the cross signifies the union of all peoples through their faith in Christ, and that the writing symbolises the word of God, 'not only alpha and omega, but all that lies between'.[2]

The wall crosses may be painted, incised in stone, modelled in plaster, or cast in metal and affixed, in each case at a height of ten palms (a little under 8 foot) from the ground such that they are at once open to view and out of the way of casual injury. According to Durand they serve three purposes.

> First, as a terror to evil spirits, that they, having been driven forth thence, may be terrified when they see the sign of the cross and may not presume to enter again. Secondly, as a mark of triumph, for crosses be the banners of Christ, and signs of his triumph. ... Thirdly, that such as look on them may call to mind the Passion of Christ ... The twelve lights placed before these crosses signify the twelve apostles who have illumined the whole world ... and whose teaching hath dispersed the darkness ...[3]

A further twelve crosses are often placed around the outside of the church.[4]

TOP RIGHT Consecration cross, Thompson, Norfolk.
ABOVE Bishop anointing cross, from a 16th-century missal.

Stages of the ceremony, from a pontifical of 1520

8. Pews

Lowering our attention to ground level, we find the seating available in the nave changing over time. Early congregations usually stand when they are not kneeling, and where there is seating it consists of stools and simple forms, without back-rests. By the later Middle Ages pews* begin to appear, although early ones may be little more than benches.[1]

From the start it is customary for men and women to sit separately, with women usually but not always on the north side of the central aisle, a practice perhaps related to the position among the rood figures of the Virgin Mary, who is always on that side. A vestige of this arrangement is seen in modern weddings, with the bride's party being seated to the north.[2]

> 1459 For amendinge of 2 mens pewes & 1 womans pew with 1d for nails & candels ... 7d (St Michael, Cornhill)

> 1596 To Fowlk Browghton for timber to make sleepers for the boording of the eight longe seates for women on the northe side of the church 2s 6d, and for saweing thereof 6d. (St Michael in Bedwardine, Worcester)[3]

One bold husband who presumes to sit with his wife causes a stir at St Alphage, London Wall, in 1620.

> Whereas we finde ... Mr Lovedaie and his wife sittinge together in one pewe, and that in the ile where men usually do and ere did sit, we hold it most inconvenient and most unseemely, and do thinke it fit that Mr Chancellor of London be made acquainted with it [so] that order maie be had for removing these inconvenients, we having sent for the said Mr Lovedaie to have come unto us into our vestry who refuseth to come unto us.

The stand-off is resolved by the vicar diplomatically inviting both Lovedays to sit in his pew.[4]

Even worse, at Wimborne Minster 'there sits many men and women together which are not husband and wife' (1629). A few years later the Bishop of Norwich's vicar general complains that at West Walton, Norfolk, 'men and women do sit in the seats or stools ... promiscuously together, whereby there is no decency or order observed', and he orders the churchwardens to place 'the parishioners' on one side and 'all their wives or women' on the other.[5]

While such division by gender often proves hard to enforce it persists in some places into relatively modern times. A parish magazine of *circa* 1893 carries the following notice relating to St Andrew, Blofield, Norfolk.

---

* The *OED* derives the word from Old French *puie*, meaning parapet, balustrade or platform.

The rector earnestly requests those who at divine service occupy free seats in the church, to observe the ancient custom of the parish, by which men sit on the north side and women on the south side of the nave. This excellent custom, so conducive to order and devotion, has been scrupulously observed by parishioners for more than 300 years, and it is earnestly hoped that strangers (and others) will conform to it.[6]

It is worth noting that this applies only to the 'free seats', those occupying family pews presumably being at liberty to dispose themselves as they wish.

Some churches also have a pew set aside for women being churched after childbirth. This may be known as the midwives' pew, it being customary for the midwife to accompany the woman to church.

1465 For making of the chirching pewe ... 8d (St Andrew Hubbard)

1617 For making a new pew for the midwives ... £2 5s (St Margaret, Westminster)[7]

However, in several churches the midwives' pew is near the font and it is perhaps associated with baptism rather than (or as well as) with churching.[8]

Segregation also occurs on the basis of age, wealth and social status, with unmarried females sometimes having their own place to sit.[9]

1499-1502 For a pew makeing in the loft for the maidens ... 8d (St Andrew Hubbard)

Backless pews, early 15th century, Cawston, Norfolk

1597 For a bord of 13 foot long and nails for a sete for jentle wimen ... 16d (St Martin, Leicester)

1624 For two formes for the poore to sit on ... 4s (St Mary the Great, Cambridge)[10]

At Great Dunmow, Essex, a complaint arises in 1612 because 'parishioners ... intrude into seates above theire quality'. Similarly at St Ebbe's, Oxford, the wardens step in when an ale bearer and a cobbler move themselves up 'into a higher seate ... not so fit for them ... because that in showe of the worlde they nowe sit above their betters'. At Nettlebed, Oxfordshire, the wardens relocate one Robert Gomme from a good pew because he has fallen in the world, having 'formerly had an hundred accers of grounde belonginge to his house, but now is reduced to twelve accers'.[11]

At St Edmund, Salisbury, an order of 1629 seeks to ensure that the poor sit in the right place.

All the poore of the new almeshouse and all other the church poore shall sit in the church ... upon formes set of purpose for them. And the church-wardens are to see who are missing, and to keepe backe that weekes pay unless they can excuse it. And that the formes may be knowen and not sate upon by others, there shalbe these wordes painted in great red letters upon the forme, *For the Poore*. Neverthelesse old John George, and John Fudges, and Susan Beckett, and such others as have already used stooles may use their former places, if it prove not inconvenient.[12]

Servants, too, may have their allotted place, although it does not ensure good behaviour.

1619 To the carpenter for mending the servants pewe at the lower ende of the churche and for brackets for them ... 2s 2d (St Bartholomew Exchange)

1744 Resolved and agreed, that the three pews under the galery, late Mr Joseph's, be for the use of the maid servants & that the men servants which used to sit in those pews be removed into the old christening pew, some inconvenience having lately arose by their siting intermixt. (Hackney, Middlesex, vestry)[13]

Such pews are usually at the 'lower' or west end of the church, the favoured seating being towards the east end, nearer the clergy and altar and activity of the service, and perhaps to God. Such places are usually occupied by office holders and the rich.

The churchwardens often have a pew to themselves and naturally ensure it is well looked after.

1610 To Goodwife Wells for salt to destroy the fleas in churchwardens pew ... 6d (St Margaret, Westminster)

1621 To Mr Angel for a cortin and matinge and stoffinge the cherch-woodens seet ... 8s 6d (St Bartholomew Exchange)[14]

Good pews are also reserved for local notables such as mayors and aldermen, considerable expense being incurred to make them comfortable and impressive. The mayor's sword and mace also need to be accommodated, as does his wife.

1569 For makinge Mr Alderman a newe pewe and for a locke thereto ... 28s | For 2 boulsters for the seates ... 5s 4d (St Michael, Cornhill)

1633 To Mr Webb uphoulster for his workes done about my lord maior pewe and my ladyes ... £9 4s | To the carver for carving the sword case and two beasts [a lion and a unicorn] ... £2 5s | To the painter for painting and gildinge the sword case ... £2 | 1634 To the gilder for gildinge the beasts at the lord maiors pewe and coulering the doore in the wall ... 13s 4d (St Christopher le Stocks)

1641 G. Pettybone for ye iron frame to set Mr Maiors maces in ... 4s | Painting ditto ... 8d (St Edmund, Salisbury)

1661 For triming up Mrs Mayresses seate ... £1 18s 8d (St Peter Mancroft, Norwich)[15]

Other favoured places are typically paid for, private individuals renting or buying their own seat or pew. At St Mary, Reading, in 1581 a scale of fees is agreed comparable to those in a theatre, 8d a year being payable for the 'opermoste' seats, 6d for the 'next' seats, 4d for the 'seconde and therde' seats, down to 1d for one 'in the seconde range'. At St Mary, Lancaster, in 1710 it is ordered that 'the manner of sale of the seates' is to be by auction, the asking price to fall until somebody bids.[16]

Pew rental is found at least as early as 1409, occurs fairly widely before the Reformation, and becomes commonplace thereafter. While it may sit uneasily with the Christian idea of everyone being equal before God, the income that arises proves irresistible to many parishes.[17]

Places are usually secured for a year or for a lifetime. At Somerton, Somerset, in 1652 'Henry Pate ... nominated Joan his wife and Mary his daughter to be the persons by whose lives he will hold the seate he bought of ye parish ye last yeare, being ye seate next above the vicars wives seate'. Sometimes payment is for the ground only, the parishioner organising construction of the pew themself. At Somerton in 1696, 'Henry Penny buyeth as much ground as to make two seates joining to the font and payeth 5s for one life.'[18]

Because of gender segregation husbands often pay a separate sum for seats for their wives, two of the entries below not therefore being as notable as they sound.

c. 1517 Of William Kalyngale for changinge of his pew ... 8d | Of John Halfpeny for changinge his wives ... 4d (St Edmund, Salisbury)

1549 To the joiner for making and mending of Mr Dobbes pew and his wife ... £4 10s 8d (St Matthew, Friday Street)[19]

Hanging or flapped seats (as *right* at Tintinhull, Somerset) are sometimes attached to the end of a pew, often to accommodate a child or servant. Receipts at St Edmund, Salisbury, in 1651 include 'Mrs An Carter hanging seat for servant 1s', 'Mrs Batter wido a clap seat fixt to her owne for servant 6d', and 'J. Flood ... clap seat for children 6d'.*[20]

Servants may also be otherwise accommodated.

> 1573 Making of a sete before John Friers pewe & Richard Gawntletes for there servantes to set on ... 4d | 1661 Mistris Turblefield a place for her selfe & another for her man ... 15s (St Thomas, Salisbury)[21]

Over time some seats come to be seen as pertaining to particular properties, while others pass on to the next generation.

> 1672 Of Joseph Dunn for his pew belonging to the house wherein he now lives, being the second seat on the south side ... 4d | 1678 Of Thomas Nicholson for his seat in a pew adjoining upon the wall under the buckets, where his father Christo. Nicholson did formerly sit ... 4d (St Nicholas, Durham)[22]

Occasionally a parishioner pays for the erection of a new gallery and as a result is deemed to own the freehold of pews installed there. Such is the case with William Etches at Holy Sepulchre, Northampton, in 1782, and on his death nine years later the pews are put up for sale like any other piece of property. At Ulverston, Lancashire, in 1812 various gallery pews are 'let to the highest bidder, for a term of five years', at a public auction at the White Hart inn. A pew at Bradford is offered for sale in 1851, a newspaper advertisement noting encouragingly that 'the antici-pated alterations in the parish church will no doubt materially increase the value of Pews and Sittings'.[23]

The privatisation of pews becomes apparent in various ways, beginning with the appearance of doors and locks.

> 1466 To a carpenter for mending of the pewes and dores ... 5s 6d | 1467 To a smith for making of a lok to maister Stokker's pew ... 8d (St Michael, Cornhill)

> 1628 Two lockes for Mr Thatchers pewe, one for his seate & the other for his cubbord ... 1s 10d (St Edmund, Salisbury)

> 1736 For a lock with 12 keys for the farmers wives pew ... 6s 6d (Leyton, Essex)[24]

---

* *Clap seat* is probably comparable to *clap-door*, defined by the *OED* as a door or gate which shuts when slammed or which swings to of itself.

Attending church on Christmas morning 1661 Samuel Pepys notes without particular comment that 'at the door of our pew I was fain to stay, because that the sexton had not opened the door'. A while later at St Martin, Leicester, 'to prevent the charge of locking and unlocking the seats', the churchwardens are ordered 'to cause keys to be made, and given to the persons placed in these seats'.[25]

In addition, pews may be marked with numbers or with the names of those entitled to sit in them.

1554-58 For a skin of parchment to write mens names upon ther pewes ...
4d (Lambeth, Surrey)

1569 For paintinge numbers upon pewes ... 6d (St Matthew, Friday Street)

1624 To Jonathan for marking the seat doores ... 2s 6d (St Mary, Reading)[26]

In a few places pew renting has the incidental advantage of leaving records that afford us a glimpse of the changing cast of parish life. Among the 16th-century pew receipts of St Edmund, Salisbury, for example, we find the following.

Hamon the brewer | Owdall the cooper | The crossebowe maker
The foyster* in ye Market place | Robert girdler | Symon Glover
John Maltman | Robert organmaker | John Alen the shomaker
William skinner | Nicholas Taillor | John West ye taner
William tapster | Drewe the wever | Bryan the woodcarver [or 'caryer']
The goodwife of the Blew Bore | One called Margery
A woman sitting under the clock | A Northern man in Castel strete
George Hogeskyns | James Sweetaples | The widowe Bright.

At St Thomas in the same city and period we find, among others, 'Jacob the boucher', 'John the cooke upon the Ditche', 'Percival the painter', 'Margery silke-woman', 'the sope maker' and 'William the spurrier' (spur maker).[27]

Like the above, most parishioners pay simply for particular places in ordinary pews, but the rich naturally want more: their own pews with space, comfort and a degree of privacy. Often they also wish to display their wealth. The result is the box pew which in places develops into a 'parlour' or 'manorial' pew. These are effectively private sitting-rooms, with sides sometimes 6 foot high and their own carpets, armchairs, sofas, tables, curtains, shutters and windows, and occasionally even a fireplace. Some of the grandest are elevated and separate from the main seating area, appearing rather like opera boxes.[28]

Such comforts alarm some clerics, Bishop Corbett of Norwich inveighing against them in an address to his clergy in 1634.

Stately pews are now become tabernacles, with rings and curtains to them.
There wants nothing but beds to hear the word of God on: we have casements,

---

* *Foister*. A cheat (particularly at dice), sharper or pickpocket. It was a new term at this time. Indeed, this instance (1543) predates the earliest one in the *OED* by a decade.

Two Yorkshire manorial pews
UPPER Milbanke pew, Croft on Tees. LOWER Bolton pew, Wensley.

locks and keys, and cushions; I had almost said bolsters and pillows; and for those we love the church. I will not guess what is done within them, who sits, stands, or lies asleep, at prayers, communion, &c., but this I dare say, they are either to hide some vice or to proclaim one; to hide disorder, or proclaim pride.[29]

Writing in 1708, Sir Christopher Wren notes another objection.

A church should not be so fill'd with pews, but that the poor may have room enough to stand and sit in the alleys, for to them equally is the gospel preach'd. It were to be wish'd there were ... no pews, but benches; but there is no stemming the tide of profit, and the advantage of pew-keepers ...[30]

The problem is exemplified a few years earlier at Thame.

1701 We present Mrs Frances Striblehill for ingrossing & makeing two several seates into one large pew & keeping the same locked up ... for her sole & only use which will hold at least twelve persons whereby she has excluded several credible and sufficient inhabitants ... from sitting therein.[31]

A third objection is noted by Gilbert White at Selborne: 'nothing can be more irregular than the pews of this church, which are of all dimensions and heights, being patched up according to the fancy of the owners'.[32]

In addition the arising sense of entitlement to a particular place leads to numerous disputes.

As early as 1287 the Synod of Exeter hears that 'parishioners have often quarrelled on account of seats in churches, two or more persons claiming one seat'. At Terrington, Yorkshire, in 1553 a band of men come into the church in service time 'arayed with swords, bucklers, pikes, staves, ironforks and other weapons'. Their leader Richard Barton, wielding a pitchfork, violently ejects a churchwarden's wife from her accustomed pew and then breaks it into pieces. At Congleton, Cheshire, in 1576 a mare is reportedly led into the church to foul a contested pew, although in the event it 'did not dunge in the said pewe but very nere unto it'. And at St Ebbe's, Oxford, in 1584 a woman complains that when she tried to take her place at evening prayer another woman called Barbara

jostled further into the seate and wolde not let her come into her owne place there, whereupon this respondent sayed unto her, if yowe will not let me come into mye owne seat I will sit upon yor lappe ... and thereupon grewe further wordes of inconvenience betwene them, as *whore* and *basterd* & suche like ...[33]

A short time later the Bishop of Rochester has to adjudicate between a Mr Eliott and a Mrs Twist who both claim a particular pew in Eltham church. He manages to be even-handed by ordering that Eliott is to have the pew and Mrs Twist the place where it stood.[34]

A row at Richmond, Surrey, is less easily resolved. In July 1624 a Mr George Savadge breaks open a pew built by a Mr Hickman and his father and replaces their lock with his own. To reclaim the pew the vestry have Savadge's lock and then Savadge himself forcibly removed. He appeals to the Bishop of Winchester, who orders that Savadge and his wife are to have possession. The vestry in turn appeal, but in vain, so they have the pew demolished, on which Savadge takes the matter to the court of star chamber. The upshot is unknown, except that the vestry are forced to pay over £18 in legal costs, raised by subscription among their number.[35]

In the face of such strife the following seems a good investment.

1622 Paid for drawinge of a map for as conserning the seats for to have the parish in good order ... 4s (Holy Trinity, Chester)[36]

As a result of such problems, and the principled objections indicated above, pew renting comes under attack during the 19th century. 'For what is the history of pues,' asks J. M. Neale in 1841, 'but the history of the intrusion of human pride, and selfishness, and indolence, into the worship of God?' Nonetheless the practice survives in some places into the 20th century.[37]

Questions of ownership aside, much work goes into creating and maintaining pews.

1504-07 To Arnolde Lokear for 23 irnes [irons] to sette candels on for the pewes ... 20d (St Andrew, Canterbury)

1556 Paid John Fleming ... for sawinge of 300 of planks for seates in ye churche ... 4s 6d (Eltham, Kent)

1571 Michel Wigner & his boye 38 daies ... makinge of newe pewes at the east end of the church &c. ... £3 3s 4d | 3 li. of candels for him to worke with ... 12d (St Thomas, Salisbury)[38]

The following adjustments appear rather pointed.

1592 For making Mrs Wiseman's pew-door wider ... 1s 4d (St Laurence Pountney)

1621 For enlarging ye seate where Mrs Sparrow setteth ... 2s 6d (St Mary the Great, Cambridge)[39]

Some pew ends are embellished with fine carvings, including the ornamental finials known as poppy-heads.

1571 For the carvinge of 27 poppee heeds ... 36s (St Martin in the Fields)

1572 For the cutting of the 7 beastes for to stand on the new pewes ... 9s (St Matthew, Friday Street)[40]

Further expense may be incurred to ease the devotions of the occupants.

1538 For mats for the parishioners to kneel upon when they reverenced their Maker ... 4s 4d (St Margaret, Westminster)

1571 For a long mat for the poor to knelle on ... 8d (All Hallows Staining)[41]

Pews may also be provided with straw for warmth and comfort. At Barrow on Humber, Lincolnshire, the parish clerk is responsible for having a load delivered to the church stile before Easter and Christmas each year and then laying it in the seats.[42]

Clockwise from upper left
Poppy head and hare, Combs, Suffolk.
Bench end, Crowcombe, Somerset.
Straw hassock, Dorset.
Bench elbow, All Saints,
South Elmham, Suffolk.

9. Pulpit, hour glass, lectern

Ahead of the pews, usually where the nave meets the chancel, and north of the central aisle, stands the pulpit (from Latin *pulpitum*, scaffold, platform, stage).

Pulpits are recorded at least as early as the 14th century, but they only become commonplace after the Reformation, which brings with it an increased emphasis on preaching and other communication between minister and congregation. They are usually reached by steps or a ladder, perhaps with a rail for support.[1]

> 1575 For a longe iron to go up by into the pulpit ... 3s 2d (St Ethelburga, Bishopsgate)

> 1605 For mending the door and ladder for the pulpit ... 6s 7d (Mortlake, Surrey)[2]

The extra element in the following sounds promising.

> 1721 For stairs to the pulpit and a trap door ... 12s 6d (Hawkshead, Lancs)[3]

Light is provided for the preacher to read by and so that he can be seen the better, being particularly necessary at evening services and in the darker months.

> 1567 For a kandlesticke to hange upon the pulpit ... 3d (St Martin, Leicester)

> 1597 For kandles for Doctor Crooke his sermons ... 5s 3d (St Peter, Cheapside)[4]

There is often a finely made pulpit cushion on which to rest the bible. Materials used include 'greene kersey' and 'perpetuana'* (St Bartholomew Exchange), 'yellow serge' and 'Padua serge' (Youlgreave; St Oswald, Durham), and 'feathers' or 'flocke' for the stuffing (St Nicholas, Durham; Wandsworth). There may also be an ornamented pulpit cloth. At Chester-le-Street twelve yards of 'sparkie velvet' (spotted with gold or similar material) are used for one.[5]

After the Reformation there may also be an hour glass to regulate the length of sermons, held by one of a variety of fittings and perhaps having an accompanying light.[6]

> 1564 For an hour-glass, that hangeth by the pulpit, when the preacher doth make a sermon, that he may know how the hour passeth away ... 1s (St Katharine Cree, Leadenhall Street)

> 1581 For a turned piller to set ye hower glass upon ... 8d (Bishop's Stortford)

> 1602 For a sandglasse ... 18d | To William Maye for setting of a litle borde by the chauncell dore for the sandglasse to stand on ... 2d (Hartland, Devon)

---

* *Kersey.* A coarse narrow cloth woven from long wool, perhaps originally made at the village of that name in Suffolk. *Perpetuana.* A woollen fabric, apparently named in reference to its ability to endure.

1603 To the smithe for mendinge the houreglas candlesticke ... 2d (St Mary, Reading)[7]

Popular 17th-century preachers are sometimes encouraged by congregations to turn the glass and preach for a second hour, but in time glasses of shorter duration appear. They are presumably a welcome sight to many.

c. 1664 Three glasses, one running an hour, another three quarters, and a third half an hour. (St Giles without Cripplegate, inventory)

1716 For a 20 minute glass ... 1s (All Saints, Newcastle)[8]

Queen Victoria goes slightly better, having an 18 minute glass installed when the Chapel Royal at the Savoy is refurbished in 1867.[9]

In the 17th century 'two-decker' pulpits appear comprising a desk below, for conducting the service and reading the lesson, and a pulpit above, sometimes topped with a sounding board to help project the preacher's voice.

1641 For making of the sounding board ... 18s (St Clement, Ipswich)

1689 To Mr Starling for painting and gilding the sounding board and polpitt ... £3 (St Benedict, Norwich)[10]

Hour glass fittings at Chelmondiston, Suffolk (*left*) and Compton Bassett, Wiltshire

Bulbous elaboration is common, both on any board and on the pulpit itself.

1606 For a cover for the pulpit ... with 5 turned bobbs ... 11s (Holy Trinity, Chester)

1723 For knobs for ye pulpit ... 11d (Duffield, Derbyshire)[11]

UPPER
Sounding board,
Lenham, Kent,
dated 1622 but
possibly earlier.

LOWER
Jacobean pulpit,
Chesterfield,
Derbyshire.

There is also the less common 'three-decker' in which a clerk's desk is added at the bottom. At Whitby, Yorkshire, there is a mechanical contrivance for raising or lowering the floor of this section so that, whether the clerk is tall or short, he can always be seen and heard.[12]

Hogarth's 'The Sleeping Congregation', 1736, showing a two-decker pulpit complete with pulpit cushion, hour glass and sounding board. While the minister preaches, his usual position is occupied by a clerk with a roving eye.

If not part of a two or three-decker, a reading desk or lectern may stand across from the pulpit, usually on the south side of the central aisle. Sometimes its upper part is of brass and in the form of an eagle, symbol of St John the Evangelist, carrying the word of God on its outstretched wings.

> 1560 For skowring ye eagle & candell stickes ... 10d | For mending of ye eagle's taile ... 16d (Holy Trinity, Coventry)

> 1686 Paid Zachary Gower for bringing the eagle to towne and carrying it back to church ... 1s 6d | Gave the men that helped to carry it to the carte and carrying it up to the church ... 6d (Redenhall, Norfolk)[13]

Eagle
lectern,
1518,
St Mary
the Virgin,
Wiggenhall,
Norfolk

10. Mass: a digression before entering the chancel

Before proceeding east into the chancel it is worth noting some changes over time in the handling of the central act of Christian worship known as communion or the eucharist (from the Greek for 'thanksgiving') as celebrated in the service called mass (from Latin *missa*, dismissal, from *mittere,* to send, probably relating to the dismissal of the congregation at the service's end).

Christians believe that, as a result of being consecrated by a priest, the bread and wine used in the service become the body and blood of Christ, hence one alternative name used for the bread: the host, from Latin *hostia*, victim, sacrifice. It is also often referred to as the sacrament, from Latin *sacrare*, to consecrate, and as the eucharist.

In 1215 early differences of view as to whether these changes are merely symbolic or involve a change 'in substance' are addressed at the Fourth Lateran Council. It affirms the doctrine of Transubstantiation – that the eucharistic elements (bread and wine) are indeed converted in substance. This naturally raises the perceived importance of the mass, along with that of the clergy and of the eastern end of the church where the ceremony is performed. One result is that, to protect the mass's mystery and sanctity, this part of the church comes to be screened off from the relatively worldly arena that is the nave: hence the name chancel, from Latin *cancelli*, bars of lattice work.

The same council rules that all Christians should receive the sacrament at least once a year, at Easter. In practice most people merely fulfil this minimum requirement, and when they do so they receive bread but not wine because communion 'in both kinds' (bread and wine) comes to be restricted to the clergy.* They may also be kept out of the chancel, receiving the bread, in the form of a wafer, at the junction between nave and chancel, although practice varies on this point.[1]

The result is that in the later Middle Ages the average person's experience of the central action in the church's life is very limited. They participate actively only once a year and are largely barred from the part of the church where the transformation of the elements is believed to take place. The service is conducted in a language (Latin) they do not understand and often *sotto voce* such as to be barely audible in the nave.

---

* Anxious to suppress any sense of Christ being divided into parts, the medieval Church insists that he is present in his totality in both bread and wine. 'By the power of the sacrament there is contained under … the species of the bread, not only the flesh, but the entire body of Christ' (Thomas Aquinas, *Summa Theologiae, c.* 1270). 'Let priests ... take care when they give the holy communion ... diligently to instruct [those receiving] that the body and blood of our Lord is given to them at once under the species of bread' (Council of Lambeth, 1281). According to William Lyndwood, an eminent 15th-century authority on Church law, two reasons for administering only bread are first, 'on account of the danger that the blood [wine] could easily be spilt', and second, that 'it would not be decent or secure' to consecrate and administer the large quantities of wine needed in populous parishes. Such justifications notwithstanding, the restriction evidently increases the sense that the celebrating priesthood stands apart from and above the laity.

Communion in both kinds (*left*) and in one kind only

They are, however, expected to be present at mass each Sunday, when the best they can do is to look on through the gaps in the rood screen as the service unfolds. The climax is the 'elevation', when the priest holds up the bread, indicating that it has been transformed into the body of Christ and offering it to God while also exhibiting it for human adoration. Alternatively the parishioner may sit or kneel in the nave and be alerted that the elevation is about to take place by the ringing of a small bell known as the sacring bell. As *The Lay Folks Mass Book* explains,

Looking in and on, *c.* 1470

Then is time nigh of sacring, | A little bell he will to us ring.
Then is reason that we do reverence | To Jesus Christ's presence,
That may loose all baleful bonds. | Therefore kneeling hold up thine hands,
And with inclinacion of thy body, | Behold the elevation reverently.[2]

Whether such limitations reduce the importance of the mass to the ordinary churchgoer, or whether paradoxically its being mysterious and remote renders it the more valued and effective, we cannot of course know. In addition it should be noted that, as seen earlier, in most churches masses are regularly performed at side altars which are relatively accessible and allow parishioners a closer view of proceedings.[3]

Reformer Thomas Becon sees the elevation as the 'most wicked and abominable' part of the mass and mocks all involved.

They believe that bread which the priest heaveth above his head to be Christ ... Therefore kneel they down unto it, knock their breasts, lift up their hands, worship and honour it. When the bell once rings, if they cannot conveniently see, they forsake their seats and run from altar to altar, from sacring to sacring, peeping here and touting there, and gazing at that thing which the pilled-pate priest holdeth up in his hands. And if the priest be weak in the arms, and heave not up high enough, the rude people of the country in divers parts of England will cry out to the priest, 'Hold up, Sir John, hold up; heave it a little higher.' And one will say to another, 'Stoop down, thou fellow afore, that I may see my Maker: for I cannot be merry except I see my lord God once in a day.'

There is in fact more at stake than merriness, it being believed that seeing the host brings protection for the rest of the day from hunger, blindness and sudden death.

Becon also takes aim at the marginal role assigned to the laity.

Christ's ordinance is not that one standing at an altar should eat, devour, and munch up altogether alone, but that a multitude should receive the sacramental bread and wine together. 'Take ye,' saith our saviour Christ, 'eat ye, and drink ye all of this.' He saith not, 'Take thou, Sir John, eat thou, and drink thou all alone.'[4]

A Protestant view of the elevation, from the 1570 edition of John Foxe's Book of Martyrs. With metaphorical fanfare the wafer is raised. Among the tonsured clergy gathered round, one holds a sacring bell and another a holy water bucket with an aspergillum (sprinkle).

11. The chancel before the Reformation

If we stand alongside a pre-Reformation parishioner looking through the gaps in the rood screen into the chancel, we see a stage set for the drama of the mass.

Against the east wall is the high altar, so called to distinguish it from any side and other altars found elsewhere in the church. It is usually made of stone, or at least has a stone *mensa* (Latin, table) or surface slab which has to be consecrated before mass can be celebrated on it. In preparation five crosses (representing the five wounds of Christ) are incised indicating places to be anointed, one at each corner and one in the centre. There also needs to be a 'sepulchre' or enclosed hollow space within (or perhaps below) the *mensa* to serve as a resting place for relics, ideally relating to the saint to whom the church is dedicated.

The ceremony, performed by the bishop, is described by Thomas Becon.

> At ye four corners of ye altar he shall make four crosses with holy water. ... [He] shall go seven times about the altar, and seven times he shall wash the table of the altar, or altar stone, with holy water, having a holy water sprinkle made of hyssop. ... In the four corners of the sepulchre, wherein ye reliques are laid, the bishop shall make four crosses with ye cream [chrism] and ye reliques shall be laid up in a bag with three grains of franck-encense, and put again in the sepulchre. ... The stone, which is called the table, shall be made meet [fitting], and laid upon the altar, and ... the bishop shall anoint it with oil in five places, and likewise shall he afterward do with the cream ... The bishop also shall confirm the altar in the forehead or forefront with a cross of cream, and shall burn franckencense upon the altar in five places. After all these things be done, ye altar shall be covered with fair cloths, and the priest may now lawfully sing mass upon it, when he will.[1]

Another account adds that the relics are laid up on the preceding night and borne to the altar in procession with garlands carried before. Prior to the interment the bishop prepares plaster with holy water, and, having placed 'the little vessel of reliques in the grave of the altar', he sings an antiphon, 'Ye have a resting place under the altar of God, O ye saints, intercede for us to the lord Jesus Christ, &c.' Later he lays on the plaster and places a stone on the sepulchre opening, ready for masons who are in attendance to 'make firm'.[2]

Placing relics,
from an early 15th-century pontifical

Anointing altar front, 1520

As Becon indicates, the altar is covered by a rich cloth. This is sometimes referred to as a carpet, in the now obsolete sense of a thick fabric used to cover tables, beds, et cetera, and it is kept in place by a hair-cloth beneath.

> 1519 For 3 yerdes of hereclothe ... to covere the heye auter ... 12d (Lambeth)

> 1552 Three carpetes for the communion table, one of blew clothe of golde, another of red velvet with roses and starres, and ye thirde of blew silke with lions of golde. (St Benet, Gracechurch Street, inventory)[3]

Upon the cloth sit candlesticks and sometimes (but not always) a cross.[4]

> 1516 I bequeth two tapers of 2 li. of wax every peece, to be kept on the two greate candlesticks before the highe aulter to burne at time of Gods divine service the terme of 30 yeres. (will of Thomas Burston, Milton by Gravesend, Kent)[5]

Above the altar is suspended the pyx, a container made of wood, metal or ivory, sometimes in the shape of a dove. It contains the reserved sacrament – a consecrated wafer kept securely out of reach in this way but ready in case it should be necessary to carry it at short notice to the sick or dying. It usually hangs on a chain operated by a pulley and is protected by a canopy or veil of fine fabric. It should have a lock – the Lateran Council of 1215 orders that the sacrament be kept securely such that it might not 'be reached by rash and indiscreet persons and used for impious and blasphemous purposes' – and the wafer within should be renewed every Sunday.[6]

> 1478-80 For mending of the boxe that the sacrament hangith in ... 6d (St Andrew Hubbard)

> 1525 For 12 yerds of chening to henge up the sacrementes over the auter ... 2s 2d (Prescot, Lancs)[7]

LEFT Pyx in the shape of a dove, French, early 13th century. The small door on its back conceals a cavity into which the wafer is placed. RIGHT 15th-century pyx with a ring on the top and a lock on the side. It was found near Exning church, Suffolk, in 1845 along with altar candlesticks, probably having been buried at the time of the Reformation.

To the north of the altar there should be an image of the church's patron saint, often upon a corbel or within a niche beside the east window, and to the south there may be a corresponding image of the Virgin Mary.[8]

Near the altar, perhaps in the south-east corner of the chancel, is a piscina (Latin for fishpond), a stone basin used for the ritual washing of the vessels used at mass. Nearby, probably recessed in the chancel's south wall, are sedilia (from Latin *sedere*, to sit), a series of stone seats, usually three in number, for the use of the priest, deacon and sub-deacon during the ceremony. In addition there may be wooden seats or stalls towards the west end of the chancel for the use of the clergy and perhaps also of a few high status parishioners.

The chancel may also have a low side window, usually on the south side and below a larger one. In the 19th and early 20th centuries a number of theories were advanced to explain these apertures – for example that they were to enable lepers to receive communion, or for firing arrows out of should the church be attacked – but it is now thought that they were simply for ventilation, a pressing need given the enclosed nature of the pre-Reformation chancel and the large quantities of candles and incense burnt here. The seriousness of the problem is indicated by a cost incurred at the funeral of John Paston at Bromholm Priory, Norfolk, in 1466.

> To the glaser for takin owte of 2 panes of the windows of the churche for to lete owte the reke of the torches at the dirige and soldering new of the same ... 20d[9]

ABOVE. LEFT Figure of patron saint (St Peter) in its traditional position, Wilmington, Sussex. RIGHT Low side window, Branscombe, Devon.

BELOW Piscina and sedilia, Alfriston, Sussex.

Opposite the sedilia, in or against the chancel's north wall, there may be an Easter sepulchre, representing Christ's tomb. On Good Friday each year a cross and the host (representing Christ's body) are placed inside it (the *depositio*) and on Easter Sunday they are retrieved (the *elevatio*), in re-enactment of the burial and the resurrection.*

Its location here may arise from a wish to imitate the holy sepulchre in Jerusalem, early pilgrim accounts, such as that of Arculf of Gaul in the late 7th century, describing Christ's sepulchre as being cut in the rock on the north side of the tomb.[10]

In a few cases it further echoes the original by being a permanent stone structure, ranging from a simple arched recess in the wall to an elaborately carved monument set against it.† However, most Easter sepulchres are temporary wooden ones that can be put up and taken down each year.[11]

> 1426 For the sepulcre, for divers nailes & wires & glu ... 9d ob. | To Thomas Joynour for makinge of the same sepulchre ... 4s (St Mary at Hill)

> 1536 For a peece of timber for the sepulcer ... 10d | To the joiner for working of the timber in the sepulcer ... 14d (St Mary the Great, Cambridge)[12]

Most wooden versions probably take the form of a gabled coffer or chest.

> 1549 The sepulchre chest that stode in the quere sold for 20s. (All Hallows the Great, Thames Street)[13]

Such a coffin-like form accords with their role as a resting place for a body. Moreover, they are commonly set upon wooden frames that resemble in some respects the biers used to carry corpses and the hearse frames set about them at funerals.‡[14]

> 1554 For a frame to set the sepulker on ... 2d (St Mary, Shrewsbury)[15]

Alternatively they may be placed upon stone tombs, which are sometimes designed with this function in mind, local eminences liking to associate their own sepulture with that of Christ.

> 1514 My body to be buried within the quere ... on the north side, where as the sepulcre is accustomed to stande, in the wiche place I will a tombe of marble to be made, with my picture and myn armes garnisshid theron, with a vawte rising up by the wall, coming over the same stone of marble, so that at Easter time the sepulcre maye be there set to thonour of allmighty God. (will of Robert Morley, Glynde, Sussex)[16]

---

* The ceremonies are described on pp225-229 and pp233-235.

† Traditionally such structures have been considered Easter sepulchres, but more recently it has been suggested that some may have been built as 'tombs of Christ', not least because their openings are not large enough to allow for the ready insertion and removal of an altar cross. If this is correct they may have been used in Easter ceremonies, but their main purpose was to represent Christ's burial place throughout the year.

‡ On biers and hearses see pp333-342; also p489 for a sepulchre turned into a bier.

Two Sussex sepulchres: Selmeston (*left*) and Alfriston. The former is dated 1532 and, like many others, is a personal tomb designed with Easter use in mind.

Many sepulchres are aptly adorned with carved or painted panels featuring figures from the resurrection story, for example sleeping soldiers, representing the guard set to watch the tomb, and one or more angels, representing the angel which rolled back the stone from its door. Often the angels are four in number, suggesting one at each corner.[17]

1518 To a smith for hokes & staples for the 4 angelles on the sepulcre [etc] ... 6d (St Mary at Hill)[18]

A particularly elaborate sepulchre is given to St Mary Redcliffe, Bristol, by Nicholas Canynges in 1470. It has a cover, is 'well gilte with fine golde', and includes the following elements.

Heven, made of timber and steined clothes.
Hell, made of timber and iron worke, with devells the number of 13.
The holy goste coming out of heven into the sepulchre.
An image of God Almighty rising oute of the same sepulchre.
4 knightes armed, kepinge the sepulchre with their wepons in their hands.
4 peir of angels winges for 4 angels made of timber and well peinted.
Belonging to 4 angels, 4 chevelers [wigs].[19]

Easter sepulchres at Patrington, Yorkshire (*left*) and Holcombe Burnell, Devon (*above*), with details on the facing page.

The inscription at Patrington, on either side of the veiled recess, reads 'Alleluia, Alleluia.'

12. The chancel after the Reformation

If we return after the Reformation several changes will have occurred, although in some parishes the process takes many years. Any images, including that of the patron, have been removed. The sepulchre is no longer set up at Easter. Stone altars have given way to wooden communion tables. As for mass, the term itself is now considered to have Romish connotations and gives way to 'communion'.* The service is conducted in English. Those taking part do so slightly more often,† and they receive both bread and wine, reflecting the belief that everyone, not just the clergy, should communicate directly and fully with God. The resulting increase in wine consumption leads to the replacement of slender chalices with larger communion cups.[1]

> 1571 Paid John Ions [Jones] goldsmith for changing the chalice into a
>   cup ... £1 15s 5d (St Petrock, Exeter)[2]

There is less certainty as to where the bread and wine are received and the position of the altar or table, these things entering a state of flux in the century or so after the Reformation as conservatives and reformers seek to impose their differing views.[3]

When and where reformers hold sway the table, as they prefer to call it, is moved westwards, to the lower end of the chancel or into the nave, and is sometimes orientated west-east, rather than north-south, such changes reflecting their belief that communion is not a miraculous re-enactment but merely a commemorative supper. In addition, if the floor of the chancel or its eastern end had previously been raised above that of the nave it may be lowered to reduce the sense of hierarchy.

> 1576 To Patrick ... for 5 days worke 2s 6d & to Danalt Holland for 3 days
>   & halph [half] to make the quier even 21d. | For 6 women to carry the
>   earth to level the quere at several times ... 18d (Holy Trinity, Chester)[4]

When the more hierarchically inclined have their way – notably in the 1630s under Archbishop Laud – the importance of the table or altar is underlined by having it placed firmly at the east end of the chancel. It is also protected by a rail, the bars of which are set sufficiently close to keep out marauding canines. In 1636 Bishop Wren of Norwich orders that there should be rails 'from the north wall to the south wall, neere one yarde in height, so thick with pillars that dogs may not get in'. Two years later his successor enquires whether rails are 'close enough to keepe out little dogs or cats from going in and prophaning that holy place, from pissing against it, or worse'.[5]

---

* The 1549 edition of the Book of Common Prayer refers inclusively to 'The Supper of the Lord and the Holy Communion, commonly called the Mass', but 'mass' is omitted in later editions.
† According to the 1552 Book of Common Prayer, 'every parishioner shall communicate at the least three times in the year, of which Easter [is] to be one'.

Laud himself relates a case in point in Cambridgeshire.

There happened ... in the town of Tadlow a very ill
accident on Christmas-day, 1638, by reason of not
having the communion table railed in ... For in sermon
time a dog came to the table, and took the loaf of bread
prepared for the holy sacrament, in his mouth, and ran
away with it. Some of the parishioners took the same
from the dog, and set it again upon the table. After
sermon, the minister could not think fit to consecrate
this bread; and other fit for the sacrament was not to
be had in that town; and the day so far spent, they
could not send for it to another town: so there was no
communion.[6]

The importance of the altar is often further underlined by raising the floor level.

1636 To James Prat for making & setting up the railes before ye commu-
nion table ... 45s | For fetching the said railes from Bungay ... 1s 4d |
For a days worke to Joseph Goody in helping to raise ye floore in the
chancell, where ye communion table standeth ... 1s (Stockton, Norfolk)[7]

After the Restoration in 1660 things settle down and the Laudian arrangement
becomes the norm, with the rail before the altar serving as a convenient place at
which to distribute the bread and the wine.

Receiving communion at the altar rail, 1717

The Reformation also heralds the end of rood lofts, at the chancel's junction with the nave. As for the screen below, in some churches it is removed or reduced, giving the parishioners in the nave a relatively clear view of the altar.

> 1574 For making the particion of the chauncell lower [etc] ... 53s 6d (Hawkhurst, Kent)

> 1577 To Nobbe ye sexton for making clean of the churche after the putting down of the particon between the chauncell & churche ... 6d (Bungay)[8]

According to William Harrison in his 'Description of Britaine' (1577), 'wheras there was wont to be a great particion betweene the quire and the body of the church, nowe it is either very small or none at all'. However, many screens survive, the official position being that where there is 'a comely partition betwixt the chancel and the church' it should be retained, and 'where no partition is standing' one should be made (royal order, 1561).[9]

13. The vestry

The church's vestry, provided it has one, is often located near the chancel. As the name indicates its primary use is to store the clergy's vestments and to provide a robing and disrobing space, serving in effect as the church's backstage.

> 1750 A looking glass for the vestry ... 1s (St Martin, Salisbury)[1]

It is also used for other storage

> 1588 For new articles because the myse had eaten up the other in the cubberd in the vestrye ... 4d (All Hallows Staining)[2]

and for church meetings, with the result that 'the vestry' comes to be used to indicate a group of parishioners who meet and take decisions regarding parish affairs.

Those meeting or otherwise spending time here need to be kept warm.

> 1536 For 2 bushels of coles for the vestre agenst Cristmas ... 6d (Lydd, Kent)

> 1648 For a paire fire irons for the vestry ... 3s | More for fireshovel, tongs and bellowes ... 4s (Fulham, Middlesex)

> 1829 For turf for vestry fire ... 1s 6d (Chipping, Lancs)[3]

Any chimney may need attention from time to time.

> 1773 For a boy going up ye vestry chimney ... 3d (Tooting, Surrey)[4]

Other needs also arise.

> 1621 For on urinall in the vestry ... 2d (St Bartholomew Exchange)

> 1657 For biskett & writing paper for the vestry ... 1s 6d (St Christopher le Stocks)[5]

Any efforts to create comfort may fall short. On 8th March 1736 the vestry of St Mary, Bury St Edmunds, retires to the Three Tuns 'on account of its being damp and cold' in the church, and many another meeting is similarly adjourned.[6]

14. Organs and other musical instruments

During the Middle Ages ordinary parishes may simply use a pipe or two to establish pitch at the start of singing, but during the century or so prior to the Reformation many acquire an organ. After the Reformation, however, the number of organs declines markedly under the influence of puritans, who tend to regard church music much as they regard images, as a sensual and therefore decadent distraction from the real business of worship.[1]

> 1548 To Betts of Wetherden for removinge of the orgaynes ... 5s 4d
> (Boxford, Suffolk)

> 1570 To a bricklear for mending the place where the orgaines stood ... 18d
> (St Clement Danes, Strand)[2]

The process is patchy and localised, and some organs remain in place, but it is only after the Restoration that they come to be uncontentious and widely found again.

There are three basic elements in the construction of early organs: the bellows or other wind-raising device; the chest, with pipes of differing lengths attached so as to produce different notes; and the keyboard, which controls the admission of wind into the pipes.[3]

The larger versions are called positives, from the fact that they occupy a fixed position. Smaller, portable versions, which can be played in procession or at outdoor entertainments, are known as portatives.

> 1517 Payed unto Joyes orgayenmaker in parte of payement for a new paier of smale organes called portatifs beside the stuff of the olde organes to him delivered ... 23s 5d (St Andrew, Canterbury)[4]

Positive and portative organs, from the Peterborough Psalter, early 14th century

Old Parish Life

As seen earlier, before the Reformation any organ may well be in the rood loft. If so, and it survives the loft's removal, it may well be relocated to a new one constructed at the west end of the church and incorporating timber from the earlier loft.[5]

A new organ is a major investment, the following being just a few of the costs incurred at St Edmund, Salisbury, in 1567.

> To Thomas Milbridge for caryenge of 2 letters to ye organ maker of South Molton ... 5s
>
> Bought of Hary Bekingame 3 skore fote of elmen borde to make the bellos ... 3s
>
> 2 dosen of shepes skins & 4 calves skins* ... 12s
>
> A white wine caske to make ye pipes ... 2s 6d | 2 yerdes of Jene fustian† and 2 yerdes of pampillon to cast ye pipes upon ... 2s 6d
>
> A pan to make fire in ... 1d | 4 sackes of coles ... 16d | Dry wood ... 20d
>
> Iron work ... 6s 11d | Pound of wier ... 11d
>
> Halfe a hondred of dry borde ... 3s 4d | 12 nailes ... 2d | 2 hondred of golde ... 12s
>
> 7 wenscottes ... 34s | Ye porters for lodinge of them ... 3d | Ye caryenge home ye wenscottes ... 3s | At ye gate for custome ... 6d
>
> Collars [colours] to paint with ... 6d | Painters oile ... 4d
>
> To ye organ maker for makinge of ye organs ... £12
>
> Walter Crede for ye makinge of the roddes & iron work for the curtains of the organs ... 18d
>
> Thred, inkell,‡ ringes & makinge of the curtains ... 16d | Cordes to ye same ... 6d
>
> Seate for the organs for Bluet to sit and playe ... 6s 8d[6]

There also tends to be a good deal of expenditure on tuning and maintenance over the years.

> 1521 Paid Winsborough the monke of Crists Churche [Canterbury] for mending the grete organes ... 3s 4d (St Mary, Sandwich, Kent)
>
> 1525 To the organmakers servant for skoring of the pipes of the organs ... 4d (St Martin Outwich)
>
> 1532 To ye organ maker for a reward for tuening of ye pipes ... 12d | Spent on him & divers of the cumpany at ye ale howse ... 6d (St Mary at Hill)
>
> 1542 For fetching of the orgon makers tools from Baldok ... 8d (Bishop's Stortford)

* Also for the bellows.

† A twilled cotton cloth, its name apparently derived from Genoa in Italy. Later shortened to 'jean'.

‡ *Inkle.* A kind of linen tape.

1550 To John Howe for mending of ten pipes and other falts that the rats had eaten in our organs and for candell and coles ... 10s 3d (St Benet, Gracechurch Street)

1641 To Mr Hayward of Bath for making the organ musical ... £1 10s (Somerton, Somerset)[7]

The stated and apparent trades of some of those employed is notable, those who work with leather often attending to the bellows.

1472 To William Plomer and William Sadeler for amending of the windbagge of the organes ... 6d | For a skinne to the same ... 3d (Andover, Hants)

1525 To Thomas Crown, shomaker, for mending of owre organnes ... 27s 8d (All Hallows Staining)

1565 To Mr Tanner for mendinge the bellies of the great organs ... 3s 4d (Ludlow)[8]

Those who play the instrument also need paying. They include children, monks, and one of the great composers of the Tudor age.

1460-65 To Thomas the childe for pleyinge at the orgonnes ... 4s 4d (St Andrew Hubbard)

1513 To a blak frier in Estir holidais for to pley atte orgayns ... 16d (St Mary the Great, Cambridge)

1536 To Thomas Tallis for half [a] yeres wages ... £4 (St Mary at Hill)[9]

Payment may come with conditions attached.

1756 March 29th. Agreed that Mr Wm. Bolton be organist so long as he behaves well at £10 per annum. (St Martin, Leicester, vestry)[10]

Every organist needs someone to operate the bellows, a menial job often done by a recipient of parish charity.

1524 To the 3 almesmen, to every of them 2d for theire weke when they do blow the organs ... 8s 8d | 1527 To Balaham for blowing of the organs for a year ... 8s 8d | 1529 For blowing of the organs in the Christemas holydays when Balaham was sike ... 4d (St Mary at Hill)

1549 To a man that blew the bellowes to the mender of the ... orgaynes for 2 days and a halfe ... 12d (St Edmund, Salisbury)

1557 To Jerarde the bedeman for his wages for blowinge of the organ bellowes for one yere ... 2s (Mere, Wilts)

1714 [Ordered] that John Ballards blind daughter be organ blower ... (St Giles without Cripplegate, vestry)

1754 Sarah Palmer blowing the organ bellows 1 quarter and keeping the curtains a year ... 15s 6d (Hackney, Middlesex)[11]

Painted pipes and part of the case of a celebrated organ at Framlingham, Suffolk.
The organ was built by Thomas Thamar in 1674 but the case is believed to be older.

While the process is referred to as 'blowing', the bellows are operated by hand, and a rope or cord or wooden staff may be involved.

1529 For a rope for the bellowes of the orgons ... ob. (St Mary at Hill)

1537 For a staffe for the belowes ... 4d (St Mary the Great, Cambridge)

1542 For a corde to blowe our lady organs ... 1d (Ludlow)[12]

In addition to or instead of an organ, from at least the early 18th century churches use a range of smaller instruments to accompany singing, the bassoon being a popular choice.[13]

1751 Gave Ben. Jones to buy reeds for ye basoon ... 3s (Youlgreave, Derbyshire)

1769 To a base vile ... £2 2s | 1781 For repairing the bass viel ... £1 1s (East Budleigh, Devon)

1809 For 2 clarinets for the choir ... £5 5s (Edenbridge, Kent)

1826 For fiddel strings ... 7s (Helpston, Northants)[14]

Angelic musician in stone, north porch,
Barton le Street, Yorkshire

15. Clocks and chimes

Leaving the main part of the church we move to the tower or steeple, commonly located at the west end and where any clock is probably to be found.

The way up may be dark and precarious.

1549 For a ladder to go up to the clok ... 4d (Ludlow)

1554 For a li. of candells serving to light me to the clocke ... 2d ob. (Wandsworth)[1]

Clocks are recorded in cathedrals in the 13th and 14th centuries and during the 15th century are installed in a number of parish churches.[2]

Properly 'clock' indicates a device which sounds the hours, and perhaps its divisions, by strokes upon a bell, deriving as it does from Continental terms for a bell (French *cloche*, German *glocke*). However, early records also refer separately to 'chimes'. For example, in his will of 1463 John Baret of Bury St Edmunds bequeaths 8s a year to the sexton of St Mary's in the town, 'to kepe the clokke, take hede [heed] to the chimes, [and] winde up the peis and the plummes* as ofte as nede is, so that the seid chimes faile not to go'. According to one authority 'chime' refers specifically to 'the mechanism striking the quarters or playing a tune of more than four notes', although in church accounts it is used more loosely.[3]

Most early chimes involve a rotating barrel on the surface of which iron pins or pegs are set in sequence, much as musical notation is set on a page. The tune to be played is first pricked out (written or set down by means of pricks or notes) by a musician, and then the chime-maker can get to work.

1638 To Mr Heardson the organist for prickinge the tune to the chimes ... 6s 8d | For my selfe and my horse to go to Hereford to fetch John Silvester to make the chimes ... 5s | Paid John Silvester for makeinge the chimes ... £6 10s (Ludlow)

1739 Paid Prick for cleaning the chimes and putting on 'Britain strike Home' ... 12s (St Mary, Bury St Edmunds)

1794 Paid Mr Whitehurst's bill for setting a tune on the chimes – 'God save the King' ... £5 5s (All Saints, Derby)[4]

Once installed the barrel is driven by a lever from the clock, and as it revolves each pin trips a key that causes a hammer to strike on a particular bell. Chimes may be located at a distance from the clock and connected to it by wire. In some cases the striking is done by mechanical figures of men called Jacks, those striking the quarters being known as Quarter Jacks.

1498 For the setting of Jak with the hanging of his bell & mending his hand ... 4d (St Lawrence, Reading)[5]

---

* *Peise.* Weight used to move the mechanism of a clock. *Plumb.* A lump of lead used as a weight in a clock, from Latin *plumbum*, lead (a plumber originally being one who dealt or worked in lead).

19th-century clock face on the tower at Cullompton, Devon

FACING PAGE. UPPER Two Suffolk Jacks. The one at Blythburgh (*left*) probably dates from 1682 or earlier and formerly held a hammer in his left hand. Jack the Smiter of Southwold (*right*) dates from the 15th century. LOWER 15th-century clock face inside the church at Raunds, Northamptonshire, with the 24 hours marked around the circumference. The earliest church clocks probably only had interior dials in this way, but payments for exterior ones occur at Rye in 1515 and at St Lawrence, Reading, six years later.

The installation of a clock and dial at St Mary, Reading, is recorded in detail in 1611.

> To Robert Duglas the clockmaker for coming twise to confer about the clocke before it was agreed on ... 2s
>
> For takinge downe of the plancke oute of the belfrie which was for the dial ... 6d
>
> For sawinge the plancke and for caringe of him to the joiner ... 1s
>
> To the joiner for makinge of the frame for the dial [etc] ... 10s 6d
>
> To Milksop for two sheetes of leade waiinge [230] poundes, and for five poundes of solder ... 30s
>
> To Prince for makinge the frame that the clocke standithe on and the timber which he founde ... 10s
>
> To Hill the mason for makinge a scaffold to set up the dial and for findinge of cordes, and for his worke ... 10s
>
> For hookes and hinges for the clock house doore ... 1s 1d
>
> To the painter for paintinge the hande of the dial after it was set up ... 1s 6d
>
> To Richard Redwarde for iron worke ... 2s 6d
>
> To the clocke maker ... £13
>
> For the clocke makers diet and his mans for tenne daies ... 14s

'Two purses to gather monie with' are also purchased and almost the entire cost of the clock – just over £40 – is covered by contributions from parishioners. These range from 45s from 'Alexander Blagrave, gent.' down to 4d from John Tanner.[6]

As with organs, looking after clocks is an ongoing effort.

> 1546 For mendinge of the barrells that the chime goeth with, to the smith at the west bridge ... 12d (St Martin, Leicester)

> 1564 For a roler to save ye rope of ye clock from freting ... 6d (St Edmund, Salisbury)

> 1597 For mendinge the clock ... 15s | For candles that nighte the clock was broughte home ... 1d | For carrienge and recarrienge the clock by water to London and home againe ... 12d | For a lock and keye, and two staples, and a haspe for the bell-loft dore, because no bodie but the clerke shoulde meddle with the clock ... 9d (Wandsworth)

> 1651 A pound of wire for the clock ... 1s 4d | The smith and his boy for coming over to mend it ... 3s 8d | For mending him again when the rogue pulled him in peeces ... 1s | For carrying the wheeles on my back to Oxford three times to mend ... 1s (Yarnton, Oxon)

> 1701 May 9th. [Agreed that Robert Crow] shall have twenty shillings a yeare for keepeing the clock, *if he do it well*. (Soham, Cambs, vestry)[7]

Rye, Sussex
The present face and original quarter boys were added to the clock in 1760.
The portly cherubs on duty now are fibre-glass replicas of the originals.

Bells

1. Sanctus and sacring

Before looking at the main peal of bells in the belfry it is worth noting two others which are usually located elsewhere in the church and which, before the Reformation, inform parishioners about the performance of mass.

The first is the sanctus bell, so named because it is rung when the sanctus, at the end of the preface to the mass, is sung or spoken, beginning with the words *Sanctus, sanctus, sanctus* (Holy, holy, holy). The bell's main function is to alert those within earshot – for example anyone dallying in the churchyard – that the service is taking place so that they may enter the church.

Sometimes it takes the form of a handbell but usually it is a hanging bell of intermediate size.

> 1479-81 For naile to amende the wheele of the sanctus bell ... ob. (St Mary at Hill)

> 1518 For a rope to the litell sanctus bell ... 4d (St Mary the Great, Cambridge)[1]

It may be with other bells in the belfry.

> 1552 In the steple five great belles and a sanctes bell. (Henley, Oxon, inventory)[2]

Alternatively, if the church has one, it may be in the bell-cote. Usually cotes house one or two bells and are located at the western or eastern end of the chancel roof, with a rope running down into the chancel so that the bell can be operated by one of those assisting at mass. After the Reformation the same bell is often used in a similar way, being rung immediately before divine service to summon people to church.

Bell-cote at west end of chancel: Binsey, Oxfordshire, by Francis Grose, 1775

ABOVE Ringing the sanctus bell, from an early 14th-century manuscript.
BELOW Sacring bell, Salhouse, Norfolk.

There is also the sacring bell which, as seen earlier, is rung just before the climax of mass, the elevation, when the consecrated host is held up by the priest at the altar. Usually it is small and rung inside the church, being either hand-held or fixed high up and operated by a cord. A common fixing point is on or near the top of the rood screen, where it is well placed to sound out across the church.

> 1447 A litell bell hanging in the chancell by the quere dor for to ring sacring. (Thame, inventory)[3]

The bell serves the practical purpose of alerting those in the nave that the elevation is about to take place so that they may show due reverence. In addition, one or more large bells in the belfry may be tolled to alert the parish more widely. Where this is done the sacring bell perhaps serves an additional purpose in providing a cue to the belfry ringer.[4]

> At the elevation of the body of the Lord let the bell be rung on one side [i.e. tolled], so that the people who do not have leisure to attend mass each day may, wherever they are, whether in the fields or in their houses, bend their knees. (Council of Lambeth, 1281)

> Let the parishioners be earnestly exhorted that, at the elevation of the body of Christ, they ... kneel down and adore their Creator with all devotion and reverence. And for this purpose let them be warned beforehand by the ringing of a little bell, and at the elevation itself let the great bell be struck thrice. (Synod of Exeter, 1287)[5]

2. Belfry

The main belfry is in the steeple or tower – indeed, much of the point of a church tower is to hold bells high up so that their sound rings out across the surrounding countryside or town.[1]

> 1594 It was agreed that our gret bell should be cast againe and not so much the tune of the bell was cared for as to have it a lowd bell and heard far. (St Lawrence, Reading)[2]

The bells may be rung from the ground or from a raised gallery or loft reached by a ladder or stairway.

> 1580 For makinge the plowmen drinke when they fot [fetched] timber to make the belle-lofte ... 20d (Minchinhampton, Glos)

> 1619 Cariadge of timber from Bentlie wood ... 7s 6d | Nicholas Perrie for buildinge the ringinge lofte ... £12 | A locke and two keyes for the bell lofte doore ... 2s 6d (St Edmund, Salisbury)[3]

In some places turf is placed below the bells to deaden the noise within the belfry.

> 1709 To Robert Webb for cutting turf ... 5s | For carrying ye turf into ye steeple ... 1s (Quainton, Bucks)

> 1720 For two loads of sods to lay under ye bells ... 2s 6d (Duffield, Derbyshire)

> 1751 For sodding bell house floor ... 2s (St Mary, Lancaster)

> 1803 For covering the floor in the upper bell loft with turf ... 6s (St Giles, Northampton)

In the last case at least this proves a serious mistake. When the bells are re-hung it is discovered that the floorboards and supporting beams have almost rotted away as a result of damp.[4]

The belfry, Stevington, Bedfordshire

ABOVE Ringing chamber, Felmersham, Bedfordshire.
BELOW The way up: at Felmersham (*left*) and at Flitton in the same county.

3. Casting, installation, tuning

In acquiring new bells or recasting existing ones the first stage is to agree terms with the founder.

> 1631 For drawinge the articles of agreement between the bell-founder and our selves and for makinge a bonde ... 1s 3d (Ludlow)[1]

Then comes the casting, which may be done at the founder's or in the parish.

> 1648 To Francis Goare for goeing to Mr Tompson for the keye of the vicarage barne doare for casting of the bells in the saide barne ... 2s 6d (Castle Cary, Somerset)[2]

Sometimes a pit is made in the churchyard, and occasionally the church itself is used.

> 1591 To Cudbert [Fisher] for going to York to buy metal ... 3s 4d | For woode for drying the mold ... 12d | For 1 gallon of ale at the drying of the mold ... 5d | For casting the bell ... £3 7s | To Will. Ripley for that laide out about the bell casting ... 41s 5d | For flags for his fornaces ... 8s | Bearing of horse dung to the bell casting ... 3s 4d | For going to Ripon to fetch one cable ... 4d | For ale and brede for draweing the bell into the steple ... 3s 2d | To Vincent Owthwaite for paveing the church where the bell was casten ... 2s (Kirkby Malzeard, Yorks)[3]

Details from the 14th-century Bell-Founder's Window at York Minster. LEFT A man with a long angled tool shapes the clay mould as it is turned by a second man. RIGHT Two boys operate the bellows of a furnace while a man with a club-shaped tool guides the molten metal into the mould.

Some costs at Ludlow in 1624 give a sense of the effort and upheaval involved.

To John Crowe for a gable [or possibly cable] to let downe the bells ... £2 5s 8d

For a peece of timber to make a barrel to wind downe the bells ... 1s 6d

To Frauncis Bibb for makinge the barrel ... 1s 6d

To Frauncis Bibb, for three dayes worke and a half to make redy a prop of 24 foot longe and draweinge him up in the steeple and placinge him there and for draweinge up a barrel and planks and boords to stand upon to wind the bells downe and up againe [etc] ... 6s

To people to carry up the pole to make the prop in the steeple, and the barrels to drawe downe and up the bells, from the widowe Groves house to the church ... 8d

To Burd and Brompton for draweinge downe the bells to be cast and draweinge them up againe ... 2s 8d

For wier for the chimes ... beinge most of them broken with takinge downe the bells ... 3s 4d

To Frauncis Bibb for making a scale to way the bells ... and for raising up the bells to way them and helpinge to way the bells and for nailes to make [the] scale ... 3s 10d

To Ribalds for throweinge out of stones out of the place where the bells were cast and for makinge it cleane ... & for makinge up a wall of stone that was broken downe into Davies garden to make the site of the furnace ... & for fillinge up the pit againe where the bells were cast [etc] ... 13s 8d

To Thomas Davies & Wm. Posterne for the house to cast the bells in ... 6s 8d[4]

Casting new bells from the old ones in this way is common. At the church which serves as the chapel of Merton College, Oxford, five bells are cast into eight in 1657, greatly vexing diarist Anthony Wood, who is convinced not only that the new bells are inferior but that Darby the bell-founder 'stole a great deal of mettle' in the process.[5]

Various methods are used to transport large bells to and from foundries. Within towns a sledge may suffice.

1510 For the cariage of 2 belles to the fownders ... 2s | To 6 porters to helpe them on the slede ... 6d (St Mary at Hill)

1603 To make the folke drinke for drawing the bell forth & backe from the founders ... 2s 8d | Mendinge of the slead we borrowed for ye bell ... 10d (St Edmund, Salisbury)[6]

For longer journeys other methods may be required, sometimes including construction of a bespoke vehicle.

1541 To John Whell wright for making of a carte and axling of the whelles [etc] ... 12d | For meat and drinke for 4 men that went with the carte ...

14d | For horsemeat of 15 horses that went with the bell the ... first day and night at Uppingham ... 2s 9d | For horsemeat of 15 horses for 2 nightes and a day ... in Lecester ... 5s 8d (St John the Baptist, Peterborough)

1613 To John Coleman to hoist out the bells at Barnestaple keye ... 2s | To Philip Nicholl for carrying the bells to Northam from Barnestaple in a boate ... 7s 6d (Hartland, Devon)

1641 To John Addamson and Jasper Greene for helping down the riven bell ... 1s | To Jasper Greene and his son for making a waine fit to carry the bell to Lincoln, for their day's work ... 2s | To Mr Chapman for making 2 waine felfs* for the bell to lie in ... 8d (St Mary, Barton on Humber, Lincs)[7]

When the journey is cross country ox power is often employed.

1557 For drinking for them that went forth that caried the bells to Ashe Priors ... 5d | At Larksbere the Sonday for 5 men's supper & fetching of a yoke ... 21d | For meate for the oxen for four daies ... 17s 4d | For the shoeing of Thomas Hall's eight oxen ... 5s 4d (Woodbury, Devon)

1558 For the diners of those wiche went with the bell in Wigan ... 9d | At night for drinking ... 5d | For the mete of the oxen and horses long as they were in Wigan ... 18d (Prescot, Lancs)

1608 For meate, drinke & lodging for myselfe, William Hills & the carryers & meate for their oxen when the bells were fetcht from Hatche ... 21s 6d | For 6 oxen to help the carryers to bring the bells some parte of the waye because they did want helpe being over loaded ... 3s 6d (Cranbrook, Kent)[8]

The beginnings and ends of journeys involve particular challenges.

1676 When the great bell was taken downe ... for ashe wood for rowlers ... 4s | For soape for the rowlers ... 6d (Houghton-le-Spring, co. Durham)[9]

Adjustments may need to be made so that bells can be manoeuvred in and out.

1557 For laying againe of thre flowers [three floors] after the bells were had up, and for nailes to fasten the bourds ... 11d (Woodbury)

1639 Robert Slaitor mason for takeing down ye steeple window to let out the bell and setting up againe ... 6s (All Saints, Newcastle)

1684 For drink when the bells were carried away ... 6d | Unto Henery Burt for beating the hoal in the steepel ... 2s 6d | Unto William Chouney for helping of him ... 1s (Woking, Surrey)[10]

---

* *Felf.* Alternative spelling of *felloe*, one of the curved pieces making up the outer rim of a wheel. Here apparently indicating pieces placed in the wain to cradle the bell.

Moving the tenor bell for recasting, Broad Clyst, Devon, 1937.
Four foot in diameter and weighing nearly a ton, it was originally cast in 1768 by
Thomas Bilbie of Cullompton, one of a well known family of founders. It is inscribed,
'I to the church the living call | And to the grave do summon all.'

The progress of one set of bells is recorded in a note in the parish register of
Gillingham, Kent.

The 21st February, 1699 [old style], being Wednesday, the bells of this
parish were taken down in order to be new cast. They lay in the church porch
till March the 11th following ... They were carried to the copperas house
by William Smith his teame, and put on board Thomas Smith his hoy.
He set saile for London Wednesday the 13th of March. They were weighed
at London Friday the 15th. ... The new bells were cast May the 15th 1700
by Philip Wightman, bell founder. He lives at the figure of the five bells on
Windmill Hill, neere More-fields, London. The new bells were weighed
May 24th ... There was added 511 pounds of mettle to the new bells.
They were brought from London to the copperas house May the 27th.
Brought to the church the same day. The 29th they were pulled up into the
steeple. They were hung on Wednesday, Thursday, Friday and Saturday
June 1st ... The new treble was filled with flip,* Friday May 31, in William
Smith's yard called the Court Lodge and there drunk out the same day.[11]

---

* A mixture of beer and spirit sweetened with sugar and heated with a hot iron. The
name may derive from the fact that it is 'flipped' or whipped up into froth.

Tuning bells is a skilled task involving chipping or shaving away the brass to achieve the particular note or tone required.

> 1565 To Thomas Whithede for 8 daies worke for himself and his man in chipping the bells ... 21s 4d (Lambeth)

> 1588 Paid the firste of December at the vewinge of a newe bell at Mr Motes house, at which time we had with us a musicion to sounde the bell ... 13d | Paid to ye waites of the cittie that took paines to take the note of our belles & to go to Mr Motes to take the note of the newe bell then cast ... 18d | Spent upon a company [of] other musicions to take a further note of the same bell ... 12d (St Michael, Cornhill)

> 1657 Spent on the belfounder & his son in Chester, they being here six dayes to see the bells hanged, and to chip them to make them tuneable ... 9s 4d (St Mary on the Hill, Chester)[12]

The excess metal arising may be sold: in 1656 St Edmund, Salisbury, receives 5s 'for the dust of the tuneing of the bells'.[13]

The right note can be elusive. The last of the Bilbies is said to have committed suicide in 1813 'because he could not get the Cullompton bells in tune'.[14]

4. Hallowing

In medieval times bells are hallowed before use. The ceremony is similar to baptism and is conducted by the bishop or his deputy. Godfathers and godmothers, often of high status, are enlisted, a name is bestowed, the bell is carried to the font, washed, anointed with holy oil, and blessed. The following extracts from a 13th-century form of benediction give a sense of the elaborate solemnity involved.

> First let litanies be said. Then let the bishop say, 'O God, make speed' &c. Next let the bishop make exorcism of water, saying, 'I exorcise thee' &c. ... Then shall he sprinkle the bell with blest water, saying, 'Asperges,' 'Thou shalt sprinkle', &c.

There follow a prayer and the singing of seven psalms and an antiphon. 'And when it shall have been sung, let them wipe the bell with a linen cloth.' Then comes another prayer.

> 'God ... grant that this vessel prepared for thy church may be sanctified by the holy ghost, and that by its stroke the faithful may be invited to their reward. And when its melody shall have sounded in the ears of the people, may devotion of faith increase in them, may all the snares of the enemy be driven far away, may the crashing of hail, the storm of whirlwinds, the rush of tempests, be moderated; may perilous thunders and the blast of winds become healthfully modified and suspended; may the right hand of thy might overthrow the powers of the air, and, hearing this bell, may all impure spirits tremble and fly as if before the ensign of thy sacred cross.'

Amid further prayers and antiphons the bishop anoints the bell with chrism, 'seven times without, four times within'. It is then raised over a censer in which incense and myrrh are burning, 'so that it may collect all the smoke'. Finally the bishop, raising his hand, asks that the blessing of God, Christ and the holy ghost 'ever abide upon this bell to call the faithful to divine worship throughout all ages'.[1]

A range of costs may arise.

1468 Paid the suffragan [assistant bishop] for hallowing of the bells ...
6s 8d | For wine for the suffragan ... 12d | Reward to his clark ... 8d | For bering water to the bells ... 2d | For shetes washing that wer fowled with the bells ... 2d (Great Yarmouth, Norfolk)[2]

In later periods, too, the installation of bells is usually marked by celebration. According to Gilbert White, when a new peal is installed at Selborne in 1735, one bell being donated by Sir Simeon Stuart, 'the day of the arrival ... was observed as an high festival by the village, and rendered more joyous, by an order from the donor, that the treble bell should be fixed bottom upward in the ground, and filled with punch, of which all present were permitted to partake'.[3]

The bishop makes the sign of the cross with chrism upon the bell,

and the censing, both from a pontifical of 1520

5. Supernatural powers

As the prayer quoted above makes clear, once they have been hallowed bells are believed to possess supernatural power to combat evil spirits and so to quell the storms which those spirits are thought to raise. The rationale is set out in *The Golden Legend*, compiled *circa* 1270 by Jacob de Voragine and later translated by William Caxton.

> The evil spirites that be in the region of the air doubte moche when they heare the trompes [trumpets] of God, whiche be the belles rongen ... And this is the cause why the belles be ronge when it thondreth, and when grete tempestes and outrages of wether happen, to the ende that the fiendes and wicked spirites shold be abashed and flee, and cease of the moving of tempest.[1]

As a result a church's bell-ringers are often set to work.

1457 For drink given to the ringers when it thundered ... 1d (Yeovil, Somerset)

1464 For bred and drinke for ringers in the gret thundering ... 3d ob. | 1507 For bread and drink for the ringers ... at night in the thundering ... 1d | To the sexton for drink when it thundered ... 1½d (St Mary, Sandwich, Kent)

1519 For ringing when the tempest was ... 3d (Spalding, Lincs)[2]

In his *Survey of London* John Stow describes an incident at St Michael, Cornhill, related to him by his father Thomas, who died in 1559. It suggests an association between the devil and thunderstorms, and perhaps that the evil one is indeed disturbed by the sound of bells. (The drawing is of the church's steeple in 1421.)

> I have oft heard my father report, upon St James night, certaine men in the lofte next under the belles, ringing of a peale, a tempest of lightning and thunder did arise, an uglie shapen sight appeared to them, coming in at the south window, and lighted on the north, for feare whereof they all fell downe, and lay as dead for the time, letting the belles ring and cease of their owne accord. When the ringers came to themselves, they founde certaine stones of the north window to be raised and scrat[ched], as if they had been so much butter, printed with a lions clawe. The same stones were fastened there againe, and so remaine till this day. I have seene them oft, and have put a feather or small sticke into the holes, where the clawes had entered three or foure inches deepe. At the same time certaine maine timber postes at Queene Hith were scrat and cleft from the toppe to the bottome, and the pulpit crosse in Powles churchyarde was likewise scrat, cleft, and overturned.[3]

Over the following centuries the beliefs which give rise to ringing against storms fall away, but the practice is found at least to the end of the 19th century.

> In conformity with an old usage, the bells in Dawlish parish church were rung during the recent thunderstorms, in the belief that 'the Spirit of the Bells would overcome the Spirit of the Lightning'.
>
> *Torquay Directory*, 9 August 1899[4]

Among their other powers, bells can dispel noxious vapours. In *Certaine Rules, Directions, or Advertisments for this Time of Pestilentiall Contagion* (1625), Francis Hering advises, 'Let the bells in cities and townes be rung often, and the great ordnance discharged, thereby the aire is purified.'[5]

They can also register calamity of their own accord: in this way the bells of Canterbury ring out at the murder of Thomas Becket in 1170, and those of distant churches toll upon the death of Robert Grosseteste, Bishop of Lincoln, in 1253.[6]

6. Used to mark time

The main use of church bells is to mark the times of services and devotions and so of times of the day. Before the Reformation this is primarily effected by ringing the Ave bell early in the morning, at noon, and in the afternoon or evening, typically in the form of three sets of three strokes. This is done to mark the recital of three Ave Marias (Hail Marys), from the greeting to the Virgin Mary at the annunciation ('Hail, thou that art highly favoured'), and the identity of the proclaiming angel is reflected in the common use of Gabriel as a name for individual bells.[1]

> 1524 Paid George Nicoll for tolling of ye Ave bell for Cristmes quarter ... 10s (Lydd, Kent)[2]

In 1512 the vicar of Cropredy, Oxfordshire, gives a sum 'in redy money' to the churchwardens on condition that, among other things, they provide 'for evermore' for someone to 'toll daily the Avees bell at sex of the clok in the morning, at 12 of the clok at noone, and at foure of the clok at afternoone'.[3]

While the Ave itself is no longer recited after the Reformation, the ringing associated with it, particularly of the morning and evening bells, persists widely over the following centuries, largely because of its practical usefulness to a population commonly lacking clocks or watches of their own.

Both before and after the Reformation the particular hours of ringing vary from place to place. The morning bell, often referred to as the day bell, is usually rung at 4 or 5 a.m. in earlier centuries but tends to creep later over time. The evening bell is usually rung at 8 or 9 p.m. and is in large part a continuation of the old curfew bell.

> 1483 [My executors are] to finde for ever after my decese a man of gude conversation to ringe daily one of the belles in the churche of Blakesley curfewe at 8 of the clocke at night and day bell at 4 or 5 of ye clock in the morning and also to kepe a clok ... and to receive yerely 13s 4d sterling. (will of John Aleyn, Blakesley, Northants)

1490 To the sexten for his rewar for ringing of the day belle ... 3s 4d |
1492 To ye sexten for ringing of korffow belle ... 3s 4d (Walberswick, Suffolk)[4]

The ringers must cope with darkness, particularly in winter.

1549 12 pound of candelles for to ring at 5 of the clocke in the morning and at 7 of the clocke in the night ... 18d (St Edmund, Salisbury)

1666 For candles for Squib to see to ring four and eight ... 1s (Wimborne Minster, Dorset)[5]

7. The curfew bell: a digression

Curfew is a medieval regulation under which fires have to be covered at a fixed hour in the evening, the name deriving from the Old French *cuevre-fu* (*couvre feu*, cover fire). At the Synod of Caen in Normandy in 1061 it is ordered that a bell be rung every evening and that on hearing it prayers should be offered and everyone should retire to their houses and shut their doors. A similar measure is introduced to England by William the Conqueror and then apparently abolished *circa* 1100. However, because an evening bell is so useful, it continues to be rung in many places.[1]

At St Mary le Bow, London, for example, a bell is 'solemnly rung' for an hour each evening so that everyone 'benighted in the fields may be able to betake themselves to the same city more quickly for getting shelter'. In addition, according to John Stow, 'the lanthornes on the toppe of this steeple were meant to have beene glased, and lightes in them placed nightly in the winter, whereby travellers to the cittie might have the better sight thereof, and not to misse of their wayes'.[2]

In similar vein the clerk of Louth in Lincolnshire is instructed to ring curfew at a regular hour, and to do so 'with 18 score pulls for this consideracion, if any man shuld go wronge in winter day in the fielde, by the sounde of the bell he may come the sooner to the toun'.[3]

The value placed on the bell is attested by gifts and bequests of land to fund it in several parishes, often known as Curfew Land. At Cropredy, Oxfordshire, it is known as Bell Land and at West Rasen, Lincolnshire, as Ding Dong.[4]

At Wokingham in 1664 Richard Palmer donates land to pay for a sexton who, from September to March each year, is to ring the church's largest bell for half an hour twice a day: at 4 a.m., to encourage people to rise to their labours, and at 8 p.m., so that 'strangers and others who should happen in winter nights, within hearing of the said bell, to lose their way in the country, might be informed of the time of night, and receive some guidance into their right way'.[5]

At St Margaret at Cliffe, Kent, at an unknown date, a shepherd who falls over the cliff in the dark survives long enough to bequeath five roods of pasture land for a bell to be rung at 8 o'clock every night during winter. By 1696 the custom has fallen into neglect, prompting a strict order from the vestry.

To prevent for the future any danger which may ensue to travellers and others being so near the Cliffe, for want of the due and constant ringing ... the said curfew bell [shall] be hereafter rung ... constantly every night in the week ... the full time of a quarter of an hour at the least, without any exceptions of Sunday nights or holy-day nights, and he that rings is to have and receive the benefit and profit of the said Curfew-Land ...[6]

According to tradition, at Barton on Humber, Lincolnshire, an elderly woman, accidentally benighted on the Wolds, and alarmed as a result, is led to safety by the sound of a bell of St Peter's church. Out of gratitude she gives land to the parish clerk on condition that he ring a bell from 7 to 8 on every evening except Sunday. This is to be done during the winter months – from the day on which the first load of barley is harvested until the following Shrove Tuesday. It continues to be rung until *circa* 1870, when it is stopped because of the nuisance it is causing to those living near the church.[7]

8. Further uses: Harvest, sermons, pancakes, fire

In many rural parishes a bell is rung specifically in relation to harvest.

> 1556 For knelling the bell in harvest for gatheringe of the pescods [pea pods] ... 4d (Louth)
>
> 1685 Ringing ye harvest bell ... 2s 6d (Eastbourne, Sussex)[1]

At Barrow on Humber the clerk is 'to ring a bell every evening about the sunsetting' from 'the beginning of harvist ... until harvist be fully ended', while at Driffield, Yorkshire, a harvest bell is rung at 5 a.m. and 7 p.m. until at least the end of the 19th century.[2]

After the Reformation another bell, rung to summon parishioners to the main Sunday service, is often called the sermon bell.

Bench end, Aspall, Suffolk

> 1575 To Aldriche for tolinge of the bell to sermons ... 12d (St Alphage, London Wall)
>
> 1628 For trussing a newe wheele broken as the sermon bell was in ringing ... 30s (St Mary the Great, Cambridge)[3]

Perhaps more inviting is the pancake bell, rung in many places on Shrove Tuesday at or about 11 a.m.

> 1640 Carpender for making a frame for the Pancake bell ... 3s 4d (St Edmund, Salisbury)[4]

It is thought to have its origin in a bell rung in medieval times to summon people to be shrived (to make confession and have a penance imposed) on this day before the onset of Lent. As shriving falls into disuse after the Reformation the bell comes to be associated instead with the making of pancakes on the same day, as 'water poet' John Taylor describes in his 'Jack a Lent' of 1620.

> By that time the clocke strikes eleven, which (by the helpe of a knavish sexton) is commonly before nine, then there is a bell rung call'd the Pancake Bell, the sound whereof makes thousands of people distracted and forgetful either of manners or humanitie. Then there is a thing call'd wheaten floure, which the sulphory necromanticke cookes do mingle with water, egges, spice, and other tragical magical inchantments, and then they put it by little and little into a frying pan of boiling suet, where it makes a confused dismal hissing ... until at the last by the skill of the cookes it is transform'd into the forme of a flap-jack, which in our translation is call'd a Pancake, which ominous incantation the ignorant people do devoure very greedily ...[5]

Writing more soberly a century later, Thomas Hearne notes that 'it hath been an old custom in Oxford for the scholars of all houses, on Shrovetuesday, to go to dinner at 10 clock, at which time the little bell call'd Pan-cake Bell rings, or, at least, should ring, at St Marie's'.

The practice persists quite widely into Victorian times, one of the bells at Wellingborough, Northamptonshire, being known by the ringers as Old Pancake and another, at All Saints, Maidstone, being called the Fritter bell.[6]

Church bells may also be rung to alert the parish to fire.

> 1670 For casting the fire bell ... £1 8s (St Mary, Warwick)[7]

Such ringing is often intentionally jangled and discordant. According to Joseph Hall, Bishop of Norwich in the 1640s, 'As we testify our public rejoicing by an orderly and well-tuned peal, so, when we would signify that the town is on fire, we ring confusedly.'[8]

9. The passing bell

Church bells also sound out melancholy tidings as they announce the deaths of parishioners. In modern times this takes the simple form of the death knell, rung after the event. In the Middle Ages, however, and continuing after the Reformation, it is customary for a bell to be rung as death approaches and arrives, the terms used reflecting the belief that death marks the start of the soul's onward journey.

> 1491 Received for ringinge of the grete belle at the forthfare [going forth] of Katherine Poez ... 12d (St Edmund, Salisbury)

> 1500 And when my body and my sowle departs, then to have the sowle bell to ring for me, in tokening calling to God for help. (will of William Dager, Walsingham, Norfolk)

1526 [List of fees] The clerke to have for tollinge of the passinge belle
for manne, womanne or childes, if it be in the day ... 4d | Item, if it be
in the night, for the same ... 8d (St Mary Woolchurch)[1]

Such ringing has several purposes ranging from the superstitious to the practical.

• To drive away evil spirits. In medieval times it is believed that the devil and
other spirits attend the bedsides of those in extremis with a view to snatching their
souls before they pass up to heaven. The sound of bells is thought to drive such
spirits away and therefore to ensure safe passage for the soul. After the Reformation
such thinking is considered superstitious and discouraged.[2]

• To encourage people to pray for the soul
of the dying person, or for their recovery. 'The
bells ought to be rung when anyone is dying,
that the people hearing this may pray for him,'
writes Durand. A foreign visitor to London
in 1602 notes that 'when a person lies in agony,
the bells of the parish he belongs to are touched
with the clappers until he either dies or recovers
again. As soon as this sign is given, everybody
in the street, as well as in the houses, falls on
his knees offering prayer for the sick person.' This purpose is also emphasized by
Church authorities. A visitation in Chichester diocese in 1638, for example, asks
each parish, 'Is there a passing-bell tolled, that they who are within the hearing of
it may be moved in their private devotions to recommend the state of the departing
soule into the hands of their redeemer [?]' In practice some at least of the prayers
offered are presumably for the earthly recovery of those stricken.[3]

• To comfort the dying. According to an idealised account of the death of Lady
Jane Grey's sister Katherine, when a prisoner at Yoxford Hall, Suffolk, on hearing
her custodian mention the idea of sending to the church for the bell to be rung,
she responds, 'Good Sir Owen, let it be so.' Even a puritan such as John Rainolds
(*d.* 1607) finds value in the custom: 'death seazing upon all parts of his body, he
expressed by signes that he would have the passing bell toll for him'.[4]

• To remind all hearers of their own mortality. A visitation in Worcester diocese
in 1662 asks whether the parish clerk or sexton takes care to admonish the living
'by tolling of a passing-bell of any that are dying, thereby to meditate of their
own deaths, and to commend the others weak condition to the mercy of God?'[5]

• To summon clergy to the bedside in case this should not already have been
done. This is suggested by canon 67 of 1604: 'and when any is passing out of this
life, a bell shall be tolled, and the minister shall not then slack to do his last duty'.[6]

As the examples above show, the passing bell is still encouraged after the Reformation, but in time it falls into widespread disuse, prompting a regretful defence
by Henry Bourne, writing in 1725.

Did we indeed imagine with the papists, that there is any virtue or extra-ordinary power in a bell, that it ... drives away the spirits of darkness, then it might justly be called Superstition, and therefore justly abolished. But when we retain the custom, only to procure the prayers of the faithful for a departing soul, it would surely be of advantage to observe it, if the prayers of a righteous man avail any thing at all ... | But how shall they then pray for him, if they know not of his departure? And how can they know that, without the tolling of the bell?[7]

At Melton Mowbray, Leicestershire, a Mr Crane, dying in about 1738, is reportedly 'the first person ... for whom the bell tolled after death, till when the custom was for it to pass before'. At King's Cliffe, Northamptonshire, the old practice lasts longer, at least until late in the same century, the bell being rung in one case for a woman who does not die as expected, but recovers.[8]

After the lapse of the old practice the term 'passing bell' continues to be used widely but now usually indicates ringing after death.

10. Post-mortem ringing

Before the Reformation bells are rung shortly after a death for much the same reasons that they are rung at the time of passing: to drive away the devil so that he cannot get his eager hands on the soul of the deceased, and to remind people to pray for that soul, the hope being that their prayers will persuade God to mitigate the pains it suffers in purgatory and speed its passage to heaven.

> 1546 I will that the bells shall ring for me 8 days after my death — a peal at masse, & another at even; & the ringers to have a penny apec every day, and the church to have for the bells 2s 8d, that my loving frends hering ye sownd of the bells may make their supplicacion to Allmighty God for me. (W. Dickins, St Mary, Northampton)[1]

It may also be believed that the sound of bells is itself effective to these ends. 'They ring so diligently for the dead,' laments reformer John Hooper in 1547, 'that they break the ropes to pull the souls out of purgatory.'[2]

An angel and
a murky devil
compete for a soul
as it rises from a
shrouded corpse,
c. 1430

After the Reformation attempts are made to restrict such ringing, Protestants considering that any attempt to intercede on behalf of the soul of a dead person is superstitious, since as far as they are concerned purgatory does not exist and salvation is achieved through faith alone. Accordingly an order of 1566, reiterated in the Canons of 1604, requires that 'after the time of ... passing' there is to be rung 'no more but one short peal'. The purpose of this peal is not stated but it may be or include the more acceptable one (to reformers) of simply informing those within earshot that a parishioner has died.[3]

Old beliefs die very slowly, however, particularly in remote areas, as is clear from the following account of a conversation with a parish clerk published in the *East Anglian* in 1894.

> Trying to find out from the clerk if he had any rule or custom when ringing the bell for the dead ... he did not seem to have anything decided to say ... But he added, which was interesting, that, 'as how Master —, and his father was clerk, used to say, that it fared to him that the properest time he reckoned to ring the bell was to do it as soon as he could when the person was dead, because, as he said, the spirit was then a roaming like ...' This seems to show that there is an idea in the people's minds that the object of ringing the bell was to lay the spirit, or to ring while the spirit was in transit from this world to another.[4]

As for the manner of ringing to announce a death, this varies from place to place, more than seventy distinct methods being found in Lincolnshire alone. The sex of the deceased is often indicated, and sometimes also their age.[5]

> In ringing the passing peal, it has been time out of mind customary, for a man that dies, to toll 12 tolls. For a woman 9 tolls. They are accounted man or woman at the age of 16 or 18 years. For young persons, a male 7 tolls, a female 6 tolls. (Leverton, Lincs, note in constables' accounts, 1692)
>
> *Knocks* for the Dead*. 3 for girl. 4 for boy. 6 for spinster. 7 for matron. 8 for bachelor. 9 for husband. (Marsham, Norfolk, ringing rules in belfry, undated)[6]

A common method is to ring 3 x 3 strokes for a man, 3 x 2 for a woman, and 3 x 1 for a child, followed in each case by a stroke for each year of their age. Durand offers a rather strained explanation of the differing numbers of strokes, involving Adam and Eve and the Trinity, but they may at root be little more than a reflection of the social hierarchy.[7]

---

* Bell strokes. Another term used is 'tellers', which is sometimes said to have given rise to the saying, 'Nine tailors makes a man.' However, the saying, alluding to the supposed inadequacy of tailors, goes back to at least 1651, whereas the use of 'teller' for a bell is not recorded before 1868 (*OED*). It seems likely therefore that an old saying was punningly and belatedly adopted with reference to bell-ringing.

11. Funerals, peals, knells

According to Durand, 'the bells ought also to be chimed when the corpse is brought to the church, and when carried out from the church to the grave.' This is echoed in the order of 1566 mentioned above, which allows a second short peal to be rung 'before the burial, and another short peal after the burial'. Henry Ellacombe, writing in the 1870s, notes that modern custom reduces death-related ringing to two occasions: 'first, after the death of a parishioner, to which the term *passing-bell* has been incorrectly transferred; and the second time, during the procession of the funeral from the house of the deceased to the church-gate, or entrance'.[1]

The meanings of other terms shift too, affording room for confusion.

Peal is a shortened form of 'appeal' and its use in the 1566 order accords with its original meaning of a call or summons made by ringing a bell. Later, however, it comes to be used more generally of any loud or prolonged ringing involving more than one bell.

Knell, meanwhile, is derived from Anglo Saxon *cnyllan*, to beat noisily. Originally it just indicates ringing or sounding a bell but it comes to be used specifically of solemn ringing in relation to a death, often involving a single bell. It may be used of ringing shortly after death, or in connection with the burial, or both.[2]

The following indicate that the custom, at least in 16th-century London, is to have a solemn knell rung for a lengthy period prior to burial and then one or more clamorous peals rung at the time of the service. They also show incidentally the valuable income parishes derive from such ringing.

> 1520 [Paid] for ringing of a knell for Mr Roches servant for 6 owres ... 6d | For ringing of the pelis at Mr Roches servantes buryeng ... 10d | Received for his knell ... 5s | Received for the pelis at that dirige and masse* ... 20d (St Mary at Hill)

> 1521 [List of fees] For a knell of 6 owres of the great bell called Russe with all ye peales of all the belles to ye dirige and masse ... 8s 8d | For an owre knell with the bell called the Trinite and a peale with 3 belles to bringe the corsse to churche ... 12d (St Michael, Cornhill)

> 1580 The 27th day of April was buried Mr Robart Colshill, ye best cloth 2s, ye whole dayes knell 2s 4d, and the six peales 12d. (St Martin in the Fields)[3]

In his will of 1528 Richard Clerke of Lincoln asks for 'no pompouse buryall, but bring my body to the grounde honestely withowt any solemne ringing of all the belles, saving one peale afore dirige and one other peale at masse, and ellys but one bell be rung continually to I be laid in the grounde in my long bedde'.[4]

---

* The later parts of the funeral service.

Those living nearby may consider prolonged knells excessive. As early as 1339 Bishop Grandisson of Exeter seeks to restrict them on the grounds that 'they do no good to the departed, are an annoyance to the living, and injurious to the fabrick and the bells'.[5]

By the late 17th century the sense of competition has become palpable.

> 1699 One howres knell for Jane Blackhead ... 2s 6d | Two howres knell for Mrs Dorothy Westbeere ... 5s | Three howres knell for Mr J. Westbeere ... 7s | Four howres and ground* for Mr Adam Aust, a stranger ... 11s | Seven howres and ground for Mr J. Ivie marchant ... 19s 6d | Nine howres and ground in the church for Mr T. Hancock batcheller ... £2 12s 4d | Fifteen howres and ground in old church for Mrs Alice Dove widdow ... £1 19s 6d (St Edmund, Salisbury)[6]

As seen above in the list of fees at St Michael, Cornhill, the amount charged may also vary with the size and status of the bells used.

> 1469 Receved of John Marham for the grete bell for his moder ... 4d | Of John Gibson for the third bell for his dowter ... 2d (St John the Baptist, Peterborough)[7]

At Cranbrook the most impressive bell is reserved on the basis of class.

> 1619 *Regulations as to Ringing of Knells, etc, by the Sexton.* Item, that he shall not ring the greatest bell for a knell for any corps neither for a solemne bell before the bringing of the corps to churche except the partie deceased had landes or were esteemed to be worth one hundred poundes or were the sonne or daughter of one of the same estate.[8]

More generously, some churches provide basic ringing at low or no cost for the poor.

> 1501 It is agreed ... that Sir John Plommers bell shall serve for all poor people of this parishe, and for none other, paying 1d for the ringing. (St Mary at Hill)

> 1546 It is agreed the smawll bell to be of charite rowng for all poverte, withe owtt costes or anye money. (St Andrew Hubbard)

> 1685 At the parish meeting ... it was ordered that every poore person that dieth having not money to pay for the ringing of the 5th bell, may have liberty to send any person to ring that bell without paying for ye same. And if the party deceased hath none to ring the bell for him nor money to pay for the same that the clarke shall ring the said bell without receiving any pay for ringing the said bell. (St Mary, Warwick)[9]

---

* For the interment.

12. Occasional ringing, for royalty &c.

While most ringing relates to religious observances, bells are also used ad hoc to mark particular events.

> 1628 To the ringers for ringing at Wm. Smithes fast'ning of the pinnackle ... 6d | 1654 To the ringers for ringing when Mr Lee the newe parson & his frindes came to towne ... 1s 6d (Ludlow)

> 1646 Ringing the race day that ye Erle of Pembrook* his horse won the cuppe ... 5s (St Edmund, Salisbury)

> 1670 [Received for] ringing at the shoomakers feast ... 2s 6d (St Thomas, Salisbury)

> 1687 To the ringers a duck hunting day ... 3s 6d (St Peter, Bristol)[1]

Occasionally the bell tower needs testing.

> 1664 Paid in beere to the ringers for a peale to trye if the tower shooke ... 1s (Wimborne Minster, Dorset)

> 1695 Gave the ringers for ringing after mending of the frame and tower that we might see and finde the falts ... 3s 6d (Lambourn, Berks)[2]

Should royalty come by they expect the bells to be rung to mark the auspicious event. There are few early records of this practice but from at least the reign of Elizabeth it occurs widely.[3]

> 1570 For ringing when the queenes majestie [did] ride about the feildes the 20th of Aprile ... 12d | 1587 To ye ringers when ye queene came to my lord his grace† ye 18th of Januarie ... 4s | For borrowinge a fowrth bell clapper ye same time our clapper beinge broken ... 8d | 1595 24 Februarii. It is agreed in vestry that the ringers for her majesties remove shall have every time of her passage here 3s, and for her majesties birthday 4s 6d, and for the coronation day 6s 8d. (Lambeth)

> 1629 For ringing the day that the kings majestie [Charles I] dined at the George ... 3s (Bishop's Stortford)

> 1680 Received of the Sherriffe of London, to give to the ringers when his majestie [Charles II] supt at his house ... 10s (All Hallows Staining)

> 1687 May 4th. Paid ringers, ye king [James II] being in town to see ye ship launch ... 10s (St Nicholas, Deptford, Kent)

> 1699 April 11th. Pay'd the ringers that day the king [William III] went twice over the ferry ... £1 (Chelsea, Middlesex)[4]

* Owner of nearby Wilton House. Ten years later the parish borrowed pulleys from Wilton for use during work in the bell tower.
† The Archbishop of Canterbury, at nearby Lambeth Palace.

Should royalty dally in the area the costs can mount up.

1603 For the ringers ... when our kinges majestie [James I] came in his
prograse for 4 daies followinge and parte of the nightes from ye 26 of
August unto the 30th ... 34s (St Edmund, Salisbury)[5]

If plans change the summoned ringers still need to be paid.

1601 To ye ringers when the queene was expected to come bye ... 6d
(Wandsworth)[6]

Bishops and other notables also expect to be greeted.

1535 To ringers agenst my Lord of Caunterburye cuming and to one man
watching for his cuming ... 7d* (Lydd, Kent)

1626 To 5 ringers for ringinge at the Countesse of Huntingdons being
at the Angell at Cristmas ... 2s 6d (St Martin, Leicester)

1716 Paid the ringers when the Duke of Marlborough went through the
town ... 6s 6d (Burford, Oxon)[7]

To avoid disappointment word may be sent ahead.

1684 Paid to the ringers when the king came by, notice being first sent
by a messenger ... 3s 6d (Kensington, Middlesex)[8]

Should the bells not be rung, a fine is demanded by a functionary such as the
king's almoner, and in some cases the church doors are sealed up in punishment.

1493 Paid to the kinges amener for faulght of ringing of the belles agenste
the kinge ... 4s 10d (St Mary at Hill)

1548 Paid to the king's amner when he would have sealed up the church
doors at the departure of the king's majesty, the 2d day of July, because
the bells were not rong ... 2s 4d (St Margaret, Westminster)

1629 Paid the lord bishop's man, because the bells did not ring when his
lordship was in town ... 6s 8d (St Michael, Coventry)

1647 For default of ringinge in harvest when the kinge came by twice ...
13s 4d (Twickenham, Middlesex)[9]

In his diary Henry Machyn records that, on the morning of 19th June 1563,
an official places a notice

on divers churche dors, because that he said that they did not ring when
that the quen went to Grenwiche, and that they shuld not open the churche
dors till that he had a nobull on [noble from] evere churche by the water
side from Tempull bar unto the Towre, but he could get nothing yet.[10]

* The lookout was presumably stationed on the church tower. The archbishop was
Thomas Cranmer.

13. Marking history

Over the centuries church bells mark many of the notable events in English history. The custom, like that of ringing for royalty, is widely recorded from Tudor times.

> 1509 To seven men that rong the bellis when the kinges grace [Henry VIII] went to Westmister to be crowned ... 1s 2d (St Mary at Hill)

> 1553 To ye ringers at ye proclamation of our soverain lady Quene Marie ... 5d (Yatton, Somerset)[1]

Bells are rung enthusiastically on news of the foiling of plots, particularly if they are Catholic ones.

> 1586 For bread and drinke for the ringers when Antony Babington and the rest of the traitors were taken ... 20d (St Botolph, Bishopsgate)[2]

The Babington plot's discovery is used to bring about the trial of Mary Queen of Scots and her execution, which takes place at Fotheringhay on 8th February 1587 and is celebrated with un-Christian glee.

> 1587 [Accounts] For breade and beare for ye ringers on ye day that the Queen of Scotts was beheaded ... 12d | [Note in register by clerk] Feb. 9th. Memerandum that we did ringe ... for joye that the Queene of Skotts that enemy to owre most noble queens majestie and ower contrie was beheaded for the which the lorde God be praised and I wold to God that all her confederates were knowne and cut off by the like meanes. (St Botolph, Aldgate)

> 1587 Ringers for joy when newes reached us of beheadinge of Quene of Scottes ... 12d (Minehead, Somerset)[3]

The failure of the ensuing Armada sent from Spain is seen as a sign of divine favour.

> 1588 Ringinge ... for the greate victorie against the Spaniardes by the mightie hande of God ... 8s (St Thomas, Salisbury)[4]

At St Andrew, Plymouth, they commemorate the event long afterwards.

> 1639 Paid ringers for ringing in remembrance of God's gracious deliverance of this land from the Spanish invasion, and for candles ... 5s 3d[5]

During the reign of James I the foiling of a further Catholic attempt, in the form of the Gunpowder Plot, is marked at parliament's church, a stone's throw from the intended scene of devastation.

> 1605 Paid the ringers for ringing at the time when the parliament-house should have been blown up ... 10s (St Margaret, Westminster)[6]

The thwarting of Catholicism is celebrated again when James II is deposed by the 'Glorious Revolution' and the Protestant William of Orange and Queen Mary II come to the throne.

1689 To ringers upon coronation day ... 12s | For their meat and drinke ... 8s | For ourselves and for 2 dozen of ale which we sent to the people at the bonefire ... 7s 6d (Prestbury, Cheshire)[7]

Among many victories marked, the following relate to those at sea, the first (by Spanish and Italian forces) at the Battle of Lepanto, the second against the Dutch, and the third at Trafalgar.

1571 For ringing for joy of the great victory that the Christians hath gotten of the Turk ... 2s 6d (St Margaret, Westminster)

1666 Spent the 10th day [of June] hearing of a victory from the sea, of the ringers, they ringing most parte the whole night ... 1s (Wilmslow, Cheshire)

1805 Nov. 19th. For ringing on account of the decisive victory obtained over the combined fleets of France & Spain in which the Immortal Nelson fell ... 10s | 1806 Jan. 9th. For 2 hours knell on account of the funeral of the ever to be lamented Lord Nelson ... 4s (St Martin, Salisbury)[8]

Enthusiastic celebration may give rise to problems. A re-cast bell at Ashover, Derbyshire, bears the inscription, 'This old bell rang the downfall of Buonoparte, and broke, April, 1814'.[9]

Mourning the death of the monarch is expected, but a particularly sombre note is struck in the case of Mary II, who dies from smallpox on 28th December 1694 at a relatively young age. Her elaborate funeral at Westminster Abbey does not take place until 5th March 1695, on which day bells are rung for her across the country.

1694-95 To Mr Greenebury for tolling ye great bell when ye late Queene Mary (of ever blessed memory) was berryed ... 1s 6d (Lambourn, Berks)

1694-95 To Charles Smith for tolling ye bell 3 hours the day that the queene was interred ... 1s (Weybread, Suffolk)[10]

The death of George III, after sixty years on the throne, also strikes home.

1820 T. Agas, tolling the bell 6 hours upon death of king ... 7s 6d (Starston, Norfolk)[11]

At Chester-le-Street the parish books note in some detail the ringing on the funeral day of William IV, albeit after an undistinguished reign of only seven years.

1837 The interment of his late majesty took place at Windsor. At Chester the bell toll'd from 9 o'clock in the morning until 12 o'clock, and from 1 till 4; the minute bell then commenced and toll'd until 9 o'clock, after which a muffled peal was rung until near one o'clock on Sunday morning.[12]

14. Maintenance

Much can and does go wrong with bells, most parishes incurring expenditure on them every year.

Baldricks often need replacing. Early ones are made by a range of traders dealing in leather.

> 1491 To Awuncelle Pouchemaker for 6 bawderikkes ... 3s 2d | 1563 Thomas Boocket ye sadler making 2 bawdrikes ... 2s 8d | 1567 George Warner ye lame glover for makinge of a bawdrick and tan lether ... 12d (St Edmund, Salisbury)

> 1518 To William Cobelar for makinge of 3 new bawdrikes ... 2s 5d (Leverington, Cambs)

> 1588 For half a horse skin for bawdricks of ye belles ... 2s | Paide ye knacker for making ye bawdricks ... 8d (Redenhall, Norfolk)[1]

Domestic items may be recycled.

> 1580 For a paire of boote leggs to mende bawdricks ... 8d (Stanford, Berks)[2]

The clappers (sometimes referred to as tongues) attached by the baldricks are another frequent casualty.

> 1517-19 To Jacobbe of Maidston for a bell clapur ... 12s 9d (Rainham, Kent)

> 1518 Paid Phelip Smith in Kinges Stret for the mending the claper of Sent Thomas bell with his marke theron and by his promas and if it breke within 7 yer after he to make it at his proper cost and charge ... 3s 4d (Lambeth)

> 1605 For making of a newe eye for the great bell clapper and mending of the flight ... 3s (Strood, Kent)

> 1608 For the mendinge of our grett bell tounge ... 7s 8d | For the carriage of the bell tounge up into the steple ... 2d (St Oswald, Durham)

> 1613 To Terne for carrying the clapper of the bell upon his shoulders to Baschurch and back again ... 6d | For the hire of a horse to go to Baschurch with the bell-clappers to mend ... 12d (St Mary, Shrewsbury)[3]

Like the bells themselves they may be turned periodically with a view to balancing out the wear on different sides.

> 1513 To John Smith ... for torning of 2 bell clappers ... 4d (St John the Baptist, Peterborough)[4]

Less frequently there are problems with the means by which the bell itself is hung and moved.

Some parts

Stock. Wooden or metal block or beam from which the bell is hung.

Gudgeon. Pivot, usually of metal, projecting from each end of the stock and enabling the bell and stock to revolve.

Cannon. Metal loop, or ear, on the top of a bell by which it is hung.

Clapper. Tongue of a bell, and possible source of the modern phrase 'like the clappers'. In early bells the clapper is attached by a **baldrick** or leather thong which goes through the eye of the clapper and through a u-shaped staple at the top of the inside of the bell. The leather does not endure well and in later bells metal is used instead.[5]

1608 To Goodman Wyborowe the carpenter for newe hanging the bells & for mending the wheles & stocks & helping up with the bells ... £3 10s | For candles for him & his men to worke by ... 10d (Cranbrook, Kent)

1609 Batten the joiner for a new wheele for the third bell ... 10s (St Edmund, Salisbury)[6]

Such work often involves the gudgeons.

1621 One dayes worke for a man for to mend the great bell when she was loose in the guginges and takeing her downe and hanging her up againe ... 1s 6d | 1623 For wedges for the gugenes... 6d (Strood)

1686-88 To Mary East, smithe ... for mending ye bell guggens ... 1s 6d | To ye said Mary for 4 bolts about the bells ... 2s (Birchington, Kent)[7]

Lubrication is often required and takes various forms.

1572 For sope for the belles that time that Mistresse Bassit was buried ... 2d (Eltham, Kent)

1575 For netesfoot oil to liquor the belles ... 2d* (St Margaret, Westminster)[8]

Elsewhere they use tallow (St Edmund, Salisbury, 1549), 'black soape and grese' (Bramley, Hampshire, 1565), 'a pint of salad oil' (Bishop's Stortford, 1579), 'a pinte of goose liker' (Ludlow, 1583), and 'two pound of hoggs grease' (Manchester, 1682).[9]

Bell ropes naturally need mending or replacing.

1547 To Thomas Season and John Tayler for shuttinge [splicing] the belle ropes at divers times, and picchinge them with piche and talow ... 4s 5d ob. (Ludlow)

---

* *Neat's foot*. The heel of a cow or ox. *Liquor*. Lubricate with grease or oil.

1554-58 For 56 fadams* of bell ropes ... 6s (Lambeth)

1659 To William Smith ropemaker for 3 stone of hempe for bellropes & carriage ... 14s | To him more for making of 4 bellropes & halfe a bellrope ... 9s | To George Wilkinson for helping to twist & twine them ... 12d (Kendal, Westmorland)[10]

Pipes are sometimes installed to reduce fraying.

1586 To Trasy for making of 9 pipes for the bell ropes to run in ... 3s | For timber for the pipes ... 6d (Mere, Wilts)[11]

Some parishes own small areas of land, usually left to them by parishioners, which provide an income to help meet the kind of costs listed above. At Barham, Kent, for example there are '3 akers of belrope land', while at Wimborne Minster there is 'one acre of meadow lying in Netherwood, called the Bell-acre, which hath ben always appertaining to the maintenance of the said bells'.[12]

15. Bell-ringers and rules

Ringing of a single bell, to mark a death or summon the congregation, is usually done by the clerk or sexton as part of their ordinary duties. For more elaborate ringing, such as at funerals or major festivals, the parish's bell-ringers assemble.

Sometimes they are paid in money

1564 To the fower ringers for their wages this yere ... 2s (Barnstaple, Devon)[1]

but often part at least of their reward comes in the form of food and drink.

1522-24 For calves heddis [heads] for the ringers for 2 yeres ... 14d | 1542-44 For the ringers brekefaste on Corpus Christi daye for 3 yeres ... 2s (St Dunstan, Canterbury)

1524 To John Tilers wyff for drink fett to the chirch for the ringers & the clarkes at divers times at high festes ... 12d (St Mary at Hill)

1724 Paid young Plumpton for beer for the ringers ... 8s 6d (Cullompton, Devon)[2]

Like others performing tasks for the parish, ringers tend to be relatively poor, so the rewards they receive serve a semi-charitable purpose. It is not always enough, however. At St Edmund, Salisbury, payments to ringers are increased in 1684 'provided they forbeare begging of any one'. At Kendal in 1834 the ringers go on strike over pay for nearly a year. Later in the same century at Tydd St Mary,

---

* *Fathom*. The length covered by the outstretched arms, from fingertip to fingertip, usually taken as a measure of 6 feet. In this case, therefore, 112 yards of rope.

Lincolnshire, the ringers down ropes after the rector stops them taking beer into the ringing chamber, and a chiming apparatus is installed in their stead.[3]

Rules for ringers adorn the walls of many belfreys. The following set, at All Saints, Hastings, is dated 1756.

> This is a belfry that is free | To all those that civil be,
> And if you please to chime or ring, | It is a very pleasant thing.
> There is no music played or sung, | Like unto bells when they're well rung.
> Then ring your bells well, if you can, | Silence is best for every man.
> But if you ring in spur or hat, | Sixpence you pay, be sure of that;
> And if a bell you overthrow, | Pray pay a groat before you go.[4]

The rules at Burnley, dated 9th June 1804, include a series of such forfeits.

> Any person attempting to ring with spurs on ... 6d
> For not attending to practise on Monday and Tuesday evenings
>   at ten minutes past eight ... 3d
> For swearing or telling a lie in the steeple ... 3d
> For a ringer coming into the steeple intoxicated ... 3d
> For divulging anything out of the steeple which may tend to produce
>   mischief ... 3d | Also to the informer ... 3d
> For overthrowing a bell ... 2d
> For ringing with the hat on ... 2d[5]

A visitor to the belfry at Pitminster, Somerset, in 1849 notices a sheet of paper affixed to the wall inscribed with the following lines.

> If aney do ware hise hat
> When he is ringing here
> He straitte way then shall sixpence pay
> In sider or in bere.

Nearby, in the same handwriting, is added: 'Mr Robert Marke gave the ringers a pitcher of sider 1847.'[6]

The fact that ringing and refreshment often go together may partly explain why vicars and church-wardens often have trouble with those involved. Writing in 1872 the Rev. Henry Ellacombe, a great authority on bells, notes with feeling that 'generally speaking, there does not exist in connection with the church, a more difficult class of men to keep in order and submission than the bell-ringers'.[7]

Ringer on pillar, Stoke Dry, Rutland

Victorian bell-ringers in Suffolk.
ABOVE At Fressingfield, date uncertain. BELOW At Halesworth, 1876.

16. Abuse and accidents

One problem that arises is incidental damage, and the culprit may be required to pay.

> 1581 Received of Mr George Bodnam for ringing and breaking of a bell rope ... 18d (Mere, Wilts)

> 1600 Sold the metal of the little broken bell which Garyes man broke ... 3s | Received of Garyes man towards the same bell ... 2s 6d (Bishop's Stortford)

> 1693 Paid Denny for mending the treble wheel which young Buxton broke purposely ... 2s (Wenhaston, Suffolk)[1]

Occasionally the chance to misuse the bells proves too tempting. In 1610, for example, John Ball of Banbury is presented 'for procuring the bell to be knoled for John Smith in mockery'. Precautions may therefore need to be taken.[2]

> 1606 For a loke and two keyes to loke the bell ropes ... 12d (Prescot, Lancs)

> 1658 To George Wilkinson for keeping the bellstrings [ropes] lockt up in the deske from jangling of boyes ... 2s 6d (Kendal, Westmorland)[3]

Similarly at Barrow on Humber the list of the clerk's duties stipulates that 'he must be carefull that no boys or idle persons jangle the bells'.[4]

At Stoke Albany, Northamptonshire, the rector Hugh Conygrave goes further, forbidding ringing by the parish's young men and finally cutting the bell ropes to prevent them (1634).[5]

At Twickenham ringing at 'unseasonable hours' causes 'very great disturbance' to the vicar, Dr Hartcliff, and provokes a stiff order from the vestry.

> 1711 Whereas ... several disorderly persons did lately in a very insolent manner ... with the help of a ladder, break into the steeple of the church and ring the bells to the intent and purpose to disturb and provoke the said Dr Hartcliff. It is therefore ordered by this vestry that for the future during the said doctor's residence in the parish, there be no more ringing of the bells for recreation (unlesse upon some solemn occasion), but two nights in a week, viz. Thursdayes and Mondayes, and not to exceed the hour of nine.[6]

At Manchester in 1679 the churchwardens complain that 'through the carelessness of the clerks ... who for their owne gaine and advantage have frequently suffered yonge youthes, and persons wholly inexperianced in ringing ... the bells have been much damaged, burst, and spoild, whereby the parish have been put to great charges in repairing of them'. They appoint 'a certaine number of ringers, who are conceived to be men expert in ringing,' but it appears that problems persist.

> 1682 For boards for mending the ringing loft floor where two boyes had fallen downe, and a bar for steeple doore ... 5s 6d[7]

Problems also arise at Holbeach, Lincolnshire.

1803 July 8th. At a vestry ... to take into consideration the misconduct of the Society of Ringers here on several occasions, but particularly on Wednesday, the 22nd of June last. Constable Pick stated that he interposed and found Wm. Clarke, bricklayer, Wm. Dean, sadler, James Blinkhorn, blacksmith, George Stuart, shoemaker, Saul Warrener, taylor, John Kames, roper, and John Bland, sawyer, and several other persons in the belfry. That there was much disorder and some of them had been fighting. ... Ordered, that in future no drinking or smoking be allowed in the belfry and that the sexton do preserve good order therein or be discharged his office. Ordered, that in future no ringing be permitted, except on proper festivals or days, without the consent of the minister and churchwardens ... and that on no occasion dumb peals and tangling of the bells be suffered at the will or caprice of the ringers on pain of their being discharged from the Society. It was also found that Wm. Clarke, George Stuart, Wm. Dean, and James Blinkhorn were the ring-leaders [!] on the above day, and they are hereby expelled from the Society and be from henceforth discharged and kept out of the belfry.[8]

More serious incidents also occur.

At the hour of vespers on New Year's Eve 1301 a clerk called Robert de Honiton goes up to the tower of St Michael, Oxford, and then falls through a trap-door as he is ringing the bells. He dies five days later.[9]

At King's Lynn in 1621 a man is 'drawn up by the rope of St Margaret's great bell, and kill'd thereby'.[10]

At Culworth, Northamptonshire, the register records the death of Edward Elsden, 'killed by a bell upon Tuesday in Easter week' 1694. According to tradition some of his blood is sprinkled on the belfry walls.[11]

On 18th January 1774, as the ringers at Bungay are on their way down from ringing a mid-day peal for the birthday of Queen Charlotte, 'the large clock weight fell upon the head of John Gibborn, one of them, who died the next day, and cut off one of the great toes of Edward Tibbenham, another of the ringers'.[12]

Those involved in bell repair and maintenance are also at risk. At All Saints, Stamford, an installation does not go well for the bell-founder's brother.

1726 To ye ringers when the bell was hung ... 5s | To John Smith for a horse to carry Mr Eayres brother home he being lamed by ye bell ... 3s[13]

Fortunately the following accident has a happier outcome.

1701 The great bell in our steple was taken down to be cast upon Friday, 27 June, and as it was coming down the pulleys broke & the bell fell to the ground & brought all before it. The man who was above to guide it was one Ezekiel Shuttleworth, a joiner in this town; he seeing the pulleys break could no ways help himself but came after it, a ladder with himself & a little crow of iron in his hand, and yet by God's great preservation had little or no harm. The great bell was recast at Wigan 6 August 1701. (Chapel-en-le-Frith, Derbyshire, note in register)[14]

17. Delight

Despite the recurring trouble and expense, and the occasional danger, churches continue to treasure their bells, and a good set may draw enthusiastic visitors, so helping a little to refill the depleted parish coffer.

> 1577 Memorandum. That this yere past two of our belles were newe cast, and were very well handled both in the casting and hanging of them. By reason wherof many strangers did come to Bramley churche to ringe, of the whiche strangers so coming at diverse and sondrie times, John Litlewoork and Thomas Wigley, being parisshenors, did gather the sum of 16s 4d, whiche money was bestowed in suche order and sorte as shall appeare in the next yere's accompt. (Bramley, Hants)[1]

In 1598 a foreign visitor observes that the English are

vastly fond of great noises that fill the ear, such as the firing of cannon, drums, and the ringing of bells, so that it is common for a number of them, that have got a glass in their heads, to go up into some belfry, and ring the bells for hours together, for the sake of exercise.[2]

Four years later another foreigner notes similar enthusiasm.

On arriving in London we heard a great ringing of bells in almost all the churches going on very late in the evening, also on the following days until 7 or 8 o'clock in the evening. We were informed that the young people do it for the sake of exercise and amusement, and sometimes they lay considerable sums of money as a wager, who will pull a bell the longest or ring it in the most approved fashion. Parishes spend much money in harmoniously sounding bells, that one being preferred which has the best bells.[3]

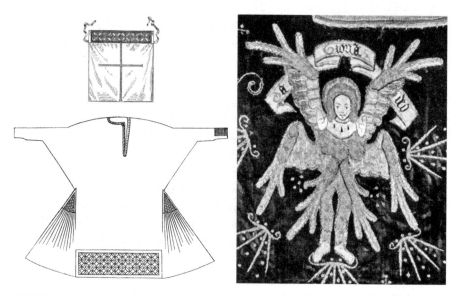

ABOVE. LEFT Amice and alb said to have belonged to Thomas Becket. RIGHT Detail of a chasuble, early 16th century. BELOW. LEFT Back of the same chasuble. RIGHT Portion of an orphrey with an angel above and St Catherine with her wheel, 14th century.

Paraphernalia, or The Church Stuff[1]

1. Vestments

The main vestments in use before the Reformation include the following.

Alb (from Latin *albus*, white). Full length white garment worn with a girdle at the waist.

Amice. White linen cloth with strings attached, originally worn over the head but often lowered to become a neck cloth.

Cassock. The ordinary clerical gown or under garment. Full length, with sleeves, usually buttoned at the front.

Chasuble. Circular or oval cape with a central opening for the head. Worn over other garments as the principal vestment of a priest celebrating mass. Decorated with **orphreys**, embroidered bands also found on copes and altar frontals.

Cope. Large flowing cape or cloak, often elaborately decorated. Worn over a cassock or surplice at festivals and in processions.

Rochet. Similar to an alb or surplice but shorter and sometimes sleeveless.

Stole (*right*). Narrow decorated strip of silk or linen worn over the shoulders and hanging down to the knee or lower.

Surplice. Loose white garment with an opening for the head and wide sleeves and reaching to the knee or lower. Often worn over a cassock.

Much day to day work goes into making and mending all these.

1462-64 To that woman lodging with Thomas Barbour for mending ye vestiments ... 3d (Thame)

1485 To Isabel Pye for making of 3 surplis & an albe ... 16d (Walberswick, Suffolk)

1566 To Anne of the vicarege for making 2 rochettes for the parishe clarke ... 6d (Saxilby, Lincs)[2]

When it comes to the show item of the cope, parishes want something impressive and invest a good deal of money.

1491 For a new cope bought by Mr Briges & Mr Hampton at London ... £9 18s 4d | To the carior for carrying of the same cope from London to Sarum ... 12d (St Edmund, Salisbury)

1525 Payed unto the brothere [? monk or monks] for 8 wekes & 3 days workin of the cope ... 23s 3d | For 3 ounces & a quarteren of fenys [Venice] golde ... 11s 11d (St Mary the Great, Cambridge)[3]

At St Peter Mancroft, Norwich, *circa* 1500 they have over forty copes including

A cope of blew velvet florishid with archangels of gold, the orpheras red velvet garnishid with marters of gold, and the cape written with letters made with perle *domine peto judicium de tua misericordia* [Lord, I beg judgement according to your mercy].

A cope of red velvet & wight satten paned, florishid with flowers in maner of running wyne [trailing vine] except the orpheras & the mide panne wich is red velvet & garnishid with dolphins of gold.

A cope of grene bawdkin* powdered with pecoks of gold, the orpheras of [em]brodery with apostells & virgins and in the cape the coronation of our lady.

In each case the gold decoration serves not only to show off the church's wealth but also to catch candlelight. Its use is not limited to copes: the church also has a set of vestments 'of blake bawdkin powderd with squerelles of gold', an alb and blue chasubles 'garnishid with crownes of gold & a lambe upon a boke of gold', and 'a single vestment for the high aulter, of red & grene bawdkin with lions & unicorns in gold'.[4]

Elsewhere, St Mary at Hill, London, has a cope decorated with 'grefons [griffins] of gold'; St Lawrence, Reading, has a blue silk chasuble 'with popingeays of gold'; and Thame has two red silk copes with 'dragons of gold'. More modestly St Dunstan, Canterbury, has '3 rocketts for men', and more soberly All Hallows, Bread Street, has 'a black velvet cope to singe the comunion at the beriall of ye ded'.[5]

Such riches need careful handling and storage and to be protected from the damp that besets most churches.

1464 In the vestrye 1 gret old arke to put in vestiments &c. (St Mary, Warwick, inventory)

1479-81 For a table & a pair trestellis to stand in the vestry, to ley the copes apon in festival days ... 2s (St Mary at Hill)

1480-82 For coles in the upper vestiary to drie the copes ... 1d (St Andrew Hubbard)[6]

Efforts may also be made to imbue them with agreeable smells.

1611 For a pound of orris-powder† to put among the church linen ... 10d (St Margaret, Westminster)

1634 For a boxe rose cakes,‡ and sweet pouder to keepe the church linin ... 2s (St Bartholomew Exchange)[7]

---

* *Baudekin.* A rich material, originally from Baghdad (whence the name by way of its Italian form, Baldacco), woven with a warp of gold thread or wire and a woof of silk. Later used more generally of rich brocades and shot silks.
† Powdered iris root, prized for its aromatic fragrance.
‡ Cakes of compressed rose petals used as a perfume for linens.

The array of vestments and their diverting decoration naturally arouse the ire of reformers. Thomas Becon attacks in particular those used at mass.

> Some have angels, some the blasphemous image of the Trinity, some flowers, some peacocks, some owls, some cats, some dogs, some hares, some one thing, some another ... This your fool's coat, gaily gauded, signifieth your pleasant fineness and womanly niceness ... But whence have ye your game-players' garments? ... Certain am I that ye have them not of the authority of the holy scripture. Christ and his apostles used no such fond coats at the ministration of the sacrament.[8]

LEFT Cope with a central image depicting the Assumption of the Virgin, late 15th or early 16th century. RIGHT. UPPER Detail of a 13th-century cope later converted into an altar cloth, Great Bircham, Norfolk. LOWER Detail of the 14th–century 'Jesse' cope showing the Virgin and Child.

2. Bread, wine and related items

Various other items required for the performance of services are also commonly found in the vestry. Several relate to the consecrated elements of wine and bread. The latter takes the form of a wafer, is served on a **paten** or shallow dish, and is often referred to as **singing bread**.

> 1465 To Jenet White for singing brede ... 3s 9d (St Michael, Cornhill)
>
> 1552 A pece of pewter made sawser wise to lay the sacramental bred in. (St Benet, Gracechurch Street, inventory)[1]

There is also the **houseling cloth** (from *housel*, an old English name for the administering of the eucharist), a long towel or sheet held before communicants to catch any bits of consecrated wafer that may fall as they receive it.

> 1501 A towell of diaper* for howseling, conteining in length 6 yerds. (Fordwich, Kent, inventory)
>
> 1535 I giff to the hie aulter the longest towell that I have to be there used at the time of Ester afore them that then schall resayve the holie sacrament in forme of bredde. (will of William Bridges, priest, Macclesfield, Cheshire)[2]

When altar rails appear, from the later 16th century onwards, the cloth is often spread over them.

The **corporal** or corporas is a smaller, square cloth on which the consecrated elements are placed during mass and with which any remnants are covered afterwards, the name deriving from the fact that it holds the body (*corpus*) of Christ.

Distinct from the wafers is the ordinary unconsecrated bread blessed by the priest after he has said mass and distributed to those who have not taken communion. This is known as **holy bread** or holy loaf and eaten as a token of friendship.[3]

> 1531 For a basket for holy brede ... 2d (Louth)
>
> 1547 For the holy lof ... 3d (St Martin, Leicester)[4]

The **wine** is served in a **chalice**, or later in a communion cup. Along with other items used at mass this needs to be hallowed before use.

> 1498 For halowing of the chalice ... 12d | For 3 men and 3 horse to bringe ye said chalice to Wells ... 10d† (Yatton, Somerset)
>
> 1554 To ye lorde sufferagan of Sarum for hallowing 2 chalesses, a pyx & 2 corporase clothis ... 2s 8d (Stanford, Berks)[5]

---

* Linen fabric woven with a small and simple pattern formed by the directions of the thread.

† The size of the party perhaps reflects a need to safeguard the valuable item.

ABOVE Houseling cloth, from an early 14th-century psalter.

LEFT Chalice, from a floor brass, Rendham, Suffolk.

RIGHT Communion cup, Mobberley, Cheshire.

BELOW Hallowing a chalice and paten, 1520.

Storage vessels are also needed, earlier ones tending to be made of leather or tin.

> 1577 For towe bottelles of lether, thone of three pints and thother of three quarts, for the communion wine ... 3s | 1586 For a pewter pottell pott* for the comunion table ... 3s 4d (Battersea, Surrey)[6]

The wine itself is of various types.

> 1529 For wine for our lady mass for the hole yere, that is to say, for 4 galons of Malmesey 5s 4d, and for 2 quartes of red wine 5d. (St Mary at Hill)

> 1596 Bastard wine for the communion ... in toto 8 quartes and a pinte at 12d the quarte ... 8s 6d (Worcester)

> 1613 For 12 gallons and a quart of Canary wine against Easter ... £1 16s 9d (Hartland, Devon)

> 1648 Paid Mrs Saintloe for 9 gallons of muskeadine [muscadine] for the sacrament this yeare ... £2 2s (St Christopher le Stocks)

> 1664 For the six bottells of Allegant [Alicant] for ye sacrament on Palm Sunday and Easter daye ... 12s (Weybridge, Surrey)

> 1667 For 4 quarts of sake [sack] at 2s quart for Whitsuntide ... 8s | For a great bottel to hold ye wine ... 1s 6d (St Mabyn, Cornwall)

> 1708 For four bottles of claret and four loaves for Whitsunday ... 8s 4d | For four bottles of tent wine and four loaves ... 12s 4d (Hawkhurst, Kent)[7]

Of these, tent is Spanish and deep red in colour, the name deriving from *tinto*, dark-coloured, but others, including Canary and sack, are white. Several are sweet including Canary, Malmsey and bastard (so named because it is mixed or adulterated).

Complaints are occasionally made about the quality. The wine used at Christmas 1607 at Smarden, Kent, is 'offensive' to several of the communicants, 'being dreggye & having some raggs in it'. At St Neot, Cornwall, in 1695 the accounts are challenged because 23 quarts provided for communion at Easter are 'so exceedingly bad and ... the church wardens have charged 2s 4d for each quart of it, whereas the wine was not really worth 12d a quart'.[8]

In some places better wine may be provided for those of higher status.

> 1573 Wine 22s 9d & bowght besides for ye masters & mistresses 7 pintes of muskodell [muscadel] 2s 4d. (St Thomas, Salisbury)[9]

The amounts consumed are often large, perhaps suggesting peculation.

> 1674 For 18 gallon and three pints of wine for the sacrament ... £3 13s 6d (St Mary, Manchester)[10]

---

* *Pottle.* Pot, tankard, or similar, especially one containing a 'pottle' (half a gallon).

3. Other ceremonial items

Holy water is scattered among the faithful with a kind of brush called an asperge or **aspergillum** (from Latin *aspergere*, to sprinkle).

> 1541 For 2 holy water sprinkelles ... 4d (St John the Baptist, Peterborough)[1]

Incense is stored in a boat-shaped vessel called a **ship**.

> 1556 For the ship to put frankincense in ... 20d (Ashburton, Devon)[2]

Clerk with bucket and sprinkle, from a 14th-century manuscript

From this it is spooned into a perforated metal **censer** in which it is burnt on glowing charcoal, the censer being swung on a chain both to stimulate combustion and to aid dispersal of the resulting fumes.

> 1530 To a tinkeler for making chenes to the sensers and mending them ... 2d (Prescot, Lancs)

> 1545 For charcolls for ye sensesse at Cristenmes ... 1d (St Mary on the Hill, Chester)[3]

Such items are often elaborately decorated. St Peter Mancroft, Norwich, has 'a shipe with an estrige [ostrich] feather stonding upon the middle' and 'a sensor of silver & parcel gilte ... with 3 libbards heeds blering ther tounges'.*[4]

Censer, from a mural, Easby, Yorkshire

According to Thomas Aquinas, the use of incense at mass has reference to two things: 'first, the reverence due to this sacrament, in order, by its good odour, to remove any disagreeable smell that may be about the place; second ... to show the effect of grace, wherewith Christ was filled as with a good odour'.[5]

Also used at mass is the **pax**, a tablet often made from precious material and bearing a depiction of the crucifixion. It is customary for it to be kissed by the celebrant and then by the other participants, its name (Latin for peace) deriving from this sign of amity.

More mundanely, after the service the sacred vessels are washed, leaving wet hands.

> 1528 Shorte towels for the preste to wipe on his hands at the lavatory,† 16. (Cratfield, Suffolk, inventory)[6]

---

* Leopards' heads with protruding tongues, to *blear* being to protrude the tongue in mockery.

† A piscina or other basin or bowl used for ritual washing during mass.

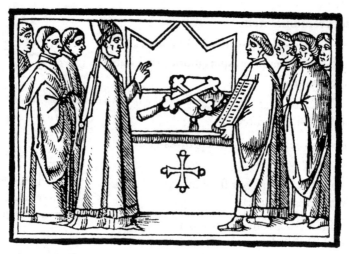

Hallowing a cross, 1520.
The attached fitting may be for placing the cross atop a pole for bearing in processions.

Other items include the **chrismatory**, for storing the consecrated oil called chrism. Typically it takes the form of a case containing three flasks for different uses, one for baptism, one for confirmation, and one for anointing the sick.[7]

1554 To Father Charlemayne for mending the chrismatory ... 6d (Worcester)[8]

Most churches have a variety of **crosses**.

1479-81 For mending of the cross that is borne abowte every day, and for mending of the mustenaunce* cross ... 3s 4d | 1527 Unto a goldsmith for burnishing of the best cross [etc] ... 3s 4d (St Mary at Hill)

1557 To the painter for painting the Lent crosse ... 12d (Bungay)[9]

On festival days parishes may parade their **relics**, among which pieces of the original cross are notably common.

1431 1 crosse of golde with 1 pece of the crosse of Criste within, the same garneshed with perry and oder stones. (St Peter, Cheapside, inventory)

1472 A combe of Seint Edmundes. | A pece of ye skoll of Seint Wolfrise. (St Edmund, Salisbury, inventory)

1500 A pax of silver and gilt with a pece of the holy crosse therein. (St Dunstan, Canterbury, inventory)[10]

The following seems modestly priced if genuine.

1495 Paid for a relike of Seint Andrews finger ... 1d (St Andrew Hubbard)[11]

---

* *Monstrance.* An open or transparent holder in which a consecrated host is displayed, often set into a cross.

4. Books

A number of books are needed for the conduct of services in a medieval parish church, all of them in Latin. The **missal** contains the various versions of mass for the whole year. The **gradual** or **grail** contains the musical portions of mass, its name taken from that of an antiphon sung at the steps of the altar (Latin *gradus*, step). The **breviary** contains the offices of the canonical hours (lauds, compline, matins, etc) said by the clergy. It is usually small in format so as to be easily portable, hence the alternative names of **porteous** and **portas**. The **antiphoner** or **antiphonary** contains the musical portions of the breviary and is the forerunner of the modern hymn book. The **manual** contains the occasional services including baptism, marriage and burial, and is named from its handy size (*manus*, hand). Also needed are the **psalter**, containing the psalms, and the **processional**, containing the litany and hymns sung in procession. There may also be a **legend** or book of readings (*legere*, to read) for use in services, often containing accounts of the lives of saints.[1]

The production of books at this time involves a great deal of painstaking labour and they are accordingly expensive.

1401 For a new missal for the church ... £4 13s 4d (Tavistock, Devon)

1509 To Frier Jeffrey for the binding and new covering and pening of one antiponer and a great legend in 2 volums ... 16s 8d (Holy Trinity, Cambridge)

1554 For the grale to singe masse apon ... 18s (Wandsworth)[2]

A range of animal skins are used for the bindings, along with wooden boards.

1531 *The costs of the Books.* For 3 buk skines, 2 stag skines & 8 shepe skines ... 18s 6d | For 21 rede skines ... 7s | For glew ... 12d | For small threde & pak threde ... 2s 2d | For a dosen of parchment skines* ... 2s 2d | For 15 vellam skines† ... 10s | To the joiner for bordes to the bokes ... 20d | To the boke binder for binding of the bokes ... 24s | To frere Peter for writing & noting the new graile & for the vellam therto ... 46s 8d | For binding the new graile & liming‡ thereof ... 9s 10d | For vellam for the great leager§ ... £3 23d | For florishing the same boke with stuff therto belonging ... £3 9s 1d (St Lawrence, Reading)[3]

The music books feature pricksong – music set down by means of pricks or notes, and so distinct from that either sung from memory or extemporised.

1469 To Sir William Barbour for prikking of a masse ... 10d (St Michael, Cornhill)

---

* *Parchment.* Animal skin dressed and prepared for writing, binding, etc.
† *Vellum.* A fine parchment prepared from the skin of a calf (cf. veal).
‡ *Limn.* Illuminate; adorn or embellish in gold or bright colour; paint.
§ *Ledger.* A large copy of the breviary.

1506 To John Cawod for a long masse prekin, writing & rewling, called
      Miserere ... 2s (Louth)[4]

Most of the above books are jettisoned at the Reformation, after which services
depend mainly on the Book of Common Prayer and the latest approved version
of the bible in English. Psalters survive but are now in English.

1598 For singinge bookes for the churche, viz. the Psames and other
      godlie bookes in fower or five partes ... 6s (Hartland, Devon)[5]

By this time the old practice of books being written out by hand, perhaps by
a friar or local monk, has largely been replaced by printing, usually in London or
at the university presses. As a result parishes often need to arrange for books to
be collected or delivered from afar.

1569 For a new bible ... 30s | For a communion boke ... 4s 8d | For
      brenging them home from Cambridge ... 4d (Bishop's Stortford)

1612 Paid at London ye 5th of Maie for a bible ... 47s 6d (Hartshorne,
      Derbyshire)

1677 Paid for one bible 45s, and for one common prayer book 14s, and
      the hoy-man for bringing them down from London 1s, [in] all ... £3
      (Ash-next-Sandwich, Kent)[6]

Hitches may occur.

1605 Paid to carry back againe the bibell that was misbeliked by the parson
      .... (Dartington, Devon)[7]

Whether the books are copied by hand or printed, costs for binding and re-
binding arise periodically. Sometimes the books are taken to the binder and
sometimes he comes to stay.

1498 To a glovar for a schep skin & a caf skin to bind bokes wyt in ye
      kirke ... 11d | To the boke binder his hire ... 21d | For ye boke binders
      bord a weke ... 10d | For ye boke binders bord and his wife a noder
      weke ... 16d (Leverton, Lincs)

1501 For mending of the best antiphoners cuvering the which the rattes
      had hurte ... 12d | 1504 To the boke binder at Ledon halle, for covering,
      binding & pesing* of 4 antifoners, a masse booke, a manewell, a legend
      in 2 foloms [volumes] & 3 grailes ... 46s 8d (St Mary at Hill)[8]

Sometimes parishes wish to smarten up the book most exposed to public view.

1601 For mendinge ye greate church bible with bosses and clasps and
      bufinge ye backe ... 1s 4d (St Mary the Great, Cambridge)[9]

* *Piecing.* Joining pieces together; repairing or patching.

Occasionally the texts themselves need attention.

1496 To the stacyener for setting of all the new feestes in to the bookes that lakked them and in to the masse bookes, & for mending, pinning, clasping of them ... 33s 4d (St Mary at Hill)

1547 For carrying up the bible to London to set in certen gospels which it lacked ... & for bringing downe the same bible agein ... 3s 4d (Great Hallingbury, Essex)

1572 To Scottowe the scrivener for mending decayed places in the bible ... 5s (Bungay)[10]

Given the large sums laid out on books, parishes are naturally concerned to prevent them from being stolen. Among the titles warranting protection are two approved by the authorities after the Reformation: John Foxe's 'Book of Martyrs', first published in England in 1563, and Erasmus's 'Paraphrases' of the gospels, which under injunctions of 1547 churches are required not only to own but to 'set up in some convenient place' so that parishioners can read it.[11]

1542 For a chain for ye bible & fixing ye same ... 3d (Great Hallingbury)

1636 For the chaines wherewith the Bookes of Martyrs are tied ... 1s 8d | For a chaine and staple to tie the booke of the paraphrases of Erasmus ... 8d (St Mary, Devizes, Wilts)

1733 Paid Mr Chubb for putting clasps, screws and chains to eleven prayer books in ye gallery ... £1 7s 6d (Fulham, Middlesex)[12]

Books, paper and binding are also needed for the parish's own records, the main uses being for its registers and accounts.

1561-63 Payed to Arthur Pepwell bokebinder in Seint Paules churcheyard at London, for this present boke to write the accomptes in 13s, and for the cariage home of him 4d. (Mere, Wilts)

1597 Paid for this accompte booke, boughte at Exon [Exeter] by John Abbatt and by him brought home for nothinge ... 3s (Hartland)

1600 A skin of parchment to wright this on ... 4d (St Thomas, Salisbury)[13]

A professional may be employed, particularly for more formal documents.

1492 To the skrevener in Lombard strete for writing of 2 dedes and the bede rowle* and for other thinges that he made for the cherch ... 3s 4d (St Mary at Hill)

1558 Paid the scrivner to write a bill to certifye ye archdeacon whether there was any anabaptist, or erroneous opinions, within ye parishe ... 1s (St Benet, Gracechurch Street)[14]

* *Bead-roll.* A list of benefactors read out regularly in church.

The following perhaps explains itself.

1741   Paid Revd. Mr Clieve for righting regester ... £2 2s (Duffield, Derbyshire)[15]

Writing materials also need to be provided.

1549   For gum, gaules [galls] and coperas for to make incke [etc] ... 3s (St Dionis Backchurch)

1609   For an ink horne,* pennes, paper & ink ... 1s 4d (Battersea)

1686   For a standish, pens, ink, and sandbox† for the vestry ... 2s (St Martin, Leicester)

1762   For ink powder ... 6d (Chester-le-Street, co. Durham)[16]

Problems may still arise. The following note is from the register of Cratfield, Suffolk, and relates to a nearby parish.

In 1594, at Halesworth, on the feast of the Nativity, commonly called Xtmas day, the weather was so cold that the rector could not thaw his ink to write down the names of the communicants.[17]

5. Lights‡

Each year every parish spends a good deal of money on lights used in services and to illuminate the church's often gloomy interior spaces. In addition, before the Reformation a great number of lights are set upon the rood loft, about the Easter sepulchre, and before images.

First wax has to be bought, often in large quantities, and then the chandler or wax-maker must mould, 'make' or 'strike' it into the required shape, perhaps adding gold foil or other decoration as a finishing touch. Sometimes the work may be done in the church, or perhaps in the church house.

1446   For waxe agen[st] Crisemasse ... 20s | For making of the waxe ... 3s | For hors-mete to the wax-maker, and his owne mete, and our mete, while we made the said waxe ... 17d (Yatton, Somerset)

1514   For 44 li. of rawe waxe bought at Sterbyriche [Stourbridge] fayer, with the caryage, for the rood lights at Midsomer and Michaelmass quarters, and for waxe to 4 torches this Madsummer ... 19s 4d | For gold foile and colours of those 4 torches ... 8d | For fire wood and meat and drink to those 4 torches making ... 10d | To the werkeman Robert Blane chaundelor for his labur in making ... 16d (Bassingbourne, Cambs)[1]

* A small portable vessel made of horn for holding ink.
† *Standish.* A stand containing ink, pens, etc. *Sand-box.* A box with a perforated top for the sprinkling of sand to blot wet ink.
‡ The discussion here is of a general nature. References to particular lights can be found in the Church, Year and Burial chapters.

Quite often women are involved.

1546 For making the churche light and the sepulchre light ... 6s | For meate and drinke to Robert Webster, Robert Worseley and Elsabeth Latham when the light was in casting, fascioning and making ... 4s 6d | To the said Elsabeth for tempering of the waxe ... 6d | To the same Elsabeth for weke yorne [? wick yarn] ... 6d (Prescot, Lancs)

1547 For making the wax for the whole yeare to Edw. Hallowood wife ... 2s 4d (Holy Trinity, Chester)[2]

Old wax is commonly recycled.

1454 For joining to geders of 3 stumped torches ... 2d (St Ewen, Bristol)

1528 To James Holt for gethering the droppeing of waxe ... 1d ob. (Prescot)

1539 Delivered to the waxchandler the old stuff of the beam light, weighing 54 lb. [For] the making of the same ... 2s 3d | Left in the waxchandler's hands, a bag of old wax, to be tried, weighing altogether, with the bag, 26 lb., whereof is tried good wax 9¼ lb., and in torch wax 11½ lb. (St Laurence Pountney)

1554-58 For making of 4 newe torches, wiche torches were made of olde torches endes and renewed with 7 li. of new waxe to them ... 6s 8d (Lambeth)[3]

Much the greatest need is for **candles**. Those used for liturgical purposes, notably at mass, should be made of beeswax, which is considered pure because of the supposed virginity of bees and because it is extracted by them from flowers, and so is seen as aptly representing the pure flesh of Christ born of a virgin mother. The wick is seen as representing Christ's soul and the flame his divinity. However, for ordinary, non-ceremonial purposes candles made of tallow (animal fat) are often used.[4]

1510 For 3 li. of talow candells for to set in the churche on Cristmas daye ... 3d ob. (St Lawrence, Reading)[5]

Church accounts indicate a few further distinctions.

1555 For cotten candles ... 6s 6d | 1589 For one virgin waxe candle ... 8d (St Michael, Cornhill)

1556 For rushe candells ... 1d (St Michael, Bath)

1556 To the wife of Thomas Pycavance for a li. of wax to make small candeles of to saye masse with and to sing matins with on Christ[mas] daye .... | For white candelles to ring with and to do serves with .... | For making of 3 surges to the alter .... (Prescot)

1571 For half a dozen of sise candelles on Christermas eve to eveninge prayer ... 8d (St Peter, Cheapside)[6]

Cotton candles are simply those with cotton wicks. Virgin wax originally denotes fresh or unused beeswax or that produced by the first swarm of bees, but later is applied more generally to any fine quality wax. Rush candles are made by dipping the pith of a rush in tallow or other grease and have little illuminating power. White candles are perhaps those made with bleached wax. Cierges (from Latin *cereus*, of wax) are candles or tapers, especially large ones used in religious ceremonies, and sizes are small candles used especially at court and in churches.[7]

Whatever their type, candles are essential early and late in the day and more generally during the darker months.

> 1511 To Sir Robert for candell to sey his matens in the morninges ... 3d (St Mary at Hill)

> 1547 For 13 li. and a half of candelles for the first mass and to ringe curfur [curfew] ... 2s 3d (Ludlow)

> 1562 Candell in ye winter nightes in ye churche ... 12d (St Mary the Great, Cambridge)

> 1707 For candles for the minister a very dark Sunday morning ... 1d (St Alphage, London Wall)[8]

The following odd entry apparently relates to a belief that they also serve to preserve woollen from moths.

> 1734 For a pound of candles to lie among the shrouds ... 6d (Ockley, Surrey)[9]

Tapers, wax candles mainly used for devotional purposes, are often set before the altar or image of a saint.

> 1529 For 3 tapers making befor our lady ... 12d (Rotherfield, Sussex)

> 1533 For three pounds wex to Sent Andrews taper and the making ... 7d (St Andrew, Lewes, Sussex)[10]

Torches provide stronger light on particular occasions.

> 1530 To the churche ... so muche money as will buy one torche, the wiche I will be used in the administracon of the blessed sacrament & at pore men's burials. (will of J. Pye, Walgrave, Northants)

> 1532 For 4 coarse torches to light on Alhalow night and at other times in the churche ... 16d (Lydd, Kent)[11]

Lights of all kinds naturally need to be supported by some means.

> 1437 For making clay balls to hold the candles at Christmas ... 1d (All Saints, Bristol)

> 1458 For 6 dishes for the auters to set the candellstikes on ... 7d (Walberswick, Suffolk)

1545 For socketts for ye candalls in ye quer ... 3d (Bungay)

1557 For pricks that the tapers stand on ... 8d (Thame)

1571 For 5 iron candlesticks to stick in the pillars of the church to set lights in at morning prayers ... 18d (St Mary, Aldermanbury)[12]

From an English manuscript of the Apocalypse, *c.* 1260

These may need repair or adjustment, or they may be embellished.

1515 For souldring two lions upon the great candelstikkes ... 6d (St Mary the Great, Cambridge)

1557 For mending one of the gret candlesticks that ye boys did breake ... 2s 4d (Bungay)

1626 To a gyner [joiner] for cutinge all the candlesticks shorter [etc] ... 2s (St Bartholomew Exchange)[13]

Once secure the lights are ready.

1503 For 2 reddes [reeds] to lythe candelles withe ... 2d (St Mary at Hill)[14]

The dripping of wax may then be a problem.

1468 To a carpenter and to a dawber for making of a thing in the north side of the chirche for dropping of candell ... 8d | 1476-78 For iren werk for the dropping of the tapirs before our lady of pitee ... 9d (St Andrew Hubbard)[15]

In due course the flames must be quenched.

1517 For snoffers of plate for to put owte the tapurs ... 5d (St Mary at Hill)

1677 For a pair of snuffers & snuff pan ... 2s (St Alphage, London Wall)[16]

Hanging lights provide more general illumination inside the church. They may be in the form of a **trendle**, a suspended hoop or wheel on which candles or tapers are fixed and which, before the Reformation, is sometimes hung in front of the rood.

1502 To John Turner* for making of the trendell ... 2s | For corde to the same ... 6d | For timber .... | For painting ... 5d | For a bolte & a swevell ... 6d (St Lawrence, Reading)

1518 Received of the goodwife Argell and the goodwife Hilles in money gadered of the parrisoners for the trendells lyte afore the rode ... 7s 9d (Lambeth)[17]

* Perhaps his occupation as well as or rather than his surname.

In some cases suspended fittings are referred to simply as candlesticks.*

1531 For 2 hanging candelstikes for the quire ... 5d (St Mary at Hill)

1621 For a brasson [brazen] candlstick with 12 branches for the midle ile ... £1 16s 6d | For a cord to hange the candlstick in the midle ile ... 10d (Ludlow)[18]

Alternatively candles may be placed within the protective casing of a **lantern**. The panels of the case may be made of glass or of horn, hence probably the alternative spelling of 'lanthorn'.

1550 For 7 foote of new glasse for one of ye lanterns ... 2s 11d | 1564 For skoringe and makinge cleane of the lantern hornes ... 2d | For a rope 30 yards longe to hange the greate lantern in ye middeste of ye churche ... 12d (St Michael, Cornhill)

1554-58 For newe horning of the church lantern ... 10d (Lambeth)[19]

There may also be a welcoming light hung near the church's entrance.

1608 To Mr Grey, clerke, for candles to the lanthorne at the churche dore in Bartholemews lane and for his paines, one yere ... 6s 8d (St Bartholomew Exchange)

1638 For candles for the lanthorne at the church gate all the winter ... 3s (St Anne & St Agnes, Aldersgate)[20]

These two London parishes are among those which provide lighting across a wider area as well.

1638-39 Nov. 22nd. To Mr Bowles for mendinge 2 precinct lanthornes ... 3s | Dec. 21st. For a case for the lanthorne at Mrs Millingtons doore ... 5s 3d | Jan. 30th. To Mr Cakebread for candles for the lower precinct ... 3s 7½d (St Bartholomew Exchange)

1646 For mending of the three greate lanthornes which did hang in three several places in the parrish ... 3s 6d | Unto Goodman Field the bellman for putting in the candles into the greate lanthornes this winter ... 3s | For 22 lb. of candles for the greate lanthornes for the winter nights ... 11s 11d (St Anne & St Agnes, Aldersgate)[21]

There may also be portable lanterns for those needing to get about on parish business, a 'dark' one having a sliding panel or other means by which the light can be concealed.

1637 For a lanterne for the sexton ... 9d (Ludlow)

1686 For a dark lanthorn for ye bellman ... 2s 4d (Bishop's Stortford)[22]

---

* Chandelier is a modern term. Its earliest use listed in the *OED* in relation to lights is in 1736, when it was considered 'modish'.

Some of the parish's expenditure on lights is offset by income, mainly from dedicated collections

> 1526 Received of men and women in the parish this yere that was gadered toward the torchis ... 4s 8d (St Dunstan, Canterbury)[23]

and from payments for the 'waste' or depletion of wax at funerals. In addition there may be the occasional sale of surplus items and ad hoc hiring out of torches.

> 1524 Received for 3 ends of torches sold ... 3s (St Andrew, Canterbury)

> 1538 Received for a torch to bring home a child from christening ... 2d (St Alphage, London Wall)[24]

6. Chests, including for the parish register

The church almost certainly has a chest, and there may be several for storing different items.

> 1504 For the making of a new chest to put torches & for iren worke of the same ... 6s | 1511 For a lok & a key [and] a peir garnettes [hinges] for a chest in the quere to ley in old wax ... 12d | 1519 To Gymbold the joiner for a chest for the vestmentes ... 13s 4d (St Mary at Hill)

> 1513 A hundred board to make a chest for the priest's song books ... 1s 4d | William Wyner for making ditto ... 1s 8d (Rye, Sussex)

> 1538 For mendinge of a lock to the coffer that kepith singing bred in ... 1d (Tavistock, Devon)

> 1633 For a chest with a locke and a key with partitiones in the chest to lay the candells in theire sortes ... 7s | 1674 For a chest to put the parish writeings in ... £1 (St Bartholomew Exchange)[1]

In some cases great effort is made to ensure security

> 1597 For a cheste, covered with black leather, and barde with iron, with five locks and keys thereunto ... £4 10s (St Margaret, Westminster)[2]

although keys may of course be lost and locks may go awry.

> 1620 To Roberte Ludlam for openinge of the church coffer ... 3d (St Martin, Leicester)[3]

The most notable items kept in the chests are the **parish registers**. These are effectively instituted by an order of 5th September 1538 issued by Thomas Cromwell which requires the parson, vicar or curate to keep

> one boke or registre wherin ye shall write the day and yere of every wedding, christening and buryeng made within your parishe for your time, and so every man succeeding you likewise. ... And for the sauff keping of the same boke the parishe shalbe bounde to provide of theire comen charges one

sure [secure] coffer with two lockes and keys, wherof the one to remain with you, and the other with the ... wardens, wherein the saide boke shalbe laide up.[4]

Parishes make provision accordingly.

1538 For a boke to write there names in that be cristened & wedded or buried acording to ye kinges injunctions ... 12d | For 6 bordes to make our churche coffer with all ... 14d | For gemows [hinges] & nailes concerning ye same coffer ... 10d | For ye makyn of ye same coffer in meat & drinke & wages to Lousemore & a man to helpe him ... 12d | For 2 lokis concerning ye same coffer, to Stebbe ... 18d (Morebath, Devon)[5]

In 1597-98, among other changes, it is ordered that the coffer is to have a third lock, each of the two churchwardens having a separate key.[6]

One problem arising from the storage of such items in churches is noted in the register of Rodmarton, Gloucestershire.

1630 If you will have this book last, be sure to aire it at the fier or in the sunne three or foure times a yeare — else it will grow dankish and rot, therefore look to it. It will not be amisse when you finde it dankish to wipe over the leaves with a dry wollen cloth. This place is very much subject to dankishness, therefore I say look to it.[7]

A regester booke of all the marriages Cryfteninges & birialles that hath ben in the parrishe of St peters in Dunwich within the countie of Suff Senc the yeare of our lord God
1539

Title page of an early parish register, St Peter, Dunwich, Suffolk.
The church itself was lost to the sea towards the end of the 17th century.

Chests at Dersingham, Norfolk (*top*) and Harty, Essex

Decorated initial letter at the start of the churchwardens' accounts of St Michael, Cornhill, 1556. Such accounts are among the parish books typically kept in chests.

7. Miscellaneous

Collection boxes and plates are often stored in the vestry.

1610 For two boxes for to gather for the poore ... 2s (St Mary the Great, Cambridge)

1656 Bought two pewter saucers to gather money in for the poore ... 2s (Hammersmith, Middlesex)[1]

Items used in church cleaning may be there too.

1511 For a long pole with a brome to swepe the church rofe ... 2d (St Martin Outwich)

1576 For a basket for carrying muck out of ye church ... 4d (Bungay)

1620 For a brush to take the cobwebbs downe ... 4d (Wandsworth)

1706 Paid for the Turk's head brush* and carriage from London to sweep ye church windows ... 3s (Rotherham, Yorks)[2]

There may also be a large **umbrella** to shield the minister as he reads the burial service. Despite the high cost churches are early adopters of this device.

1700 One umbarellowe. (Manchester, inventory)

1746 A hombrellow for the use of the vicar for burying in rainy weather ... £2 10s (Walthamstow, Essex)

1759 For an umbrella and carriage from London ... 15s (Liskeard, Cornwall)[3]

Once acquired it needs holding aloft. Often this is done by the parish clerk, but others may be paid for doing so.

1770 Jan. 2nd. Dame Lofthouse for bringing out the umbrella ... 5s | May 26th. Dame Lofthouse ½ year for umbrella ... 5s (Wakefield, Yorks)[4]

Alternatively it may be attached to a pike thrust into the ground.

1769 For a pike for ye umbrella ... 8d (Ulverston, Lancs)[5]

On a visit to Bromley church in the 1820s William Hone comes across

a capital large umbrella of old construction, which I brought out and set up in the churchyard: with its wooden handle, fixed into a movable shaft, shod with an iron point at the bottom, and struck into the ground, it stood seven feet high; the awning is of a green oiled-canvas, such as common umbrellas were made of forty years ago, and is stretched on ribs of cane.

---

* Brush with bristles extending around the top of the stem like a 'wild' head of hair. This use predates the earliest listed in the *OED* by nearly 150 years.

LEFT Umbrella in use, from an engraved writing sheet published at Chester, 1798.
RIGHT Watch-box of the type disdained by William Hone, Ivychurch, Kent.

It opens to a diameter of five feet, and forms a decent and capacious covering for the minister while engaged in the burial service at the grave. It is in every respect a more fitting exhibition than the watch-box sort of vehicle devised for the same purpose, and in some churchyards trundled from grave to grave, wherein the minister and clerk stand ...[6]

Other even more miscellaneous items may be lurking in the vestry, the following being one useful example.

> *c.* 1481 A rounde balle of laton [latten] and gilte, and a litle balle therein of irne [iron], in colde weder to make it brenning hote, and then put it inne the balle for a prest to have it in his hande in wintir. (St Stephen, Walbrook, inventory)[7]

In addition, prior to the Reformation many rural parishes keep a **plough** in the church with a light maintained above it in the hope that this will ensure good harvests. Some ploughs linger in churches into later centuries, although without the associated light. A visitation of Ely diocese in 1685 finds several, for example at Dry Drayton, Cambridgeshire, where it is ordered that 'the town plough ... be removed out of the church'.[8]

8. For secular activities: armour, fire-tackling equipment, bird nets

In medieval times and later, individuals, villages and towns are all legally required to play a part in the defence of the kingdom. As the main unit of local organisation the parish becomes involved in various ways, from constructing archery butts to kitting out soldiers to send to musters. As a result, before about 1650 some or all of the parish **armour** may be kept in the church, either stored away or put on show.

> 1567 For mending and setting up the coate armour in our lady chapel ... 6d (St Margaret, Westminster)

> 1632 For setting up a frame in the church to hange the armor upon ... 12s (Chedder, Somerset)[1]

There may also be a stash of **gunpowder**.

> 1600 For making a key to the powder chest & mending the locke ... 2s 2d (Woodbury, Devon)

> 1607 For hooping the gunpowder barrels ... 6d | 1615 [Inventory] One old carpet lying in the vestry over the gunpowder. (Chelmsford, Essex)[2]

Fortunately most churches boast a range of **fire-tackling equipment**. At the most basic level this means **buckets**, usually made of leather, which may be hanging up in a row.

> 1586 To John Franklin in Powles churchyard for 12 lether buckites ... £1 10s | For painting on the buckites the name of the churche and the churchwardens names ... 2s 6d | For 12 wooden pins to hange the buckites on [and] for nailles ... 1s 4d (St Mary Woolchurch)

> 1624 For new sowinge, mendinge, hoopinge and pitchinge twelve buckets ... 16s (Wandsworth)

Parish armour, Brington, Northamptonshire

1656 For the 30 buckets in the church and the charge of bringing them down from London ... £4 14s 2d | For painteing of the said buckets, to Ducket the painter ... 8s (St Peter Mancroft, Norwich)

1672 For a staffe to take downe and hange up the buckets ... 1s (St Christopher le Stocks)[3]

They are liable to be damaged or lost when pressed into service.

1646 Mending 23 buckets that was split at Wilton when the fire was at my Lorde of Pembrookes house ... 16s (St Thomas, Salisbury)

1650 Paid the sexton in lookeing after* the buckets which were used about the fire in Holborne ... 6d | And to the bucketmaker for mending of sixteene buckets which were broake at the fire ... 20s (St Anne & St Agnes, Aldersgate)

1678 To ye belman for going thorow town for buckets ... 2d (Manchester)[4]

Ladders are also essential, and sometimes very long.

1579 For 4 ladders ... 29s 4d | For the carriage of them ... 16d | To 2 porters to helpe with the ladders over the bridge ... 2d | To Yorke for hookes of iron to hange up the ladders on ... 4s (Lambeth)

1607 For a longe ladder beinge forty & three rounds ... 9s | 1647 Paid eight men for carrieinge the greate ladder of the church from Corve bridge ... 1s 10d (Ludlow)[5]

If stored outside they need securing.

1488 In the churchyarde ther beth 3 longe ladders lokked in a cheyne, one of 31 stares and another of 25 and another of 24. (St Christopher le Stocks, inventory)[6]

As with buckets they may be damaged or lost, and they are often marked to reduce the risk of the latter.

1664 For a marke for brandinge the ladders and poles ... 3s (St Bartholomew Exchange)

1666 Paid the bell-man for goinge about towne for the church ladders [which] were lost ... 4d (Manchester)[7]

Another vital instrument is the **fire-hook**, used to pull down timbers of burning houses to prevent fires from spreading. They are usually 20 to 30 feet long with iron rings at the ends and on the sides so that, using ropes, they can be pulled by horses or companies of men.[8]

1527 For a fire croke to help draw down the houses that are aventured with fire ... 5d (Wimborne Minster, Dorset)

* Probably here with the sense 'seeking out'.

1649 4 ropes belonging to the fire hookes. (St Giles without Cripplegate, inventory)

1654 Paid porters for carrying the iron hooke when ye fire was in Thread-needle street ... 1s (St Christopher le Stocks)[9]

Beyond such basic items, in the 1630s St Botolph, Aldersgate, boasts 'one brasse squirt to quench fire with, in a case'. By the 1650s some London parishes and wards have their own **fire engines** which, by way of leather pipes, project water onto fires from a distance.[10]

1651 For mending the wardes engine usefal against fiers [etc] ... £1 4s (St Bartholomew Exchange)

1655 Expended upon the men that went forth with the engine ... 6s 6d | Given to the men that drew the engine out and in ... 1s 6d | To Abell Hodges for working the engine at both fires ... 5s (St Giles without Cripplegate)

1661 For bringing back the engines from Whitehall, when the fire was there ... 6s (St Margaret, Westminster)

1708 For leather pipes for the engine ... £1 15s (St Ethelburga, Bishops-gate)[11]

Engines also appear outside the capital. At All Saints, Maidstone, payments are made in 1683 for 'cleaning the engines and setting them up' and for 'getting the engines out and in, and trying them'. At St Peter Mancroft, Norwich, money for one is raised by a subscription among parishioners in 1690. At Ludlow two engines are well established by 1721, when the vestry agrees that, along with three dozen leather buckets, they 'shall be kept and preserved in the Weavers Chancell of the church'. At the same time it is ordered 'that Wm. Bird have 20s per annum for keeping the engines in repair & that he shall play them the first week in every month'. At Leyton, Essex, a meeting in 1790 orders that 'the parish engine ... be brought out the next vestry and worked in the presence of the gentlemen'.[12]

Time and use naturally take their toll, however, and, in addition, during the 19th century the involvement of parishes in such civic functions declines. In 1857 the vestry of St Martin, Salisbury, resolves 'to sell the fire engine belonging to the parish, the same being in a very dilapidated condition and quite useless'.[13]

Another unlikely parish responsibility is indicated by an inventory entry at Wenhaston, Suffolk, in 1686: 'A rook-net very old.'[14]

Under the 1532-33 Acte to destroye Choughes, Crowes and Rookes the inhabitants of 'every parishe, towneship, hamlet, borough or village' are to 'make or cause to be made one nette' with which to catch the birds in question. This requirement is renewed by the 1566 Acte for preservation of Graine.[15]

1571 For a crowe nette ... 10s (Wandsworth)

1672 For mending the rook net ... 1s (Forncett St Peter, Norfolk)[16]

ABOVE Fire-hooks, Raunds, Northamptonshire. BELOW An early fire engine in use in London in 1748, with the tower of St Michael, Cornhill, in the background.

9. Payments for vermin: a digression

The 1566 Act also sets out rewards to be paid to those destroying a range of 'noyfull fowells and vermin', from bullfinches and buzzards to badgers, foxes, moles, otters and hedgehogs. Over the next three centuries such payments become a regular feature of the accounts of many parishes, particularly those in rural areas.

1577 To the clerke for killinge of crose ... 12d (Abbey Church, Shrewsbury)

1582 To the wife of George Washington, for killinge of rattes according to the statute ... 4d (Prescot, Lancs)

1626 To the otter ketchers for three otters heads ... 3s (Thatcham, Berks)

1646 To the sexton for killing an owle [etc] ... 1s 2d (St Mary, Beverley, Yorks)

1653 Thomas ap Lewis for killing two foxes in Acton Wood and bringing their heades to church ... 2s (North Lydbury, Shropshire)[1]

1662 For two bodgers heads ... 2s (Chiddingly, Sussex)

1687 To Farmer Monday for killing rooks ... 6s (St Mary Bourne, Hants)

1708 For 3 foxes, 2 cubs & the old bitch ... 13s 4d (Youlgreave, Derbyshire)

1752 For 47 hedgehogs and 1 sparrow hawk ... 8s (Barnstaple, Devon)[2]

From the 18th century onwards sparrows are the main sufferers.

1721 To the sparrow catcher for 36 dozen of sparrows ... 11s (Mogger-hanger, Beds)

1742 For 264½ dozen of sparrow ... £2 4s 1d (Kempston, Beds)

1768 Paid the boys at the workhouse 4 dousen sparrows and 3 dozen of eggs ... 11d (Northill, Beds)[3]

Some payments point to the relatively rural nature of city parishes in earlier times.

1573 To a yonge man for killinge and takinge 6 hedge-hogges ... 2s (St Martin in the Fields)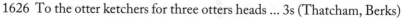

1682 For 71 doz. of moles ... £1 15s 7d (Manchester)

1812 A brood of pollcats ... 5s 6d (Battersea)[4]

Sometimes parishes provide not only reward but also materials and equipment beyond the statutory rook net.

1560 For a fox net bought this yere ... 4s 8d (Woodbury, Devon)

1679 For powder for shouting the crows ... 1s 6d (Milton Bryan, Beds)

1745 For half a bushel of oats the bird catcher used ... 1s 3d (Forncett St Peter, Norfolk)[5]

They may also pay for labour, often partly as a way of supporting poorer members of the parish.

1662 To James Barefoote being the foxe killer ... 16s (Frithelstock, Devon)

1752 To Eliz. Cooper 2 years mole catching ... £1 4s (Milton Bryan)[6]

And there may be refreshment for those involved.

1703 Paid when one fox was killed for beer ... 2s | For beer when two foxes were killed ... 7s 6d (Countisbury, Devon)

1725 For beer when we dug for the foxes in the wood ... 1s 6d (Ravensden, Beds)[7]

Some parishes even fund bird-scaring.

1697 For gunpouder as was delivered to Nicholas Clarke to fright the crowes and pigeons in the wheatefield ... 1s | For one lb. of shot ... 2½d (Milton Bryan)[8]

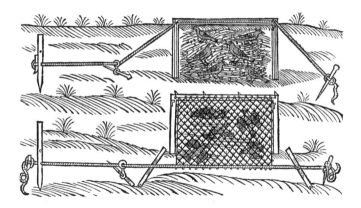

UPPER Crow net, 1590. LOWER Fox caught, misericord, Ripon Cathedral.

Upkeep

Apart from its life as a place of worship, the parish church is the scene of a great deal of mundane activity as it is cleaned, maintained and altered over the years.

1. Building repairs &c.

Churchyard trees supply some of the timber needed for repairs, but additional wood often needs to be found, purchased and transported.

> 1525 For freight of bourdis and plankes for the chirch owte of Essex to London ... 6s 8d | For 2 cartes to carry the same plankes and bourdis from the wharf to the chirchyerd ... 3s | To 4 laborers for to helpe to lade them and for the leyng of them in the chirchyerd ... 2s (St Mary at Hill)

> 1548 To Mr Barnyshe for 6 trees ... 44s | The falling of the same trees ... 2s | To Bond for his help in ye wood ... 4d | To Bond for making the [saw] pittes in the wood ... 3s 4d | To the same Bond for filling of the same pittes ... 12d | To William Carpenter for sawing of 13 tonne of timber ... 22s 4d (Baldock, Herts)

> 1640 For 3 trees for the church ... £2 | For meate for the oxen when they did fetch the trees ... 5s | For the ploughmen's supper, and in the morning ... 6s 10d | Allowed to myself Herculas Comer, for one loade ... 12s (Chedder, Somerset)[1]

Once on site the wood has to be made ready for use.

> 1608 For a timber tree bought of Thomas Hale ... 25s 8d | To Lewis Perton for makeinge a saw pitte in the churchyarde ... 8d | Unto Thomas Cheese and his men for squareinge the said tree ... 5s 7d (Worfield, Shropshire)

> 1624 Sam Sweetapple & his partner for 4 daies sawinge of timber ... 9s 4d (St Edmund, Salisbury)[2]

The repairs, alterations and additions needed range widely.

> 1500 To little Robin the carpenter for mending a defect in the canapy ... 1d (Bishop's Stortford)

> 1504 To Robert Kervar for making of a shelf in ye vestrey ... 6d (St John the Baptist, Peterborough)

> 1557 For mendinge the doors of the quere and chappelles for that they were sagged downe and therby would not open and shutte ... 6d (St Michael, Cornhill)

> 1613 Reizor the joiner for altering the pewes ... 19s (St Bartholomew Exchange)

1622　Gripp the joiner for wainskot for Sir Frauncis Knowlles seat ... 3s 4d (St Mary, Reading)

1635　Paid Roger Walker for a peece of wainescot and turned pins to hange the ministers hats ... 3s 4d (Ludlow)[3]

As some of the preceding entries show, such records of payment cast incidental light on the emergence of surnames, it often being uncertain whether a capitalised second word (Carpenter, Kervar, etc) indicates the recipient's occupation or surname or both.

1462-64　To Will Miller for cutting wood for ye churche gate ... 3d | To Richard Sawyer for sawing ye same wood ... 7d | To John Carpenter for worke about ye churche gate ... 8d (Thame)

The same set of accounts also includes payments to John Glasier, Peter Mason and Peter Tinker, along with rent received from John Sadeler and a bequest from William Carter.[4]

Stone, the other staple of church building, is also often needed, along with masons to work it.

1524　To Bonting of Romney for 2 loads of stone ... 2s | For 5 loads of stone more ... 3s 4d | For ye carying of ye 7 loads of stone ... 3s 6d | For ye labour of ye churchwardens when they went to Romney to buy the said stone ... 12d | To ye mason for ye staires of ye rood lofte ... 20s | For a load of lime for ye staires ... 6s 8d | For ye bording of ye mason and his sarvants for a holl week ... 5s 4d | To ye said mason at his going home ... 6s 8d (Lydd, Kent)

1556　To Stoker and his boye for making the buttress of the northe side of the churche, being 16 dayes at 16d the day ... £1 1s 4d (Crondall, Hants)

1593　For a honny barrell & two bowles for water for the masons ... 16d | For 1 li. of harde tallowe for the crane rope to make it slippery ... 4d (St Mary the Great, Cambridge)

1687　Goodfellow the stonecutter, side walls of the quire ... £6 13s (St Thomas, Salisbury)[5]

Hair is among various materials mixed with lime to create the mortar used in such work.

1521　For shreds to bind ye lime ... 2d (Yatton, Somerset)

1636　For 1 stone of haire for the masons aboute the pointing of the pinacle of the steple ... 8d (Ludlow)

1652　For lime and haire used about the church, and to John Sim's wife for makeing it ... 3s 4d (St Oswald, Durham)[6]

At Leverton, Lincolnshire, an ingredient apparently required for mortar or cement is collected.

> 1526 Receved for chese that was gadered in the town for ye alabaster man ... 8d | In mony that was gadered in ye towne at ye same time of them that gaffe no chese ... 14d[7]

Painters, too, can often be found at work. Many of the murals that enrich parish churches prior to the Reformation are created well before the time of surviving accounts. The more prosaic later work on the Ten Commandments and royal arms has already been seen, but even in later times there are occasional glimpses of higher things.

> 1657 Paid Griffith Edwards for drawing anew the picture of Death ... 5s (Ludlow)

> 1678 To Mr Richard Bird for his work in painting the Resurrection in oile at the west end of the chapel (ye like before being decayed) ... £6 (Beauchamp Chapel, St Mary, Warwick)

> 1698 To George Marlow for painting the roof of the church and gilding the stars ... £2 | To John Smith for nailing up the stars ... 1s 6d (St Oswald, Durham)[8]

Most painting expenses nonetheless relate to basic work.

> 1468 To a warkman that rede okerd [red ochred] and whited the chirch ... 3s 4d | For rede oker ... 5d (St Andrew Hubbard)

> 1495 To Simon dawber for whiting of the church, 5 days ... 3s (St Mary at Hill)

> 1722 Paid Mrs Field for plastering and whiteing the porch ... 14s 10d (St Peter in the East, Oxford)[9]

The following show some of the colours and materials used and the need for fire.

> 1588 Unto 4 several painters for their workemanshippe in trimminge* of ye church ... 47s 8d | For coullors bought at sondrie times ... 42s 4d | For white and red lead ... 12s 2d | For russett and Spanishe whitinge ... 13s 2d | For blackeinge, florey & Brasell† & vermillion ... 2s | For 4 sackes of coales at 9d a sacke to heat ye painters thinges and for pottes to seeth size in and for leather and fier wood ... 4s 2d (St Martin in the Fields)

---

* *Trim*. Put into a proper condition; restore or adorn.
† *Florey*. A blue pigment consisting of the scum collected from the vat in dyeing with indigo or woad. *Brazil*. A red dye, originally obtained from the hard brownish-red wood of an East Indian tree known as Sappan. The name was later used of a similar wood found in South America, and this in turn led to its use for the land of Brazil.

1593 For ashe colour that coloured ye churche ... 4d | 1608 For lambe blacke,* a pounde and a half ... 18d | For indico ... 2s | For a satchell to put the colours in ... 4d | Our charges for fetching the colours at Worcester ... 9d (Worfield)

1706 For leaf gold to gild the cherubs head &c. ... 2s 6d (Northwold, Norfolk)[10]

While such decoration may please the eye, perhaps more important is the ongoing struggle to keep the inside of the church dry. Plumbers take the lead, and like painters they need fire.

1449 To ye plomber of Kodysdan [Cuddesdon] for a watertabel of ledde ye weyyt 14 li. & mete & drinke & setting in to ye walle ... 14d (Thame)

1603 Kettle ye plumber for mending 11 sheetes of led that was sunke downe ... 2s 9d (St Edmund, Salisbury)

1612 To George Salt, plumer, for lead & work ... 4s 9d | To Mary White for fier to heate his irons ... 4d (Holy Trinity, Chester)[11]

Cannington, Somerset

Gutters, spouts and gargoyles often need their attention

1514 For mending of 2 spowtes and making of one ... 5s (St John the Baptist, Peterborough)

1522 John Hareson for iron warke aboute the garkels ... 2s 4d (Louth)[12]

although improvised solutions may be tried.

1699 A young tree to prop up ye gutter ... 2s (Eastington, Glos)[13]

---

* Probably *lamp black*, a pigment made from lamp soot. '*The making of ordinary lamp blacke.* Take a torch or linke, and hold it under the bottome of a latten basen, and as it groweth to be furd and blacke within, strike it with a feather into some shell or other, and grind it with gumme water.' (Henrie Peacham, *The Gentlemans Exercise*, 1612, p76)

The main concern is the roof itself. Sometimes the problem is serious and the work needed radical.

> 1634 March 26th. Paid and given to the master of the shippe carpenteres of the East India Company and to his men for veuing, reping up the roofe of the church, and searching it all over to see if it were sound or not and to give their opinions of it which was that it must be new builte ... £1 | April 18th. For boathire to seeke for beames for the middle roofe ... 1s | April 21st. Given the carpenters William Taylor and Nicholas Collis in earnest for the new building the middle roofe ... 2s | May 13th. Given the said carpenters men to drinke at the firste entrance of their new timber ... 1s | Paid John Godfrie ironmonger for 1000 of nailes for the leads ... 10s | [*c.* 31 January 1634-35] Paid William Taylor and Nicholas Collis carpenters in full satisfaction for the new building the middle roofe ... £95 (St Bartholomew Exchange)[14]

More often it is a case of patching and repairing.

> 1600 To Saunders the carpenter for boords and workemanship on the top of the church where it rained in ... 5s 1d (St Bartholomew Exchange)[15]

Such work is often brought on by bad weather.

> 1562 To John Younge for the nels for to nele downe the leddes that was blone up in the tempaste ... 17d (St Martin, Leicester)

> 1733 Paid Mr Thomas Gorden a bill for timber & other stuffe used to repaire the church & toppe of the steeple when the northeast corner was took off by a clap of thunder ... £5 12s 3½d (Northwold)[16]

Work on and about the steeple generally sounds perilous.

> 1550 To Thomas Season for gowinge up into the stiple 2 windy nightes to save the glase in the windowes ... 10d (Ludlow)

> 1658 To Robert Foster for himselfe & his men taking downe the little pinacles of the steeple that were ready to fall ... 4s (Loughborough, Leics)

> 1666 Paid Evan Clarke for weedinge top of the steeple ... 1s (Manchester)[17]

The following can perhaps be done at ground level, but perhaps not.

> 1562 To Vivies wife for painting of the crosse upon the steple ... 20d (Kingston upon Thames, Surrey)[18]

If those doing the work are in luck there are cramps of iron attached to the outside of the roof to aid their ascent, and perhaps a door near the top to allow egress, but first someone has to put them there.

> 1549 For making of a dore to the toppe of steple which is covered with leade ... 16d (St Michael, Cornhill)

1605 Paid John Brock for fastening the loose barre of iron on the toppe of the steepell, and for placing 300 and 30 cramps in the steepell ... £9 16s | Paid him more for placing 54 cramps in the belfery and battlements ... 20s (Holy Trinity, Coventry)

1629 To Richard Clench for 11 dayes worke with Letsome the plomer and Humfrey Collier, for the making of fire to melte lead for the fastninge of the cramps upon the pinacle of the steeple and to reach it to them and for the heating of the irons ... 6s 6d (Ludlow)[19]

Roof work often also involves an array of ropes, buckets, ladders, cradles and suspended chairs.

1541 For a bokett to cary up stuff ... 2d (St Giles, Reading)

1568 For a paire of ropes for the shinglers ... 1s 2d | For gathering rede [reed] to make a cradell for the stepell ... 8d (Eltham, Kent)

1625 1 buket paile to cary morter ... 4d | For a polley ... 12d | 1 bed cord to bind the chayer ... 12d | For a rope to hang the chayer ... 3s 2d (Ludlow)

1659 To Richard Robinson for 3 daies roughcasting of the south side of the steeple and some other places upon the higher & lower leads ... 3s 6d | To George Wilkinson for his paines in the time of the worke, in fastning of the cradle above, in drawing up and letting downe of the same ... 2s | For drinke to the workmen and other helpers in the time of worke it being troublesome ... 2s 6d (Kendal, Westmorland)

1700 Two chears to point ye steeple with. (Manchester, inventory)[20]

However careful the preparation, even experienced workmen are vulnerable.

1679 Paid by consent of churchwardens towards the burying of one Edward Sheapherd of Kirkland who was killed whilst he was workeing about the repaire of ye steeples roughcasting ... 6s (Kendal)[21]

According to antiquary Thomas Hearne, a man who had repaired the steeple of St Mary the Virgin, Oxford, is later 'killed from some steeple he was pointing, the rope breaking which drew him up in the bucket or frame prepared for him'.[22]

The weathervanes which crown many towers and steeples also need maintaining. The work (and refreshment) involved in replacing just the pole for one at Ludlow is set out in the accounts for 1577.

To John Roo the 21 of February for taking downe the pole of the weathercocke ... 3s 3d

To them that carried ladders to take downe the pole... 2d

Paid John Bewlen for a ladder that was broken ... 12d

Bread and ale for the laborers at the takinge downe of the pole ... 7d

To John Roo for his daies worcke when he chose the pole for the weathercocke ... 12d

To Hamond for fallinge the tree of the weathercocke and cuttinge of the
   same in peeces ... 9d

In ale carried to the woode at the loadinge of the pole ... 6d

In ale at the cominge home of the pole, to the wainemen ... 10d

More to Roo for squaringe the pole when he [it] came home, in the
   streate ... 12d

For ale when the pole was windinge up into the nether flore of the
   steple ... 16d

Spente more upon the laborers when they had wounde him up, at Mr
   Asbaches ... 9d

Paid Thomas Higgs for peecinge ropes that were broken hallinge up the
   pole ... 16d

To William Burges for settinge up the pole ... 26s 8d

For ale and vittualls at Richard Sherwods, spent on the laborers when
   the pole was set in his place ... 2s 8d[23]

Windows require occasional attention.

1602 To Hugh the glasier for glasses for the little squinches* of the tower
   ... 10d (Hartland, Devon)

1610 Paid the glasior for mendinge the windowe that was blowne downe
   in a great windy night ... 3s 10d (St John Zachary)

1616 To Thomas Cowley for halfe a bushel of lime slap for to pointe the
   glasse ... 2d (Mere, Wilts)

1635 To John Eve for 36 foote of new glasse in the sowth windowe to give
   more light to the minister ... 12s 6d (Bishop's Stortford)[24]

Those responsible for any damage may be identified.

1548 To the glasier for mending the hole that the dogge brake ... 5d†
   (Bishop's Stortford)

1573 For mendinge the glasse in Saint Johns chauncell, beinge broken by
   a lunatick ... 7s (Ludlow)[25]

Prevention may be tried.

1668 To Christopher Davison, wireman, for covering the vestry windows
   with wire ... £3 4s (St Margaret, Westminster)[26]

More generally, those working on the building are themselves subject to injury.

1632 To Mr Boone for curing the laborer that broke his legge in our
   church work ... £2 (St Helen, Bishopsgate)[27]

---

* *Squinch*. A slit or narrow opening in a building.

† Assuming the damage was to a window, either it was a very low one or the dog was
very bouncy.

And, inevitably, some builders are found wanting and their charges are resented.

1588 Paid to Burwell and his loiterers for 6 dayes worke ... 5s 8d (St Peter Mancroft, Norwich)

1726 Mr Harris the bricklayer his salary for doing nothing to the church this year ... 10s (St Anne & St Agnes, Aldersgate)[28]

The Pedlar's Window, Lambeth

Its origin is obscure. One old tradition, unsupported by evidence, is that it shows a pedlar who gave the church a piece of land called Pedlar's Acre (on which County Hall was later built) in return for being allowed to bury his dog in the churchyard. In 1607 it was repaired, 2s being paid 'for a pannell of glase for the windo where the picture of the pedler standes', and a century later the figure was replaced: '1703. March 6th. Paid Mr Price for a new glass pedler ... £2'. The confusion over the stick end (bottom left in the above image, published in 1827) is evidence of changes over time.

The window was destroyed by bombing in 1941 and has since been replaced.

2. General upkeep

Miscellaneous other costs arise for the upkeep of the church and parish properties.

1579 For mendinge the churche kettle ... 4d (Kilmington, Devon)

1615 For varnishing the pulpit ... 13s 6d (Newbury, Berks)

1644 For paving the place that smelt in the church, making clean noisome holes and corners in the church, and for ridding and carrying away all the old mats, which annoyed the church ... 5s (St Martin, Oxford)

1718 For shifting ye old font ... 2d (St Werburgh, Derby)

1743 Gave ye turn cock man for taking a large eel out of [a] pipe belonging to ye workhouse ... 6d (St Anne & St Agnes, Aldersgate)[1]

There are also useful additions to be made.

1548 For an edge to stay the bible upon the deske ... 2d (Ludlow)

1577 To the glasiers man for setting up a clothe to keep awaye the sonne from the preacher ... 1d (St Mary Woolnoth)

1665 For a plate of iron and nailing it on the keyhole of the north side dorre to hinder the opening of it with ones finger ... 2d (Kendal, Westmorland)[2]

Costs relating to monuments and other decorative elements appear occasionally in accounts.

1502 To Michell Wosebyche for making of 8 dragons* ... 6s 8d (St Margaret, Westminster)

1586 For glewinge of the anticks broken off from Mr Wads pewe & others at Mr Clarkes funeral by poore people assembled ... 3d (St Matthew, Friday Street)

1633 For carving of some of the angels and for some new made ... £1 18s (St Mary Woolnoth)[3]

Various minor purchases occur.

1498 For a new wheelbarowe ... 12d (St Mary at Hill)

1640 For a tumpe† for Mr Browne to stande upon ... 3d (Ludlow)

1766 For a pair of bellows for Thunder‡ ... 6d (High Wycombe, Bucks)[4]

---

* Perhaps for heraldic display of some kind. Under the then monarch, Henry VII, the red dragon of the Tudors was used as a supporter for the royal arms.

† The *OED* defines *tump* as a hillock, mound or heap, but in this case a stool or small platform seems likely.

‡ Thomas Thunder is found bell-ringing two years earlier. The purchase perhaps relates to the blowing of an organ.

And in time money may be spent on newfangled amenities and comforts.

1764 Paid the Bridge Company for water for the workhouse ... 12s | And New River Company, water for the church ... 10s (St Anne & St Agnes, Aldersgate)

1774 Two warming machines placed in two pews ... £65 4s. [Paid for by] voluntary subscription. (St Olave, Hart Street)

1831 Paid Messrs. Lees [Lee & Son] of Sunderland for airing the church by hot-water pipes ... £105 | Paid woman for carrying water and gathering wood to heat the boiler for warming the church ... 5s (Chester-le-Street, co. Durham)

1900 National Electric Wiring Co. ... £117 9s | Fitting switches, new lamps, &c. (Salisbury Electric Light Co.) ... £18 4d (St Martin, Salisbury)[5]

3. Cleaning and rubbish removal

Church cleaning may be undertaken by the clerk or sexton as part of their routine duties, or poor members of the parish may be paid to do the work.

1619 To Joane Bush and other poore folke for making cleane the church the whole yeare ... 18s 6d (St Mary the Great, Cambridge)[1]

Cobwebs in high places are a recurring problem.

1602 To a man that swept downe the dust and cobwebbes from the walles and high windowes ... being five dayes ... 5s (Lambeth)

1610 To the chimney sweeper for taking downe cobwebbes about the church ... 20d (St Bartholomew Exchange)

1624 To Thomas Howton for swepinge off the spiders ... 3s 4d (Leominster, Herefordshire)[2]

The church needs periodic washing, with ale and milk sometimes used.

1478-80 To her that washeth the chirche for 2 yere ... 6s 8d | 1480-82 For ale to make clene the chirche ... ob. (St Andrew Hubbard)

1490 To Smetams wife for washing behinde ... 6d ob. (St Dunstan, Canterbury)

1541 For sopinge of the walls within the churche, for 2 men 2 dayes ... 16d (Ludlow)

1651 For water and for several people to cleane the church ... £1 11s 10d | For coles to dry the church and parsonage house ... £1 2s 4d (St Bartholomew Exchange)

1663 J. Boden washing ye chancell and taking out ye names which ye boyes rudely set in ... 1s (St Thomas, Salisbury)

1713 To Carter for 8 gallons of milk used about ye church ... 1s (Smarden, Kent)[3]

Vestments and cloths also need attention.

1538 To my lady ancress for washing of all the corporas clothes ... 8d* (St Margaret, Westminster)

1540 To halting Agnes for whesshing of the church gear for 3 quarters ending at Ester ... 2s (St John the Baptist, Peterborough)

1633 For washing the surples 3 times & sweete water to take away ye sent of sope ... 4s (Redenhall, Norfolk)[4]

Particular steps may be required if they are the worse for wear.

1715 For lime-juice for ye comunion cloth & ye surplices ... 6d | 1730 For taking out a stain out of ye comunion cloth ... 2d (Battersea)[5]

Elbow work is required to keep metal items looking good.

1463 To ye clarkes wife for skoweringe of ye candellstickeys ... 4d (Walberswick, Suffolk)

1580 To Mother Dobbs for skoringe of the lectornes ... 12d (St Peter Mancroft, Norwich)

1624 To John Hall for scowring the flagons which Mr Peapes forgot the last yeare ... 2s (St Mary the Great, Cambridge)[6]

Just occasionally the efforts of those doing the work are recognised.

1594 For 13 yardes lacking halfe a quarter of blacke friset to make J. Pinnockes wife & her 2 children gownes, because they take great paines to make & kepe the church & lampe cleane ... 15s 4d (St Thomas, Salisbury)[7]

Meanwhile the church's exterior needs looking after.

1501 For riding [clearing] of gotters of ye church and ye gargells [gargoyles] ... 8d (Yatton, Somerset)

1506 To the bellman for sweping of the church roweff ... 5d | 1541 To Peter Pecocke for sweping the leades ... 4d (St John the Baptist, Peterborough)

1556 For picking of moss and ivy from the churche ... 10d (Bramley, Hants)

1725 To Richard Garson for clearing the church windows of ivy and pulling out the roots ... 1s (Ockley, Surrey)[8]

---

* It was perhaps thought that such items, used at mass, should be washed by a holy person, in this case an anchoress. Similar reverence is indicated by a payment at Morebath, Devon, in 1539 for 'a pere of gloves to washe ye corporas'.
† *Frieze.* Coarse woollen cloth with a nap, usually on one side only.

Some urban parishes take trouble about the approach to the church.

1560-61 To two poore folkes for making cleane of the church lane when the lorde kepers child* came thither to be christened ... 4d (St Martin in the Fields)

1608 To Eliz. Noble for sweepinge before the church the whole yeare ... 2s 8d (Holy Trinity, Chester)[9]

The churchyard also needs to be maintained, with scythe-wielding mowers often receiving refreshment as part of their reward.

1485 For lopping of the tree on the chirche yarde for caterpillars ... 2d (St Andrew Hubbard)

1556 For spredinge of mole hillocks in the churche yarde ... 8d (St Michael, Lichfield, Staffs)

1595 For cleveing and rooting of a tree that was bloen doun in the churchyarde ... 6s (Wimborne Minster, Dorset)

1639 For moweinge the grasse of the three church yards, and cutting the bowthes [boughs] of the dead trees, & bread and beere for the man ... 1s 9½d (St Anne & St Agnes, Aldersgate)

1662 To Protheroe for pulling up nettles ... 2d (Ludlow)

1663 To Thomas Gilpin ... for cutting the brambles & wood in the church yard and carrying them away ... 1s (Kendal, Westmorland)

From a Book of Hours *c.* 1300

1682 For filling up a grave sunck by the raine ... 2d (Manchester)[10]

As the last entry suggests, poor drainage is one problem found here.

1661 Paid the gravemaker for his makeing of a current for to carry away the water out of the church yard into the streete ... 2s 6d (St Anne & St Agnes, Aldersgate)

1824 Paid Flood for helping to dig cesspools in various parts of the church-yard to drain the walks ... 18s (Fulham, Middlesex)[11]

The accumulation of rubbish is another.

1567-69 To John Kirbe of Fletton for 2 days carige of mucke owt of ye churche yard ... 3s (St John the Baptist, Peterborough)[12]

---

* Future statesman and philosopher Francis Bacon, baptised on 25th January 1560-61. His father Sir Nicholas was lord keeper of the great seal.

More generally rubbish removal is a recurring cost for many parishes, particularly those in urban areas, and professional contractors are often employed.

> 1454 To the raker for caryeng away of the churche dust ... 4d (St Ewen, Bristol)

> 1621 Paid the dust man for 2 lood owt of the cherchyarde ... 1s 4d | 1640 Paid Mr Fox the scavenger* for the church ... 5s (St Bartholomew Exchange)[13]

'Dust' may sometimes include, or be a euphemism for, dung, which is a major problem. Usually it is that of animals and needs to be removed from the churchyard and other outside spaces.

> 1600 For caringe awaye the dunge at two times from the churche gate ... 9d (St Clement, Ipswich)

> 1609 For gathering horsedung ... 4d (Ludlow)[14]

In addition, human waste may need to be collected from church properties.

> 1651 The nightmen for emptieing 4 tunn of soile out of the parsonage vault at 4s 4d per tunn ... 17s 4d | 1692 For emptying the necessary house ... 7s (St John Zachary)[15]

Regular collections may be made by gong farmers, 'gong' denoting either a privy or its contents. The farmers usually work at night and may need watching to make sure they do not take advantage to skimp on the job.

> 1500 Paid to Doning, gong farmer, the 30 day of Janier, for farming of a sege [privy] in George Gysborow the clarkes chamber wherin was 5 tone at 2s the tone ... 10s | To Richard, servante with John Wolff, for watching with them to see the [tonnes] well filled ... 4d | 1536 To a man that watched ye gong farmers 2 nightes ... 8d (St Mary at Hill)

> 1577 To gong farmer for 15 tonnes carriage out of the vawte of Wm. Charleys house at 22d the tonne ... 27s 6d | For foure pounds of candells for the gong farmer for two nights .... (St Mary Woolnoth)[16]

In London boats are often used for the removal.

> 1537 Toward the making of the dong bote for the chirch ... 16d (St Mary at Hill)[17]

Occasionally women carry out such work.

> 1585 To Mother Friar for caryage of a lode of dunge ... 4d (St Mary the Great, Cambridge)[18]

---

* *Scavenger.* One employed to keep a church clean. Also an officer appointed by a ward or parish to ensure the streets are kept clean, and sometimes used of rakers and others who carry out such work.

Also needing periodic removal are the rushes which cover many church floors, at least until paved floors become commonplace in the 17th century. Rushes are usually replaced at intervals through the year, Easter, Whitsun, Midsummer and Christmas being common times, and they may also be removed when infection is feared.

1463 To ye raker for 3 lodes of rushes and duste had out of ye chirche ... 9d (St Michael, Cornhill)

1631 For carrying the rushes out of the church in the sickness time ... 5s (Kirkham, Lancs)

1661 For getting forth of all the mats, rushes and makinge the church cleane against the rushbearinge ... 3s (Wilmslow, Cheshire)[19]

Other problems arise from the weather, particularly from snow and ice in winter.

1458 To the clerk and to 2 other men to throwe oute snowe fro the ledes of the chirch atte 2 sondry times ... 5d (St Michael, Cornhill)

1739 For clearing the ice & snow away in ye late frost, several times out of the churchyard footways that people may come to church ... 5s 6d (Battersea)[20]

For some churches flooding is a recurring problem.

1673 For drink to men for removing a chest in ye vestry when water came in ... 3s (Kendal)

1673 July 19th. Being sabbath day at night there was a great flood the water was two foot high in the middle alley it were mesured so that it came into chests & wet all the writings such a flood were not known in our age before. | Cloves to sweeten the church after ye flood ... 3d (St Werburgh, Derby)

1682 April 26th. Paid the watermen in bread, beer, and brandy, that brought their boats to save the people from the flood this day ... 6s | For clearing water out of the church, mops, &c. ... 9s (Brentford, Middlesex)[21]

Extraordinary expenditure also arises when royalty and other eminent figures visit, or are expected.

1505 For makinge clene of the churcheyard agenst the king his coming ... 16d (Wimborne Minster)

1602 For flowers & rushes for the churche when the queene was in towne ... 20d (St Lawrence, Reading)

1697 Dan Buthroyde and Robert Kaye for sweeping the church walls and roofe and rubbing the seats when the bishop should have come ... 4s 6d (Almondbury, Yorks)[22]

4. Fumigation &c.

Fumigation and the introduction of agreeable smells are used at various times, whether to drive out or mask noxious airs, in celebrating a particular festival, or as part of a general smartening up when an important visitor is expected.

> 1574 For strauing hearbes against my Lord of London preached the 20 of November ... 3d | For parfuming of the church that day ... 6d | For a parfuming pan .... (St Margaret, 'Fenchurch Street')
>
> 1581 For perfume when Mrs Jerningham was beryed ... 2d (St Margaret, Norwich)
>
> 1614 For birch and herbs at Pentecost ... 16d | For herbs in Assension weeke ... 4d (St Peter Mancroft, Norwich)[1]

The most notable substance used is frankincense, an aromatic gum resin gouged from the bark of trees of the genus *Boswellia*. As seen earlier, it is usually stored in a ship and burnt in a censer which is swung to and fro to disperse the fumes. While the name is not itself exotic – 'frank' probably just indicating 'of high quality' – its spelling nonetheless poses a challenge for early writers of accounts.

> 1555 On New Yeres even, 2 ounces franke and sens ... 1d (Ludlow)
>
> 1563 Oct. 17th. For frankumsens to burne in the churche against ye masters cam to chose master mayre ... 2d (St Edmund, Salisbury)
>
> 1589 For frankensence to aire the vault ... 2d (St Michael, Cornhill)[2]

Juniper is also sometimes used.

> 1589 To Bettres Dobson and her daughter for bringinge of two burthen of jenepers to the churche ... 3d (Pittington, co. Durham)
>
> 1619 For juniper to burne in the church this yeare ... 2s (Bishop's Stortford)[3]

The following perhaps just involves opening all the doors and windows.

> 1645 To Goodman Currell for airing the church after Agerley had carried his bedding into it ... 1s (St Peter in the East, Oxford)[4]

5. Birds &c. in churches

Birds, too, seek to set up home here. Defecating from high places and fluttering about during divine service, they pose a persistent problem, the best solution being to prevent them from gaining access in the first place.

> 1536 To two men for half a day work to bord the stepill to kepe oute birdes ... 6d (St Mary the Great, Cambridge)
>
> 1542 For stopping the holes in the church where doves came in ... 8d (Louth)
>
> 1560 To Cressy for making the trellisses to kepe out crows ... 2s 6d (Worksop, Notts)[1]

Nets are sometimes set up for this purpose.

1563 To Robert Walwyn for hanginge of nets & stopping of ye windowes to kepe owt ye pigeons ... 10d (Kingston upon Thames, Surrey)[2]

They may also be used for catching the intruders.

1554 For netes to distroye the choyes [choughs] that did defowle the churche ... 18d | To Frauncisse Barret for settinge up of the netes ... 4d (Worfield, Shropshire)

1576 For a net to catche ye stares [starlings] in the church ... 6d (St Michael, Coventry)[3]

Alternatively tar or bird-lime may be spread.

1568 To Richard Caldwells man for setting lime rods in the churche to take starlings ... 16d (St Martin, Leicester)

1574 For birde lime to kach the stars about ye church ... 2d (Lambeth)

1699 For tar to catch the swifts within ye church ... 2d (St Michael, Coventry)

1759 For bird lime to catch owles in the church ... 2d (St John the Baptist, Chester)[4]

Owls are also in trouble elsewhere.

1640 For killing two owles in the church ... 1s (Worksop)

1722 For catching the owles ... 3d (Redenhall, Norfolk)[5]

Bats are another target.

1615 For killing the battes in the high roofe ... 7d (St Michael, Coventry)

1820 Paid Walter Webb & others for destruction of abought 70 bats taken in the church ... 1s (Cranfield, Beds)[6]

Those with a good aim may try shooting either with ordinary arrows or with bolts, blunt-headed ones shot from a crossbow.

1548 For a bow bought for the church and strings ... 7d | For 12 arrows and 6 bolts for the driving of daws out of the church .... (Peterborough Cathedral)

1564 For 4 boltes for to shoute a starlins ... 6d (St Martin, Leicester)[7]

Chough.

Owl poppy head, Combs, Suffolk.

Bolt.

Birds may be so troublesome that the risk of collateral damage to the fabric of the building seems worth taking.

> 1563 For gunpowder to beate ye starlings from ye churche ... 2d | 1564 To Mr Clarke for halfe a pound of gunpowder for to shout at starlings [and] Harte to shout at em ... 9d (St Martin, Leicester)
>
> 1746 For shooting sparrows in ye church, and powder ... 2s 6d (Sapcote, Leics)[8]

Sometimes the nests are destroyed as well.

> 1584 For hontinge steeres out of the churche, and polinge downe ther nestes at the same time ... 7d (St Mary, Shrewsbury)
>
> 1632 For killing of starlings and stopping their nests ... 1s (St Mary the Great, Cambridge)[9]

Birds outside on the roof may also be in the line of fire.

> 1686 To Hennery Mickleburgh for shooting of 4 dozen & a halfe of cadowes [jackdaws] off ye church ... 6s (Stockton, Norfolk)
>
> 1815 For destroying jack daws on the steeple ... 11s 8d (High Wycombe, Bucks)[10]

Hoping to avoid the need for such action, at St Mary, Sandwich, at an early but uncertain date, they pay 2s 4d 'for 23 iron pikes, that were made for to sette up on ye points of ye crosses of ye pinacles of ye stepell for [so that] ravouns shuld not stonde theron to soile ye stepell, goteris [gutters] with bones and other things'.[11]

At Wilmslow, Cheshire, various approaches are tried.

> 1670 For a new door to set up in the top of the steeple to keepe forth the pigeons from fowleinge the church ... 4s 8d | 1675 For a net to keep the pigeons forth of ye church ... 1s | 1678 For shot and powder to kill the pigeons in the church ... 2s 2d[12]

The purpose of the door is not clear, but perhaps it is to enable someone to go aloft to scare the birds away or to shoot at them.

Part of the problem is that left undisturbed in a church's high places birds deposit large quantities of dung. At Sandwich 8d is paid 'for ye carying down of culver [pigeon] dung out of ye stepell', while at Redenhall a shilling is paid 'for cleaning the steeple after ye jackdaws'.[13]

Such dung is also a resource, however, and it may be sold.

> 1680 Of Dr Bisbie for the pigeon dung out of the steeple ... 2s 6d (Long Melford, Suffolk)[14]

Alternatively dung or pigeons or both may be bestowed as a benefit in kind. At South Littleton, Worcestershire, in 1555 the parishioners find themselves short of funds and needing to replace their old Latin service books (they had been dispensed with under Edward VI but now, with Catholicism restored under Queen Mary, are required again).

> All the hole parish agreed with Sir Humfrey Acton owr vicar that he showld finde us books as long as he is vicar. And for his gentelnes, and becawse owr churche had but littell money in store and lacked many thinges in owr churche, we were all content that the seid vicar showld have all the profett of the piggens that use the stepull of owr churche for all the time that he shalbe vicar here finding us bookes. And furthur he hathe promessed that he wil be good to owr churche at the time of his deth ...[15]

A few years later at St Saviour, Southwark, it is agreed to pay the sexton, Laurence Robinson, 44s a year, along with perquisites for tolling the bell and digging graves, and he is 'to have likewise all the profits of the pigeons resorting to the church steeple'.[16]

While birds are much the most troublesome intruders, money is also occasionally spent on tackling rats and mice.

1469 For 3 rat trappes for the chirche ... 6d (St Michael, Cornhill)

1523 For milke and rattisbane for the rattes in the chirch ... 1d ob. | 1537 To the rat taker for laying of his baite ... 4d (St Mary at Hill)

1731 Spent at Halesworth in endeavouring to get the ratcatcher ... 2s (Wenhaston, Suffolk)

1762 For killing the rats in the church ... 2s 6d (Maidstone, Kent)

1777 Paid Slim for two mous traps ... 4d (Hardingstone, Northants)[17]

From *The Famous Ratketcher,* a ballad published *c.* 1616

Routine and People

Routine[1]

Before the Reformation the basic rhythm of a church's day is provided by the divine office, a daily sequence which priests are obliged to recite. It is based on the traditional monastic office which consists of Matins, the night office, which under the 6th-century rule of St Benedict is performed at 2 a.m. but over time tends to be performed later; Lauds, the morning prayer (from Latin *laudare*, to praise); Prime, the office of the first hour (dawn or 6 a.m.); Terce, Sext and None, the offices of the third, sixth and ninth hours respectively; Vespers, the evening office (from Latin *vesper*, evening, evening star); and Compline, which completes the day 'hours' (hence the name), said before retiring for the night.

In ordinary parish churches matins and vespers (or evensong) are usually marked in a public fashion, but the other hours may be observed relatively discreetly, with the clergy saying or chanting them quietly with little or no lay attendance.[2]

Distinct from this sequence is mass, performed once a day in most churches, typically in the more elaborate form known as high mass.[3]

In addition one or more private or low masses may be performed by chantry priests employed to intercede for the souls of individuals, usually on a daily basis. Such secondary masses may be performed early in the day so as to avoid overlapping with the main parish mass and so that any chantry priests are available to assist at that main service. An ordinance made at St Michael, Cornhill, in 1504 sets out that 'every priest disposed to celebrate shall say masse before the hie masse except there be a bodie present to be buried or else some other reasonable cause do let [prevent] it'.[4]

High mass is typically performed at the main altar and requires the presence of a deacon and sub-deacon to assist the celebrant. It usually involves incense and singing, with part at least of the service being performed 'by note'. At St Michael, Cornhill, all the priests and clerks 'shalbe present in the quire in theire surples singing there from the beginning of mattens, masse, and evensong unto the end of them all'. At Doncaster chantry priests attend 'daily matines, masse, and evensonge by note'.[5]

A low mass, in contrast, is typically performed at a side altar and said rather than sung, with the celebrant attended by a single server, perhaps the parish clerk or one of the church boys. It is therefore relatively discreet and, depending on where you are in the church, you might not even be aware that it is going on.[6]

If resources allow there may also be an early mass, known as the morrow mass and performed by a separate priest.* At Wakefield such a mass is said 'at 5 of the clocke in the morninge for all servauntes and laborers'. Such masses are popular with those setting out on a journey, not least because, as noted earlier, it is believed that seeing the host provides protection against sudden death for the rest of the day.[7]

The morrow mass may share an altar with one or more chantry masses, and sometimes a chantry mass serves as the morrow mass. At St Denis, York, an alderman establishes a chantry with a priest to sing for his soul between 11 and 12 each morning, but at a later date the hour is 'altered by th'advice of the parochiners' to 'between 4 and 5 in the morning ... as well as for ther commoditye as travelinge people' – that is, for their convenience as well as for that of travellers.[8]

In terms of attendance chantry masses, as largely private affairs, are likely to attract few if any parishioners, particularly if performed for the soul of someone who died long ago. On work days even matins, high mass and evensong may attract only a limited congregation comprising those of the more devout parishioners who can spare the time. On feast days and Sundays, however, things are very different, everyone in the parish being expected to attend mass and urged to attend matins and evensong as well.[9]

While there is a great deal of variation from parish to parish because of differing resources and local customs, the sequence of services on an ordinary day, in a reasonably busy church, with a morrow mass priest and two chantry priests, might be along the following lines.[10]

4.30 a.m.	First Ave bell (day bell)
5.00 a.m.	Morrow mass said at a side altar
6.00 a.m.	Mass of first chantry priest said at a side altar
7.00 a.m.	Matins in the choir, sung
8.00 a.m.	Mass of second chantry priest said at a side altar
9.30 a.m.	High mass at the main altar, sung
12 noon	Second Ave bell
3.00 p.m.	Evensong in the choir, sung
8.00 p.m.	Third Ave bell (curfew)

In summer some or all of these may occur half an hour or an hour later.

---

* Canons issued at Westminster in 1200 stipulate that 'a priest may not celebrate twice a day, unless the necessity be urgent,' so if the parish priest is to celebrate the main mass he cannot perform the morrow mass. The rule is restated in constitutions of 1367 but with exceptions made for 'the day of the nativity or resurrection of our Lord, or when one has a corpse to bury'.

Some related detail can be gleaned from a list of duties drawn up in 1462 for two of the deacons or junior clerics of Holy Trinity, Coventry. As with every church it has its own particular timetable and routine. It starts the day relatively late and the first or morrow mass is dedicated to the Trinity, presumably because of the church's own dedication. It is also worth noting that in many churches the kind of tasks referred to are carried out by the clerk or sexton rather than by deacons.[11]

> The first deacon shall every day open ye churche doors at 6 of ye clock, and deliver to ye prieste that singethe ye Trinity masse a booke, and a chalice, and a vestment; and when masse is done, see ye said booke, chalice and vestment be laid up in ye vestry.
>
> He shall ring all in to matins, with his fellow ... and bear forthe ye books for matins belonging to ye southe side of ye choir; and when matins is done, bear them in to ye vestry againe.
>
> He shall ring, with his fellow, to high masse, and sing in ye choir at ye masse; and when masse is done, see that ye chalice and ye books be locked sure in ye vestry.
>
> He shall be at ye churche again by 3 of the clock, to help to ring all in to evensong ... He shall sing evensong on ye southe side of ye choir. When evensong is done, he shall make sure ye vestry, and see that all ye books be in. He shall lock ye churche doors at a convenient hour.
>
> He shall ring the day bell, with one bell, every day.

The second deacon's duties largely mirror those of the first but afford a few further details.

> He shall be at churche every weeke day half an hour afore 7 a clock, and ring ye seconde bell.
>
> He shall every day make ready ye high altar for ye prieste to sing high masse, and fetche forthe ye masse booke and ye chalice, and see ye prieste have bred and wine, and cause a childe to attende to ye prieste at masse; and when masse is done, he shall bear up ye booke and ye chalice into their place again.
>
> He shall ring curfew every night at 8 of ye clock, and when it is done he shall serche ye churche all abowte, lest there be any person lying in any seate or corner, and then lock ye churche door sure.

Each Sunday there is more to be done.

> The first deacon shall finde one to ring a procession every Sonday, and his felow likewise.
>
> At every procession he shall bring forthe processionals* for his side of ye choir and see they be borne in to ye vestry when ye procession is done.

---

* Books containing the litany and hymns sung in processions.

He shall finde a deacon to reade ye gospel at high masse every Sunday and holy day.

He shall see ye holy cake [loaf] be cut every Sunday according to every man's degree, and he shall bear ye holy bread to serve ye people in ye northe side of ye churche, and he to go to them on ye 12th day [Epiphany] for his offering, to ye reparacione of his surplice.

He and his felow shall every Sunday and high day folde up ye albs and vestments that be used that day.[12]

The procession referred to commonly precedes high mass on this day in parish churches. In its ordinary form it just involves the carrying of a cross before clergy and choir as they make a short clockwise circuit within the church, passing down the south aisle (if there is one) to the font and returning up the nave. It may also involve sprinkling of holy water with an aspergillum upon the church's altars and the congregation, either by the parish clerk or by the minister attended by a boy carrying the holy water pot. In elaborate cases, notably on certain feast days, it involves the whole parish as clergy, choir and congregation leave the church by one door, process to the churchyard cross, return inside through another door, go round the aisles, and finally advance down the nave towards the rood screen. The celebrant wears a silk cope and the sense of theatre may be further enhanced by the swinging of censers to and fro, and the bearing aloft of banners and torches.[13]

The kind of recurring weekly routine outlined above can be seen as the first of four layers of activity that make up the life of a parish church.

The second layer is the largely moveable annual cycle of services commemorating the life of Christ, from Advent Sunday through to the Ascension, with most of the dates involved depending on that of Easter.

The third layer is the fixed annual cycle of services celebrating the feasts of saints, occurring on the same day each year, for example Michaelmas, or the feast of St Michael, on 29th September.

These second and third layers are detailed in chapter 7.

The fourth layer consists of the occasional services marking the baptism, marriage and burial of individual parishioners. These include obits, annual commemorations of dead individuals scattered through the year, typically on the anniversary of death. This layer is detailed in chapters 8, 9 and 10.

All the while, as already seen in chapter 5, there are the more mundane activities carrying on in the background: sweeping of floors, washing of linen, scouring of candlesticks, a joiner fixing a pew door by candlelight, and so on.

After the Reformation the mundane requirements continue, as does the basic pattern of three services (matins or morning prayer, mass or communion, evensong), but many other things come to an end including religious processions, most devotions relating to saints, and all attempts to intercede on behalf of the dead. This transformation is detailed in chapter 13.

People

1. Clergy

Although in practice the various terms denoting those in holy orders are often used more or less interchangeably, in theory they indicate distinct roles.

Rector (from Latin *rector*, ruler). In early use it indicates an incumbent who is entitled to retain the tithes. Later, and particularly after the Reformation, the rector is often a layman or lay body entitled to appoint a vicar to act in his or its place.

Vicar (from Latin *vicarius*, substitute; hence 'vice', 'vicarious'). In early use it indicates a person acting in place of the rector or parson, and later it indicates the incumbent of a parish where the tithes are impropriated (assigned to a lay person or body).

Parson (from Latin *persona*, personage). In early use it indicates a rector, the 'person' of the parish, but over time it slips a little in dignity and precision, coming to be used of any vicar or other clergyman.

Priest (from Latin *presbyter*, an elder). A more general term, it indicates one who performs religious functions and is particularly associated with the mass.

As seen above, before the Reformation some churches have a **morrow mass priest**, responsible for performing the first mass of the day, usually at 6 a.m. or earlier, and who may for convenience sleep in the church.

> 1487 To Sir John Plommer for the keping of the morowe mass for this hole yer ... 20s | 1526 For [a] bedsted for the preistes chamber that kepith the first mass ... 14d (St Mary at Hill)[1]

Rectors on brass memorials.

LEFT Looking devout, Harlington, Middlesex (John Monemouthe, *d.* 1419).

RIGHT Looking prosperous, Whichford, Warwickshire (Nicholas Assheton, *d.* 1582).

Reapers by
George Stubbs,
1795

Tithes are a tenth of annual produce and earnings paid by parishioners to support the church and clergy. They are divided into 'great' and 'small', the former arising from the major field crops and the latter from lambs, chickens and minor produce. It is customary for the small tithes to be allowed to the vicar, not least because they are troublesome to collect.[2]

The following extracts from a note of 'the manner of paying the small tithes' and other fees due to his office, made by the vicar of Herne, Kent, in 1621, give a sense of how in practice the clergy benefit. It should, however, be borne in mind that a great deal of local variation occurs.

> The calfe, if it be sold, the vicar's due is the tenth penny; as, if it be sold for 10s, the vicar hath out of that due to him 12d. If the owner of the calfe kill it in his house, the vicar hath due the left shoulder thereof.
>
> Grasse hath usually been taken in grasse cockes, unlesse in curtesse [courtesy] the parishioners will make it good.
>
> Of bees, the tenth measure of honey, and the tenth quantity of wax.
>
> Eggs, as the vicar and parishioners can agree, but if he will have eggs ... two eggs for every hen, and three for every cocke. The like for ducks and drakes.
>
> Geese and turkeys are to be taken for tithe at such times as they may be made fit for food.
>
> Fruits (as apples, pears, nuts, wardens [an old variety of baking pear], plums, &c.), the tenth measure as they are gathered.
>
> Out of dove houses the tenth pigeon.
>
> For their mullet nets I have compounded (and others before me) for 3s 4d, sometimes 5s, sometimes 6s 8d, for the year.[3]

Such commutation to a fixed monetary amount is common and becomes increasingly so over time.

Additional to tithes are the parsonage house, provided for the incumbent but which he is responsible for maintaining, and the glebe (from Latin *gleba*, soil), the land with which the church was originally endowed and which should provide him with a subsistence, whether by his own cultivation, by renting out, or by some combination of the two.[4]

LEFT Priest on an incised slab in a chantry, Wimborne Minster. RIGHT 'The Curate', 1790. He wears a surplice and spurs. Below him the clerk in his box sleeps with mouth ajar.

There may also be one or more **chantry priests**. While their primary role is to perform masses for the souls of particular individuals, the terms of many endowments require them also to take part in parish worship.[5]

> 1534 I will that a preist be founde to sing and say masse ... at Jesus aulter, for my sowle and all cristen sowles, and the same priste shall helpe to maintaine the servis of God in the quere, by the space of 10 yers ... (Robert Astbroke, High Wycombe, Bucks)[6]

Moreover, some chantry priests are funded not by the bequests of rich individuals but by ordinary members of the parish joining together to ensure that there are sufficient clergy to serve the needs of their church.

> 1546 Put in by the honest of the parishe. To th'entente to pray for the soules of the founderes and all cristen soules and to do divine service in the quere, and to minister to the sike of the said parishe in time of nede. (Chantry of Our Lady, South Kirkby, Yorkshire, certificate drawn up at dissolution of chantries)[7]

Parish guilds often fund additional priests in a similar way.

Curate (from Latin *cura*, care; hence 'curator'). One who has the spiritual charge of souls or of a parish. After the Reformation the term loses some of its dignity and usually denotes a deputy or assistant. This shift is thought to arise from the fact that many rectors and vicars are non-resident and appoint a junior clergyman to look after the parish's day to day affairs.

Deacon (from Greek διάκονος, servant or messenger, via Latin *diaconus*). A junior cleric who assists the priest.

Ordinations, from a 15th-century manuscript

UPPER The bishop draws down a chasuble over a priest. LOWER The bishop lays hands on a deacon with the words *Accipe spiritum sanctum*, 'Receive the holy spirit.'

Some of the pre-Reformation duties of the deacons at Holy Trinity, Coventry, have already been seen. They are also responsible for a range of other tasks, including the following, although, as noted above, in many churches such chores fall to the clerk or sexton instead, the first one in particular usually being performed by the *aquaebajulus* (water-bearer) or holy water clerk.

The first deacon shall every Sunday bear holy water in his chaldron to every howse in his warde, and he to have his duty off every man, after his degree, quarterly.

He shall see ye floor of ye choir and of ye body of ye church be sweeped every time when it hathe nede and that ye leads over ye church be made clene, and if it be a snowe to void ye guttars, lest they be stopped.

He shall at every snowe, with his fellow, void ye floor of ye steeple, and caste oute ye snowe, [to prevent] roting ye timber.

He shall see that ye clappers of ye bells hang in order and ye baldricks be sure, and if they be not, to shewe to ye churchwardens, that they may be mended in season, and to shewe to them ye bell ropes in like manner.

His fellow shall grease ye belles, and finde grease thereto, when they have nede. And they shall have ye profetts of ye bells, when they ring for any corpse or obit.

Also ye said deacon and his fellow shall ring ye bells at ye cumming of ye king and ye quene and ye prince. If they fawte [fail], they are to bear ye losse [fine].

The first deacon shall tende ye lampe, and fetche oile and rushes, where ye churchwardens will assign them.

He shall go with ye prieste when he goethe to visit ye sick, or else [another shall go] in his stead.

He shall fetche every corpse that deceasethe in his ward to churche, in his surplice, and he to have [reward] for his labour.[8]

In addition to such permanent clergy there are **visiting preachers**, particularly after the Reformation. To prevent the promotion of egregious opinions the Canons of 1604 stipulate that only those licensed are to be allowed to preach, and their names must be recorded.[9]

1615 For a booke to write in strange prechers names, as we weare commanded by the offishales ... 2d (Worfield, Shropshire)

1716 Paid at Beccles visitation for suffering a man to preach without seeing his orders ... 9s (Weybread, Suffolk)[10]

Those who come to preach expect to be rewarded.

1618 To a poore preacher for his sermon ... 3s 4d | 1657 To the minister that preached at the Elme Trees ... 2s (Battersea)

1646 Paid in the time when we had no parson to several ministers for 44 sermons at 10s per sermon ... £22 (St Mary Woolchurch)[11]

Often the reward takes the form of wine, or at least includes it.

1540 To Mr Dr Kitchin in reward for preaching on our lady day, a pike price 2s 4d, a galland of wine 8d, and his bote-hire 4d. (St Margaret, Westminster)

1574 To a preacher that made a sermon here, for his dinner and horse meat ... 3s 4d (Tavistock, Devon)

1654 For wine and bread in the vestry for strange ministers &c. ... 10s (St Bartholomew Exchange)[12]

As for what is expected of the clergy more generally, from the 11th century they are required to be celibate, although this is widely ignored until the 13th, and clerical marriage is allowed again under a law of 1548-49. They should also of course dress soberly and live exemplary lives. In 1577 Bishop Barnes of Durham orders that

> the parsons, vicars, and curates at ministracion of sacraments weare cleane and comelie surplesses, and that they abrode do weare grave, clerkely, and decent apparell, as gownes or cloaks with sleves of sad* colour, and none unsemely apparell, as great ruffes, great britches, Gascogne hose,† scalings,‡ nor any other like monstrous and unsemely apparell, only rounde cloaks when they ride [to] cast off the mier and dust may be used, but no otherwise. And we require and charge you, in the Lorde, that you by all meanes indever your selves to frame your lives and conversacion so that ye may be livelie paternes and holesome examples to your flockes in all modestie, sobrietie, faithe, zeale and godly conversacion.[13]

2. Singers

A church's clergy are expected to sing at the main services. Additional bass and tenor parts in the choir may be performed by clerks§ and singing men, who are often hired to help out at particular festivals.

1462 To 2 clerkes for singing in the chirche from Wednesday afore Ester unto the Utas¶ after, and for the borde of one of the same clerkes by the same time ... 7s 1d (St Michael, Cornhill)

---

* Dark, grave.

† Hose of great width, probably introduced from Gascony.

‡ The *OED* quotes this as the only example of the word and defines it (wisely, but not very helpfully) as 'some kind of garment'.

§ Medieval 'clerks' were those in holy orders and the term was often used of those in minor orders who sang in choirs. The position of parish clerk was filled by an individual clerk. After the Reformation the parish clerkship came to be a lay office, and while the clerk usually led the singing his role became increasingly administrative.

¶ Octave or eighth day. The terms 'octave' and 'octaves' are also used for the period of eight days beginning with the first day of a festival.

1504 To a strange clerk for singing in the queer in Ester weke ... 12d (St Mary at Hill)

1542 To Georg ye singeng man for helping ye quier the holy dayes ... 12d (St Martin in the Fields)[1]

The higher parts are naturally sung by boys.

1493 To a childe that songe a trebell to helpe the quere in Cristmas halydayis ... 12d | 1523 For 2 yerdes of wikur matt for the childrens fete ... 16d | For 6 round mattes of wikers for the clerkes ... 15d (St Mary at Hill)

1561 To the children of Powles for helpeing the quier at my Lady Bowes daughters marriage ... 5s (St Mary Woolnoth)[2]

As with preachers, singers are often rewarded with wine and other treats.

1519 For brede, ale and wine for the clerkes & the children at masse ... 12d ob. | 1523 To Northfolke and his compeny & the children when that Mr Parson gave to them a playing weke to make mery ... 3s 4d | 1524 To John Northfolke & the conductes* & the children in the play-ing weke aftur Christemas for to sport them ... 3s 4d (St Mary at Hill)

1557 2 pounde of figges for them that did helpe to singe at salve† the first Friday in the Lent ... 6d | More for brede and drinke for the singin men that did singe at salve ... 5s 4d (St Edmund, Salisbury)

1582 5¾ yardes to make Distine the boye which singeth in the quire a coate and a paire of breeches ... 7s 8d (St Thomas, Salisbury)[3]

Some of the singers of Henry VIII's chapel perform often at St Mary at Hill and are well looked after in return.

1510 For a pike 2s 8d, for 2 soles 4d, for half a side salt fish 3d, for rochis [roaches] 4d, oysters 1d, for buttur 1d, for a pie of quinsis 6d, for brede, ale, wine, erbes & a side of linge & flownders, nuttes, fire & sawce 2s 6d; for the cokes labur for dressing this diner at Mr Sudborowys for Mr Kyte and Harry Prenttes of the kinges chapell 4d. | 1522 For a galon of Gascon wine sent to John Edyalles to the kinges chappell for theire diner ... 12d | Paid on Seint Barnabis day, at the Sonn taverne, after evensong, for drinke for the kinges chappell and for the clerks of the towne ... 21d[4]

---

* *Conduct.* A hired or salaried priest or chaplain. In 1529 three men from St Mary at Hill rode to Norwich to see the parson 'to knowe his minde for the paying of the conductes wages', at which time 20d was spent on '2 lampreys for Mr Parson'.
† An antiphon beginning '*Salve, Regina*' (Hail, Queen), addressed to the Virgin Mary and often sung near or at the end of the liturgical day.

In other places harmony does not always prevail.

1749 Feb. 11th. The company of singers ... were forbidden to sing any more by the minister, upon account of their frequent ill-behaviour in the chancel and their ordering the carpenter to pull down part of the belfry without leave from the minister and churchwardens. | March 18th. The clerk gave out the 100th Psalm, and the singers immediately opposed him and sung the 15th, and bred a disturbance. (Hayes, Middlesex, note in register)[5]

Singers in stained glass, North Tuddenham, Norfolk

3. Parish clerk

Before the Reformation the parish clerk is in holy orders but later it comes to be a lay office. The Canons of 1604 require that the holder is at least 20 years old, is chosen by the incumbent, 'and known to the said parson, vicar, or minister, to be of honest conversation, and sufficient for his reading, writing, and also for his competent skill in singing, if it may be'. As this suggests, his duties include writing up the parish records, leading the singing in services, and reading the lesson. At Preston, Lancashire, one 18th-century clerk is known as 'Amen'.[1]

Other duties vary from parish to parish, and depend in part on what other staff are employed, but they may include ringing bells, attending to the clock, digging graves, and keeping a watchful eye on the church, sometimes sleeping there.

> 1563-64 John Webbe *alias* Clarke, & clarke of this parishe, was buried the 4th day of Februarye. The which John Webbe *alias* Clarke came to this parish in anno 1516, and his sarvys [service] so diligent to ye parish, that he never lay night owt of the same parish all the same time, but allwayes waiting on his sarvyse, whose soule nowe reste with the lorde, God onely be praised therfore, Amen. (St Dionis Backchurch, register)

> 1586 Agreed by the consent of the parish that William White the clarke shall keepe the clocke, belles, make cleane the church, sweepe the leddes, and ringe the bell for coverfue [curfew] and day, and shall have yearlie for his labour 13s 4d. (Steeple Ashton, Wilts)

> 1650 To Marmaduke How for making up the window in the belfree for the clarks bed and for timber boords and workmanship ... £1 1s (Waltham Abbey, Essex)

> 1693 To William Hatton for clerkship, moletakeing & writeing ... £2 1s (Billington, Beds)[2]

At Louth in 1500 the two clerks are ordered not to leave the church from the ringing of curfew until the mass priest calls them in the morning, the one exception being if they are required to accompany the parish priest when he goes to administer the eucharist to the sick and dying.[3]

Occasionally the clerk is troublesome. In 1614 Thomas Milborne of East Ham, Essex, is presented to the Church authorities for a range of transgressions.

> For spreadinge mowle hills with a shovell in the churchyard ... and for that he doth not kneele on his knees in time of devine service when as it is fittinge he should and the rather in that he is the parishe clerke who ought to give good example therby unto others that are negligent therein, and he hath often times been admonished for to kneele by the minister but he doth altogether refuse it. And for that he singeth the psalmes in the church

with such a jesticulus tone and altitonant* voice, viz. squeakinge like a gelded pig which doth not only interrupt the other voices, but is altogether dissonant and disagreeing unto any musicall harmonie, and he hath been requested by the minister to leave it, but he doth obstinatlie persist and continue therein.[4]

A more forgiving description of a clerk's vocal contribution is found in the register of Buxted, Sussex.

> 1666 Richard Bassett, the old clarke of this parish, who had continued in the offices of clarke and sexton for the space of 43 years, whose melody warbled forth as if he had been thumped on the back with a stone, was buried the 20th of Sept.[5]

The register of Totteridge, Hertfordshire, includes a tribute to a rare female clerk.

> 1802 March 2nd. Buried Elizabeth King, widow, for 46 years clerk of this parish, in the 91st year of her age, who died at Whetstone, in the parish of Finchley, February 24th. N.B. This old woman, as long as she was able to attend, did constantly, and read on the prayer-days, with great strength and pleasure to the hearers, though not in the clerk's place, the desk being filled on the Sunday by her son-in-law Benjamin Withall, who did his best.[6]

In some places a specific levy is raised from parishioners for the clerk's pay, although he may not receive all that is collected.

> 1530 Received of the parish towards the clerk's wages ... £6 18s 6d | Paid to the clerk for his wages ... £5 (St Laurence Pountney)[7]

However, the basis on which he is rewarded varies considerably from place to place and often involves fees, perquisites and contributions in kind. The 1604 Canons state simply that clerks should 'receive their ancient wages ... according to the most ancient custom of every parish'.[8]

> *c.* 1700 The clarke is to have from every farm at Easter 6d, and at Christmas 6d, or a curfew loafe.† From every tenement at Easter 4d, at Christmas 4d, or a curfew loafe ... From every house-holder at Easter, in eggs or money, 1d; bell sheaves which are three sheaves of rye, or of other corne if there be no rye. Christnings, his dinner and 2d; burials in the church yard with coffin, 1s; without coffin, 6d;‡ [etc]. (Myddle, Shropshire, from Richard Gough's history of the parish)[9]

---

* *Altitonant.* Thundering from on high, used in particular of Jupiter (*OED*). This does not, however, seem apt for 'squeakinge like a gelded pig'.

† Perhaps a reward for ringing the nightly bell. The 'bell sheaves' mentioned further on are perhaps similarly explained.

‡ The higher fee for coffined burial reflects in part the greater labour involved. See below, pp347-350.

Grave-digger, perhaps the clerk or sexton, South Mimms, Hertfordshire,
by Francis Grose, 1787

4. Sexton

In larger parishes there is also a sexton. The name is a contraction of sacristan, but while this suggests a keeper of sacred things, in practice sextons tend to carry out menial tasks such as bell-ringing and grave-digging. The tomb of Hezekiah Briggs (*d.* 1844) at Bingley, Yorkshire, records that 'He was sexton at this church 43 years, and interred upwards of 7000 corpses,' while at St John the Baptist, Chester, Benjamin Carter (*d.* 1808) 'is supposed to have buried 8000 corpses'.[1]

As with clerks, the duties can be quite varied. The following, in condensed form, are some of those set out at Faversham in 1506.

i. The sextayn or his sufficient depute every night shall lie in the churche stepill.
ii. And every night he at 8 at clok shall ring couvrefewe by the space of oon quarter of an hour with suche a bell as of olde time hath be accustomed.
iii. He every day in the morning in somer shall open the churche doores at 5 at clok, and in winter at 6 at clok. ...
vi. He every werke day shall toll three times to the morow masse, with the 4th bell at 5 of the clok in somer and at 6 at clok in winter ...
vii. He shall make provision for the lighting of the lampe in the quier before any prest go to masse and so to see it continue as long as any masse is to be songe ther. ...
ix. He shall fill the holy water stoppis [stoups] in the body of the churche with freshe water as often as nede shall require, and every day in the morning [is] to see the churche made clene for skomering [from defecation] of dogs.
x. He every weke shall make cleen the body of the churche, and the crosse aisles, from dust or other filthes, and also on the even of every principal feast, and brushe away all the cobwebbis and make cleen over and about all the auters, walles and windowes ...
xi. If their com any bestis into the churcheyerd by escape or non closure of the churche walles then the sextayn or his depute shall drive them out in as hasty time as he can.[2]

At Loughborough a similar role is played by a 'bellman'. His duties include:

First to lie in ye cherch and to come at 8 of ye clok at night in winter and somer to ring curfew and then to go to bed. ... Also to light the candelles in ye cherch every holyday as custom has been used. To blow ye orgens at matins and mass and evensong as has been of custom afore time. To help to ring to service if need be. To sweep ye cherch thorow and to clen every seventh day and every Hallow even. To sweep ye pillars to and of ye cherch as hy as he can rech with a long banner pole and wher cobwebbs and dost does hang on ... To go every Friday abowt ye towne to bid [parishioners to] pray for all Christian soles as of custom has been used at 6 of ye clok in somer and 7 of ye clok in winter. Also to set ye hearse of every corpse.[3]

In later periods sextons are quite often women, widows sometimes taking over the role from deceased husbands.

> 1690 April the 22th. Rebekah Dowse (the late sexton's widow) was chosen sextoness for one year upon condition that betweene this and Midsomer next she lay aside her alehouse. (Hackney, Middlesex, vestry)

> 1763 Sep. 25th. Elizabeth Ager is this day appointed sexton of this parish in the room of her late husband, to continue in the place so long as she shall behave herself obediently and honestly towards me, dutifully and orderly about the church, quietly and contentedly under the clerk, and no longer; but then to be displaced and another to be appointed in her room. [Signed] Tilly Walker, vicar. (Holy Sepulchre, Northampton, vestry book)[4]

In some London parishes it becomes more or less customary for the sexton to be female. At St Anne and St Agnes, Aldersgate, twelve women hold the post between 1660 and 1890, their combined tenures amounting to some 175 years.[5]

Hester Hammerton

On 2nd March 1730 she and her brother are helping their father Abraham, sexton of Kingston upon Thames, to prepare a grave in an old chapel on the south side of the church when the chapel collapses as a result of their digging too close to a pillar. Abraham and another man are killed at once, but after lying buried in the ruins for three hours (or seven, depending on the account) Hester and her brother are dug out alive. She succeeds her father as sexton and holds the post until her own death sixteen years later.

The sexton is always paid less than the clerk: at St Mary at Hill in 1514, for example, the former receives £2 a year and the latter £6.

At Houghton-le-Spring, county Durham, the 'anciently accostomed' fees due to the sexton are set out in 1658.

> By each plow 2d; by each cottage a ob. yearly. For a christning 2d; for a grave making in the quire 6d; in the church 4d; in the church yard 2d. And upon good will each householder to give him buns at Christmas and eggs at Easter yearly.[6]

Goodwill is not always earned or forthcoming. At St Andrew, Plymouth, the parish receives no income for bells or burials during the last two months of 1606, the accounts noting in explanation that 'Ye sexton ran away with ye money'. Five years earlier Francis Whitacres, sexton of Stepney, is dismissed for various faults including 'not looking dutifully unto the bells' and telling one of the churchwardens to 'shake his eares among dogges'. The same parish later suspends another sexton who 'demeaned himself in a very uncivil and disorderly manner towards the parishioners & hath been a contemner & scoffer of them that are godly & also hath been very negligent in the performance of his place' (1647). Meanwhile St Martin, Leicester, dismisses its sexton 'for getting a bastard child on the body of Margaret Weston, haveing a wife of his owne' (1643).[7]

Other sextons provide long service, none more impressively than William Hill of Crowland, Lincolnshire. The following letter recounts a visitor's encounter with him in 1782, some nine years before Hill's death.

> I walk'd about the churchyard and had much talk with the sexton who was very merry, digging a grave. I found him a pleasant, intelligent, facetious fellow, and could not help being highly entertained with his humour and drollery. Afterwards he pointed to the cottage where his wife was who had the key of the church. When there, I congratulated her on having so cheerful a husband. She say'd indeed he was a very good man, and a good scholar, that he had formerly been an assistant schoolmaster, as well as sexton, that he had also been the easiest person in the world, excepting one year of his life, during which period he continually fretted day and night. I ask'd the occasion, heard it was misfortune. — What misfortune? — Loss of sight! — Well, be thankful he is recovered and got well again. — Yes, sir, say'd she, he is well to be sure, but has never got the better of his blindness, nor has he been able to see for 18 years past. The woman astonish'd me. I inquired repeatedly if she really meant the man whom I saw digging the grave, for I had been prating with the poor fellow some considerable time, and he never once lamented his want of sight, or even threw out the most distant hint of his being blind, but kept shoveling up the earth, and talking with as much ease as it is possible to conceive, and without a murmur or complaint. It is a fact that the man has been sexton

at Crowland 22 years, and has done the business of a sexton 17 years since his blindness ceased to distress him. It was occasioned by a cold he caught one severe winter, when he was obliged to travel about in the snow, on foot, to many places, in search of some person to officiate for a Mr Benson, the gentleman who formerly had the living — and what is equally extra-ordinary, that very gentleman was blind, but had nevertheless done the duty of his church every Sunday, when well, for 30 years preceding his death ...

A tablet raised to Hill's memory some years later records that 'he could walk in and about the town, and could go in the church yard [and] find each and every grave he was desired to point out'.[8]

Better known is Robert Scarlet, 'Old Scarlet', who dies in 1594, well into his nineties, having been sexton of St John the Baptist, Peterborough, for many years.

1541 Gevin to Skarlet for setting the herse ... 2d | 1563 To Scarlet for making cleane the churche yard ... 8d | 1564 To Robert Skarlett for his paines taking for this whole yere in keping and clensing the leades and other necessary business abowte the church ... 3s | 1572 To Scarlet being a poore olde man and rising oft in the nightes to tolle the bell for sicke persons, the wether being grevous, and in consideracion of his good service, towardes a gowne to keepe him warme ... 8s[9]

He is employed at the church but also digs graves in the cathedral, apparently being responsible for the burial there of two queens, Catherine of Aragon in 1536 and Mary Queen of Scots in 1587. Such is his renown that his portrait is later displayed in the cathedral with the following verses below.

You see old Scarleit's picture stand on hie
But at your feete there doth his body lie.
His gravestone doth his age and death time show
His office by theis tokens you may know
Second to none for strength and sturdye limm,
A scare-babe mighty voice with visage grim.
He had inter'd two queenes within this place
And this townes householders in his lives space
Twice over: but at length his own turne came
What he for others did for him the same
Was done: no doubt his soule doth live for aye
In heaven, though here his body [is] clad in clay.[10]

Robert Scarlet, after a portrait in Peterborough Cathedral.
There have been several versions and the original likeness,
a mural, is said to show a taller, leaner figure.

5. Dogwhipping and congregation control

Tucked into Scarlet's belt is a whip for keeping dogs out of church. The role of dogwhipper pre-dates the Reformation but comes into its own after it as the chancel becomes more accessible to intruders. The work may fall to the sexton, or someone else may be appointed.

1504 To fader Yanne for the keeping of the whipe for beting the dogges oute of the churche ... 16d (St Margaret, Westminster)

1621 To Roger the dogwhipper ... 10s (St Mary the Great, Cambridge)

1627 To Bury for lashing the dogs out of the church for one quarter ... 1s (Smarden, Kent)

1650 To old Elton* for keepin dogs out of the church for a whole yeare ... 4s (Battersea)

1806 Paid Fewkes dog flogger ... 10s (St Martin, Leicester)[1]

Occasionally the whip-hand is female.

1647 To Richard Hodgson's wife for whipping dogs ... 2s (Barnsley, Yorks)

1726 To widow Sandys 1 years sallery for whipping ... 5s (Ulverston, Lancs)[2]

The post is generally used as a way of providing employment for one of the parish poor.

1588 To a poore man that whipped the dogges ... 4d (St Martin, Salisbury)[3]

At Chislet, Kent, two acres of land called Dogwhipper's Marsh are rented out, the tenant paying 10s a year to a person for keeping order in the church during divine service.[4]

A whipper naturally needs a whip. At Ludlow it has bells attached, perhaps with the humane intention of alerting the dogs so that the whip will not need to be used.

1560 For a belle and whipcorde to make a whip to drive dogges out of the churche ... 1d ob. | 1569 For 2 belles for the whip ... 4d[5]

In some parishes clothing is provided for the wielder.

1618 For a jerkin to Edward Johnson according to ancient custom for whiping dogs out of the church ... 6s 4d (Bray, Berks)

1713 To Thomas Ranson ye dog whipper for a coat cloth and trimming and making ... 15s 6d | For a whip and shoes mending ... 8d (Burnsall, Yorks)

1793 A coat and waistcoat for Dog-man ... £1 3s 4d (North Lydbury, Shropshire)[6]

---

* Thomas Elton had been whipping dogs at Battersea since at least 1614.

Tethered dog in stained glass, and one on the roof which got away,
both at Huntingfield, Suffolk

At Mullion, Cornwall, there is a small latchet door at the bottom of the church's south door for the easier ejection of dogs, and at Youlgreave, Derbyshire, there is a designated dogwhippers' pew until 1868.[7]

Not that dogs are always unwelcome. On Whitsunday 1640 the church of Antony, Cornwall, is struck by lightning during divine service. A contemporary account of the impact notes that it 'instantly kill'd a dogge at the feet of those who were kneeling in the chancel to receive the sacrament, and likewise another without the church at the bell-free doore', suggesting that dogs are familiar figures around the church.[8]

A story recorded by Philip Thicknesse in his guide to Bath for 1778 also suggests they are free to come and go.

> [Bishop Warburton] declared, that being at the Abbey church one Sunday, when a certain chapter in Ezekiel was read in which the word *wheel* is often mentioned, that a great number of turnspits, which had followed the cooks to church, discovered a manifest alarm, the first time the reader uttered the word *wheel*; but upon its being repeated twice more, they all clapt their tails between their legs, and ran out of the church.[9]

Their alarm is understandable as the words 'wheel' and 'wheels' occur ten times in Ezekiel chapter 1, verses 15 to 21. Meanwhile in Lincolnshire,

> Thomas Peacock, who died in 1824, was always accompanied to Northorpe church by his dog. There was a little pew just within the chancel arch, on the south side, in which the animal was confined. It went by the name of The Hall Dog Pew.[10]

Nor are canines the only source of trouble, children – and particularly boys – also needing attention.

> 1600 Paide ... for a presentment ... touching the boyes playing at dice in the churche ... 1s 8d (All Hallows Staining)

> 1619 Paid Rafe Coney for whippinge dogges out of church & over seeinge wicked & unruly children in church ... 12d (Holy Trinity, Chester)

> 1635 [To Giles] for keeping out the dogges and keeping in the boyes ... 10s | 1649 For rods for keepinge quiet of the boyes ... 2d (St Andrew, Plymouth)

> 1725 In expenses at Tiverton about the boys that made a disterbains in the church ... 2s 4d (Cullompton, Devon)

> 1747 For going about to fright children from play in service time, great complaints being made ... 2s (Almondbury, Yorks)

> 1765 [Ordered] that the churchwarden do every Sunday cause two of the bearers or such persons as they shall think fit to attend in the church in the forenoon and afternoon during the time of divine service, to prevent noises and disturbances usually made by boys and beggars ... | 1769 [Ordered] that iron spikes be placed on the doors opening to the middle aisle of the church, to prevent boys from climbing over the same ... (St Giles without Cripplegate, vestry)[11]

Children sitting in a gallery are a particular concern, not least because the temptation to drop things on those below may prove too great.[12]

> 1664 Paide Ric. Fidler for keepinge the boyes in order in the gallary ... £1 (Battersea)

Richard (perhaps known familiarly as Dick) Fidler is an unfortunately named schoolmaster.[13]

An eye may also need to be kept on the churchyard.

> 1611 To John Gurland for keeping the boys from the churchyard walls at the funeral of the Earl of Dunbar .... (St Margaret, Westminster)

> 1822 Paid Farr for attending in the churchyard to see that no mischief be done to the church and the monuments by the children ... 5s (Fulham, Middlesex)[14]

A more general problem is that of parishioners of all ages sleeping in church, particularly during sermons.

> 1705 For walking in ye church on ye Sunday to keep people from sleeping, and whipping of ye dogs ... 2s 6d (Almondbury)

> 1736 [Agreed] that 13s a year be given to George Grimshaw, of Rooden Lane, for ye time being, and a new coat (not exceeding 20s) every other year, for his trouble and pains in wakening sleepers in ye church, whipping out dogs, keeping children quiet and orderly, and keeping ye pulpit and church walks clean. (Prestwich, Lancs, vestry)[15]

At Sutton-on-the-Hill, Derbyshire, Samuel Lygoe is paid 5s a year for dog-whipping and he is also 'to prevent any one sleeping in the church by wakeing them with a white wand'.[16]

6. Beadle &c.

Some parishes appoint a beadle who may undertake similar tasks. At Basingstoke in 1691 he is to

> attend in the church in the time of divine service, both at morning and evening prayer and sermons, and then and there keep the children and youth in due order and from playing and making of noises, and also to drive dogs out of the church, and to assist the churchwardens in any other disturbance that shall there happen.[1]

A contributor to *Notes and Queries* recalls attending Handsworth church, near Birmingham, as a boy in about 1830.

> The beadle, an old man, attired in his official costume, somewhat resembling that worn by the celebrated Mr Bumble, used to make the rounds of the church during service carrying a stout wand, surmounted with a gilt knob or ball. This instrument he used in waking up sleepy boys or girls. The unruly ones he admonished by a smart tap on the head, which could be distinctly heard all over the church.[2]

Beadles also act as parish messengers and punish petty offenders. As public representatives of the parish they are dressed rather more smartly than dogwhippers.

> 1678 For the beagle's coat, and triming and makeing ... £1 4s 3d (St Nicholas, Durham)

> 1730 For the beadles cloaths ... £5 6d | For the gold lace ... £1 11s 6d | For a hat and stockings ... 14s 6d (Fulham, Middlesex)

> 1847 For three cocked hats, with gold trimmings, for the three beadles ... £6 (St Leonard, Shoreditch)[3]

At Leyton, Essex, in 1718 Robert Snow is chosen as beadle on a salary of £5, his main task being 'taking up of vagrants, and other who [are] likely to be chargable to this parish'. At Mortlake seventy years later John Andrews is elected to the post on the same salary, 'with usual cloaths, and he was ordered to keep the parish clear of beggars, and to give an account of all soldiers seen lurking about in the lanes and fields of this parish at unseasonable hours'.[4]

In some places the office has the descriptive name of bang-beggar.

> 1705 [Accounts] For making bangbeger coate ... 3s 6d | For bangbegers staf ... 1s | 1710 [Vestry] Ordered that old Ed Peters be made bang-begger for the said parish, his pay to be eighteenpence by weeke & a coat against Christmas. | [Accounts] Making ye bangbegers coat & a new hat ... 5s 2½d (St Werburgh, Derby)[5]

Some parishes also employ one or more **pew-openers**. At Tooting, Surrey, Mary Wren is elected to the post in 1813 on a salary of £10 and continues opening pews until her death nearly forty years later.[6]

A parish beadle tidies away street life
After a painting by David Wilkie, 1823

7. Churchwardens

The churchwardens are responsible not only for maintaining the church and managing all expenditure but also for making sure parishioners attend divine service on Sundays and other holy days. In addition they have the primary responsibility for informing the Church authorities of faults and offences within the parish.[1]

There are usually two of them, appointed each year at Easter, at which time the old wardens give up their accounts to parish scrutiny. According to the Canons of 1604, they 'shall be chosen by the joint consent of the minister and the parishioners, if it may be: but if they cannot agree ... then the minister shall choose one, and the parishioners another'. However, the custom in the City of London and some other areas is for both wardens to be elected by the parishioners.[2]

Occasionally those chosen are women: at St Petrock, Exeter, for example, the wardens in 1426 are Alice Cooke and Alice Pyppedon.[3]

Wardens are almost always unpaid,* their only tangible reward being food and drink enjoyed in connection with parish business, beginning when they are chosen and ending at the giving up of their accounts.[4]

> 1559-60 Payed the 14th of March at the gevinge of the accompt of the other yeres, for kracknells 6d, for figges, reasons and almonds 12d, for apples 3d, for a wine 16d, for sewgar 7d, for bere and ale 4d. (St Martin in the Fields)
>
> 1602 For a pottle of sack which was drunke in the chauncell of the auditors and others at the giveinge up of the laste churchwardens accounte ... 2s (St Mary the Great, Cambridge)
>
> 1632 To Edmund Brodbanks wife for cakes and beer, for fire and wood, on the reckoning day ... 15s (Cratfield, Suffolk)[5]

The following includes a nice literal use of a phrase later applied figuratively.

> 1625 Cakes when Ambrose West gave up his accompt ... 16d | Ditto at the summing up of the booke ... 16d (St Thomas, Salisbury)[6]

During their time in office churchwardens tend to spend a good deal of further parish money on eating and drinking, some instances appearing more justified than others.

> 1561 Paid at divers times for myn own drinkin ... 12d | For a drinkinge another time for Master Benbow and me ... 2d (St Andrew Hubbard)
>
> 1600 For wine & nuttes when we sat at Mr Knightes about our present-mentes ... 18d (St Martin in the Fields)[7]

* The following is a rare exception: '1788. Payed Richard Hall for doing the office of church warden ... £1 1s' (Woodbury, Devon). They do also sometimes pay themselves for carrying out particular tasks – some examples are on pp151, 153, 382, 398, 468.

In some parishes the abuse becomes more or less flagrant, the following being just a few of the entries for St James, Westminster, in 1723.

> April. Expences with the scavengers, to bring them to account and receive their balance ... £1 9d
>
> May 3rd. At Champion's after rating of the scavenger's book ... £1 12s 6d
>
> May 28th. At Milner's on the king's birthday ... £3 15s
>
> June 17th. At Baldwin's after a vestry, on an inquiry for a pall stolen ... £1 6s
>
> July 25th. At Solaro's for a visitation dinner ... £9 12s
>
> August 1st. At ditto on the king's accession day ... £3 16s
>
> Oct 20th. At Champion's on the coronation day ... £3 17s 6d
>
> Oct 31st. At Milner's on treating the gentlemen of St Bartholomew's Hospital ... £15
>
> Nov. 29th. At Milner's on the king's landing from Holland ... £1 5s[8]

Eventually some parishes lose patience.

> 1703 June 3rd. It was agreed on by a general consent that hereafter there should be no money spent in eating and drinking upon the parish charge upon any peremptory day, and that the churchwardens be allowed only 4d a man out of the public stock for their refreshment. (Kendal, Westmorland, vestry)[9]

The position is onerous, nonetheless, and those chosen are often reluctant, so that many parishes institute a fine for those refusing to serve. In 1568 St Mary the Great, Cambridge, sets it at 10 shillings, but too many people prefer to pay than to serve and in 1621 they raise it to £2. At St Bartholomew Exchange a Mr Gibson pays £5 in 1615, 'for the which he was freed from beinge churchwarden of this parishe for ever', and in 1630 Thomas Mustard pays the princely sum of £20 'to be freed of all offices that this parish can impose upon him'. At St John Zachary a few years later William Symonds gets away with paying only £5 'to free him from all offices', but that is perhaps 'because he could not write nor rede' and so would have been of limited use.[10]

While most churchwardens act responsibly and do their best, some let the parish down, as the following presentments indicate.

> 1623 Robert Forde *alias* Pullen, one of the churchwardens, is very often drunke. Since he was churchwarden, he was drunke at Petworth, and lay abroad all night in the strete. And a little before that he was drunke, and lay all night upon the hill going to Arundel, and lost his corne that he was carrying to market. (Sutton, Sussex)
>
> 1625 We present our old churchwardens for not giving up theire accompte at Easter last to the parish, and for selling the lead of the steeple away. (Tortington, Sussex)[11]

8. The vestry

As seen above, traditionally parishioners are involved once a year in electing churchwardens and approving their accounts. During the 16th and 17th centuries this oversight is extended in response to the increasing complexity of the parish's finances as, in addition to its ecclesiastical functions, it takes on a growing role in local government and in consequence imposes an array of charges upon house-holders. During this period the term 'vestry' comes to be used both for parish meetings – the vestry being where they are often held – and for the parishioners as a decision-taking body. It is a common custom for the minister to act as the vestry's chairman, but his presence is not formally required and his right to preside is occasionally challenged.[1]

i. Business

Vestry meetings typically focus on building repairs, poor relief and the setting of rates. They also grapple with a wide range of other pressing local issues, the following being a few examples.

> 1593 August 26th. Mr Welles our parsonne moved the parrishe abought the woman that Mr Cox kepeth in his chambar to serve him, & for that it is very suspicious for him to kepe hur so, it is agreed that the churchwardens shall admonishe him to put hur awaie before Sondaie next ... (St Margaret, Lothbury)

> 1738 Sep. 8th. It was unanimously agreed that if any person hereafter shall hang cloaths to dry in the churchyard they shall be prosecuted for a nuisance, and that Curtis the sexton do give notice to the several persons concern'd and likewise to Francis Reynolds to keep his hog out, otherwise it will be pounded, and himself prosecuted for the same. (Fulham, Middlesex)

> 1752 [Agreed that] Thomas Earle being a lunatick to be got into Bedlam. (Tooting, Surrey)

> 1823 June 25th. [Agreed] to employ one or more persons to root up and destroy the deadly night shade throughout this parish. (Minchin-hampton, Glos)[2]

In addition to electing churchwardens the vestry may choose those holding a number of other positions. For example, on Easter Monday 1797 the parishioners of St Peter Mancroft, Norwich, are summoned to elect not only two wardens but also two sidesmen to assist them, a pew-opener, a bellows-blower, an organist, an upper sexton, an under sexton, a clerk, four overseers of the poor, and twelve auditors.[3]

Like more or less everything else that happens in the parish, such meetings are an excuse for consumption, sometimes modest, sometimes less so.

1653 For 4 gallons & a pint of sacke for the vestry ... £1 13s (St Christopher le Stocks)

1656 For 5 kidds burnt at ye several meetings ... 10d (St Mary, Leicester)

1677 Tobacco & pipes & beere when the vestry met ... 2s (St Thomas, Salisbury)

1756 For a rump of beef, a loin of mutton and leg of veal for the parish meeting ... 9s (Otterton, Devon)[4]

ii. Composition

Vestries are usually divided into two types, open and select.

In theory an **open vestry** includes all the rate-paying householders. It is thus a relatively inclusive body in the context of the times and provides large numbers of people with an early experience of democracy and a direct say in how their money is spent. However, women are usually excluded, proceedings may be unruly, and the 'openness' may be superficial, with proceedings dominated by a small number of the more substantial householders.

As the name suggests, a **select vestry** is made up of a limited group, ranging from a handful to thirty or more, almost always men. Its members are known by a range of names in different places, for example the 'select men' or 'the masters of the parish'. Sometimes the term used indicates their number, for example 'the three men' at Morebath, Devon, or 'the twelve' and 'the four and twenty' respectively at Pittington and Houghton-le-Spring, county Durham.[5]

The initial choice of select vestry members may be made by the parishioners as a whole. However, it is common for those members then to retain the position for life and, when one dies, for the surviving members to choose the replacement.

As their affairs become more involved many parishes move from an open to a select approach. The shift occurs most markedly in London, where by 1638 a majority of parishes have made the change. At St Botolph, Aldgate, it happens in 1622, at which time the 'better sort' of the parishioners, supported by the minister and wardens, successfully petition the Bishop of London to allow a group of forty-eight to 'be appointed continually to be vestrymen' to run affairs. The reasons they give include 'the great confusion and disorder' of parish meetings and 'the ignorance and weakness in judgment ... of some of the parishioners that have resorted thither' – that is, of newcomers and transients.[6]

Some parishes seek to combine the benefits of the two approaches. At St Andrew, Holborn, 'the receipts and disbursements of the churchwardens ... are every year given up publicly before the whole parish', but 'some affairs belonging to the church are consulted upon and ordered by the rector and churchwardens, and a selected vestry of twelve persons, grave and ancient inhabitants, men of approved honesty and good discretion'.[7]

iii. Corruption

At their best select vestries provide continuity and orderly and well informed management of parish affairs. However, over time their lack of accountability tends to lead to corruption, a point made in emphatic style by Daniel Defoe in the 1720s.

> There is not a greater abuse in the world than that of select vestries ... [They are] never renew'd but by one at a time, as the old ones drop off, [and] they are sure to choose none in their room, but those whom they have mark'd for their purpose beforehand; so rogue succeeds rogue, and the same scene of villainy is still carried on, to the terror of the poor parishioners.

As he also observes,

> Nothing is so profitable to these gentlemen as parish repairs. If the church is new beautify'd, painted or whitewash'd, whip they come upon you with a church rate, and where two hundred pounds has been expended, twelve hundred shall be collected ... Nay, there are some parishes, where church-wardens tho' they went in as poor as rats, have come out too rich ever to be poor again ...[8]

St Martin in the Fields is a notorious case in point. In the later 16th century it moves from an open to a select system and by the 18th century the abuse is patent. In 1742 a House of Commons committee finds that there has been an 'extravagant increase of expence' on candles after a vestry member began to supply them. Much of the money supposedly spent on communion wine has been for 'white wine, oranges, sugar, butter, and glass bottles'. One of the royal glaziers testifies that the parish is paying a vestryman glazier considerably more than the king pays for similar work. Meanwhile, among disbursements 'on account of the poor', £3 3s has been paid 'to the Duke of Somerset's park-keeper for a present of venison' and £5 12s 6d 'on a dinner upon the gentlemen who were judges of the organ'.[9]

Despite such evidence, and later challenges by unhappy parishioners, the vestry at St Martin's is not reformed until 1834.

iv. Disorder &c.

More generally the deliberations of both types of vestry may be undermined by the kind of problems that can beset any meeting.

> 1610 [Ordered] that everie vestrieman ... shall sit still and not remove or go from place to place to talke with any, or sittinge in his place to have any talke with any others, but to give eare to that which is in hand that it may be the better heard and answered, so that one man may make answeare at one time and every man one by one to shewe his minde and to make answeare one after another and not five or six to speake at once ... (Lambeth)

1744 Feb. 10th. Several things were mentioned about three children that were irregularly brought to our parish and left at the overseer's house, and Peter Moor's house, and the mentioning the same ... led to nothing but wrangling and passion on this affair, without anything being done in relation to the same. (All Saints, Hastings, Sussex)[10]

Occasionally the passion gets out of hand.

1813 July 24th. It appears by the report of the vestry clerk of this parish that at a meeting of the parishioners held at the workhouse ... on Wednesday evening last, that the vestry book was forcibly and in a most outrageous manner taken from him, and the records and resolutions for nearly two years torn out and defaced ... (Stoke Damerel, Devon)

1823 Feb. 6th. The greatest tumult and disorder now began to be manifested in opposition to Dr Gwynne (who had been elected chairman). The uproar and confusion continued without intermission for more than an hour, when a scene of riot prevailed which became seriously alarming ... many persons getting upon the tables, even over the backs of others, and thus endeavouring to force their way to the top of the room to place Mr Rennoldson in the chair. The great pressure and suffocating heat added to the vociferation and menacing attitude of various parties [and] caused the greatest terror and alarm in the vestry room. A cry of *Murder* was heard and, lives of several vestrymen appearing to be in serious danger, the chairman was requested to disperse the meeting. He thereupon read the Riot Act ... and ... ordered the meeting in a legal way to separate ... whereupon the officers ... from the police department in Worship Street were called in [and] the meeting was with some difficulty dispersed. (Bethnal Green)[11]

Partly as a result of such scenes, and the corruption outlined above, during the 19th century vestries are deprived of their civil powers by a series of Acts culminating in the Local Government Act of 1894.[12]

FACING PAGE
Satirical views of select vestries, 1795 (*above*)
and 1806 (*below*, by Thomas Rowlandson)

'These select vestries ... have their charity feasts and official banquets too, and gorge and guzzle most sumptuously at the public cost. ... At Norwood [Middlesex] ... each gorged and guzzled in one day more than went to support a shivering pauper for 3 months. ... Oh! for the pen of Cervantes, or the pencil of Bunbury or Hogarth, to exhibit the gang as they deserve.'
(*Sunday Times*, 13 April 1828 p2)

A GOOD THING *or* SELECT VESTRY REPAST

A SELECT VESTRY

Adoration of the Magi, alabaster, Nottingham school, 15th century

Matthew 2:1-12 describes an unspecified number of 'wise men from the east' who bring gold, frankincense and myrrh. The later tradition of three magi probably arises from the number of gifts. In addition they come to be identified as kings - hence their crowns here - emphasising the message of earthly power humbling itself before the new dispensation.

The Old Parish Year

Many of the festivals outlined below are moveable, being dependent in most cases on the date of Easter. In order to create a simple sequence Easter has been taken to fall on 5th April, not far from the middle of the possible range (22nd March to 25th April). Dates assigned to moveable festivals are given in square brackets, with the basis for determining them following in round brackets.[1]

Two general and well known points about the shape of the traditional year are perhaps worth making. First, the major festivals, while ostensibly Christian in origin, are profoundly rooted in the cycle of the seasons, Easter for example mirroring nature's own 'resurrection' with the arrival of spring. Second, their clustering in a 'ritual half year' from Christmas to Midsummer, or from winter solstice to summer solstice, also bears witness to the influence of nature, leaving largely clear as it does the period required for the great annual task of a rural community, harvest.[2]

January 1st New Year's Day

The day coincides with a minor festival, the Feast of the Circumcision, based on the account in Luke 2:21 of Christ's circumcision eight days after his birth. The new year itself is scantly celebrated by the Church, perhaps from reluctance to encourage any revival of the licentious revelry with which it tended to be marked in pagan times. In later centuries bells are sometimes rung.

> 1756 For ringing the old year out and the new one in ... 5s (Ecclesfield, Yorks)[1]

At Sutton-in-Ashfield, Nottinghamshire, in 1638 two men get into trouble 'for unreasonable ringing [of] the bells in their church upon New Years daie [at] which time there was a fire made in their church and ale druncke there'.[2]

January 6th Epiphany

Traditionally Twelfth Night is the evening of 5th January, preceding Twelfth Day on the 6th, and together they mark the end of the season of Christmas celebration.

Twelfth Day coincides with the feast of Epiphany, from the Greek for 'manifestation', which commemorates the appearance of Christ to the Gentiles in the form of the Magi.

In some churches it may be marked by a ceremony, akin to a nativity play, in which the Magi and the star they follow are represented. The accounts of Great Yarmouth include several references to such a star, the amount spent being lost in most cases.

> 1465 Making a new star .... | Paid for leading the star, 3d, on the twelfth day. | 1506 For hanging and scouring the star .... | A new balk line to the star, and rising the star ... 8d | 1512 For a line called a nine-thread, and six-thread line, to lead the star ....[1]

The following Victorian description of the ceremony is largely conjectural, based as it is on accounts of the 'Stellae Festum' or Feast of the Star celebrated on the Continent in medieval times. It involves kings in addition to magi.

> The Magi, represented by two priests, entered the church by the west door, and proceeded up the nave until, on approaching the chancel, they perceived a star hanging before the great crucifix on the rood loft, whereupon they exclaimed, 'Behold the star of the East.' The star, moving back by means of lines and pulleys, led them to the high altar, where, on drawing aside a curtain, a living child would be discovered, representing the infant saviour. At the same time three priests dressed as kings, and attended by servants bearing presents, met, from different directions, before the altar. The offerings having been made to the child, the kings and magi engaged in prayer before the altar until a boy, representing an angel, addressed them with the words, 'All things which the prophets said are fulfilled,' and then the festival concluded with chanting.[2]

[January 12th] **Plough Monday** (first Monday after Epiphany)

Plough Monday marks the start of the ploughing season and more generally is the day on which agricultural toil resumes after the feasting of Christmas. In some rural areas, mainly in and near East Anglia, it is celebrated with the drawing of a plough around the parish while money is gathered. Before the Reformation the proceeds often go to support a plough light hanging in the church. After the suppression of such lights in 1538 the custom persists in some places, but with the money going towards general church funds or the costs of carousing instead.[1]

> 1538 Receved for ye plow light ... 3s 6d | 1539 Receved of ye gathering on Plow Monday ... 4s 6d (All Saints, Tilney, Norfolk)

> 1611 [Paid] for ayle on plowmunday ... 12d (Leverton, Lincs)[2]

Ploughing in
Suffolk, 1888.
FACING PAGE
The Magi
approach the
Virgin Mary,
whose broken
figure lacks
the child she
once held.
Tympanum,
12th century,
Bishopsteignton,
Devon.

In 1560 ten men of North Muskham, Nottinghamshire, perhaps enjoy themselves too much as they end up in trouble 'for plowing in the churchyarde, and misusinge themselves in the churche upon plowe daie last'.[3]

In addition, before the Reformation the ploughs kept in some churches, and others besides, may be blessed either on the Monday or on the preceding day, Plough Sunday. In the 1540s John Bale, a prominent reformer, refers to 'censinge the ploughes upon Plough Mondaye' and criticises the old Church for using frankincense 'in the ... conjuring of their ploughs'.[4]

In later centuries any religious elements disappear. The following account, written in 1854 and relating to Northamptonshire, suggests that proceedings may nonetheless be colourful.

> Sometimes five persons precede the plough, which is drawn by a number of boys with their faces blackened and reddled.* Formerly, when the pageant was of a more important character than now, the plough was drawn by oxen decorated with ribbons. The one who walks first in the procession is styled the Master, and is grotesquely attired, having on a large wig; two are gaily bedizened in women's clothes; and two others have large hunches on their backs, on which are sewed the knave of hearts; these two are called Red Jacks, or Fools. Each of the five carries a besom, and one of them a box, which he rattles assiduously among the spectators to obtain their donations, which are spent at night in conviviality and jollification. In some instances they plough up the soil in front of the houses of such persons as refuse their contributions.[5]

* *Reddle* or *raddle*. Mark (a sheep etc) with red ochre.

Some coastal towns mark the day in a manner adapted to their concerns. At Kingston upon Hull a play featuring Noah and his ark is staged in Holy Trinity church by a guild of master mariners and pilots. A ship features in the play itself and, before or afterwards, is pulled around the streets of the town accompanied by musicians and minstrels.

> 1483 To Noah and his wife ... 1s 6d | To Robert Brown playing God ... 6d | To the Ship-child ... 1d | For mending the ship ... 2d | Straw for Noah and his children ... 2d | To a man clearing away the snow ... 1d | Mass, bellman, torches, minstrels, garland, &c. ... 6s | Straw and grease for wheels ... ¼d | To the waits* for going about with the ship ... 6d
>
> 1494 For three skins for Noah's coat, making it, and a rope to hang the ship in the kirk ... 7s | Making Noah's ship ... £5 8s | Two wrights a day and a half ... 1s 6d | Rigging Noah's ship ... 8d
>
> 1529 For a pair of new mitens to Noye ... 4d | Nicholas Helpby for writing the pley ... 7d | Taking down ship and hanging up again ... 2s | Wine when the ship went about ... 2d[6]

February 2nd **Candlemas**, or the Feast of the Purification of the Virgin Mary and of the Presentation of Christ in the Temple

The feast is based on the account in Luke 2:22-39 of Mary taking the infant Christ to Jerusalem to present to God forty days after the birth, 'when the days of her purification according to the law of Moses were accomplished'. While they are in the temple a devout man called Simeon recognises Christ as the saviour and describes him as 'a light to lighten the Gentiles'. This gives rise to a ceremony involving the lighting, blessing, and carrying in procession of candles, and so to the popular name 'Candlemas'. A rite emphasising the triumph of light is also naturally apt at a time when winter darkness is finally beginning to recede.

> 1458 For making 4 torches agenste Candelmas ... 2s (Yatton, Somerset)
>
> c. 1500 A thing to bere holy candle in on Candlemasse day, for the prieste. (St Margaret Pattens, inventory)[1]

Every parishioner brings to church a candle which is blessed, it being believed that this endows it with demonifugal power, as the following prayer from the Sarum Missal makes clear.

> Bless, O lord Jesus Christ, this creature of wax ... and pour thy heavenly blessing upon it by virtue of the holy cross, that as thou hast granted it for the use of men to dispel darkness, so ... in whatsoever places it shall be lighted or set up the devil may depart, and tremble, and flee away pale, with all his ministering spirits ...[2]

---

* A small body of wind instrumentalists maintained by a city or town at the public charge.

The candles are then carried in procession and afterwards made an offering to the priest. Thereafter they may be set to burn before an image of the Virgin Mary in the church.

The proceedings lend themselves to a degree of pageantry, as in the case of the Guild of St Mary at Beverley, Yorkshire.

All the bretheren and sisteren shall meet together in a fit and appointed place, away from the church, and there one of the gild shall be clad in comely fashion as a queen, like to the glorious Virgin Mary, having what may seem a son in her arms; and two others shall be clad like to Joseph and Simeon; and two shall go as angels, carrying a candle-bearer on which shall be twenty-four thick wax lights. With these and other great lights borne before them, and with much music and gladness, the pageant Virgin with her son, and Joseph and Simeon, shall go in procession to the church. And all the sisteren of the gild shall follow the Virgin, and afterwards all the bretheren, and each of them shall carry a wax light weighing half a pound. And they shall go two and two, slowly pacing to the church, and when they have got there the pageant Virgin shall offer her son to Simeon at the high altar, and all the sisteren and bretheren shall offer their wax lights, together with a penny each. All this having been solemnly done, they shall go home again with gladness.[3]

After the Reformation the feast survives but as a celebration of Christ's presentation rather than of Mary's purification, and it is shorn of its pageantry and the blessing of candles.[4]

Villagers carrying candles to church, by Simon Bening, *c*. 1550

Confession and
absolution,
from *The Crafte
to Live Well and
to Die Well*,
1505

[February 17th] Shrove Tuesday (the day before Ash Wednesday)
The day is named from the custom of people being shriven – making confession
and having a penance imposed – in preparation for Lent. As Abbot Aelfric notes
in a sermon on the preceding Sunday, about the year 1000,

> Now is a clean and holy tide drawing nigh, in which we should atone for
> our remissness. Let therefore every Christian man come to his confessor
> and confess his secret sins.[1]

The custom of eating pancakes on this day has already been seen in relation to
the pancake bell (pp103-104) and appears to have a practical explanation in the
eating up of milk, eggs and fat before the fast of Lent.

Another widespread custom is that of cock throwing. Dutch visitor William
Schellinks describes two versions of this 'entertainment' as he finds it in 1662.
In London apprentice boys take a cock with a string tied to one foot to an open
space, attach the string to a spike placed in the ground, and charge people a penny
to throw a cudgel at the bird from a distance, anyone who manages to kill the bird
receiving it as their prize. In the country proceedings are crueller still: 'they bury
a cock with only its head above ground, and blindfold a person and turn him two
or three times round himself, and then he tries to hit the cock with a flail, and
the one who hits it or comes closest to it gets the prize'.[2]

Writing much later, R. S. Downs gives a fuller account of the first version.

> The owner of the bird would put him in training some time before Shrove
> Tuesday by throwing sticks at him, in order to accustom him to the
> threatened danger, that by springing aside he might avoid the missile.
> When the time arrived for the sport to commence, the cock was placed in
> position, a stake with a cord attached to it was driven into the ground, the
> other end of the cord being fastened to one of the cock's legs, which, while
> allowing the bird sufficient freedom to enable him to hop about, at the same
> time prevented him making his escape. ... A crease was marked off at a
> distance of twenty-two yards, at which the person stood who threw at the
> bird. He was allowed three shies at the cock for twopence, and if he knocked

A victor,
c. 1340

him down, and could run up and catch the bird before he recovered his
legs, the thrower won the cock, or its equivalent in money. The cock, if
well trained, would elude the sticks hurled at him for a long time, and thus
gain a considerable sum of money for his master. Sometimes, however, the
poor creature was fastened by two cords, one on each leg ... and it was shied
at for mere wanton cruelty to see who could knock him over first.[3]

The origin of the practice is unclear. One suggestion is that the cock, symbol
of St Peter, is punished for the saint's denial of Christ three times 'before the
cock crow'. This is alluded to in an epigram upon a cock at Rochester by Restoration
poet Sir Charles Sedley.

> May'st though be punish'd for St Peter's crime,
> And on Shrove-tuesday perish in thy prime.[4]

Whatever the origin, churches are happy to profit from the practice.

1531 Reseved of ye cocke money ... 17d (Badsey, Worcs)

1622 Received for cocks at Shrovetide ... 12s | 1628 Received for cocks
in towne ... 19s 10d (Harrow on the Hill, Middlesex)[5]

On Shrove Tuesday 1665 children at East Bergholt, Suffolk, throw at cocks
not only in the churchyard but also in the church.[6]

During the 18th century, however, polite opinion turns, and at Hayes, Middlesex,
in 1754 the vicar tries to have the practice stopped.

> Feb. 27th. Being Shrove Tuesday, divine service was performed in the after-
> noon, and no care was taken to prevent the throwing at cocks, rioting, and
> swearing in the churchyard, at the same time: though I gave previous notice
> of the same to the churchwardens and the magistrate, and desired that it
> might be prevented for the honour of God and a public good; but his answer
> was this: 'I know no law against throwing at cocks, even in the churchyard.'[7]

In the same year the bellman at Wakefield is paid sixpence for 'crying no throwing at cocks', and a similar payment is made at High Wycombe twenty years later.

1774 Feb. 14th. Paid Daniel Pearce, for crying down the cocks being thro'd at in the churchyard &c. on Shrove Tuesday ... 3d[8]

In 1778 the *Lewes Journal* reports:

It is with great pleasure we can inform the public that the barbarous practice of throwing at cocks is now so universally exploded in these parts, that Shrove Tuesday did not produce a single instance of those acts of riot and cruelty by which this day was long and shamefully characterised ...[9]

Not that being thrown at is all cocks have to worry about on this day. At Knotting, Bedfordshire, two churchwardens get into trouble for allowing cockfighting in the chancel on Shrove Tuesday for three years running, 1634 to 1636.

In or about the sacred place where the communion table stands, there were fighting cocks brought thither and cock fightings there held, and many persons assembled to behold the same, and to bet and lay wagers thereon; and ... they, Bourne and Hewitt, and a son of Bourne, and Mr Alvey, minister of Knotting, and some of his sons, and many others, both youths and men and others, were present as actors and spectators, and laughed and sported thereat, and most profanely abused the said consecrated place.[10]

[February 18th] **Ash Wednesday** (6½ weeks before Easter Day) and the beginning of **Lent**

The word Lent is derived from Old English 'lencten' and refers to the lengthening of days as spring approaches. It is observed as a fast in memory of Christ's forty days in the wilderness and lasts for that period plus six Sundays.[1]

It is ushered in by Ash Wednesday, so called from the use of ashes in church on this day. Traditionally the ashes are those of the palm (or a home grown substitute such as yew or box) used on Palm Sunday in the preceding year. At Holy Trinity, Coventry, it is the duty of one the deacons to 'see ye palm be burned for ye ashes that shalbe dealte on Ashe Wensday'.[2]

The following account of the pre-Reformation form of the ceremony is from *The Doctrine of the Masse Booke*, published in 1554.

When the prieste hathe absolved the people, then must there be made a blessinge of the ashes ... by the prieste, being turned towards the east. 'Almighty eternal God ... vouchsafe to better sanctifie these ashes, which because of humilitie, and of holy religion, for ye clensing out of our trespaces thou hast appointed us to cary upon our heades after the maner of the Ninivites.* And grant that thorow the invocacion of thy holy name, all

---

* On Jonah carrying God's warning to the people of Nineveh that they would be overthrown, they put on sackcloth and fasted to avert His wrath, and their king 'sat in ashes'. (Jonah chapter 3)

they that beare them upon their heades for the obtaining of thy mercy, may merite of thee to receave forgivenes of all their trespaces, and so this day to begin their holye fastinges, that in the day of the resurrection they may deserve with purified mindes, to approch to the holye Easter, and receave eternal glorye in ye world to come ...'

Holy water is sprinkled on the ashes and further prayers are said.

Then let them distribute the ashes upon the heades of the clarckes and of the lay people, the worthier persons making a signe of the crosse with the ashes, saying thus, *Memento homo quod cinis*. Remember man that thou art ashes, and into ashes shalt thou returne.[3]

In addition to this general observance, according to old custom those requiring public penance go to church early in the morning, barefoot and bareheaded. They prostrate themselves, are sprinkled with holy water, have ashes placed on their heads, and are assigned a course of penitential works and prayer. They are then led outside and are barred from entering the church again until Maundy Thursday. However, this rite is usually described as conducted by the bishop or his deputy and occurring in cathedrals, and it probably happens seldom if at all in parish churches.[4]

Public penitents bow in submission and are led out of church, from a pontifical, 1520

Rood and images covered in Lent: detail from a Book of Hours, late 15th century

The arrival of Lent also sees the church itself taking on a sombre, penitential appearance as its images are covered. According to Sarum rules this is done on the following Monday, the first in Lent, but in later times it tends to be done on Ash Wednesday.[5]

> 1465 To the bellman, for clothing the images in Lent ... 3d (Great Yarmouth, Norfolk)

> 1527 To the 2 clerks for hanging up of the Lent cloths upon Ashe Wednesday ... 2d (Wimborne Minster, Dorset)[6]

The cloths used appear in many inventories.

> 1512 In a cheste withoute the quier dore ... 26 olde steined clothes for to cover with the images in the church in Lente. (Faversham, Kent)

> 1547 A clothe to hange before the roode in Lent painted & another for to cover the 12 apostelles. (St Mary Magdalen, Old Fish Street)[7]

The rationale is set out by Thomas Becon, writing in 1542.

> This time of Lent, which is a time of mourning, all thinges that make to the adornment of the church are either laid aside or else covered, to put us in remembrance that we ought now to lament and mourn for our souls dead in sin, and continually to watch, pray, fast, give alms, and do ... other works of penance ...[8]

In some cases, however, the idea of an image fast is undermined as the veils themselves come to be 'stained' (painted) or otherwise decorated with images.

> 1466 *Coverings for images.* 1 steined in the chapell before our lady with a lily and our lady therin. | 1 before Synt Katerine steined with the image of Synt Katerine therin. | 1 before Synt Nicholus with his image steined therin. | 1 rode clothe steined with the passion of our lorde. (St Stephen, Coleman Street)

> 1488 *Vaile Clothes.* 1 clothes with the image of Seint Cristofre to cover Seint Cristofre. (St Christopher le Stocks)[9]

The cloth covering the rood, high up in the centre of the church, is often operated by a pulley.

1557 For putting the rope into the pulley in the ruffe of the church, to
    drawe up the clothe before the crucifix ... 2d (Bungay)[10]

There is also a larger Lenten veil or curtain hung between the choir and the
altar to screen the latter from view. It is hung a few days after Ash Wednesday, on
or about the following Sunday, the first in Lent, and then remains in place until
Wednesday in Holy Week, only being raised at certain festivals and whenever the
gospel is read at mass. As with the other cloths it is sometimes plain, sometimes not.[11]

1448 A white veile for the croce in Lent time. And another white veile to
    be hanging in the chauncell befor the hy auter in Lenten time. (Thame)

1529 A cloth of Adam and Eve to draw before the high altar in time of
    Lent, called the Veil. (Long Melford)

At Long Melford they also have an altar cloth for Lent, 'painted about with
whips and angels'.[12]

Away from church parishioners face a period of abstinence, as *The Popish
Kingdome* relates.

Then (O poore wretches) fastings long approching do appeare:
In fourtie dayes they neither milke, nor fleshe, nor egges do eate,
And butter with their lippes to touch, is thought a trespasse great ...[13]

An Act of 1548 is one of several codifying the rules for fasts.

No person or persones, of what estate, degree, or condicion he or she be,
shall ... willinglie and wittinglye eate any manner of fleshe ... upon any
Fridaye or Satterdaye, or the Embringe dayes,* or in any daye in the time
commonly called Lent, nor at any suche other daye as is or shalbe at any
time hereafter commonly accepted and reputed as a fishe daye within this
realme of Englande ...[14]

In 1562-63 a further Act, designed to support the navy and fishermen, adds
Wednesday to the fish days, although this is later repealed. It also sets out a
scheme for two types of licence to allow people to eat flesh on the prohibited days.

The first type is for those willing to pay, with the cost varying according to
rank. Every lord or lord's wife 'shall paie to the poore mens boxe within the
parishe where they shall dwell' 26s 8d, payment to be made within six days of
Candlemas. The fee is halved for a knight or knight's wife (13s 4d) and halved
again for those of more modest station (6s 8d). Such payments do not bring total
freedom: 'no licence shall extende to the eating of any beef at any time of the
yere, nor to the eating of any veale ... from the Feast of St Michael tharchaungell
[29 September] unto the firste daye of Maye'.

---

* *Ember days.* Days of fasting and prayer observed in the four seasons of the year, being
the Wednesday, Friday and Saturday after the first Sunday in Lent, Whitsunday,
Holy Cross day (14 September) and St Lucia's day (13 December).

If the practice makes a mockery of abstinence as a religious duty, it does at least provide much needed funds.

> 1635 Received of Mr Lemotte, Mr John Fountaine, Mr John Millward, Mr Fowster, 6s 8d a pece for thire several licences to eate flesh this last Lent ... £1 6s 8d (St Bartholomew Exchange)

The Act also sets out the terms for a second kind of licence for those who are unwell.

> All persons whiche by reason of notorious sicknes shalbe inforced for recoverye of helthe to eate fleshe for the time of their sicknes, shalbe sufficiently licensed by the bishoppe of the dioces or by the parson, vicar or curate of the parishe ... whiche licence shalbe made in writing ... and not endure longer than the time of the sicknes.[15]

A note in the register of Wedmore, Somerset, records a particular case.

> 1632-33 March 1st. Whereas upon my owne certaine knowledge my wife lying now in childbed is very weake and sick, and by eating of fishe she may very much if not altogether endanger her life, I, Mathew Law, being vicar of the said parish of Wedmore, do, as much as in me lieth, licence and authorise her to eat flesh according to the forme and effect of the statute in that case provided ...[16]

Parishes also have a role in enforcing the rules. In 1596 the churchwardens of St Alphage, London Wall, pay a Mr French and a Mr Dager 'to look for meat in cookes shopes & taverns' to ensure that 'fasting nightes' are observed. In the same year the wardens of Henley on Thames present three men to the Church authorities, one 'for roasting a pig in his house', one 'for seethinge [boiling] 2 pec of bacon', and one for 'roasting a shoulder of veal'.[17]

The restrictions are revived by royal proclamations up to 1687, and the laws remain on the statute book until 1863, but after 1688 no serious attempt is made to enforce Lenten abstinence.[18]

March 25th **Annunciation of the Virgin Mary**, or **Lady Day**

Nine months before Christmas, a day commemorating the angel Gabriel's announcement to Mary of the conception of Christ in her womb (Luke 1:26-38). Until 1752, when the calendar changes, it is also the day on which the official year begins.

FACING PAGE
The Annunciation depicted on the spandrels of the south porch, East Tuddenham, Norfolk.
On the left the Virgin Mary, the pot of lilies before her symbolising purity.
On the right the angel Gabriel unleashes the momentous news.

[March 29th] **Palm Sunday** (one week before Easter Day)[1]
The start of Passion or Holy Week, and a commemoration of Christ's entry into Jerusalem on the Sunday before his crucifixion, as recorded in John 12:12-14.

> On the next day much people that were come to the feast, when they heard that Jesus was coming to Jerusalem, took branches of palm trees, and went forth to meet him, and cried, 'Hosanna: Blessed is the King of Israel that cometh in the name of the Lord.' And Jesus, when he had found a young ass, sat thereon.

Before the Reformation the day sees one of the most involved celebrations in the Church year, falling into three parts – the blessing of palms, a procession with the palms, and mass. Apart from its Christian significance, the blessing and bearing of foliage on this day are also of course a rite of spring.

The following account is based largely on the Sarum Missal, but in many small parishes the festival is almost certainly celebrated a good deal more simply.[2]

First, palm leaves and branches – or a locally available substitute such as yew, box or willow – are gathered.

1541 For fetching one bundell of palme agenst Palme Sonday ... 2d
(Lydd, Kent)[3]

In preparation for the blessing they are placed in two piles in the church, one on the altar, for the clergy, and one on the altar steps, for the laity.

Early in the service of benediction the account of Christ's entry into Jerusalem is read from St John's gospel, after which a priest wearing a red cope exorcises and blesses the palm and it is sprinkled with holy water and censed. It is then distributed in readiness for the procession while anthems are sung, including one beginning, 'The children of the Hebrews, carrying olive branches, went to meet our Lord, crying out and saying, *Hosanna in the highest*.' Meanwhile the sacrament or host, representing the body of Christ, is also readied for the procession. The Missal directs that it is to be carried 'by two clerks of the second rank', along with the church's relics, in a portable shrine supported by two poles. More simply it may be held aloft in a monstrance by a single priest. In addition it may be protected from the elements by a canopy.[4]

1533 For garlandes for them that bare the canope ... 6d (St Mary at Hill)

1541 For pointes to thy [tie] the canapy that is cared over the sacrament on Palme Sonday ... 2d (St John the Baptist, Peterborough)[5]

Those present move out into the churchyard in two separate processions in symbolic re-enactment of Christ's entry into Jerusalem. They may use the church's north door if it has one, many such doors being closed up in later times after religious processions have fallen foul of the Reformation.

The first procession represents Christ and his disciples and includes the sacrament preceded by two banners and an unveiled cross. The second procession represents the crowd and includes the choir and parishioners holding palm branches and preceded by a priest bearing a veiled cross.

1533 For bering of the 2 crosses ... 2d (St Mary at Hill)[6]

According to Thomas Becon, the veiled cross signifies the 'clouds and shadows of the old law' and the unveiled one 'Christ already come ... in this world'.[7]

The processions take different routes towards the first 'station', which the Missal says is to be 'in the extreme east of the north side of the church' and for which the churchyard cross, decorated with flowers and branches, may serve. Once the procession representing the crowd has arrived the deacon reads the account from St Matthew's gospel of Christ riding into Jerusalem on an ass. It tells of his being greeted by 'a very great multitude', who spread garments and branches in his path

LEFT North doorway, useful for processions, seen through the south one, Littlebury, Essex. RIGHT Blocked north doorway, East Dean, Sussex. FACING PAGE Palm Sunday on tympanum above south door, Aston Eyre, Shropshire.

LEFT. UPPER Relics carried in procession, from a pontifical of 1520,
giving an idea of one way the sacrament and relics may be carried on this day.
LOWER Woodcut from the Sarum Processional, showing some of the elements
involved in proceedings, including the two piles of palm. Clergy are indicated by
circles representing their tonsured heads.

RIGHT Bench-end showing a cross-bearer, perhaps the parish clerk, Trull, Somerset.

and cry out, 'Hosanna to the Son of David, blessed is he that cometh in the name of the Lord' – at which point the other procession, representing Christ, arrives.

After the reading three clerks step forward and sing a series of prophetic texts, and the choir and the officiating priest sing responses.[8]

In some service books this part of the ceremony is elaborated by the addition of a boy dressed as a prophet who stands in a conspicuous place and sings further prophetic texts, the first being, 'O Jerusalem, look to the East and see; lift up thine eyes, O Jerusalem, and see the power of thy king.'[9]

In describing the church of Long Melford as it was before the Reformation, a parishioner, Roger Martyn, recalls 'a boy ... signifying a prophet as I think' who 'sang standing upon the turret' (a brick tower on the north side of the church serving the rood loft). He adds that the boy pointed 'with a thing in his hand' to the sacrament carried in the procession and representing Christ.[10]

The accounts of several parishes, mainly in London, include payments relating to these prophet figures. They suggest that the roles ascribed by the rubrics to the three clerks and the boy are sometimes played by children and sometimes by adults.[11]

> 1540 To the childern that played the proffetes on Palme Sonday ... 2d (St Alphage, London Wall)
>
> 1540 To Loreman for playing the prophet on Palme Sonday ... 2d* (St Lawrence, Reading)[12]

The prophets may wear wigs and false beards and hold scrolls or boards identifying themselves by name.[13]

> 1519 For bred, ale and wine and dressing of the proffettes ... 20d | 1525 For the hire of the haires for the profette on Palme Sondaye ... 6d (St Stephen, Walbrook)
>
> 1530 For papur for the profettes on Palme Sonday in ther hondes ... 1d | For heres, berdis and garmentes ... 12d (St Mary at Hill)[14]

Platforms may be erected to give them due prominence, or a railing may be added to a section of roof.

> 1524 For a quarter† that was for the frame over the north dore of the chirche, that is for the prophettes on Palmesonday, & workmanship ... 3d | 1536 For making of ye stages for ye prophettes ... 6d (St Mary at Hill)
>
> 1540 For setting up the railes upon the leds on Palme Sunday ... 3d | 1545 For setting up the railes for prophetes ... 2d (St Mary Woolnoth)[15]

* Some years later 'Loryman', apparently the clerk, is paid 'for carryeng out the rubbish' when the altars are taken down under Queen Elizabeth. Assuming it was the same man, one wonders what he made of all the changes affecting the church in his lifetime.
† A piece of wood four inches wide by two or four inches thick, used for partitions etc.

Before leaving the first station the two processions join together and the veiled cross is taken away. Depending on how elaborately the ceremony is enacted, the combined procession then continues with anthems and readings around further stations in the churchyard, the general progress being clockwise from north, north-east or east to west. Another common station, apart from the cross, is the church porch. It may serve for the second station, which the Missal describes as being 'on the south side of the church'. Here 'seven boys, from a very elevated position, shall sing, "All glory, laud, and honour | To thee, redeemer, king, | To whom the lips of children | Made sweet hosannas ring."'[16]

In some places it is customary for these singing boys, or someone else occupying an elevated position, to cast down cakes and flowers on the children in the crowd below, who rush to retrieve them. Roger Martyn recalls that on the parishioners 'coming near the porch a boy, or one of the clerks, did cast over among the boys flowers, and singing cakes,* &c.' According to a disapproving Protestant commentator, 'Then cakes must be cast out of the steple, that all the boyes in the parish must lie scambling together by the eares, till all the parish falleth a laughing'.[17]

Thomas Becon, in his *Potation for Lent* (1542), describes the scene and offers an explanation of its significance.

> Then the people goeth somewhat further unto the church-doorward, and there standeth still. ... Immediately after, certain children, standing upon an high place right against the people, sing with a loud voice a certain hymn in the praise of our saviour Jesus Christ, which beginneth, *Gloria laus*. ... At the end of every verse the children cast down certain cakes, or breads, with flowers. ... The children which sing betoken the faithful Christian men in this world, which ought to be simple and humble in heart as a child is ... The continual exercise of godly virtues is signified by the flowers ... Mercy toward the poor people ... is signified by the casting down of the cakes.[18]

The flowers can also be seen more literally as a further echo of the boughs and branches cast before Christ as he entered Jerusalem.

The cake and bread are recorded in parish accounts.

> 1518 For cake for the children on Palme Sunday ... 1d (St Andrew, Canterbury)
>
> 1540 For singing cakes at palme tide ... ob. (St Andrew, Lewes, Sussex)[19]

In some parishes an angel appears, although at what stage in the proceedings is not clear.[20]

> 1535 For the hiring of a paier of wings, a here [wig], and a crest for an angel on Palme Sonday ... 8d (All Hallows Staining)[21]

---

* 'Wafer bread used for the mass was commonly called *singing bread*, or *singing cakes* ... because used in singing mass, but this kind of bread was also used ... as other confectionery.' (H. J. Feasey, *Ancient English Holy Week Ceremonial*, 1897, p59)

LEFT
Turret at Long
Melford, Suffolk,
on which the boy
'prophet' appeared.

BELOW
Prophets
(Amos and Isaiah)
complete with
impressive beards,
Holme,
Nottinghamshire.

On the Continent the procession sometimes features a figure of Christ trundling along upon a donkey.

A wooden asse they have, and image great that on him rides,
But underneath the asses feete, a table broade there slides,
Being borne on wheeles, which ready drest, and all things meete therfore
The asse is brought abroade and set before the churches doore ...[22]

However, there appears to be no evidence of such figures appearing in parish processions in England.

The procession usually ends at the west door, which is opened from within after the priest strikes it with the foot of the processional cross – 'to declare', according to Becon, 'that our ingress and entering into heaven cometh only by Christ and by Christ's death'. If the church does not have a west door the south one is used. If the sacrament is in a shrine, the priests carrying it stand on either side of the doorway and raise it aloft for the people to walk under as they go back inside, each one bowing his or her head as they pass beneath the body of their saviour.[23]

Not everyone takes it all entirely seriously. In 1556 at Brampton, Huntingdonshire, when the vicar opens the church doors using the shaft of the cross, one parishioner calls out, 'What a sport have we towards. Will our vicar ronne at the quintine* with God Almightie?'[24]

Once all are inside they kneel as the cloth which has been covering the rood during Lent is drawn up by a pulley and the anthem *'Ave rex noster'* (Hail, our king) is sung. The other crosses in the church are also uncovered.

1504-08 For Sandewich corde† for to pulle uppe the cloth before the rode on Palme Sonday ... 4d (St Dunstan, Canterbury)[25]

In the mass that follows the entire story of Christ's Passion is sung or recited from the gospel of St Matthew, the performers using three tones: high or alto for the words of the Jews or the disciples; middle or tenor for Matthew's narrative; and low or bass for the words of Christ.[26]

1447 Paide on Palme Sundaye for brede & wine to the reders of ye Passion ... 3d (St Peter, Cheapside)

1509 For a quart of bastard, for ye singers of the Passhion on Palme Sondaye ... 4d (St Lawrence, Reading)[27]

As seen earlier, the performers are sometimes located in the rood loft.

After the service the people return to their homes, some bearing crosses newly fashioned out of the blessed palm, now assumed to have protective powers, and the church's crosses are covered again.

---

* *Quintain.* Game or exercise involving tilting with a lance or pole at a target.
† Not in the *OED*. Evidently strong and, given the name, perhaps originally for maritime use.

[April 1st] **Wednesday in Holy Week** (the Wednesday before Easter Day)
During mass, St Luke's account of the crucifixion is read (Luke 22 and 23:1-49), and at the words 'the veil of the temple was rent in the midst' the Lent veil concealing the altar is let fall. At Exeter Cathedral, and perhaps elsewhere, a deacon advances and tears the veil asunder with his hand.[1]

In the evening, and on the following two evenings, the office known as Tenebrae is sung. Its name, Latin for 'darkness', is thought to derive from the extinguishing of lights as the service progresses.[2]

1556 For wax candull that wer burned the Wensday, Thursday & Friday before Ester at ye Tenebrees ... 6d (Stanford, Berks)[3]

John Mirk, in his *Festial*, written in the 1380s, gives a detailed account.

The service of these three nightes is don in darkenes. The which service makethe mind how Judas betrayed Crist, and how the Jewes comen with fors and armes as prively as they could, for drede of the people. Wherfor to this service is no bell rongen, but a sownde made of tre* wherby each Cristen man and woman is enformed, for to come to this service without noise making. ...

Also at this service is set a herst† with candull burning, after as the use is some places more, some less, the which be qwenched each one after other, in schewing how Cristis disciples stelen from him when he was taken, each one after other. But when all be quenched, yet one [light is left], the which is borne away a while, while the clerkes singen Kyrie eleisons and the verses ... which betokeneth the woman that made lamentacion over Cristis sepulcur. Then, after this, the candell is broght ageine, and all others at it [are lit]. The which betokeneth Crist, that was for a while ded and hid in his sepulcur, but soon after he rose from death to life, and gave light of life to all them that were quenched by despaire.[4]

Tenebrae hearse,
15th century

* i.e. wood, in the form of a rattle or clapper. Mirk suggests that wood is used to put people in mind of the cross on which Christ suffered and because Judas subsequently hung himself on a tree. The term 'Judas bell' may refer to such a device, perhaps being applied because it is false i.e. not a real bell: '1495. For mending of Judas bell ... 1d' (Dartmouth, Devon). Clappers are mentioned in several inventories recording the fate of church goods in Lincolnshire after the Reformation: 'Clappers, Judaces and a sepulker – made awaie and broken in peces' (Skillington); 'Chrismatories, paxes, clappers, with such other trumperie were burned in the market place' (New Sleaford). † *Hearse*. A large, triangular candlestick upon which tapers are set for the service. '1540. For a triangle to set candles apon in tenable weeke ... 4d' (Bramley, Hants). The word is also used for a rectangular structure set around corpses for funerals.

As Mirk mentions, the number of candles involved varies. The Roman use is 15 candles (as *right*) but in England there are usually 24 or 25. One custom is for there to be 24 of yellow wax, representing the twelve prophets and the twelve apostles, and a single one of white or bleached wax, representing Christ. As the office progresses, the yellow ones are extinguished until the white taper alone remains, and it is then hidden behind the altar, leaving the church in darkness.[5]

At this point in some churches a sudden noise is made with books, or by the beating of desks or stamping of feet. This is usually held to symbolise the convulsion of nature at Christ's death, although Mirk offers a different explanation.

> The strokes that the priest giveth on the boke betokeneth the clappes of thunder that Crist brake hell-gates with, when he come thither ...[6]

According to Herbert Thurston, writing in 1914,

> Historically speaking a much more prosaic account must be given of this noise. When the public recitation of office was concluded, the abbot or presiding prelate always gave the signal for the monks to move out of the choir by knocking the bench, or by one of those wooden clappers ... used for this purpose. There is little doubt that the noise at the end of Tenebrae has no other origin than this. The pious imaginations of the mediaeval liturgists sought for mystical meanings everywhere and found them ... Thus many of our most beautiful pieces of symbolism are certainly after-thoughts which never entered into the mind of the framers of the ceremony ... but ... the symbolism is true ...[7]

From the account in *The Popish Kingdome* it seems the opportunity may be exploited by those wishing to let off steam.

> Three nightes at midnight up they rise, their mattens for to heare,
> Appointed well with clubbes and staves, and stones in order there:
> The sexten straightwayes putteth out the candles speedely,
> And straight the priest with rustie throte, alowde begins to cry.
> Then furious rage begins to spring, and hurlyburly rise,
> On pewes and deskes and seates they bounce, and beate in dredfull wise:
> Thou wouldst suppose they were possest, with sprightes and devils all ...[8]

After this hubbub the hidden candle is brought forth and the church's lights are kindled again.

FACING PAGE Maundy Thursday: Christ institutes mass and washes the feet of his disciples, from the Gospels of St Augustine, late 6th century

[April 2nd] **Maundy Thursday** (the Thursday before Easter Day)

Observed as a commemoration of the Last Supper, at which Christ instituted the mass and washed the feet of the disciples.

> As they were eating, Jesus took bread … and said, Take, eat; this is my body. And he took the cup … saying Drink ye all of it, for this is my blood …
>
> Matthew 26:26-28

> He riseth from supper, and laid aside his garments, and took a towel, and girded himself. After that he poureth water into a bason, and began to wash the disciples' feet, and to wipe them with the towel wherewith he was girded.
>
> John 13:4-5

The word Maundy probably derives from Latin *mandatum*, commandment, with reference to John 13:34 ('A new commandment I give unto you, that ye love one another'), the washing of feet being emblematic of such devotion. In medieval times the day is also known as Sheer Thursday, probably in reference to making clean or clear, whether of the soul by confession or of the church's altars, which are ritually washed on this day. John Mirk suggests that it refers to the shearing of hair: 'For in old fathers dayes men wold … shear … their heads, and clip their beards, and so make them honest against Easter Day.'[1]

The main ceremonies of the day are four.

i. Reconciliation of penitents, excluded from the church since Ash Wednesday. According to the Sarum Missal, after various preliminaries they are led into the church and towards the altar. 'Then shall they all prostrate themselves, and the clerks in the quire shall say the seven penitential psalms, with *Glory be to the Father* etc'. After several collects the penitents are formally absolved, at which point 'all shall rise from their prostration, kissing the benches or the ground', and solemn mass is performed. However, as noted with regard to the exclusion on Ash Wednesday, such reconciliation is usually described in relation to cathedrals and probably does not occur much if at all in parish churches.[2]

ii. Consecration of the holy oil known as chrism. The oil for use in the diocese during the following year is blessed in the cathedral by the bishop or one acting for him and distributed to parish priests for use in their churches.[3]

iii. Washing of the feet of the poor, in imitation of Christ's example. This is performed in cathedrals, and by English monarchs until the late 17th century, but there is little evidence of its occurring in parish churches.[4]

iv. Stripping and washing of altars occurs in at least some parish churches. All the coverings and ornaments are removed and each altar is washed using wine and water and a brush of thorny wood.

1529 A pinte of wine to washe the awters ... 1d (Dartmouth, Devon)[5]

Mirk explains the symbolism.

The besom that it is washen with betokeneth the scorges that beat his [Christ's] body and the thornes that he was crowned withall. The water and the wine that it is washen with betokeneth the blood and the water that ran downe after the spere from Cristis heart that washed his body.[6]

Once washed the altars remain bare until Easter Saturday, emblematic of a season of penitence and a stark visual reminder of the abandonment experienced by Christ as his crucifixion approached.

Also on this day, during mass, two additional hosts are consecrated and reserved for use on Good Friday, when by tradition no mass is performed. One is for the priest and the other is for placing in the Easter sepulchre, as will be seen below.[7]

Penitents led back into church; oil brought for blessing; the bishop washing the feet of the poor

The Virgin Mary
holds her dead son,
east window,
East Harling,
Norfolk,
15th century

[April 3rd] **Good Friday** (the Friday before Easter Day)

Commemorating the crucifixion and entombment of Christ, 'Good' in this case probably indicating 'holy', or perhaps the benefits received by mankind as a result of Christ's sacrifice on this day.[1]

The two most noted elements in the day's services are the veneration of the figure of the crucified Christ upon a cross, known as creeping to the cross, and the placing of the cross, along with the host or sacrament, representing Christ's body, inside the Easter sepulchre, representing his tomb.

The following is an account of the elaborate ritual performed at Durham before the dissolution of the monasteries.

Within the abbey church of Durham upon Good Friday [there was a] marvelous solemne service, in the which ... after the Passion was sung* two of the eldest monkes did take a goodly large crucifix all of gold, of the picture of our saviour Christ nailed upon the crosse, lyinge upon a velvet cushion [and brought it] to the lowest greeces [steps] in the quire, and there betwixt them did hold the said picture of our saviour, sittinge on every side of [it upon their knees], and then one of the said monkes did rise and went a prettye way from it, sittinge downe upon his knees with his shoes put off very reverently, [and] did creepe away upon his knees unto the said crosse and most reverently did kisse it. And after him the other monke did so likewise, and then they did sit them downe on every side of the said crosse and holdinge it betwixt them, and after that the prior came forth of his stall, and did sit him downe on his knees, with his shoes off, and in like sort did creepe also unto the said crosse ...

All the monks then follow the prior's example while the choir sings a hymn.

* The account in St John's gospel, read or sung in services on this day.

Creeping
to the
cross,
1520

The service beinge ended the two monkes did carrye [the cross] to the sepulchre with great reverence, which sepulchre was set up in the morninge on the north side of the quire nigh to the high altar before the service time, and there did lay it within the said sepulchre, with great devotion with another picture of our saviour Christ, in whose breast they did enclose with great reverence the most holy and blessed sacrament of the altar, censing and prayinge unto it upon theire knees a great space [and] settinge two tapers lighted before it, which tapers did burne unto Easter day in the morninge ...[2]

While there is little evidence of 'creeping' in parish churches, it certainly occurs in some, the offerings made sometimes being called 'creeping silver'.[3]

> 1524 Received on Good Friday in money for creping to the cros ... 14½d (St Margaret Pattens)

> 1557 Received for crepeing ye crosse at Ester ... 3d ob. (St Mary the Great, Cambridge)[4]

Offerings may also be made in kind: one 16th-century reformer laments that on Good Friday the people 'offered unto Christe egges and bacon to be in his favour', while another condemns 'crepinge to the cross with egges and apples'.[5]

The other notable feature of the ritual, the Easter sepulchre, appears very widely. As seen earlier, it is usually a wooden structure set up on Good Friday and dismantled or removed after Easter Sunday.*

> 1520 For setting up of God's house, and for taking it down again ... 4d (St Margaret, Westminster)

> 1557 To Thomas Season ... for 3 dayes worke in settinge up the sepulcre ... 18d (Ludlow)[6]

* For an account of its physical features see pp74-76.

A rare
survival:
a wooden
sepulchre,
Cowthorpe,
Yorkshire

While it is in place the sepulchre is usually set about with richly decorated hangings. At Durham it is 'all covered with red velvet and embrodered with gold'. In the 1430s Lady Bardolph leaves a 'purple gown with small sleeves' for use on the sepulchre at Dennington, Suffolk, and seventy years later Richard Butler leaves 'my best redde coverlet' to the one at Earl's Colne, Essex.[7]

Inventories show that the cloths used are sometimes decorated with appropriate images.

1488 2 clothes for the sepulchre, oon with the Passion ... (St Christopher le Stocks)

1552 A sepulker clothe stained with the resurreccion ... (St Nicholas Cole Abbey)[8]

Parish accounts provide some details as to the means by which they are secured.

1498 For tenter hookes* to the sepulcre [etc] ... 1d ob. (St Mary at Hill)

1536 For nailes, pins and thred to heng the sepulcur ... 2d (St Mary on the Hill, Chester)[9]

* Hooks set on the bars of a tenter, or wooden frame on which cloth is stretched, to hold the edges of the cloth and so achieve sufficient tension.

They also show the occasional need for repair.

> 1527 For an eln of fine linnen cloth to amend the sepulture cloth wherat it was eiton with rattes ... 12d | To a bedmaker for mending & sowing the same ... 12d | To Mr Wolf for painting & renewing the images in the same cloth ... 5s (St Mary at Hill)[10]

Further fabrics may be provided for the interior. At St Dunstan in the East they have 'a shete to laye in the sepulture', while at Poole in Dorset the cross is placed upon a pillow and both are then covered with a towel.[11]

Often the sepulchre is set around with tapers which may be fixed to a frame or beam.

> 1527 For 8 pound of waxe for sepulchre lights ... 4s 4d (Hagworthingham, Lincs)

> 1529 For mending of the beme of the sepelker leyte ... 4d (St Andrew, Lewes, Sussex)

> 1530 For makyn of a frame to set tapers in afore the sepulker ... 12d (Stratton, Cornwall)

> 1544-46 For makeing the iern to set the sepulcre light in ... 16d (St Martin, Oxford)[12]

At least one light, the 'sepulchre light', usually burns constantly before it until Easter morning, and in some places a light is set inside the sepulchre along with the cross and the host.[13]

> 1557 For 2 little tapers for the sepulcre ... 2d | For makinge the toppe of one of them anewe after it was burnt out in the sepulcre ... 1d (Ludlow)[14]

At Walberswick lights may be placed, aptly enough, in a funeral hearse.

> 1463 To William Alkok ... in parte of payement for ye herse abowt ye sepulcre ... 6s 8d | 1472 To Edmund Wrytte for skoring of ye kandel-stekes and watcheng of ye herse at Estren ... 12d[15]

The importance of the sepulchre to parishioners and clergy is seen from the fact that lights for it feature often in bequests.

> 1487 To the support of 8 tapers burning before the sepulchre at Easter, until the last mass on Easter day, two sheep. (Richard Meryweather, Sibertswold, Kent)

> 1509 I will a taper of 3 li. wex to bren before the sepulture of our lorde ... at the time of Easter, that is to saye from Goode Fridaye to Thursdaye in the Easter weke ... (Alice Bray, Chelsfield, Kent)

> 1519 10 bee hives to meintein the sepulture light, which 10 bee hives shall be in custody of ye church wardens. (Sir John Pollard, parson, Luddington in the Brook, Northants)

1543 I give unto the sepulker light a browne cowe of the value of 12s, the which cowe I will schulde be set unto one pore man my nebur, and he to pay yerely for the same cowe & calfe unto the churchewardens upon midlent Sunday yerely 20d. (T. Goodman, Bradden, Northants)[16]

Given the heavy use of lights, it is not surprising that when a piece of white cloth of gold 'that wente abowte ye sepoulter' is sold by St Dionis Backchurch in 1550 it is described as 'sore droped with wex'.[17]

Not everyone approves of all the expense bestowed on sepulchres, Thomas Becon for one seeing it as a sign of the Church's corruption.

Christ was buried in a poore monument, sepulchre, or grave, without any funeral pompe. Antichrist is buried in a glorious tombe, well gilt, and very gorgeously set out, with many torches and great solemnitye, and with angels gloriously portured,* that beare his soule to heaven ...[18]

After the cross and host have been deposited inside, the sepulchre is watched over day and night until Easter morning. This may be done partly out of general piety and partly in remembrance of the watch kept on Christ's tomb by soldiers – indeed, at Orleans the watchers are dressed as such. However, there are also practical motives: the combination of tapers and rich hangings poses an obvious fire risk; the cross, and the pyx in which the host is placed,† may be valuable; and the faithful coming to pray at the sepulchre may need to be prevented from getting too close, to which end any surrounding hearse is useful.[19]

With tapers all the people come, and at the barriars stay,
Where downe upon their knees they fall, and night and day they pray:
And violets and every kinde of flowers about the grave
They straw, and bring in all their giftes, and presents that they have.
The Popish Kingdome[20]

Payments for watching the sepulchre occur each year in many parishes, with a fire sometimes lit in the church to furnish the watchers with warmth and light.

1488 For fire and drinke at wacching of the sepucre ... 4d (St Andrew Hubbard)

1538 To Barns and his sonne for 2 nights watcheing abowte the sepulture ... 8d | In bred and drink for them ... 2d (St Andrew, Canterbury)

1543 To Vulfray the clerke for watching on Easter eve ... 2d (Worcester)[21]

At Holy Trinity, Coventry, the sepulchre is watched by the second deacon on the night of Good Friday and by the first deacon 'on Estur even, till ye resurrection be don'.[22]

* On sepulchre angels see p76.
† The priest places 'the cross in the sepulchre, along with the Lord's body in the pyx' (Sarum Missal).

[April 4th] **Easter Eve**, or **Holy Saturday**

On this day all the lights in the church are extinguished, perhaps in token of the eclipse of the sun that accompanied the crucifixion, and new fire – the holy fire – is created and hallowed. An old custom is to create this new fire using a burning glass so that it emanates directly from the heavens, with sparks struck from flint serving as a fallback method in cloudy weather.[1]

According to the Sarum Missal the fire is to be kindled 'close to the font', an apt location symbolically as the kindling constitutes a rebirth of light.

At Holy Trinity, Coventry, the second deacon's duties include going to the churchwardens to 'cawse them to provide for coles that ye halowd fire shalbe of, and [he] shall see ye coles be laid on ye sowthe side of ye font, and ... conveniantly kindled against ye priest coming to halow ye fire'.[2]

As this indicates, it is also a practical location as the hallowing involves sprinkling holy water from the font upon the fire. Incense is also hallowed, after which 'a censer shall be filled with coals together with incense, and the new fire shall be censed'.[3]

This fire is then used to light the church's largest and most important candle, the paschal, from Latin *paschalis*, 'relating to Easter'. It is usually substantial and is seen as an emblem of Christ, sometimes being made from 33 pounds of wax in allusion to the years of his life. In practical terms it provides light for the watch kept in the church through the night of Easter Eve.[4]

In large churches it can assume gigantic proportions. According to the diary of Henry Machyn, at Westminster Abbey in 1558 it consists of '300 pounds of wax, and ther was the master and the wardens of the waxchandlers [with] 20 more at the making, and after[wards] a great diner'.[5]

In parish churches it tends to be relatively modest.

1529 For the making of the pascal, weighing 22 pounds ... 1s (St Laurence Pountney)

1555 For nine pounde of wax for ye pascall and for bringinge ye same from Canterbury and strickinge [moulding] ... 10s 2d (Lydd, Kent)[6]

In some churches it is set in a basin which may be suspended from the roof.[7]

1498 Payed for the pascall bason and the hanging of the same ... 18s |
   For 7 pendaunts to ye same bason and the caryage from London ... 3s
   (St Lawrence, Reading)

1529 Making the pan that the pascal stands in [etc] ... 3s (St Laurence Pountney)[8]

More often it is placed on a large standing candlestick on the ground in the form either of a seven-branched candelabrum or of a single column or post.[9]

1546 A standerd of tree painted with a crowne of golde for the pascall. (St Peter, Cornhill, inventory)

1546-52 For painting of the pascall post ... 6d (Bletchingley, Surrey)[10]

The paschal blessed by a deacon, from an 11th-century manuscript

However the candle is placed, ropes and pulleys may be needed to raise it and perhaps also to keep it from toppling.

1455　For 1 rop to ye paschal ... 3d (Walberswick, Suffolk)

1515　For 2 poleys for the pascall ... 3s (Lambeth)[11]

The stock or stand is often painted or otherwise decorated to look like the lower part of a candle, so increasing the paschal's apparent height. Such a base is known as a Judas, being false, like its biblical namesake, and yielding no light.*[12]

1517　To James Calcote for painting of Judas ... 6d (Lambeth)[13]

At Durham the entire structure is nearly 70 foot high, apparently reaching to 'within a mans length to the uppermost vault roofe of the church', there being 'a fine conveyance through the said roofe of the church to light the taper'.†[14]

* On some other meanings of Judas in relation to church lights see note on p552.
† One authority refers innocently to the Durham paschal as 'a magnificent erection', and while it may be impious to notice the fact, this towering structure raised and venerated at the heart of a spring festival is on one level at least a phallic fertility symbol. Its role – noted further on in the main text – as the source of new light for all the other candles in the church can be seen as progenitive, and the practice of dipping it several times into the font (symbolic of birth) and dropping its wax into the water hardly undermine such an interpretation. It is, in this aspect, the church's Maypole.

According to the Sarum rite, the paschal is blessed

> by the deacon, vested as for a procession, facing north, and standing at the
> step of the quire, accompanied by two candle-bearers, one on his right
> hand, one on his left, both turning towards him, and holding unlighted
> candles. ... | The deacon shall put incense into the candle or into the candle-
> stick in the form of a cross ...[15]

Traditionally five grains are inserted. One explanation of their significance,
mentioned by Durand in the late 13th century, is that they are symbolic of the
five wounds inflicted upon Christ's body at the crucifixion.[16]

> At this point the candle shall be lit from the new fire, and ... then shall
> the candle-bearers light their candles throughout the church.

Once lit the paschal is not to be extinguished 'till after compline on the day
following' and it 'shall burn continuously throughout Easter week at matins, and
at mass, and at vespers', as well as on subsequent Sundays and other holy days.
It is only removed on Ascension Day or the day after, in token of the fact that
Christ, of whom it is a symbol, has then departed the earth.[17]

There follows the blessing of the font and its water, during which the priest
'shall divide the water with his hand in the form of a cross', and say, 'O Lord, let
every unclean spirit depart far hence, let the whole malice and fraud of the devil
stand afar off.' Then, making the sign of the cross at intervals, he says, 'Let it be
a living + font, a regenerating + water, a purifying + stream, so that all who are
to be washed in this laver of salvation may obtain the favour of perfect purification,
through the operation in them of the holy spirit.'

He proceeds to cast water 'with his hand out of the font into the four quarters'.
He breathes upon the font three times, causes drops from a candle to fall into it,
and dips the candle into the middle of the font, in each action making the sign
of the cross, and he says, 'Here let the stains of all sins be blotted out ...'[18]

Anciently the paschal itself may be dipped, but the Sarum rubric refers simply
to a candle, perhaps for the practical reason that dipping a heavy and towering
paschal candle would be difficult. As a result smaller alternatives may be used: at
St Andrew Hubbard in 1510-12 payment is made 'for a pound taper for halowing
at fonte'.[19]

Just as the church's lights are extinguished and renewed on this day, so too
parishioners often put out the old fires in their houses and bear home with them
from the church a new light lit from the hallowed fire, believing it to have protective
power.

The Popish Kingdome gives as usual a slightly sceptical account of the day's
proceedings.

> On Easter Eve the fire all is quencht in every place,
> And fresh againe from out the flint is fetcht with solemne grace:
> The priest doth halow this against great dangers many one,

A brande whereof doth every man with greedie minde take home,
That when the fearefull storme appeares, or tempest blacke arise,
By lighting this he safe may be, from stroke of hurtfull skies:
A taper great, the paschal named, with musicke then they blesse,
And franckensence herein they pricke, for greater holynesse:
This burneth night and day as signe of Christ that conquered hell,
As if so be this foolish toye suffiseth this to tell.
Then doth the bishop or the priest the water halow straight,
That for their baptisme is reserved ...[20]

[April 5th] **Easter Day** (first Sunday after the first full moon after March 21st, the approximate date of the spring equinox)

The Venerable Bede derives 'Easter' from Eostre or Eastre, a pagan goddess whose festival was celebrated by the Anglo-Saxons in the spring, but no other early source supports this, and it may simply derive from old words for East. Either way, the name indicates a festival marking the arrival of spring.[1]

In the morning the drama of Christ's death and resurrection is completed with the opening of the sepulchre and the return of the cross and host to the high altar.

At Durham the ceremony is performed between 3 and 4 in the morning. Two of the oldest monks retrieve the image of Christ, 'representinge the resurrection, with a crosse in his hand, in the breast wherof was enclosed ... the holy sacrament'. They raise it up for all to see then carry it to the high altar 'upon a faire velvet cushion all embrodered, singinge the anthem of *Christus resurgens* [Christ is rising again]'. Having placed it on the middle of the altar they kneel, 'senceing it all the time' while 'the rest of the whole quire' sing the same anthem.

There follows a procession in which the two monks carry the image on the cushion around the church. On its progress 'a most rich canopye of purple velvet tached [secured] round about with red silke' is held over it by 'four antient gentlemen belonginge to the prior'. Meanwhile 'the whole quire [wait] upon it with goodly torches and great store of other lights, all singinge, rejoiceinge and praising God most devoutly till they came to the high altar againe, wheron they did place the said image, there to remaine until the Assencion day'.[2]

According to the Sarum rite, once the host (representing Christ's body) has been returned to the altar, above which it is suspended as usual in a pyx, 'then all the bells shall be rung in a clash' and an anthem is sung. Afterwards 'all the crosses and all the images shall be uncovered throughout the church, and the bells shall be rung for matins in the usual way'.[3]

Prior to the Reformation a simpler version of these ceremonies, or something similar, is probably performed in many parish churches.

In some places the usual symbolic representation of the resurrection merges with re-enactment. According to *The Bee hive of the Romishe Churche*, written by a Dutch Calvinist in 1569 and translated into English ten years later,

They put him in a grave [the sepulchre] till Easter, at which time they take him uppe againe, and sing *Resurrexit, non est hic, Alleluia*: He is risen, He is not here, God be thanked. Yea and in some places they make the grave in a hie place in the church ... and there do walke souldiours in harnesse, as bright as Saint George, which keepe the grave, till the priests come and take him up: and then cometh sodenlie a flash of fire, wherwith they are all afraid and fall downe: and then upstartes the man, and they begin to sing *Alleluia* on all handes, and then the clocke striketh eleven.[4]

Churchwardens' accounts suggest the occasional performance of similar dramas in English parishes, although it seems they may be separate from the sepulchre rite and take place on specially erected stages, probably outside. In the first example following the 'rosen' or resin may be for a burst of light similar to the 'flash of fire' above. In the last example it is joined by *aqua-vitae* or ardent spirits, presumably used to foster flames.

1507 To Sybel Darling for nailes for the sepulcre & for rosen to the resurrecion pley ... 2d (St Lawrence, Reading)

1519 A skinne of parchment & for gun powder for the play on Ester day ... 8d | Brede & ale for them that made ye stage at Ester & other things that belongeth to ye play ... 14d (Kingston upon Thames, Surrey)

1522 For a coate made when the Resurrection was played, for him that in playing represented the part of Almighty God ... 1s | For making the stage for the Resurrection at Easter ... 3s 4d (Rye, Sussex)

1557 Paide to the players upon Ester Daye in the mornenge ... 16d | For aqua vite, and rosen, and for nails for the skaffolde ... 5d (St Martin in the Fields)[5]

William Lambarde (*d.* 1601), recalling pre-Reformation times, records a regular performance at Witney, Oxfordshire, although he does not say whether it occurred on Easter Day itself.

In the dayes of ceremonial religion they used at Witney to set forthe yearly in maner of a shew, or enterlude, the Resurrection of our lord and saviour Christe, partly of purpose to draw thither some concourse of people that might spend their money in the towne, but chieflie to allure by pleasant spectacle the comon sort to the likinge of popishe maumetrie [mummery]; for the which purpose, and the more lively thearby to exhibite to the eye the whole action of the Resurrection, the preistes garnished out certein smalle puppets, representinge the persons of Christe, the Watchmen, Marie, and others, amongest the which one bare the parte of a wakinge Watchman, who (espyinge Christ to arise) made a continual noise, like to the sound that is caused by the metinge of two stickes, and was therof comonly called *Jack Snacker of Witney*.[6]

Parts of the story re-enacted sometimes include the visit of Mary Magdalen and other women to the sepulchre, known as the *visitatio sepulchri*. According to one account this involves three deacons, 'with their heads in the manner of women', coming through the middle of the choir towards the sepulchre, where they are met by 'a boy, clothed like an angel'. On the deacon representing Mary telling him that they seek Jesus of Nazareth, the angel replies, 'He is not here, but is risen,' and departs. Then a priest, impersonating Christ, appears and calls Mary's name. She throws herself at his feet, crying 'Rabboni' (Master), to which he responds, '*Noli me tangere*' (Touch me not). Having told the women not to be afraid he conceals himself and they, moved to joy by his words, sing 'Alleluia, the Lord is risen'.[7]

Performance of the *visitatio* may be relatively rare in England, but in her will of 1503 Agnes Burton leaves 'to the service of the sepulcre' at St Mary Magdalen, Taunton, 'my red damaske mantell and my mantell lined with silke ... to thentent of Mary Magdaleyn play'.[8]

Not everyone is convinced of the value of such dramas, or indeed of that of the more commonly performed sepulchre ceremony. In the view of John Hooper, writing in 1547,

> The ploughman, be he never so unlearned, shall better be instructed of Christ's death and passion by the corn that he soweth in the field, and likewise of Christ's resurrection, than by all the dead posts that hang in the church, or are pulled out of the sepulchre with *Christus resurgens*. What resemblance hath the taking of the cross out of the sepulchre, and going a procession with it, with the resurrection of Christ? None at all: the dead post is as dead, when they sing, *Iam non moritur*, as it was when they buried it with, *In pace factus est locus eius.**[9]

In other ways too the ritual is challenged. According to John Foxe, at Easter in 1554 someone evades the attention of the watchmen guarding the sepulchre at St Pancras in Cheapside and removes the crucifix and pyx 'before the priest rose to the resurrection: so that when after his accustomed maner he put his hande into the sepulchre, and saide very devoutely, *Surrexit non est hic*, he found his words true, for he was not there in deede'.[10]

Foxe and Hooper and their fellow Protestants have their way of course, Easter sepulchres and the accompanying ceremonies being notable casualties of the Reformation.

Meantime, under the old dispensation, John Mirk encourages parishioners to treat Easter as a new beginning in their hearts as in their hearths.

> It is the maner [custom] this day at Easter for to take fire out of the hall that has all the winter burnt with fire and blacked with smoke. It shall this day be arrayed with green rushes, and sweet flowers strewed all aboute, shewing

---

* *Iam* ... Now he dies not. *In pace* ... His place is made in peace.

a high example to all men and women that, right as they make cleane the howse all within, bearing out the fire and strewing flowers, right so ye shall cleanse the howse of your soule, doing away the fire of lechery and of deadly wrath and of envy, and strew there sweet herbes and flowers, which be vertues of goodnes and of mekenes, of kindness, of love and charite, of peace and of rest: and so make the howse of your soule able to receive your God.

Christ emerges from the tomb as the guarding soldiers sleep.
Stained glass, All Saints, Pavement, York, late 14th century.

This is particularly important because Easter is when many parishioners receive communion for the only time in the year. 'For Christ's love,' Mirk adds, 'each man search well his conscience and cleanse it, that he may be able to receive his saviour.'[11]

As for the church, after the drama of the day the sepulchre is often left in place until the following Thursday, its emptiness in the meantime serving as a triumphant reminder of the resurrection.[12]

The same scene in alabaster,
Nottingham school, 15th century

[April 13th & 14th] **Hocktide** (second Monday and Tuesday after Easter Day)
It is customary on these days to raise funds for the church by stopping members
of the opposite sex as they pass along public roads, although the origins of the
custom and of the name of the festival are both obscure.* Originally those stopped
are tied up and have to pay to be released, but a gentler later form involves setting
a rope across the road, with only the threat of binding deployed. The change may
be related to ecclesiastical objections on grounds of decency: in 1450 the Bishop of
Worcester deplores hocking for being '*occasione plura oriuntur scandala, adulteriaque,
et alia crimina*,' the occasion of many scandals, adulteries, and other crimes.[1]

The women usually do the binding and gathering on the Monday, with the
men following next day. In some places only the married women are involved,
perhaps in the hope of reducing the incidence of mischief.

> 1498 Received of hok money gadered of women ... 20s | Received of hok
> money gadered of men ... 4s (St Lawrence, Reading)

> 1499 Resseved of diverse wifes & maidens to save them from bindinge in
> Hok Tuesday ... 5s (St Edmund, Salisbury)

> 1518 Received of Mistres Sabyn, Mistres Butt, Mistres Halhed & other
> wifes of money gatherd by them on hockmondaye ... 20s (St Mary the
> Great, Cambridge)

> 1560 Received on hockmondaye of the wemen that they gathered for the
> churche ... 13s 6d | Received on hocktuesdaye of the men that they
> gathered ... 23d (Portsmouth, Hants)[2]

As this suggests, the women are always much more successful than the men.
Presumably this is partly because they have the advantage of going first and partly
because men at this time generally have more money to give, to say nothing of
whether the female gatherers are more persuasive in their appeals.

The parish may pay for food and drink, sometimes as an encouragement and
reward for those gathering, sometimes for more general celebration and fund raising.

> 1484 For baking of the brede at hoketide ... 5d | For brewing of the hoking
> ale ... 16d | 1530 Received of the hoking ale at diverse bonefiers ...
> 16s 10d (Bishop's Stortford)

> 1497 For 3 ribbes of beef to the wives on hokmonday, & for ale & bred
> for them that gadered ... 16d (St Mary at Hill)

> 1556 For meate and drinke for the women & men that did gather at
> Hoctide ... 7s (St Edmund, Salisbury)[3]

---

* 'Few words have received so much etymological and historical investigation as
Hock-day, Hocktide, Hock Tuesday, Hock Monday. But the origin has not yet been
ascertained.' (*OED*)

Like many merry customs hocking falls into general disuse after the Reformation, although it continues in some places at least into the late 17th century. At St Peter in the East, Oxford, for example, it is revived periodically when funds are particularly needed, the last instance being in 1677, when £4 10s is raised.[4]

April 23rd St George's Day

The day is established as the feast of the Christian warrior St George as early as 1222, and in the later Middle Ages his cult becomes increasingly popular. One result is the proliferation of images and altars of St George in parish churches, often funded by guilds established in his name. Another result is processions or 'ridings' held on this day in a number of large towns and cities. The best documented example, and perhaps the most elaborate, is at Norwich.* On the preceding day, 22nd April, a special evensong is celebrated in the cathedral, and the day itself sees the procession through the city, during which the cathedral bells ring out.[1]

The central figure of 'the George' consists of a man dressed as the saint and riding on horseback. His clothes change over time, but a 1469 'inventory of precious things' kept in a chest in the cathedral includes 'one gown of scarlet say' for him along with 'a coat armour beaten with silver'. There are also 'two white gowns' for his henchmen and 'four banners with the arms of St George for the trumpeters'.[2]

A guild order of 1471 sets out that 'the George shall go in procession and make a conflicte with the dragon'. The latter may breathe fire, or at least make threatening noises: some years earlier a payment is made for 'playing in the dragon with gunpowder', which sounds precarious. One or more angels may also appear, and by the 1530s the figure of St Margaret has been added, riding on a horse and referred to as 'the Lady'. In 1534 'half a hundred oranges' are given 'for borrowing a gown and kirtell for the Margaret'.[3]

The following are some of the costs incurred by the guild in 1522.

For 12 pair gloves for angel, henchmen, standerdberer, footmen, and
    2 pleyers in the dragon ... 14d
For the crosse bering, with other lights in the time of procession ... 8d
To them that went in 3 angel weeds ... 6d
To 4 men in albs, bering the canapy over the George ... 4d
To the clerks, for singing in the time of procession, and at diner, and
    at sooper ... 2s
To the 4 waits of the cite ... 6s 8d | To 2 other minstrells ... 16d
Also to 2 monks of the monestery, for using of ther albs ... 2s
To the sexton of the seid place, for ringing and other things ... 2s

---

* While the account that follows does not relate directly to parish life, it gives a sense of the cult of St George and the pageantry associated with him, both of which were found in more modest form at parish level.

St George slays
the dragon as
a damsel prays
for his success,
by the Master of
Sir John Fastolf,
c. 1430

To the pleyer in the dragon and his man, for ther labor ... 12d

To the banner berer ... 4d

To a saddeler, for borowing of a horse harnes for the George, and trimming of the same ... 4d

For mending of an angel wings that was broken, and the iron to the same ... 13d

For newe pointing, hooping, and newe reparing of the dragon ... 6s 6d

Also for a reward to him that browte the George's horse, and for leding home agein ... 4d[4]

The procession ends at the cathedral where all the guild members offer up wax at the high altar before taking part in a mass in honour of St George, the monarch and the guild.

Other notable St George processions occur at Leicester, Coventry, Chester and York, and more modest ones take place in parishes across the country, for example at Little Walsingham in Norfolk and Lostwithiel in Cornwall.

While the celebrations are only marginally religious, most fall victim to the Reformation, religious guilds being abolished in 1547 and processions forbidden. At Norwich the guild manages to survive as part of the city corporation, but there remains the problem that the procession pays honour to saints. In 1559 they therefore agree that 'there shall be neither George nor Margaret', but there is a reprieve for the dragon, which 'for pastime' may still 'come and shew himself as in other years'. He survives in one form or another into the 19th century, being known as 'Old Snap'.[5]

Elsewhere the day comes to be marked less colourfully, but with bells ringing out across the country for its patron saint.

> 1673 Paid the ringers on St George's day as accustomed ... 4s (St Werburgh, Bristol)
>
> 1712 Given to the rengers apon Sand Gorge is day ... 5s (Eastchurch, Kent)[6]

May 1st **May Day**

The best description of traditional May celebrations, marking the beginning of summer, comes from the lively but disapproving pen of Philip Stubbes. It appears in his *Anatomie of Abuses*, first published, appropriately enough, on 1st May 1583.

> First, all the wilde-heds of the parish, conventing together, chuse them a Grand-Captain (of all mischiefe) whom they innoble with the title of my Lord of Mis-rule, and him they crowne with great solemnitie, and adopt for their king. This king anointed, chuseth forth twentie, fortie, threescore or a hundred lustie guttes like to himself to waighte upon his lordly majestie, and to guard his noble person. Then everie one of these his men he investeth with his liveries, of green, yellow or some other light wanton colour. And as though that were not (baudie) gaudie enough I should say, they bedecke themselves with scarfs, ribbons & laces hanged all over with golde rings, precious stones & other jewels: this done, they tie about either leg 20 or 40 bells, with rich handkercheifs in their hands, and sometimes laid acrosse over their shoulders and necke, borrowed for the most parte of their prettie mopsies & loving Besses, for bussing them in ye dark.
>
> Thus all things set in order, then have they their hobby-horses, dragons and other antiques, together with their baudie pipers and thundering drummers to strike up the devils daunce withall. Then marche these heathen company towards the church and churchyard, their pipers pipeing, their

drummers thundring, their stumps dauncing, their bells jingling, their handkercheifs swinging about their heds like madmen, their hobby-horses and other monsters skirmishing amongest the route: and in this sorte they go to the church (I say) & into the church (though the minister be at praier or preaching), dancing & swinging their handkercheifs over their hede in the church like devils incarnate, with such a confused noise that no man can hear his own voice. Then the foolish people, they looke, they stare, they laugh, they fleer, & mount upon formes and pewes to see these goodly pageants solem[ni]zed in this sort. Then after this, about the church they go again and again & so forth into ye churchyard, where they have commonly their somer-halles, their bowers, arbors, & banqueting houses set up, wherin they feast, banquet & daunce all that day, & (peradventure) all the night too.[1]

The dance referred to is of course the Morris dance, from 'moorish', of or relating to the Moors. A 'hobby' is a small horse so the term 'hobby horse', while useful, is tautologous. According to Francis Douce, it 'was represented by a man equipped with as much pasteboard as was sufficient to form the head and hinder parts of a horse, the quadrupedal defects being concealed by a long mantle or foot-cloth that nearly touched the ground. ... [From] the horse's mouth was suspended a ladle for the purpose of gathering money from the spectators.'[2]

In some places the summer lord or lord of misrule takes the form of Robin Hood. At Kingston upon Thames he is attended not only by Morris dancers but also by the familiar figures of Maid Marian, Little John and Friar Tuck.[3]

1507 For painting of a bannar for Robin Hode ... 3d | For a goun for the lady ... 8d | For belles for the dawnsars ... 12d

1508 For little John's coat ... 8s

1509 For silver paper for the Mores dawnsars ... 7d | For kendall* for Robin Hode's coat ... 1s 3d | For 3 yerds of white for the frere's coat ... 3s | For 4 yerds of kendall for Maide Marian's huke† ... 3s 4d | For 2 paire of gloves for Robin Hode and Maide Marian ... 3d | For 6 brode arowes ... 6d | To Maide Marian for her labour for two years ... 2s

1519 Shoes for the Mores daunsars, the frere and Maide Marian at 7d a paire ... 5s 4d

1521 Eight yerds of fustian‡ for the Mores daunsars coats ... 16s | A dosen of gold skinnes§ ... 10d

1523 Hire of hats for Robin Hode ... 16d | Paid for the hat that was lost ... 10d

* A type of green woollen cloth manufactured in Kendal, Westmorland.
† A cape or cloak with a hood.
‡ A kind of coarse cloth made of cotton or flax.
§ Possibly gilt leather, pliable enough to accommodate the movements of the dancers.

1524 Received at the church ale and Robin Hode, all things deducted ... £3 10s 6d

1529 For spunging and brushing Robin Hode's coats ... 2d

1536 Five hats and 4 purses for the daunsars ... 4½d | 4 yerds of cloth for the foole's coat ... 2s | 2 ells of worstede for Maide Marian's kirtle ... 6s 8d | To the fryer and the piper for to go to Croydon ... 8d[4]

ABOVE Piper, hobby horse and dancers,
from a painting of the Thames at Richmond, early 17th century.
BELOW Robin Hood, Will Scarlet and Little John, from a ballad printed in 1700.

As this shows, the parish funds these entirely secular festivities which not only help to bind the community together in celebration of the arrival of summer but also provide an opportunity to raise money for the church. The £3 10s raised in 1524 is a substantial sum, and such profits are sometimes augmented by hiring out costumes and performers, which is presumably why the friar and the piper are heading to Croydon.

> 1588 [Received] for the lone of Robin Hoodes clothes ... 18d (St Columb Major, Cornwall)

> 1595 Paide to one for the carrying of the Morris coats to Maidenhed ... 4d | 1612 Received of the churchwardens of Bisham [for] loane of our Morris's coats and bells ... 2s 6d (Great Marlow, Bucks)[5]

The earliest known performance of a Robin Hood play is in 1427, and from the 1470s onward they are adopted widely as a means of raising parish funds.[6]

> 1536 Received of John Marys & of his company that playd Robin Hoode ... 38s 4d | 1538 Received of Robin Hoode & of his men ... £3 10d (Stratton, Cornwall)[7]

In the 1530s reformer Hugh Latimer, then Bishop of Worcester, while travelling sends word ahead to a town that he intends to preach there next day, only to arrive and find the church door locked. On enquiry he is told, 'Sir, this is a busye daye with us, we can not heare you, it is Robin Hoodes daye. The parishe are gone abroade to gather for Robin Hoode'. Latimer's dismay is not eased by the fact that in his eyes Hood is 'a traitoure, and a thefe'.[8]

It seems likely that, rather than acting out any extended drama, Robin and his fellows often merely lord it over the feasting and dancing. In many places the celebrations are simpler still, involving games and good food, and of course the gathering of funds.

> 1499 Received of Symand Smyttes wife and Lymken barbers wife of money by them gadered with Virgins upon May day ... 6s 7d ob. | 1518 Given by the children of the May-game ... 8d (St Margaret, Westminster)

> 1538 *Expenses of the Maye Feast.* To Reynolds the butcher for mete ... 15d | For a calf ... 2s | For a quarter of mutton ... 16d | For halfe a shepe ... 12d | To John the cook ... 6d | To Mother Watt for salt and honey ... 7d | [To the same] for brewing ... 6d | For wood ... 6d | For turning the spit ... 1d | To the minstrels all that day ... 6d (Great Dunmow, Essex)[9]

Churches sometimes also pay for the most patently pagan element in the celebrations, the Maypole.

> 1613 To Robert Brandin for makeinge the Maypole ... 4s (Lowick, Northants)[10]

Maypole, from a ballad printed *c.* 1675

Philip Stubbes, unhappy again, describes the harvesting and erection of the pole.

Against May, Whitsonday or other time,* all the yung men and maides, olde men and wives run gadding over night to the woods, groves, hills & mountains, where they spend all the night in plesant pastimes, & in the morning they return bringing with them birch & branches of trees, to deck their assemblies withall ...

But the cheifest jewel they bring from thence is their May-pole, which they bring home with great veneration, as thus. They have twentie or fortie yoke of oxen, every ox having a sweete nose-gay of floures placed on the tip of his hornes, and these oxen drawe home this May-pole (this stinking idol rather) which is covered all over with floures, and herbs bound round about with strings from the top to the bottome, and sometime painted with variable colours, with two or three hundred men, women and children following it with great devotion. And thus being reared up, with hand-kercheefs and flags hovering on the top, they straw the ground rounde about, binde green boughes about it, set up sommer halles, bowers and arbors hard by it. And then fall they to daunce about it like as the heathen people did at the dedication of the idols, wherof this is a perfect pattern, or rather the thing itself.

I have heard it credibly reported (and that, viva voce) by men of great gravitie and reputation, that of fortie, threescore, or a hundred maides going to the wood over night, there have scarcely the third part of them returned home againe undefiled.[11]

---

* While the celebrations of early summer typically begin on 1st May they occur over a period. In his diary Henry Machyn refers to a 'May game' before the queen at Greenwich in June 1559.

Between the Reformation and the Restoration Maypoles become a battle-ground as the puritanically inclined seek to excise them from national life. John Stow records the destruction in 1549 of a pole which had long been raised near St Andrew Undershaft in London and which, when not in use, was stored 'under the pentises of one rowe of houses' in nearby Shaft Alley.

> One Sir Stephen, curat of St Katherine Christs Church, preaching at Paules Crosse, said there, that this shaft was made an idol, by naming the church of Saint Andrew with the addition of *under that shaft* ... I heard his sermon ... and I saw the effect that followed: for in the afternoone of that present Sunday, the neighbours and tenants ... over whose doores the saide shaft had laine, after they had dined to make themselves strong, gathered more helpe, and with great labour raising the shaft from the hooks, whereon it had rested two and thirtie yeares, they sawed it in peeces, everie man taking for his share so much as had laine over his doore and stall, the length of his house, and they of the Alley divided amongest them so much as had laine over their alley gate. Thus was this idol (as he termed it) mangled, and after burned.[12]

Three years later 'a goodly May-pole' appears in Fenchurch parish, along with Morris dancers and the figure of a giant, but on the same day the lord mayor causes it to be taken down and broken.[13]

Sometimes such poles are afterwards put to practical use.

> 1635 Paid Anthony Thorne and others for taking down ye Maypole and
> making a town ladder of it ... 3s 10d (Cerne Abbas, Dorset)[14]

In 1644 parliament orders that all Maypoles be taken down, referring to them as 'a heathenish vanity, generally abused to superstition and wickedness'. The most famous casualty is the one in the Strand in London, but in 1661, as a sign of loyalty to the restored monarchy, a new pole is installed 'in the very same pit where the former stood, but far more glorious, bigger and higher than ever'. It is made in two parts and is so long that it is thought 'landsmen (as carpenters) could not possibly raise it', so twelve seamen are employed, bringing 'cables, pullies, and other tacklins, with six great anchors'. It is 'jointed together, and hoopt about with bands of iron,' and then decorated with a 'crown and vane with the kings armes richly gilded' on the top and a structure 'like a balcony' about the middle.

> This being done, the trumpets did sound, and in four hours space it was advanced upright, after which being established fast in the ground, six drums did beat, and the trumpets did sound again, great shouts and acclamations the people gave, that it did ring throughout all the whole Strand; after that came a Morice dance finely deckt, with purple scarfs, in their half-shirts, with a taber and pipe the antient musick, and danced round about the Maypole ... Little children did much rejoice, and antient people did clap their hands, saying, golden dayes began to appear.[15]

LEFT
Embroidery,
early 18th
century.
BELOW
Printed
textile
c. 1770.

Elsewhere there is less hoopla, but the same result.

> 1661 Laid out for the Maypoles ... £2 13s 6d | 1662 Spent upon Wildgoose
> for mesuring the Maypole ... 3d | To Goodman Badger for pitching and
> graveling about the Maypole ... 7s 2d (St Peter in the East, Oxford)[16]

Not everyone is happy at the return of the poles. Anthony Wood records the
short-lived opposition in Oxford.

> 1660 *May 1st.* May poles, May games. A May-pole against the Beare
> in Allhallows parish, set up on purpose to vex the Presbyterians and
> Independents. Dr Conant, then vice-chancellor, came with his beadles
> and servants to have it sawed downe, but before he had entered an inch
> into it, he and his party were forced to leave that place.[17]

At Rostherne in Cheshire a nonconformist minister, Adam Martindale, opposes
the return with greater determination, and is exceptional in prevailing.

> The rabble of prophane youths, and some doting fooles that tooke their
> part, were encouraged to affront me, by setting up a May-pole in my way
> to the church ... I would not, for a time, seeme to gratifie their spitefull
> humour by taking notice of it; but in due season, when their youthfull rage
> was somewhat cooled, and there was no colour to say what I spoke proceeded
> from passion, I tooke occasion to preach upon Proverbs i 22, *How long,*
> *ye simple ones, will ye love simplicity?* &c.; and after I had laid before them
> many other things of greater weight, I calmly reproved their folly in erecting
> a May-pole in that way they had done; told them, many learned men were
> of opinion that a May-pole was a relique of the shamefull worship of the
> Strumpet Flora in Rome; but however that was, it was a thing that never
> did, nor could do good; yea, had occasioned, and might occasion, much
> harme to people's soules; and I thinke I also told them of their sin in doing
> such a thing (though it were granted to be harmelesse in itselfe) on purpose
> to affront me, their spiritual father and pastour. ...
>
> Not long after, my wife, assisted with three young women, whipt it
> downe in the night with a framing-saw, cutting it brest-high, so as the
> bottome would serve well for a dial-post. This made them almost mad,
> and put them to the trouble of piecing it with another fowle pole; but it
> was such an ugly thing, so rough and crooked, as proclaimed the follie and
> povertie of those that set it up, so that they were content it should be
> taken downe ...[18]

[May 11th-13th] **Rogation Days** (Monday, Tuesday and Wednesday. Preceded by Rogation Sunday, the 5th Sunday after Easter Day, and followed by Ascension Day or Holy Thursday.)

> Now comes the day wherein they gad abrode, with crosse in hande,
> To boundes of every field, and round about their neighbours lande:
> And as they go, they sing and pray to every saint above ...
>
> *The Popish Kingdome*[1]

The Rogation Days (from Latin *rogare*, to ask) have their origin in processions and prayers ordered in about 470 by Mamertus, Archbishop of Vienne in Gaul, to seek divine protection against earthquakes and other perils. Over time two further elements are added: the seeking of divine favour for the harvest, aptly enough given the time of year; and the confirmation of the bounds of the parish, in a time before reliable maps. As a result the process is also known as **perambulation** (a walk around, from Latin *per* and *ambulare*) or **beating the bounds** (from the practice of beating at certain landmarks on the boundary to impress them upon the memories of those involved).

Originally the processions occur on the Rogation Days, but in time they often occur on Ascension Day instead. The period is also called **Cross Week**, from the custom of carrying a cross in the procession, and **Gang Week**, from the act of 'going' about.

A sermon in a late 15th-century manuscript, but perhaps written earlier, sets out some of the pitfalls for the parishioners who take part, the preacher bidding them

> not to come and go in procession talking of nice tales and japes by the way or by the fieldes as ye walke, or to bacbite your even [fellow] Cristen. Or to go more for pompe and pride of the worlde than for to plese God, or for helpe of theire owne sowles. Soche processions are but vaine and litell worthe for the help of man. But ye sholde come mekely and lowly with a good devocion, and follow your crosse and your belles in your bedes bidding and good prayers, that almighty God will the rather through your prayers stint the grete perils and mischeves that ben among mankinde, and to bring you to the bliss.[2]

Another early homily sets out the purposes of the prayers offered.

Firste that God sholde withestande the batell of owre enemies bothe bodily and gostly. For in that time of the yere the devils and other wicked spirites are moste besy abowte for to drawe a man in to sinne and wrechednes. And holy churche prayethe that Criste sholde kepe the tender frutes that be done on the erthe to mans helpe, and so sholde all Cristen pray for the same …

Also in these processions baners and crosses ben borne and belles rung that the spirites that flye above us in the air as thike as motes in the sonne sholde flee awey from us, when they see baners and crosses on lofte, and hearing the belles ring. For like as a king hath in his hoste [army] baners and trompettes and clarions to the drede of his enemies, righte so in like wise almighty God that is king of all kinges hath belles for his clarions and for his trompes, and a cross raised for his baner.[3]

The *Golden Legend* adds that

in some churches, and especially in them of France, [it] is accustomed to bear a dragon with a long tail filled full of chaff or other thing. The two first days it is borne before the cross, and on the third day they bear it after the cross with the tail all void, by which is understood that the first day before the law, or the second under the law, the devil reigned in the world. And on the third day of grace, by the passion of Jesus Christ, he was put out of his realm.[4]

According to Durand, on the first two days the dragon's tail is 'long, erect, and inflated', but once he has been relegated it becomes 'empty and depressed'.[5]

While the dragon represents the devil, Christ is sometimes represented by a lion. At Salisbury Cathedral the processions feature a dragon upon a pole and a lion banner, while the banners listed in an inventory for St George's chapel, Windsor, in 1385 include '*unus draco, et unus leo, pro processione in Rogationibus*'. Such banners may also feature at parish level, but as for stuffed Rogationtide dragons, the lack of evidence for them in churchwardens' accounts tends to suggest that they do not appear widely in England.[6]

In some cases those carrying the cross and banners, usually poor members of the parish, are paid for their trouble.

1503-07 For the banneres bering about the feldes in theis 3 yeres … 23d (Bassingbourne, Cambs)

1542 To Barett for 3 dayes bering of the cross at gangtide … 3d (Bishop's Stortford)[7]

As already seen, religious processions are banned in 1547, but injunctions issued by Queen Elizabeth in 1559, at the start of her reign, make an exception of perambulations. 'The curate and the substantial men of the parish' are to walk the bounds each year. At 'certain convenient places' the curate

shall admonish the people to give thanks to God … for the increase and abundance of his fruits upon the face of the earth, with the saying of the

103rd Psalm, *Benedic, anima mea* [Bless [the lord], O my soul] etc, or such like. At which time also the same minister shall inculcate these or such sentences: 'Cursed be he which translateth the bounds and doles* of his neighbour.'[8]

In a letter to one of his archdeacons in the following year Edmund Grindal, Bishop of London, stresses that any 'popish' elements are to be omitted.

For avoiding of superstitious behaviour ... give notice and commandment within your archdeaconry, that the ministers make it not a procession, but a perambulation; and also that they suffer no banners, nor other like monuments of superstition to be carried abroad; neither to have multitude of young light folks with them, but the substantial of the parish, according to the injunctions; the ministers to go without surplices and lights; and to use no drinkings, except the distance of the place do require some necessary relief; and to use at one or two convenient places the form and order of prayers and thanksgiving appointed by the queen's majesty's injunctions.[9]

Eleven years later, as Archbishop of York, Grindal endorses the singing in English of two psalms (103 and 104), but reiterates that the perambulation must be performed 'without wearing any surplices, carrying of banners or handbells, or staying at crosses, or other such like popish ceremonies'.[10]

Being much attached to the old ways, the parish of Stanford, Berkshire, ignores the new rules and in 1564 its wardens are summoned to speak with their archdeacon 'for caryeng a stremer in Rogacion weke'.[11]

Female involvement is rare but when it occurs it too is frowned upon. In the same year it is complained of one Essex vicar that he allows several parish women to take part both in the perambulation and in the 'good friendly dinner' afterwards, and when in 1575 the Bishop of Winchester enquires of his clergy 'whether women go about' with the perambulation it is clearly a question requiring the answer 'no'.[12]

More generally the authorities encourage perambulations, and parishes face trouble if they fail to perform them.

1589 Paid to Doctor Stanup for a fine for that the perambulacon about the parish was not kept the yere before ... 3s 4d (St Ethelburga, Bishopsgate)

1635 Paid to the consistory court for not goinge to the uttermost bounds of the parish every Rogation weeke ... 22d (St Mary on the Hill, Chester)[13]

Various methods are used to try to impress landmarks along the boundary upon the memories of those taking part, particularly upon the memories of the young of the parish, almost always boys. Sometimes they are provided with wands with which to beat the bounds.

1725 For 2 bundels of willow wands for ye boyes ... 5s (St Giles without Cripplegate)[14]

* *Translates*. Takes away or removes. *Doles, dools*, *dewels*. Boundary marks or landmarks such as posts or stones.

In 1661 Pepys is pleased to see boys processing 'with their broomestaffes in their hands, as I have myself long ago gone'.[15]

Often the boys are given 'points', which Sir John Hawkins, writing in 1776, explains as follows.

> Points were anciently a necessary article in the dress, at least of men ... They were bits of string about eight inches in length, consisting of three strands of cotton yarn, of various colours, twisted together, and tagged at both ends with bits of tin plate; their use was to tie together the garments worn on different parts of the body ... With the ... doublet or jerkin buttons were introduced, and these in process of time rendered points useless; nevertheless they continued to be made till of very late years, and that for a particular purpose. On Ascension-day ... it was the custom at the commencement of the procession to distribute to each [boy] a willow wand, and at the end thereof a handful of points ... which were looked on by them as honorary rewards long after they ceased to be useful, and were called *tags*.[16]

On the rare occasions that girls take part they are usually given ribbons.

1598 For 4 dozen of pointes to geve to boyes to remember the circuite of our parishe ... 8d (St Bartholomew Exchange)

1663 For points for the boys ... 5s | For ribbons for the girls ... 8s (St Mary Woolchurch)[17]

Sometimes it is the boys rather than the bounds that are beaten.

1670 Given to the boys that were whipt ... 4s (Chelsea, Middlesex)

1747 Paid to the boys for being wipt at ye dewels ... 11d (All Saints, King's Lynn, Norfolk)

1747 On Ascension Day, after morning prayer at Turnworth church, was made a publick perambulation of ye bounds of ye parish of Turnworth, by one Richard Cobbe, vicar, William Northover, churchwarden, Henry Sillers and Richard Mullen, overseers, and others, with 4 boys; beginning at the Church Hatch and cutting a great T on the most principal parts of the bounds. Whipping ye boys by way of remembrance, and stopping their cry with some half-pence, we returned to church again ... (Turnworth, Dorset, note in register)[18]

At Purton, Wiltshire, in 1733 coins are thrown for the boys to retrieve and keep as their reward, in one case leading to a fight, but there is no whipping. Instead readings are made from the bible and crosses are cut on trees.[19]

At Epping in 1762 the preferred methods are 'bumping' individuals against any upright landmark and placing them in any declivity. 'Put into the pond Wm. Hatt. ... Put into the ditch Thos. Webb, Thos. Wakefield.' When they come to one ash tree, however, 'John Penson hit his hat against it twice and his — once, the tree standing in such a manner that nobody could be bumpt at it.'[20]

At Windsor in 1801 payments are made 'for creeping through sundry arches' (3s) and 'for swimming through the ponds' (5s). Money is also spent on 'use of planks to lay over ditches in Goswells and three men to fetch, carry and take them home'.[21]

At St Martin, Salisbury, twenty-five years later the costs include

> For ribbons and rods for the boys ... 7s | Mr Burch for money thrown away ... 3s 6d | 8 boys for their attendance ... 8s | Boy for going through the water ... 1s 6d[22]

Writing in 1833 the vicar of Scopwick, Lincolnshire, recalls a method formerly used there.

> At different points there were small holes made in the ground ... and the boys who accompanied the procession were made to stand on their heads in these holes, as a method of assisting the memory; and several persons are now living, who, by this expedient, can distinctly remember where every hole was placed.[23]

In London and other urban centres boundary points are often less memorable, prompting parishes to install physical markers.

> 1653 To Edward Huckwell, mason, for eleven stones to set out the bounds of the parish, at 7s 6d the stone ... £4 2s 6d (St Margaret, Westminster)

> 1659 To Mr Slade the plummer for some leaden markes set up at the parish boundes ... 8s 9d (St Bartholomew Exchange)[24]

The incursions involved in perambulations are not always appreciated. In 1503 Thomas Walterkin, a hermit 'of St Michael besides Highgate', brings a case in the court of star chamber against the vicar of St Pancras, complaining of assault by about forty 'riotours and evil disposed persons'. He had been in his garden with his servants 'in peasible maner there laboring' when the intruders arrived 'with billes and staffes and other wepons', broke down the pales of his garden and orchard, 'and unlawfully entered into the same'. One of the intruders, William Chadwike, struck Walterkin on the arm with a bill, 'and wold have murdered him except he had escaped ... into the stepill of his said hermitage'. The intruders then entered the hermitage and 'toke away two aulter clothes, a surplis, and a boke called a grail, with other stuff'.

In their defence Chadwike and the vicar claim it is all a vexatious slander. The incident happened 'in the Rogacion weke' when, 'according to the lawdabull custome of Englond', a procession had traditionally gone about the parish with prayers, at least until the hermit and his predecessors had set up the hermitage and 'stopped the procession way ... by meanes of making of pales and dikes'. On the day of the incident Chadwike had 'curtesely entretid' Walterkin to let them pass.

> And then the saide hermite having a grete clubbe by him in his garden & two other with him with clubbes ... sodenly toke the saide clubbes and strake at the saide Chadwike over the pale with the violence of whiche stroke the

saide hermite brake divers of his pales, and afterwards divers of the saide parishe pulled downe serten pales for the saide parishe to passe with theire procession and so departed peasibly that wey ...[25]

Other problems are more easily resolved.

1748 For a sash pane at Mr Upjohn's the boys broke on Holy Thursday ... 10d (St Anne & St Agnes, Aldersgate)

1784 Paid for the boys breaking two panes of glass at perambulation ... 5s (St Martin, Leicester)[26]

Apart from confirming the bounds, perambulations also promote community spirit and provide an opportunity to give food and drink to poorer members of the parish, as George Herbert explains in *The Countrey Parson* (1652).

The countrey parson is a lover of old customes, if they be good, and harm-lesse ... Particularly, he loves Procession, and maintains it, because there are contained therein four manifest advantages. First, a blessing of God for the fruits of the field. Secondly, justice in the preservation of bounds. Thirdly, charity in loving walking, and neighbourly accompanying one another, with reconciling of differences at that time, if there be any. Fourthly, mercy in releeving the poor by a liberal distribution and largesse, which at that time is or ought to be used. Wherefore he exacts of all to be present at the perambulation, and those that withdraw, and sever themselves from it, he mislikes, and reproves as uncharitable, and unneighbourly ...[27]

Churchwardens' accounts show that, as the decades pass, the provision of food and drink tends to become increasingly liberal.

1560 For bread and drink for the parishioners that went the circuit the Tuesday in the Rogation-week ... 3s 4d | 1595 For bread, drink, cheese, fish, cream, and other victuals, when the worshipfull of the parish, and many others of the poorest sort, went the perambulacion to Kensington, in this hard and dere time of all things ... £7 10s (St Margaret, West-minster)

1679 *The charges of the perambulacon* ... For a surloine of beefe ... 14s 8d | For two legs of veale ... 13s | For 10 chickens ... 2s | For dressinge the meate ... 15s | For wine ... 18s | For bread & beere ... £2 7s 6d | For lemons and oringes ... 2s 6d (Leyton, Essex)

1684 Paid Mr Dowse for a possessioning dinner ... £4 7s | Mr Cox at the half-way house for meat, bread, beer and cakes ... £2 16s | Rob. Phipps for bread and beer at ye Black Jack and Shovell ... 4s 6d | For 2 bottles of Canary, which we had in Peckham lane ... 4s | To make ye boys drink when we came home ... 1s | More ye same day with ye gentlemen of ye parish at Mr Dowse's after dinner ... 8s 6d (St Nicholas, Deptford, Kent)

1725 Ascension Day, in ale and buns as usual ... 13s 4d (Liskeard, Cornwall)[28]

The costs can get out of hand. At Deptford in 1712 they spend nearly £15,
the wardens explaining slightly sheepishly in the accounts that 'a great number of the
parishioners' were present. Other wardens make the most of the opportunity.[29]

1667 The procession dinner for the parish at the Green Man was spent ...
£5 10s | And a bottle of sacke for me ... 2s (Leyton)[30]

At Windsor in 1801 they spend £3 13s on 'musick' for three days and £2 10s
on 36 gallons of beer distributed in the market place. The total bill is almost £20.[31]
As a result some parishes clamp down, Malvolio style.

1679 [Ordered] that for the future there be no cakes and ale eaten or drunk
on perambulation days, upon the parish account, although it hath been
usual or customary formerly. (St Giles without Cripplegate, vestry)[32]

Other parishes get quite cross when those occupying land and property along
the way fail to provide customary refreshment. In Essex in 1608 one John Owting
of Great Waltham is presented to the Church authorities because

he refuseth to make provision for the perambulation which hath bin done
time out of minde, and before time his wife and family have very disdain-
fully cast water upon the minister, and this time of perambulation the said
Owting did very desperately offer to strike our minister with his hedging bill
[on his] going to his house with the rest to require the customary refreshing.[33]

At Yapton, Sussex, in 1621 they present ten such offenders. One farm 'was wont
to give a dinner upon every Thursday in the Rogacion weeke to the greatest number
of the people of the parrishe, and now there is nothing given'. Several others
'missed to give a cake' and a Mrs Oglander 'missed to give 2 cakes and a cheese'.[34]

The vicar's account of a three day perambulation at Cuckfield in 1629 makes
no mention of refreshment, but spirits are sustained by the singing of psalms at
regular intervals.

Upon Monday morning May 11, meeting in the churchyard, and setting
ourselves in order processionwise, we began to sing the 24th Psalme and
so went over the stile at the south east end of the church yard singing
downe the lane ...

At the end of the Wednesday,

We came to Nashe gate againe where we began. Where thanking God for
his mercie and praising his holy name by singing the 67 Psalme we came
along through the park and lanes till we came to the churchyard where
setting ourselves in order as we did at the first we went singing lustily and
with a good courage towards the vicarage the remainder of the 85 Psalme
beginning at the 7 verse. | Blessed be God.[35]

[May 14th] **Ascension Day** or **Holy Thursday** (Thursday after Rogation Sunday)

Commemorating the ascent of Christ into heaven as witnessed by the apostles forty days after the resurrection (Acts 1:3-11).

As seen above, while not one of the Rogation days, Ascension Day is often used for perambulating the parish bounds, and it is otherwise marked as a feast. There may be a procession with torches and banners to mark Christ's entry into heaven: at Salisbury Cathedral it is headed (as on the preceding day) by a banner featuring a lion, now taking precedence over a sag-tailed dragon, emblematic of the triumph of Christ over the devil.[1]

Woodcut from the Sarum processional showing the lion banner and the dragon

1527 For bering of the stremer and ringing upon Assencon day ... 4d (St Giles, Reading)

1555 For garlandes for the quere on Holy Thursdaye ... 4d (St Michael, Cornhill)[2]

Before the Reformation the ascent to heaven may be embodied by raising the cross from the altar up to the roof of the church, and in some places while this is happening a representation of the devil is made to descend.

> Then comes the day when Christ ascended to his fathers seate,
> Which day they also celebrate, with store of drinke and meate. ...
> And after dinner all to church they come, and there attende.
> The blocke that on the aultar still, till then was seene to stande,
> Is drawne up hie above the roofe, by ropes, and force of hande:
> The priestes about it rounde do stand, and chaunt it to the skie,
> For all these mens religion great, in singing most doth lie.
> Then out of hande the dreadfull shape of Satan downe they throw,
> Oft times with fire burning bright, and dasht asunder tho,
> The boyes with greedie eyes do watch, and on him straight they fall,
> And beate him sore with rods, and breake him into peeces small.
>
> *The Popish Kingdome*[3]

> Upon Ascension day, they pull Christ up on hie with ropes above the clouds, by a vice devised in the roofe of the church, & they haule him up, as if they would pull him up to the gallowes: and there stande the poore priests, and looke so pitifully after their God, as a dogge for his dinner.
>
> *The Bee hive of the Romishe Churche*[4]

These accounts relate to practice on the Continent, but according to Abel Wantner, writing *circa* 1713, something similar was done at Gloucester Cathedral 'in the time of popery'. He notes that there are 'two round holes ... on each side the roofe of the presbiter* from whence (in those times aforesaid) they drew up with weyers every Assention day the representation of our blessed saviour Jesus Christ, in imitation of his ascending into heaven'.[5]

Whether many parish churches manage as much is not known.

Also on this day or the next the paschal candle, lit at Easter, is put out and removed to mark the fact that Christ, of whom it is a symbol, has departed the earth.[6]

After the Reformation the candle, processions and theatricals are no more but the day is still marked as a major festival.

The Ascension (*left*) and Pentecost (*right*), in the east window at East Harling, Norfolk, 15th century, in both cases showing the Virgin Mary with the apostles

[May 24th] **Whitsunday** or **Pentecost** (7th Sunday after Easter Day), and **Whitsun**†

Commemorating the descent of the holy spirit upon the disciples during the Jewish festival of Pentecost, as described in Acts chapter 2.

> And when the day of Pentecost was fully come, they were all with one accord in one place. | And suddenly there came a sound from heaven as of a rushing mighty wind, and it filled all the house where they were sitting. | And there appeared unto them cloven tongues like as of fire, and it sat upon each of them. | And they were all filled with the holy ghost, and began to speak with other tongues ...[1]

* *Presbytery*. Originally the part of a church, especially of a cathedral, reserved for the clergy. Often used to denote the eastern part of the chancel beyond the choir.
† 'Whitsun' generally being used to indicate either the weekend that includes Whitsunday or the week beginning on that day.

In the Middle Ages, and to some extent later, Pentecost is a common time for baptisms to be performed, and the name Whit probably derives from the wearing of white robes by those being baptised.[2]

> 1556 For watar for the font at Whit sonteye ... 1d (St Matthew, Friday Street)[3]

Before the Reformation a striking feature of divine service on this day in some churches is the appearance of the holy ghost or spirit. Usually it descends from the roof space in the form of a dove, the symbolism arising from the account of Christ's baptism in Mark 1:9-10.

> Jesus came from Nazareth of Galilee and was baptized of John in Jordan. | And straightway coming up out of the water, he saw the heavens opened, and the spirit like a dove descending upon him ...

According to *The Bee hive of the Romishe Churche*, the bird's appearance is noisily heralded.

> Upon Whitsunday ... they send downe a dove out of an owles nest, devised in the roofe of the church: but first they cast out rosin and gunpouder, with wilde fire, to make the children afraide, and that must needes be the holie ghost, which cometh with thunder and lightening.[4]

It seems likely that a model bird rather than a living one is usually deployed, although *The Popish Kingdome*'s account seems to suggest both.

> On Whitsunday, white pigeons tame, in strings from heaven flie,
> And one that framed is of wood, still hangeth in the skie.[5]

There are only a few references to the practice in church accounts.

> 1500 John Leeke lating doun the holy gost at divers times ... 12d | 1517 Rob Boston for the holy gost apering in the kirke roffe ... 2s (Louth)

> 1540 For wire to set up the holy goste ... 1d (St Mary on the Hill, Chester)[6]

William Lambarde, born in 1536, recalls something more elaborate at the old St Paul's Cathedral.

> The like toye I myselfe (beinge then a child) once saw in Poules churche at London, at a feast of Whitsontide, where the cominge downe of the holy gost was set forthe by a white pigeon, that was let to fly out of a hole, that yet is to be seene in the midst of the roofe of the great ile, and by a longe censer, which descendinge out of the same place almost to the verie grounde, was swinged up and downe at suche a lengthe, that it reached with the one swepe almost to the west gate of the churche, and with the other to the quire staires of the same, breathinge out over the whole churche and companie a most pleasant perfume of suche swete thinges as burned thearin ...[7]

A 1552 inventory for the cathedral includes 'A greate large sensoure all silver with manye windowes & battilments used to sense withall in the Penticoste weeke in [the] bodie of the chirche … at the procession time'. At an earlier date the *Liber Albus* (1419) records that on Monday in the same week the mayor, alderman and others attend a service at the cathedral and, as they stand before the rood screen and the hymn *Veni, Creator Spiritus* ['Come, creator spirit'] is sung, the figure of an angel (perhaps a boy or man dressed for the part) is lowered from above swinging a censer.[8]

Censing angel on spandrel, Salle, Norfolk

At a more prosaic level, Whitsun is often a time for renewing the rushes which cover the church floor.

1612 To goodwife Stepinge for 2 bundles of rushes at Whitsontide for the church ... 4d (Strood, Kent)[9]

In some places Whitsun is also the occasion for plays, pageants and processions. A notable instance of the last occurs at Leicester, where each year parishioners from other churches in the city process to St Margaret's, as John Nichols relates in his history of Leicestershire.

There used formerly to be a solemn procession from the collegiate church of St Mary de Castro to that of St Margaret, every Whit-Monday, in which the image of the Virgin Mary was carried under a canopy borne by four persons, with a minstrel, harp, or other musick, and twelve persons representing the twelve apostles, each of whom had the name of the apostle whom he represented written on parchment fixed on his bonnet; and fourteen persons bearing banners, with the virgins in the parish attending. When they came to St Margaret's, among other oblations there were two pairs of gloves, whereof one is said to be for God, the other for St Thomas of India. A similar procession was, on the same day, made from St Martin's church to St Margaret's, viz. the image of St Martin was carried thither, with twelve persons representing the apostles, and twelve banners, &c., but no musick, or any canopy carried over St Martin.[10]

Church accounts add some details.

1498 Paid at Whitsuntide for bread, ale, and flesh for the apostles and others ... 3s 4d | 1512 For mending a silk streamer which was torn on Whitson Monday ... 4d | 1516 Paid to the 12 apostles and the bearers of banners and other things done at Pentecost [etc] ... 5s 8d (St Mary)

1555 For the offeringe that lacked at Seint Margaret at Whitsonday &
drink ther for the virgins ... 12d | 1557 For 3 galons of ale & 4d in kakes
at Seint Margarets ... 19d | For the bearing of the cross & banners ...
14d (St Martin)[11]

As this illustrates, having been banned under Edward VI in 1547, religious
processions are revived under Queen Mary in the 1550s. However, they do not
long survive Elizabeth's ascent to the throne: at Leicester the last sign of the
Whitsun procession is in 1560, and in the following year the 'banner cloths' of
St Martin's are sold for a mere two shillings.[12]

More generally Whitsun is marked by secular feasting, including dancing, the
appearance of minstrels, and the occasional bear.

1563 To the minstrels for playing at Witsontide ... 5s (Marston, Oxon)

c. 1575 Ringers for ringinge at the Whitson dawnce ... 4d (St Edmund,
Salisbury)

1613 Paid men to fetch Shelderden with his bears at Whitsuntide, but
he refused to come because there was cocking* ... 1s 3d | Paid Mr
Horden to fetch Brock, who came with his bears and was paid 6s 8d
because Shelderden refused to come. (Congleton, Cheshire)[13]

Such attractions are of course an opportunity for raising funds.

1505 Received of the maidens gadering at Whitsontide by the tre† at the
church dore ... 2s 11d (St Lawrence, Reading)

1556 Received of John Feshpole & Thomas Maye that there cheldren
gatherd in the towne at Whitsontide & of Steven Thorneton that
he gatherd ye same yere being lorde of misse rule ... £5 19s 8d (Melton
Mowbray, Leics)

1593 Gathered in the Whitson weeke over & above all charges for the
childrens daunce ... 22s (St Thomas, Salisbury)[14]

In particular Whitsun is the most common time of year for holding a **church
ale**.

1558 For wheate & flower for Whitsunday at super ... 4s 6d | For a
barrell of bere ... 22d | For a pound of peper ... 20d | For mace ... 2d |
For mutton & veale ... 8s 8d | For a quarter of lambe ... 6d | To mother
Johnson for ale ... 8d (St Mary, Reading)

1580 We made of oure Whiteson ale ... £3 5s (Minchinhampton, Glos)[15]

Ales are also held more generally during May – in which Whitsun usually
falls – but they can occur through the year, including in Lent.

___

* i.e. a rival attraction, reducing his prospective takings.
† Perhaps some kind of bower.

1493 [Received] of a cherch ale made on Pentecost Sonday ... 12s 10d |
Of a cherch ale made in harvest ... 9s | Of a cherch ale made on
hallmesday [Hallowmas or All Saints' Day, 1 November] ... 11s 8d
(Cratfield, Suffolk)

1533 Received of the Maye ale, costes and charges alowed ... 31s 5d
(Wing, Bucks)

1555 To Sparrowe's wyff for making of the cake and of appulcake agenst
the ale kept in Lent ... 11d (Long Melford)

1595 Received of the profit of the Midsemer ale last past ... £6 3s 4d
(Great Marlow, Bucks)[16]

Neighbouring parishes often attend each other's ales in a reciprocal effort to
boost takings.[17]

1472 Paid at a cherche ale at Yoxford ... 6d | At a cherche ale at Blybur
[Blythburgh] ... 2s 6d | At a cherche ale at Hallyssword [Halesworth]
... 16d (Walberswick, Suffolk)[18]

At Mere, Wiltshire, two ales bring in more than £17 in 1559-1561, accounting
for some 80 per cent of all the money received by the churchwardens in the period.[19]

The food and drink may be served in or about the church or church house,
or in a private dwelling borrowed for the purpose.

1506 To Macrell for making clene of the church against the day of drinking
in the said church ... 4d | For flesh, spice and baking of pasteys against
the said drinking ... 2s 9d ob. | For ale at the same drinking ... 18d
(St Lawrence, Reading)

1534 To Joanna Langford for occupying of her howse to drink our ale ...
6d (Stratton, Cornwall)[20]

At Seale, Surrey, in 1592 the merriment lasts for five days, during which time
they pay musicians and a drummer and consume nine barrels of beer. Further
payments are made for 'spice and frutte', for 'gunne powder', and 'to Goodman
Shrubbs wife for helpinge all the time'.[21]

Among the games played at such gatherings is pigeon-holes, which seems to
involve rolling balls under arches which resemble the holes in pigeon lofts or dovecotes.

1621 Paid Goodwife Ansell for the pigeon holes ... 1s 6d | 1624 Cleared
by pigeon holes ... £4 19s (Brentford, Middlesex)

1622 For making a new paire of pigeing-holes ... 2s 6d (Chiswick,
Middlesex)[22]

Often proceedings are presided over by a king and called a King Ale. At St
Ives, Cornwall, there are a 'kinge and quene of the somer game', while at Mere,
Wiltshire, there is a Cuckow or Cuckoo King.[23]

The merriness of ales naturally upsets puritans and reformers, and in his *Anatomie of Abuses* (1583) Philip Stubbes articulates their moral view.

> The church-wardens ... provide half a score or twenty quarters of malt ... which malt being made into very strong ale or beere, it is set to sale, either in the church or some other place ... | In this kinde of practise, they continue ... swilling and gulling, night and day, till they be as drunke as apes, and as blockish as beasts. ... | If all be true which they say ... they repair their churches and chappels with it, they buy bookes for service, cuppes for the celebration of the sacrament, surplesses for Sir John, and such other necessaries. ... These be their excuses ... But if they daunce thus in a net, no doubt they will be espied.[24]

Richard Carew, writing of Cornwall *circa* 1600, paints a more indulgent picture and provides some further details.

> For the church-ale, two young men of the parish are yerely chosen by their last foregoers to be wardens, who, deviding the task, make collection among the parishioners of whatsoever provision it pleaseth them voluntarily to bestow. This they employ in brewing, baking, and other acates [delicacies] against Whitsontide; upon which holydayes, the neighbours meet at the church house, and there merrily feed on their owne victuals, contributing some petty portion to the stock, which, by many smalls, groweth to a meetly greatness ... Besides, the neighbour parishes at those times lovingly visit one another, and this way frankly spend their money together. The afternoones are consumed in such exercises as olde and yong folke (having leisure) do accustomably weare out the time withall.
>
> When the feast is ended, the wardens yeeld in their accounts to the parishioners, and such money as exceedeth the disbursments is laid up in store, to defray any extraordinary charges arising in the parish, or imposed on them for the good of the countrey, or the princes service. Neither of which commonly gripe* so much, but that somewhat still remaineth to cover the purses bottome.[25]

He adds with regret that 'of late times, many ministers have by their ernest invectives ... suppressed the church-ales as licentious', and while they continue in some places they become increasingly rare over the following decades. William Prynne, writing in 1646, laments their decline.

> I finde that in some places the people have bin perswaded to leave them off, in other places they have bin put down by the judges and justices, so that now there are very few of them left: but yet I finde that by church-ales heretofore, many poore parishes have cast their bells, repaired their

---

* Grip, grasp.

The Cotswold Games, an elaborate example of summer festivities, held in Whitsun week each year. Woodcut, 1636.

towers, beautified their churches, and raised stocks for the poore; and not by the sins of the people (as some humourists* have said) but by the benevolence of people at their honest and harmlesse sports and pastimes, at which there hath not bin observed so much disorder, as is commonly at fairs and markets.[26]

A similar note is struck by John Aubrey, writing *circa* 1670 of Wiltshire two generations earlier.

There were no rates for the poore even in my grandfather's daies: but for Kington St Michael (no small parish) the church ale at Whitsuntide did their businesse. In every parish is, or was, a church howse, to which belonged spits, crocks, &c., utensils for dressing provision. Here the howsekeepers met, and were merry and gave their charitie: the young people came there too, and had dancing, bowling, shooting at buttes, &c., the ancients sitting gravely by, and looking on. All things were civil and without scandal.[27]

* Those affected by humours and so subject to quirks or obsessions.

[May 31st] Trinity Sunday (1st Sunday after Whitsunday)

Celebrated as a festival in honour of the Holy Trinity of the Father, the Son and the Holy Ghost or Spirit. In Christian theology they are seen as one God existing in three persons with one substance.[1]

The Trinity,
Flemish,
c. 1469

[June 4th] Corpus Christi (Thursday after Trinity Sunday)

Feast commemorating the institution of the sacrament of the eucharist, *Corpus Christi* being Latin for 'the body of Christ'.

Until the Reformation the main feature of the festival is a procession in which the pyx, containing the consecrated bread or host, is carried under a canopy around the parish. Preparations for the day may include construction work.

> 1472-74 For ale to the carpenter that made the crosse ... 1d | To the plummer for the leding of the crosse ... 2s 6d (St Andrew Hubbard)

> 1547 For makinge the canapie over the sacrament upon Corpus Christi day, and pins and tackes to the same ... 10d (Ludlow)[1]

In London, St Margaret Pattens has 'a canapie serving for Corpus Christi day, to bere in the procession over the sacrament, with 4 staves and angelles concerning to the same', while St Peter, Cornhill, has 'a pall of red damaske for the sacrament upon Corpus Christi day, fringed about with Venice golde and red silke, and 4 painted staves thereto belonging'.[2]

During the procession torches are carried and the church bells ring out.

> 1457 To the ringers for ringing on the feast of Corpus Christi while the procession went round the town ... 1d (Yeovil, Somerset)[3]

ABOVE Corpus Christi procession, from the Spinola Hours, Flemish, *c.* 1510. The inscription on the canopy refers to the transformation of the host (*panis angelorum*, the bread of angels) into *cibus viatorum*, the food of pilgrims.

RIGHT Popish procession, perhaps at Corpus Christi, from the 1570 edition of John Foxe's Book of Martyrs.

In Coventry 'all the bretheren and sisteren' of the Guild of Corpus Christi are required to 'be clad in livery ... and ... carry 8 torches around the body of Christ, when it is borne through the town'. In addition the guild has 'three waxes, a cross, with a spear, and four banners, for the procession'.[4]

Parishioners taking part may be joined by additional clergy and singers hired for the day.

> 1534 To 8 priests to a procession on Corpus Christi day ... 2s 8d | To
> 2 clerks ... 8d | To the children that singeth ... 8d | To children to
> bear 4 candlesticks, 2 sensers and the ship ... 8d | For bearing of the
> cross ... 4d (St Nicholas, Bristol)[5]

At St Mary at Hill, London, the host is attended by its own bell and by up to eight men bearing torches, while four further bells accompany the canopy. The parish's precious copes are carried and three men bear crosses garlanded with flowers. Further garlands are provided for the choir, for 'Mr Doctor and the parish priest', and for the rest of those taking part.[6]

Roses are often used in the garlands, at least in London.

> 1492 Paid on Corpus Cristi day for garlandes of roses & of wodroffe for
> the quire & the torche berers ... 13d (St Andrew Hubbard)

> 1505 For rosis to make garlonds for them that bare torches ... 3d (All
> Hallows Staining)[7]

Corpus Christi is also a common occasion for putting on pageants and plays. At a parish level these are likely to be fairly modest.

> 1492 In cost of bread and ale on Corpus Christi day to the players ... 8d |
> 1516 For 4 ratilbagges and visers bought for the players ... 20d | 1528
> For painting cloth for the players, and making their tunics ... and for
> making staves for them, and crests upon their heads ... 9s 9d | 1537
> For a pair of silk garments for King Herod ... 1d | 1555 For a pair of
> gloves for him that played God Almighty ... 2d (Ashburton, Devon)[8]

In some cases scenes are acted out or tableaux are presented on moveable stages or platforms called 'pageants'. These are often mounted on carts and sometimes incorporate machinery related to the particular scene or tableau. In 1514 two men are brought before the court of star chamber for vandalism in Bungay 'on the Fridaye at night next after Corpus Christi day', at which time they 'brake and threw down five pagents' belonging to the inhabitants, 'that is to say heven pagent, the pagent of all the world, Paradis pagent, Bethelem pagent, & helle pagent, the which wer ever wont tofore to be caryed abowt the said town upon the said daye in the honor of the blessed sacrement'.[9]

June 23rd and 24th **Midsummer Eve** and **Midsummer Day, or the Nativity of St John the Baptist**

> Then doth the joyfull feast of John the Baptist take his turne,
> When bonfiers great with loftie flame, in every towne do burne:
> And yong men round about with maides, do daunce in every streete ...
>
> *The Popish Kingdome*[1]

Midsummer is a time of decorating churches with greenery, although this is more often recorded in urban parishes, where it is liable to be paid for, rather than in rural ones, where summer's abundance is all around. In addition new rushes and straw may be brought in for the floor and pews.

> 1491 At midsomer for birche & flowers for the churche & the dore ... 6d (St Andrew Hubbard)

> 1505 For mowing of grasse for the chirch agenst midsomer with drinke to the carters of the same ... 4d (Bishop's Stortford)[2]

As at other festivals earlier in summer, mock kings and queens or lords and ladies may preside. At Wootton, Oxfordshire, in 1584 the churchwardens are presented to the authorities for failing to report 'evell rule done in the churche by the lord and the ladie on Midsomer day'. Their agreeable response is that 'there was no lord or ladie this yeare in Wootton parishe, but on Midsomer daye laste at evening prayer the youthe were sumwhat merrie together in crowning of lordes'.[3]

Away from the church it is a time of bonfires, those in London being famously described by John Stow, writing towards the end of the 16th century.

> In the months of June and July, on the vigils [eves] of festival dayes, and on the same festival dayes in the evenings after the sunne setting, there were usually made bonefiers in the streetes, every man bestowing wood or labour towards them: the wealthier sort also before their doores neare to the said bonefiers, would set out tables on the vigils, furnished with sweete breade, and good drinke, and on the festival dayes with meates and drinks plentifully, whereunto they would invite their neighbours and passengers [passers by] also to sit, and be merrie with them in great familiaritie, praising God for his benefites bestowed on them.[4]

Roger Martyn, born *circa* 1525, notes similar hospitality in describing Long Melford as it was in his youth.

> On St James's even [24th July] there was a bonefire, and a tub of ale and bread then given to the poor, and before my doore there was made three other bonefires, viz. on Midsummer even, on the even of St Peter and St Paul [28th June], when they had the like drinkings, and on St Thomas's even* ...

---

* Either 2nd July (eve of the feast of St Thomas the Apostle) or 6th July (eve of the translation of St Thomas Becket).

And in all these bonefires, some of the friends and more civil poor neighbours were called in, and sat at the board with my grandfather, who had at the lighting of the bonefires wax tapers with balls of wax, yellow and green, set up all the breadth of the hall, lighted then and burning there before the image of St John the Baptist, and after they were put out, a watch candle was lighted, and set in the midst of the said hall upon the pavement, burning all night.[5]

Writing in 1725 Henry Bourne records a similar spirit still in evidence.

On the eve of St John the Baptist, commonly called Midsummer-Eve, it is usual in the most of country places, also here and there in towns and cities, for both old and young to meet together, and be merry over a large fire, which is made in the open street. Over this they frequently leap and play at various games, such as running, wrestling, dancing, &c. But this is generally the exercise of the younger sort; for the old ones, for the most part, sit by as spectators, and enjoy themselves and their bottle. And thus they spend the time till mid-night, and sometimes till cock-crow.[6]

¶ After Midsummer the ritual year sees a long lull during which the main concern, in rural parishes at least, is the gathering in of harvest. Fairs are held, providing informal entertainment, but in churches the period is punctuated by only relatively minor festivals.

August 1st **Lammas**

From the Anglo-Saxon *hlaf-maesse*, loaf mass. Traditionally the day on which loaves of bread made with the first ripe corn of the year – the 'first fruits' – are consecrated at mass.

> 1557 For garlondes and flowers on Lammas
> daye ... 2s 6d (St Peter, Cheapside)[1]

August 15th **Assumption of the Virgin Mary**

Feast celebrating the immaculate assumption of the body and soul of the Virgin Mary into heaven.

> 1525 For ringing ... on our lady day the
> Assumpcion [etc] ... 12d (St Mary at Hill)

> 1539 On the assumption of our lady for a
> taper of 2½ lb. in the rood loft ... 1s 8d
> (St Laurence Pountney)[1]

A natural casualty of the Reformation, it is omitted from the 1549 Book of Common Prayer.

The Assumption, Nottingham school alabaster, 15th century

Harvest scenes.
UPPER
Printed on cotton,
c. 1805.
LOWER
Woodcut, from a ballad of 1630.

¶ There is no fixed service of thanksgiving for **harvest** until one is introduced by West country vicars in the 19th century, but less formal celebrations are commonly held. In 1622 the parson of Rustington, Sussex, is presented 'for not making our drincking at harvest last past for the parishioners ... which is a custome in our parrishe'. According to Henry Bourne, writing a century later,

> When the fruits of the earth are gather'd in ... it is common, in the most of country places, to provide a plentiful supper for the harvest-men, and the servants of the family, which is called a Harvest-Supper ... At this the servant and his master are alike, and every thing is done with an equal freedom. They sit at the same table, and converse freely together, and spend the remaining part of the night in dancing, singing, &c. without any difference or distinction.[1]

September 29th **Michaelmas**, or **the Feast of St Michael the Archangel**

Not generally marked in a notable way in parish churches, but an important date in the secular calendar, falling half-way through the old style year (25th March, Lady Day, being its start).[1]

October 31st **Hallows' Eve**

November 1st **All Hallows' Day**, also known as **Hallowmas** or **All Saints' Day**

Feast in honour of all the saints, *hallow* being a holy personage, from Old English *halga*.

November 2nd **All Souls' Day**

Commemoration of the souls of the faithful departed.

While formally separate, All Hallows and All Souls tend to merge into a single festival for the dead, held at an appropriately dark time of the year. While the saints are duly honoured, the main focus is on remembering the parish dead, with All Hallows, and in particular its evening, serving as the eve or vigil of All Souls.

In old times a bellman, perhaps arrayed in black, may perambulate the parish, ringing to remind people to pray for those in purgatory.[1]

> 1539 To ye bellman for All Sowles ... 1d | 1540 To ye bellman for All Cristen Sowles ... 1d (Bungay)[2]

It is also common practice to ring the church's main bells for the souls of the dead, necessary preparations being made in advance.

> 1530 To Frenche for 2 new bell ropes against Halontide ... 3s 2d (Lydd, Kent)

> 1540 To Ryc Alberd & his brother for mending of ye belles ageyns Hallomes ... 12d (All Saints, Tilney, Norfolk)

> 1556 [Received] of the maids upon All Hallow day at nighte towards the bell roops ... 2d (Stanford, Berks)[3]

The main ringing is usually on the night of All Hallows, leading into the morning of All Souls, and those involved naturally need warmth, refreshment and light.

> 1528 For a quarter of coles against All Hallowtide ... 4d (St Alphage, London Wall)

> 1549 For a chese for ye ringers at Halowmes night ... 4d (North Elmham, Norfolk)

> 1557 For candles of Alhalowen night for the church ... 3d (St John the Baptist, Bristol)[4]

At Holy Trinity, Coventry, the duties of the first deacon include going 'on All Halowe day at even among ye pepell' to 'geder money off them for ye ringars that ring for all Cristen solls'. At Hagworthingham, Lincolnshire, Robert Neve gives 10 shillings in 1533

> upon this condition, that the churchwardens ... shall buy and give yearly to the ringers upon the even of All Saints yearly 6 gallons of ale, or else to brue or cause to be brued one strike of malt yearly and the profit thereof to be all to the ringers the same night ...[5]

The following may indicate enthusiasm in the ringing.

1481 For the mending of candelstickes standing before the grete crosse the whiche were broken with ringing on All Sowles night ... 2d (St Edmund, Salisbury)[6]

Meanwhile a hearse, a frame set about corpses at funerals and holding tapers and candles, may be erected and rites performed as for an individual corpse.

1526 For ye light for ye herse for Sowlemesse Day & ye even ... 4d (Bungay)

1533 For All Halowes dirge ... 20d (Wing, Bucks)[7]

Mass for All Souls, including a hearse and draped coffin,
from the Belles Heures of Jean de France, duc de Berry, *c.* 1405

It is also customary in some parishes for money to be given to the poor.

1534 Paide on Alsollen day to poore peopull in the churche ... 3s 4d (Lydd)[8]

After the Reformation All Souls' Day is removed from the Church calendar and the authorities seek to suppress the associated practices that they consider superstitious, in particular the ringing for the dead. The following is a typical enquiry made to that end.

> 1551 Item, whether the parson, vicar, or curate observe All Souls Day (as it was called), and use to say dirige, openly or secretly, for the dead and permit ringing of bells upon the same day, or night before, as it was used after the popish and superstitious order. (Bishop Hooper, interrogatories for Gloucester and Worcester dioceses)[9]

In the same vein, in 1569 the Bishop of Norwich orders that

> upon All Saintes daye and other like times, ther be no ringing of belles after evening prayer, or any other superstitious ceremony used, to the maintenaunce of poperie, or praying for the dead, and that if any such shalbe henceforth used, the same with the names of such as shall offende therein, to be presented to the ordinary.[10]

Those detected find themselves in trouble.

> 1564 Roberte Stringfellowe to appere ... for suspicious ringing on All Soules Day at night last and to declare his felloes that rong with him that night. (Kirkby Overblow, Yorks)

> 1565 Spent at Lecester being somoned for ringing of All Hallodaye at night ... 10d (Melton Mowbray, Leics)[11]

The wish to commemorate the dead, and to speed the progress of their souls through purgatory, lingers nonetheless. One puritan, describing the state of the Church in England *circa* 1566, includes among old ways that persist 'the tolling of bells at funerals and on the vigils of saints, and especially on that of the feast of All Saints, when it continues during the whole night'. When the men of Wanstrow, Somerset, are forbidden to ring on All Hallows in 1568, some of the parish women do it instead, their cunning defence being that as females they are 'lawless', or outside the law. In the same year Thomas Buck is charged in a court in York that

> upon Allhallowes night last past he did go with one Thomas Shepperd, under sextone of Rippon, to the most parte of the house[s] of Rippon, and begged money and candels for suche personnes as did that night ringe the bells of Rippon. Suche money, candels, and other thinges as they got, they brought to the said ringers, and there drunke ayle in the said churche with parte of the money they got, and the reste they and the said ringers did bestow of good chere abrode in the towne the same night.[12]

A decade later the people of Weaverham, Cheshire will still 'not be staied from ringinge the bells on All Saints daie'.[13]

November 5th **Gunpowder Treason**

After the failed attempt by 'malignant and devilish papists' to blow up parliament in 1605 a law is passed ordering everyone to attend church on 5th November each year, when a prayer of thanksgiving 'for this most happy deliverance' is to be read. It also becomes customary to ring church bells to celebrate the day.[1]

> 1606 To the ringers the 5th daie of November ... 3s 4d | For one gallan of ale to the ringers the same daie ... 6d (St Oswald, Durham)
>
> 1613 For candles and drink for the ringers, Nov. 5 ... 1s 4d (Wimborne Minster, Dorset)[2]

There may also be bonfires and general festivity.

> 1647 5 November for ringing [etc] ... 2s 7d | 5 November for a man to wach in the church yard for keping the boyes from brecking the glas windes ... 8d (St Clement, Ipswich)
>
> 1684 Nov. 5th. For meat and beere for the ringers ... 10s | For a seam of wood for the bunfire ... 1s | To Mrs Yealdom for candles ... 6d (Tavistock, Devon)
>
> 1715 To Mr Floyd for half a hogshead of beare on Gunpowder Treason Day ... £1 3s 8d (Cranborne, Dorset)[3]

November 17th **Accession day of Queen Elizabeth**

Between 1568 and 1602 the day is marked with widespread celebration, particularly in London. It is known as 'the queen's day' or 'the queen's night', and often in error as the 'coronation' day. It is also coincidentally the feast day of St Hugh.[1]

> 1575 For bred, drinck and cheese for ringing of St Hewes daye in rejoysing of the quenes prosperous range ... 2s 8d (Bishop's Stortford)
>
> 1577 To the ringers upon the coronatione day and for a carte loode of wood to make a bonefire ... 4s 9d (Worfield, Shropshire)
>
> 1594 For a candle on the coronation day of our gracious queen. God long continue her in health and peace to raigne over us. So be it, Amen ... 1d (Great Wigston, Leics)
>
> 1600 For wine and suger, bread and chease, beare and cakes, spent on ye crownuation night at ye church, on ye parish and ringers ... 9s (St Stephen, Walbrook)[2]

[November 29th] **Advent Sunday** (nearest Sunday to November 30th, the feast of St Andrew)

The start of the ecclesiastical year, heralding as it does the coming (Latin *adventus*) of Christ. In earlier centuries Advent, running from this day until the start of Christmas Day, is kept as a fast like Lent, albeit with less strictness.[1]

December 6th **St Nicholas**

Before the Reformation the feast of St Nicholas, the patron saint of children, is marked in cathedrals and some parish churches by the election of one of the choristers as a boy bishop. His rule usually runs until the evening of 28th December, Holy Innocents' Day, which commemorates Herod's ordering of the slaughter of young children in the hope that the infant Christ would be among their number.

The putting of children first during this period serves as an apt riposte to Herod's action. The young bishop is assisted by other church boys as his clergy, and to complete the role reversal adult clergy sometimes perform the menial tasks usually undertaken by the boys.

In a tract published in 1649 John Gregory details the by then obsolete custom, and in particular its enactment at Salisbury Cathedral.

> The *Episcopus Choristarum* was a chorister bishop chosen by his fellow children upon St Nicholas daie. ... From this daie till Innocents daie at night [he] was to bear the name, and hold up the state of a bishop, answerably habited with a crosier or pastoral-staff in his hand, and a miter upon his head ... The rest of his fellows from the same time being, were to take upon them the style and counterfaict [counterfeit] of prebends* ...
>
> Upon the eve to Innocents Daie, the chorister bishop was to go in solemn procession with his fellows *ad altare Sanctae Trinitatis et omnium Sanctorum* [to the altars of Holy Trinity and All Saints] *in capis, et cereis ardentibus in manibus*, in their copes, and burning tapers in their hands, the bishop beginning, and the other boyes following.

While the other boys sing, the bishop 'fumeth the altar first, and then the image of the Holie Trinitie'. Afterwards,

> The bishop taketh his seat, and the rest of the children dispose of them-selves upon each side of the quire, upon the uppermost ascent, the canons resident bearing the incense and the book, and the petit canons the tapers, according to the rubrick.† ...
>
> And all this was done with that solemnitie of celebration ... that no man whatsoever, under the pain of Anathema,‡ should interrupt or press upon these children at the procession spoken of before, or in anie other

---

* Cathedral canons. Originally a 'prebend' was land which provided funds to pay the stipend of a canon but in time the word came to be used both for the tenure of such a benefice and for the office holder.
† Canons resident were the senior canons who lived within the cathedral close or precinct. Petit or petty canons were, as the name suggests, of secondary rank. It is not clear whether it was the real canons or the boy substitutes who carried out the tasks described.
‡ The great curse of the Church, cutting off a person from communion and formally handing him over to Satan.

part of their service in anie waies, but to suffer them quietly to perform and execute what it concern'd them to do.

And the part was acted yet more earnestly, for Molanus* saith, that this bishop in some places did ... receive rents, capons,† &c. ... And it seemeth by the statute of Sarum, that he held a kinde of visitation ... More than all this, Molanus telleth of a chorister bishop in the church of Cambrai, who disposeth of a prebend which fell void in his month ...

In case the chorister bishop died within the month, his exequies were solemnized with an answerable glorious pomp and sadness. He was buried (as all other bishops) in all his ornaments ...

The custom doth verie much appear to have taken its rise from the Romish, but how anciently, I must confess, I know not. ...

It seemeth indeed to suit well ... that the memories of the young Innocents should be kept in store by a holiedaie of children ...[1]

Gregory's researches had been prompted by his coming across 'a monument in stone' in the cathedral 'of a little boye habited all in episcopal robes, a miter upon his head, a crosier in his hand, and the rest accordingly'. Having been obscured 'under the seats near the pulpit' it had lately been moved 'to the north part of the nave, where now it lieth betwixt the pillars, covered over with a box of wood, not without a general imputation of raritie and reverence, it seeming almost impossible to everie one, that either a bishop could be so small in person, or a childe so great in clothes'.[2]

There is in fact considerable doubt as to whether the monument is that of a boy bishop, not least because diminutive effigies sometimes served to indicate not that the dead person was small but that their heart alone was buried beneath. Sadly there is also reason to doubt the following agreeable story related by John Aubrey.

The monument
in question

The tradition of ye choristers, and those that show the church is, that this childe-bishop being melancholy, the children of ye choire did tickle him to make him merry, but they did so overdo it that they tickled him to death: and dying in his office and honour, here was this little monument made for him, with the episcopal ornaments, e.g. mitre, crosse, and cope.[3]

---

* Joannes Molanus (1533-1585), Catholic theologian.
† Often used for payment in kind of rent.

Away from Salisbury, the custom is recorded as early as *circa* 1200 at St Paul's in London and around 1220 at York Minster. At Heton, near Newcastle, in 1299 a boy bishop says vespers before Edward I, then on his way to Scotland, and the king gives the considerable sum of 40 shillings to the boy and his companions.[4]

At York in 1367 it is ordered that the boy selected as bishop should be the one who has served longest in the church and is most useful, provided that he is '*corpore formosus*' (of body finely formed). In 1390 it is added that he should have a good voice. Six years later the boy so qualified is one John de Cave, and the cathedral accounts give a detailed picture of his tenure, including a great supper held on the eve of Innocents' Day.

> Bread ... 7d | Lord's bread ... 4d | Ale ... 21d | Veal and mutton ... 9d ob. | Sausages ... 4d | Two ducks ... 4d | Twelve chickens ... 2s 6d | Eight woodcocks and one plover ... 2s 2d | Three dozen and ten field-fares ... 19d | Small birds ... 3d | Wine ... 2s 3d | Spices ... 11d | Sixty wardens [pears] ... 5d ob. | Honey ... 2d ob. | Mustard ... 1d | Flour ... 2d | Two pounds of candles ... 2d ob. | Fuel ... 1d. ob. | To the cook ... 6d

Over the following weeks the bishop pays a series of visits to monasteries and noble households in the surrounding area accompanied by a servant, a 'seneschal' or steward, and four singers. They visit Bridlington, Fountains Abbey and Leeds, among other places, dining and collecting donations along the way.[5]

The custom spreads from cathedrals to a number of parishes. At St Nicholas, Bristol, a list of duties drawn up in 1481 states that 'the clerke and the suffrigan [are] to dresse uppe the bisshopes sete ageniste Seinte Nicholas daye'. On 5th December the mayor and corporation attend evensong. They return next day for mass and to hear the boy bishop's sermon and receive his blessing. After dinner they receive him at the guildhall, where he and his fellows sing and are treated with bread and wine, and all then return to the church to attend the bishop's evensong.[6]

There is more scattered evidence in the inventories of many churches, mainly but not always in large cities.

1470 A miter for Seint Nicholas of white damaske embrodred with bells of gold. (St Margaret Pattens)

1473 A litell chesebyll for Seint Nicholas bisschop. (St Mary, Sandwich, Kent)

c. 1500 A cope for the boy that is the bishope paned yelow & blew. (St Peter Mancroft, Norwich)[7]

There is also occasional evidence in parish accounts.

1500 To the child bishop at Cristenmes for 1 paire cloffs [gloves] ... 1d | 1505 For making the child bishop see* ... 6d | 1506 Paid the child bishop at Cristenmes ... 6d (Louth)

---

* Presumably in the sense of a bishop's throne or seat of authority.

1522 For the bishoppes dinner and his company on Saint Nicolas day ...
2s 8d | To old John Clerke for his labor in going with the bishoppe ...
12d (Lambeth)

1530-32 Receved on Saint Nicolas even with the bischope ... 4s 10d (St
Andrew, Lewes, Sussex)

1535 Unto the goodman Chese, broiderer, for making of a new miter for
the bishop against Saint Nicholas night ... 2s 8d (All Hallows Staining)[8]

In 1541 the custom is banned by royal decree.

Whereas heretofore diverse and many superstitious and childishe observations have been used, and yet to this day are observed and kept in many
and sondry parties of this realm, as upon Sainte Nicholas, Sainte Catherine,
Sainte Clement, the Holy Innocentes, and such like, children be strangelye
decked and appareled to counterfaite priestes, bishops, and women, and so
ledde with songes and daunces from house to house, blessing the people,
and gatheringe of monye, and boyes do singe masse, and preache in the
pulpit, with suche other unfittinge and inconvenient usages, rather to
the derision than to any true glory of God, or honour of his saints; the king's
majestie therefore minding nothing so moche, as to avaunce the true glorye
of God without vaine superstition, willeth and commaundeth, that from
henceforth all suche superstitions be loste and cleerlye extinguished
throughowte all this his realmes and dominions, forasmoche as the same
do resemble rather the unlawfull superstition of gentilitie,* than the pure
and sincere religion of Christe.[9]

Like other old customs it is revived under Queen Mary, as Henry Machyn
records in his diary for 1556.

The 5 day of December was Sant Necolas even, and Sant Necolas went
abroad in most part in London singing after the old fassion, and was reseived
with many good pepulle into ther howses, and had muche good chere as
ever they had, in many places.[10]

Not everywhere, however.

Gertrude Crokehey dwelling at St Katherines by the Tower of London, and
being then in her husbandes house, it happened in the yeare 1556 that the
popes childish St Nicholas went about the parish, whiche she understanding,
shut her dore against him, not suffering him to enter into her house.
    Then Doctor Mallet hearing thereof, and being then master of the said
St Katherines, the next daye came to her with twenty at his taile, thinking
belike to fray [frighten] her, and asked why she woulde not the night before
let in St Nicholas and receave his blessing, &c. To whom she answered

* i.e. of the Gentiles or heathens.

thus, 'Sir, I knowe no St Nicholas (said she) that came hither.' 'Yes,' quoth Mallet, 'here was one that represented St Nicholas.' 'Indeede sir (said she), here was one that was my neighbours childe, but not St Nicholas, for St Nicholas is in heaven. I was afraide of them that came with him to have had my purse cut by them, for I have hearde of men robbed by St Nicholas clerkes,' &c. So Mallet perceiving that nothing could be gotten at her handes, went his way as he came, and she for that time so escaped.

John Foxe, *Actes and Monuments*, 1583[11]

After the accession of Elizabeth the custom falls away again, this time for good.

Nativity scene, east window, East Harling, Norfolk, 15th century

December 25th **Christmas Day**

In comparison with the prolonged and elaborate commemoration of Christ's death at Easter, the parish celebration of his birth at Christmas is relatively simple. The day is distinguished by having three masses performed, one at midnight, one at daybreak, and one in the morning. According to Aquinas this is 'on account of Christ's threefold nativity'. First 'his eternal birth, which is hidden in our regard, and therefore one mass is sung in the night'. Second 'his nativity in time, and spiritual birth, whereby Christ rises *as the day-star in our hearts* (2 Peter 1:19), and on this account the mass is sung at dawn'. Finally, his 'temporal and bodily birth ... and on that account the third mass is sung in broad daylight'.

Meanwhile, in the depths of midwinter, the church is ablaze with lights symbolic of the triumph of new life over darkness.

> 1505 For a dossen of candell to set about the churche upon Cristenmasday in the morning ... 12d (St Margaret, Westminster)

> 1548 For 2 pound of tallow candells on Cristmas night ... 4d (Wandsworth)[1]

Before the Reformation particular attention is paid to the rood and its loft.

> 1516 For making of the high cross light agen Crismas ... 1s 5d (Banwell, Somerset)

> 1544 23 pounds of wax for the rood loft against Christmas ... 2s 5d (Rye, Sussex)[2]

Holly may be placed before the central figure of Christ upon the cross, emblematic of the belief that from his sacrifice springs life eternal. At Reading small candles are set in the bush in the manner of a modern Christmas tree.[3]

> 1506 Paid Macrell for an holy bush before the rode ... 2d | For sysis [sizes] to the holy bush at Christmas ... 9d (St Lawrence, Reading)

> 1532 For holly for the rood against Cristmas ... 2d (St Nicholas, Bristol)[4]

In some churches the star of Bethlehem is represented.

> 1461 To John Benet for the stars to hang before ye rode at Crismas ... 20d (Thame)

> 1559 For a quarte of oyell for to burne in the star on Christmas daye in the morninge ... 10d | For a line to hange the star by ... 4d (St Mary Redcliffe, Bristol)

> 1608 Nov. 28th. To a tinker for makinge the candlesticks for the star and nailing them on ... 12d | For a cord for the star ... 6d | For a pully with iron staples & hooke ... 9d | For a glass lanthorne for the star ... 7s | To Rafe Davies joiner for makinge the star ... 7s | To Nicho. Hallowood for paintinge the star ... 4s (Holy Trinity, Chester)[5]

At St Mary on the Hill, Chester, the moon appears as well and there is a special decoration made of holly and referred to as 'the holyn'.

A Christmas congregation by Adelaide Claxton (1858-1905), with greenery around the pillars and numbers on the pews

1540 Nails & timber to make the mone undur the holyn ... 4d | For making a skaffolde to take downe the mone ... 2d | 1556 For a man for putting up of the rope to the hollen ... 1d | 1557 For making of a star ... 20d | For the penting & gilding of the same star ... 20d | For wier to the star ... 2d ob. | For a rope to the star ... 9d | For a man to get the rope in to the pulley ... 2d | For candells for the star and the holyn ... 3s[6]

More generally greenery is placed around churches.

1465 We gave to children to gadr ivy ... ob. (Thame)

1540 To the bellman for ive and holye at Christemas ... 2d (Ludlow)

1566 To Goodman Plommer the 24th day of December for to buy holly for the churche and for packthred to binde up the same ... 9d (St Mary Woolnoth)[7]

At Holy Trinity, Coventry, one of the deacons 'shall hang ye wires over ye hy awter at Cristemas with ive and candels'.[8]

In the late 16th century John Stow notes similar decoration around London.

Against the feast of Christmas, every mans house, as also their parish churches, were decked with holme [holly], ivie, bayes, and what soever the season of the yeare aforded to be greene. The conduits and standardes in the streetes were likewise garnished ...[9]

Visiting church on 23rd December 1660 Samuel Pepys notes 'our pew all covered with rosemary and baize'.[10]

In addition new straw and rushes may be strewed in honour of the day.

1488 For strawing ye quire at Crismase ... ob. (Thame)

1583 For 2 bundles of rushes at the birth of Christe ... 4d (Allhallows, Hoo, Kent)[11]

In some places frankincense is, appropriately, burnt.

1556 For haulf a pound of frankinsenc bought againste Crismas ... 4d (Eltham, Kent)

1579 Coles and fronkinsence againste Christmas ... 14d (St Edmund, Salisbury)[12]

And bells are rung.

1554-58 For candilles for the ringers on Cristmas even ... 5d (Lambeth)

1666 For the ringinge of Christmas Day ... 2s (Manchester)[13]

The ringing may get out of hand. At Graffham, Sussex, in 1626 a number of servants are presented 'for that they upon Christs birth day last past almost all the night following rung the bells in our church very disorderly so that we could not sleep quietly in our beds'.[14]

At Dewsbury, Yorkshire, the custom is

to toll what is known as the Devil's Knell immediately after midnight every Christmas morning. Immediately the clock has struck midnight the tenor bell is raised and tolled for an hour, then settled, and four fours struck on it. There is then struck on the bell a number of strokes corresponding to the year of our Lord. The four fours are the particular knell for the devil.[15]

This day of the devil's vanquishing is also one on which many people take communion.

1577 For 7 quarts of Malmesie and breade upon Christelmas Day ... 3s 7d (St Alphage, London Wall)[16]

Wine is provided too for the clerks and other singers.

1497 In brede & wine & coles on Cristmas day for singars ... 5d (St Andrew Hubbard)

1522 For a quarte of swete wine on Cristemas day in the morning for the priksong singars ... 5d (St Andrew, Canterbury)

1546 A pottle of bastard for the clerks on Christmas Day ... 8d (Rye)[17]

Carols are sung, latterly in church but in earlier times largely with the singers going from house to house around the parish. From entries in church accounts it is often hard to tell which is involved.[18]

1524 To John Byche for priking of 5 carell books ... 5s | 1533 To the clarks for the singing of the carrolls ... 16d | 1555 On Christemose day at night to ye clarke for singinge of ye carolls ... 8d (All Saints, Bristol)[19]

The type of light in the following perhaps suggests singing about the town.

1556 To William Powis ... for a linke of 3 li. and 3 quarters to light at after evensonge, to singe carolles at the same time ... 12d (Ludlow)[20]

At Myddle in Shropshire Richard Gough (born 1635) notes that when he was young 'there was a custom ... that upon Christmas day, in the afternoone after divine service, and when the minister was gone out of the churche, the clarke should sing a Christmas carroll in the churche'.[21]

According to Henry Bourne, 'the reason of this custom' of singing carols 'seems to be an imitation of the *Gloria in excelsis*, or *Glory be to God on high*, &c. which was sung by the angels, as they hovered o'er the fields of Bethlehem, in the morning of the Nativity'.[22]

Meanwhile the story of Christmas may be enacted in some form. At Lincoln Cathedral sixpence is paid in 1406 for gloves for the Mary, Angels and Prophets on Christmas morning, suggesting a Nativity play of kinds, perhaps performed by the choristers and clerks.

According to *The Popish Kingdome*, describing customs on the Continent,

> A wooden childe in clowtes [clothes] is on the aultar set
> About the which both boyes and girles do daunce.[23]

Something similar may occur in English parish churches, but if so it has left few traces, and there is no indication of subject matter in the entries below.

1479 To the players that playd in the church at Cristemesse ... 20d (St John the Baptist, Peterborough)

1533 Rewarded and alowed to the pleers of Crissmas game that pleyd in the said churche ... 2s (Ashburton, Devon)[24]

The following is slightly more suggestive.

1524 For makeing the frame for the angels upon Cristmas day ... 4d | 1525 For 1 lb. of sysses [sizes] for the angels at Cristmas ... 9d (St Lawrence, Reading)[25]

Perhaps the angels, candles in hand, are fixed aloft as below parish members, including shepherds with a few well-behaved sheep, act out the humble event in a manger which, in the Christian view, changes everything.

A while later such a scene might be accompanied by the words of Luke's gospel read from the 'Great Bible' of 1539, the first version in English to be used in all parish churches.

> And lo, the angel of the Lord stode harde by them, and the brightnes of the Lord shone rounde aboute them, and they were sore afrayed. And the angel saide unto them, 'Be not afrayed. For beholde, I bringe you tidinges of greate joye, that shall come to all people. For unto you is borne this daye in ye citie of David a saveoure which is Christ ye Lord. And take this for a signe: ye shall finde the childe wrapped in swadling clothes, and layed in a manger.' | And streight waye ther was with the angel a multitude of heavenly soldiers, praising God and sayinge, 'Glory to God on hye, and peace on the erth, and unto men a good will.'[26]

Shepherds shield their eyes against the angel's brightness, by Simon Bening. From a Book of Hours, *c.* 1530.

The nativity, condensing the biblical account and placing the angels and their message of peace inside the manger. From a book of meditations, 1635.

RITES of the LIFE CYCLE
Baptism and Churching

Baptism

1. The ceremony

Derived from the Greek for 'to immerse or bathe', baptism is the first of the seven sacraments.* It marks the entrance of an individual into the Church and is performed at the font which is usually located near the church's main entrance. According to Ottobuono, a papal legate to England in the 1260s, 'to those coming into the *mare magnum* [great sea] of this world, manifestly full of shipwrecks, baptism must be regarded as the first plank of safety to support us to the port of salvation'. Changing metaphors he adds that it is the gate through which all must pass in order to enjoy the grace of the other sacraments, so 'any error in regard to it is *maxime periculosis* [most dangerous]', and great care must be taken to ensure that a child does not die before receiving it.[1]

In early periods it is customary for baptisms to occur at Easter and Whitsun, but by the time of the Reformation they are performed throughout the year, typically within a day or two of the birth. The mother is not usually present, being at home, lying in and waiting out the customary period of a month or so after the birth before being churched.[2]

A Book of Ceremonies, compiled in about 1540, outlines the stages of the pre-Reformation ceremony, largely following the Sarum Manual, and explains their significance. It should be noted that the service is conducted almost entirely in Latin.[3]

The preliminaries take place at the church door. First the minister makes a cross upon the child's forehead to indicate 'that he is come to be professed and ... dedicated to Christ crucified'. He makes a second cross 'upon the breast ... signifying that it is not enough to confess Christ with mouth openly unless he doth steadfastly believe in heart inwardly'. He puts hallowed salt into the child's mouth, 'to signify the spiritual salt, which is the word of God, wherewith he should be seasoned ... that thereby the filthy savour of stinking sin should be taken away, preserving him from corruption'. He makes a third cross upon the child's forehead, 'adjuring the devil to depart, and no more to approach to him'.

Then the minister 'wetteth with spittle the nose thurles [nostrils] and ears of him that shall be baptized ... signifying thereby the grace and godly influence descending from heaven which, by the operation of the holy ghost, openeth our

---

* The other universal ones being confirmation, the eucharist, penance and extreme unction. In addition, for those choosing them, there are matrimony and the taking of holy orders.

nose to take the sweet odour and savour of the knowledge of Christ and our ears to hear his word and commandments'.

He makes a fourth cross 'in the right hand of the infant, which cross should in all our life time admonish us valiantly to defend, resist and withstand the crafty assaults of our enemy the devil'. Then, as the minister blesses the child in the name of the Father, Son and Holy Ghost, he takes it 'by the right hand and biddeth it enter into the church, there to be admitted as one of Christ's flock and congregation'.

Those gathered proceed to the font where the minister asks for the name of the child to be baptised. He follows this with a series of further questions, the first of which is '*Abrenuntias Satanae?*' (Forsakest thou the devil?), to which the godparents and others present answer on the child's behalf, '*Abrenuntio*' (I forsake him).

The minister anoints the child with holy oil, 'before upon the breast and behind between the shoulders'. The first signifies 'that our heart and affection should be wholly dedicate[d] to Christ', and the second 'that we should be steadfast, stout and strong to bear the yoke of our Lord'.

After further questions and answers the minister 'calleth the child by the name and baptizeth it in the name of the Father and the Son and of the Holy Ghost, putting it into the water of the font and taking it out again, or else pouring water upon the infant, whereby the person christened hath ... remission of all his sins by the operation of the holy ghost'. As a result the child is 'washed from sin' and may 'walk in a new, pure and godly life'.

After baptism the child is anointed with holy oil upon the head, 'as the supreme and principal part of man, signifying thereby that he is made an Christian man'.

The child is then 'clothed in a white vesture' called a chrisom which signifies 'Christian purity and innocency'.

Finally the minister 'putteth a candle light in the right hand of him that is baptized, in token that he should through all his life time show before all men a light of good example and godly works, that he may be always in a readiness ... to meet our Lord and receive the fruition of everlasting joy'.[4]

From
*The Crafte to
Live Well and
to Die Well,*
1505

East window, Tattershall, Lincolnshire, *c.* 1482. As in the preceding image the three figures on the right are probably the god-parents.

A briefer and less reverent account of the priest's actions is given in *The Popish Kingdome*.

A number great of crosses first he makes and lustilye,
He blowes out sprightes, commanding them with cruel words to flye.
The foole beleeves the infantes yong, with sprightes to be possest,
Whom faithfull Christian people here begat, and parents blest,
Then thrustes he salt into their mouth, anointing all the while,
The infantes tender eyes, and eares, with stincking spittle vile.
This done his oile and creame he takes, and with discretion small,
Anointes the shoulders of the childe, and eke [also] his brest withall.
The crisome then he calleth for, wherein he fast doth foulde
The little soule: and makes him in his hande a taper houlde.[5]

Originally the chrisom is a cloth placed over the child's head to prevent the early removal of the holy oil or chrism, hence its name. Latterly, however, it is a small robe, as indicated in *The Popish Kingdome*. After the baptism it may be worn by the child for a period, variously said to be seven days, a month, or until its mother comes to be churched, and at that time the mother donates it to the parish.

1524 Received of the barbours wife at her chirching a cresom and 2½d.
    (St Margaret Pattens)[6]

Should the child die within this early period the cloth may be wrapped about it as a shroud.

After the Reformation the ceremony is adjusted in various ways, being performed entirely in English and typically on a Sunday or other holy day. In addition the 1552 Prayer Book omits the exorcism, the anointing with oil, and any reference to the chrisom cloth, although use of the cloth persists for some time, and the term 'chrisom child' continues to be applied to those dying in early infancy.[7]

1665-66 John Gant's child being a creesam was buried Feb. 25. (Halstead, Essex)[8]

It is sometimes said that in early times the church's north door, known as the Devil's Door, was left open during the service to speed satan's departure from the child. While this would be consistent with the beliefs that inform the pre-Reformation rite, and with the association of the devil with north, there appears to be no evidence of its ever having been done.[9]

Nonetheless, even at a much later date it is held to be ominous if a child does not cry when sprinkled or immersed during the service. According to Charlotte Latham, writing of West Sussex superstitions in 1868,

The water sprinkled on an infant's forehead at the font must on no account be wiped off, and it must cry at the christening, or ill luck will follow. The hold which this last superstition has, even upon educated people, is extra-ordinary. It is believed that when the child cries the evil spirit is in the act of quitting it, and I was lately present at a christening in Sussex when a lady of the party, who was grandmother of the child, whispered in a voice of anxiety, 'The child never cried; why did not the nurse rouse it up?' After we had left the church she said to her, 'Oh! Nurse, why did not you pinch baby?' And, when the baby's good behaviour was afterwards commented upon, she observed, with a very serious air, 'I wish that he had cried.'[10]

Francis Grose, in his *Provincial Glossary* (1787), notes simply, 'A child, who does not cry when sprinkled in baptism, will not live.'[11]

Water is cast upon the head of a well-wrapped child,
from *A Booke of Christian Prayers*, 1578

2. Steps taken to avoid children dying unbaptised

Because baptism is considered so important for the soul's salvation, the priest is sometimes summoned urgently when it is thought the child may die before it can be brought to church.

> 1679 Thomas the son of Laurence Wright & Elizabeth his wife was in case of great necessity baptized privately at his house the 31st of March. Memorandum, I was sent for & called out of bed about 12 of the clock in the night & in 30 years I was never sent for in the night upon such an occasion. (Drinkstone, Suffolk)
>
> 1689 Richard ye son of William How & of Elizabeth his wife was baptized 15th day of September. Called out of church in midst of sermon to baptize it, be[ing] likely to die. (Thornton, Bucks)[1]

To the same end midwives are instructed in performing the ceremony.

> 1569 Feb. 16th. George Bourne the son of William Bourne was christened at home by mother Wryte the midwife of the parish and in the presence of 9 other honest women of the parish then beinge present accordinge to the lawe thorowe great pearill and dainger. (Bobbingworth, Essex)[2]

Writing *circa* 1400, John Mirk tells parish priests to teach midwives to have clean water ready.

> And though the child but half be born, | Head and necke and no more,
> Bid her spare never the later | To christen it and cast on water ...
> And if the woman then die, | Teach the midwife that she hie [hasten]
> For to undo her with a knife, | And for to save the child's life
> And hie that it christened be, | For that is a deed of charity.

He adds that the water and vessel used should both be burnt, or the water should be taken at once to the church and cast into the font. This echoes rules set out by Archbishop Edmund in 1236: 'If a child in case of necessity has been baptized by a layman at home, let that water ... be either thrown into the fire, or carried to church in order to be poured into the baptistery, and let the vessel be burnt, or deputed to the use of the church.'[3]

The account of one midwife who steps in survives in the records of the consistorial court of Rochester diocese.

> 1523 Oct. 14th. Eliz. Gaynsford, obstetrix [midwife] ... 'I, the aforesaid Elizabeth, seeing the childe of Thomas Everey, late born in jeopardy of life, by the authorite of my office, then being midwife, did christen the same childe under this manner, *In the name of the Fader, the Son, and the Holy Ghost, I christen thee Denys ...*' [She is asked,] Whether the childe was born and delivered from the wife of the said Thomas, whereto she answereth and saith, that the childe was not born, for she saw nothing

of the childe but the hedde, and for the perell the childe was in, and in that time of nede, she christened as is aforesaid, and cast water with her hand on the childe's hede. After which so done, the childe was born, and was had to the churche, where the priest gave to it that christenden that lakked, and the childe is yet alyf [alive].[4]

Mirk remarks on the importance of not christening twice, and it is notable in the above case that the priest makes good only the parts of the rite not already performed by the midwife. The following also suggests caution on this point.

1564 Memorandum, that whereas a child was founde by the highe waye, and, by estimation, not 3 weeks olde, the father nor yet mother founde ne [nor] knowen, being uncertaine whether that were christened or not, I, Sir William Meane, by the advise of Mr William Pounde ordinarie, did baptize the child in my cure and churche of Thatcham, at the evening prayer, on a Sondaye, John William godfather, and Elizabeth Robinson and Elizabeth Gassard godmothers, the 15 day of ... October. (Thatcham, Berks)[5]

Sometimes the outcome is not so good.

1566-67 Jan. 26th. John, son of John Gillam, founder, was baptized at home by the midwife and died bringing to church. (Ardingly, Sussex)[6]

Elizabeth Gaynsford perhaps chose the name she did because the birth was partial and the child's sex not evident, it being possible to take Denys as male or female, Denis or Denise. The same motive may lie behind the choice of the name Creature bestowed in some parishes upon children baptised at home.

1547 The 27th of Aprile there were borne 2 children of Alexander Beerye, the one christened at home, and so deceased called Creature, the other christened at church called John. | 1548 11th day of June there was baptized by the midwife, and here buried, the childe of Andrew Partridge, called Creature.* (Staplehurst, Kent)[7]

The involvement of midwives is not universally countenanced. In injunctions issued in 1577 Bishop Barnes of Durham insists

that no midwifes, nor any other women, be suffered to minister baptisme ... And we charge and commaunde you ... to present the names and surnames of all suche women as shall take in hande, or enterprice, to baptize, or at the childes birthe use supersticious ceremonies, orizons, charmes, or develishe rites or sorceries.

---

* Creature as a Christian name does, however, appear in other register entries with no indication of extremity. For example, 'Creature ye base borne daughter of Sander Hadds & Elizabeth Huntsmell' is christened at Chislet, Kent, in 1637, and forty years earlier Creature Winborne is married at Ardingly, Sussex.

He is more conciliatory towards those left unbaptised as a result.

> If any infant die without publique baptisme first to it ministered ... the same is not to be condemned or adjudged as a damned sowle, but to be well hoped of, and the body to be interred in the churche yarde, yet without ringinge or any divine service or solemnity, because the same was not solemnely professed and received into the churche and congregacion.[8]

In 1604 the rubric of the service is adjusted so as to allow for baptism 'in private houses in time of necessity' only 'by the minister of the parish, or any other lawful minister that can be procured', after which time there is little evidence of baptism by midwives. The following is perhaps a late exception, although the midwife's role may simply be in providing information to the minister.[9]

> 1730 Robert, daughter of William Thompson, baptised 15 Feb., the midwife mistaking the sex, *ebrietas dementat* [out of her senses with drink]. (Bishopwearmouth, co. Durham)[10]

3. Some register entries

Most baptism entries in parish registers are simple and predictable, but occasionally extra information is included. For example the place of baptism may be changed.

> 1633 Baptised Susan, daughter of Anthony Blackmore of Linfield. By reason of greate waters they could not carry it to their owne parish. (Newick, Sussex)

> 1678 Edward, the son of Thomas Stannard and Elizabeth his wife, was baptized the third day of December, at home, being a cold, frostie, snowie day. (Laxfield, Suffolk)[1]

The weather is not always to blame.

> 1581 The 11 of February was christened Edwarde the sonne of Clement Bright which was don in Westgate church because ye keys of St Peters could not be founde. (St Peter, Canterbury)[2]

Among other register entries the following are striking.

> 1662 Anne, supposed daughter of Sir Jeremiah Smithson, fathered of ye said Sir Jeremiah in the church, baptised 9 April. (Forcett, Yorks)

> 1690 Baptised Elizabeth, daughter of Francis and Anne Comber. This child was heard crying in the wombe before it was borne. (Wadhurst, Sussex)

> 1747 Sep. 8th. Cunozoa Almsbury baptized. This child was exposed and preserved by dogs which defended it from the swine. | Oct. 10th. Cunozoa Almsbury buried. (Winchcombe, Glos)[3]

Churching of women

In early Christianity the mother is held to be unclean for a period after giving birth and presents herself at the end of that time in order to be readmitted to the church. Traditionally, following the example of the Virgin Mary, this occurs on the fortieth day after the birth, although later the period of exclusion may be shortened.[1]

According to the Sarum rite the woman is blessed before the church porch. After various prayers she is sprinkled with holy water by the priest who says, 'Thou shalt purge me, O Lord, with hyssop,' before leading her by the right hand into the church.[2]

It is customary for the woman to wear a veil, usually white, and she may bear a candle, apparently in reference to the bearing of candles at Candlemas, the celebration of the Virgin Mary's churching.

> 1485 1 candlestike to stande afore childwifes.* | 1500 A clothe stained for the purificacion of women. | A coverlett for child-wife. (St Dunstan, Canterbury, inventories)

> 1546 2 candelstickes of latten for wemens purifying. (St Peter, Cornhill, inventory)[3]

Over time the emphasis tends to move away from purification and towards the giving of thanks both for the birth and for the woman's survival of its perils.

> 1636 For an ell of Holland† to make a cloth for women to give thankes after their childbirth ... 4s 6d (Wilmslow, Cheshire)[4]

This shift is registered in the headings given to the service in the first Reformation prayer books, 'The Order of the Purification of Women' in 1549 and 'The Thanksgiving of Women after Childbirth' in 1552.

A change also occurs in relation to the chrisom cloth. In 1549 'the woman that is purified must offer her chrism, and other accustomed offerings', but three years later only 'accustomed offerings' are mentioned. Nonetheless, a payment in lieu may still be expected, and in a few cases a cloth itself is still given.[5]

> 1576 Of the painters wife upone Fisherton Bridge for her crisom 6d, and for her offering ob. | 1585 Whores wife churched the 15 of November, her crisom in cloth, her offering 6d. | 1587 The hatmakers wife beneth the Queenes Armes, her crisom 4d, her offering 2d. | Memorandum for the chrisom sold, 3d. (St Thomas, Salisbury, 'Chrysom Book')[6]

The same book shows that, in cases where the child has already died, a basic offering is usually still made but payment in respect of the chrisom is rare, perhaps indicating continued use of such cloths in burial.

---

* In the sense of wives who are or have recently been with child.
† A linen fabric from that country.

1581 Richard Batts wife churched the 29 of June, neither offering nor crisom. The child is dead. | 1581-82 John Flude wife churched the 7 daye of February, her crisom nothing, her offering ob. The child is dead. | 1582-83 Richard Marshe wife churched the 7 daye of January, children dead, her offering ob.[7]

In both the 1549 and 1552 prayer books the ceremony takes place inside the church. Usually a seat or pew is set aside for the woman being churched and she is accompanied by other wives and the midwife.

1597 To John Hardin for makinge a natt [mat] for the wives to knele on when they come to be churched ... 2d (Pittington, co. Durham)

1819 For making the churching pew ... £2 9s 9d (Chipping, Lancs)[8]

Some women evidently dislike the ceremony, or at least refuse to take it seriously. In 1597 Jane Minors of Barking is presented to a Church court 'for keping her child unbaptised a whole month', the offence being aggravated by the fact that

she very unwomanlike came to be churched at the end of the said month, together with her child to be baptized, and feasted at a taverne 4 or 5 howres in the forenone, and [in the] afternone came to the churche, rather to be seene than upon any devotion, as it seemed; for whilst the minister was burieng a corps, she went owte of the churche, unchurched, unto the taverne againe. And when she was spoken unto by the clerk to returne to churche againe & to give God thanks after her deliverye, she answered it was a ceremonye.[9]

Others bridle at the requirement to be veiled, perhaps in part because it harks back to the idea of purification. In 1602 a Mrs Collins of South Benfleet, Essex, is presented for coming

very undecently & contrary to order, unto the church, without kercher,* midwife, or wives; & placed herselfe in her owne stoole, not in the stoole appointed: by the which she shewed herselfe derisiouse, in coming so like a light & common woman ...[10]

At Wolverhampton in the 1630s it is alleged of a Mrs Pinson that,

being demanded by the priest why she did not wear a veil, she answered she would not, and being told by the priest that he was commanded by the ordinary not to church any but such as came thither reverently and lowly in their veils, she in the church, after prayers ended, scornfully pulled off her hat and put a table napkin on her head, and put on her hat again, and so departed from the church.[11]

---

* *Kerchief.* A cloth used to cover the head, from French *couvrir* (to cover) and *chef* (head).

Marriage

1. Restrictions

Traditionally marriage is prohibited in and around three periods of the year roughly corresponding to times of supposed fasting: Advent, in preparation for Christmas; Lent, in preparation for Easter; and a period from Rogation Monday, in preparation for the Ascension.*

> 1665 Christopher Mitchell and Anne Colcot, married, 4 June, by permission of Sir Richard Chaworth, it being within the octaves of Pentecost. (Twickenham, Middlesex)[1]

In later periods only the prohibition relating to Lent is strictly observed.[2]

Additionally, to avoid clandestine proceedings, the wedding must take place during the day. According to orders issued in 1322, it should be undertaken 'with reverence, in the daytime, and in the face of the church, without laughter, sport, or scoff'. Canon 62 (1604) orders the minister not to perform the service 'at any unseasonable times, but only between the hours of eight and twelve in the forenoon, nor in any private place, but either in the ... churches or chapels where one of [the parties] dwelleth'. In 1886 the hours are extended to 3 p.m.[3]

Marriage is allowed from the ages of 12 for a girl and 14 for a boy.

> 1603-04 George ffetyplace, gent., about the age of 14 years, and Mary Dutton, about the age of 15 years, were joined together in holy matrimony Feb. 14. (Sherborne, Glos)[4]

---

* The Sarum Missal gives the periods as: from the first Sunday in Advent to the octave of the Epiphany (13th January i.e. the eighth day after 6th January, counting inclusively); from Septuagesima (the 70th day before Easter) until the octave of Easter Day; and from Rogation Monday until the day after Trinity Sunday (the Sunday being the octave of Pentecost).

However, if the parties are under 21 they need the consent of parents or guardians and in practice teenage marriages are rare.[5]

In 1653 an Act touching Marriages raises the ages to 16 for boys and 14 for girls, but this law lapses after the Restoration and the lower ages obtain once more and remain in force into the twentieth century.[6]

Following the injunctions of God to Moses in Leviticus chapter 18, the union cannot be with anyone too closely related, whether by blood or marriage. Before the Reformation canon law forbids marriages within the fourth degree of consanguinity (by blood) or affinity (alliance by marriage), first cousins lying within the fourth degree. After the Reformation the position remains broadly similar but the rule becomes that marriage is only allowed between those who are 'without the Leviticall degrees'. For the sake of clarity a table of prohibitions is drawn up in 1563 and it is ordered that it be set up in every church for all to see. It contains all the obvious exclusions, but is slightly less restrictive than the medieval regime and does not include marriage between cousins.[7]

2. Banns

The final hurdle is the issuing of banns, or proclamations, of the marriage on three Sundays or other holy days in the parish church or churches of both intended parties, so that anyone knowing of any impediment may come forward.[1]

Occasionally they do so with apparently good cause

> 1655 Jane Sutton of Maidstone did the 5th day of December except against the proceeding to marriage of Henry Robins and Katherine Solmon for that as she saith the said Henry Robins did solemnly promise her the said Jane Sutton to make her his wife, and upon the 12th day of January 1655 he the said Henry Robins had carnal copulation with her the said Jane Sutton, whereby as she saith she the said Jane is with child. (Maidstone, Kent, note in register)[2]

although if the dates are correct and new style the pregnancy looks improbably long. In other cases opposition to the planned match appears less reasonable.

> 1585 Henry Marshall and Joanna Brewer ... were contracted together, and afterwardes the said Henry sold the said Joane unto one Edward Croxen for 10s, and for that the 10s was not paid the said Henry did forbid the banes. (Great Warley, Essex)[3]

A visitation in 1511 hears that at Wye in Kent Thomas Bocher and Agnes Halke

> were contracted togider and purposid to solemnise matrimony in the face of the churche, and they were axid oones [asked once] openly in the churche. But one Richard Halke, not being content with the same, going aboute to let [hinder] matrimony, menaced the preest and said 'If you ax them any more here I will stik thee,' and in like wise the parishe clerke [so] that he durst not come owt of the churche nor churcheyard of [for] a great while.

The objector is summoned to answer before the Archbishop of Canterbury and the marriage goes ahead.[4]

A rather different problem arises at West Walton, Norfolk, in 1782, when the intending bride has the banns read without consulting the groom, who is not so keen. As a result she is fined 6s 8d 'for mocking the church'.[5]

Here too the 1653 Act touching Marriages brings in a short-lived change which ends at the Restoration, ordering that the banns be published either on

> three several Lords-days then next following, at the close of the morning exercise, in the publique meeting place commonly called the church or chappel; or (if the parties so to be married shall desire it) in the market-place next to the said church or chappel, on three market-days in three several weeks next following, between the hours of eleven and two.[6]

In the puritan-leaning town of Boston, Lincolnshire, the secular option is widely adopted, two thirds of banns between 1656 and 1658 being proclaimed in the market-place rather than in the church.[7]

3. The usual ceremony

The medieval ceremony with the man taking the woman's right hand, from a late 14th-century manuscript

The most commonly used pre-Reformation form of the marriage ceremony is set out in the Sarum Manual and Missal. While it is largely familiar from the modern form, there are notable differences. The marriage is to take place 'before the door of the church, or in the face of the church'. As now the woman is to stand on the left side of the man, 'the reason being that she was formed out of a rib in the left side of Adam'. In plighting her troth the woman promises to be 'bonere et buxum,* in bed et at bord'. In presenting the ring the man commits to endow her 'with all my worldly catell' (in the old sense of goods and property). He takes the bride's right hand and places the ring first

> upon the thumb ... saying, *In the name of the Father*; then upon the second finger, saying, *and of the Son*; then upon the third finger, saying, *and of the Holy Ghost*; then upon the fourth finger, saying, *Amen*, and there let him leave it ... because in that finger there is a certain vein, which runs from thence as far as the heart ...

---

* *Bonaire*. Gentle, courteous, kind. *Buxom*. Obliging, pliant, obedient; according to the *OED* the modern sense of 'comely' only appears from the late 16th century.

Only after the marriage service has been completed do the couple proceed into the church, 'as far as the step of the altar', where they kneel as those gathered pray for them. There follows a nuptial mass, during which, after the sanctus,

> the bridegroom and bride shall prostrate themselves in prayer at the step of the altar, a pall being extended over them, which four clerks in surplices shall hold at the four corners, unless one or both shall have been previously married and blessed, because in that case the pall is not held over them, nor is the sacramental blessing given.

The Church's involvement does not end here, for 'on the following night, when the bridegroom and bride have gone to bed, the priest shall approach and bless the bed-chamber'. He proceeds to two further blessings, one 'over the bed only', the other 'over them in bed', before sprinkling them with holy water. Only then does he depart.[1]

After the Reformation, among other adjustments, the marriage ceremony moves into the body of the church, the ring is placed upon the bride's left hand, and the bed-chamber visit is omitted.[2]

4. Smock marriages and other variations

While most marriages follow the established form, occasionally innovation is called for.

> 1575-76 Februarye the 5th day, Thomas Tilsey and Ursula Russel were maryed; and because the saide Thomas was, and is, naturally deafe, and also dombe, so that the custom of the form of marriage used usuallye amongst others which can heare and speake, could not for his part be observed; after the approbation had from Thomas the Bishope of Lincoln, John Chippendale, doctor in lawe and comissary, as also of Mr Richard Davye, then mayor of the towne of Leicester, with others of his brethren, with the reste of the parishe; the saide Thomas, for expressinge of his minde, steade of words, of his owne accorde, used these signes: first, he embraced her with his armes, and tooke her by the hande, put a ringe upon her finger, and laide his hande upon his harte, and upon her harte, and helde up his hands towards heaven; and to shew his continuence to dwell with her to his lives ende, he did it by closinge of his eyes with his hands, and diggine out the earthe with his fote, and pullinge as though he would ringe a bell, with diverse other signes approved. (St Martin, Leicester)

> 1832 Nov. 5th. Christopher Newsam married Charity Morrell. Charity Morrell being entirely without arms, the ring was placed upon the fourth toe of the left foot, and she wrote her name in this register with her right foot. (St James, Bury St Edmunds)[1]

A more general but short-lived innovation occurs during the Commonwealth when, under the 1653 Act, the ceremony is performed by justices of the peace, although in some places other office holders also preside.[2]

> 1654 May 17th. James Finch, single man, of Weathersfield, and Ann Clay, single woman, of Shafford, were married by the right worshipful Arthur Barnardiston, Esq., justice of the peace. (Castle Hedingham, Essex)

> 1656 April 24th. Roger Harrison and Elizabeth Pettit married. They were married by Captain Jenner. | July 1st. David Hart and Ceselie Hammond were married by Captain Stapley. (Wartling, Sussex)[3]

Another departure from usual practice arises from the popular but unfounded belief that if a woman marries in her smock or shift, or in a sheet, then the groom is not responsible for any debts she may have incurred. The idea seems to be that in shedding prior worldly goods, in the form of clothes, she also sheds her old legal persona and with it any outstanding liabilities.[4]

> 1547 August 4th. Here was wedded early in the morning Thomas Munslow Smith and Alice Nicols, which wedded to him in her smock and bareheaded. (Much Wenlock, Shropshire)

> 1723 June 24th. Leonard Pybus, of Ilton, and Sythe Horner, of Masham, were married by banns published. The woman, to prevent the creditors coming on her new married husband for the debts contracted by the former husband had nothing to cover her nakedness during the solemnizing of the wedding but her shirt. (Masham, Yorks)[5]

The custom is also the subject of newspaper reports.

> On Tuesday sen'night was married at the parochial chapel of Saddleworth, Abraham Brooks, a widower, of about 30 years of age, to Mary Bradley, a widow of near 70, but as the bride was a little in debt the bridegroom obliged her to be married in her shift, and the weather being very severe threw her into such a violent fit of shaking as induced the compassionate minister to cover her with his coat whilst the marriage was solemnised.
>
> Prescott's *Manchester Journal*, 12 February 1774[6]

The *Annual Register* records a case in Cumberland in June 1766 in which the positions are reversed, although it is still the woman who divests.

> A few days ago, a handsome well-dressed young woman came to a church in Whitehaven to be married to a man, who was attending there with the clergyman. When she had advanced a little into the church, a nymph, her bride-maid, began to undress her, and by degrees stript her to her shift; thus was she led blooming and unadorned to the altar, where the marriage-ceremony was performed. It seems this droll wedding was occasioned by an embarrassment in the affairs of the intended husband; upon which account, the girl was advised to do this, that he might be intitled to no other marriage-portion than her smock.[7]

5. Some register entries &c.

As with entries of baptism, those of marriage are usually spare and functional, typically providing no more than the names of the parties and the date of their union. Occasionally, however, hidden stories emerge.

> 1641 September. Thomas Blacket married the 23 day to his dame Marie Green (she did love him in his master's time). (St Andrew, Newcastle)

> 1748 Edward Aggs of Shouldham & Mary Fane. Memorandum. Aggs was a married man, & a few days after his marrying his wife came big with child & claimed him. To such lewdness & dissoluteness are we arrived in this polite age of free thinking. (Walpole, Norfolk)[1]

The registers of Stixwold, Lincolnshire, offer a cautionary tale.

> Francis Fawcett, of the age of 93 years, marryed to Anne Hemidge, of the age of 21 years, upon Saterdaie, the 27th daie of January, 1621.

> Francis Fawcett, the above named, was buryed the 8th day of February, 1621, having been but 12 daies married.[2]

The *Derby Mercury* tells a similar story in 1753, but in reverse and with more detail.

> *Jan. 12th.* Last Saturday, at the chapel of Sheldon, in the High Peak of Derbyshire, were solemniz'd the nuptials of a widow gentlewoman of that place, of about eighty years of age, to a young lad (by the consent of his parents) of about fourteen.* As she was render'd incapable of walking, by a complication of disorders, she was carried in her chair, from her house to the chapel, about a hundred yards distant, attended by a numerous concourse of people; where the ceremony was performed with becoming seriousness and devotion; after which she was re-conducted in the same manner, the musick playing, by her orders, the Duke of Rutland's Hornpipe, before her; to which (as she was disabled from dancing) she beat time with her hands on her petticoats, till she got home, and then call'd for her crutches, commanded her husband to dance, and shuffled herself as well as she could. The day being spent with the ringing of the bell, and other demonstrations of joy, and the populace (mostly miners) being soundly drench'd with showers of excellent liquor, &c. that were plentifully pour'd upon them. The new-marry'd couple, to consummate their marriage, were at length put to bed; to the side of which, that well-polish'd and civiliz'd company were admitted; the stocking was thrown, the posset drank, and the whole concluded with all the decorum, decency and order imaginable.

---

* According to the parish register the bride was a decade younger. '1753. Jan. 6th. The man about 14 years of age. Married, Cornelius White and Ellen Dale. The woman 70.'

Jan. 26th. We are informed that last Sunday dy'd at Sheldon near Bakewell the old gentlewoman who was marry'd the 6th instant to a young lad aged about fourteen, as mention'd in a former paper. Her corpse was brought to Bakewell church on Tuesday last, where she was handsomely interr'd, and a funeral sermon preach'd on the occasion, to a numerous and crowded audience, by the Rev. Gentleman who had so lately perform'd the nuptial ceremony.[3]

Plate 5 of 'A Rake's Progress' by William Hogarth, 1735, set in old Marylebone church

Death, Burial and Beyond*

1. Visitation of the sick

For those too unwell to attend church, the sacrament of the eucharist is carried to them, usually in a pyx. Before the Reformation this is done with a good deal of ceremony. According to rules laid down by Archbishop Pecham in 1279, the priest is to wear a surplice and stole, a light is to be carried before him, and a handbell is to be rung 'to excite the people to due reverence, who are discreetly to be informed by the priest that they prostrate themselves, or at least make humble adoration, wheresoever the king of glory is carried under the cover of bread'.[1]

> 1478-80 To Saunder while we were clerkless to bere a torche with the housel [eucharist] ... 1d (St Andrew Hubbard)
>
> c. 1521 For bad and broken silver to mend the pyx in which the body of Christ is carried to the infirm ... 18d | To the goldsmith for repairing the said pyx ... 1s | 1544 For silk for making of on purse for to bere the sakarment in to seke folke ... 7d | Paid Alson Fendyk for making of the same purse ... 8d (Leverton, Lincs)
>
> 1532 For a litell bell to go a visiting ... 3d (St Nicholas, Bristol)
>
> 1546 For a gret lantorn to bear light before ye sacrament ... 6d (North Elmham, Norfolk)[2]

---

* In the extracts from wills in this chapter the name of the relevant parish – usually the home parish of the testator – is given where known. However, where it seems clear that the action or actions mentioned occurred entirely elsewhere – for example observances performed in a religious house – the parish name is placed within square brackets.

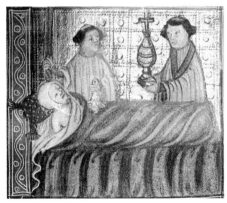

At the bedside, from English manuscripts, *c.* 1400 (*left*) and *c.* 1370.
FACING PAGE Carrying the sacrament to the sick, from the Nuremberg Chronicle, 1493.

On the return journey, if the sacrament has been consumed, the light is extinguished, the bell is silent, and kneeling is not required.[3]

After the Reformation the bell and light are no more, but items essential for communion are still taken.

> 1579 For wine to go to sicke folks ... 4d (Mere, Wilts)

> 1713 For a tin box, to carry ye chalice in, and bread, for administration of ye holy communion to ye sick in ye parish ... 2s 6d (St Peter, Bywell, Northumberland)[4]

2. Extreme unction

When death is expected the priest returns to the bedside attended by one or more clerks and armed with the eucharist, holy water and holy oil. To begin with he holds or sets up a crucifix before the dying person's face and tells them to 'looke thereupon and comfort thee therewith'.[1]

> 1522 Rob Cornford for painting crucifix of wode for seke pepull ... 12d (Louth)[2]

He proceeds to ask a series of questions, known as 'the seven interrogations', in an attempt to ensure that the person about to face divine judgement has acknowledged their faults and made a clear affirmation of their faith in the central Christian tenets. The following version is from the Sarum Manual and includes some supplementary questions.

> Brother, art thou glad that thou shalt die in Christian faith?
> Do thou acknowledge that thou hast not well lived, as thou shouldest?
> Art thou sorry therefore?
> Hast thou will to amend thee, if thou haddest space of life?

Believe thou in God, father almighty, maker of heaven and of earth?

Believe thou in the father and son and holy ghost, three persons and one God?

Believe thou that our lord Jesus Christ, God's son, was conceived of the holy ghost, and took flesh and blood of our lady Saint Marie, and was born of her, she being mother and maid?

Believe thou that he suffered pain and death for our trespass ... and died for thee on Good Friday, and was buried?

Thank thou him therefore?

Believe thou that thou may not be saved but through his death?[3]

Provided he or she can still communicate, the dying person is supposed of course to answer 'Ye' or 'Yea' to each question in turn, and it seems unlikely that many have the strength to demur or argue the toss at this stage, even if they should be so inclined.

According to the Manual, the priest then says,

While thy soul is in thy body, put all thy trust in his passion and in his death, and think only thereon, and on no other thing. With his death medil* thee, and wrap thee therein, not thinking on thy wife, nor on thy children, nor on thy riches, but all on the passion of Christ, and have the cross before thee and say thus: 'I wot [know] well thou art not my God, but thou art imagined after him, and makest me have more mind of him after whom thou art imagined. Lord, father of heaven, the death of our lord Jesus Christ, thy son, which is here imagined, I set betwen thee and my evil deeds, and the desert of Jesus Christ I offer, for that I should have deserved and have not.' ... And say: 'Into thy hands, Lord, I betake my soul, for thou God of truth boughtest me,' and say so thrice.[4]

A tract on the art of dying adds another prayer which gives a sense of the deathbed as a battlefield upon which forces of darkness and light contend for the passing soul.

Dear brother, I commend thee to almighty God, and commit thee to him, whose creature thou art ... Know you never that [which] is horrible in darkness, that grunteth and flameth fire, that punishes in torments ... that foul Satan with all his servants. In his coming against you, agast [frighten] him with the presence of holy angels, and flee he unto the darkness of everlasting night, unto the great troublous sea of hell. Our lord arises and his enemies be disparted [scattered] about ...[5]

From a mural of
the Last Judgement,
Stratford upon Avon

---

* *Meddle*. Concern or busy oneself.

Only when death is immi-
nent, and the priest is satisfied
that the soul is ready for its
journey, does he proceed to
anoint the dying person with
holy oil. He dips his right hand
into the oil and makes with it
the sign of the cross upon the
eyes, ears, nostrils, mouth,
hands and other parts. According to Durand, 'This unction
is applied ... especially on those
parts in which the five senses
chiefly reside, that whatever
sins ... may have [been] committed by means of these may
be abolished by virtue of this
unction.' The priest then ad-
ministers the eucharist, known
in this use as the *viaticum*, from
Latin, 'provision for a journey'.[6]

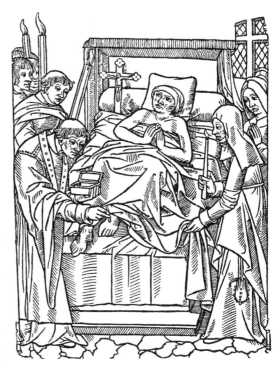

Meanwhile at the church the passing bell may be rung, one of its purposes
being to drive away any evil spirits that lurk by the bedside ready to snatch the
departing soul.

After the Reformation the dying are still visited, the articles of faith are
rehearsed, and communion is administered, but the act of anointing is omitted
from the Prayer Book of 1552 and later editions. More importantly, with the waning
of the medieval cast of mind, the sense of a great battle for the soul slips away.[7]

ABOVE
Anointing a
dying man, 1503.

RIGHT
A late 17th-century
deathbed. The open
window may reflect
a belief that the
departing soul
needs a way out.

The priest sprinkles holy water over a shrouded corpse as it is lowered into a shallow-looking grave, having been carried there in a reusable coffin. Meanwhile an angel gathers the departing soul, which thus eludes the clutches of the devil. From a Book of Hours by the workshop of the Bedford Master, French, *c.* 1440.

3. Burial before the Reformation*

According to the Sarum rite the body is washed immediately after death with warm or tepid water and then rubbed all over with balsam and spices before being placed in a linen winding sheet. It is then laid upon a bier and carried to church preceded by a cross-bearer; a boy carrying holy water; two acolytes or attendants bearing lighted tapers; the sexton or clerk, ringing a handbell to prompt those within earshot to pray for the deceased; and finally clerks and the parish priest singing psalms.[1]

> 1552   A litell liche bell that went before the corps. (Hallow, Worcs, inventory)
>
> 1556   To Phelyp tinker for the mendinge of the corps belle ... 12d (Ludlow)[2]

The biered corpse is surrounded by friends of the deceased, or members of his or her guild, bearing torches and wax lights, and is followed by the chief mourners who are dressed in black cloaks and hoods.

Once inside the church the bier is set down in the chancel if the deceased was in orders, or near the east end of the nave if not, in both cases with the corpse's feet to the east. The bier is covered with a pall around which are placed large free-standing candlesticks, typically one at each corner or one at each end and one on each side. Alternatively, if the church has a hearse to set about the corpse, lighted tapers may be placed in it.

The body is now ready for the Office for the Dead to be performed.

This begins with **vespers**, held on the evening before the burial and often known as **placebo** from the opening of the service's first antiphon, *Placebo Domino in regione vivorum* (I will please the Lord in the land of the living).

The body remains in the church overnight and early in the morning **matins** and **lauds** are chanted, this part of the office being known as **dirige** (or dirge) from the opening of the antiphon *Dirige, Domine, Deus meus, in conspectu tuo viam meam* (Direct, Lord, my God, my way in your sight).

The **commendatio animarum** (commendation of souls) is then sung over the corpse while the priest goes into the churchyard and marks out the place for the intended grave by digging the shape of a cross in the ground, having first sprinkled it with holy water.[3]

He returns to the church and, while the grave is being dug outside, mass for the soul of the dead person is celebrated. This too has its popular Latin name, **requiem**, from the introit *Requiem aeternam dona eis, Domine* (Rest eternal grant them, Lord).

While the Sarum Manual indicates only the requiem mass, in early use and in more elaborate later cases it may be preceded by one or two additional masses, usually of the Trinity and of the Virgin Mary. In his will of 1463 John Baret of Bury St Edmunds directs that 'on the day of my intirment' there is to be sung 'a messe of prikked song ... in wurshippe of oure lady' at 7 a.m. with 'ye messe of

---

* For the use of bells in relation to death and burial see pp104-109.

requiem' to follow 'forthwith'. In other cases the mourners may retire for breakfast after the earlier observances and return for the requiem mass.[4]

After mass the bier is carried into the churchyard and the clergy and mourners stand around the grave, which is blessed, censed and sprinkled. The body, wrapped in its winding sheet but usually not coffined, is lowered into the grave, again with the feet to the east, while the clerks sing a psalm.

As the body is lowered the priest sprinkles it with holy water again. According to John Mirk, this is done so that 'fiends schal have no post in his grave'. Rather worryingly he adds that 'it is often seen that fiends have post to trouble a corpse that hath not his full sacrament of holy church'.*[5]

Prayers are then said for the forgiveness of the sins of the deceased, and if he or she had previously obtained an absolution, written upon a parchment scroll, the priest places this upon the corpse's breast.†

> 1527-28 I charge and require myn executours that all my letres of pardons, whiche lie in my cypres chest, which standith upon my compting bourde, be buried with my body. (John Gonne, Eastbourne, Sussex)[6]

Further prayers follow, then the priest strews earth upon the body in the form of a cross, and, as those around sing another psalm, the grave is filled up with soil. The procession then returns to the church, penitential psalms being sung as it goes.

While this level of ceremony is common in cathedrals, ordinary parish burials may be carried out a good deal more simply. Churchwardens' accounts provide little indication of what is involved, but that itself tends to suggest relative simplicity.

One variation is that the body may rest at home rather than in the church until the burial day, and placebo at least may be performed there. As much is made clear in an order issued by Archbishop Stratford in 1343.

> It is a devout custom of the faithful to observe night-watches, in behalf of the dead before their burial, and to do it sometimes in private houses, to the intent that the faithful there meeting together and watching, might devoutly intercede for them with God: but by the arts of Satan this wholesome practice of the ancients is turned into buffoonery and filthy revels; prayers are neglected, and these watchings are become rendezvous for adulteries, fornication, thefts, and other misdoings. As a remedy for so rife a disease, we ordain that when ecclesiastical men have performed the memories [rites] of the dead, none for the future be admitted to the accustomed night-watches in private houses, where dead corpses often remain till their burial, the relations and such as say psalters for the dead only excepted, under the pain of the greater excommunication ...[7]

---

* In similar vein Odericus of Siena, writing *circa* 1215, notes that holy water is cast into tombs to deter demons, who would otherwise vent their rage upon the bodies of the dead.

† 'On opening old graves, some of these very "absolutions", as they were sometimes called, have been found quite whole and readable'. (Daniel Rock, *The Church of Our Fathers*, vol 2, 1905, p387)

In his will of 1526 Richard Russell of Helpston, Northamptonshire, leaves 4d 'to the ringers at the caryge of my corsse to the church at masse time', that is, on the morning of the burial day. In 1544-45 Robert Peche of Aldingbourne, Sussex, leaves 2d a piece 'to 5 of my pore neighbours at my funeral day ... to feche me at home, berying each of them a taper in ther handes'.[8]

On the other hand, lying of the corpse in the church overnight may be expected, for example for members of the clergy, who tend to favour fuller rites and for whom the church is in a sense home. Richard Oliver (*d.* 1535), a particularly pious member of the clergy in York, stipulates in his will that he is to be buried at Holy Trinity Priory. Beforehand, however, once his body is cold, it is to be taken to his own church of All Saints, North Street, where it is to be set in the middle aisle, 'and there to abide' and have dirige and mass performed before being carried to the priory. Widows are to be paid 2d each to watch over it after 9 o'clock at night, and there is to be 'no revell of ... young folkes'.[9]

4. The campaign for salvation: an introductory outline

It is believed that the soul of each individual faces its own particular judgement at the moment of death and then, when the world comes to an end, will be reunited with its body to face the general or Last Judgement, at which the fate of every soul will be revealed before an assembly of all mankind.

The purposes of the burial procedure outlined above are clear: to mark the passing of the deceased in a dignified way; to inter the corpse before it becomes noxious; to mark it as that of a Christian and otherwise leave it in a state of readiness for the Last Judgement; to ward off any evil spirits that may be lurking (whether to sport with the corpse or snatch the departing soul); and to seek God's mercy for that soul. There remains, however, much more to be done to ease the passage towards heaven.

While it is believed that those free of sin pass straight there, and that those guilty of mortal sin pass straight to hell, the majority are guilty of venial sins (from Latin *venialis*, forgivable) which need to be purged through suffering before admission to heaven can be granted. As noted earlier, this purging takes place in an intermediate place or state called purgatory (from Latin *purgare*, to make clean), and one's stay there is no trivial matter: according to Thomas Aquinas and other medieval theologians, the smallest pain in purgatory is greater than the greatest pain on earth.[1]

Those who live good lives and are penitent before death should of course suffer less, but no one can face the prospect too confidently – not least because to do so would involve the sin of pride. The medieval Church does, however, hold out two main ways in which you can reduce your suffering in purgatory by actions taken in anticipation of death: arrange to have prayers and masses performed for your soul by those left behind, and leave instructions and funds for good works. There are no set levels for either: in theory the more observances performed, and the greater the charity bestowed, the more the soul will be helped, but there are no guarantees and at no point can anyone feel assured that enough has been done.

The result is a mini economy of salvation as those with financial means seek to accumulate as much spiritual credit as they can in order to settle their dues and make their stay in purgatory as short and as comfortable as possible. In many cases there is doubtless a secondary, social motive in the wish to assert status and display wealth conspicuously. The only certain beneficiaries, however, are the poor, who receive a great deal of charity, and the Church, which is paid handsomely for the performance of a range of observances. Indeed, the idea of purgatory is a highly effective means of raising Church income, the Protestant Hugh Latimer labelling it 'purgatory pick-purse'.[2]

From the individual's point of view the sense that an investment is being made is often explicit in the wording of wills.

> 1517 And for as much as with good prayers and almes dedes the soule is delivered fro everlasting deth, therfor I will that at the day of my burying I may have a trentall* songe for my soule, my fader [father's] soule, and for all my brethern and sistern soules, and for all Christen soules ... I will that ... every pouer man that cometh have a peny and a loffe, to pray for my soule and the soules afore rehersed ... And if goodes will not reche to that, I will that my executours do as they think most best for me. (Sir Arthur Vernon, priest, Nether Seale, Leics)

> 1533 The residew of my goodes not before bequethed I put them to ye disposicion of my executors, they to distrebute and dispose them in dedes of charite where as they shall thinke it most nede for the welthe of my sowle, all my good frendes sowles, and all good cristen sowles ... (Robert Garrad, Ixworth, Suffolk)[3]

Nor does this end once your corpse is in the ground, at least not for those who can afford an ongoing campaign. There are also post-burial commemorations to be arranged. These typically repeat elements of the burial service, with masses said for the soul, but of course no body to inter. They usually take place in the first month after death, during which time it is traditionally believed that the soul may still be lingering in the vicinity of the body and so stand in need of help on its journey.[4]

> 1544-45 I [will] that the curat say dirge every Friday for my soule unto the month day, and he to have for his paines 2d, and the clark 1d to ring the great bell. (Robert Peche, Aldingbourne, Sussex)[5]

Particular emphasis is placed upon the **month's mind**, performed 30 days or a month after death. For those who can afford it this is followed by a **twelve-month's** or **year's mind** which often recurs as an annual commemoration called an **obit** (from Latin *obire*, to go down, perish, die), and is funded either for a limited number of years or for eternity.

---

* *Trental.* Set of thirty requiem masses.

5. Seeking salvation: the details

i. Masses

The following is a typical and relatively modest instruction.

> 1543 I will that therbe song or said ye day of my buryeng for my sowle and all christen sowles 6 masses with placebo and dirige and at my monthes mind 6 masses and in like manner at my yeres mind. (Thomas Ryckeward, Southease, Sussex)[1]

If wishing to go beyond the standard requiem mass, but without vast outlay, a promising option is the **Mass of the Five Wounds of Christ**. According to the rubric of the Sarum Missal it was instituted by Pope Boniface the VIIIth or IXth after a visit by the archangel Raphael, and is particularly useful because 'if it be said on behalf of the soul of a deceased person, directly after it has been said completely, that is to say, five times, that soul shall be freed from punishment'.[2]

> 1541 I will have at ye day of my funeral and burying 5 masses of ye five woundes to be celebrated and done for ye helth of my sowle and all cristen sowles. Item, I will have at my monthes minde other 5 masses of ye 5 woundes and at my yeres minde other 5 masses of ye 5 woundes. (Joan Taylor, Kingston, Sussex)[3]

For those who can afford more, the usual thing is to commission masses to be said or sung in sets of thirty called trentals.

> 1514 I will that at the day of my sepulture be had in song a trentall of masses and another at my monthes minde and also another at my twel[ve]monthes minde. (Robert Morley, Glynde, Sussex)[4]

A notable elaboration is **St Gregory's trental** which is spread over a year and involves the celebration of three masses within the octaves of each of ten major feasts: Christmas, Epiphany, Candlemas, Annunciation, Easter, Ascension, Pentecost, Trinity, and the Nativity and Assumption of the Virgin Mary. A priest is also to recite placebo and dirige daily throughout the year. It is a considerable commitment and comes at a price.[5]

> 1517-18 I bequeth to a discrete preest to sey the great trentall of Saint Gregory for my soule and all Christen soules 40s. (William Jurdayn, Wilmington, Sussex)[6]

Another hopeful option is a mass at or of **Scala Caeli** or Celi. The name derives from a vision granted to St Bernard, while he is conducting a requiem mass, of a heavenly ladder (*scala caeli*) on which angels are conducting to heaven the souls of those released from purgatory on account of his prayers. In due course special status is granted to masses said at the church of Scala Caeli outside the walls of Rome where the vision is said to have occurred, and in 1500 Margaret, mother of Henry VII, obtains a papal grant of the same advantages for masses performed at her son's chapel at Westminster. Subsequently similar grants are made to other establishments in England, including the Lady chapel of St Botolph, Boston, Lincolnshire, and the church of the Austin Friars in Norwich. Those wishing to give their souls an edge can therefore pay for a priest to travel to one of these favoured places. A lesser option is to have a 'mass of Scala Caeli', containing certain special prayers, performed locally.[7]

> c. 1458 I will put an able prest of good conversacon to singe & pray for my soule atte Scala Celi in Rome by the space of an hoole yere & 30 daies. (Sir Edmund Mulsho, [Newton, Northants])[8]

> 1513 I will have incontinent [without delay] after my dedde day one trentall songinge for my sowle of 30 messes at the Scala Celi at Westminster and for my frends sowles, by an honeste monk of the same place, with licens of his abbatt. (Thomas Wyssett, [Upton, Norfolk])

> 1529 I will ther be done for my soule 5 masses of the 5 woundes of our savior Jesu Criste & one masse of Scala Celi. (Richard Goose, Naseby, Northants)[9]

Alternatively you can simply go for quantity, an option open only to those with substantial means.

> 1395 I bequethe £18 and 10s for to singe and seye 4,400 masses for my lord Sir Thomas West his soule, and for myn, and for alle cristene soules, in the most haste that it may be do[ne], withinne 14 night next after my deces. (Alice, Lady West; burial at Christchurch Priory, Dorset)

> 1417 I bequeath for 3,000 masses to be celebrated for my soul in three days immediately after my death, £12 10s. (Richard Weyvyle, Rodmell, Sussex; burial 'in the great church' of St Pancras Priory, Lewes)

> 1537 I will that imediatly after my deceas myn executors do give to one thowsand preestes, every of them 11d to say placebo, dirige and masse for my soule and all Christian soules ... (George Talbot, 4th Earl of Shrewsbury; burial 'in the parishe churche of Sheffield')[10]

The following acknowledges that finding sufficient priests to perform so many services in a short time will require the sending of messengers to churches and religious houses in the surrounding area.

> 1412 I bequeath for celebrating a thousand masses for my soul within the octave after I shall pass away from this world, together with the expenses of divers horsemen in arranging the matter aforesaid, 100s. (John Testwode, Trent, Somerset)[11]

More generally, while ordinary priests will serve for whatever is done in your parish church, you may wish to supplement their efforts by having monks, nuns, anchorites and hermits intercede for you as well, the prayers of such holy men and women having particular weight.

1519 To the ancres in the churchyard to the intent she shall pray for my soul and all Christian souls, 4d. (William Perkin, Faversham, Kent)

1531 To Sir Gregory heremite of Weldon to singe for my sowle 5 masses of ye 5 woundes of our lord, 20d. (Richard Bawe, Northants)

1534 I bequeth to every house of freres within the countie of Sussex 10s to singe a trentall of masses ... immediately after my deceas for my soule ... (Edward Markewyk, [Hamsey, Sussex])[12]

ii. Works of Mercy and the prayers of the poor

Another way to obtain spiritual credit is to perform one or more of the Corporal Works of Mercy. Traditionally these are seven: feeding the hungry; giving drink to the thirsty; harbouring the stranger; clothing the naked; visiting the sick; ministering to prisoners; and burying the dead. The last is from the apocryphal Book of Tobit, but the rest derive from Christ's account of the blessed in the parable of the sheep and goats in Matthew 25:35-36.

For I was an hungred, and ye gave me meat. I was thirsty, and ye gave me drink. I was a stranger, and ye took me in. Naked, and ye clothed me. I was sick, and ye visited me. I was in prison, and ye came unto me.

Some are evidently harder to undertake by means of bequests than others, and most testators focus on providing food, drink and clothing. The standard approach is to give one or more of these, and perhaps money, to poor people to attend your funeral, in return for which they are expected to pray for your soul. This not only increases the quantity of intercession made on your behalf but also its quality, the prayers of the poor being considered particularly effective because of the special place they hold in Christian teaching. As an additional benefit their presence swells the scene, enhancing the funeral as a demonstration of your social status.[13]

1411 I desire on my burial day that twelve torches and two tapers burn about my body, and that twelve poor women, holding the said torches, be cloathed in russet, with linen hoods, and having stockings and shoes suitable. (Joane, Lady Hungerford, Farleigh Hungerford, Somerset)

1511 I will that mine executour shall provide 7 blak gownes for 7 poor men, 5 smockes for 5 poor women, and 10 paire of shoes for 10 poor men and women, at my burying. (Agnes Morley, St John the Baptist, Lewes)

1525 I will that there be at my burying 24 poor men to holde 24 torches in the service time and every one of them to have a blak gowne and a hood and 12d for his labour. Also I will that my executours dele at my burying [in] 2d dole £20 and that they cause every man, woman and child before the dole [to] knele on their knees and to say the prayer of de profundis, and such that cannot, they to say one pater noster, one ave and one crede for my soule. (John, Lord Marney, Layer Marney, Essex)[14]

Those receiving alms in this way, known as beadsmen, are often represented on tombs. For example in 1439, giving instructions for her planned resting place in Tewkesbury Abbey, the Countess of Warwick seeks to be surrounded by figures of the poor at prayer for her soul for ever: 'and all abowt my tumbe, to be made pore men and wemen in their pore array, with their bedes in theire handes'. Similar but less durable are the 'hundred bedemen in mourning, with their bedes in their hands', made in wax and set about the hearse at the funeral of the 2nd Duke of Norfolk at Thetford Abbey in 1524.[15]

While the provision of food and drink serves two self-interested purposes – earning credit for works of mercy and increasing the 'prayer load' – the particular instructions of some testators suggest a genuine wish to provide well.

> 1529 Every person that shall be at my beryall shall have 2d. Also I will that every house in the town shall have a chese, & the porest house the best chese. (Myles Roos, Naseby, Northants)

> 1544 I will there shal be brewed ageinst my buriall 4 quarter of malt, 3 bullocks killed, 6 shepe, 3 calfs, 6 pigs, & hens & capons as nede shalbe, & 3 quarter of brede corne, that all comers may be releved ... to crye to God for me by prayers. (Edward Martin, rector, Old, Northants)

> 1549-50 I will that my wheate that is in the barne be threshed oute and that my executours shall make of the same breade and pasties for the poore folkes of the said parish and in every pasty to be 4 heringes with reasons and siropp ... (Robert Otes, vicar, Firle, Sussex)

> 1559-60 I will the people to be refreshed at my buriall with bread and drink and 2 good cheses and at my monthes mind with bread and drink and 2 good shepe. (Thomas Gwr, Beddingham, Sussex)[16]

Bequests for prisoners and the sick are less common, but these less conspicuous works of mercy are sometimes remembered.

> 1487 I bequeith to the prisoners of Newgate and Ludgate, Kinges Bench and Marshallsee, to every of those places to be praid for, 20d. Also, I bequeith to bedred folkes and other poor householders, as well men as women, dwelling within London and without in the suburbs of the same, and moste specially suche as have knowen me and I thaym, 40s. (Elizabeth Browne, née Paston; burial 'within the churche of the Blak Freris within Ludgate')[17]

John Coote of Bury St Edmunds manages to more or less cover four of the works and to do so with a degree of modesty, omitting the common custom of having a bellman going around the parish to solicit prayers for the donor's soul.

> 1502 I will that at my burying day there be delte 40s in brede at my dore, or else in some other convenient place. Also I will the day before my thirtyday 6s 8d to be delte in bedred [to bedridden] men or women,

and ther where it shall be most nedefull; and also the day afore or the
day after my thirtyday the prisoners in the jaile to have as moche mete
and drinke as cometh to the valewe of 2s; and the day of my thirtyday
I will neither ringing nor belman goinge, but this to be don in secrete
manner under this forme afore rehersed.[18]

UPPER Beadsman and woman in alabaster, seated on a lion and sheltered by the feet
of the tomb effigy of Sir John de Strelley (*d.* 1501), Strelley, Nottinghamshire.
LOWER Visiting the sick and ministering to prisoners, All Saints, North Street, York.

ABOVE Feeding the hungry, Tattershall, Lincolnshire, *Cibo* being Latin for 'I feed.'
BELOW & FACING PAGE Six of the works of mercy from *A Booke of Christian Prayers*, 1608: feeding the hungry, giving drink to the thirsty, harbouring the stranger, clothing the naked, visiting the sick, and ministering to prisoners.

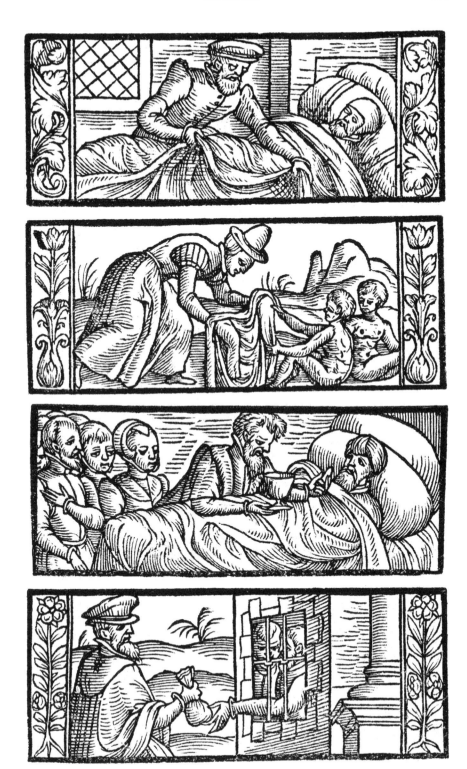

iii. Pilgrimages by proxy

Further spiritual credit can be gained by arranging for someone to travel to one or more holy places on your behalf and there say prayers for your soul.

1429 I wil and ordeine that three preestes be hired to go on pilgrimage for me, one to Jerusalem, another to Rome, the thriddete to Seint James in Galice and to Seint Michelles Mount in England,* for the whiche pilgrimage I assigne £50, and more if it nedeth, and [they are to say] masses every day, whenne they be disposed and may have place, time and leiser [leisure] to do it, and to praye in special for my sowle, my fader and moder sowles, my ancestres sowles, and for all cristen sowles; and also to saye every day placebo and dirige and commendacon ... (Sir Gerard de Braybroke, [Danbury, Essex]; burial at Colmworth church, Bedfordshire)

Figure, possibly of a pilgrim, Youlgreave, Derbyshire

1504 I will that as soone as my executor may know that any troste man that is a preste of this cuntre have an eryn [errand] to Rome, that he shall give unto him a certein money, to singe for my soule, and for the soules of my good benefactors, 5 masses at Rome, at such places as moste mede† is at. (Thomas Herynge, [Walsingham, Norfolk])

c. 1530 [To my] cosen Harrisons wyf at London my best girdell under this manner, that she will go a pilgrimage to our lady of Walsingham‡ and there to offer for me a nobell, my best kirtell, and my best gown. (Margery Everingham, [Gravesend, Kent])[19]

---

* Santiago de Compostela in Galicia, Spain, supposed resting place of the remains of St James, and St Michael's Mount, Cornwall, where in 495 AD fishermen reportedly saw the archangel Michael standing on the rock.

† *Meed.* Recompense, reward, in this case spiritual.

‡ The shrine to the Virgin Mary at Walsingham, Norfolk, the most popular of all pilgrimage destinations in England after Canterbury.

iv. Other bequests to ensure remembrance and prayers

For those of modest means a gift to the parish will ensure you are listed in its bead-roll, a list of benefactors read out regularly in church, at which time the congregation is exhorted to pray for those named.

> 1526 I bequethe one shepe to be praide for in the bead role ... (Elen Chapman, Denton, Northants)
>
> 1540 To the church of Lilford £6 13s 4d so that the inhabitants of Lilford put me in the bedroll by the space of twenty yeres & to cause me to be prayd for especially by name. (John Elmes, Lilford, Northants)[20]

You can also leave money to pay for vestments and altar cloths and have your name or coat of arms stained or embroidered upon them. While this appears vainglorious, and at odds with Christian humility, it may serve a practical purpose, reminding the officiating priest and others that you are the donor and so to say prayers for your soul.

> 1501 To the churchwardens ... two altar cloths of white, my name and arms to be stained upon every of them, all to the value of 13s 4d. (John Isaak, Patrixbourne, Kent)
>
> 1525-26 I will there shalbe geven toward the bying of a sute for deacon and sub-deacon ... £6 13s 4d, and I will there be a scriptur on the back of either of the said vestments desiring the parisheners to pray for my soule. (William Abell the elder, Erith, Kent)[21]

The following unusual request may be aimed at putting the testator and his family in the minds of those who are in the chancel offering up prayers.

> 1519 I will that my picture and my wifes and my childern shalbe painted in the bacside of the wall behinde the rode. (Thomas Pellet, Steyning, Sussex)[22]

v. Longer term intercession: month's minds and obits

While you may be released from purgatory quickly, it is prudent to provide against a long haul. The standard option, as noted earlier, is to have further observances performed for your soul a month after death, and perhaps twelve months after as well. Sometimes such secondary services are more extensive than those relating to the original burial – for example, Richard Adames of Fletching, Sussex, asks for 'a trigintall [trental] of masses at my buriall' but 'two trigintalles' at both his month's and his year's minds.[23]

If you can afford it, you may then have a recurring annual service or obit either for a specified number of years or for eternity.

> 1508 I will 3 score moder shepe to finde a obite in the said churche as long as the worlde standeth ... (John Palmer the younger, High Halstow, Kent)

1521 I will that mine executours ... by the space of twenty yeres next ensuing after my deceas, shall cause a solemne obit or anniversarye by note to be kepte and mainteined by the vicar, prestes and clerkes at Cukfeld, in the parishe churche there, aboute such season or time of the yere as it shall happen me to deceas, that is to saye placebo and dirige overnight and masse of requiem [on] the morowe ... (Edmund Flowre, Cuckfield, Sussex)

1538 I will have an obit yerly in our lady chauncell at Bosham, and therto I geve a cow and 2 ewes. Also I geve 2 ewes, and the profit of them shall finde ringers to ring at my saide obit at dirige and masse. (John Estoke, Bosham, Sussex)[24]

As these bequests suggest, like month's or year's minds obits largely mimic the original burial. Not only are dirige and mass performed but bells are rung, as if for a death; a hearse may be set up, as if there is a body to bury; and a bellman may go about the parish to solicit prayers for your soul, as he did on your burial day.

1463 I wil that the belle men have 4d to go yeerly abowte the town at my yeerday for my soule and for my faderis and my modrys. (John Baret, Bury St Edmunds)

1517 I bequeth ... 2 kine [cows] for the maintenance of one annuell obit, and to be rented at the discrecion of the church wardens for the most merit of my soul, wherof I will the curet ... to have ... at my said obit 8d, and other prest 4d, the clerk 2d, the belman a penye, for light 2d, for making the hers 1d ... (Humfrey Hyberdam, Boxgrove, Sussex)[25]

There may also be a dole for the poor.

1528 Also yerlye for ever to kepe ... an obit for my sowle & the sowles of my frends & yerly to despose at the said obit for ever 10s in manner and forme folowing, that is to saye to the parishe prest ther for his besynes that day & for the names of me & my frends in the beadrolle 12d, to the parishe clarke 3d, to every preste that dwelleth within the towne of Ketring being present 4d, to 6 yeoman clarks 12d, to 4 children that singe versicles & rede lessons 4d, to the belman 1d, to the profit of the bells 8d, to the ringers for ther labors in money 8d & to drinking 4d, to every poore body in the almes howse 1d, and halfe a pounde of waxe to burne abowt ye herse ther, & the residew of the said 10s to be bestowed amonge poore folkes ... (W. Fleckton, Kettering, Northants)[26]

Sometimes the dole occurs separately from the anniversary, Good Friday and All Souls being common choices.

1530 I will that ... yerely ... ther be given in almes to the pore people upon All Soules day 10s, and also likewise upon Good Friday 5s, it to be disposed wher need is ... (Hugh Schawe, skinner, Boston, Lincs)[27]

And while obits themselves are usually kept on the anniversary of death, sometimes another date or period is stipulated, Lent being popular.

> 1493 I will my obite be kepte yerely on Shere [Maundy] Thursdaye with prestes and clarkes singing, reding, and prayeing, and at after noone that same day at the washeing of the auters there to have bred and ale. (Richard Longeman, High Halstow)[28]

The following are a few examples of related payments received by the parish.

> 1516 For the use of the best cross at the obit of Johanna, late wife of John Ford, and others ... 20s (Ashburton, Devon)

> 1544 For torches burning at ye obbett of Robert Payne ... 4d (Bungay)

> 1557 At the monethes minde of Thomas Perkins, for twelve tapers, two torches, and the best paule ... 2s 6d (St Helen, Abingdon, Berks)[29]

vi. Chantries: intercession through the year

Another option is to provide funds for one or more priests to intercede for your soul throughout the year in a form of endowment known as a chantry. This is of course much more expensive but the level of intercession is correspondingly greater, a mass typically being said for your soul every day, usually at a side altar. As with obits, chantries can be established for a specified number of years or – provided your bequest is sufficient – for eternity.

> 1501 I will that a good and vertuose prest rede and singe for me after my decesse the space of 7 yeers; and if he be not vertuose, I prey you that be mine executors let him be changed. (Nicholas Talbot, Great Berkhamsted, Herts)

> 1532 An honest prest shall from the daie of my burying singe in Withecombe ... for 15 yeres, praying for the soules of my father Richard, my mother Phelep, my sowle, [etc] and after the same 15 yere to the end of the world, as my wife and children executors will answer before God at the dredfull daie of jugement. (James Hadley, Withycombe, Somerset)[30]

The Last Judgement, English, *c.* 1485

6. Guilds*

For those of relatively modest means a degree of intercession can be achieved by joining one of the guilds which are to be found in most parishes in the later Middle Ages.

Many guilds have other functions as well – typically supporting lights in the church, holding an annual feast, and giving alms to the poor – but almost all provide benefits for members when they die.

These vary but often include guild officers and members coming to your house and keeping watch over your body, and the guild's expensive lights may be brought and set about your corpse.

> When one of the bretheren dies the officers shall summon a third part of the bretheren, who shall watch near the body, and pray for his soul, through the night. ... It is also ordained by the bretheren and sisteren of the gild that, when any of them dies, the wax† ... together with eight smaller ones, shall be carried from the church to the house of him that is dead, and there they shall be kept alight before the body of the dead until it is carried to the church ... (Guild of the Holy Cross, Stratford upon Avon, Warwickshire)

> On the death of a brother or sister within the city, not only shall the dean bring the four wax lights which are called 'soul-candels', and fulfil all other usual ceremonies, but the banner of the gild shall be brought to the house of the dead, and there openly shown, that men may know that the dead was a brother or sister of the gild, and this banner shall be carried, with a great torch burning, from the house of the dead, before the body, to the church. (Guild of St Michael on the Hill, Lincoln)

> [1284] If any man wishes, as is common, to keep night-watches with the dead, this will be allowed, on the condition that he neither calls up ghosts, nor makes any mockeries of the body or its good name, nor does any other scandal of the kind ... And never shall any woman, unless of the household of the dead, keep such a night-watch. (Guild of the Palmers, Ludlow)[1]

At Wiggenhall, Norfolk, on the river Ouse, several guilds promise to seek out your body if you go missing. In addition, as often happens elsewhere, they will pay for the funeral should your goods or wealth not be sufficient to cover the cost.

> What brother or sister die, and he may not be broughte to the hergdes [earth] with his owne catelle [goods], he shall be broughte with the broderhedes. And if he be drowned in water, he shall be sought 6 mile about, and the lighte be broughte before him to the kirke. (Guild of the Holy Trinity)

---

* Most examples of guild rules in this section are from ordinances provided as part of a survey carried out in 1389, although a few are of earlier or later date as indicated.
† A light maintained in the church before the cross to which the guild was dedicated.

If he be perichee [perished] by water or by land, then shall his gild brothers gare seke him 3 mile aboute, and bringe him to cristen mennes bereinge, if he be not in power of his own catelle; and ye light be brought before him to ye dirige, and to ye kirke ... (Guild of St Peter)[2]

Fellow guild members are often expected to accompany the corpse to church in this way and they are always required to attend the funeral, usually on pain of a small fine. In addition they must pray for your soul and perhaps make a modest offering for it.

All the bretheren of the gild are bound to follow the body to church and to pray for his soul until the body is buried. And whoever does not fulfil this shall pay one halfpenny. (Guild of the Holy Cross, Stratford upon Avon)

It is ordained ... that every brother and sistur be redy to go to ye kirke, wen any brother or sistur is ded ... and that every brother offer a ob., and that each brother giff a halfpeny worth of bred for his soule ... (Guild of St Peter, Wiggenhall)[3]

After the funeral most guilds will arrange for one or more masses to be said for your soul. In the following case this is akin to a month's mind.

[1494] *Special obit.* When any broder or sister of this gilde is decessed oute of this worlde, then, within the 30 dayes of that broder or sister, in the chirch of Seint Poules, ye steward of this gilde shall do ringe for him, and do to say a placebo and dirige, with a masse on ye morowe of requiem, as ye common use is. At the which masse the alderman of ye gilde, or his depute, shall offer 2d for the same soule, and to ye clerke for ringing 2d, and to the belman for going aboute ye town 1d. The said dirige to be holden on ye Friday ... and the masse on the morowe. All this to be don on ye coste and charge of the gilde. (Guild of St Katherine, Stamford, Lincs)[4]

Many offer greater quantity. The Guild of the Assumption at Wiggenhall will have nine masses performed for your soul, the Guild of St George the Martyr at King's Lynn sixty, and the Guild of the Resurrection at Lincoln 'as many masses ... as there are bretheren and sisteren in the gild'.[5]

In addition you will be included in a collective obit performed on the annual guild day.

[1494] *General obit.* The same daye when the generall feste is holden, at afternoone, in the ... chirch of Seint Poules, shalbe done and said a placebo and dirige for all the sowles of the bredern and sisters that ben past in this gilde, and ther to ring 3 peeles; with masse of requiem on the next morowe, with as many peeles. At the which masse the alderman of the gilde, or his depute, shall offer 2d. And at the said dirige, the stuarde of the gilde shall see that they that seye the said dirige shall have brede, chese and drincke, and the ringers also, and he shall giff the clerke for his ringing 2d, and the bellman for going aboute the town 1d, and brede, chese and drincke. (Guild of St Katherine, Stamford)[6]

Such annual services are also recorded in guild accounts.

1512 Paid at ye dirige in churche kept for all ye brothers & sisters ... 5s 4d | 1523 To the sextens for ringing at dirige by 2 yers ... 4d (Guild of All Saints, Wymondham, Norfolk)

1545 The prestes, the decon and sexton singing dirige and masse for the soules of the brethers and sisters of Jesus Masse ... 22d | For the herse ... 2d | For the blacke awter ... 2d | The grete bell ... 12d (Guild of Jesus Mass, St Edmund, Salisbury)[7]

Beyond this, larger and richer guilds may have their own chapel and employ their own priest to pray and say masses for members in an ongoing fashion, acting in effect as co-operative chantries.[8]

1530 To a prest singing for ye brethers & sisters souls by a quarter of a yere ... 13s 4d (Guild of the Holy Trinity, Wymondham)[9]

Further to boost intercession for any recently deceased member, the Guild of St Peter at Bardwell, Suffolk, provides a 'sepulchre light' which, after the funeral, is set upon the grave in the churchyard and kept burning for at least a month, and sometimes for as long as a year, the aim being to remind passers by to pray for the soul of the person interred below.[10]

Occasionally a guild may also provide for the funerals of poor people and strangers, thus engaging in a credit-earning work of mercy on behalf of guild members.

If any poor man in the town dies, or if any stranger has not means of his own out of which to pay for a light to be kept burning before his body, the bretheren and sisteren shall, for their souls' health, whosoever he may be, find four waxes, and one sheet, and a hearse-cloth to lay over the coffin until the body is buried. (Guild of the Holy Cross, Stratford upon Avon)[11]

7. After the Reformation

Impressive and reassuring as all this may be, by the time of the Reformation there is a growing sense that the Church is effectively running a lucrative salvation racket. The charge is summed up in *The Popish Kingdome*.

Give money, and thy tombe amid the church shall placed bee,
Or in the queere, so that no raine or wet shall trouble thee.
Give money, then, and store of psalmes and dirges shalt thou have.
And eke [also] with great lamenting shall the corps be borne to grave.
Give money and thou shalt be blest, with store of trentals soong,
And yearely in remembraunce had, with soule peales duely roong.
Give money, and upon thy tombe a princely hearse they set,
Still smokt with franckensense, and all with holy water wet.

Give money, and of all thy vowes discharged shalt thou bee,
And eke with Gods commaundements they shall dispence for thee.
All things for money will they do ...[1]

Alongside the rejection of such 'corruption', one of the central changes brought about by Protestant reformers is the rejection of the idea of purgatory. Instead they believe the soul is freed from sin by faith alone. Obits and other attempts to intercede for the souls of the dead are therefore pointless, and indeed superstitious. Considerable simplification of the ritual surrounding death is a natural consequence, and in the Prayer Book of 1552 the burial service is so reduced that it can be performed at the church stile and the graveside without it being necessary even to take the body inside the church.[2]

Nonetheless, the following account of a well-to-do post-Reformation burial, written by antiquary Francis Tate in 1600, suggests that some of the old ways persist. It also shows that by that time individual coffins are becoming commonplace among those who can afford them.[3]

When life beginneth to forsake the bodie, they which are present close the eyes and shut the mouth, according to the custom of the Jews, Grecians, and Romans ... Then is the body laid forth ... upon a floore in some chamber, covered with a sheete, and candles set burning over it on a table day and night, and the body continually attended or watched. Though the custom of burning candles be now grown into disuse, being thought superstitious ... there is yet in use amongst us such kinde of candles, which, because they were in former times applied to this kinde of use, do beare the name of Watche Candles. ...

Amongst us there is not any set and determinate time how long the corpse should be kept, but as seemeth best to the friends of the deceased. ...

The appointed day for the funeral being neere, the body is wrapt up with flowers and herbes in a faire sheet, and this we call Winding a Corpse. ... After this, the body is put into a coffin of wood or stone, or wrapped in lead, and sometime there is put up with it somethinge which he principally esteemed. ...

On the day of the interment the body is brought forth of the chamber, where before it lay, into the hall or great chamber, and there placed till the mourners be reddy and marshalled ... The body is laid with the face upright, and the feet towards the doore. The coffin or beare [bier] is covered with a sheet, over which lieth a blacke cloth or a blacke velvet covering, round about which are hanged the armes of the party that is dead, and so he is carried towards the grave. ...

The corpse is taken up and carried either by poor people chosen out for the purpose, or by the servants of him that is dead. They and the rest of the servants clothed in blacke go before the corpse, his kinsfolk and familiar friends followe after in blacke gownes and hoodes. ... Then they carry the body the best and most convenient way to the grave, and neither into the market place nor other streets for [to avoid] ostentation; and if they be barons or men of high degree, they are set under an herse covered with blacke.* ...

The body being thus interred, the banners and scutchions are hanged and set upon pillars in the churche ...[4]

Further paring back of the rite occurs in the mid 17th century under puritan influence, but after the Restoration a degree of elaboration returns with the revised Prayer Book of 1662. Its rubric explicitly sets out the option of taking the corpse into the church for the first part of the service, and indeed seems to expect that this will be done.[5]

Perhaps the best account of a post-Restoration funeral is that by François Misson, a French Protestant who settled in London in 1685 and published an account of England in 1698. In particular he describes the process of burying in woollen, required under a law of 1678.

There is an Act of Parliament which ordains that the dead shall be bury'd in a woollen stuff, which is a kind of thin bays, which they call *flannel*; nor is it lawful to use the least needleful of thread or silk. (The intention of this Act is for the encouragement of the woollen manufacture.) This shift is always white, but there are different sorts of it as to fineness, and consequently of different prices. ...

After they have wash'd the body throughly clean, and shav'd it, if it be a man, and his beard be grown during his sickness, they put it on a flannel shirt, which has commonly a sleeve purfled† about the wrists, and the slit of the shirt down the breast done in the same manner. ... The shirt shou'd be at least half a foot longer than the body, that the feet of the deceas'd may be wrapped in it, as in a bag. When they have thus folded the end of this shirt close to the feet, they tie the part that is folded down with a piece of woollen thread ... so that the end of the shirt is done into a kind of tuft. Upon the head they put a cap, which they fasten with a very broad chin cloth; with gloves on the hands, and a cravat round the neck, all of woollen. That the body may lie the softer, some put a lay of bran, about four inches thick, at the bottom of the coffin. Instead of a cap, the women have a kind of head-dress, with a forehead-cloth.

The body being thus equipp'd, and laid in the coffin ... they let it lie three or four days in this condition; which time they allow, as well to give the dead person an opportunity of coming to life again, if his soul has not quite left his body, as to prepare mourning, and the ceremonies of the

* On the changing nature of hearses see pp336-342 below.
† *Purfle*. Adorn with a border of threadwork or embroidery; trim with gold or silver lace, fur, etc.

funeral. They send the beadle with a list of such friends and relations as they have a mind to invite; and sometimes they have printed tickets, which they leave at their houses.

A little before the company is set in order for the march, they lay the body into the coffin upon two stools, in a room, where all that please may go and see it; then they take off the top of the coffin, and remove from the face a little square piece of flannel, made on purpose to cover it, and not fastened to any thing ... The relations and chief mourners are in a chamber apart, with their more intimate friends; and the rest of the guests are dispersed in several rooms about the house. When they are ready to set out, they nail up the coffin, and a servant presents the company with sprigs of rosemary. Every one takes a sprig, and carries it in his hand 'till the body is put into the grave, at which time they all throw their sprigs in after it.

Before they set out, and after they return, it is usual to present the guests with something to drink, either red or white wine, boil'd with sugar and cinnamon, or some other such liquor. Every one drinks two or three cups. Butler, the keeper of a tavern,* told me that there was a tun of red port drank at his wife's burial, besides mull'd white wine. Note: No men ever go to women's burials, nor the women to the mens; so that there were none but women at the drinking of Butler's wine. ...

The parish has always three or four mortuary cloths of different prices, to furnish those who are at the charge of the interment. These cloths, which they call *palls*, are some of black velvet, others of cloth with an edge of white linen or silk a foot broad, or thereabouts. For a batchelor or maid, or for a woman that dies in child-bed, the pall is white. This is spread over the coffin ... They generally give black or white gloves and black crape hatbands to those that carry the pall; sometimes also white silk scarves.

Every thing being ready to move, (it must be remember'd that I always speak of middling people, among whom the customs of a nation are most truly to be learn'd,) one or more beadles march first, each carrying a long staff, at the end of which is a great apple or knob of silver. The minister of the parish, generally accompany'd by some other minister, and attended by the clerk, walks next; and the body, carry'd as I said before, comes just after him. The relations in close mourning, and all the guests two and two, make up the rest of the procession.

The common practice is to carry the corpse thus into the body of the church, where they set it down upon two tressels, while either a funeral sermon is preach'd, containing an elogium upon the deceased, or certain prayers are said, adapted to the occasion. If the body is not bury'd in the church, they carry it to the church-yard ... where it is interr'd in the presence

* The Crown and Scepter in St Martins-street. [Footnote in original English edition.]

of the guests, who are round the grave, and do not leave it 'till the earth is thrown in upon it. ...

Among persons of quality 'tis customary to embalm the body, and to expose it for a fortnight or more on a bed of state. After which they carry it in a sort of a waggon made for that purpose,* and cover'd with black cloth, to the place appointed by the deceased. This cart is attended by a long train of mourning coaches belonging to the friends of the dead person.[6]

Mourners, from a ballad published in 1685, around the time that Misson was writing

8. Some parts of the process in more detail

i. Covering the body

The body is wrapped, usually at home, in a sheet or shroud, the process being referred to variously as sewing, winding or socking.

> 1543 The best sheet I will have for my soking shete, the which hath a blewe thred at the one end. (Simon Mew, Eastbourne, Sussex)

> 1558-59 I will and give to 4 honest matrones enlapping my bodye in linnen clothe ordeined for that purpose 12d a pece. (George Haile, rector, Clayton, Sussex)[1]

As with other parts of the burial process, in the case of strangers and the poor the parish usually pays, one result being that details are recorded in the accounts.

> 1571 To Stones wife for watching with Russalls wife and soweng of her ... 13d | To Mother Masone for helping of her to sowe her ... 5d (St Mary Magdalen, Pulham, Norfolk)

---

* i.e. a hearse in the modern sense.

1598 For a winding sheet for Ralph Tomson ... 22d | For winding him ... 4d (Leverton, Lincs)

1603 For 2 ells of canvas to wind a man that died in the street ... 2s (St Alphage, London Wall)[2]

The sheet or shroud is secured above the head and below the feet, either by tying of its ends or by a separate cord, and may be sewn centrally along its length. Usually it is white, which, according to John Mirk, shows that the deceased 'was cleane shriven, and cleansed of his sins by contricion of herte and by asoiling [absolving] of holy church', and it may be marked with a cross.[3]

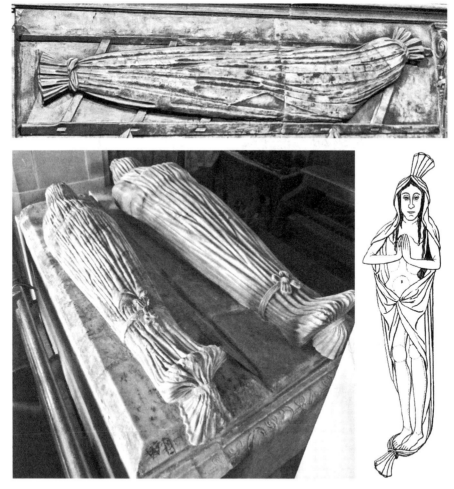

UPPER Shroud on one of the Foljambe monuments at Chesterfield, late 16th century.
LOWER. LEFT Tomb of Thomas Beresford and his wife at Fenny Bentley,
Derbyshire, thought on the basis of style to be 16th-century (albeit he died in 1473).
RIGHT From a brass memorial to Thomasina Tendring, Yoxford, Suffolk, 1485.

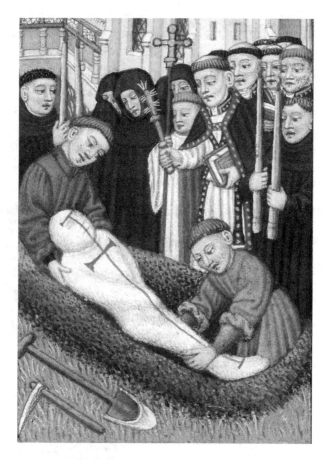

By the Master of Sir John Fastolf, from a Book of Hours, *c.* 1430

The pall or burying cloth is a separate item, laid over the body or coffin at the funeral but then removed and reused.

> 1538 For sponging and drying the second pall ... 1d (St Mary the Virgin, Oxford)

> 1669 For a blacke [cloth] to lay upon the dead corpses, for the use of the parishners ... £1 17s (Wilmslow, Cheshire)[4]

Inventories indicate that they are often of rich material and are sometimes decorated.

> 1486 A grene silke cloth for to serve for the pulpit and to ley upon ded corsis of the parish with serpentes therein. (St Margaret Pattens)

> 1552 A pall cloth of black damask with a crosse of white damask. (St Mary Woolnoth)

> 1553 A buring clothe of blew bodkin [baudekin] branched with gold. | A buring clothe of ould blacke velvet with Katherins whelles. (St Mary at Hill)[5]

As Misson notes, it is customary for the parish to charge for their loan.

> 1578 The 27th of Maye was buried John Wharton the queenes mowle-ketcher, the best cloth ... 20d | 1587 April 15th. Buried Oliver Twist,* worst cloth ... 2d (St Martin in the Fields)

> 1624 Receaved for the church cloth at the buriall of one out of the Angel ... 1s (St Ethelburga, Bishopsgate)[6]

There may be a smaller one for children and perhaps one designated for those of lowly status.

> 1547 2 burying clothes, one of clothe of gold for men and the other of blacke velvet for childerne. (All Hallows the Less, Thames Street, inventory)

> 1552 1 beryall cloth of gold for children. | 1 beryall cloth of silke for ye power and for sarvantes. (St Dionis Backchurch, inventory)

> 1689 A handsome black buriall clothe for a man's corps, being 3 yrds and a ½ long ... £1 1s | Another of ye same clothe for a youth's or child corps, 2 yrds near in length ... 12s (Wenhaston, Suffolk)[7]

In some places a cloth is provided without charge for the bodies of the poor.

> 1613 Mrs Gundry hath given a silke cloth to the church to be a covering for the corps of the poore when they are brought to be buried. (Wimborne Minster, Dorset)[8]

At Gillingham in Kent a cloth for the poor is bought by subscription. In 1742 it is in the care of Widow Jenner, schoolmistress, who is to charge a shilling for its use to those who are not poor, and two shillings in rainy weather.[9]

ii. Burial in woollen

As seen above, in order to protect the domestic wool industry an Act of 1678 requires that every corpse is buried in the material. Replacing similar legislation passed twelve years earlier which had been widely disregarded, the Act states that after 1st August

> no corps of any person or persons shall be buryed in any shirt, shift, sheete or shroud or any thing whatsoever made or mingled with flax, hempe, silke, haire, gold or silver, or in any stuffe or thing other than what is made of sheeps wool only, or be put into any coffin lined or faced with any sort of cloath or stuffe or any other thing whatsoever that is made of any material but sheeps wool only, upon paine of the forfeiture of five pounds of lawful money of England ...

---

* The name also occurs in a baptism register entry at Shelford, Nottinghamshire: '1567. May 10th. John Twiste sonne of Oliver Twiste.'

Each parish is required to keep a register recording whether burials comply with the Act

> 1678 For a larg paper booke for ye registering burials in woolen ... 14s (Manchester)[1]

along with written affidavits confirming the same. The affidavits are to be provided within eight days of the burial by 'the relations of the party deceased or other credible person', and are to be made 'under the hands and seales of two or more credible witnesses'.

It seems, however, that not everyone takes the matter seriously.

> 1682 Dec 7th. Frances Pickeings widow of the parish of Helmdon was then let downe into her grave made in the churchyard of the village aforesaid. Let the beadle take notice that within 8 days after ye funeral obseqyes of Frances Pickeings affidavit was brought from a neighboring minister that the abovesaid Frances Pickeings was shrowded only in a winding sheet made of the Fleece of good Fat Mutton. (Helmdon, Northants)[2]

The affidavits and the wool both need to be paid for, by the parish in the case of the poor.

> 1678 For a certificate that Widow Mansfield was buried in woollon ... 2d (St Werburgh, Derby)

> 1712 For wool for to lay on Anne Pearce in her cofin by way of a shroud ... 6d (Swainswick, Somerset)

> 1750 Paid Garviss for geting ye man that was drown'd out of ye river ... 9d | For bringing him to the church ... 6d | Expences going to Ashford for the coroner ... 8s | For wool for the man that was drowned ... 1s 6d (Holy Cross Westgate, Canterbury)[3]

The Act sets out that the money collected for breaches of the law is to be divided, one part going 'to the use and benefit of the poore of the parish', the other to the person who informs of the breach. In effect this means that provided a relative tells the parish that the law has been broken the fine is halved.[4]

> 1678 Received of the executors of Mr William Browne, he being buried in linen, contrary to law, they informinge paid the half of the forfeiture ... £2 10s (Hammersmith, Middlesex)

> 1682 Given to several poore people ye mony that was received for burying the Lady Bright in lining [linen] which was ... £2 10s (Battersea)[5]

Over time the law comes to be widely disregarded, but it is not repealed until 1814.[6]

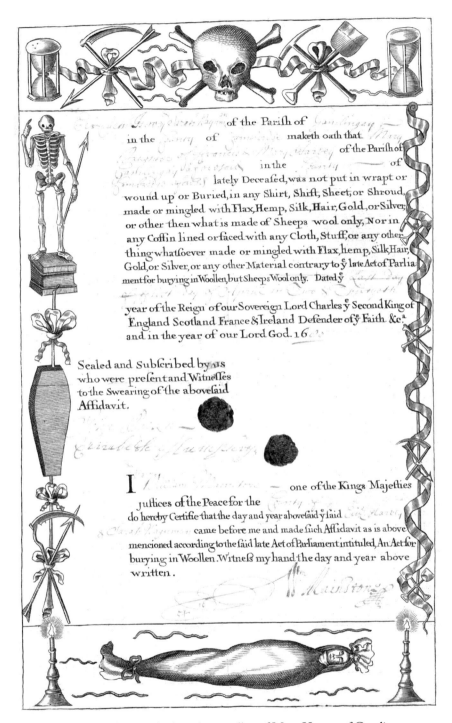

Affidavit confirming the burial in woollen of Mary Harvey of Gamlingay,
Cambridgeshire, 1680, including worms about the shrouded corpse

iii. Coffins &c.

Before the 17th century most coffins for interment are for the well-to-do. They are also used occasionally for bodies thought to be infected, the following, occurring in a notable plague year, perhaps being a case in point.

> 1593 Received of Mr John Heybourne for the buriall of his childe in the church yard in a coffin ... 3s 4d (St Alphage, London Wall)[1]

There are also lidless parish coffins in which bodies are placed in their shrouds or sheets for carriage to the grave but which, after the burial, are returned to the church for future use.

> 1524 For mending of the cofin that lieth on the bere ... 2s ob. (St Giles, Reading)

> 1626 To Curtes ye carpenter for two coffins to carry ye deade corpes in ... 6s (St Mary Coslany, Norwich)[2]

The Reading entry above is the earliest instance recorded in the *OED* of the modern, burial-related sense of 'coffin', which had previously been a more general term for a basket, chest, case or box.

At Louth a list of duties for the bellman, drawn up in 1521, says that 'he shal bere and convey the chest or chests as nedes shall require to every place in the towne wher any corse is or corses as it shall happen'.[3]

Some parishes also have smaller versions for the corpses of the young.

> 1562-64 To Couke the carpendar for a couffin for the youthe ... 3s 4d (St Andrew Hubbard)[4]

A shed or other structure may be built to provide shelter.

> 1569 For a newe coffin for the use of the parishe ... 5s | More for making of a penthowse in the churche yarde for the keping drye of the said coffin ... 6s 8d (St Alphage, London Wall)

> 1578 Agreed that Ric. Bowdler, then churchewarden, withe the advice of workemen shall cawse to be set up at the charge of the said parishe a shedde or pentehowse upon the north side of the churche where the old shedde stoode for the kepinge dry of the laders and coffens: and that serten hookes of iron be set in the said wall for to bere the same laders & coffens, and ... also to provide three new coffens of sundry biggenes to carry the deade to the grownde etc. (St Bartholomew Exchange, vestry)[5]

During the 17th century the use of personal coffins spreads down the social scale

> 1618-19 Feb. 18th. Andrew son of William Beast, lookingglassmaker, in the churchyard at the hether end, coffined. (St Peter, Paul's Wharf)[6]

and increasingly parish coffins are used only for the poor.[7]

> 1636 For a newe comon coffin and a new beere to carry poore people to church [etc] ... £1 1s 6d (Mortlake, Surrey)

1649 For a coffing to be remaining to the parishe for poore people ... 2s 6d (Battersea)[8]

Where space is a problem, notably in the case of burials inside London churches, the parish may insist on flat-topped coffins, as at St Mary Colechurch, where in 1615 the vestry proscribe 'ridged' coffins so that if necessary two corpses may be interred in a single grave.[9]

The following is an oddity, perhaps being a precaution against premature burial.

1590 Dec. 27th. Leonard Thickpenny, minister of Enfeld, brought from the Kinges bench in a coffen with a flap to open, with a writing on it in verse. Laid at Ledenhall gate by night. (St Peter, Cornhill)[10]

In time individual coffins are provided for the poor as well, although in the first case below it seems infection may be suspected.

1651 For a coffin for Goodwife Peche ... 4s 6d | For carying her bedding to aire ... 2d (Holy Cross Westgate, Canterbury)

1690 For a coffin for a poor man ... 5s 6d (Houghton-le-Spring, co. Durham)[11]

There is also the occasional burial in leather. Thomas Hearne mentions that in the past 'many persons of distinction, instead of coffins, were wrapt up in leather ... and 'twas in such leathern sheets, or bags, that others were put that were laid in the walls of churches'. In his will dated 1644 Richard Ferror of Thurne, Norfolk, orders 'that my dead body be handsomely trussed up in a black bullock's hide, and be decently buried in the church yard ... at the chancell's end'. He then signs off rather nicely: 'And thus I take my leave of the world. *Deo Gloria, amicis gratia, mihi misericordia* [Glory to God, thanks to friends, mercy to me.] Amen.'[12]

iv. Carrying the body

Whether or not it is coffined, for carriage, and while at rest during the funeral, the body is often placed upon a bier.* In form this is similar to a stretcher, with handles at each end for the bearers. It may also have legs, and these may fold upwards so as to tuck away when the body is in transit.

1506 To Thomas Couper wright makin 2 beers, nailes & sawing ... 20d (Louth)

1625 Mr Christopher Wormall, churchwarden ... did at his charge give unto the churche a stronge and comely newe beere to carrie the dead corps to the grave, all framed and made of wanescott with turned postes or pillers. (Lambeth, vestry book)[1]

---

* Derived from an Old English word for to bear or carry and in early use spelt *baere* or *bere*. It is thought that the modern spelling, which the *OED* records from 1611, may have been adopted in imitation of the French *bière*, coffin.

As with parish coffins, there may be a smaller version for children

1562 To Nicolas Corder for ye making of a childe bere and for nailes for
it ... 4d (Long Melford)[2]

and provision may be made for storage.

1579 Mending of the beare house ... 10s 6d (St Thomas, Salisbury)

1592 For a rope to hang up the beere ... 8d (St Andrew, Canterbury)[3]

If the bier lacks legs, when in church it may be rested upon a small table or
stool at each end. A similar arrangement may be used for a coffin in the absence
of a bier, such tables coming to be known as coffin stools.

1638 Two joined stooles to set dead corps on ... 5s (Gateshead, co. Durham)

1641 For 2 short formes to set a coffin
upon in time of prayers in the church
... 3s 8d (St Oswald, Durham)[4]

At St Edmund, Salisbury, the fees due to
the sexton include the use of such supports.

1651 For moving the stone & placing it
there againe, diging ye grave & stools
... 4s 8d | For making a grave in the
church yard & setting his stools ... 1s[5]

Sometimes, usually in the case of the poor, the parish pays those carrying the
corpse, whether on a bier or otherwise.

1531 For bringing of a ded corse to towne that was found ded in haygarthes
in the great snow ... 4d (Louth)

1569 For caringe a dead corps to church oute of the Palace ... 4d (St
Margaret, Westminster)

1649 For the burying of Jonas Heywood his wife that died at 9 Elmes,
for bringing her by water & foure poore women that laid her into the
boate & carried her out ... 4s 3d (Battersea)[6]

Coffins borne aloft
UPPER From the title page of John Weever's *Ancient Funerall Monuments*, 1631.
LOWER By Richard Bentley, a tailpiece for Thomas Gray's
'Elegy written in a country church yard', 1753.

FACING PAGE. UPPER Coffin stools in a domestic setting, before the body
is carried to church, by Hogarth, 1732. LOWER Bier, East Ruston, Norfolk.

v. The hearse

As seen above, once inside the church the body upon the bier is set down where the chancel meets the nave or, if the deceased was in holy orders, in the chancel itself. In either place it may in earlier periods rest under or within a hearse, an item possessed by some parishes and already referred to several times.

The word derives from French and Latin terms for a harrow (*herse* and *hirpex* respectively). Its earliest use in an ecclesiastical context is thought to be for the triangular frame designed to hold candles at the Tenebrae services in Holy Week. The name may have been adopted because of a resemblance between the shape of the frame and that of an ancient harrow, and/or because the frame's numerous candle-holding prickets resemble a harrow's spikes or teeth.[1]

'Hearse' also comes to be used for various structures relating to burial, the name perhaps being borrowed from the Tenebrae candle-holder because originally the main function of these structures is to hold lights. Such burial hearses may be divided into five broad types.[2]

1. A free-standing wooden enclosure holding tapers around the body. It also serves to keep people – and perhaps dogs – at a distance from the corpse. In her will of 1391 Margaret, Countess of Devon, asks for 'no other hearse than plain bars to keep off the press of people'.[3]

2. A frame set over the body, primarily to support a pall, sometimes fitting onto or forming part of a bier. A bier given to South Wootton church, Norfolk, in 1611 has an upper section in the shape of a bail – a half-hoop for supporting the cover of a wagon or cradle – apparently designed to hold a pall over the (then still usually uncoffined) corpse. That similar structures were in use in pre-Reformation times is evident from the tomb of Richard, Earl of Warwick, in the Beauchamp chapel in St Mary, Warwick. The 1454 contract for the tomb requires 'an hearse' of latten to be constructed 'over the image [effigy], to beare a covering to be ordeined'.

In addition the shape and size of the draped structures in many funeral depictions in medieval manuscripts suggest the use of square or angled supporting frames.[4]

The main point of this type of hearse being to support a covering, provision for lights is secondary. The Beauchamp monument has fixtures for them at the corners, but separate from the frame. One common solution is to place free-standing candlesticks around the draped hearse. Another is to pay poor people to stand holding lights.

UPPER The Wootton bier. LOWER The Warwick tomb.
FACING PAGE. Enclosure hearses. LEFT From a 15th-century Book of Hours.
RIGHT Mass for the dead, by the Master of Sir John Fastolf, *c.* 1430.

Presumed pall-supporting hearses. While the concealed structures could be coffins it seems likely they are frames designed to hold the cloth neatly over the corpse whether it is coffined or not.

RIGHT From an English Book of Hours, *c.* 1490, with beadsmen holding torches.

BELOW From a Flemish Book of Hours, *c.* 1460, with standing lights and a beggar seeking alms.

3. An elaborate temporary structure created for a grand funeral. This is the one type of hearse of which detailed descriptions survive, but it is not generally relevant to practice in parish churches. The illustration *below* is of the one erected in Westminster Abbey for the funeral of the abbot, John Islip, who died in 1532, and shows the elaboration sometimes involved. Such structures often remain in place until the month's mind, as happens in Islip's case: on the funeral day his body is buried in a chapel, but 'undernethe the herse was made a presentacion of the corps covered with a clothe of golde of tissewe', and 'the herse with all thother things did remaine there still until the monthes minde'.[5]

Also at Westminster Abbey, a 'very somptiouse herse' features prominently at the funeral of Queen Mary in 1558. It has 'lightes to the nomber of a thousand and more' and comprises eight squares or sections.

> On the upper parte of the 8 great postes stood 8 archangels of waxe, and under them 8 great skochiones of armes ... All the eight square of the herse was garneshed and set with angelles, morners, and quenes in their robes of estate maid of waxe ... The eight postes were covered with blake velvet, and on every post a skochion of sarsenet wrought with fine gold ...[6]

Two years later the hearse at the funeral of Francis Talbot, Earl of Shrewsbury, has 'a bredth of black velvet' all round it, 'and to all the nether edge of the said velvet was fastened a valance of sarsenet, written with letters of gold SIC TRANSIT GLORIA MUNDI [Thus passes the glory of the world]'.[7]

Such grand hearses become an increasingly rare sight, although they appear occasionally in later times.[8]

Use of the more modest hearses usually found at parish level also wanes after the Reformation as elaborate obsequies are discouraged. At Rippingale, Lincolnshire, the 'herse lightes' are destroyed in 1561 along with other anachronistic items, and in the 1570s Bishop Barnes of Durham orders 'that all balkes or herses, wherupon lightes or serges were in time of poperye used to be set' are to be 'utterly removed'.[9]

4. A permanent metal version set on or around a tomb. The above types 1 to 3 used at funerals are typically made of wood and no early examples are known to have survived. Types 1 and 2 are, however, sometimes imitated in metal in permanent memorials used for obits and other post-burial observances, and a few of these can still be seen. That of Thomas Fitzalan, 5th Earl of Arundel (*d.* 1415) in the Fitzalan Chapel at Arundel (*below left*) echoes type 1 and the one in the Beauchamp chapel at Warwick echoes type 2, while that of Sir John Marmion (*d.* 1387) at West Tanfield, Yorkshire (*below right*) contains elements of both.

5. A mobile version, used to carry the body. By the mid 17th century the word has acquired the more modern sense of a vehicle for carrying a coffin to or at a funeral. A notice of 1672 concerning a coach service between Oxford and London concludes: 'These are farther to give notice that the aforesaid Thomas Moor hath a hearse, and all things belonging to it, convenient for the carrying of dead corps to any part of England.'[10]

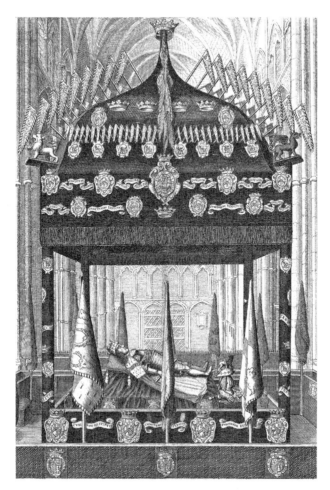

The funeral of George Monck, Duke of Albemarle, 1670

UPPER An old style hearse (type 3) erected in Westminster Abbey. Like another notable 17th-century example, that erected for James I in 1625, it is distinguished from medieval versions by a lack of lights and a heavy emphasis on personal heraldry. LOWER A 'chariot' or new style hearse used in the procession, in this case carrying an effigy rather than a corpse.

References to hearses in parish accounts and ordinary wills do not of course bother with the above distinctions, but in most cases they probably relate to types 1 (a taper-holding enclosure) or 2 (a pall-supporting frame), or to hybrid structures incorporating elements of both.[11]

> 1533 For making of an new herse and the bords and nails therto ... 15d (Lydd, Kent)

> 1554 For pitche to blacke the herse ... 2d ob. (Stanford, Berks)

> 1590 For mendinge one of the hearse feete ... 10d (St Mary the Great, Cambridge)[12]

Occasionally one or more crosses are fixed upon the frame.*[13]

> 1535 I geve to the said church [Frindsbury, Kent] a cross to stand upon the herse at buryings and obetts and other times upon our lady aulter.† (Richard Brawdrib, priest)[14]

As for the lights around the body, the first of the following entries perhaps relates to those mounted on the hearse itself while the others appear to relate to free-standing ones set round about.

> 1504-06 Received of Sir John Pesmeth for ... 4 herse tapurs for the olde parson [etc] ... 2s 8d (St Andrew, Canterbury)

> 1522 Mathew Tynkelare mending grett candilstikis to herses ... 8d (Louth)

> 1556 For 2 standinge candelle sticke of irone for a hearse [etc] ... 3s 4d (Eltham, Kent)[15]

Hearse lights are often mentioned in wills. The following all relate to Kent, the first incidentally indicating the lying of the body in the church overnight.

> 1509 I will 5 prestis besides the parsone at my burying and 8 torches which I will schalbe light and brenn at the time of my going to churche all the waye betwene my house and the churche and also schall brenn aboute my herse all the dirige time and masse of requiem on the morowe. (Alice Bray, Chelsfield)

> 1521 To the ... churche ... a cow to finde light aboute the herse when poor people schalbe buried. (Thomas Kinge, Milton by Gravesend)

> 1527-28 I will they set abowte my herse 12 tapers of 2 li. a pese, four score penny candels, 7 torches, these to be borne aboute my herse at my month daye ... (Sir Thomas Newsam, Milton by Gravesend)[16]

The other major recurring hearse-related cost is for the large cloths placed upon them. These are often made of rich material.

* Examples can be seen on p271 and p336.
† A fitting allowing different uses in this way can be seen on p130.

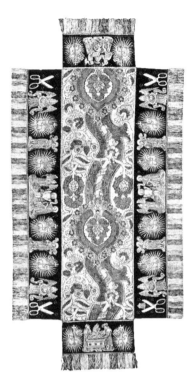

Palls or hearse-cloths belonging to the Vintners' Company (*left*)
and Merchant Taylors' Company (*right*)

1521 For 3 yerdes of purpell velvet for our herse clothe ... 36s | For the
reband of silke goinge abowt the herse clothe ... 3s 4d (Lambeth)

1550 2 hearse clothes thone of clothe of golde & thother of red fustian
of Naples. (St Andrew Hubbard, inventory)[17]

Sometimes they are decorated, as the following inventory entries show.

1475 A cloth of blac worstede for the herse with a white crosse improwdered
in 5 places with the name of Jesus Christ. (High Wycombe, Bucks)

1542 A herse clothe, blewe velvet enbroderid with pelicans. (St Stephen,
Coleman Street)

1552 1 herse cloth of gold with Saint Georgs crosses. | 1 olde herse cloth
with armes imbrothered with Venys gold. (Greenwich, Kent)[18]

The decoration may be apposite.

1523 I will that my executours shall cause a bawdkin* or a pall of blake
velvet to be made to cover the herse with all in our lady church, and

---

* As previously noted, *baudekin* is a type of material but it seems to be used here to
indicate a cloth, presumably made of such material rather than of black velvet.

therupon I will have an image of the Blissid Trinitie wrought with golde, and a ded man lyeng before Him in a winding shete; and at the sides I will have 4 angels wrought with golde and nedill warke, with candilstikkes in ther handes, as though they gave reverence to the Trinitie; and my name written under the fete of the ded man, for a memorial. (will of Dame Joan Thurescrosse, Kingston upon Hull, Yorks)

1552 One herse clothe of black velvet with dede mens heddes. (All Hallows the Great, Thames Street, inventory)[19]

Other examples of cloths with writing upon them include one given by Alice Chester in about 1480 to All Saints, Bristol, which has 'a scriptur in gold' reading *Orate pro animabus Henrici Chester & Alicie uxoris eius* [Pray for the souls of Henry Chester and Alice his wife].'[20]

More modestly, in his will of *circa* 1403 William Elwell of Battersea provides for 'one new cuverlet to cover the hearse over the bodies of the sorrowing poor'.[21]

Strictly speaking the term 'hearse cloth' should be used for cloths placed upon the hearse in this way. However, some of the other examples given may reflect the looser usage that develops over time whereby the term comes to be used for any cloth placed over a corpse or coffin.[22]

1552 An herse cloth to lay upon corps to the buryinge. (St Mary Abchurch, inventory)[23]

Some inventories of this period list different sizes of cloth, suggesting placement directly onto coffins or corpses.[24]

1552 An herse clothe of blake velvet and clothe of gold. | A litell herse clothe of cremsen velvet for children. (All Hallows Staining)

1552 A hers cloth for men & women of cloth of golde wrought with imbrodered work. | A hers cloth for children of purple velvet with images of children about the same. (St Magnus Martyr, Thames Street)[25]

vi. Blacks

Further cloths are sometimes draped around the church for sombre effect and for a fee.

1587 Received for the funeral of Sir Henry Gates, for the blacks about the church ... £1 (St Margaret, Westminster)

1596 Received for hanging of black cloth about the church at the buriall of Mr Lee ... 10s (St Alphage, London Wall)[1]

In the following case the parish pays a large sum in a show of respect for 'their late worthy vicar, who filled that office for the space of 43 years'.

1797 For hanging the church with black cloth for the funeral of the Rev. Thomas Keighly ... £24 12s (Leyton, Essex)[2]

vii. Lights

Funerals are also a time of great expense on lights beyond those set about any hearse. It is believed that candles that have been blessed have demonifugal power, warding off the devil, and more generally lights can be conceived as a defiance of darkness and a figuring of the hope that the dead do indeed live on.[1]

Those paying for a funeral are often charged for 'waste of wax', the reduction of the various lights as a result of their use.

> 1458-60 Received for wasting of 2 torches at Wetherleis dirige ... 4d (St Andrew Hubbard)

> 1491 At the burying of William Caxton, for 4 torches ... 6s 8d | 1496 2 tapers for the man that died in Tothill-street ... 2d | 1510 At the burying of my Lady Vampage 8 torches ... 8s | At the burying of Robert the Hermit 4 tapers ... 4d (St Margaret, Westminster)

> 1543 For the shorte torches and clothe at the buriall of Agnes Puffington ... 6d | 1546 At the buriall of Katherin Golightly for the smalle lightes, two torches and the clothe ... 18d (St Martin in the Fields)

> 1558 Received of Thomas Jakson for the wast of two taperes at ye berryall of his boye ... 4d (Wandsworth)[2]

After the Reformation such use of lights tends to decline, partly as a result of the formal reduction of burial rites and partly because of a related but more gradual falling away of belief in the power of earthly actions, props and ritual to secure advantages for the souls of the dead.

viii. Choosing where to be buried

The socially elevated sometimes stipulate in their wills not only where their corpse is to be taken to for burial but also what is to be done along the way.

> 1369 My body to be buried in the chapel of Walsingham, before the image of the blessed Virgin, and thither to be carried with all speed, having one taper at the head and another at the feet where it rests the first night. Also I will that a dirige shall be there said, and in the morning a mass, whereat a noble shall be offered for my soul; that two torches be carried along, one on one side, and the other on the other side, which are to be lighted at passing through every town, and then given to that church wherein it shall rest at night. Likewise I will that the chariot in which it be carried shall be covered with red cendall,* with the lion of my arms thereon, and my helmet at the head: and to every church wherein it may rest all night the like cloth of cendall with my arms thereon, to be left. Also I will that every morning there shall be given to the poor

* *Sendal.* 1. A thin, rich, silken material. 2. Fine linen, used especially as a shroud. (*OED*)

of that place as much dole as my executors may think fit, and that on the day of my funeral no other cover be laid on my body than that of red cendall, with the lion of my arms, with my helmet, and also a taper at the head and another at the feet, and on each side a torch. (Sir Bartholomew Burghersh)[1]

The following suggests that it is customary for churches in which bodies lie overnight on their journey to charge for the loss of wax through the night hours.

> 1538 To every parishe church through whiche my body shalbe caryed towards my burying 6s 8d, and if my body rest in any churche one night, then to that churche 20s, so that they cleame no waxe ne other thing for my coming to the said churche. (Sir John Fitzjames, [Bruton, Somerset])[2]

More commonly, parishioners request where in the church or churchyard they are to be interred. Prior to the Reformation favoured locations within the church include before the rood, Christ's suffering on the cross being seen as the gateway through which humanity may pass to immortal life, and near an image or altar of a particular saint – usually the Virgin Mary – whose protection and intercession are sought. More mundanely, requests are often made to be buried near the seat or pew occupied when alive, or near the grave of one's father, mother or spouse.

> 1488 I leave my body to be buried in the parish church of Sandall before the altar of the blessed Mary the Virgin in the south part, at which altar I ordain that one chaplain shall celebrate annually for ever to pray for my soul and the souls of Elizabeth my wife [etc]. (Thomas Savile of Hullinedge, Yorks)[3]

> 1514 ... in the southe ile ... directly afore the windowe of the 7 werkes of mercy. (John Mongeham, St Mary at Hill)

> 1520 ... before the pictor of Saint George. (William Winsby, Greenwich)

> 1521 ... before oure lady and Josep. (Robert Wodgrene, Allhallows, Hoo, Kent)

> 1540 ... at my pewe dore. (John Pinchester, Plumstead, Kent)

> 1543 ... in the middell passe, before the rode, at my father's feet. (William Jeffray, Chiddingly, Sussex)

> 1545 ... in our lady chapell whereas I have used to sit at service time, right under the foote of the image of our lady there. (John James, West Malling, Kent)[4]

Members of the clergy sometimes seek to lie as close as possible to the place where mass will continue to be performed above their bones.

> 1500 ... in one of two places as can be thought most convenient by my frends, either before the high awter in the chauncell ther, so that my feet

may be under the preests feet standing at masse, or els under the steppe coming in at the church dore, so that every creature coming in at the same dore may trede upon my buriall. (Gilbert Carleton, vicar, Farningham, Kent)

1511 ... in the chancel ... before the blessed sacrament, so that the priest may stand upon my breast at the beginning of his mass. (Richard Ashelworth, rector, St Alphage, Canterbury)[5]

Gilbert Carleton's desire to have a traffic of feet passing regularly over his grave is echoed in lay requests to be buried in or near the porch, in particular beneath the place where the faithful stand as they dip their fingers and cross themselves before entering the church.

1500 To be beried in the south porch of [St Mary's] Gravesend under the holy water stopp as nye the church dor as it may be. (Richard Mikylhalf, Gravesend, Kent)

1526 ... next unto [as near to] the holy water stoke as may be so the people may tredde & come over my grave or sepulture. (H. Goodwin, Irchester, Northants)[6]

In Kent those stipulating churchyard burial often seek proximity to the yew or 'palm' tree, perhaps seeing it as a symbol of everlasting life and certainly creating harder work for gravediggers.

1517 ... beside the palm tree, next to the grave of my father. (Robert Langley, St Nicholas at Wade)

1542 ... in the churchyard nere unto the gret ewe tree there. (Thomas Chapleyn, Dartford)

1542 ... under the ewe tree. (John Stake, Lewisham)[7]

The following is a reminder of the effects of the Reformation.

1550 [In the churchyard,] nere unto the place where the crosse stode. (John Jefferye, East Hanningfield, Essex)[8]

ix. Charges and costs

The fees charged by the parish for a grave depend partly on its location. The chancel is the most prestigious and, when available, the most expensive, but it may effectively be reserved for the clergy and members of prominent local families. The body of the church comes next, followed by the porch. Last comes the churchyard, where most parishioners are interred and which is always the cheapest option: indeed in some places, particularly in earlier periods, it is provided free. The amount charged also depends on whether or not the body is coffined, in part because this makes it heavier to handle and requires the digging of a larger grave.

1613 The churchwardens shall have for the ground for every man or woman that shall be buried in the church ... 20s | For the ground ... in the chauncell ... 26s 8d (St Saviour, Southwark)

1613 Everyone that shalbe buried in the church shall paye breakinge of the grownd ... 10s | In the church porch ... 6s 8d | In the church yard with a coffin ... 3s 4d | In the church yard without a coffin ...12d (St Alphage, London Wall)[1]

The fees at St Saviour's, later Southwark Cathedral, are unusually high. The typical rate for an ordinary grave inside a church is 6s 8d, although it ranges from about double that to about half, and there are exceptions high and low.

1502 Resseived de Thomas Hont for breking of grounde within the chirche for his dowghter ... 13s 4d (St Mary at Hill)

1570 For breaking the ground in the churche for burieng Mr Barley ... 6s 8d (Bishop's Stortford)

1584 For Widowe Batmans grave ... 6s 8d (St Mary, Reading)

1706 For breaking ye ground in ye church for Priscilla Whitefoot ... 3s 4d (Cardington, Shropshire)[2]

At Louth in the early 16th century you would pay 6s 8d for burial inside the church but 3s 4d in the porch. At Battersea the rate inside the church is 6s 8d until 1620 when, in an attempt to stem overcrowding, it is raised to 13s 4d. Less conventionally, at All Hallows Staining in 1498 they receive 'a kinderkin of ale ... for breking of the grounde in the churche' for a burial.[3]

Sometimes there are lower fees for children, perhaps prompted by the practical consideration of grave size.

1614 For a buriall without a coffin in ye churchyard, 8d. | If the partie be not above 12 years old, then 6d. (Chelmsford, Essex)[4]

Wherever the grave may be located it is customary to charge outsiders double.

1631 Received for the ground in the middle ile for one Mr Whitaker a stranger 30s, for the great bell 10s, and for peals 2s, all being double duties ... £2 2s (St Bartholomew Exchange)[5]

The higher fees for intramural burial reflect not only the more limited space available and the greater prestige but also the fact that more work is involved. Pews may need to be moved and reinstated

1495 Paid for a carpenter for taking up the pew for beryeing of Casson ... 5d (St Andrew Hubbard)[6]

and paving stones taken up and replaced with care. At Kendal in the late 17th century the churchwardens agree to pay the female sexton, Debora Wilkinson, 2s 6d 'for every coffin in the church ... she or her deputy in takeing up of flaggs in the church or lying them downe to place them leveally & in good order, breaking none of them'.[7]

The parishioners of Burnley are also concerned about the effect on their floor, as they make clear in a petition to the Bishop of Chester in 1636.

For & towards the repaire of the church & chancell there is but paid 20d a corps by those that inter their dead in either place, which small summe causeth verie manie to presse to bury there & throngs the church & chancell with many graves, and by often takeing up of the flagges causeth the floore to be verie uneven by the earth shrinking as ye bodies consume.*

The bishop replies with an instruction that from now on the wardens are to allow 'no buriall in the bodie of the church under a noble nor in the chancell but for an angel'.†[8]

One way of creating more intramural space is to construct large vaults beneath the church. Places in these may command a premium, not least because they afford scope for a family to secure its own area in which its members can be buried together over a long period. At Battersea in 1779 fees payable to the vicar and wardens for a place in the vaults of the then recently rebuilt church amount to £6 16s 6d for a parishioner and £10 10s for an outsider, halving in each case for the interment of children. For 'a vault parted off for the use of a family (8ft. 6in. by 7ft. 4in.), walls included', the fees are £31 10s, with £2 2s payable every time it is opened.[9]

In addition to such fees for ground or space a charge is made for any gravestone supplied by the parish.

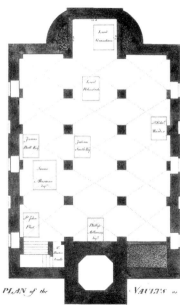

PLAN of the VAULTS as

Executed under **BATTERSEA CHURCH**

by Jos: Dixon Surveyor.

. 1500 Received of my Lady Morland for a stone to lay upon her husband ... 13s 4d (St Margaret, Westminster)

1588 Received of John White for burieng his father in the churche ... 6s 8d | Also of him for an alter stone bought of ye parishe to laye upon his father ... 4s (Bramley, Hants)[10]

---

* This incidentally suggests that uncoffined burials were still common at this time.
† The double reference – to gold coins and social/moral/celestial status – is presumably intended. The standard value of a noble was 6s 8d. An angel, so named because it bore the figure of St Michael the Archangel killing a dragon, was originally worth the same but by this time its value stood at 10 or 11 shillings.

There may also be a separate fee payable to the person who digs the grave or arranges the digging.

> 1546 Every man that is buried in the churche must paye for the grave ... 6s 8d | And to the clarke for ye pit making ... 2s (St Andrew Hubbard)

> 1634 [Sexton's fees] For making a grave in the church 2s. | For making a grave in the churchyard, the corps being coffined 1s. | For making a grave in the churchyard, the corps being uncoffined 6d. (Burford, Oxon)[11]

Gravedigging,
Ecton, Northants, 1749

If not receiving such a fee direct the digger needs to be paid by the parish for what can be thirsty work.

> 1682 To Isaac Archar for ringing ye bell and digging Richard Longman's grave ... 2s | To Morly for ale which Isaac had when he made Richard Longman's grave ... 2d (Swainswick, Somerset)[12]

Burying outside in cold weather is particularly hard work.

> 1607-08 Edward Terrill, a fool or innocent ... was buried upon Wednesday the 13th day of Januarie. The ground in the church yard so hard frozen that it could hardilie be pearced with a mattock or pickaxe. Note. The Thames frozen over. (Tottenham, Middlesex)

> 1680 Paid Philip Burnell extraordinary for makeinge of graves in the frost to prevent takeing up grave roomes in the church ... 8s | More to Philip Burnell for his extraordinary paines in make[ing] 22 graves in the hard and long frost which must otherwise have beene made in the church ... 7s 4d (Manchester)[13]

Apart from the charges for ground and digging, and those for cloth, lights and bells outlined earlier, there are also commonly fees to be paid to the minister for conducting the service and to the clerk for registering the burial. Although such work is not rendered more arduous by intramural burial or by the use of a coffin, both may attract higher fees, presumably as a kind of expenditure tax designed to discourage these choices and to boost income.

> 1613 *The Parson's duties.* For burialles in the church ... 4s | For burialles in the church yard with a coffin ... 2s | For burialles in the churchyard without a coffin ... 12d (St Alphage, London Wall)

> 1644 For buriails in the upper churchyard 1s 10d, whereof to the minister
> 6d, to the clerke 4d, to the sexton for the bell and gravemaking 8d, to
> the parish 4d. (St Giles without Cripplegate)[14]

The minister and others may also be available to lend dignity as your corpse
is brought to church, but if so there will be a price to pay.

> 1613 [Burial in the church] For the service of a minister if he fetch the
> corps ... 16d | But if he fetch not the corps ... 8d | For the service of a
> clarke if he fetch the corps ... 12d | If he fetch it not ... 6d | For the service
> of a sexton if he fetch the corps ... 8d | If he fetch not the corps ... 4d |
> The foure bearers whether they beare the corps or not, so they give
> attendance ... 16d (St Saviour, Southwark)

> 1644 For the attendance before the corps to the church or church-yard
> 3s [whereof] to the minister 2s, to the clerk 8d, to the sexton 4d. And
> whosoever please may have the minister, clerk, or sexton alone. (St Giles
> without Cripplegate)[15]

x. Burying promptly and digging deep

Bodies are usually buried within three days of death, and sometimes within a few
hours, largely out of concern that they will become noxious.

> 1575 The 31st daie of Julie ... was one buried at St James that was so
> noisom that he was not to be brought to the church ... (St Martin in
> the Fields)

> 1657 Thomas Warde of Broxey fell sicke on Satterday in the afternoone
> and laid speechless till he died upon the Lordes day at night beinge the
> 23th of August and was buryed the 25th day of the same: and his body
> was somewhat corrupted at his buriall being kept so longe. (Hackness,
> Yorks)[1]

In 1621 the vicar of Rainham, Essex, is presented to the Church authorities
because 'he did suffer a childe this summer to lie three dayes unburied after it was
dead until it did stinke'.[2]

With this concern in mind, graves are supposed to be dug to a certain depth,
often 6 foot, but not always.

In 1542 at St Stephen, Coleman Street, the list of duties drawn up for the sexton
states that 'he shall make the pittes for dead bodies depe inough for corrupte
heyers,* that is to say for men and women 4 fote deep and for children 3 fote deep'.[3]

In 1613 at St Saviour, Southwark, 'it is ordered that the gravemaker shall
make every man and womans grave (if there be a coffin) 5 foot and an halfe deep

---

* i.e. sufficiently deep that corrupt airs will not emerge.

if the ground will serve; if without a coffin, foure foot and a halfe.' For a child's grave the respective depths are 4 foot and 3½ foot.[4]

In 1638 the parish of St Edward, Cambridge, reports that all is well in the churchyard, with 'graves diged east and west about 5 foot deepe, and the bones of the dead ... piously used as besemeth Christians', but several other Cambridgeshire parishes report as a failing that the graves 'are not six foot deep'.[5]

The following vestry orders show some of the variety of practice in and around London in the 18th century. The common resort to stacking is evident in the first entry.

> 1721 November. That the graves be dug six feet deep where it may be done and to be filled up every night and two feet of earth to be left on the upper corpse in each grave to avoid infection. (St Giles without Cripplegate)

> 1732 July 31st. Complaint being made that the graves were not dug deep enough and therefore were very offensive. It was ordered that for the future every grave shall be dug seven feet deep, and that the grave-digger shall have two shillings for his trouble. (St Helen, Bishopsgate)

> 1751 April 2nd. Ordered, the charge for digging every grave the common depth, that is four feet, 1s. For every foot deeper than four feet, 1s. (Woolwich, Kent)[6]

Occasionally an individual requests particular depth. In his will of 1695 Oxford antiquary Anthony Wood asks that his body be buried in Merton College chapel 'deeper than ordinary', and he may not be alone in his wish to lie far below.[7]

> 1743 The gravemaker for an Extraordinary Deep Grave in the church for Mr Seagood ... 1s (St Anne & St Agnes, Aldersgate)[8]

xi. Overcrowding

The relentless influx of bodies to be buried, particularly in old churches and populous parishes, makes those responsible keen-eyed for any spare nooks that may remain.

> 1614 Nov. 19th. Emanuel Francklin, buried in ye chancel under ye communion table close up to ye commandementes: ther is roome for sum small bodie. | 1614-15 March 7th. Ann wife of Mr Andrew Windsor, buried in ye upper end of ye chancel next unto ye tombe but one: there is roome left for 2 more upon her. (St Olave, Hart Street)

> 1801 N.B. I this day discover'd a large vault in the north west corner of St Nicholas Acons church yard which is now empty and will hold twenty or more coffins. ... John Wickes, April 12. (St Nicholas Acons)[1]

Adding (or finding) a vault helps ease space problems for a while, but eventually it too will fill up.

1688 Paid for removing the corpes in the vault to make way for more ...
  5s (St John Zachary)[2]

The problem is most acute in London. At St Laurence Pountney in 1808 the vestry agree

1st. That it is expedient to adopt some measures to economize the soil of the church ground and church yard for the future, by directing the graves to be dug to a greater depth than heretofore.

  2d. That the sexton be ordered in all cases, excepting where by special desire the deceased is to be buried upon some of his or her relations previously interred ... to dig to the depth of ten feet, if possible and with safety to the surrounding walls, for his encouragement in which he shall receive over and above the customary fee, one shilling per foot, for every foot so dug beyond the depth of five feet ...

While the order refers to 'he' the sexton expected to dig this deep is a woman, Dorothy Carr.[3]

Thirty years later another London parish also looks to go deep.

1838 For digging a grave 18 feet deep in the back church yard for the poor ... £2 10s | Paid Mr Line for carpenters work and materials to shore up the grave in back church yard and cart away the rubbish ... £11 11s 11d (St Mary, Aldermanbury)[4]

In 1850 a parliamentary inquiry into burial hears a string of grim reports relating to London parishes. At St Andrew, Holborn, two graves are always kept open for the bodies of paupers and are 'never covered in until thought sufficiently full'. At St Giles in the Fields bones disturbed in digging new graves are routinely removed to a large communal pit. In the vaults of St Andrew by the Wardrobe 'as many as seven or eight coffins have been placed in one grave of 12 or 13 feet in depth'. Meanwhile at St Mildred, Poultry, one those reporting to the inquiry is denied access to the vault, being told by the sextoness, Mrs Knipe, that 'no one ever dared to enter ... till the large trap-door had been raised for many hours'.[5]

  Such caution is well founded. In September 1838 Thomas Oakes, gravedigger of St Botolph, Aldgate, is killed soon after descending into a deep pauper's grave by the noxious vapours emanating from the cadavers all around. A local fish-dealer who tries to save him suffers the same fate: according to a witness, 'the instant he stooped down to raise the head of Oakes he appeared as if struck with a cannon ball, and fell back ... and appeared instantly to expire'. At the inquest it emerges that both Oakes and his predecessor had been 'in the habit of burning straw, and using other means, to dispel the impure air' from graves before entering them.[6]

  The inquiry of 1850 is soon followed by Burial Acts which bring to an end interment in such inner city churchyards.[7]

xii. The gravemaker's tools

The most basic of these are for the digging.

> 1548 For a spade for to make graves … 7d (Bishop's Stortford)

> 1564 To Grimes for a picke axe … 2s (St Michael, Cornhill)

> 1711 Grinding the spade for the grave diger … 6d (St Alphage, London Wall)[1]

A range of further equipment may also be required.

> 1573 Making of a crowe bare of irone, whiche is for removing of grave stones … 6s 4d (St Thomas, Salisbury)

> 1653 For a scuttle for the gravemaker to gather up bones … 1s (St Mary, Warwick)

> 1700 Four biers, one shovel, two speads, two mattocks, six long planks for sides of graves and four for ends, and some small boards. Two small ladders for graves, eight long ladders, one carte. Three wheele barrows, one iron croe. (Manchester, inventory)

> 1777 For bells rops & coffin rops … £1 4s (Hardingstone, Northants)[2]

ABOVE
Headpiece
from Bills of
Mortality, 1665.

RIGHT
Coffin ropes
in use, from
the Trivulzio
Book of Hours,
c. 1470.

9. Miscellaneous fees: the mortuary, and for corpses passing through

In addition to charging for ground, burial, lights, et cetera the pre-Reformation Church also often extracts a fee called a mortuary or corpse-present, in theory to recompense the parish or incumbent for any tithes or offerings left unpaid at the time of death. The requirement is set out by Archbishop Winchelsey in 1305.

> We ordain that if a man at his death have three animals or more among his chattels, of what sort soever they be, the second best be reserved for the church where he received the sacraments while alive, the very best being kept for him to whom it is due by law.[1]

The allusion is to the feudal rule that, upon a tenant's death, the lord of the manor has the right to choose his best beast as a tribute known as heriot. Local customs vary, however, with the 'best beast' often being provided to the church.[2]

> 1402 I bequeath my best beast in the name of my mortuary. (John de Burgh, Halifax, Yorks)

> 1526 For my mortuary my best horse with bridell & saddell. (Robert Tyghe, Maxey, Northants)[3]

In some places the animal or animals are driven before the corpse on the burial day, hence the name 'foredrove' used in Essex.

> 1504 I bequeth for my for drove at the day of my burying 2 shepe. (Alice Humbringle, Great Wakering)

> 1517 And for my foredrove I bequeth a trotting grey colt of 2 yeres of age. (John Garyngton, Mundon)

> 1518 I bequethe to the highe aulter ... for my tithes necligently withholden or forgotten 10s and to the parsone to praye for me. A horse to be driven afore my body on the day of my burying for amendes in the same church. (Thomas Geffery, East Hanningfield)[4]

In the following case there is a quid pro quo.

> 1530 To be buried in the church of Cowling aforesayed in ye midell alley wherfor I bequeth to ye church a cow to be driven to church with me at my beryall. (Richarde Browne, Cooling, Kent)[5]

Those who do not own animals may be expected to give a garment instead. As much is clear from a dispute at St Just in Roseland, Cornwall, in 1396 which ends up in the court of chancery.

> Whereas the custom of the parish, used of ancient time, is that when any man or woman ... dieth, the parson shall have the best garment of the person so dying in the name of a mortuary, and there died a woman called Desyra, widow of one Jakke-John ... and the best garment she had, to wit, a red surcoat worth 6s 8d, belonged to the parson by the custom aforesaid,

this was carried over the body to the church ... when there came [Alan Bugules] with force and arms, to wit, with club and knife, within the churchyard ... and took and carried away the garment ...

The culprit had previously intervened after the death of Jakke-John himself, carrying off 'a young steer worth 6s 8d' which had been due to the parson as the second best animal of one 'having beasts'.[6]

The custom comes to be widely resented, not least because it is often abused, money or goods being taken in relation to those with little to their name.

> 1517 8d, for the mortuary of a poor fellow at the barber's. (All Saints, Oxford)[7]

As a result a law of 1529 greatly restricts the practice, so that the most that can be demanded is 10 shillings, and children, married women, and those with 'movable goodes' worth less than 10 marks are all exempt. Subsequently mortuaries are less widely claimed, although some clergy are unabashed.[8]

> 1634 I buried Alice Whitesides, Feb. 22d, who being but one weeke in the parish of Ripe, died as a stranger, for whose mortuary I, John Goffe, had a gowne of Elizabeth her daughter, price 10s. (Ripe, Sussex, register)[9]

In many places mortuaries are claimed into the 18th century, and the practice persists into the 20th.[10]

The parish may also demand and receive a fee simply for offering to provide burial to a corpse passing through on its way to be interred elsewhere. There appears to be no legal basis for the practice, but it occurs widely, with bells sometimes being rung to make clear that the parish is ready and willing.

> 1627 Paid to the ringers at the passage of the Bishop of Bath and Wells, his corpse ... 1s | Received for the passage of the corpse of the bishop ... 6s 8d (Basingstoke, Hants)

> 1637 To the sexton for tolinge ye bell when a corpes came through the towne and to him that brought word of the corpes ... 1s 6d | Received for a corpes goeinge through the parish ... 6s 6d (Lambeth)

> 1668 May the 8th ye Lady Ford came thro' ye towne & paid all dutye to ye minister, clerk & sexton for proffering to burie her. (Godalming, Surrey)[11]

10. Burial of the excommunicated, nonconformists, &c.

Those who have been excommunicated stand literally outside the communion of the Church and so are not entitled to Christian burial. Canon 68 of 1604 obliges the minister to bury any corpse 'except the party deceased were denounced excommunicated *majori excommunicatione* [with the greater excommunication], for some grievous and notorious crime, and no man able to testify of his repentance'. The final words provide a useful way out, however, for the excommunication does not need to be lifted: all that is required is testimony of a change of heart and a minister prepared to accept it.[1]

> 1615 Nov. 24th. Hester Ashfield buried, being an excommunicated person, in the church yard, according to ye lxviii Cannon therein provided. (Eltham, Kent)[2]

Such burials tend nonetheless to be downgraded in one or more ways. They may take place in a remote or otherwise unfavoured part of the churchyard, perhaps after dark, and the usual rites may be withheld.

> 1575 Richard Chreswell of Ashe died excommunicate the 6th of July about 10 of the clocke in the night and was buried the 9 of the same month like an infidell without any christian ceremonie ... (Sutton-on-the-Hill, Derbyshire)

> 1595 Margaret Bakewell, a maid of Aukmanton [Alkmanton], buried excommunicated 14th of October being Sunday, after sun setting. (Longford, Derbyshire)[3]

Any such indulgence can lead to problems if the Church authorities consider it unjustified. The presence of the body of an excommunicated person may be held to desecrate the churchyard, provoking an interdiction under which no more burials are allowed until the space has been reconsecrated or at least reconciled, a cumbersome and costly process requiring the attendance of the bishop or a deputy.[4]

A bishop sprinkles holy water as he reconciles a church, from an English pontifical, early 15th century

> 1598 Dec. 15th. Robertus Eyre ... | Upon the buriall of the said Robert Eyre being an excommunicate recusant, our buriall was interdicted; in the time of the inhibitian, before it was released these persones followinge died, and were buried at other churches as followeth. [There follow entries for eight burials elsewhere.] (Chesterfield, Derbyshire)

> 1615 William Radhouse the elder, dying excommunicated, was buried by stealth in the night time in ye churchyard, ye 29th day of January, whereupon ye church was interdicted a fortnight. (Weedon Bec, Northants)

> 1615 Paid at Bury court for dismission fees for ye buriall of old Mistris Tostwood, being a recusant excommunicated ... 2s 8d (Mellis, Suffolk)[5]

Where indulgence is not shown, other places of burial need to be found.

1610 Oct. 1st. Henry Turner a prophane drunkard died excommunicate and was buried in the highe way to the terror [of] drunkards. (Salehurst, Sussex)

1619 August 20th. Izable Keames of the Park Side, widowe, deceased the 18th day of August, and was buried in the hall orchard nere unto the church wall upon the west side thereof, the 20th day of August, being an excommunicated person. (Albrighton, near Wolverhampton)

1664 Dec. 31st. Infant Knight & Mary Watson, being excommunicated, buried in a garden. (St Nicholas, Newcastle)[6]

Burial rites are also often limited, adjusted or refused for members of dissenting Christian sects such as Anabaptists, who oppose baptism in infancy, reserving the rite for those old enough to profess their belief.

1681 Feb. 25th. George Piper, an Anabaptist, tumbled in ye ground. (Warleggan, Cornwall)[7]

Antagonism is also shown towards Quakers, who reject church trappings and believe that God works directly through the 'inner light' of an individual.

1653 Richard Cockerell died on Wednesday the 14th day of September and was buried the next day being Thursday and there was many of them they call Quakers at his buriall. And Mr Prowde did exhorte and argue with them at the grave ... (Hackness, Yorks)[8]

Unsurprisingly they often bury their dead elsewhere.

1669 September. Anthonie Peniston, Quaker, buried his mother like a dog in his garden. (Saffron Walden, Essex)

1702 Nov. 30th. Calab Rous, son of Nathanael Rous, merchant. Carried away to the Quakers burial ground. (St Dionis Backchurch)[9]

Catholics, too, may receive only grudging and constrained interment.

1585 April 23rd. Mr Cuthberte Dawny ... a papist, buried without any solemnitye. (St Michael le Belfrey, York)

1642 Rose, ye wife of Robert Lunford, was buried ye 23 of December. She was a recusant papist. She was buried in the night without the church ceremonies. (North Elmham, Norfolk)[10]

Gypsies occasionally fare better.

1533 Receved of the gypcous for breking of the ground in the churche for one of ther company ... 7s 6d (Lydd, Kent)

1768 Old Bridget, the Queen of the Gypsies, buried August 6th. (Dulwich, Surrey)[11]

11. Burial of suicides and other criminals

A similar range of outcomes occurs in relation to those who have committed suicide. Here too grounds for leniency are sometimes found. In 1615, granting a licence for the burial at St John Zachary of Anthony Gurlinge after he has strangled himself with a bridle, the Bishop of London notes that he was

> a youthe of ye age of but 15 yeares or thereabout, so as he had not sufficient discretion for the orderinge of ye course of his life, nor was so capable of good or evil as persons of ripe & full years, and ... before ye committing of this fact was ... honest, sober & of good conversacon, one that resorted dutifully to church & was diligent in ye hearing of God's word preached, and descended of good & godly parents ...

Burial is allowed 'in some outward parte' of the churchyard 'nere one of the walls' and is to be carried out 'privately, without solemnitie or prayers'.

A similar licence is granted in 1633 at St Anne and St Agnes, Aldersgate, in the case of Dorothy Eden, an elderly widow 'much possessed with melancholick humours'. Having stabbed herself with a knife 'she lived full foure dayes ... and in that time shewed and expressed great sorrowe and repentance'. In particular she told Mr Pecke, the curate, that her offence 'did proceede from her troubled conscience for her many sinnes and because she could not serve God with that purity as she desired', and as a further sign of repentance she received 'the holy sacrament of the Lord's supper'. As she had otherwise been 'a woman religiously disposed, and of good life and conversation', churchyard burial is granted, to be carried out 'privately, without pompe or solemnity or much companie'.[1]

The following register entries also show, or seem to show, suicides being interred within churchyards, although sometimes in less favoured parts and without ceremony.

> 1597 Anne Rutter a singlewoman drowned herselfe & was buried the 4 daie of Julie on the north side of the church. (Drypool, Yorks)

> 1722 July 15th. Amy Levit, felo de se,* was buried without Christian burial. (Helpston, Northants)

> 1765 Nov. 21st. Thomas Todd, buried behind the church, a suicide. (Wolsingham, co. Durham)[2]

In his diary Anthony Wood records another instance.

> 1674 *Feb. 2nd, Candlemas day.* Mr Martin Rosenstand, a Dane, sojourner in Mrs Mary Mumford's house Oxon, neare the Theater,† hanged himself about 4 or 5 in the morning. Buried the next day following at night about

---

* Latin for 'felon of himself', the felony or crime being murder.
† The then recently erected Sheldonian Theatre. The house was opposite the King's Arms, on the corner of modern day Broad Street and Parks Road.

10 or eleven privatly (no body present but the carriers and clerk of the parish) in Magdalen parish churchyard close under the wall ... aet. 21 or 22. He with his yonger brother of a good family in Danemark, both the civillest men that ever came into that house: no sign of discontent ever appeared in him, never seen to be angry, very modest, apt to blush etc.[3]

Beyond this, Christian burial is traditionally allowed to those held to have killed themselves while in a state of insanity, mirroring the distinction in common law between those considered guilty of the wilful murder of themselves and those held not responsible by dint of lunacy.* While this charitable distinction is absent from a rubric added to the Book of Common Prayer in 1662, which states that the burial service 'is not to be used for any that ... have laid violent hands upon themselves', in practice it is usually applied, with a legal ruling on the point often cited in justification.[4]

1694-95 Feb. 6th. John Garland, gent., a stranger, in the church behind the churchwardens pew. He shot himselfe with a pistol being distracted. (St Peter, Cornhill)

1724 Oct. 31st. Elizabeth wife of Benjamin Brown labourer who hanged herself being a lunatic was (by virtue of ye coroners warrant) permitted to be thrown into a grave. (Waltham Abbey, Essex)

1754 June 1st. Henry Jordan, cord-wainer. He cut his throat with a razor, & was brought in by ye jury a lunatick, & orders were given by ye coroner for him to have Christian burial. (Yaxley, Hunts)[5]

Those of high status may even be given an honoured place.

1719 August 23rd. Sir Peter Gleane, bart., was buried in the chancel, who hanged himself August 21st, but brought off by the jury as *non compos mentis*, and so had Christian buriall. (St George, Canterbury)[6]

However, in many cases, particularly in earlier periods, burial in church ground is not permitted.

1284 Laurence Ducket, goldsmith, having grievously wounded Raph Crepin in west Cheape, fled into [St Mary le] Bowe church, into which in the night time entered certaine evil persons, friendes unto the said Raph, and slue the said Laurence lying in the steeple, and then hanged him up, placing him so by the window, as if he had hanged himselfe. And so it was found by inquisition, for the which fact Laurence Ducket,

---

* In law the important practical difference was that the goods of the former were forfeited to the crown but those of the latter were not. As a result juries often ruled that the deceased was insane in order to protect the interests of his or her beneficiaries.

being drawne by the feete, was buried in a ditch without the Citie. (John Stow, Survey of London)*

1629 May 8th. John Goldsberrie buried in the feeld. He poisoned himselfe. (St Olave, Hart Street)

1644 Paid to the coroner for sitting upon the bodye of William Belt ... 3s | To the man that digged his grave in the highway, and who carried him thither ... 2s 6d (St Giles in the Fields)[7]

The last case points towards the full and more severe traditional punishment for suicide involving burial at a crossroads and a stake driven through the heart.

1573 Thomas Maule found hunge on a tree by ye wayeside after a druncken fitte April 3. Crowners queste [coroner's inquest] in churche porche April 5. Same nighte at midd nighte burried at ye nighest crosse roades with a stake in him, manie people from Manesfeilde [attending]. (Pleasley, Derbyshire)[8]

A fuller account of such a burial, also showing the matter dealt with quickly, appears in a note made by the parish clerk in the register of St Botolph, Aldgate. The following is slightly condensed from the original.

1590 Memerandum that a crowners quest was pannelled in our parish church the 7th day of September to examen how Amy Stokes the wife of Lewis Stokes a sawyer did come by her deathe, who hanged her selfe in her chamber over a saw pit in Mr Ansell his yard [on the same day] abowte the ower of 9 of the clocke in the forenoone ... She had cast a cord abowte a beame, fasteninge it to the beame and puttinge the same with slidinge knot abowte her necke, as it apeared standinge upon a three footed stoole which with one of her feete she had thrust from her, and so hanged her selfe, her feete standinge bent upon the floor or bords of the chamber. And being found by the jurie that she falling from God had hanged or murthered her selfe, judgment was given in the church by the crowner that she should be carried from the howse to some cross way neare the townes end and there that she should have a stake dreven throughe her brest and be buried with the stake to be seene for a memorial, that others goinge by, seeinge the same, might take goode [warning against] comittinge the like fault. And the said

* 'But shortly after,' Stow continues, 'by relation of a boy, who lay with the said Laurence at the time of his death, and had hid him[self] there for feare, the truth of the matter was disclosed'. As a result 'a certaine woman named Alice, that was chiefe causer of the said mischiefe, was burned', and a number of men were hanged. 'The church was interdicted, the doores and windowes were stopped up with thornes, but Laurence was taken up, and honestly buried in the churchyard.'

Amy Stokes was so buried in the cross way beyond Sparrows corner*
the said 7th day of September ano 1590, abowte the owers of 8 or 9
of the clocke at night. She was abowte three score yeares owld.[9]

The most celebrated instance of such a punishment occurs on 31st December
1811 after John Williams, suspected of the Ratcliff Highway murders, commits
suicide while in prison awaiting trial. His body is placed on an angled platform
above a cart (*opposite*) so as to expose it as fully as possible to view as it is paraded
through the streets. Above his head, fixed in holes at the top of the platform,
are tools used in the murders: on one side a mallet or hammer (referred to in
contemporary accounts as a 'maul' or 'mall'), and on the other a ripping chisel.
Below them, crossways, is a crow bar found in the house of one of the victims,
and below that the stake, serving as an unforgiving pillow for the dead man's head.
After processing slowly around the scenes of the murders, the cart moves west
along Ratcliff Highway and up Cannon Street, until it reaches a crossroads where
'a hole five feet long and as many deep' has been prepared.

The crowds of spectators collected here were beyond calculation, the houses
covered — the windows were filled, and the tops of coaches, waggons,
and carts were literally swarming with people ... As the body approached,
a murmur of contempt and execration was heard from all quarters, which
rose to a shriek of satisfaction when two men mounted the platform, and
unceremoniously hurled the remains of the monster ... into his last earthly
receptacle. The hole being too short to permit the body to lie at full length,
it was crammed down in rather a contracted position; the stake was then
handed to the person appointed to drive it through the body of the suicide,
which he did with several blows from the mall ... The earth was then
thrown into the hole, together with some unslaked lime, and the paving
stones were immediately restored to their former situation.

National Register, 5 January 1812[10]

What is thought to be the last such burial occurs eleven years later, on 26th
June 1823, after Abel Griffiths, aged 22, shoots his father and then himself in
the drawing room of his father's house in Maddox Street (no. 4). This time the
burial is conducted with relative secrecy, partly because the jury's verdict that
Griffiths was of sound mind is widely disputed, and partly for fear that family
and friends might seek to rescue the corpse. Such a rescue is indeed carried out
a few days after the interment, three of the dead man's friends digging up his
body and bundling it into a hackney coach. Subsequently they gain permission
for it to be interred in the burial ground for the poor of St George's, Hanover
Square, although no ceremony is observed and the burial service is not read.[11]

A few days later, on 8th July, the law concerning the burial of suicides is changed.
The gruesome traditions are set aside, but interment in the night-time is required.

* At the south end of Minories on the east side, where it meets Rosemary Lane.

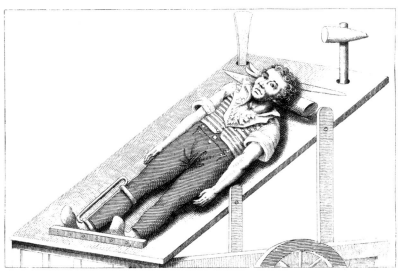

A Correct likeness of JOHN WILLIAMS, *the supposed murderer of the Marrs & Williamsons Families.* December the 8th & 19th 1811.

It shall not be lawful for any coroner, or other officer having authority to hold inquests, to [direct] the interment of the remains of persons, against whom a finding of *felo de se* shall be had, in any public highway, but [they] shall give directions for the private interment of the remains ... without any stake being driven through the body of such person, in the churchyard or other burial ground of the parish ... such interment to be made within twenty four hours from the finding of the inquisition, and to take place between the hours of nine and twelve at night. | Provided nevertheless, that nothing herein contained shall authorize the performing of any of the rites of Christian burial on the interment of the remains of any such person ...[12]

As for other criminals, they may be interred in churchyards, but usually in unfavoured parts and without ceremony.

1578 Richarde Kendall, a prisoner in the bishopes prison, which came from Doncaster, buried the thirde day of April without any solemnitye, savinge that the curate and clerke and other persones were by and presente at his buriall. (St Michael le Belfrey, York)

1631 Thomas Laceby, a prisoner, prest to death, buried in church yard on the north side the steeple the 23th day of April. (St Mary on the Hill, Chester)[13]

Quite what to do in such cases may be a matter for discussion.

1705 Gave George Woolley for tolling the bell to call the parishioners together about burying the woman that was executed ... 1s (All Saints, Stamford, Lincs)[14]

12. Delaying burial: the coroner and bodies arrested for debt

Where a death is unexplained or suspicious the coroner needs to be paid to hold an inquest or, as it is usually phrased, 'to sit upon the body'. If that body has already been buried it may need disinterring for inspection.

> 1633 Paied John Cooke for digging up the corps for the crowner ... 6d (St Martin, Salisbury)
>
> 1650 Received of mony wich was found in a drowned man's pocket which was tooke up at 9 Elmes ... 11s | Paid the coroner 13s 4d for sitting upon the drowned man. | Laid out 3s 1d upon the jury. (Battersea)
>
> 1842 [To the carpenter for] opening the coffin of a child disinterred by order of the coroner ... 1s (St John the Baptist, Chester)[1]

At Widdecombe in Devon an old practice is observed of leaving a body where it is found until the coroner has inspected it *in situ*. If he has to be summoned from a distance an eye needs to be kept on the body in the meantime.

> 1734 For two men to watch by Thomas Greep after he was found dead, for two days, each man 1s per day, comes to 4s. | And for three men to watch by him by night for two nights time, at 1s 6d each man, comes to 9s. | Paid Roger Hannaford for two seames of wood which was burnt by the watchmen, and for the straw made use of by the watchmen ... 1s 6d | Paid John Smerdon of Rowdon for riding to Exeter to fetch the coroner ... 5s | For the coroner's fee ... 13s 4d[2]

On rare occasions burial may also be delayed if the deceased was in debt. Francis Tate, writing in 1600, is sceptical: 'Some say, that the creditors may stay the body of their dettor from burial, till they be fully satisfied their debt ... but I thinke no man ever heard any such thing practised in Englande.' While there appears to be no support for such a step in law, it is sometimes attempted.[3]

> 1659 August 30th. Humphrey Dakin, buried about 2 of the clock in the night, feareing an arrest. (Alstonfield, Staffs)
>
> 1689 The corpse of John Matthews, of Fawler, was stopt on the churchway for debt August 27. And having laine there fower days, was by justices warrant buried in the place to prevent annoyances — but about six weeks after it was by an order of sessions taken up and buried in the churchyard by the wife of the deceased. (Sparsholt, Berks)[4]

Perhaps the most notable case involves Don Pedro Ronquillo, Spanish ambassador to England. After his death in 1691 his body is placed in a coffin in Westminster Abbey and it is still there when John Macky visits over twenty years later: 'Poor Don Pedro ... is like to have the honour of lying unburied amongst the English kings for ever; his corps being arrested by his creditors, and kept in this chappel above ground till his relations redeem it'. Nothing appears to have changed in 1764 when Horace Walpole observes to a friend that, should bankruptcy strike, 'you will lie above ground in a velvet coffin, like the Spanish ambassador's in Westminster Abbey'. The body is only removed and returned to Spain in 1811.[5]

Meanwhile in 1784 the body of Sir Barnard Turner, a former sheriff of the City of London, is 'arrested after it was put into the hearse, in the street, for a considerable debt', but the matter is compromised and the elaborate funeral procession is allowed to proceed, complete with military escort, muffled drums, and plumes of expensive ostrich feathers.[6]

13. Particular practices: burial at night and of bowels

As seen above, burial at night sometimes occurs in the case of Catholics and other outsiders, and from 1823 it is the required form for suicides. It is also often used in earlier periods in times of plague and in individual cases where contagion from the corpse is feared.

> 1621 May 23rd. Mr Ambrose Gurney, in the chaunsell at 11 of the clok at night because of his infirmity. (Eltham, Kent)

> 1823 Paid for bringing dead bodies 10s, candles 5s 4d (buried at night when the small pox was so bad here). (St Mary Bourne, Hants)[1]

Otherwise night burial tends to be restricted to those of higher social status whose estate or relations can bear the cost of the extra lights.

> 1628 Nov. 13th. Ninian Burrell, gent., who died at London; buried by torchlight. (Cuckfield, Sussex)

> 1690 Nov. 1st. Sir M. [Mark] Guyon was buried about 10 o'clock in ye evening, by torches, without a sermon; there was about half a score coaches, and about 30 or 40 men had black gowns and caps; they carried torches to light the coaches. There was one breadth of black cloth hung round the chancell, and ye pulpit was covered with black, and the great bible. (Coggeshall, Essex, diary of Joseph Bufton)[2]

However, relative parsimony may also be involved as night burial provides a way of having a distinguished interment without the expense of elaborate heraldic trappings.[3]

Another high status departure from the norm is burial of the bowels only in the parish where death occurs, the rest of the body being embalmed and transported for interment in the home or ancestral parish.

> 1577 Received ... for the buriall in the quire of Mrs Abingtons intralles and for ringinge then ... 6s (St Martin in the Fields)

> 1628 June 21st. Wm. earle of Devnshier, his bowels buried in ye evening. (St Botolph, Bishopsgate)

> 1638 Sir Edward Clarke, knight, steward of Reading, his bowells interred in St Marie's, his body carried to Dorchester in Oxfordshire, Jan. 11. (St Mary, Reading)[4]

14. Three grand funerals

The following long lists of selected costs illustrate in a more concerted way the kind of elaborate funerals provided for well-to-do commoners in various periods. The first example is that of Norfolk squire John Paston, who died in London in 1466, and exemplifies the pre-Reformation way of doing things. His body is carried via Norwich to Bromholm Priory, near the north-east coast of Norfolk.

The journey to Norfolk

To the prest that cam with the cors from London ... 3s 4d

To 12 pore men bering torches from London to Norfolk
be 6 day 1s, takinge eche of them on the day 4d, and for
3 dayes in going homeward takinge every day 6d

For bred and ale for 12 men that bare torches ... 13d ob.

At Norwich

The 4 orders of friers ... £8 | For the herse ... 40s

To 38 prests at the dirige at Norwich, when the cors lay
ther ... 12s 8d

To 39 children with surplices within the church and
without ... 3s 4d

To 26 clerks with 4 keepers of the torches, eche of them
2d ... 3s 4d

To the clerk of St Peter's of Hungate* his felaship for
ringing when the cors was in the church ... 12d

To the clerks of St Peter's and St Steven's for the ringers
ageyn [against] the cors ... 2s

For wine for the singers when the cors was at Norwich ...
20s

To the Prioress of Carow ... 6s 8d | To a maide that came
with her ... 20d

At Bromholm Priory

To 9 monks, eche of them 6s 8d ... £3 | To 14 ringers ... 7s

To 2 men that filled the grave ... 8d | To a dole ... £5 13s 4d

For a cope called a frogge† of worsted for the Prior of
Bromholm ... 26s 8d

To the Prior of Bromholm for malte spent at the
interment ... 40s

To the baker for 310 eggs ... 19d

Given among the men of the bakehouse ... 20d

Tomb figures,
Warwick, 1454

---

* A church in Norwich. Six years earlier Paston had paid for it to be rebuilt.
† *Frock*. A long habit with large open sleeves; the outer dress of a monk.

For 6 barells bere ... 12s

For a roundlet of red wine of 15 gallones, &c. ... 12s 11d

For 8 peces of peuter lost of the priors ... 20d

For fish the day after the interment ... 6s 10d

Vitelles bought by Richard Charles [apparently for feasting at Bromholm]

For 27 gees ... 17s | 27 franked* gees ... 6s 8d

70 caponnes ... 17s 7d | 41 pigges ... 13s 10d

49 calves ... £4 13s 4d | 28 lambes ... 27s 2d

22 sheep ... 37s 5d | 1300 eggs ... 6s 6d

20 galons milk ... 20d | 8 galons creme ... 2s 8d

4 pints of butter ... 4d | 14 galons of ale ... 2s

To Herman, fleying bests [? flaying beasts] by 3 days, 2s, and to John Foke by 3 days, 20d

Lights

To the parson of St Peter's for his fee of the wax abought the cors, besides 2 candels of 1 lb. and 1 hert candel of a pound ... 20d

To Skolehouse, wax chandeler, for making of the herse at Bromholm ... £22 9s 8d

To Gresham the London carrier in full payment for the chandeler of London ... £5 19s

To the glaser for takin owte of 2 panes of the windows of the churche for to lete owte the reke of the torches at the dirige, and soldering new of the same ... 20d

To Skolehouse in part of his bille for torches and wax made at Bromholm, for to brenne upon the grave ... 4 marks

For light kept on the grave ... 10s†

Miscellaneous

To the keeper of the inne where mine husband died, for his reward ... 20s‡

To Daubeney, for to kepe the yere day at Bromholm the first yere after his dethe ... £8 2s 4d

To the viker of Dalling for bringing home of a pardon from Rome, to pray for all our frends sowles ... 8s 4d | For a blacke gowne to the said viker ... 8s[1]

* Fattened in a frank or pen.

† Perhaps comparable to the 'sepulchre light' provided at Bardwell, Suffolk: see p322.

‡ This part of the account was written by Paston's widow Margaret.

Over a century later, on 29th December 1580, John Dudley, a kinsman of the Duke of Northumberland, dies in London. When he is buried on 12th January at Stoke Newington the pre-Reformation trappings of monks and dirges are gone, but the process is elaborated in other ways.

The Expences of the Funerall

To Doctor Smithe and Doctor Hector at the opening of the bodie ... £2

To the clarcke of the parishe at London, for the fees of the churche for burieing the bowells ... £1 6s 6d

To a poore man that made an epitaphe ... 10s

To the ringers of the bells at Newington ... 6s

The charges of the hearse, and the valte in the churche at Newington ... £3 11s

To two tippstaves there attending ... 2s

The Diet at the Buriall

Three barrells beere ... 13s | Strong beere one barrell dim. ... 12s 9d

Claret wine one hogshead ... £4 5s | Sack, muskadell, and malmezie, 10 gallons ... £1 | Rennishe wine two gallons ... 5s 4d

One thowsand and a half of billets* ... £1 | Two loades coales ... £2 8s

Floure for pies and breade, 32 bushels ... £3 16s

For bacon and other cates† and necessaries bought by Percivall ... £6 15s 4d

To Mr Haynes for freshe fishe ... £2 5s | To a fisherman for 4 pikes ... £1

Two boxes of wafers ... 5s 4d | Two gallons of mustarde ... 8d

Three gallons and a half of creame ... 4s 8d

Paiments made to Cookes and others

To a master cooke, 6 under cookes, and ten turnbroaches‡ ... £3 3s 4d

The dressing up of the house at London ... 7s 10d

To a woman for washing, scowring, and watching at London ... 2s

Paiments for Blackes, and others

To the draper for blackes ... £166 5s

To Henrie Goodladd for making of the poore men's gownes ... £2 8s

To Browne for making the men's coates ... £3 14s 4d

To the shoemaker ... 18s 6d

To the tailor for making garments for women ... £6 11s 8d

To the browne baker§ for horse bread ... £1

To the smith for shoeing of horses ... 14s 9d

Mourning cloth is provided for 105 persons and runs to just over 300 yards.[2]

* Thick pieces of wood cut to a suitable length for fuel.

† *Cates, Acates*. Purchased provisions. Often used to indicate fine food.

‡ Turnspits, *broach* being a pointed rod of wood or iron used for roasting meat etc.

§ At this time bakers of brown bread and of white bread formed separate companies.

By the early 18th century the commercialisation of death is well advanced. The following are some of the charges made by the Company of Upholsterers for the burial of Andrew Card, senior bencher of Gray's Inn, at St Andrew's, Holborn, in 1732.

Wrapping and enclosing the body

A large sarsenet sheet to wrap the body in ... £2 10s

Men to help move the body downstairs ... 6s

An elm coffin, lined with a fine sarsenet quilt, a pink'd ruffle, a sarsenet pillow run with green inscar, and his body put up with sweet powders ... £2 10s

A superfine pinked shroud ... 5s 6d

A leaden coffin with a leaden plate of inscription ... £6 6s

6 men to carry in the leaden coffin & put the body in ... 6s

A large elm case, covered with rich black velvet, 4 pair of chaced handles gilt & finished with the best nails close drove all round ... £15

4 men to carry in the velvet case to put the leaden coffin in, & fix it up ... 4s

Displaying the body

A large newe velvet pall laid over his body ... £1

A bail round the body covered with plumes of fine ostrich feathers ... £2 2s

A large majesty escutcheon* with the crest and mantling painted on silk to put up at the head of the corpse ... £3 3s

8 large plate candlesticks on stands round the body ... £1

A coffin lid covered with velvet & adorned with plumes of fine black ostrich feathers on the body ... £1 1s

The house in mourning

A room for his body hung in deep mourning with velvet, the floor covered ... £10

The next room for company, hung in mourning with black cloth, the floor covered ... £3 10s

The passage & stairs hung in mourning ... £2

53 plate sconces for the rooms, passage & stairs ... £2 13s

43 lbs. of wax lights and tapers ... £5 14s 8d

8 dozen of buckram escutcheons for rooms, passage & stairs ... £12

8 dozen of crests to intermix with the escutcheons ... £8 8s

An achievement† for the house with the outside frame in mourning ... £3 10s

---

* *Escutcheon.* In heraldry, the shield or shield-shaped surface on which a coat of arms is depicted, from Latin *scutum*, shield. A majesty escutcheon is one bearing the royal arms.

† 'A square or diamond-shaped panel or canvas with a deceased person's armorial bearings, affixed to his or her house during mourning or placed in a church'. Also more generally 'an escutcheon or other armorial device, especially one granted in recognition of a distinguished feat'. (*OED*)

Procession and hearse

6 bearers that brought the body out of the house & put it into the hearse & afterwards bore it to the grave ... 12s

A man in mourning to carry the coffin lid of feathers before the hearse ... 2s 6d

4 porters at the door in proper habits to walk before the hearse ... £1 4s

2 men to light the porters at the door ... 2s

A hearse & six horses ... £1

Covering for ye hearse and velvet housings for ye horses ... £3 15s

23 plumes of fine black ostrich feathers for ye hearse and horses ... £3 10s

24 buckram escutcheons, 12 shields, 6 shafferoons,* 24 long pencills,† 24 crests & 8 banners on buckram with the arms on both sides, for hearse and horses ... £13 6s

12 bearers with velvet caps and truncheons to attend the hearse and horses ... £1 4s

8 mourning coaches & six horses ... £7 8s

9 cloaks for coachmen ... 9s | 18 hatbands for ditto and postillions ... £1 7s

15 pages in mourning to attend the coaches ... £1 10s

100 white wax branch lights & 100 men in mourning to carry them ... £27 10s

100 pair of black gloves & 101 knots for lightmen and [the] man that carried the lid of feathers ... £7 11s 6d

Miscellaneous

Tickets printed from a new copper plate to invite the company & men in mourning to deliver them ... 15s

4 servants in mourning to attend the funeral ... 10s

At the church

100 yards of pressed baze ... £8 6s 8d

6 dozen of buckram escutcheons ... £9

12 silk escutcheons for the pulpit ... £3

9 yards of superfine fine black cloth for the pulpit, reader's and clerke's desk ... £8 2s

---

* '*Chaperonne.* An old French word, signifying a hood, whence ... it is become the name of those little shields, containing Death's Heads, and other funeral devices, plac'd upon the foreheads of the horses that draw hearses at pompous funerals, vulgarly now call'd, by corruption, *Chaperoons*, or *Shafferoons*, because these devices were anciently fastned to the chaperonnes those horses us'd to wear with their other coverings of estate' (James Coats, *A New Dictionary of Heraldry*, 1725, pp72-73). The modern meaning of chaperone is thought to be a figurative application, the accompanying protector shielding a young woman's modesty in much the same way that a hood shields the face.

† *Pencel.* A small pennon or streamer.

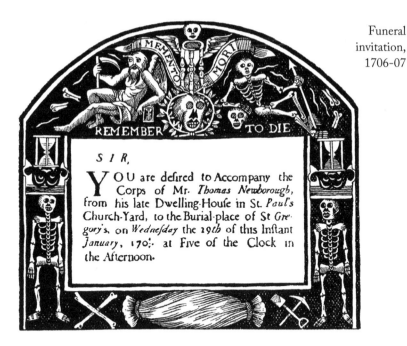

Six pair of black gloves for the parish bearers ... 6s
Paid the parish dues of St Andrews ... £2 14s 4d
Paid the information for burying in velvet ... £2 10s
Paid the stonecutter ... £2 4s | Paid the bricklayer ... 10s 6d
Gave the stonecutters man & labourer for expedition ... 2s
Paid the men for emptying the vault of water &c. ... 7s 6d.

The total bill amounts to £269 7s 11d.[3]

15. The alternative of a modest end

It should be added that some people look for their passing to be observed and commemorated after a humbler fashion, resisting expectations of elaboration and extravagance.

1393 To be buried in the chancel of Oundell, if I die there, with an honest stone to cover me, & that my body be buried immediately after my death, & that five candles of wax & no more be placed round my body in the form of a cross. (Richard de Treton, rector, Oundle, Northants)

1522 To be buried within the church yarde ... nexte the holy water stopp where Kateryn my moder lieth. An obett 13s yerely in hands of churchwardens, they to have 20d, and so the reste of the money to be by them imploed so that I have no pompe of torches nor grete ringing of belles, but that there be brede and ale at the dirige to make the neighbors and poor people for to drinke. (Richard Broke, Greenwich, Kent)[1]

The Parish and Those in Need

The Parish Poor

1. Legal responsibility

Following the dissolution of the monasteries, and the loss of their charitable provision, a series of laws formalises and extends the role of the parish in caring for the poor. At first the aim is to do so by way of voluntary donations, each parish having to set up a poor box and ministers being required to solicit alms from the congregation. This approach proves inadequate, however, and Acts of 1598 and 1601 confirm a compulsory system of collection and provision which remains largely in place until the 19th century.[1]

Under the 1601 Act each year every parish is to appoint 'overseers of the poore', comprising the churchwardens and two, three or four 'substanciall housholders'. These overseers are to set the able-bodied, including children, to work by providing 'a convenient stocke of flaxe, hempe, wooll, threed, iron, and other necessarie ware and stuffe'. As for those who are 'lame, impotente, olde, blinde' or otherwise unable to work, parents, grandparents and children have the first responsibility to provide for them, but in the absence of such support the overseers are to provide 'the necessarie reliefe'. To meet these two responsibilities – setting the able to work and caring for those who cannot work – the overseers are to raise 'such competent sum and sums of money as they shall thinke fit' by taxing inhabitants, householders, landholders and tithe owners.

> 1631 Received and gathered by a tax which was intended for a stocke to set the poore on worke ... £7 2s 6d (Lambeth)

Anyone who refuses to pay may be imprisoned or have their goods sold.

> 1637 For a warant for those that would not pay to the poore ... 1s (St Bartholomew Exchange)

Separate accounts are to be kept, to be made up each year and presented to two justices of the peace, who are effectively the overseers of the overseers.[2]

> 1609 For a paper booke for accounts for poore ... 18d (Holy Trinity, Chester)[3]

In practice, however, in many parishes some or all of the expenditure on the poor appears in the main churchwardens' accounts rather than separately.

2. Badges

To ease the administration of such relief, and to reduce abuse, parishes may require their poor to wear badges.

1601 For badges to the poore folkes ... 2s 4d (Houghton-le-Spring, co. Durham)

1616 For a mowld & castinge of badgs for the poore ... 5s (St John Zachary)[1]

An Act of 1555 requires 'such poore folkes' as are licensed to beg to 'weare openly ... bothe on the breast & the back of ... their uttermost garment, some notable badge or token'. A later Act (1696-97) applies more widely, requiring all those entitled to receive poor relief to wear, 'in an open and visible manner', on 'the shoulder of the right sleeve of the uppermost garment', a badge or mark comprising 'a large Roman P, together with the first letter of the name of the parish or place whereof such poor person is an inhabitant, cut either in red or blew cloth'.[2]

1697 [Ordered] that the churchwardens do provide 400 brass badges, and set the same upon pieces of red cloth, for the pensioners to wear, pursuant to Act of Parliament lately made for that purpose. (St Giles in the Fields, vestry)

1698 To the Widow Still, that was kept back from her for neglecting to wear the badge ... 2s (Cowden, Kent)

1749 For marking the poor, putting on the letters ... 8d (Swainswick, Somerset)[3]

3. Forms of charity

Provided they do as required the parish almsfolk receive regular pensions. The parish also makes a range of more ad hoc payments to the poor more generally, for example distributing money at particular festivals and in hard times.

1554 On Christmas Eve. Paide to the poore of this parishe in the alyes and in the streate side in Birchen lane and in the churche yarde, to some 12d, to some 20d, and to some 2s a pese ... £2 7s (St Michael, Cornhill)

1556 Geven to the pur in mony apon gud Friday ... 8s 5d (Strood, Kent)

1664 To the poore of the toune in the frostie weather ... 13s 6d (Metfield, Suffolk)[1]

Money is also given to individuals in particular need.

1642 To Mrs Mabbs, a poet's wife, her husband being dead ... 1s (St Giles in the Fields)

1661 [To John Lambert] for losse of his pigge ... 1s 6d (St Mabyn, Cornwall)

1700 To Hugh Moulsey that was out of work and like to fall into despaire ... 3s 6d (Camberwell, Surrey)

1715 To Goody Pricklove to help her to pay her husbands fees & discharge him out of prison ... 2s 6d (Leyton, Essex)[2]

1723 Gave Sarah Justice being very bad of the blowes and bruises her husband gave her ... 1s (St Ethelburga, Bishopsgate)

1728 Paid Wm. Belchers wife who lies in and her husband run away ... 5s (Walthamstow, Essex)

1772 Paid Wm. Griffin in ye snow for want of bisness ... 5s (Marholm, Northants)[3]

Often payments are related to illness or disability.

1550 Given to lame Agnes when she was seke in harvest season ... 4d (St Martin, Leicester)

1576 To Roger Yonge, his tonge was cut oute ... 2s (Holy Trinity, Coventry)

1640 To Tottenham-court Meg, being verie sicke ... 1s (St Giles in the Fields)

1667 To dumbe Grace ... 2s (Holy Cross Westgate, Canterbury)[4]

1668 To Daniel Ogiles his boy being sick of the smal pokes ... 6d (St Giles, Northampton)

1725 To Thomas Wager a sick man that lay at my door ... 1s (St Giles without Cripplegate)

1778 Gave Joseph Hollis being bit with a mad dog ... £1 11s 6d (High Wycombe, Bucks)[5]

The parish may also provide grain or bread and cheese to the poor generally.

1552 For the expences of Thomas Spysall, Alexander Lamb, Thomas Payne, when they did ride into Lincondeshire [Lincolnshire] to buy corne for the pore ... £2 16s 1d (Brightlingsea, Essex)

1644 For scales to weigh the poores bread ... 4s 6d | 1697 Paid Mr Skinner the cheesemonger for cheese for the poore for one yeare ... £5 4s (St Bartholomew Exchange)

1693 Paid Mr Bensted, baker, for a yeare's bread given to ye poor on Sondays, being ye gift of Sir Thomas Hunt ... £2 12s | 1699 Charges in prosecuting Wm. Bensted at the quarter sessions at Kingston for makeing the poor's bread too light ... 7s 6d (Camberwell)[6]

Occasionally individual appetites are indulged.

1756 Gave Blind Hannah to buy tobacco ... 1s (St Anne & St Agnes, Aldersgate)

1788 Dec. 6th. Let Grace Lovel have 13 quarts of brandy at 2s per quart ... £1 6s | Ditto 1 gallon of wine ... 7s | Dec. 10th. For a coffin for Grace Lovel ... 13s (Puxton, Somerset)[7]

Clothes are one basic need to be met.

1656 Paid Widow Hazard to buy her a wastcoate ... 6s (St Bartholomew Exchange)

1679 For scouring Will Thomas his britches ... 2d (St Peter in the East, Oxford)

1709 For a speckled hankercher for Rucks garle ... 7d (Holy Cross Westgate, Canterbury)

1725 Gave Goody Little for footling* Mary Cat's stockings ... 6d (Smarden, Kent)

1725 For cutting out of shirts and smocks for ye poor ... 4s 2d (St Giles without Cripplegate)

1748 To a ramskin for old Downs breeches, and making ... 3s 9d (Otterton, Devon)

1750 Lent Mr Jos. Taylor to buy him a shirt, 3s, when he came again to be cloathed with a pretence that he had been stript of all. (St Anne & St Agnes, Aldersgate)[8]

Shoes are another.

1592 For seven paire of shoes for the 7 almsfolks ... 9s 8d (Thatcham, Berks)

1626 For a pair of shoes for the girl that went into the country ... 1s (St Laurence Pountney)

1749 For a pennard [pennyworth] of nailes to naile the litle boys sheows ... 1d (Kingston, Sussex)[9]

Wood and coals may be provided, for warmth in winter and for cooking.

1554 At Michellmas. Paide for 78 sackes of coales given to the poore of this parishe in alyes and streate side, in the churche yarde, and to other that had greate nede ... £2 3s (St Michael, Cornhill)

1603 Paid Nicholas Hunt for felling 5 trees of the almshouseland for the almsfolk ... 12d | Paid Goodman Coxheade for the carters drinking when they brought in the 12 loades of wood for the almsfolk ... 2s (Thatcham)[10]

Some parishes have their own coal houses.

1628 For erectinge the shed in the churche yard to laie the poores coales ... £9 7s 4d (St Bartholomew Exchange)

* Presumably mending the foot part, although not in the *OED* with this sense.

1756 [Ordered] that the shed in which the coals for the poor are kept be repaired, but only in such manner as will just serve to keep the coals from being carried away by the populace. (St Giles without Cripplegate, vestry)[11]

Help may also be given towards various costs around the home.

1678 For sweeping Goody Bungays chimney ... 2d (Redenhall, Norfolk)

1687 Given Ellen Ems when the flood had been in her house ... 1s (St Werburgh, Derby)

1752 Bought for Dame Wilmershurst one tin kettle, one paire of belowes ... 3s (Icklesham, Sussex)[12]

Apart from organised accommodation in almshouses and workhouses, the parish may occasionally allow individuals to stay on Church property.

1563 Paide to Goodman Grenne a blinde man dwellinge in the churche yarde for 52 weekes at 2d the weeke graunted him by a vestreye. Summa ... 8s 8d | 1564 Paide to the olde blinde man at his departinge ... 2s (St Michael, Cornhill)

1698 Paid keeping Benjamin Cotton before he was put under the vestry stairs and for straw to lay him on ... 7s 6d (St Alphage, London Wall)[13]

Sometimes, however, the parish is less accommodating.

1585 Sep. 19th. It is agreed that widdoe Hawse shall not have her pension which is nowe 32s 4d but shall remaine in the churche wardens handes till suche time as she dothe avoid owt of the vestrye which she must do forthe withe. (St Margaret, Lothbury, vestry)

1592 For 2 sitacions for Dorathie Geaffes being in the bellfry ... 9s 6d (Cranbrook, Kent)

1612 [Presentment] Old Scott for lying in the church porche and keepinge fire there to the annoyance of the people. (King's Sutton, Northants)[14]

Over time the total expenditure on particular individuals can be substantial. For example at Cowden, Kent, between 1658 and 1694 a widow called Elizabeth Skinner receives some £230 in money with over £60 more being spent on clothing and care. It is not therefore surprising that parishes sometimes seek to avoid responsibility for individuals who are troublesome, or potentially expensive, or both.[15]

1653 Spent about that wicked woman Conoway ... £2 3s 3d | Given Widdow Conoway to cleere herselfe of the parish forever ... £2 (St Bartholomew Exchange)

1687 Paid Thomas Keeling for keeping away ... 1s (St Werburgh, Derby)

1739 Gave Margery Croydon to get rid of her ... 1s 6d (Walthamstow)[16]

4. Encouraging work

As noted above, the 1601 Act also places great emphasis on encouraging the able-bodied to work. The parish itself plays a direct part, employing poor parishioners as sextons and dogwhippers and in other menial work around the church.

> 1601 3 broomes to ye almes folkes to swepe ye church with ... 6d | 1608 To the almes folkes for helpinge to make cleane the church ... 12d (St Mary the Great, Cambridge)

> 1617 Geven to the poore that carried Hollawayes wife to be buried ... 4d (Lambeth)[1]

It may also help those who seek to make a living from crops

> 1757 Feb. 5th. Gave Jno. Baker to buy seed to sow some land he rents, but was not able to pay for seed this hard winter ... 3s 6d (St Giles, Northampton)

> 1767 For 5 bushell of barley for Bennett the blind man to sow his field ... £1 (High Wycombe, Bucks)[2]

and from livestock.

> 1699 Paid for a cow & summering grass for widow Mounsford ... £4 15s (St Werburgh, Derby)

> 1712 Lent Abraham Cornes by ye parishoners consent, £3 to buy him a cow. (Smarden, Kent)

> 1732 For fatting Widdow Cloke's hogg ... £1 10s (Icklesham, Sussex)[3]

The preparation of clothing materials and the making of clothes are widely encouraged.

> 1664 For 1 lb. of yarne to set Kempshall's wife at worke with the knitting needles ... 2s 6d | Paid her for the knitting of one paire of stockings ... 1s (Battersea)

> 1714 Gave Warren for to buy her [an] engine to wind silk ... 4s 6d (St Ethelburga, Bishopsgate)

> 1716 Mary Norfolk to buy her a wheel to set her a spining ... 1s (St John Zachary)[4]

Parishioners may be helped to acquire the necessary skills.

> 1647 For teaching Godwife Hamonds children to knit ... 1s (Redenhall, Norfolk)

> 1717 To John Wards daughter while she was learning to spin ... 2s | To Mary Ward while her daughter learned to spin soft Jarsey ... 2s (Youlgreave, Derbyshire)

1733 For teaching ye dume boy to mend shews, for 8 weeks ... 8s (East Budleigh, Devon)

1818 Agreed that a person shall be engaged to learn one person in every poor family to make gloves. (Burford, Oxon, vestry)[5]

The young may be helped to become apprentices or servants or to find other work.

1612 Paid for the apparelling of James Smith, and placing him as apprentice with John Turner of Buxted ... 32s 6d (Cowden, Kent)

1659 Paid to Mr Cooper tayler to cloathe & teach Philip Kemp the trade of a tayler ... £10 | 1778 Mrs Burton for 1 year board of Sarah Jones & teaching her the business of a Mantuamaker ... £10 (Leyton, Essex)

1714 Given with Mary Lacys boy to go to sea ... 20s (East Budleigh)

1751 Clothing from head to foot Ann Perkins that she may go to service ... 9s 6d (St Anne & St Agnes, Aldersgate)[6]

Others are helped to set up in trade or business on their own account.

1644 Given to John Bash towards ye buying of a boat ... 6s 6d (Lambeth)

1662 To George Burton senior towards the buying of commodities to load his horse, to keep forth a trade therewith, for his better livelihood ... 5s (Smarden)

1693 Paid Lucye Bartholomew (a parish childe) bound to a herbwoman in Newgate market by order of the overseers, to set her up in her trade and encourage her ... £1 10s | To Lucye Bartholomew (formerly a parish childe) for strewings and greens at Christmas ... 10s (St Bartholomew Exchange)[7]

At St Anne and St Agnes, Aldersgate, they are particularly active in this way.

1726 Gave Miles to set him up a bird merchant ... 5s | 1739 Gave Mrs Rand to set her up to sell oysters ... 5s | 1748 John Gillis to buy brushes &c. to set up shoe cleaning ... 1s | 1757 To Eliz. Kirby to buy baskets & to set her up in the green grocery ... 5s | To Mary Sutterfoot to set her up as an orange merchant ... 4s | To Robert Witherhill to set him up in his bussiness as a wire sive maker ... 8s[8]

Placing someone in a workhouse is a less satisfactory solution for all concerned.

1727 For whiping Susan Hawley at the workhouse ... 1s (St Nicholas, Deptford, Kent)

1736 For carrying Dame Ragg to ye workhouse ... 2s (Walthamstow, Essex)

1750 To the poor in the workhouse for puddings &c. at Christmas ... 3s 3d (St John Zachary)[9]

5. Encouraging marriage

Sometimes the parish pays quite large sums to bring about the marriage of poor female parishioners, perhaps out of simple charity, perhaps with a view to avoiding responsibility for their maintenance in years to come.

> 1739 April 25th. Paid for the marriage of Susan Hall and having her away ... £4 15s 4d (St Mary Bourne, Hants)

> 1744 Spent fetching of John Smith and marring him to Black Moll ... £4 3s 6d | Gave Black Moll to go to Gillingham ... 1s (East Malling, Kent)

> 1774 Gave James Morton of Thame to marry Rebekah Burkett ... £2 13s 6d (High Wycombe, Bucks)[1]

Care is required in the case of one apparently reluctant bridegroom, who is possibly being forced into wedlock having caused a pregnancy.

> 1647 Paid for wages spent upon the man that watched John Pickle all night and the next daie till he was married ... 1s (Great Staughton, Hunts)[2]

The following counter case appears to be a one-off.

> 1830 Paid to stop Couling from having a wife ... 4s (Yarnton, Oxon)[3]

Sometimes men approach the parish with an offer. Marriage is not mentioned in the following case and the proposal does not appear to be romantically inspired.

> 1591-92 Feb. 27th. At this vestry ... came Jeames Fawcet of Islington & moved us the inhabitantes of this parishe that he might have our good willes to have from us Elzabeath Lavender widow to his owne howse and also to have her pencion with her during her life, and promized to be bounde in ten pound bond to kepe her so longe as she lived so [provided] that he might have her saide pencion and her goodes, & the parishe agreed to it, & the 28th daie he sealed his bond of ten pound & caried her goodes awaie in a longe cart & caried her in a dung cart, & so finished ye mattar. (St Margaret, Lothbury)[4]

6. In sickness

When the poor become ill the parish may not only make gifts of money (as seen above) but also pay for care and treatment.

To start at the top.

> 1695 Given Widdow Parrie to go to the doctor with her sore eyes and for a horse to carry her ... 9s 6d (Lapworth, Warwickshire)

> 1712 For pulling out Betty Hanckes tooth ... 6d (St Alphage, London Wall)

> 1754 For cureing young Finch's scalded head ... £1 1s (Walthamstow, Essex)[1]

Hands occasionally need attention, and legs are a common problem.

1646 To Shotton the lame glazier to carry him towards Bath ... 3s (St Giles in the Fields)

1670 To Mr Twist for cureing William Thurstons leg which was burnt by falling into fire ... 5s (Redenhall, Norfolk)

1714 For mending Mary Goodwin's wooden leg ... 2s 6d (St Ethelburga, Bishopsgate)[2]

Some cases end badly.

1680 To Susan Nation in lameness ... 2s | To Curry the chirurgeon [surgeon] for her ... 2s | To keeping of Susan Nation at Bridgwater ... 5s | To Mr Haviland for cutting off Susan Nation's leg ... £4 | For stretching her forth and shrouding her ... 3s 8d | For 4 porters to carry her to church ... 2s 6d (North Petherton, Somerset)[3]

Bone-setters are occasionally employed.

1676 Mr Edward Barnard, for setting broken bones for the yere ... £1 (Minchinhampton, Glos)[4]

Letting of blood is used against a variety of illnesses.

1686 For blooding Margery Milward ... 6d (St Werburgh, Derby)

1736 [Gave] ye blind woman in the workhouse to be bleeded ... 3d (St Anne & St Agnes, Aldersgate)[5]

Among conditions needing attention, the itch (scabies) is very common.

1737 For a pot of ointment to cure Kirby of the itch ... 1s | 1749 To the matron to lay out for the curing the itchy folks ... 1s (St Anne & St Agnes, Aldersgate)[6]

Some other disagreeable problems are not named.

1687 To Goody Write for 3 weeks lodgings for her trouble in makeing Cleere Sewell clean in his loathesome condition when nobody else would ... 6s (Redenhall)

1727 Paid Mr Ingram for curing Hannah Batson of the foul disease ... £1 3s (St Alphage, London Wall)[7]

Other afflictions include the fits.

1697 Ye parish maid, being troubled with fits, to carry her into ye country ... 1s | And to buy herbs for her ... 1s (St John Zachary)[8]

Those with smallpox are carefully confined, and if they are lucky the parish may pay for someone to look after them.

1670 To Jeffery Cookes widow while she lay sick of the small pox and to her keeper for lookeing to her then ... £1 1s 3d | For an old sheete for Jeffery Cookes widow to lie in when she was sick ... 1s 6d | For carryeing Jeffery Cookes widow ... to the churchyarde to be buried ... 10s 6d (Redenhall)

1752 For eating and drinking to Dame Driver while she was at Mrs Walters when the small pox was there ... 4s (Edenbridge, Kent)[9]

More general support is also provided.

1531 To Ric. Robins for spice & ale & candelles abowte his moder while she lay sike ... 4d (Morebath, Devon)

1765 For fisick for Mary Hendy ... 6d | For a fowl for her when sick ... 6d (St Mabyn, Cornwall)

1784 To rum for Ben when ill ... 1s (Marholm, Northants)[10]

When the case is intractable, large amounts may be spent on an apparent expert.

1657 To a surgeon for coming from London to looke on a parish child ... 10s (Battersea)

1783 Expenses on bargaining with conjuror from Skipton to cure Matthew Hudson's daughter ... 1s | 1784 Astrological doctor for Hudson's daughter ... 12s 6d (Bramley, Yorks)[11]

Alternatively the person affected may be taken to a hospital, although provision is limited and admission far from certain.

1624 For carying Lame Zacharie to and from ye hospital ... 1s 6d (Lambeth)

1731 To Dame Duck being lame ... 1s 6d | For a horse and cart to carry Dame Duck to the hospital ... 2s 6d (Walthamstow)

1747 For a coach to bring James Walford to the hospital and back there being no room ... 2s | For Jacob Strolger's petition & a chair to ye hospital but refused, he died in the workhouse that night ... 2s (St Anne & St Agnes, Aldersgate)[12]

7. Mental illness

Among the saddest entries are those relating to mental illness.

1653 Spent on the mad doctor for Rumneys daughter ... 1s (St Bartholomew Exchange)

1687 For a small colte lock for Mary Thorpe, she being distracted ... 10d (St Nicholas, Deptford, Kent)

1689 Paid for Thomas Waltham being distracted ... 5s | Charges for bleeding Thomas Waltham and watching him in the cage,* and carring him to Bridewell ... £1 13s (Ealing, Middlesex)

* A place of confinement for petty malefactors.

1713   Paid two women for wakeing one night and tenting [attending] Hellen Ley two days ... 2s 4d | For fillicking to bind her arms ... 3d | For a cord to bind her down in bed ... 1s 4d | For a staple to locke her to ... 1d | 1726 Spent about Hellen Ley being lunatick, on ye men that assisted George Clark to break ye door being fast bolted on ye inside supposeing she had been dead ... 1s 6d | For ale and meat for her that night ... 6d | For ale to make her a caudle when she fainted ... 3d | To Dr Wooley for bleeding Hellen Ley ... 6d (Youlgreave, Derbyshire)

1761   To myself sitting up all night with a mad-woman ... 4s (Leyton, Essex)[1]

Sufferers in London, and sometimes from further afield, may end up in Bethlehem Hospital, located in Bishopsgate until 1675, when it moves to a new building in Moorfields. Securing admission for a parishioner is an involved and expensive process, and the costs do not end there.

1672   For a warrant to receive Old Day into Bethelem [etc] ... 4s 6d | For a bond which was sealed to pay 5s per weeke to Bethelem ... 1s | Spent on the steward and porter of Bethelem ... 2s | Paid William the sexton for charges he laid and his own time spent in bringing the old man to Bethlem ... 7s | For fower weekes and one day for Thomas Day's being in Bethlem ... £1 9d | Paid the chirurgeon in Bethlem for him ... £1 | Paid to Mr Francklin in charges for burying Thomas Day as per bill ... £1 5s (St Christopher le Stocks)

1756   For coach hire for Susannah Inkpen a lunatick & to her being admitted into Bethlehem ... £3 2s 3d (St John Zachary)

1762   To get the certificate sign'd to put Hannah Britton in Bethlam ... 2s | And more to put her in a strait waistcoat ... 1s (St Anne & St Agnes, Aldersgate)[2]

8. Death and its costs

When the end comes the parish also pays for the burial.*

1676   Given Darby Robins in labor ... 1s 6d | A sheet to wind her in ... 1s 6d | Ye midwife & taking away her child ... 2s | Thomas Brookhous for buring her ... 1s (St Werburgh, Derby)

1729   For coffin, shroud and bearers for John Death from ye workhouse ... 12s (Walthamstow, Essex)[1]

Costs met often include refreshment for those attending the funeral.

---

* Some similar entries, illustrating the burial process, can be found in the preceding chapter.

1635 For one pottle of sacke & one dozin of cakes at ye buriall of Margarett Dunne ... 4s | For bread & beere at ye buriall ... 3s | To a woman of Beckles for winding her ... 6d | To foure bearers which carried her to church ... 2s | To John Bird for ringing the bell & making the grave ... 12d (Stockton, Norfolk)

1673 For 2 gallons of burnt claret, 2 quarts of ale & rosemary given away at ye funeral of ye Widow Lidcott ... 8s 3½d (All Hallows Staining)

1731 For a shroude for Mary Backwell ... 8s 8d | For a coffing ... 9s | For a quarter barrel of syder ... 7s | For bread ... 2s | For 14 pound of cheese ... 3s 2½d | For a quartern of tobaca and two peniworth of pipes ... 6d | For ringing the bell and diging the grave ... 3s (Weston super Mare, Somerset)[2]

Sometimes the parish is rewarded by a bequest, or at least recoups some of its outlay through the sale of goods after death.

1588 To Mr Hypperson [the curate] for the burying of Betteris Taller [Beatrice Taylor] ... 4d | To 2 women that did dresse the said Betteris to be brought to the churche ... 12d | To them that did beare the said Betteris to the churche ... 16d. | *Receits for the stuffe of Betteris Taller* ... For a paier of bellows ... 2d | For a littell ketell ... 21d | For a red petticote ... 2s (St Mary Magdalen, Pulham, Norfolk)[3]

In 1656 the vestry of St Margaret, Lothbury, order

that none hereafter should be admitted a pensioner except they subscribe to give theire goods at theire death to ye parrishe or to restore in moneyes the valleiwe of what they have received from the parrishe, the like order to be bindinge to those that are at this present time pensioners ... Unlesse they subscribe thereunto theire pensions to cease.[4]

9. Children

It may not only be goods that are left to the parish.

1630-31 To Goody Ingrom for a shroud ... 18d | To 4 men to bringe her to church ... 16d | To the men that loaded her goods to ye cart ... 6d | For bringing away the goods ... 12d | To the woman that keepe the children, for meat for them ... 2s | Which children were put to keepe upon Friday the 11th of Februarye, the one to Mercer, to other to Marmaduke Parker ... 6s 4d | March 28th. To Goody Parker for keeping Goody Ingromes girle till it died ... 9s (Lambeth)[1]

As this illustrates, the care of children may fall directly to the parish if the parents die or disappear or are unable to provide adequately.

1641 To Hart for nursing of a poore childe almost starved to death by the mother in Maypole-lane ... 9s 9d (St Giles in the Fields)

1712 For 1 lb. of wool to bury old Trooper in ... 6d | For wood and small beer for Trooper's children ... 1s | For meat and milk for Trooper's children ... 3s 5d (Cowden, Kent)[2]

What to do in such cases gives rise to a good deal of discussion.

1665 Spent at the Dogg taverne aboute disposeing of the poore children ... 1s 8d (St Christopher le Stocks)

1773 Nov. 21st. Agreed in publick vestry held on this day in the parish church ... that John Jones a poor boy maintained by the parish is to be settled as here followeth, vizt. that every householder shall keep this boy for half a year according to lots — first half year to be allowed fifteen shillings, second half year twelve shillings and six pence, and for every half year after two shillings and six pence less, till he shall be able to get his living; only ye parish to keep him in whole clothing and reasonably to be alowd if ye boy shall be sick. (Mainstone, Shropshire)[3]

Outsiders

1. Laws against beggars and vagabonds

Given the range of costs that the parish incurs in relation to its own poor, it is not surprising that it is wary of impoverished strangers who might settle in the area and add to the burden.

This defensive attitude is supported by a series of laws. Under an Act of 1388 beggars are forbidden to leave the place where they are living, and if they cannot be maintained there or nearby they are to be sent back to their place of birth. In similar vein an Act of 1530 orders that those unable to work be licensed to beg only within a particular area. Anyone begging without a valid licence is to be whipped or set in the stocks. If anyone 'hole & mightie in body & able to laboure' is found begging he is 'to be tied to the end of a carte naked and be beaten with whippes' through the town or other place 'till his body be blody by reason of suche whipping'. He is then to give his oath to return, without delay and by the most direct route, 'to the place where he was borne, or where he last dwelled [for] three yere & there put him selfe to laboure, like as a trewe man oweth to do'.[1]

Harsher still, the 1572 Acte for the Punishemente of Vagabondes orders that anyone over the age of 14 and adjudged a rogue, vagabond or 'sturdy begger' (that is, an able bodied one who could work for their living) is to be 'grevouslye whipped, and burnte through the gristle of the right eare with a hot iron of the compasse of an inche about, manifestinge his or her rogishe kinde of life'.

1572 Sep. 8th. This day in this towne was kept the sessions of gaile deliverye and here was hanged 6 persons and seventene taken for roges and vagabonds and whipped abowte the market place and brent in the ears. (Kingston upon Thames, Surrey, note in register)

If they are over 18 and persist in offending they are to be adjudged felons and are therefore liable to the death penalty.

Some exceptions are made, including for 'cockers or harvest folkes that travaile into any countrey ... for harvest worke' and for soldiers and travellers who carry passports or licences from specified authorities.

As for those under 14, if found to be rogues they 'shalbe punished with whippinge or stockinge' (placing in the stocks).[2]

The 1572 Act is superseded by one of 1597. The grisly ear burning is now omitted but anyone found guilty is to

> be stripped naked from the middle upwards, and shall be openly whipped until his or her body be bloodye, and ... forthwith sent from parish to parish by the officers of every the same, the nexte streighte way to the parish where he was borne ... And if the same be not knowen, then to the parish where he or she last dwelte ... there to put him or her selfe to labour as a true subject ought to do ... After which whipping the same person shall have a testimonial ... testifying that the same person hath bene punished according to this Acte ... and the place whereunto such person is limited to go ...

Those who fail to comply may be whipped again and placed in a house of correction or common gaol, and if they 'appeare to be dangerous' or 'will not be reformed of their rogish kind of life' they are liable to 'be banished out of this realme'.

An exception is made for 'every seafaring man suffering shipwracke ... having a testimonial' from a justice of the peace, such a traveller being allowed to pass by the most direct route to the place stipulated in the testimonial and to receive relief on his way. Children under the age of seven are also altogether excepted.[3]

Wandering beggars, one blind, from ballads printed in 1640 and 1695 respectively

The leniency regarding branding does not last. Addressing the problem of how to identify persistent offenders, an Act of 1603 orders that they 'be branded in the lefte shoulder withe an hot burninge iron of the breadth of an Englishe shilling, with a greate Romane R upon the iron ... to be so thoroughlie burned and set on upon the skinne and fleshe, that the letter R be seene and remaine for a perpetual marke upon such rogue duringe his or her life'.[4]

Essentially, therefore, while the post-Reformation parish is required to look after its own poor, it is to hurry impoverished outsiders on, the intention being that if possible they should return to the parish of their birth, which has the responsibility for setting them to work or providing for them if they are incapable.

2. Charity to strangers

Strangers with a pass or other recommendation are best placed to receive assistance on their way.

1596 Geven to a pore man that had a licence in the churche ... 4d | Geven to another pore man that reald [railed] in the churche because he could get nothing ... 3d (Melton Mowbray, Leics)

1608 Given to two poor criples having testimonials for to collect in the churches for their reliefe ... 10d (Chester-le-Street, co. Durham)

1716 To 7 poor sailors by pass to pay for their lodging, it being night ... 2s (St John Zachary)[1]

Others too may be helped.

1555 Geven to a pur child that lay in the street ... 4d (Strood, Kent)

1566 To a naked man in the churche ... 4d (Worcester)

1567 For meate & fire for the pore woman that was borne in a barowe ... 3d (Kilmington, Devon)

c. 1624 Paid a blind woman that was carried about upon a horse ... 6d (Chedder, Somerset)

1631 Given to one Brian of Herefordshire, a poor man gathering for fire ... 12d (St Martin, Oxford)[2]

1691 Given a poore relique of a clarke ... 1s (St Bartholomew Exchange)

1705 Paid ye waygoing woman to buy a coat for her child ... 2s (Holy Cross Westgate, Canterbury)

1711 Given a soldier who pretended to be an officer ... 1s (Hargrave, Northants)

1725 To a stranger with 2 small children, lay all night at my door ... 2s (St Giles without Cripplegate)[3]

From a ballad printed in 1635

3. The stories of those on the move

Among those passing through the parish, some have, or at least claim, a strong individual reason for being on the move and seeking charity.*

Fire and water are often cited.

> 1684 To a poor man who lost his wife, 3 children, and 9 servants by fire ... 1s (Chester-le-Street, co. Durham)

> 1697 Given unto several Cornish people that were undone by the breaking in of the sea ... 2s (Worle, Somerset)[1]

As is human violence.

> 1727 Gave for relief of John Butler, without a permit pass from Somerset-shire for himself, his mother and 2 children more, his father being robbed and murthered, and afterwards his house set on fire by ye rogues that robbed him, who also cut and burnt the flesh of several of the family to make them confess where the money was laid ... 3s (St Nicholas, Deptford, Kent)[2]

Some are sick or disabled or have suffered terrible injury.

> 1574 To a lame man that led a blind man ... 6d (Leverton, Lincs)

> 1618 To three men whose tongues wear cut out ... 3s (Newbury, Berks)

> 1623 By gift to a poor woman that had a wolf on her arm ... 6d† (St Laurence Pountney)

---

* Scepticism regarding such stories is evident in the 1597 Act. Among those to be judged rogues and vagabonds it includes 'all seafaring men pretending losses of their shippes or goods on the sea' and all those who 'wander abroad begging, pretending losses by fire or otherwise'.

† *Wolf.* Malignant growth or ulcerous disease such as lupus (Latin for wolf). At All Hallows Staining the same woman received 4d.

1665 To a traveller and his wife that had no leggs ... 6d (East Budleigh, Devon)

1689 To a poor man burnt by lightning and thunder ... 6d (Starston, Norfolk)[3]

Some of the many wandering soldiers are also maimed.

1608 Given to a soldier that had but one legge and one arme ... 4d (Thatcham, Berks)

1708 [Paid] faif solgars whach had one arm apis ... 1s (East Budleigh)[4]

Relatively generous help tends to be given to impoverished clergymen, of whom there are also many.

1626 Paid to a poore minister making moane for relief ... 1s (St Katharine Cree, Leadenhall Street)

1649 Paid a minister that had lost his sight, and his guide ... 12d (Chedder, Somerset)[5]

Poverty and upheaval in Ireland see many people flee, particularly after a massacre of Protestants in the autumn of 1641, and parishes naturally look favourably on co-religionists driven out by Catholics.

1641-42 To Simon Digby, once a cheife constable in Ireland, whose house was burnt by ye rebels ... 1s | To John Steward and Thomas Steward, Irishmen, whose father & mother were murdered by the rebels, & their goods carried away ... 12d (Stockton, Norfolk)

1649 Paid a man that came from Ireland that had lost his limbs ... 6d | Unto 4 several distressed companies of Irishe people in one week ... 3s 8d (Chedder)[6]

Many others have suffered losses at sea, shipwreck being common.

1677 Given two seamen that were cast away comeing from Burbados ... 1s (St Anne & St Agnes, Aldersgate)

1680 To James Mills, John Brown and Peter Gray whose ship sprung a leak ... 6d (East Budleigh)[7]

Others have been plundered while at sea.

1573 To 5 maryoners that were robbed by pirates ... 12d (Leverton)

1619 To a poore man of Hull robd by the Danes on the seas, who had a letter patent ... 12d (Pittington, co. Durham)

1673 To 6 poore seaman whose shipe they said the Duch had taken ... 1s (St Ethelburga, Bishopsgate)[8]

Apparent sufferers at the hands of the Turks appear widely.

1609 Given to two poore men, being some time taken captives by the Turkes, and their tongues cut out ... 8s (Hartland, Devon)

1642 Gave two women whose husbands were slaves in Turkey ... 1s | To a merchant who had 2 sons in slavery in Turkey ... 1s 6d (Stroud, Glos)[9]

Foreigners themselves may receive help far from home.

1633 Gave a poor starving Frenchman ... 2s (All Hallows Barking)

1673 Given to a Dutch man which had his house burnt by the French armie ... 1s (Quainton, Bucks)

1675 Given to an Italian captain that suffered shipwracke ... 4d (Leek, Staffs)[10]

Out of the way parishes may spend little on travellers and itinerant beggars, but those in large towns and cities, and on busy routes, are likely to face an array of demands each year.

1636 An Irish gent undoon by pirats ... 1s | A poor scholler that had bin lunatick ... 6d | A poore man that had been taken by the Turks ... 6d | A poor gent undoon by suits of lawe ... 6d (Mortlake, Surrey)

1669 To decayed gentleman & travellars in the whole yeare ... 12s 6d (St Edmund, Salisbury)[11]

Over time, even in remote counties, a certain weariness sets in.

1678 To two more poor travellers that had endured great losses ... 1s 6d (Church Pulverbatch, Shropshire)

1689 Given to some passengers [passers by, pedestrians] that came with a passe ... 1s. | It is agreed on us six men* that no such thing be done any more in this parish. (Uffington, Shropshire)

1732 April 14th. It is resolved and agreed that no churchwarden or other parish officers shall after ye date hereof give or allow … any of ye parish money ... for any persons pretending to be Turkey slaves or for any wandering persons claiming relief without due authority ... (Sandridge, Herts)[12]

4. Whipping

While charity may be given, many of those who arrive in the parish are treated as beggars and vagabonds and dealt with accordingly. Costs relating to their whipping typically fall in the town or constable's accounts, but sometimes the parish pays.

1601 For whipping of Gillian Anderson … being a merchantes daughter of Newcastle, and for her pass ... 6d (St Bartholomew Exchange)

* i.e. by a select vestry.

1601 To Andrews for whipping the vagrants for one whole yeare ... 5s 4d (St Mary Woolchurch)

1609 For whipping a man and carrin of him to the next tithing* ... 4d (Chudleigh, Devon)[1]

Incongruously, money may be given before or after the whipping.

1582 Paid to Jone Fittricke ... 12d | Paid for her whippinge ... 6d (Eltham, Kent)

1602 Given to Robert Moodee for wippin two pore folkes ... 2d | And gave them when they were wipped ... 2d | Given to Tomlyn's boy for whipping a man and a woman ... 2d | And gave them when they went ... 2d (Melton Mowbray, Leics)[2]

Such punishments are also recorded in some parish registers.

1621 John Ripplaye a vagrant and a wandring begger of a lowe stature, brown headed and somewhat bleare eyed, aged about fiftye years, was this 14th day of April ... openly whipped at Stokeslay ... for a wandringe begger ... (Stokesley, Yorks)

1658 April 26th. Here was taken a vagarant one Mary Parker, widow, with a child and she was wipped according to law, about the age of thirty years, proper of personage, and she was to go to the place of her birth that is Gravesend in Kent, and she is limited ten days, and to be turned from tithing to tithing till she comes to the end of the said jorney. (Godalming, Surrey)

1695 Feb. 12th. Alice and Elizabeth Pickering, wandering children, were whipped publicly according to law, and sent with a pass to Shrewsbury, the place where they were born. (Brentford, Middlesex)[3]

5. Encouraging or forcing departure

Apart from administering the legal punishment, the parish often takes steps to make sure that the peripatetic poor do leave. In its gentlest form this involves giving money on condition of departure.

1623 Given to a poore woman to rid ye parish of her ... 2s 6d (Lambeth)

1740 Relief to the travelling woman's girle, as yearly, who promis'd not to come again ... £1 6d (Ockley, Surrey)[1]

Those who are ailing may be particularly unwelcome.

1682 Gave to a sick man to send him away ... 2s (Bromley St Leonard, Middlesex)

---

* A small rural administrative division, originally a tenth of a hundred (a hundred being a division of a county having its own court).

1740 Gave a woman & two small children to go from town having the small pox on them ... 6d (Towcester, Northants)[2]

Stronger action may also be taken.

1622 To Constable Bagley to hunt roggs and beggars out of ye parishe ... 6d (Abbey Church, Shrewsbury)

1683 Paid at several times for routing the beggars out of the farmers barnes ... 5s (Twickenham, Middlesex)

1692 Paid for a warrant to remove the old raggwoman out of the parish ... 1s (St John the Baptist, Chester)

1730 Charges in gitting the Irich women away to Ireland ... £1 1s (Leyton, Essex)[3]

The physically and mentally unwell are not exempt.

1657 For sendinge back Katherine Jones a cripple to Worcester ... 6d (Ludlow)

1682 Paid the sexton's wife for getting a sick woman out of the parish ... 1s 6d (St Christopher le Stocks)

1718 To Atkins and Mitchell to lead a lame woman out of the parish at eleven of clock in the night ... 2s | 1735 Gave the watch men that sent a mad woman out of the parish in the night time ... 1s (St Anne & St Agnes, Aldersgate)[4]

Physical removal occurs widely. The accounts give no sense of any compunction about it, although there is no way of knowing whether those carrying it out are similarly detached.

1595 For a caryenge awaie a poore boy that laye under a stall ... 2d (St Michael, Cornhill)

1596 To Micaell Hayward for taking of a pore woman in a cart from town to town ... 16d (Cratfield, Suffolk)

1604 For carying away beggers from the chirche ... 10d (St Stephen, Walbrook)

1724 For removing Francis Poulton from Mr Garnetts barne to Weston beyond Boldock being so rotten of ye pox as not able to walk or ride, and for all charges and other expenses ... £1 9s 3d (Walthamstow, Essex)[5]

6. Death and burial

A stranger about to die is particularly unwelcome because of the prospect of dealing with the body and paying for its burial.

1665 Given a man to carry away a sick man for feare he should die in the streetes within this parish ... 1s (St Alphage, London Wall)

1736 Expenses getting a poor woman out of the parish that was going to drown herself ... 1s | 1740 [Given to] a man almost dead to gitt him away ... 5s (Leyton, Essex)[1]

The anxiety is recorded by Anthony Wood in Oxford.

1679 *Dec. 21st and 22nd.* Extreame cold weather. A poore man died with hunger and cold: he began to die in St Clement's parish, but the parishioners discovering it ... carried him under Magdalen Tower in St Peter's parish East to die there and so save the parish two or three shillings to burye him.[2]

A corpse is similarly unwelcome.

1688 Gave a waterman to carry a drowned man away that lay to and again[st]e the shoar ... 6d (St Nicholas, Deptford, Kent)[3]

The following show some of the burial costs relating to poor outsiders that parishes are so keen to avoid.

1582 For a shete and for bearers to carie a poore Irishe woman to church which died in Faukes Halle [Vauxhall] ... 20d (Lambeth)

1588 For a shroud for a poor man which died within this parishe, which was caryed from tithinge to tithinge ... 16d | For bread and drinke for them which took payens for bringing the same poor man to the grave ... 6d (Milton Abbot, Devon)

1671 For burying of a waygoeing woman which died at Goodman Childs barn ... 3s 6d (Holy Cross Westgate, Canterbury)

1725 For striping and cleaning a stranger found dead in the street ... 1s (St Giles without Cripplegate)[4]

Parishioners of means sometimes cover or contribute towards the costs, burial of the dead being the last of the Corporal Works of Mercy, although such charity becomes less common after the Reformation.

1477-79 Received of John Jacob for the observaunce in the churche for a Spaynarde that was slaine ... 5s | 1487 Of Robert Walding, for a man of Caleyes [Calais] buried in the greate chirch yard ... 3s | Of Margarete Bull for the buriall of a strange childe ... 2s (St Mary at Hill)

1555 Received of Mr Whytlege for the beryalle of a strange man in the churche ... 6s 8d (Ludlow)[5]

A number of deaths occur on the homeward journey that the itinerant poor are required to make, as seen above at Milton Abbot and as parish registers record.

1615 Feb. 12th. Katherine White, a Scottish woman being a stranger, having a passe to travel homeward, fell sick by the way, and being brought hither upon a barrow from Winleston, extream sicke, died here, and was buried. (Merrington, co. Durham)

1622 John Tibneham was buried the 26 day of Marche and he was brought with a pass the 25 day of Marche from Parham in a carte by the offesseres of Parham with a paier of pothokes [pot-hooks] abought his necke & he ded depart his lyf presentle after he was laid downe ... and his pass was to send him to a town whiche by the name was named Stok Ashe. (Framlingham, Suffolk)[6]

The deaths of many children are also recorded.

1558 A strange boy begging here died and was buried ye first day of July. (Redenhall, Norfolk)

1652 Jan. 25th. One William Grimes (as he said), a beggar boy, that knewe of no place of his habitation that ever he had. (Laxfield, Suffolk)

1741 August 2nd. Sarah —, a child that died in her mother's arms in the street. (St Dionis Backchurch)[7]

7. Baptisms

More happily a child is sometimes born to those passing through and is baptised.

1695 Paid for gossips* for a poor travelling woman's child ... 3s (Birchington, Kent)[1]

Here too, however, the parish may be wary, knowing that for the rest of the child's life they may be liable to provide for it.

1723 Susannah, daughter of Moses and Mary Cooper, travellers, born in Martin [Merton], and the poor woman being desirous to have it baptized, though she had lain in but a week, carried it in her own arms to Martin church, to tender it to me to baptize it there on Sunday last, being June ye 30th. But Justice Meriton being informed by the constable of her being in the porch with that intention, went out of his seat in time of service to her, and took hold of her, and led her to the court of his house, being over against the church, and shut the gate upon her and her husband, and let them not out till sermon and service were over and I was gone home, and made the man's mittimus† to send him to the house of correction if he would not cary his wife and child out of the parish without being baptized, and consequently registered there, which being forced to comply with, she brought up her child to me, to my

---

* *Gossip*. Godfather or godmother. From Old English *godsibb*, *sibb* meaning akin or related (cf. siblings), denoting the spiritual affinity of the baptised child and the godparent.
† From Latin 'we send', a warrant issued by a justice of the peace etc committing a person to custody.

house on this day, being Tuesday, July 2nd, complaining of her hard usage, and passionately desiring me to baptize it, which I did by the name above in the presence of her husband, my wife, and Dr Elir Pitchford. | Edward Collins. (Memorandum in register, Wimbledon, Surrey)[2]

8. Gypsies

Hostility is also shown towards the wandering groups who begin to arrive in England in the 15th century from northern India. Known as Egyptians, shortened to gypsies, from a mistaken assumption as to their origins, they are widely mistrusted and an Act of 1530 orders them to leave the realm within sixteen days, 'upon paine of imprisonment and forfeiture of their goodes and catells'.[1]

A harsher law of 1554 condemns their 'develishe and noughty practises'. They are now given twenty days to depart to avoid forfeiting 'goodes and cattels', but should they still be here after forty days they shall be adjudged felons and 'suffer therfore paines of deathe [and] losse of landes and goodes'. They can, however, avoid such penalties if within twenty days they 'leave that noughty, idle and ungodly life and company' and either enter the service of an honest inhabitant or 'honestlye exercise' themselves 'in some lawfull worck or occupacion'.[2]

A further Act of 1562 widens the scope to include anyone born within the realm who is found in company or fellowship with those 'vagaboundes commonly called or calling themselves Egiptians, or counterfaiting, transforming or disguising themselves by their apparell, speeche or other behaviour like unto suche' for the space of a month, either 'at one time or at several times'.* This Act remains in force until 1783.[3]

In spite of such measures, numbers of gypsies remain and others arrive. As already seen in relation to burial (p358), the parish may turn a blind eye to their illegal status.

> 1581   April 2nd. Margaret Bannester, doughter of William Bannester, goinge after the manner of rogishe Egyptians, was baptised. (Loughborough, Leics)

> 1687 June 2nd. King and queen of the jepsies, Robert Hern and Elizabeth Bozwell, marid. (Camberwell, Surrey)

> 1735   Paid Mr Woods bill for a jepseys lying in and burying the child … 13s 10d (Leyton, Essex)[4]

In other cases they are less fortunate.

> 1592 Simson, Arington, Fetherstone, Fenwicke & Loncaster were hanged, being Egyptians, 8 August. (St Nicholas, Durham)[5]

---

* 'The counterfait Egiptian girle' is among over a hundred plague victims buried at St Mary's, Bury St Edmunds, in September 1637.

¶ Most worrying of all those arriving in the parish are pregnant women and those with infants that they plan to abandon, because any child so born or left is liable to become the parish's responsibility. Burying a stranger costs a few shillings and is quickly done. Providing for a child until it can work, and then being responsible for it should it face poverty and sickness in later life, are liabilities of another order.

Foundlings

1. Children found, alive and dead

Children are abandoned in every parish across the country, but the problem is greatest in London. The church itself may be chosen as the place of leaving.

> 1635 May 29th. Alice, a child found at the church doore. (St Benet, Paul's Wharf, baptism)[1]

To avoid detection it is often done at night, the leaver knowing that the church will be attended to early next morning. Alternatively advantage may be taken of some other aspect of church activity and routine.

> 1661 Mary Aldermary, a child, was left in a pewe in the church at a finurall [funeral] the 27th and baptized the 28th of June. (St Mary Aldermary)

> 1750 March 25th. Mary Penn, foundling, baptised. This child was found tied up in a cloth, and hung to the ring upon the south door of Penn church, about 8 o'clock p.m. by William Baker, as he was coming out of the church after the ringing of the curfew bell. (Penn, Staffs)[2]

The parish can then be relied upon to see that the child is looked after.

> 1582 Sep. 2nd. Wheras a child was left in the church porch on Sonday the 26th of August last with a note left wretten in the breast of it, that it was a Christian sole named Jane ... we call her Jane. | It is agreed that for the same child ther shalbe a nurse providid (for as small a charge as maybe) and the mony for it, as also for necessary clothes, shalbe disbursed by the church warden who shall kepe accompt of the same charge. (Stepney, Middlesex, vestry)* [3]

In addition, at a less practical level, mothers may feel that in extremis the best they can do for their child is to place it under God's protection.

Other busy places where the child will soon be found may be chosen instead, as the following baptism entries show.

> 1644 Oct. 22nd. John Cole that was laid on the needle mans stall. (St Mary Colechurch, Poultry)

> 1696 July 3rd. Penelope, a female child, taken up under the Cock alehouse in Sherborne Lane. (St Mary Woolnoth)

* Agreeably, those signing the order include 'Affabell Partridge'.

Study by Hogarth for a headpiece used on letters raising funds for the Foundling Hospital, *c.* 1739. On the left one infant has been abandoned and another is being left beside a gate. On the right children emerge from the hospital bearing the tools of various useful trades.

> 1707 Sep. 17th. William, a child found at the Lamp Office door Sep. 8. (St Mildred, Bread Street)

> 1713 Oct. 4th. John, reputed son of Catherine Cartwright of Leckhamstead, found hanging in a basket on the gates which open out of the great yard into the highway. (Thornton, Bucks)[4]

The houses of the rich or eminent are sometimes selected, presumably in the hope that the occupants will provide for the child directly or at least be well placed to ensure that the parish does so.

> 1597 Nov. 2nd. Giles Woolnoth, a manchild, found laide at the gate of the Lady Ramsay. (St Mary Woolnoth)

> 1638 Nov. 16th. Steven Christopher, a child that was laid at Sir William Middletons dore. (St Christopher le Stocks)[5]

On the other hand an obscure place may be chosen, presumably with a view to delaying discovery.

> 1643 April 25th. This day William Bryan, being fishing with an angle rod, found in the river a new borne woman child, folded up in an old cloth. (St Helen, Auckland, co. Durham, note in register)

> 1681 July the 4 there was a child found in Wessmede under a hayrick, and it was baptized at this parish church the 10 of July ... and it was named Sarah. (Northmoor, Oxon)[6]

As seen earlier in the case at Stepney, explanatory notes are sometimes left with the child. The following examples were found by a Victorian rector in an old oak chest in the tower of St Matthew, Friday Street.

[*c.* 1680] To the overseers of the parish, | Humbly shewing the resons of exposing this child: his father being latly taken by the Turkes of Algieres, and now a slave, his mother, not able by reson of her poverty to bring him up, is constrained to do after this manner to her great trouble and greife, and assures you that when God shall please to restore her husband back then to fetch him back and owne him and pay all charges for his keeping. Pray baptise him and call his name Thomas.

1713, January 14. | Robert Staples is my name; | My parents being very poor | Were forced to lay me at your door.

The latter note proves in vain as the register records the child's burial on the same day.[7]

Such a fate is all too common among those left.

1630 Matthew, an infant, left alive in ye shambles on High Ongar faire day at night, lived a month, & was buried ye October 10th. (Chipping Ongar, Essex)

1672 Provideing a nurse for the child found in Deanes Court ... 3s 9d | For a coffin for it ... 1s | And given the nurse & her daughter for carrying it to the grave ... 1s 6d (St Anne & St Agnes, Aldersgate)[8]

Sometimes the child is already dead when left.

1725 August 15th. A female child, left dead in a band box* in Three Nun Alley, the 14th, was this evening privately deposited in church yard next ye wall by the west gate. (St Christopher le Stocks)[9]

In such cases, under an Act of 1624, if the child is illegitimate the mother is liable to suffer death as for murder unless she can produce a witness to its having been stillborn. The parish may pay towards the costs of seeking her.[10]

1644 For a warrant to my lord chief justice to find out the mother of a child that was laid at the church door dead ... 2s (St Peter in the East, Oxford)[11]

2. Attempts to avoid responsibility

If a child is found alive, the parish may try to avoid the consequences.

1663 For removinge a child out of the parish that was left one night ... 3s 6d (St Bartholomew Exchange)[1]

Money may also be spent pre-emptively to the same end.

1647 Given to a poore woman that would have left her child in the church ... 2s | 1653 Paid Wards daughter for saveing the parish from a child at Mr Nurses doore ... 1s (St Bartholomew Exchange)

* A slight box of cardboard or very thin wood covered with paper, originally for 'bands' or ruffs but also used for collars, hats and millinery in general.

1664 Paid to watch a child endeavoured to be put on the parish by ye churchwardens of St Mary Woolnoth ... 1s (St Mary Woolchurch)[2]

The following shows the level of vigilance sometimes maintained.

1698 Dec. 14th. Abraham Gubinant was chosen warden for one year and he is every night to see that no children be left in ye street till ye watch be set and likewise be up in ye morning at five o'clock about ye same business for which he is to receive five pounds for his years service. (St Mary, Aldermanbury, vestry)[3]

3. Baptism

Should such efforts fail the parish must arrange for care and a christening.

1592 Sep. 22nd. Olyfer a base borne child that was taken up at Mr Barker's door was baptized before nine or ten witnesses at prayer time. (St Olave, Hart Street)[1]

Baptism may already have been performed of course, but if not the person leaving a child may place salt with it to indicate as much (salt being used in the ceremony). However, even if no salt is left the parish is likely to baptise the child anyway because the sacrament is considered vital to the child's spiritual well-being. According to canons issued in 1195,

When a child is found exposed, and it is not known that he has been baptized, let him be baptized, whether he be found with salt or without; for that cannot be said to be iterated which is not known to have been done before.[2]

The following shows this approach in practice.

1618 Oct. 26th. Elizabeth Acon. This child was found in the streete at one Mr Withers dore in St Nicholas lane upon the ninteenth of this present month of October being as it was supposed some two monthes old but we not knowing whether it was baptized before or no, baptized it by the name of Elizabeth Acon after the name of this parishe. (St Nicholas Acons)[3]

4. Naming

As several of the examples above show, the names bestowed on foundlings often include reference to the parish which now stands in loco parentis.

1588-89 Feb. 2nd. Vincent Antholins, so named because he was found in the church porch upon St Vincent's Day. (St Antholin, Budge Row)

1637 Feb. 2nd. John Mildred, a child found in a hand basket at ye Connter [Poultry Compter] gate. (St Mildred, Poultry)

1661 Sep. 6th. Faith Dionis, a foundling. | Charity Dionis, a foundling. | Grace Dionis, a foundling. (St Dionis Backchurch)

1683-84 Feb. 17th. Robert Alhallows, a parish child laid in the upper corte in Bread strett whear the widdow Planners coffy house is. (All Hallows, Bread Street)[1]

Among foundlings looked after in 1632 by St Bartholomew Exchange (in Bartholomew Lane, off Threadneedle Street and opposite the Royal Exchange) are Bartholomew Exchange, Bartholomew Needle, Mary, Bartholomew and Lawrence Threadneedle, and Mary and Mercy Bartholomewlane.[2]

The name of the finding place may also be incorporated.

1585-86 Jan. 19th. Steven Barge, a child found in the Barge* behind a currant bush. Who was his father or mother we knowe not. (St Stephen, Walbrook)

1604-05 March 8th. A man child that was lefte in Watlinge Street in ye night, that was named at ye baptisme Felixe† Watlinge. (All Hallows, Bread Street)

1660 Sep. 23rd. Ann Angell a poore child found in Angell Alley. (St Anne & St Agnes, Aldersgate)

1694-95 Jan. 5th. Cardinall Woolnoth, a male child, taken up in Cardinalls Cap Alley. (St Mary Woolnoth)[3]

1702-03 Feb. 12th. John Jerusalem a foundling at ye back dore of ye Jerusalem taverne. (St James, Clerkenwell)

1724 Jan. 15th. Mary Carfax, a foundling. (St Martin, Oxford)

1768 Dec. 16th. Edward Shambles, a deserted child, named from the place where he was left. (Romford, Essex)[4]

The following contains a whole life story, brief and sad.

1708 Spent at ye cristening of a child taken up in Mutton Court in Maiden Lane and cristened Sarah Mutton, & at ye White Hart agreeing with the nurse at Hoxton to keep it, & for victuals ... 2s 6d | For a rug to lap ye child in ... 3s | And gave ye nurse when ye child was in a fit to get it some thing ... 1s | 1709 For a coffin & shroud for Sarah Mutton ... 2s 8d | The grave making ... 1s 8d | Spent on the women & in drink ... 2s | For bringing the child from Hoxton ... 2s (St John Zachary)[5]

Other circumstances relating to the discovery may also be used, in some cases disconcertingly.

---

* Barge Yard, off Bucklersbury and close to the church.
† *Felix* in Latin meaning fruitful, fortunate, auspicious.

1611 Job rakt out of the Ashes, being borne the last of August, in the lane going to Sir John Spencer's back gate, and there laide in a heape of seacole ashes, was baptised the first daye of September following, and died the next day after. (St Helen, Bishopsgate)

1640 Spent on the gossips at the christning of Stephen Oilbut, found in the Barge yard upon an oile butt ... 3s 6d (St Stephen, Walbrook)

1690 For cloaths for Mary Basket a foundling ... £1 | For buring Mary Basket ... £1 (St Bartholomew Exchange)

1714-15 March 6th. Laurence Underbench, infant. (St Botolph, Bishopsgate, burial)[6]

Not to mention

1616-17 Feb. 11th. Strangely Found (a child found in Islington fieldes). (St James, Clerkenwell, burial)[7]

At St Mary Woolchurch more or less any circumstance will serve.

1646 April 23rd. A child found at Mr Sawyers in the street on a place to whet knives and was named Edward Sharp. | 1649 April 14th. John Wallstone, a male child found in the ally by the church door laid on a stone in the wall. | August 28th. Henry Penny, a male child about the age of 3 years was found in our parish with a penny in his hand. | Dec. 27th. There was a male child found at Mr Paschalls stall before day and was named John Beforeday being St John's day. | 1650 April 7th. John Bynight, a male child left in our parish at Mr Garretts doore. | Nov. 9th. Mary Evening, a female child found at Mr Morris doore in Cornhill. | 1651-52 Feb. 16th. Edward Munday, found on a Munday night at Mr Wrights stall. | 1653-54 Jan. 7th. Mary Gold, a female child found on a goldsmith's stall in Lombard Street. | 1678-79 Feb. 8th. Robert Entry, found in Dr Tabor's entry.[8]

Among biblical names bestowed, that of Moses, found beside a river in 'an ark of bulrushes' (Exodus 2:3), is a natural choice, and his brother Aaron also appears.

1586-87 Jan. 8th. A childe that was left in Watlinge street within our parish and that was named Moses Outecaste becawse it was so found and not knowen from whence it cam. (All Hallows, Bread Street)

1629 Dec. 26th. Moyses and Aaron, two children found in the street. (St Gregory, by St Paul's)

1669 March 28th. Moses, a child found within the forest of Bolland. (Chipping, Lancs)[9]

The following also suggests faith.

1698 June 12th. Providence, an infant whom her father and mother abandoned; but God will take care of her. (Wolstanton, Staffs)[10]

5. Seeking out the parents

The sense of acceptance indicated in the last entry is not typical. In most cases the parish makes a determined effort to identify and track down the mother, and sometimes also the father.

> 1583 Paid unto Wm. Dikinsone, officer, for going with a yong child to seke out his parentes and for his borde at 2s 4d ye weke ... 32s 8d* | 1639 For examining of a woman taken upon suspition to be the mother of our last foundling and for keeping her a while in Bridewell ... 7s 2d (St Stephen, Walbrook)

> 1644 For a warrant for the wench that left her childe in the parish ... 4d | For a horse to ride after her ... 2s 2d (Holy Cross Westgate, Canterbury)

> 1697 Expended looking after† ye woman that left her child at the Three Blackbirds ... 2s 9d | Expended in finding out the mother of a child left at John Gifford's: the same day whipt in Bridewell ... 4s 6d (St James, Bristol)[1]

Richard Gough, historian of Myddle in Shropshire, is himself involved in tracking down the mother of a child left in the parish. At nearby Shawbury he learns

that some two weeks earlier a poor travelling woman had been delivered before moving on to another village, Greensell, where the child was baptised. At Greensell he finds a servant who remembers giving 'a peice of a greene sey‡ apron to wrappe the childe in'. Next day the child is sent for and the apron piece is found about it. As a result of Gough's sleuthing Myddle escapes responsibility, the magistrates ordering Shawbury to provide for the child.[2]

Apart from such individual enquiries, the parish may publicise.

> 1717 For proclaiming ye child that was left in ye church porch in Shrewsbury, Bridgnorth & Wenlock ... 2s 6d (Cardington, Shropshire)

> 1734 Paid the bell man for calling a foundling ... 1s (All Saints, Newcastle)[3]

---

* The figures suggest that the errand lasted fourteen weeks.
† Almost certainly here with the sense 'seeking out'.
‡ *Say.* A light, twilled cotton fabric.

One way of doing so, in London at least, is to place a notice in a newspaper.

1715 To the nurse for the christning of Eliz. Church, 1s, and for putting
her into the Daily Courant, 3s 6d. (St Anne & St Agnes, Aldersgate)[4]

Fairly large rewards are usually offered, reflecting the high cost to the parish of looking after foundlings.

On Saturday the 15th instant, there was drop'd a Female Child about a month old, on a Dunghill in the passage leading to Crosby Square in the parish of St Hellen in Bishops-Gate-Street. Whoever discovers the parents, or the person who drop'd the same, shall have 40s reward …

Daily Courant, 19 September 1705

Dropt on Sunday evening last, in St Gregory's parish, the south-side of St Paul's, a child of about two years old; whoever will discover the owners of it to the church wardens of the said parish shall have 40s reward. | N.B. The following was stuck on the back of it, when found: 'In the name of God, Amen. To those good people who shall receive the poor bearer hereof. As there are none under greater want and necessity than my self, having 3 more very small children besides this, rather than have it starv'd, I'm oblig'd to leave him to God's Providence, and your care. He's born in wedlock, his name is James; the Lord preserve him, and (if he lives) give him his grace; and (I hope) for the sake of the Lord Jesus Christ you will bring him up and educate him in an honest employ, whereby he may be able to get his livelihood. The Lord preserve him, and you.'

Post Boy, 17 April 1712

Sometimes the search is successful.

1635 Paid Goodwife Perkins for keeping a child left in Castle yard …
2s 2d | Spent on a woman which did thinke she did know the child …
6½d | To Goodwife Porter for inquiring out the mother … 4s | For a warrant for the mother … 1s | Spent the same day & given the mother when she fetcht away the child … 5s (St Christopher le Stocks)

1658 To Aris ye watchman for discovering the mother of Phillip Zacharie a child left upon Mr Wallis stall … 15s 6d (St John Zachary)[5]

In other cases the child is retrieved voluntarily.

1661-62 Joanna Christopher a child laid to ye charge of ye parish was baptized March ye 20 & afterward fetched away April ye 2nd by ye aforesaid childs mother who declared the name to be Clara. (St Christopher le Stocks)

1697 Sep. 7th. Jonas Woolnoth, a male child taken up at Mr Foley's door. [In margin:] This child was taken away by Mr May, the grandfather. (St Mary Woolnoth, baptism)[6]

6. Care

Unless the mother is found the parish must arrange for the child to be looked after.

> 1623 Paid goodwife Goose for keeping a child left at ye churchwardens doore ... 16s 6d (Lambeth)

> 1717 Paid Widdow Pigg for clothing ye child that was left in ye porch ... 5s (Cardington, Shropshire)[1]

When long term care is needed London parishes often send their foundlings away from the city.

> 1636 For keepinge the child founde at the church doorc until we could get a nurse for it in the contry ... 3s 2d | To Anne Hall dwellinge at Hardnige [sic] fowre miles beyond St Albons a month's pay before hand for that child ... 6s | 1640 For my horse hire and my owne meate in goinge to Ware and Hartford, and to Standon, to see the nurse children ... 10s (St Anne & St Agnes, Aldersgate)

> 1695 Spent in going to see the parish children at twice, their nurse being like to die, and gave to the nurse in her illness ... 20s 4d | Bought two bibles for ye children ... 7s (St John Zachary)[2]

The following shows the attachment that may arise.

> 1633 Paid Judith Feverstone dwellinge at Chelsfield in Kent hard by St Mary Cray for nursing of three children, Bartholomew Exchainge, Larance Threndedle and Mary Threndedell: she hath a fowerth which doth live with her whose name is Mercey Bartholomewlane but she is 16 or 17 yeares of age the which the parish doth pay nothing for nursing her because she is old enough to go out to servis but goodwife Feverston will not part from her but will rather keepe her for nothing ... so the parish doth pay for nursinge the other 3 children at 20d a weeke which cometh to £13 and more allowed her for clothing of them £3 for the yeare and 6s for bringing up the 3 children to London, which is in all ... £16 6s | 1635 April 1st. Paid Judith Fetherston for the clearing of the parishe of anie farther charge with Mercie Bartholomewlane ... £2 10s (St Bartholomew Exchange)[3]

At some point the parish tries to find a permanent home or position for any child left in its care.

> 1593 Paide to myselfe William Hammon this accomptant by order of a vestrie holden in this parishe the 29 day of April to thende I should keepe, maintaine and bringe up orphan Michaell, a foundlinge in this parishe, and for that I shoulde for ever discharge the parish of her [sic] and to that effect to give my bond for the same ... £6 13s 4d (St Michael, Cornhill)

1601-03 For the diet and keeping of a poore childe left upon the parishe ...
13s 7d | To Christofer Courte for keeping of the poore child with diet
for sixe weekes ... 4s | To the said Christofer for takeing the said child to
be his apprentes according to an agreement with the parishenors ... 20s |
For makeing of a paier of indentures* for the boye ... 12d (Worcester)[4]

Pregnant Women

1. Encouraging or forcing departure

Given the parish's anxiety about becoming responsible for poor and abandoned
children, it is not surprising that it views female outsiders who are pregnant with
suspicion. Should they be alone and apparently unmarried, this is likely to be
compounded by strong moral disapproval.

As in dealing with those looking to abandon infants, the easiest option is often
to pay in the hope that the woman concerned will go away.

1635 Given to three great bellied women to passe them away ... 2s 3d
(St Christopher le Stocks)

1659 Given to a poor gentlewoman big with child to get her gone ... 2s 6d
(Bromley St Leonard, Middlesex)

1724 Gave [John Lord's wife] to go off with her great beley ... 16s (Leyton,
Essex)[1]

The parish may take other steps, although what is involved is not always made
clear.

1614 To watchmen to kepe a woman with childe from the porches ... 18d
(St Peter Mancroft, Norwich)

1638 To cleer the parish of a woman that cried out at Mr Carletons doore
in the night ... 2s 6d (St Christopher le Stocks)

1642 For sending a woman away by water that was great with child &
like to be delivered ... 1s (Battersea)

1675 Given Mr Kirke to passe away a greate bellied woman, ready to be
delivered in ye streete ... 6d (St Nicholas, Deptford, Kent)

1723 Paid to get a poor big bellied woman out of the parish, she being very
sick & like to become chargable to the parish, being pushed out of
Cripplegate parish by their beadle ... 3s 6d (St Alphage, London Wall)[2]

In some cases the manner of removal is spelt out.

---

* The contract in two parts by which an apprentice is bound to his master.

1628 Paid two poor women for carrying a big-bellied woman out of the parish ... 1s | Paid to the woman herself ... 6d (All Hallows Barking)

1647 For sending a woman greate with child out of this parish to St George's parish in Southwarke, for men to carry her in a chaire ... 8s (St Anne & St Agnes, Aldersgate)[3]

The sums involved add up.

1664-65 Paid in my 1st & 2d yeare in putting out of sick persons and big bellyed women ... £1 3s 6d (St Christopher le Stocks, account of Thomas Pratt)[4]

Most of the women concerned probably need all the help they can get, but some no doubt take advantage of parish anxiety.

1657 To Anne Walker for her lodging for 23 weekes at 8d per weeke, to keepe her from laying her childe in ye parrish ... 15s 4d (St Stephen, Walbrook)

1676 To a woman pretending to be in labour ... 1s | And to a watchman to see that she did not come againe ... 1s | 1739 Getting a woman pretending groaning out of ye parish ... 1½d | 1764 To a woman with child said to have lain in our parish, to carry her home — a cheat ... 6d (St Anne & St Agnes, Aldersgate)[5]

2. Support

If, in spite of such efforts, a woman from outside the parish manages to give birth while within its bounds, she may at least find that some support is provided.

1575 To the poore woman that were broughte abed in the alleye ... 3s | Unto Nicholas Payne for kepinge of the saide poore woman in his house ... 3s 4d (St Michael, Cornhill)

1588 Paide to a woman brought a bedde at our churche dore to comforte her ... 5s (St Peter, Cheapside)

1606 Paid the nurse for the child borne at Ship Alley gate ... 6s | For straw for the mother of the child to lie on ... 6d | For carrying away the straw after she had gone ... 2d (St Alphage, London Wall)

1637-38 Dec. 10th. Paid Ezekiell Cakebread for cariage of a woman in labour to the cage 12d, for straw 1s 4d, for reliefe 6d. | Dec. 13th. For bread and wine at the christninge of the child ... 1s 6d | Dec. 29th. To widow More for 4 weekes keepinge the woman in childbed ... £1 12s | Jan. 6th. Given her at her goinge away ... 2s 6d (St Bartholomew Exchange)

1722 A woman that was allnight at ye Woolpack door in labour ... 2s 6d (St John Zachary)

1735 For nursing the traveling woman as was brought abed at Hollises 2 weekes and victuals for the nurse ... 10s | For beer and bread and cheese for the woman when she was delivered ... 3s | The midwife ... 4s 6d | For keeping the woman 2 weekes and necessarys for her in her lying inn, washing, sope, fireing, use of linen, bed and other things, she being lowsy and having the itch spoiling ye bed and beding ... 15s | Giving the woman when she went away and hireing a messenger to go with her out of the parish towards Marlow ... 4s | Expences at baptising the child and in procuring godfathers ... 1s 6d | Paid the minister for baptizing the child, and clark ... 1s 6d (High Wycombe, Bucks)[1]

Often things do not end well, nonetheless.

1661 To Elizabeth Sothern a woman havinge no habitation delivered of a child in our parish, for food, fier, straw and one to tend her till she was abell to go away ... 18s 6d | To the reader, clarck, sexton and coffin for the buriall of dittos child ... 7s | Given Elizabeth to be gone as soone as she was able ... 3s (St Bartholomew Exchange)

1709 To a woman to send her away, her child being dead ... 4s (St Dunstan in the West)[2]

Bastards

More generally the parish fears the arrival of any illegitimate child, whether a foundling or not, and whether born to an outsider or to a parishioner.

The terms used for such children in register baptism entries are usually disapproving and sometimes blunt.

1560-61 Jan. 1st. Bridget & Elizabeth the daughters of adultery. (Chesham, Bucks)

1578 Feb. 15th. Sinallfus Heath, suspected bastard. (St Nicholas, Durham)

1585-86 Feb. 4th. Marye Fabian, begotten of George Fabian, base borne & of his owne servante & in his owne house. (St Michael, Cornhill)

1633 Jan. 28th. Nicholas the sonne of Rebecca Cock filius populi.* (Petersham, Surrey)

1725-26 Feb. ye 6. Jane ye spurious and illegitimate daughter of Eliz. Easy. (Rampton, Cambs)[1]

Only occasionally is tolerance shown.

1683 Feb. 22nd. Craddock Bowe, love begot. (All Saints, Newcastle)

* Son of the people (Latin).

1703 Dec. 18th. Ezekiel, natural son of Ezekiel Painter of St Clements Danes in com. Middlesex & Barbara Beaumont of this parish single-woman. (Stoke Poges, Bucks)

1715 Sep. 15th. Peter, a chance child up the hill. (Richmond, Surrey)[2]

The children themselves may be marked out for life not just by the stigma attaching to illegitimacy but also by the disapproving names bestowed upon them.

1609 Dec. 17th. Flie-fornication, the bace son of Catren Andrews. (Waldron, Sussex)

1612 May 30th. A base child Repentance, ye daughter of Richard Stanard and Ann Cutting. (Cratfield, Suffolk)[3]

Some of the names given are more generous.

1590 Dec. 31st. Fortuito, a bastard from Loxford Barne. (Barking, Essex)

1783 Feb. 23rd. Charity and Virtue twin bastards of Elizabeth Tye. (Toft Monks, Norfolk)[4]

The writers of many registers also show blunt disapproval of the mothers.

1564 August 12th. Johannes filius meretricis.* (Chelsea, Middlesex)

1574-75 Feb. 6th. Sara Willson, the daughter of a strumpett whose name was Mary Willson. (St Nicholas Acons)

1589 Jonas, a bastard son of that ancient harlot, Elizabeth Duckett, of Poplar. (Stepney, Middlesex)[5]

As for the place of birth, it is often a last resort.

1591 A bastard out of Yardington was baptized 12 May, a travellinge woman brought a bed in the streete. Hard harted people. (Aston by Birmingham, Warwickshire)

1610 June 4th. Agnes Price, base born in a barn. (Chelsea)

1727 Aug. 10th. Owen son of Owen Harris & Isabel Ellis, a bastard child born in ye churchyard. (St Mary le Bow)[6]

Regarding such children the parish has two main concerns – the risk of moral contagion and the likelihood of having to pay for their support. At a court hearing in 1606, concerning the prospect of a local woman having a bastard, the case put by the inhabitants of Castle Combe, Wiltshire, connects the two.

By this licentious life of hers not only Gods wrath may be powered downe upon us inhabitants of the towne but also her evil example may so greatly corrupt others that great and extraordinary charge ... may be imposed upon us.[7]

---

*John, son of a prostitute. Hence *meretricious.*

A parish has four main ways of avoiding such costs. First, it can encourage the mother or prospective mother to leave, whether she is a parishioner or not.

> 1759 Paid to get rid of Mr Suttons servant she being big with child ... £1 1s (Walthamstow, Essex)[8]

Second, if the child was born elsewhere, they can seek to pass the problem on to the relevant parish.

> 1610 July 22nd. This day warninge was given by the vestry to John Godfrey of Lambeth Marshe for avoidinge of Elizabeth Salter beinge in his howse with childe by one of the Courte as she confessed. And the said Elizabeth was also warned to avoide the parishe with [the] childe, and John Browne, constable of the said Marshe, was also warned to avoide her and her said childe to Westminster where it was borne at or before the last day of this month. (Lambeth)

> 1658 To John Haymon for reterning Ridles basterd to Topsham ... 9s 11d (Littleham, near Exmouth, Devon)

> 1729 Charges carrying Jane Sarcher alias Hardmore, Mary Dennis' bastard child, to Cliff in Kent being ye place of its birth ... 15s (Walthamstow)[9]

Third, they can seek to force the parents to provide for the child, magistrates being able, under a law of 1575, to charge the 'mother or reputed father' of a bastard 'with the paymente of monie weekely or other sustenacion'. To this end the mother is often questioned closely as to the identity of the father, sometimes revealing a hidden tale.[10]

> 1580 April 25th. Dorathye Atkinson, daughter to Margarett Atkinson, unmaryed, and begotten, as she did confesse in the time of her laboure, before the wives there present, by one Roger Huton, coverlett weaver. (St Michael le Belfrey, York)

> 1633 Oct. 23rd. Alexander, son of Katherine, wife of Alexander Tuckey of Poplar, begotton she affirmed in the field on this side the mud wall near the Gunne, about 9 of the o'clock at night. The father she knew not, but the said Alexander, by them that brought the child to be baptized, requested that it might be recorded in his name. (Stepney)

> 1680 Sep. 22nd. Susan, bastard of Elizabeth Godly, widow, begotten as she saith by Muzzell. (Cuckfield, Sussex)[11]

Midwives are expected to try to extract this important information, as is clear from a licence to practise granted to Bridget Kirby of Cropredy, Oxfordshire, in 1726.

> You shall not deliver any privately or clandestinely to conceal the birth of the child. If you help to deliver any whom you suspect to be unmaryed you shall acquaint the ecclesiastical court ... and before you yield your assistance

or helpe you shall perswade and by all lawfull means labour with them to declare who is the father of the said child ...[12]

Once the parish has a name a search may be set on.

> 1728 Paid at London for a warrant and charges indeavouring to take up Edward Turner putative father to Mary Trottles child ... 2s 6d (Walthamstow)

> 1803 Expenses endeavouring to take a man for a bastard child, 2 days, 3 persons ... £3 8s 11d (Lapworth, Warwickshire)[13]

Money then needs to be extracted. In and around London in the later 18th century £10 seems to be the going rate.

> 1768 Received by cash of Thomas Troughton on account of Mary Wethers being with child by him ... £10 15s (St Mary, Aldermanbury)

> 1774 Mr Ridge to accept £10 from John Godman for the bastard child sworn to him by Eliz. Best & that he be discharged from all expenses of the said child. (Tooting, Surrey, vestry)[14]

The parish's fourth and final option is to place pressure on the father to marry.

> 1724 Spent in taking the man that got Sarah Coningsby with child ... 2s 6d | In charges for putting him in the Comptor and marrying them the next day at the Fleet ... £1 2s 6d (St Alphage, London Wall)[15]

In the following case the man himself comes forward with an offer.

> 1775 August 24th. Thomas Maxwell applied to this vestry and proposed to marry Mary Sanders a poor woman of this parish whom he stated was with child by him, if they would give him forty shillings, pay the marriage fees, and clothe her. And being asked if he had any settlement, he stated that he belonged to the parish of St Luke's Old Street. The church warden [was] directed to enquire into the truth of this settlement and if found correct to give him the sum of three guineas on his marrying the said Mary Sanders. (St Helen, Bishopsgate)[16]

As with foundlings, if a solution cannot be found there are ongoing costs for the parish to meet.

> 1579 Paid to Whicke the 2 of August for keping the bastard childe of his dowghter Alice ... 10s 1d (Bungay)

> 1635 To the Widdow Huntingford for keeping of a base born child [for 3 months] ... 19s 6d | For a coate for the bastard ... 3s 1d | For makeinge of two wasequets for the bastard ... 4d (Seale, Surrey)

> 1709 Paid Widow Haslip for keeping Deaths bastard child ... 3s (Walthamstow)[17]

Disorder

1. Bringing problems to light: Visitations and presentments

Generally the old parish is an orderly and peaceful place, and most parishioners do what is expected of them most or all of the time, but there are of course exceptions.

The Church's main method of keeping a check on disorder is by **visitations**, inquiries and inspections which look into the practical and spiritual affairs of each parish, usually conducted under the auspices of the archdeacon. While the process changes over time, and varies from place to place, there are two main types, **parochial** and **general**. The different emphasis of each is summed up by Edmund Gibson, writing in the early 18th century.

> As the proper work of parochial visitation is to inspect places, with regard to repairs, so ... the chief business which remains to general visitations, is the inspection of persons, with regard to manners.[1]

Each parish is typically subjected to a parochial visitation every few years – the Canons of 1604 stipulate every three years, although that is not always achieved. Having been notified in advance it is visited by the archdeacon or his surrogate accompanied by the registrar and perhaps by other officers. They inspect the church, churchyard, parsonage and any other parish buildings, along with service books, vestments and vessels. Minor issues are addressed and afterwards the archdeacon through the registrar issues instructions for further action to be taken, the church-wardens being required to certify by a given date that these have been followed.[2]

In medieval times such visits may also concern themselves with manners and morals, but in later times the focus is very much on church fabric and paraphernalia.[3]

Faults identified at parochial visitations may be followed up at general visitations. These are sittings of the archdeacon's court to which representatives of many parishes are summoned. They are usually held once or twice a year, in spring and autumn, and provide a means of making more regular checks across the diocese than can practicably be achieved by time-consuming parochial visits. Typically the court is set up at the west end of a large church located within the part of the archdeaconry being 'visited' so as to reduce travelling for those summoned.[4]

> 1556 Expenses of the 4 men,* the priest & the warden for apperanse to the Arssedecons visitacion holden at Totnes ... 20d (Dartington, Devon)

> 1570 Expendid in goinge & cominge to & from the visitacon or general holden at Elye laste of the two churche wardons, the curate, ye two queste men† & the two ferye men, beinge owte three dayes in the same busines with ye hire of ye same water men & theire boate ... 18s 1d (Leverington, Cambs)[5]

* A select vestry.
† *Questmen.* Churchwardens' assistants, sidesmen.

The surviving fittings of a church court, west end of north aisle, St Nicholas, King's Lynn

The process begins with the provision in advance of written articles of inquiry, or questions for the parish to answer upon. These vary to some degree and reflect the particular concerns of the archdeacon and the times. At the visitation itself the parish delivers its answers to the articles along with any **presentments**, formal statements notifying the authorities of faults and offences, whether of an individual or in relation to the church.

The Canons place the onus for drawing up presentments on the churchwardens. However, they add that, because wardens are often reluctant to court trouble by reporting their neighbours, the 'parson and vicar ... may themselves present'. In addition the Canons encourage the framing of presentments before setting out. Gibson, when Archdeacon of Surrey, underlines the point, instructing wardens that he will insist upon

> the framing your presentments at home, where you will have time to consider your duty and your oath ... And by proceeding in this deliberate way, you will ... put an end to those disorders which are unavoidably occasioned by the framing of presentments at the time of the visitation.[6]

Also required to appear before the court are individuals accused in presentments of more serious offences. They are summoned by an official called the **summoner** or **apparitor**, who brings messages and orders from the Church authorities. Sometimes this leads to angry confrontation. At Chardstock, Dorset, a parishioner threatens to cut off the tail of the horse of anyone who summons him (1412). At St Mary Woolchurch in London a parishioner threatens the apparitor himself, reportedly saying, 'Thou horson knave, withoute thow tell me who set thee awerke to summon me to the courte, by Goddes woundes, and by this gold, I shall breke thy hede' (1522). At Tollesbury, Essex, the wife of John Pigbone 'wolde have beaten or hurt the apparitor with a bill' on his trying to summon her husband (1588), and at Brewham, Somerset, three men waylay the apparitor and give him a beating, their aim being to render him incapable of making any further visits (1632).[7]

For the accused who do attend there are several possible outcomes. The case against them may be dismissed for lack of evidence, or they may be allowed to leave with a warning if the offence is relatively minor and they admit to it. Alternatively, if they deny the charge, they may be given the chance to purge themselves of the accusation by producing, on a specified day, a given number of respectable parishioners as 'compurgators' prepared to swear to their veracity or innocence.[8]

Not that everyone is always convinced.

> 1638 We present[ed] Cornelius Eager and Elizabeth Wilson heretofore for a notorious crime of incontinence and the said Elizabeth is dismissed upon her purgation which yet we verily believe to be guilty of the crime and do marvel at the boldness of her compurgators for takeing so rash an oath. (Tydd St Giles, Cambs)[9]

Failing any of the above ways out, the accused will be required to perform a penance or, in the case of extreme or persistent offence, they will be excommunicated.

At longer intervals, usually every three or four years, the bishop conducts his own visitation of the whole diocese, and he also presides over his own court. Parishioners are, however, much more likely to come into contact with the visitations and court of the archdeacon, who acts as *oculus episcopi*, the 'bishop's eye', within the more local area.[10]

Most of the examples given in this chapter come from the records relating to the visitation process, in particular from presentments, which detail a wide range of trouble and strife.

LEFT A long-fingered archdeacon makes his views known at a visitation, from a manuscript of *c.* 1370. RIGHT A summoner, from the Ellesmere Chaucer, *c.* 1410.

2. Misbehaviour in church

According to the Canons of 1604, 'the names of all those which behave themselves rudely and disorderly in the church' are to be presented, although some of the offences involved seem harmless enough.[1]

Richard Boundy of West Thorney, Sussex, 'doth unreverently behave himself in time of divine service by leaning upon one elbow or his hand and the other in his pocket and sleeping' (1626). More impressively, at Ferring in the same county a parishioner is accused of 'extreme sleeping' (1613), while at Dodford, Northants, the vicar complains of being disturbed in prayer when a sleeper lets outs 'a very loud and beastly fart which caused laughter in the people' (1625). At Shelley, Essex, a presumably long-winded preacher is disturbed 'in the sermon time' when one man encourages another to tell him 'that his roast meate did burne' (1613).[2]

Similarly trivial is the case of Elizabeth Harris of Burnham, Essex, who 'refuseth to kepe her seate in the church', her excuse being that she had been placed in a pew with a woman who 'hath a stronge breth' (1578). Two other Essex women are more deliberately provoking. At Downham Joanna Towler 'came into our church in mans apparell upon the Sabaoth daie in the service time' (1596), and at Grays Thurrock a decade later Catherine Banckes does the same, 'to the contempte of religion, therby dishonouring God & disturbinge the minister & the congregation'.[3]

Other parishioners also seem to be looking for trouble.

1590 [Two men] for behaving themselfs disorderlie in churche in service time, in piping, dauncing and playing, Mr Hudesley ther vicar being then preaching. (Aldborough, Yorks)

1623 Gilbert Wimperie [and two others] for trailinge of Katherine Smith alias Colton up & downe by the heeles in the chapel. (Harby, Notts)

1634 Elizabeth Godman, for pulling downe the May boughes, in a rude scornfull manner, which were brought into the churche to adorn it. (Wivelsfield, Sussex)

1639 Sargent Winckfeild ... for ... casting things at the maides in sermon time and sticking feathers on a maides wastcoate. (Steeple, Essex)[4]

Where such petty offences are concerned the Church's disapproval is by this period not widely feared. John Stiles of St Peter-le-Bailey, Oxford, refuses to stop his boy from breaking the church windows and gives 'flowtes & mockes to those that [ad]monish him for the same' (1584). Susanna Cooke of Little Baddow, Essex, is presented 'for hanginge her linnen in the church to dry, and when our minister Mr Newton told her of it, she [said she] might hang her rags there as well as the surplisse and bad him do his worst' (1636). A few years later, during prayers at St Olave, Silver Street, London, Elizabeth Bateman 'did not kneele and did talke to them in the next pewe to her & [when] she was admonished by the sexton who was sent by the churchwardens she very scornfully answeard, *Oh! let them present me.*'[5]

Occasionally there is violent physical contact. At Hawkhurst, Kent, William Ele 'dragged the wife of Rob. Tryer of Benenden out of a seat in the church, and after doing so maliciously threw her to the ground' (1502). At Theydon Garnon, Essex, a Mr Browne gets upset when, after mass, the clerk Richard Pond does not come to him first with the pax to kiss, so he 'took it, kissed it and then broke it in two pieces over the head of the said R.P. causing streams of blood to run to the ground' (1522). At Worcester John Symons is indicted 'for fighting in the churche apon Eastur daye' (1567), and at Slaugham, Sussex, Richard Woods is presented 'for breaking Thomas Mutton's head in the churche' (1600).[6]

Women sometimes find a subtler way to make their point. Bridget Barret of Wivelsfield is presented 'for thrusting of pinnes in the wife of John Dumbrell in the church in time of divine service, and for other irreverent behaviour' (1637). She admits the main offence but claims it was because Mrs Dumbrell 'sate downe in her lap'. In Nottinghamshire Johanne Halome also claims merely to have been reacting: she admits pricking Lucie Wentworth with a pin but only after Wentworth first 'came over her backe and marred her apparell in the stall where she was set' (1587).[7]

Pins can also serve to deter men with things other than God on their mind, as Samuel Pepys discovers on wandering into St Dunstan in the West during service time on an August day in 1667.

> Stood by a pretty, modest maid, whom I did labour to take by the hand and body; but she would not, but got further and further from me, and at last I could perceive her to take pins out of her pocket to prick me if I should touch her again; which seeing, I did forbear, and was glad I did espy her design.[8]

The appetite for drink gives rise to other problems.

1603 Thomas Dancke ... for that upon St Stephen's day being druncke he came into the church, and in time of divine service spued there. (Iden, Sussex)

1618 Richard Bowerman ... for that on Whitsunday he, having received the communion the forenoon, went to the ale-house in the afternoon and there continued drinking excessively from the time that he had dinner till evening prayer was half ended, and then came into the church and most loathsomely vomited up in his pew the abundance of his stomach, which flowed in the middle aisle, to the disturbance of divine service and the great offence of the congregation, himself being churchwarden. (Reculver, Kent)[9]

Urination also occurs. In the first case below it is probably the best that can be hoped for.

1627 John Kibbitt ... for that in prophane manner in time of the sermon upon a Sundaye, in the afternoon he did — in the church into the hat of one that sate by him. (Leigh, Essex)

1638 Richard Love for makeing water in the church in the time of divine service. (St Peter, Wisbech, Cambs)

1638 John Beard ... for — out of the steeple upon some of the parishioners heads. [He claims it was accidental:] Being in the steeple ringing amongst many others, he did make water which fell upon the heads of some of the parishioners. (Fryerning, Essex)[10]

More serious in the Church's eyes is the behaviour of those who have been excommunicated and yet seek to enter the church.

1632 For carrying Roger Price out of the church he being exco. ... 3d (Chelmsford, Essex)

1667-68 Memorandum that on Septuagesima Sunday being the 19th day of January one Francis Drury an excommunicate person came into the church in the time of divine service in ye morning and being admonisht by me to begon, he obstinately refused whereupon ye whole congregation departed & after the same manner in the afternoon the same day he came againe & refusing againe to go out, the whole congregation againe went home, so that little or no service perform'd that day. I prevented his further coming in that manner as he [was] threatened by order from the justice upon the statute of Queene Elizabeth concerning the molestation & disturbance of publiq preachers. | Wm. Carrington, rector. *O tempora, O mores.* (Scotter, Lincs, note in register)[11]

Other intruders are also understandably unwelcome.

1660 Paid in prosecuting Soloman Eeles the quaker for coming into the church naked in ye time of Mr Calamy's preaching January 1st ... £1 5s 10d (St Mary, Aldermanbury)[12]

3. At weddings and funerals

Weddings are occasionally subject to pointed interruption.

1602 William Gilchrist ... for that upon Sunday, being the 27th of June last, when there was a marriage to be solemnized, he ... in derision of holy matrimonye, got a boughe hanged with ropes endes & beset with nettles & other weedes, & carried the same in the streate & churchyarde before the bride ... (West Ham, Essex)

1605 Edward Row ... for that he at the marriage of Thomas Brock and Rebecca Foster, did fasten a paier of hornes upon the church-yard gate ... (Grays Thurrock, Essex)

1639 Ralph Brooke ... for wearing a great paire of hornes upon his head in the churchyard when Henry Hall and his wife were going to be married, shewing thereby that the said Hall was like to be a cuckold. (Arlington, Sussex)[1]

The following seems relatively good-natured.

1599 John Wilkins for going about the street in woman's apparel, being the parish clerk at that time. [His explanation to the court is] that at a marriage in a merriment he did disguise himself in his wife's apparel to make some mirth to the company. (Whitstable, Kent)[2]

At King's Sutton, Northamptonshire, the minister twice has trouble performing funerals, apparently arising in the first case from a principled objection to the pared back post-Reformation form of the service.

1617 Anne Chapman ... for a scolde, that wheras the minister was attentive and waited at the church stile to meete a corps and according to the form set downe in the booke of common prayer to burye it: she contemptuously raginge, blasphemouslie swearing by the lords wounds and bloud, to his great greafe and the congr[eg]ations, disturbed him as he was reading divine service at the grave. She caused the men to carrye the corps from the grave and swore that unlesse he would come into the church and read prayers to it she would bury him alive.

1619 Humphery Justice for disquieting the minister being present in the churchyard attending to bury a corps. The grave being made and the corps being coming neare to the church stile, the said Justice came like a mad man to the grave and scrabled in the earth with his hands and feet into the grave and filled the grave halfe full of mould [earth], do what the minister could to resist him, and because the minister did resist him for filling the grave (the corps being at hand) the said Humphery shouldered him and abused him until the clarke came to stay his fury, for the which the said Humphery departed and went to a justice of peace with false tales ...[3]

The following suggests boredom rather than malign intent.

1608 John Howet [admitted] that he beinge at the funeral sermon of Mr Hotofte ... did sowe womens clothes together & that he was incouraged so to do by Thomas Fryer of Carcolston who held theire garments whilest he this respondent did sowe them together. (Flintham, Notts)[4]

4. Involving animals and birds

Fortunately dogs cannot be presented, but their owners sometimes are.

> 1543 John Ellis ... did give his dogge holy brede, and so did contemne the hole ceremonie of holy brede. (White Notley, Essex)

> 1579 Rouland Bell ... will not suffer his doge to be whipped out of the churche in time of devine service, but kepithe him uppe in his armes, and gevithe frowarde words. (Brancepeth, co. Durham)

> 1600 John Heaves ... for sittinge disorderly in the chancel with a dog on his knee. (Beddingham, Sussex)

> 1617 Thomas Tailer ... for misbehavinge himselfe with his dogge in the church in time of divine service. [In his defence he says that] his dogge being fightinge or quarrellinge in the church with another dogge he this respondent did take his dogge into his armes. (Hawton, Notts)[1]

William Palmer of West Pennard, Somerset, ties a dog to a bell-rope and makes it run around during evening prayer, causing 'a stir and a laughing ... thereby' (1616). Five years later Thomas Collins of Buckland St Mary takes his dog to church on Palm Sunday with a block of wood tied to it so as to create a clatter, prompting the rector to stop mid service and order dog and owner to leave.[2]

Worse happens at Canterbury Cathedral. According to an account published in 1644,

> One of the great canons or prebends, in the very act of his low congying [bowing] towards the altar as he went up to it, in prayer time, was (not long since) resaluted by a huge mastiffe dog which leapt upright on him once & againe, and pawed him in his ducking saluting progresse & posture to the altar, so that he was fain to call out aloud, *Take away the dog, Take away the dog.*[3]

Other creatures also appear. On Christmas Eve 1570 at Wolsingham, county Durham, the minister objects to the presence at morning prayer of a crow, brought to church by a young labourer. Things are not helped by another man putting 'a strawe crosse in her mouth to see how she could flye'.[4]

Nine years later John Goldring, rector of Langdon Hills, Essex, is in trouble about his sheep, but he at least has a good excuse.

> A little after Candelmas last his servantes endevoringe & procuring to have his shepe saved from the coveringe of the greate snowe, which at that time so greatly did fall, both by nighte and by daye; and his servantes beinge not able to bring them into anie howse, and havinge a care to have them saved, they havinge the keye of the church doore of Langdon hilles, nere which church his shepe were then pastured; they then locked the same shepe into the church, where they were 2 dayes, first and last, beinge workinge

dayes; and then by greate labor & paines his servantes, when the fall of the snowe was ended, they put them into another place, & made clene the church: all which was done for greate & extreme necessitie sake, & not in anie contempte.

He escapes with a fine of 6s 8d, to be given to the poor of the parish.[5]

On the other hand contempt seems certainly intended in the case of Walter Cushman of Buxted, Sussex. In addition to maintaining 'divers popish errors' and carrying letters between Catholics 'in the time of the queen majestys danger', he also 'led his horse up and down in the church, and about the communion table in the chancel' (1588).[6]

A similar motive perhaps lies behind the following in the same county.

1603 Joan Golding ... for baptizing a cat. (Winchelsea)[7]

5. In the churchyard

Game playing and merry-making in churchyards are frowned upon, particularly if they take place during divine service.

A parishioner of Boughton, Nottinghamshire, is presented because 'he set up a Maye pole in the church yard' (1585), while at Childwall, Lancashire, two men are excommunicated 'for pipeinge' there 'upon the Saboath day' (1592). More eccentrically, at North Stoke, Oxfordshire, Henry White is in trouble for 'runninge after maidens in the churcheyarde' (1584).[1]

The IDLE' PRENTICE at Play in the Church Yard during Divine Service.

A beadle prepares to interrupt play, from Hogarth's Industry and Idleness series, 1747. The plate incidentally shows the overcrowded state of London burial grounds at this time.

At Goring in the same year the wardens are presented 'for dauncing and bowlinge in the churcheyard' and for suffering bowling there by others. Enthusiasm for the sport is also suggested by the case of Peter Dudley of Salford: he is 'a common talker in the churchyard' at Manchester 'at the time of divine service, beinge an assembler of a number of them to talk of his bowlinge' (1592).[2]

Football is popular too. At Great Baddow, Essex, 'there was so muche noise' from a game in the churchyard one Sunday evening 'that the minister could not be heard' (1598). At Warsop, Nottinghamshire, six men admit 'playinge at footebale' not only in the churchyard but also in the church (1612).[3]

An early game of cricket occurs at Boxgrove, Sussex.

> 1622 I present Raphe West, Edward Hartley, Richard Slaughter, William Martin, Richard Martin junior, together with others in theire company whose names I have no notice of, for playing at cricket in the churchyard on Sunday, the fifthe of May, after sufficient warning given to the contrary, for three special reasons: first, for that it is contrary to the 7th article;* secondly, for that they use to breake the church-windowes with the ball; and thirdly, for that a litle childe had like to have her braines beaten out with a cricket batt.† | And also I present Richard Martin senior and Thomas West the old churchwardens for defending and maintaining them in it.[4]

Fighting is a recurrent problem. The preamble to an Act of 1551 notes that lately 'many outragious and barbarous behaviors and acts have bene used and committed by diverse ungodlie and irreligious persones by quarrelinge, brawlinge, frayinge and fightinge openly in churches and churchyardes'. It decrees that in future anyone who 'shall smite or lay violent hands upon any other, either in any churche or churcheyarde … shalbe demed excommunicate'. If anyone shall 'maliciouslye strike any person with any weapon' in those places, and be convicted of the fact, he is to 'have one of his eares cut off, and if the person or persons so offendinge have none eares … then he or they [are] to be marked and burned in the cheeke with an hot iron, having the letter F therein, wherbye he or they may be known and taken for Fraymakers and Fighters'.[5]

The threat of such punishments does not always deter.

> 1611 Francis Leake for strikinge Roger French in the church yard upon a holiday coming from service vidzt. giving him a boxe on the eare. (King's Sutton, Northants)

---

* The relevant visitation articles are not thought to have survived. However, the seventh article of another visitation six years later relates to the good order of churchyards, including the absence from them of quarrels, fighting and play.
† This is the earliest use of 'cricket bat' recorded in the *OED*.

> 1617 I, Humphrey Wheatly, vicar of the parish of St John the Baptist in
> Thanet, do present Winter Churchman of the same parish, weaver, for
> striking of Leonard Browne, parish clerk, in the churchyard of St John's
> aforesaid, who would not desist from beating him till I myself came and
> pulled him from the said Leonard, lying under him. (Margate, Kent)[6]

Occasionally such encounters are fatal.

> 1589 Lawrence Middleton, gent., who had his deathes wound in the
> churchyard, was buried 29 April. (St Gregory, by St Paul's)[7]

On a moonlit night in 1742 a local butcher waits in Rye churchyard in Sussex
to attack a man called Lamb, but in a case of mistaken identity stabs the town's
mayor instead. The culprit proceeds to run about the streets shouting 'Butchers
should kill lambs!' Not surprisingly he is soon caught, and a short time later is
hanged on a gibbet erected in a nearby marsh.[8]

6. Absence from church and profaning the sabbath

i. The rules

Under an Act of 1558 attendance at church on Sundays and other holy days is
compulsory.

> All and every person and persons inhabiting within this realme ... shall
> diligentlye and faithefully, having no lawfull or reasonable excuse to be
> absent, endevour themselves to resorte to their parishe churche or chapel
> accustomed ... upon every Sondaye and other dayes ordeined and used to
> be kept as holy days, and then and ther to abide orderlye and soberly during
> the time of the common prayer, preachinges or other service of God ther
> to be used and ministred; upon paine of punishement by the censures of the
> churche, and also upon paine that every person so offending shall forfeite
> for every suche offence twelve pens, to be levied by the churchewardens
> of the parishe ...[1]

Not everyone is happy. A Ramsgate lighterman called Browne is presented
in 1581 for complaining that 'It was never merry England since we were impressed
to come to the church.' Nonetheless the requirement is reinforced by the Canons
of 1604.

> The churchwardens or questmen of every parish, and two or three or more
> discreet persons ... shall diligently see that all the parishioners duly resort
> to their church upon all Sundays and holy-days, and there continue the
> whole time of divine service; and none to walk or to stand idle or talking
> in the church, or in the church-yard, or in the church-porch, during that
> time. And all such as shall be found slack or negligent in resorting to the
> church ... they shall earnestly call upon them; and after due monition (if
> they amend not) they shall present them to the ordinary of the place.[2]

Further laws are prompted by growing concern that the old Christian observance of Sunday as a day of reflection, sobriety and rest is being eroded. Under an Act of 1625

> there shalbe no meetings, assemblies or concourse of people out of their owne parishes on the Lords day ... for any sports or pastimes whatsoever; nor any bearebaiting, bullbaiting, enterludes, common playes or other unlawfull exercises or pastimes used by any person or persons within their owne parishes ...

Each offence incurs a fine of 3s 4d, to be used for the poor of the parish, and any offender failing to pay is to be 'set publiquelie in the stocks by the space of three houres'.[3]

Two years later an Act 'for the further reformacion of sondry abuses committed on the Lords day' orders

> that no carrier ... nor waggonmen ... nor carremen ... nor wainemen ... nor drovers with any cattell shall ... travel upon the said day, upon paine [of forfeiting] twentie shillings for every such offence; or if any butcher ... shall ... kill or sell any victual upon the said day, that then every such butcher shall forfeit and lose for every such offence the somme of six shillings and eight pence ... All which forfeitures shalbe imployed to and for the use of the poore ...[4]

A law of 1677 prohibits work much more widely, enacting that

> no tradesman, artificer, workeman, labourer or other person whatsoever shall do or exercise any worldly labour, busines or worke of their ordinary callings upon the Lords day ... and that every person being of the age of fourteene yeares or upwards offending ... shall for every such offence forfeit the summe of five shillings. And that no person or persons whatsoever shall publickly cry, shew forth or expose to sale any wares, merchandizes, fruit, herbs, goods or chattells whatsoever upon the Lords day ... upon paine that every person so offending shall forfeite the same goods ...[5]

ii. Breaches 1: Work

Many of those presented for breaching the sabbath and other holy days are engaged in agricultural work, animals, crops and the weather having of course no regard to the Christian calendar.

> 1581 Thomas Deale for being absent from common prayer on the Sabbath day, and for grinding with his wind mill. (Margate, Kent)
>
> 1607 Edmund Hall ... for moweing of grasse upon Midsomer day. (Lullington, Sussex)

Mower,
undated,
by Francis
Place
(1647-
1728)

1611 Samuel Chittenden for ploweing on St Mathews day the most parte
of the day 21 Nov. [He pleads that] he did worke & go to plowe on the
day, not knowing that it was holy day, for there was no warninge thereof
given in the churche of Smarden, neither was there any bell tolled.
(Smarden, Kent)

1623 John Abington ... for killing of a porker upon Sunday the 7th of
September which he sold the next day at Selmeston faire. (Laughton,
Sussex)[6]

1623 Robert Hogsflesh, for turning of pease in his field upon a Sabbath
day in harvest last past, betweene morning and evening prayers. (Up
Marden, Sussex)

1638 Widdow Porter for knocking and heckling* of hempe upon one
Sunday in September last. (Sutton, Cambs)

1639 Robert Levett for bringing home of sheep on horseback on the
Saboth day. (Holy Trinity, Ely)[7]

Also attending to a harvest that will not wait are the 'many parishioners' of East
Mersea, Essex, who 'went ... to cart' one Sunday in 1594 'to a wreck happening
at sea'.[8]

---

* *Heckle*. Prepare flax, hemp, etc, with a hackle or hackling machine, splitting,
straightening and combing the fibres in preparation for spinning.

Similar restrictions apply to a range of fast days. In the 1640s a puritanically inclined parliament orders additional fasts, and one parish at least does its best to detect anyone defiantly working in the fields on those days.

1641 Paid Richard Barke & Thomas Swann for watching on ye toppe of ye steeple on a fast daye ... 1s | Paid Thomas Swann for watching on two fast dayes ... 2s (Hartshorne, Derbyshire)[9]

Those offering items for sale are also likely to be in trouble.

1597 Thomas Tonge for selling bread and beere in the time of divine service. (Smarden)

1608 Edward Burgesse for that he kepeth his shop windowes and doores open the holy daies, uttering his wares to the example of many, his shop being neere adjoining to the church. (Benenden, Kent)

1625 George Bennet, Henry Fleshmonger,* [etc], butchers, for selling meate in the time of divine service. (St Olave, Chichester)

1751 January 6th. [Ordered] that the butchers, chandlers, and other shop-keepers of this parish, who presume to keep open their shops and sell their goods on Sundays contrary to Decency and the known laws of this kingdom, be prosecuted for the same, in order to prevent so scandalous a practice for the future, and that notice of this order be published in the church. (Twickenham, Middlesex, vestry)[10]

At St Giles, Colchester, barber Robert Barkham 'dothe not comme to the churche upon hye Sondays, nor holy days, but is lurking at home, and every body that wille go to him to be shaven, he is redy to shave them ... as though they were his commone workinge days' (1543).[11]

iii. Breaches 2: Recreation &c.

Others spend their time hunting, shooting and fishing.

1584 Thomas Harwell ... for huntinge on the Saboth daye. [His response:] Some times on the Sab-aoth daye he hath beene abrode at service time to hunte and nowe & then to finde hares but is sorrie for it and promiseth hereafter not to commit the like offence. (Islip, Oxon)

1614 Robert Lacie ... for catchinge of larkes in time of divine service. (Attenborough, Notts)

1617 Richard Kempe ... for ferritinge ... (Mansfield, Notts)

* The surname is presumably not coincidental.

1634 James Lee ... for beating [baiting] of eale stringes ... (Farndon, Notts)

1634 Thomas Bynns ... for seeking ducks nestes and geese nestes ... (Everton, Notts)

1636 John Naylor ... for hunting of conies [rabbits] upon a Sonday. [He confesses that he did,] but was at both morning and evening prayers the same day. (Slaugham, Sussex)[12]

Baiting of animals is popular.

1584 Robert Cave, William Brasse and William Blythe ... for baitinge of a bull on the Saboath day in service time. [Cave affirms] that they did baite the bull but not in service time. (Tuxford, Notts)[13]

Parishioners are also drawn away from church by various other recreations and sports.

1611 Raph Dixe [and three others] for playing at cards in time of divine service upon the sabbath day. (Banbury, Oxon)

1633 Godfrey Banustie ... for challenging others unto the cudgells upon the Sabboath daye, as the common fame and report is. (Mansfield Woodhouse, Notts)

1634 William Gyde ... for playing at skittolles on Sunday, and, being required to leave, obstinately he would play at that game. (Lambourn, Berks)

1638 Elizabeth Perrie, Margaret Feild, Elizabeth Crisp, and our clarks daughter ... for being sporting at the bowling greene in time of divine service. (St Peter, Wisbech, Cambs)

1675 William Weaver ... a constant player at ninepinnes on the Sabbath day. (Lullington, Sussex)[14]

The following large payment suggests alacrity to suppress such enjoyments, at least under the Commonwealth.

1658 To Richard May for informing of one that played at trap-ball on the Lord's day ... 18s (St Margaret, Westminster)[15]

Other trouble arises in relation to music.

1613 Gervase Whitehead for cominge to Clifton and alluring the people to prophane Gods service by playinge upon a paire of bagpipes. (Clifton, Notts)

1622 Nathaniel Wyhall for not resorting to our parish church; but he doth not only absent himself, but being a drummer doth draw away our youth on the Sabbath day to unseemly pastimes, as, namely, he going drumming with them following him about the island on the Sabbath days in the time of divine service. (Birchington, Kent)[16]

Piper, drinker and drummer, from 17th-century woodcuts

And dancing.

1598 William Haynes ... for that upon Sondaie before Michaelmas in the time of afternoone service he was dancing with minstrels on a grene by Thomas Harris his howse. (South Benfleet, Essex)

1623 One William Witcher of Boxgrove, fidler, cometh every Sunday from his owne parish to Yapton, and causeth divers of other parishes, some-times 30 or 40 in a day, to accompany him to Yapton on the Sundayes and there spend the best part of the day in dauncing. Whether they come to church in time of divine prayer or no we know not, but many youth in Yapton, when they should be in the church on those Sundayes to be catechised,* are then attending on him to daunce ... (Yapton, Sussex)[17]

Alehouses are another problem.

1611 John Whighton for haunting ale-houses in the time of service and sermon time, and being admonished to come unto the church by the churchwardens and sidesmen he refused, saying he would not follow a company of dog-whippers, and so would not come at all. (Whitstable, Kent)[18]

---

* A catechism (instruction by way of a series of questions and answers) was included in the 1549 Book of Common Prayer. Ten years later royal injunctions ordered that 'every parson, vicar, and curate shall upon every holy day, and every second Sunday in the year, hear and instruct all the youth of the parish, for half an hour at the least before evening prayer, in the Ten Commandments, the Articles of the Belief, and in the Lord's Prayer, and diligently examine them, and teach the Catechism set forth in the Book of public prayer.' The Canons of 1604 include a similar order but for 'every Sunday and holy day'.

Some parishes take an active approach.

> 1693 Spent upon several of the inhabitants that assisted in goeing about to the alehouses on Sondays ... 2s | 1700 Paid on searching the alehouses on ye Sabboth ... 4d (Camberwell, Surrey)

> 1743 Paid for visiting ye publicans and barbers to prevent tipling and shaving in time of divine service ... 2s (St Anne & St Agnes, Aldersgate)[19]

Searches are also sometimes made of private houses, but they are not always meekly endured.

> 1592 [The wife of Robert Goodier] wold not suffer the churchwardens and swornemen to come into her howse to see what guests were there at sermon time and gave bad speeches to them. [She is excommunicated.] (Manchester)

> 1658 Received of Joseph Piers for refusing to open his doores to have his house searched on the Lorde's daie ... 10s (St Giles in the Fields)[20]

Some of those absent from church simply want a lie-in.

> 1543 John Jonsone, a shomaker, kepeth his bed upon the Sondaies and other holy days at time of mattens and masse, as it were a hounde that shuld kepe his kenell, havinge no respecte to God nor saint. (St Giles, Colchester)[21]

Others are less innocently occupied, although in the following case it seems the main objection may be to the timing.

> 1628 Lambert Comber ... for beating his wife on the 29 of June last, being sabbath day, in time of divine service. (Slaugham)[22]

iv. Excuses

Those in financial or other trouble may use it to explain their absence.

> 1596 William Seare, for a negligent comer to the church. [In court he says that] by reason of many debts and sums of money, wherein he is indebted to divers men, he hath been enforced to refrain coming to the church lest he should be arrested. (Herne, Kent)[23]

Other excuses seem more far-fetched.

> 1617 Richard Hogbean ... for being absent from church two Sundays, the 5th and 12th of October last past, for fishing both days. [In court he explains that his brother,] being then very sick and much desiring and longing for eels, requested him to catch him some if it were possible. [He adds that] he was not about the business of catching the same eels above the space of two hours on either day. (Chislet, Kent)[24]

A harvest
fondle,
from a
Book of
Hours,
c. 1300

7. Fornication

Among offences unrelated to the church, fornication is of particular concern both because it tends to unsettle the social order and because it may result in illegitimate children who become a burden on the parish.

> 1619 Robert Dawkes behaved himselfe incontinently towards the wife of Mr Foster atturney & towards his maide called Katherin Wady also, as is reported publiquely in the towne of Banbury. The maner was by putting his hand under their clothes & lifting them up to feele their privities. | The wife of the said Robert Dawkes doth behave herselfe troublesomely against the wife of the said Foster being her seat fellow by jusselling & pushing her as she goes by her in time of divine service. (Banbury, Oxon)

> 1621 We present unto you Elizabeth Williams, for running up and downe the countrey with a deboyst knave, saying he was her husband; but after excommunication ... she confessed he was run away with her, and that he was none of her husband, and that she was with childe by him, and, as she confessed, fell over a stile by mischaunce and so spoiled it. | 1622 Also we present Margaret Cardy, for playing the harlot with an Irisheman at Petworth. (Graffham, Sussex)[1]

Some offenders are particularly energetic, as at Kennington, Kent, in 1511.

Richard Ricard ... hauntithe suspiciously the house of Thomas Hawters and wold have gone away with the saide Thomas wife over the sea. ... | The saide Richard and Elizabethe May, wife to Robert May, kepe no good rule insomuche that it is suspectid he hathe a childe by her in her husbonds absence. | The said Richard hathe had 2 childerne with 2 sisters, daughters of Robert Ilkok, Elizabeth and Margery, that they confessid bothe. ... | The said Richard and Alis Title his gossippe live suspiciously togider daiely. ... |

The said Richard and Agnes Attwelle were taken togider suspiciously and so continewe. ... | The wife of William Cristoffere [would have] bene ravished by the said Richard if one of her neighebors had not come into the shoppe. ... | Richard Ricard [and others] proposid to have slaine the vicare if he had come there where they were ... and he wold have done it because the vicare wold not holde withe him in his lewdenesse.[2]

Barns are a natural resort for those looking to escape parish eyes.

1511 Thomas Monsone, M. Mays clerk, and Elizabethe the wife of Robert May live suspiciosly insomuche that in a barne she provoked the yong man & said, clipping him aboute the middelle, 'do now with me what ye wille'. (Kennington)

1581 We presente Robert Adam on being found with one Fraunces Nobell and Fridewith Tayler, the wife of one Richard Taylor &c. in his barn after dark. (Smarden, Kent)[3]

More generally immodesty in women is frowned upon.

1599 Joan Bigges, single woman ... for that lately she did weare mans apparell and also in time of harvest last in a wild manner turned up her cloathes and showed those partes that should be hidden, willing the company to looke what a clock it was if they had any skill of the diall. (Grantchester, Cambs)

1639 Susan Seamer ... for her most shameful and ordinary filthy and impure speeches and obscene songs and immodest behaviour, such as we shame to relate. (Birchington, Kent)[4]

Given the widespread propensity to report such offences, we may admire the restraint of the wardens of King's Sutton, Northamptonshire, in the face of a series of standard questions about the parish's morals: 'As for bauds, fornicators and incestuous persons we cannot say certainly we know any. As for suspicions we are loath to trouble our consciences with such uncertenties.'[5]

Adam and Eve,
bench-end,
Osbournby,
Lincolnshire

8. Magic and witchcraft

Very occasionally a parishioner is presented for practising witchcraft or for seeking magical assistance.

1463 Robert Mabley is accused of bewitching the fish nets. (Leverington, Cambs)

1582 Goodwife Swane, for that she is vehemently suspected to be a witch, and she herself hath reported that she can make a drink, which she saith if she give it to any young man that she liketh well of, he shall be in love with her. And that she hath threatened one of her neighbours and upon words fell out with her, and told her that she would make her repent her falling out with her. And it is come to pass this same woman her neighbour hath never been well since. (Margate, Kent)

1594 Joan Bettison ... widow, publicly infamed (as it is said) for witchcraft. [She explains] that she divers times within two yeres last past when she was required to helpe cattle that were forspoken [bewitched] did for their recovery use 15 pater nosters, 15 aves and three credes in honour of the father and the son and of the holie ghoste, and that therupon the cattle amended, and for everie of them she had usually a penie, poore folkes excepted of whome she tooke nothinge, denienge that she used in that behalfe anie other ceremonie and [she said she] was taught this by her late grandfather ... Enjoined upon paine of lawe that she hereafter do not take anie such matter upon her. (Bilsthorpe, Notts)

1599 We present Thomas Ward [for seeking] helpe at sorcerers handes. [He explains that] having lost certein cattell & suspecting that they were bewitched, he went to one Tailer in Thaxted, a wisard, to knowe whether they were bewitched or not, & to have his helpe. (Purleigh, Essex)[1]

The last case seems particularly hard in light of the following cost openly incurred by churchwardens elsewhere.

1583 Layed forthe in going to Burfield to the cunning woman for to make enquire for the comunione clothe and the 2 other clothes that were loste out of the church ... 16d (Thatcham, Berks)[2]

The accounts at Gateshead provide glimpses of what may befall those suspected of witchcraft.

1649-50 Going to the justices about the witches ... 4s | The constables for carying the witches to jaole ... 4s | Carying the witches to Durham [etc] ... 4s | Paid at Mistris Watson's when the justices sate to examine the witches ... 3s 4d | Trying the witches ... £1 5s | A grave for a witch ... 6d[3]

The laws against witches are repealed in 1736 but accusations of witchcraft continue long after that date, as do tests designed to establish the truth. The popular

'Catch-22' one of placing a supposed witch in a pond to see whether or not she floats is recorded in the register of Monks Eleigh, Suffolk.

> 1748 Dec. 19th. Alice, the wife of Thomas Green, labourer, was swam, malicious and evil people having raised an ill-report of her for being a witch.[4]

Another type of test takes place inside churches.

One Susanna Hannokes, an elderly woman of Wingrave near Aylesbury, was accused by a neighbour for bewitching her spinning wheel, so that she could not make it go round, and offered to make oath of it before a magistrate; on which the husband, in order to justify his wife, insisted upon her being tried by the church bible, and that the accuser should be present. Accordingly, she was conducted to the parish church, where she was stript of all her cloaths to her shift and under-coat, and weighed against the bible; when, to the no small mortification of her accuser, she out-weighed it, and was honourably acquitted of the charge.

Gentleman's Magazine, February 1759[5]

　　The rationale of the swimming test is explained by James I in his *Daemonologie* (1603): because witches 'have shaken off them the sacred water of baptisme, and wilfully refused the benefite thereof ... the water shall refuse to receive them in her bosome'. The rationale of the bible test is apparently that the word of God will always outweigh the work of the devil. Alternatively, in both cases the simple belief may be that witches, as spirits, have no weight.[6]

'A strange and most true trial how to know whether a woman be a witch or not', from *Witches Apprehended, Examined and Executed*, 1613

9. Abusing churchwardens and ministers

The role of churchwardens and their assistants in enforcing the rules naturally leads to the occasional insult.

> 1622 We present John Cooper of our parrish, gentleman ... for vilely abusing Jeffery Woods, one of the sidemen, because [he] said he would present the said John Cooper for some misdemeanours, for which cause and no other John Cooper threatened to spend his blood with Jeffery Woods, and reviled him with many vile, filthy and opprobrious termes, calling him *rogue* and *rascall*, *knave*, *villaine* and *divell*, and in a beastly manner spitt in his face. (Felpham, Sussex)

> 1626 We present ... Thomas Michell for giving the churchwarden evil words in the church — he was *a proud jackanapes*.* (Rudgwick, Sussex)[1]

The clergy are also targets. In most cases the abuse is limited to mockery, verbal and otherwise.

At West Ham, Essex, one night in 1589, some parishioners nail a pair of horns on the door of their curate whom they take to be 'jealiouse over his wif'.[2]

Twenty years later at Benenden, Kent, several parishioners go out of their way to discomfit the vicar, Vincent Huffam. Huffam himself presents the main offender, William Watts, for, among other things,

> His calling my wife Dalila in the churchyard imediately after morninge prayer last Sunday, and often times before, and Whitstable Gyll [Jill]. | His disturbinge of me in the time of catechisinge, affirminge me not to be his lawfull minister. | [Saying] that I preache nothing but Esop's fables [and] that I am the idlest fellow in Kent or Sussex. | His ridiculous behaviour at the time of divine service and sermon, by laughing and other unseemly gesture in the church. | His ridiculous and unseemly gesture towards his minister whensoever he meets him.

The problem seems to have arisen because Watts blamed Huffam for presenting him for going 'a hunting with hounds' on holy days.[3]

In other cases, too, abuse arises from a minister doing his job. At Elsdon, Northumberland, having been sentenced to perform a penance, Parcivall Reede takes against the parson, Isaac Marrowe, when he will not let him off.

> 1637 When as he could not prevaile, he did breake forth into violent and outragious termes to and against Mr Marrowe, and told him 'he cared for never a preist of them all'; and at another time, upon the like occacion, in disgracefull manner, did call him *base preist* and *stinkeing custrell*,† and did pull him by the beard and uttered divers other reproachfull wordes against him.[4]

---

* One behaving like a pet ape or monkey, acting impudently, assuming absurd airs, etc.

† *Custrell*. A worthless or contemptible person, a knave, a rogue.

At Towersey, Buckinghamshire, it is a churchwarden who causes the trouble.

1608 *Imprimis* ... John Thornetone hath misuseth me the curat of Towersy
being a ministere of the word of God and a bachelere of arts by callinge
me *jackesauce* and *welsheroge*, and by chalengeinge me to ye fields, and
by reportinge to his neighbours that he kept every day in the weeke
servants and slaves better men than I. | *Item 2.* That he hath railed
against me on the 25 day of March callinge me *you saucie pratlere* ...[5]

At Stondon Massey, Essex, the insults come from one lower in the social order.

1614 Upon the fowerth Sundaye in Lent ... John Demaunder, dawber
and log cleaver, in the presence of the most parte of the parishioners,
presentlie after the ende of morning prayer that daye, not far from the ...
church ... said that the minister was a contentious disquiet person, and
that usuallie at everie good time he tooke occasion to treble [trouble]
and fall out with somebodie, to disquiet the whole parishe; and added
that he was fitter to have made a lawyer than a minister: moreover he said
whereas he shold be a lantherne of light to leade men to God, he was
a lantherne of light to leade them to the devil ... Then passinge alonge
toward the parsonage, beinge but a dawber as above is said, he tooke
the upper hand of him, walkinge in the path, and bravinge him and
geeringe him in the face, settinge his teeth at him, usinge these words
and often repeatinge them: *Strike if you dare. Strike me if you dare.*[6]

Occasionally violence is threatened. At St Just in Roseland, Cornwall, on
Christmas Day 1396, in a dispute about mortuary payments,* one Alan Bugules
threatens to kill the parson 'before all the parishioners'. He confronts him again
in church on the following Twelfth Day.

Alan would have chased the parson out of his chancel by the windows,
saying to him, that he should not pass out by the body of the church because
that belonged to the parishioners and not to him, wherefore the said parson
was very glad to escape secretly while others of the parish treated with the
said Alan.[7]

Two centuries later, at Aldborough, Yorkshire, the minister reproves 'certaine
disgised persons' for bringing rushes to church in what he considers an irreverent
manner. On hearing of this while in the alehouse, Robert Rodes alias Scotson hires
a gun from another man there, giving him '2d to have a shot', and heads for church.

So soone as ever the minister had ended his sermon, and before he stirred
his foote ... Scotson discharged his gunne, aiming directly over the minister,
either to hit him, as it was reported, or to afray him, and indeed the paper
wherewith the gunne was ramed [a]light[ed] very nighe him when he was
comed out of the pulpit.[8]

* Also referred to on pp355-356 above.

Actual violence against ministers is rare but does occur. At Deighton, Yorkshire, in 1575 two men set about the curate, 'beinge but willed by him to leave of the unlawfull game of bowlinge in the churchyarde'. One of the men beats him 'grevowslie', and it emerges that on a previous occasion the other had 'hurt' him 'with his dagger'.[9]

At King's Sutton, Northamptonshire, in 1610 a married couple, Hugo and Denise Holland, bid the minister Mr Smith 'kisse his horse under the taile, and saithe the world was never merrie since priests were married,' adding for good measure that Smith's wife, 'the first night she was married to him, gave her selfe to the divell'. Later, as Smith is walking to the church one evening, they 'use many reproachfull words as *reprobate* & *bloodsucker*' towards him, and Denise 'tooke uppe stones & hurt the said Mr Smith and drewe blood on his face'.[10]

Worse happens at Gamlingay, Cambridgeshire, where Elie Barnes is presented for 'striking & doing violence to Robert Humphrey, curate, in breaking his leg & afterwards wishing it had been his neck' (1686).[11]

10. Religious punishments: penance and excommunication

While individual parishioners can be brought before the Church authorities for a wide variety of offences, should they choose not to appear when summoned there is little the Church can do, having itself no practicable authority to arrest or detain anyone. Its courts also have only limited options in terms of punishments, depending almost entirely on two, penance and excommunication, although in early periods they also have recourse to corporal punishment, usually in the form of whipping around the parish church or churchyard.[1]

Penance is the usual penalty for first and relatively minor offences. It involves confession of the fault, typically performed standing in church during divine service, the following being a few examples in Cambridgeshire in the 1590s.

1594 William Drew: 'Good neighbors I acknowledge and confesse that I have offended Allmightie God, and by my evil example you all, for that I suffered Richard Peareson my servant to carrie a sheeperacke* to the pasture on the Sabboth daie before morninge praire, for which I am verie hartelie sorie'. (Newton)

1594 Daniell Large: 'I did harbor Joane Andrewe, alias Vertue Anderson, in my howse, she beinge delivered of a child there, doing thereby as much as [in] me did lie to cloake that her filthie acte'. (Holy Trinity, Ely)

1595 Elizabeth Bowltell: 'I did make discords betwene neighbor and neighbor, and also I have beene a pratlinge gossipe, goinge from one howse to another to tell tales and lies'. (Babraham)[2]

Sometimes the confession required is elaborate, as with the following, performed at St Nicholas, Durham, on Easter Day 1570.

* *Sheep-rack.* A rack from which sheep feed.

A confession to be made by Charles Shawe, for slandering Bartram Mitforth, in St Nicoles Church in linen apparell ...

'Beloved neighbours, I am now comen hither to shewe my self sory for slanderinge one Bartram Midforde, namely in that I called him openly "beggerly harlot* and cutthrote", sayinge that he was "a covitous snowge",† and [that] such as he by God's worde ought to be weeded out of the Comenwelthe. I acknowledge that thus to slander my Christian brother is an heinouse offence, first towardes God, who hathe straightly forbidden it in his holy lawes, accomptinge it to be a kinde of murderinge my neighbour and threatninge to punishe it with hell fire and the losse of the kingdome of heaven. Also the quene's lawes, against which I have stubbornely stande [stood], doeth grevously punishe all slanderers, backbiters and sowers of discorde, debate, hatred and disquietnes, to the shame of the offenders and feare of others. Againe, my unruly tonge, if it were not punished, it wolde not only set mo[re] of you on fire, but also it wolde [em]bolden others to do the like. Wherefore, as I am now called backe from mine inordinate doinges by this correction, with my cost and shame, so I beseche you all to be witnesses with me that I am sory from the verrey bottome of my harte for this and my other like offences against God, the quene's majestie, and the said Bartram Midforde, promisinge before God, and you here present, that I fully intende to amende my outragious tonge and wilfull behaviour ...'

Afterwards the curate provides a certificate to the Church authorities confirming that Shaw 'hathe don his pennans ... in our parish's churche, barfett and baredded [barefoot and bareheaded] ... upon his knees, upon Ester daye'.[3]

Sometimes the bearing of a candle is required. In 1527 Margaret Hurd of Appleby, Leicestershire, is punished for defaming one Richard Conk. She is to ask his forgiveness during divine service in front of the curate and nine or ten parishioners and is also to be chastised by the curate in a corner of the churchyard and to process barefoot and dressed in white around the yard 'with a candle worth one penny in her hand'.[4]

Often the offender has to stand in the church in a white sheet, sometimes holding a rod or wand, these trappings being provided by the parish.

1666 A white sheet for penance ... 1s 6d (Gateshead, co. Durham)

1682 Paid Robert Lever for bringinge Eliz. Cooper to do penance and putting on ye sheet ... 8d (Manchester)

1714 To procure sheet and wand for Peter Longworth standing penance ... 1s | 1735 For washing the parish sheet for Club's wife to stand penance in ... 2d (St John the Baptist, Chester)[5]

---

* *Harlot* in the original sense of a beggar or vagabond or in the slightly later sense of a scoundrel or rogue.
† *Snudge.* A miser, a niggard, a sneaking or sponging fellow.

The wearing of such a sheet is typically required in cases of fornication. At Headcorn, Kent, in 1592 Alice Gorham has to appear 'penitentlye cloathed in a whit sheete' in church during divine service on two Sundays and ask forgiveness for committinge 'ye most detestable and abominable sinne of filthy lust and fornicacon'.[6]

Some cases are felt to be so serious that they require a more public humiliation than can be achieved in and around the church.

> 1595 *Parte of pennaunce injoined unto Elizabeth Farnam of Stapleford.* The sayed penitent shall upon Satterday next comeinge, beinge the 16th day of October now instant, cloathed in a white sheete downe to the grownde, with a white wand in her hand, and haveinge papers pinned, the one upon her breste and the other upon her backe, declaringe her abhhominable offence, resort unto the bull ringe in Cambridge and there shall stand from ten of the clocke in the forenone until one of the clocke in the afternone of the same day, desiringe the people that so shall behold her to pray to God for her & to forgive her ...

On the next Sunday she is to stand in the same way in the church porch

> from the second peale to morninge prayer until the readinge of the second lesson ... at which time the minister there shall ... fetch her into the church with the psalme of *Miserere* in Englishe and place her in the middle ally there aparte from all other people, where she shall penitently kneele until the readinge of the gospel, at th'end wherof the minister there shall cause this penitent to say and confesse as followeth, viz.: 'Good neighbors I acknowledge & confesse that I have offended Almighty God & by my evil example you all, for that I have broken his divine lawes & commaundementes in committinge the most shamefull & abhominable sinne of fornicacion, for which I am moste hartely sory' [etc].[7]

Such ordeals may prove too much, whether physically or in terms of the shame.

> 1597 June 23rd. Margaret Sherioux was buried ... She was enjoined to stande 3 market daies in the towne & 3 Saboath daies in the churche, in a white sheet, with a paper on her back & bosome shewinge her sinne (namelie for unnatural incest with her owne father). Her father the like, & her husbande, for beinge bawde. She stood with them one Saturday & one Sonday, and died ye nexte. (Croydon, Surrey)[8]

In other ways too things may not go to plan.

> 1595 We present Ric. Thornton, for that upon Sondaie being the first daie of December last, he did publiquely encourage an adulteress (who was then doing penance) to go forward & to returne againe to her former folly, the morrowe after, as freshe as ever she did: who being reproved by one of the sidemen, for giving such lewd counsel and encouragement to sinne, hath very uncharitably abused the said sideman with reprochefull speaches. (West Ham, Essex)

1702 Jan. 31st. George Cason did his penance for committing fornication with Mary Johnson, but showed no sign of penitence, rather to the contrary. (Great Whelnetham, Suffolk, note in register)[9]

Those able to pay can often buy their way out of performing a public penance. For example, a man sentenced in 1569 to 'stand in Romford market ... in a white sheate and a rodde in his hande, and in his parish of Leyton' is excused on condition of giving 10 shillings each to three poor Cambridge scholars and another 10 shillings toward repairs of Leyton church. Nearly a century later Thomas Finch of Buttsbury, in the same county of Essex, is sentenced to do penance in church, presumably for fornication, but objects that, because he is a married man, it 'would much impair his credit among his neighbours'. He offers instead to pay £10, 'to be bestowed on charitable uses', and the court accepts.[10]

From the 17th century onward penances become increasingly rare, but they continue to be imposed occasionally at least into the 1880s. In one late case, at Cheltenham in 1847, hundreds of people gather in the church in hope of seeing the full ritual.[11]

The galleries were filled by a motly assemblage of both sexes, every seat and pew in the vicinity of the communion table was crowded with occupants, and the venerable old structure presented more the appearance of a theatre, or a cock-pit, than of a place of Christian worship. Fortunately for public decorum and decency, all this eager curiosity was doomed to disappointment. ... There were no bare feet, no white sheet, no lighted tapers, but a simple form of recantation was read over and subscribed to, and the crowd ... finding there was no fun to be seen, quietly dispersed.

Cheltenham Examiner, 20 October 1847[12]

Those who refuse to perform penance, or are persistent offenders, or whose sin is considered most serious, are punished with **excommunication**. There are two levels: under the lesser the offender is deprived of the right to attend services and receive the sacraments; under the greater he or she is excluded from all contact and involvement with the Church and fellow Christians.[13]

Ministers are supposed to denounce periodically in church those excommunicated and to remind parishioners not to associate with them. In 1628 the Archdeacon of Taunton writes on this point to the vicar of Luccombe, Somerset, regarding three longstanding offenders.

The next Sabath day or holiday ... at the time of divine service before the whole congregation assembled you shall publiquely denounce ... Walter Pugslie, Moses Pugslie and John Anton for aggravated persons and also then and there you shall admonish all Christian people by virtue hereof that they and any of them henceforth eschewe and avoid the society, fellowshippe and company of the said persons and that they neither eate, nor drink, buy, sell, or otherwise by any manner of means communicate with them, being members cut off from all Christian society ...[14]

In practice most excommunicants are not shunned, although those seen with them may themselves get into trouble: in 1635 a man is presented 'for sitting and conversing with Marjory Burges and keeping company with her ... she being then an excommunicate person'.[15]

Because the Church has few alternative sanctions, excommunication is often imposed for minor offences, as in the following cases in Lancashire in 1592.

> George Grundie ... for talkinge in the church. (Leigh) | Humfrey Sesbridge and Gilbert Wasse ... for standinge in the street at service time and givinge the churchwardens evell wordes. (Ormskirk) | Nicholas Low, tailor ... a comon swearer. (Wigan) | Christofer Bodon and his wife ... do not live together. (Winwick)[16]

Such overuse naturally tends to undermine excommunication as a punishment. However, even those not filled with fear for their souls are likely to find it at least inconvenient, for example if they wish to marry, and probably unsettling, for example if they wish to know that when they die they will receive a Christian burial. Most therefore end up doing what the Church requires of them in order to have the sentence lifted.

11. Fines

The parish may also impose fines for a number of offences under various laws of the realm, which in most cases require the money collected to be used for the benefit of the poor.

Many such fines relate to breaches of the sabbath and other holy days under laws discussed earlier* and otherwise.

Some of these relate to simple non-attendance.

> 1580 Received ... of certaine parishners as forfeitures for their absence from devine service ... 5s 6d (Battersea)[1]

Others to those who work and trade.

> 1569 Received of a collier for sellinge coales on Candillmas daye ... 2s 3d | Of a bargeman sellinge woode on the Saboath daye ... 12d (St Margaret, Westminster)

> 1646 Received of Mr Hooker for brewing on a fast day ... 2s 6d (St Giles in the Fields)

> 1695 Received of Mr Waggett the coffee man for keeping open house on the Lords daye ... 5s (St Bartholomew Exchange)[2]

---

* In summary, the main ones are: 1558, 12d for failing to attend church; 1625, 3s 4d for indulging in sports and pastimes; 1627, 6s 8d for butchers and others selling goods; 1677, 5s for a wider range of work. For more detail see pp420-421 above. Generally the amounts recorded in parish accounts tally with those stipulated in the legislation, but not always, as will be evident from some of the examples given in the text.

Having fun can also be expensive.

1626 Received of H. Asson and of Alexander Trite for playing at nine
pins in the Mill Common in service time ... 2s (Windsor, Berks)

1644 Received of Mr Hooper that he had of defaulters in a suspected
bawdie house, on the fast day ... 12s (St Giles in the Fields)

1647 Received of John Joslin for boys playing on the Lords day ... 3s
(Waltham Abbey, Essex)[3]

The parish also does well out of those who drink alcohol or allow drinking
on their premises.

1641 Received of the vintner at the Catt in Queene-street, for permitting
of tipling on the Lord's day ... £1 10s | 1644 Received of three poore
men, for drinking on the Sabbath daie at Tottenham-court ... 4s (St
Giles in the Fields)[4]

In addition, getting drunk at any time, not just on the sabbath, is an offence
under a 1606 Acte for repressinge the odious and loathsome sinne of Drunckennes.
Those convicted are required to pay 5 shillings to the churchwardens for 'the use
of the poore of the same parishe'. At Bakewell, Derbyshire, a note in the register
sets out 'how ye 5 shillings which Wm. Warlow paid for his drunkenness was
divided, Sep. 5, 1624'. There are no fewer than thirty-seven recipients, including
Widow Vallance and 'Noton's lame boy', who each receive 2d.[5]

From the title page of a satire on drunkards, 1648

Swearing is also illegal. In 1623 An Acte against Swearing and Cursing imposes a fine of 12d. If the offender will not or cannot pay they are to be 'set in the stocks by three whole houres', although those under the age of twelve are to be let off with a whipping. In 1650, under the Commonwealth, a scale of charges is introduced: for the first offence lords and above pay 30s, baronets and knights 20s, esquires 10s, gentlemen 6s 8d, and everyone else 3s 4d. In 1694 a further Act notes that previous measures have been ineffectual but nonetheless sets lower charges: servants, day labourers, soldiers and seamen are now to pay 1s, everyone else 2s.[6]

> 1645 Received of John Seagood, constable, which he had of a Frenchman for swearing three oathes ... 3s | Received of Mrs Thunder, by the hands of Francis Potter, for her being drunke, and swearing seven oathes ... 12s (St Giles in the Fields)[7]

The following underlines the value to the parish of such income

> 1711 Paid three watchmen for giving information of a man that swore and was drunk ... 1s (St Alphage, London Wall)[8]

although the zeal may be overdone.

> 1701 Returned to Sarah Bowley being falsely accused for swearing ... 8s (All Hallows Staining)[9]

Other miscellaneous payments for transgressions also come the parish's way.

> 1618 Received of Mr Richard Talboyes by reason his wife was brought abed of a childe before he was married unto her ... 10s (Lambeth)

> 1631 Received of Mr Thomas Jesson which he allowed me to give to our poore in bread because he — against the wall ... 12s (St Bartholomew Exchange)[10]

A less typical use of such money is recorded in the register at Tollesbury, Essex.

> 1718 August 30th. Elizabeth, daughter of Robert and Eliza Wood, being ye first childe whom was baptized in the new font which was bought out of five pounds paid by John Norman, who some few months before came drunk into the church and cursed and talked loud in the time of divine service, to prevent his being prosecuted for which he paid by agreement the above said five pounds.

The font bears an inscription: 'Good people all I pray take care, | That in ye church you do not swear, | As this man did.'[11]

12. Civil crime and punishment

As its receipt of various fine money indicates, from Tudor times onwards the parish becomes increasingly involved in civil affairs, including the maintenance of law and order. Often this sees it paying or contributing towards administrative costs, and it may reward constables and others for work done.

1583 To the constable to the carryinge of the pirats to the gyle [jail] ... 6d (Dartington, Devon)

1696 For a quart of wine for the constable carrying a sturdy beggar to Bridewell for breaking Old Kemps head ... 1s 6d (St Ethelburga, Bishopsgate)

1746 Paid the coroner for coming to the hiway man that was shot ... £1 1s | Mr Wyborn for the use of the room where the hiway man lay ... 5s | 1770 [Vestry] April 2nd. Ordered that there be two pair of handcuffs provided for ye use of ye two constables of this parish ... | 1771 [Accounts] Paid ye smith for two pair of handcuffs ... 7s (Leyton, Essex)

1801 Paid John Davis, the Chelsea watchman & tollman at the bridge, for apprehending a man with stolen turkeys ... £2 12s 6d (Battersea)[1]

It is not clear whether the following payments are to constables or to parishioners acting unofficially.

1615 To Rob. Cawlton for fetching one Finlinson againe and carrying him before a justice for getting a dwarfe with childe ... 3s (Youlgreave, Derbyshire)

1672 To Buck for hunting the whores out of the parish ... 6d (St James, Bristol)

1751 Mr Hewes for conducting a highwayman to Chelmsford ... £5 17s 3d (Walthamstow, Essex)[2]

The parish may also maintain or contribute towards a place of confinement for minor offenders called a **cage**.

1624 To Pickering the beadle for mending the cage, being rated upon every parish in the ward ... 2s 8d (St Bartholomew Exchange)

1676 For covering for ye cage ... 1s | For tar to tar it ... 3s 6d | 1677 To Edward Paine, bricklayer, for ye underpinning of ye cage ... 6s (St Nicholas, Deptford, Kent)

1676 Paid a porter for carrying a woman to the cage ... 6d (St Christopher le Stocks)[3]

Similarly it may provide or contribute towards instruments of punishment, although the punishment itself is usually inflicted by the civil authorities.

In some cases **stocks** are erected near the church as a suitably public setting for exemplary punishment.

1616 To two porters for drawing up the stocks into ye churchyard ... 6d (St Alphage, London Wall)

1698 Paid ye constable for carrying a drunkard to ye stox ... 4d (All Saints, Newcastle)

1775 For setting up the stocks in the church yard ... 1s (Edenbridge, Kent)[4]

ABOVE Stocks before Kensington church, mid 18th century. In the sky left a kite flies. BELOW Stocks, pillory and whipping post, Wallingford, Berkshire.

There may also be a **whipping post**.

1637   Paid Thomas Durban and Richard Smith, constables, for settinge up the whippinge-post and for carryinge Peakeman's wench to prison ... 12s (Chedder, Somerset)

1735   For scourging a woman ... 1s 4d (St Peter, Bywell, Northumberland)

1799   Paid the blacksmith's bill for irons for the stocks and whiping post ... 13s 9d (Hutton, Somerset)[5]

A whip is naturally required, and disguise may be provided for those doing the whipping.

1646-48   For a frame and a whip that hangs in the church for drunkards ... 1s 2d (Mortlake, Surrey)

1659   For a fresh vizard, whip and perriwig ... 12s (Hammersmith, Middlesex)[6]

The parish may also boast a **cucking** or **ducking stool**,* the usual means of punishing female scolds but also sometimes used to punish troublesome men.[7]

---

* While the terms tend to be used interchangeably they are technically distinct. If true to its name a cucking-stool should be bottomless, as with a close-stool (to *cuck* meaning to void excrement), the offender being fastened in place and then exposed humiliatingly to public view and/or conveyed to be ducked. A ducking-stool may have a bottom but must of course be suitable for ducking, whether by way of a pulley or by attachment to one end of a tiltable plank.

1499 To Splatt for mending of the scoldinge stoole ... 8d (Chudleigh, Devon)

1614 Collected for makinge of a cuckingstoole ye summe of thirtene shillinges and sixpence. (Lambeth, vestry)

1679 For mending ye cuckstoole & for a cheere for ye same .... (Bakewell, Derbyshire)[8]

One use of such a stool is noted in the register of Kingston upon Thames.

1572 On Tewsday being the 19 day of this monthe of August — Downing wife to — Downing gravemaker of this parishe she was set on a new cukking stolle made of a grett hythe [height] and so browght abowte the market place to Temes bridge and ther had 3 duckinges over hed and eres becowse she was a common scolde and fighter.[9]

ABOVE Chairs used at Sandwich (*left*) and Scarborough. BELOW One in action.

13. Complaints against ministers

Returning to Church affairs, we pass from the conduct of parishioners to that of the clergy, who are expected to live exemplary lives, as set out in the Canons of 1604.

> No ecclesiastical person shall at any time, other than for their honest necessities, resort to any taverns or alehouses ... Furthermore, they shall not give themselves to any base or servile labour, or to drinking or riot, spending their time idly by day or by night, playing at dice, cards, or tables, or any other unlawful games ... having always in mind, that they ought to excel all others in purity of life, and should be examples to the people to live well and Christianly ...[1]

Naturally many fall short, and some then find themselves presented to the authorities. A visitation in Kent in 1511 hears that the vicar of Patrixbourne 'kepithe Alice Claringbole and doeth adultery'. Less happily the priest at Swalecliffe, Sir James Comer, 'doeth stand herkening under menes windowes at 10 of the clock in the nighte' and 'drawithe to one Johan Potters wife and she cannot be rid of him'. The vicar of Littlebourne 'sometime is maliciouse and lokithe on his neighbors with a grim and sower contenance whereas they thinke him, God knowethe, no hurte'. At Linsted they lack a vicar and the role is filled by Sir Robert Downe, a soul or chantry priest, but 'the said Sir Robert is a dicere, a kardere & a tenis player and gevithe ille example to many'.[2]

Tristram Tildesley, minister of Rufforth, Yorkshire, is presented *circa* 1581, his faults including that on various occasions in the preceding years he

> hath daunced amongst light and youthfull companie both men and women at weddings, drinkings and rushbearings ... and especiallie upon one Sonday or holidaie ... in his dauncing or after wantonlye and dissolutelye he kissed a maid or yong woman then a dauncer in his companie, wherat divers persons were offended and so sore greved that ther was wepons drawn and great dissention arose or was like to arise ... | [On another occasion] he did not only permit and suffer a rushbearing within the churche and churchyard of Rufforth wherat was used much lewde, light and unsemelye dauncing and gestures very unfit for these places but also he himselfe ... very unsemelye did daunce, skip, leape and hoighe gallantlye as he thought in his own folishe and lewde concepte in the churchyard amongst a great multitude of people where he was derided, flowted and laughed at ...[3]

Dancing also gets John Birkbie, rector of Monkton Moor, into trouble. His other faults include wearing 'verie undecent apparell' and being 'divers times in the night time ... taken abroade in the towne of Rippon ... with lewde women' (1567).[4]

Such loose living is a common problem. At Gainford, county Durham, they present the minister Ralph Smith. One churchwarden reports that he 'liveth very ungodlie and naughtilie with ... Carr's wife', while another adds that he 'doth use to play at dice, cards and tables, and ... to sweare great and grevous oathes in his play' (1586). The rector of Great Warley, Essex, is presented and then suspended from office because, on the night of 2nd January 1596-97, 'he did to the scandal of his calling and offence of good Christians behave himselfe very dissolutely and wantonly in the parish of Kelvedon etc in taking upon him to be a lord of misrule or Christmas lorde etc amongest certein yongelinges'. At Broughton, Buckinghamshire, the minister is presented for getting drunk and 'making lewd attempts upon women' (1662).[5]

A more involved case emerges in a letter of 1596 to the Archdeacon of Essex. It is written by one Joseph Bunting, who, having previously defended the vicar in question, Mr Mercer of Little Wakering, now seeks to alert the archdeacon to his shortcomings.

A hidden hand, by Hogarth, 1732

> Seeing that neither your good and godly instructions, nor all your gentleness, mildness nor long sufferance ... will do no good of him, but rather maketh him worse, and more shameless now than before, I trust your worship shall ... be a meane to avoide or gitt him out of the ministrye, which he doth most shamefully staine ... This Mercer [has defiled the church] since Easter last, in being dronk at the least 30 times since that time, & when he is dronk in singing most filthye and bawdye songes, in being madde when he is dronk, hallowing and whisseling up and down the streates to the great trouble of his neybours, in monstrous beating his wife, in brawling with all the ale wifes ... in drinking in his own churche porche with roges & beggars a hole daye together, and his ordinary companye is tinkers & pedlers. He did drink at Reyligh [Rayleigh] this somer 16d in sallett [salad] oile, and [is] of his word and promise most unfaithfull and frevolous, with many hundreths more faults. But these ... I am ashamed to rehearse to your worship because I have bene a speaker & writer for him too often ...[6]

Many complaints regarding the personal behaviour of ministers are mixed up with concerns about their conduct of services and their religious leanings. The vicar of Eardisley, Herefordshire, is presented for several faults: for being a usurer, for buying and selling goods, for not using chrism at a baptism, for conducting a clandestine marriage, for celebrating mass twice in one day, for failing to administer the last rites, and for living suspiciously with two female servants, Agnes and Isabel, who ring bells and assist him at mass, which is 'against ecclesiastical honesty' (1397).[7]

At Barnard Castle in 1587 the conduct of the priest, Thomas Clark, prompts the wardens to lock him out of the church. Subsequently they make a series of accusations against him.

He did not at all crosse the children in the foorhed when he christened them ...

He refused to christen one John Cooks of Barnard Castell child upon a worke day, wher he had christened others that was welthye mens children ...

He maried one Warton of Eggleston in the parish of Middleton and Janet Sayer, of the parish of Startforth, upon the night, about Candlemas last, at what time ther horses was set in the church by the space of the said mariadge, and bothe the said maried folkes and ther compeny wer riddin away longe before day. ... Both the said Warton and Janet Sayer was handfest or betrowed with others.

[He married] an unknown tinkler with a girle of 12 yere olde, neither being of that parish ... for 2s 6d ... when as the curat of Startforth had refused to mary him ...

He also refused to minister the communion to one John Shaw, beinge sike ...

He was also a week away before Magdalen day last, at which time ther was 2 corses to be buried ...

He also refused the last rogacion dayes to go or walke the perambulacion of their parish, according to the quenes injunctions ...[8]

14. Dilapidation

i. Church

Most presentments are made by churchwardens, but they are themselves liable to be in trouble if, during a visitation, the church is found wanting, either through disrepair or because required articles are lacking.

The following notes relating to a visitation in the diocese of Ely in 1685 give an idea of the sorry state of things in some parishes and also of the critical eye cast. It is thought they were made by the chancellor of the diocese, assisted by his clerk, as he travelled from parish to parish.

Great Abington. The whole church pitiful and thatcht and that extream ill, great holes in it at which ye pidgeons come in. Once a handsome church now a dismal one.

Long Stow. The church a pidgeon-house, the parish plough in it. ... The chancell is a wofull case, the windows and dore broken. The surplice, communion plate and clerks bible and common prayer booke stolen and ye chest broak.

Meldreth. Seats broaken miserably. The chancell in a sad pickle. The graves uncovered. The gravestones lie about ye church and great heapes of other stones and dust.

Oakington. The church lies in great neglect like a barn or dovehouse. ... A pitifull carpet. ... A sad pulpit. The font nasty. ... This is ye most scandalous parish and worst in ye diocese for ye people are most vile.

Sawston. The chancell a dungeon, the windows stopt up with pease-straw. ... The dore so broken that hogs may creep under it. ... The font nasty and no plug. The churchyard weedy and full of elders, the walls thereof want coping, the hogs have rooted up the graves. Vicaridge-house turned to an ale-house and a sign upon ye dore ...

Toft. A very dangerous crack in the steeple. Many great cracks in ye chancell quit thoro [quite through]. Ye walls lean extreamly. No way but to sequester ye living.[1]

As this suggests, problems commonly arise in relation to the chancel, its upkeep being the responsibility of the rector, who may not live in the parish, and after the Reformation is often a lay person or body. There is little that can be done other than to make a presentment.

> 1575 The chauncell is oute of reparations and the raine raineth into the churche, and it fell downe 7 yeres since and slewe the parishe clarke, and thoughe it have bene verie often presented yet the sworne men [select vestry] saye they can never get any amends any waye. (Huddersfield, Yorks)

> 1625 I present Roger Barwicke, improprietary [lay impropriator] of the parsonage of Upmarden, for suffering the chancel there to be so far gone to ruine that unless speedy order be taken to compel him to repaire the same it is likely in short time to fall doune. And it is now so undecently and beastly kept both in healing [roofing] and otherwise that through the pigeons dung and other filth in the same the people are not able to endure the ill and noisome smell thereof when they come into the same, but are inforced to stop their noses or carry flowers in their hands to prevent the ill smell thereof. And I further heard him say that it should fall to the ground before he would repaire the same, or words to the same effect, being a most uncharitable and unchristianlike speech for any man to use concerning the house of God. Anthony Gray, vicar. (Up Marden, Sussex)[2]

Towers and steeples are also much subject to decay, their state sometimes being such as to render bell-ringing hazardous.

> 1607 The steeple ... is much decayed and rotted with raine, and dothe rocke & shake the roofe of the churche when the bells ringe, whereby as [the wardens] think the shingles are shaken off the church and the tiles off the chauncell ... (Little Laver, Essex)

> 1628 The steeple ... is greatly decayed and ruinated insomuch as the sexton of that church is in great feare and danger of the fall thereof at such times whenas he rings or tolls the bell for the calling of the parishioners together for the hearing of divine service ... (Staines, Middlesex)[3]

Such fears are not fanciful. At St Edmund, Salisbury, in 1653 the vestry

> find the tower to be so cleft with shaking, by meanes of the ringing of the belles ... that we cannot without great danger of the towers falling downe suffer any peale to be rung againe, and therfore to give ease to the said tower, it is now ordered that the churchwardens do take downe all the belles in the tower except the greatest bell to call the people together and the treble to ring at 5 a clocke in the morning ...

Even these precautions are not enough. A week later, on 26th June, when the church is full,

> the maine pillars did bulge out, and sensiblely shake. The cleftes in the walles were seen to open and shut with ringing the sermon bell ... so that nothing but the very hand of God did keep the stones and timber from falling until the next morning [when] his one people were all secure at home, and then he so sweetly ordered the fall of the tower that (albeit many workmen were about it that day) neither man, woman, nor child, received any hurt therby.[4]

At Wye, Kent, in 1686,

> the minister being at prayers with the congregation perceived the bell ropes to shake, there being no winde then, and immediately warned the congregation of the imminent danger, and they all ran out, and immediately the steeple fell down.[5]

While roof decay is most feared, many other problems are also reported.

1502 A glasse window is broke open [on the] sowth side of ye church, throwgh ye which winde does harme and spills our lights in ye rode lofte. (Acrise, Kent)

1554 Our glasse windows are broken as well in the chancel as in the body of the churche so that with doves and other fowl we be trobled in the time of divine service. (Trumpington, Cambs)

1579 Ther churche's dore is broken, so that swine or other beasts maye come in to the churche. (Seaham, co. Durham)

1606 Our communion table is covered over with pigeon dung. (Reculver, Kent)

1637 The pavement of the church is uneven in most places and broken in divers places, most part of it of rough stone, a great deal of it fitter for the gripp [gutter] of a cowhouse than the house of God ... The crosse which was upon the east end of the chancel is broken down, and instead thereof the towne's armes are set up as if it were the towne's church and not Christ's. (All Saints, Northampton)

1685 The church seems to leane toward the south ... and so does ye chancel. (Pitsea, Essex)[6]

Building fabric apart, various items within the church may be found wanting.

1511 There is great nede of books. ... There lakkithe a beere to cary dede men to theire graves. (Chilham, Kent)

1573 The boke of common prayer is torn ... The poore mens boxe is not in all respects well. (Luddenham, Kent)

1684 The ten Commandments are to be made anew, for they are quite out. (Leigh, Essex)[7]

ii. Churchyard

Problems caused by animals in churchyards have already been seen.* A range of other nuisances emanate from humankind.

Some relate to trade of various kinds. At St John the Baptist, York, a mass of offal, dung and animal bones spills into the churchyard from a butchers' shambles, attracting dogs and birds so that it is scarcely possible to conduct services (1416). At Sheppey, Kent, there is a 'noyfulle' lime kiln (1511). At Haltwhistle, Northumberland, a parishioner 'hath a doore issueing into the churchyard, and hath ... made a common stackyard for hay and strawe in the churchyard, and pleadeth custom [seeks buyers] for the same' (1627). At St Peter, Chester, the doors of three tippling houses open onto the yard, with the result that it is 'so abused as to become loathsome, so that no person will allow a friend to be buried there' (1636). At All Saints, Northampton, the tombstones are used 'for the butcher lads to whet their cleavers against', while also serving as 'skulking places for loiterers' (1795).[8]

Many yards are used for laundry. At Sturton, Nottinghamshire, 'there is a well and batting block ... for washing clothes', not to mention 'a muckhill' (1638). At St Laurence Pountney, London, clothes are dried and servants beat carpets against the tombstones (1681, 1791). At St Oswald, Durham, women use the yard for bleaching and spinning (*c.* 1575).[9]

Churchyards also commonly serve for answering nature's call. At St Botolph, Colchester, the occupants of houses opening onto the yard, and their children, 'do their easements' there (1633). At All Saints, Northampton, it is 'basely defiled with excrements and it appears that there is usual evacuatinge against the church walls' (1637). At St Bartholomew Exchange, near the Bank of England, a payment in 1601 'for making cleane the pissinge place at the south church dore and along the wall' is one in a series.[10]

iii. Upshot: dealing with the authorities

Once a problem with the church or churchyard has been reported, the wardens have to deal with the court and officials of the archdeacon or bishop, giving rise to a range of costs. They also have to remedy the problem.

* See p7.

1586 To Roberts the somener for somening the church wardens to Ashforde
for certaine faults that Mr Commissary* found in the church. First, for
that we had not a bible according to the order set downe, for lacke of a
poormans boxe, the glass windowes mended and scowered, the church
dore a newe locke and a key, and a cover for the fonte ...
20d | For two horsis and theire meate ... 3s 4d | For the two
churchwardens dinnere there ... 18d | For two horsis to
ride againe to Ashforde to apere before Mr Commissary,
who said unto the churchwardens whie should you not do
pennaunce for that the thing above said were not had and
done ... 3s 4d | More for theire two dinners ... 18d | For a
newe bible ... 42s | For making of the poormans boxe,
a locke and a key to the same, for a cover for the fonte
[etc] ... 5s 8d | For making clene of the glass windowes in the church
and mending of them ... 14s | For making of a bar of irone for the
church dore and for mending the hooke to hang the bar on ... 14d | To
Mr Craynemer for writing out the pennaunce and certifieng the courte
... 16d (St Andrew, Canterbury)[11]

In addition they must clamp down on misdemeanours.

1634 Spent when we were called to Wells for not preventing bowlers
playinge in the churchyard ... 6s | 1635 Spent when I was called to Wells
to prevent those that played fives in the churchyard ... 17d (Locking,
Somerset)[12]

If deemed to have failed in their duties wardens risk being excommunicated,
and whether it happens or not there is likely to be a cost.

1600 For stayinge of an excommunication for not mendinge of the
steeple ... 16d (St Peter, Cheapside)

1626 Paid by Robert Jordan to the ordinary at Oxford for ye churchwardens
excommunication for not settinge up the church porche dore upon
notice given ... 4s 6d (Burford, Oxon)[13]

15. Thefts from churches

With their valuable contents churches are natural targets for thieves.

1531 For mette [meat] for the theff that stalle [stole] the pyx ... 4d (St
Margaret, Westminster)

1546 For hors-hire to Newbury for th' enditing William Paytfer that
stall the chalice ... 6d (St Lawrence, Reading)[1]

---

* *Commissary*. Church official exercising jurisdiction as the representative of a superior
authority such as an archbishop, bishop or archdeacon.

At times of vulnerability the parish may pay someone to keep watch overnight.

1477-79 To William Paris for wacching in the churche in time of making of the vestry, by 16 nightes ... 16d (St Mary at Hill)

1716 Watching in the church for several weeks by night, by order of Dr Tipping, when the man sent a letter to the doctor that the church was to be rob'd and going with Mr Acton to the man in prison to know ye truth of it ... £4 9s 1½d (Camberwell, Surrey)[2]

Lead is a particular target.

1567 To 2 men that watched the lead in the church 2 nights after the fall of the rooffe ... 16d (Worksop, Notts)

1567 To one of the kepers of Newgate for bringing Father Stone to be examined before Mr Southcote touching the leade stolen from the vestry ... 12d (Lambeth)

1648 To two men to carry the piece of the pipe of lead which was stolen off the vestry back to church. It was found in Mrs Doulman's pond ... 1s (St Giles in the Fields)[3]

Even material that is hard to access may be taken.

1633 Upon the first day of August or there aboute there was a great clock plum stolen out of the steeple, which was eight or nine stone weight. Sum strong body did steal it or else it could not have been carried away for I could not lift it with one hand. (North Wingfield, Derbyshire, note in register)[4]

In October 1801 at Deptford it is found that a gang of young men have been burrowing at night from the churchyard into the vaults, from which they have removed the lead of over forty coffins, leaving a trail of bones and mangled corpses in their wake. On one occasion during a thunderstorm their light gutters, leaving them to spend a fearful night in darkness among the dead.[5]

One targeted theft prompts a heartening response from the young of the parish.

1534 Ye 20 day of November ... betwixte that Friday & ye Saterday a theffe with a ladder gat up apon this churche & pulled up ye ladder after him & sette ye ladder to ye tower window & brocke oppe that window & so gat in to ye bells & fro ye bells came a downe in to ye churche & with a fire box strake fire & to prove this he left his fire that he strake fire with all behind him & [it] was fownd & then broke oppe ye stoke coffer & ye other grete coffer & toke away ye challis that was in ye stoke & Sent Sidwell his shoe of silver & no other thing & so gat owt to ye quire dore & pulled ye quire dore after him: so upon this ye yong men & maidens of ye parishe dru themselfe togethers & with theire geftis & provision they bought in another challis without any charges of ye parishe. (Morebath, Devon)[6]

Thieves are also prepared to stoop low.

1623 Taken out of the poores box when it was robd ... £1 2d (Lambeth)[7]

A number of thefts occur around the time of the Reformation, when the sense of the church and its objects as sacred is being undermined, offenders perhaps feeling that if church goods are to be plundered by the state they may as well get in first.[8]

1548 Shortly after the feast of Easter the church was robbed, the pore mennes chest broken, the best copes and vestements and all other things worth the conveying away, stolen by the thefes. This year also ... a pore mennes chest was provided again after that it was broken. | 1552 This year, the night before the conversion of St Paule, two of the churche windowes was broken by thefes. The Tuesday at night folowing they or other came again & brake open the vicares copher & robbed it. They also caryed away the pore mennes chest into the fielde and brake it & robbed it. (East Ham, Essex)

c. 1552 [While] Thomas Hutton [churchwarden] lay on his death bed, our churche was robbed, and there was stolen out of it a faire cope, an awlbe, a vestment, 4 surplices, a towel, a latten senser, and all the clothes that lay of the communion table, with all other implements that was in the churche the which was any thinge handsome* to be carried away. (Little Ilford, Essex)[9]

In trying to trace culprits and recover goods parishes spread word as best they can.

1541 To Master Tie 10s and Marten 2s ... riding to London with a bill of the juells of the churche whiche were stolen, to ley for the same with the goldsmithes ther and also to inquire of certen suspect persons ... 12s | To John Witton going to Hastings with a letter to Petite ther concarning the seid goods and for watching at home after the churche was robbed ... 4s 10d | For thexpencs of Robert Robin, Simon Gason and William Baroughe going to Romney for the examinacon of certen suspect persons for steling of the seid goods ... 12d (Lydd, Kent)

1710 Paid for putting the church regalia into the Gazette and Postman ... 15s (Lambeth)[10]

At Fulham they not only advertise but also take precaution against future theft.

1649 For printing several bills to have found out the basins which were stolen ... 1s | To a bedell for dispersing them to several shops in London ... 1s | For two new pewter dishes to be used for collections instead of the basins ... 5s | For graving on them an inscription for Fulham Church ... 2d[11]

* In the now obsolete sense of suitable or handy.

16. Bodysnatching

Corpses too are worth stealing, because of their value to those studying anatomy. Writing in 1724, Oxford antiquary Thomas Hearne notes that it is

> a common practise nowadays for young physicians to rob church yards, tho' even churches are still less safe, many clarks, as 'tis said, in London, and other great places, being confederate with the physicians. But 'tis for young people, especially young women, that they generally seek, which sometimes they mistake, and take up old women. So that I remember that about twenty years ago ... a pretty young woman being buried in St Peter's church yard in the East. Search was made in the night time for her body, but they mistook her grave, and took up one goody Beecham, an old woman who had been bed-maker of [St] Edmund Hall, and was buried at the same time. This old woman they had convey'd out of the church yard, but being some way or other disturbed as they were going along, they drop'd her, and set her in her shroud, bolt upright, just under Edmund Hall against the wall, where (before day) in the morning she, being seen, frighted some people, who knew nothing of the matter.[1]

As Hearne suggests, complicity on the part of those employed by the parish is a recurring problem.

In December 1777 the gravedigger of St George's, Bloomsbury, John Holmes, and his assistant, Richard Williams, are tried at Guildhall for stealing the corpse of Mrs Jane Sainsbury who had died two months earlier. At the trial, according to the *Morning Chronicle*,

> Mr Eustanton, who lives near the Foundling-hospital, deposed, that on going by the Foundling-hospital about eight o'clock in the evening, with some other gentlemen, they met the prisoner, Williams, with a sack on his back, and another person walking with him. Having some suspicion of a robbery, he stopped Williams, and asked him what he had got there? To which the prisoner said, 'I don't know,' but that pulling the sack forcibly off his back, the prisoner begged to be let go, and said he was a poor man just come from harvest. Mr Eustanton untied the sack, and, to his great astonishment, found the deceased body of a woman, her heels tied up tight behind her, her hands tied together behind, and cords round her neck, forcibly bending her head almost between her legs. The horror they were all in at such a sight prevented them from securing the other person, who ran off, but they secured Williams and took him to the Round-house, where he was well known to be the assistant grave-digger to Holmes, and went by the name of Bobby.

Next day Eustanton and others go with a constable to question Holmes while he is at work digging in the churchyard. He denies knowing Williams and claims not to recall any burial having taken place within the last few days.

However, by the appearance of the mould [earth], they insisted on his running into the ground his long iron crow, and then they discovered a coffin, only six inches under ground, out of which the body had been taken. This appeared on strict enquiry to be the coffin of a Mrs Guy, who had been buried the preceding Wednesday, very deep. The gentlemen present not yet satisfied, examined the ground farther, and then discovered another coffin, out of which the body of Mrs Jane Sainsbury had been stolen, and whilst this examination took place, Holmes was detected in hiding in his pockets several pieces of shroud which lay contiguous to her grave.

The two culprits are sentenced to six months in prison and 'to be publickly and severely whipped, twice in the first and last week of their imprisonment, from Kingsgate-street, Holborn, to Dyot-street, St Giles's, which is full half a mile'. In the event it seems they are spared whipping, reflecting the half-hearted attitude of the authorities towards the crime.[2]

Bodysnatchers by Hablot Knight Browne ('Phiz')

In 1828, in the wake of the notorious case of Burke and Hare in Edinburgh, a committee of the House of Commons takes evidence on the trade in bodies, and the witnesses from high to low concur on the importance to grave-robbers of having inside help. According to Sir Astley Cooper, president of the Royal College of Surgeons, 'the sextons and gravediggers are always in pay, as far as I have heard; indeed, I have no idea of their being able to procure a body, except occasionally, without it'. A bodysnatcher, identified only as 'A.B.', is asked whether 'the grave-diggers and sextons ever wink at the practices of those who raise the bodies?', to which he replies that 'you cannot do it without bribing those people ... If you are friends with a gravedigger, the thing will be all right ...'[3]

Various methods are used to try to protect individual corpses from such efforts. They may be buried in iron coffins which can be locked, bolted and even soldered fast; a protective iron railing called a mortsafe may be installed, covering the grave permanently; or a great weight may be placed over the grave while it is still fresh: at Pannal, Yorkshire, the parish rents out an extremely heavy medieval stone coffin for this purpose for a guinea a fortnight.[4]

The parish may also provide more general protection. A.B. tells the committee that his work is 'very dangerous' and that 'every ground in London is watched by men put into them at dark, who stop till daylight with fire arms'. At St James, Clerkenwell, they employ such watchmen at great expense, but it is not enough: as a former churchwarden tells the Commons committee, 'We were obliged to raise a wall, which was 16 or 18 feet high. We were obliged to increase it 12 feet, because with all the vigilance we could use, persons were continually entering the churchyard.'[5]

Mortsafes at Warden, Northumberland, late 19th century

London's riverside villages are particularly vulnerable, being relatively populous, and so providing a reliable supply of bodies, while also being discreetly accessible from the night Thames.

> 1823   Paid Callaway and Hawkins for watching the churchyard, the Resurrection Men being expected down ... 5s (Fulham)

> 1823   Watching churchyard ... £40 15s | Watchman's ammunition ... 5s | 1826   Lanthern for watchman ... 4s 10d | 1827   Brace of pistols for watchman ... £1 15s | 1829   Watchman's coat ... £1 18s (Battersea)[6]

While it is a dark business, Charles Fèret, writing at the end of the 19th century, relates one light-hearted encounter.

> So much were the people of Fulham terrorized by these body snatchers that it was once the custom for the friends of a deceased person, buried at All Saints, to guard the grave for some time after the interment. In the early years of this century, William Tomlin got a frugal living by minding the churchyard at night. On one occasion, about the year 1825, some boys were commissioned to 'watch' a grave. 'Billy' Tomlin, not relishing the idea of his business thus passing out of his hands, donned a white sheet and, making some hideous gesticulations, swooped down on the group of amateur grave-watchers, who, for dear life's sake, fled before the awful vision. 'You make a pretty set of watchmen,' cried old Billy as he cast aside his ghostly attire and revealed his identity to the boys. From that time forth, William Tomlin is said to have encountered no further competition in his office of grave-watcher.

An Anatomy Act passed in 1832 dramatically reduces the trade, but the fear lingers, one elderly Fulham resident telling Fèret that 'as late as 1846 I have known people to watch bodies for a month'.[7]

Vulnerable from the river: Battersea church, looking north-east towards Chelsea, 1750

HISTORY INTRUDES

While the parish and its church embody continuity they are subject to gradual change in all periods. In addition their rhythms and ways are dramatically interrupted twice, first by the Reformation in the mid 16th century and then, a hundred years later, by the Civil War and Puritan rule.

A sympathetic depiction of the Reformation, with Henry VIII and
Thomas Cranmer in attendance as superstition is replaced by true religion.
Frontispiece of Gilbert Burnet's history, 2nd edition, 1681.

Part 1: The Reformation

A: Under Henry VIII

In its early stages the Reformation affects the parish only modestly. An Act of 1533 ends the payment of Peter's Pence* to Rome. Another in the following year declares Henry VIII to be 'the supreme head of the Churche of England', and royal injunctions of 1536 order the clergy to declare openly in church that the pope's 'power and jurisdiction' have been abolished for 'most just causes'.

The injunctions also set in train the general demystification or dis-enchantment of religion by ordering that the clergy are not to 'set forth or extol any images, relics, or miracles for any superstition or lucre, nor allure the people by any enticements to the pilgrimage of any saint'. Instead parishioners are to be told that 'it shall profit more their soul's health, if they do bestow that on the poor and needy, which they would have bestowed upon the said images or relics'.

In addition the use of English in worship is to be encouraged. Every parson is to provide a bible 'in Latin, and also in English, and lay the same in the choir, for every man that will to look and read thereon', and parents and employers are to be admonished to teach their children and servants the creed, paternoster ('our father' in Latin; the Lord's prayer) and Ten Commandments 'in their mother tongue'.[1]

Such changes are reinforced by a second set of injunctions issued in October 1538. These require 'one book of the whole bible of the largest volume, in English' to be set up in each church 'in some convenient place' where parishioners can easily read it for themselves, with the cost to be split equally between parson and parish.

> 1539 For the half-part of the bibell, accordingly after the king's injunction ... 9s 9d (St Margaret, Westminster)
>
> 1540 For making a deske to set on the bibill ... 6d | For 2 stapulls for the chaine of the said bibill ... 2d (St Mary Woolnoth)[2]

The creed, paternoster and Commandments in English are now to be recited regularly in church so that the entire congregation 'may learn the same by heart'. Meanwhile a range of 'superstitious' practices are to be suppressed.

> Ye shall ... exhort your hearers to the works of charity, mercy, and faith ... and not to repose their trust ... in any other works devised by men's phantasies besides scripture, as in wandering to pilgrimages, offering of money, candles, or tapers to images or relics, or kissing or licking the same, saying over a number of beads, not understood or minded on, or in such-like superstition ...
>
> Such feigned images as you know ... to be so abused with pilgrimages or offerings ... ye shall ... forthwith take down and delay,† and shall suffer

---

* A tax of that amount upon every householder having land above a certain value, collected by parishes and passed to the papal see.

† *Delay* in the sense of withhold something or keep it back.

from henceforth no candles, tapers, or images of wax to be set afore any image or picture, but only the light that commonly goeth across the church by the rood-loft, the light before the sacrament of the altar, and the light about the [Easter] sepulchre, which for the adorning of the church and divine service ye shall suffer to remain, still admonishing your parishioners that images serve for none other purpose but as to be books of unlearned men that can [know] no letters ... which images, if they abuse for any other intent than for such remembrances, they commit idolatry in the same, to the great danger of their souls.[3]

As a result, most of the lights in churches are removed, along with any images visited by pilgrims, such as those of Our Lady of Walsingham and Our Lady of Ipswich, both of which are brought to London and burnt.[4]

The injunctions also order that any observances relating to Thomas Becket be 'clean omitted', apparently because he is seen as an embodiment of resistance to royal interference in Church affairs. A proclamation of November 1538 goes further: from now on Becket 'shall not be esteemed, named, reputed, nor called a sainte ... and ... his images and pictures, through the whole realme, shall be putte downe, and avoided out of all churches, chapelles, and other places'.[5]

1539 To Sir Richard Charnell for correkyn ye service of Thomas Beket* ... 2s | For bread & drink for him in ye time of doing it ... 2d | To John Pack for racen [erasing] the windows of Beket & transposin of stained clothes that Thomas Beket was on ... 3s 4d (Bungay)[6]

Imagery associated with the papacy, including the tiara or triple crown, is also expunged in some churches.

1538 The painter for the puttinge out of Seint Gregoryes three crownes ... 2d (St Edmund, Salisbury)

1541 To the glasier for taking down of the Bishop of Romes hede ... 4d (St Mary the Great, Cambridge)[7]

The assault on the old ways is seen too in local injunctions such as those issued by Nicholas Shaxton, Bishop of Salisbury, in 1538. His clergy are ordered

that ye suffer no night watches in your churches or chapels, neither decking of images with gold, silver, clothes, lights, or herbs; nor the people kneel to them, nor worship them, nor offer candles, oats, cake-bread, cheese, wool, or any other such things to them ...

Shaxton also scorns objects revered by 'ignorant people, under the name of holy relics'. Items of this kind which he says have 'already come to mine hands' include 'stinking boots, mucky combs, ragged rochets, rotten girdles, pild purses, great bullocks horns, locks of hair, and filthy rags, gobbetts of wood, under the name of parcels of the holy cross, and such pelfry [trash] beyond estimation'.[8]

---

* i.e. altering the form of service so as to omit his name.

Another popular custom, that of the boy bishop, is banned by royal decree in 1541, the king being minded 'to avaunce the true glorye of God without vaine superstition'.[9]

More generally a number of parishes remove items which are out of step with the new spirit of the times. Some no doubt do this on principle, those involved sharing the reformist view, while others perhaps act out of prudence, fearing that what is not sold now may be seized later.

> 1542 Received ... for ye silver that was upon the crosse that the reliques wherin ... 19s 2d | Of Mr Nicholls for ye silver shoes wiche wer upon ye brown rodes fete ... 10s | 1543 For a purse and 2 combs that were reliques in ye churche ... 3s (North Elmham, Norfolk)[10]

Some zealous officials and private individuals take things literally into their own hands. In 1540 Edmund Cranmer, Archdeacon of Canterbury and brother of Thomas, reportedly removes three tapers burning before the sacrament in St Andrew, Canterbury, along with a coat from the rood, 'and did violently break the arms and legs of the rood'. Two years later, at St Mary Northgate in the same city, one John Toftes takes down the image of the Virgin Mary, 'and had her and the tabernacle home to his house, and there did hew her all in pieces'.[11]

The other major religious change of the period, the dissolution of the monasteries – the lesser in 1536 and the greater three years later – has little direct impact on parishes, although some take advantage of the resulting availability of paraphernalia and building materials.

Madonna and child,
Winchester Cathedral,
probably vandalised in 1538

> 1538 For the organs and the ornamentes that came from Woburn ... £9 | For meate & drinke when we went for the organs to Woburn, & for workemen ... 2s 7d | For a glasse windo boght at Woburn ... 3s 4d (Wing, Bucks)

> 1541 For a lode of free stone at Walsingham Abbey, wiche lie ther yet still ... 16d | To ye mason for going to Walsingham ... to see ye free stone ... 6d (North Elmham, Norfolk)

> 1545 For carteing the pulpett from Osney [Abbey] ... 3d (St Martin, Oxford)[12]

In addition an Act is passed in 1545 for the dissolution of chantries. However, little is achieved to this end before the king's death, and his own underlying religious conservatism is clear from his will, dated 30th December 1546, which includes a bequest of '£600 sterling per annum in land to the Dean of Windsor, that he may order masses for his [the king's] soul continually'. It is also reflected in his burial, which takes place with the old observances. He dies on 28th January 1547 at Whitehall Palace where, after embalming, his body lies in state. During this period, according to the chronicle of Charles Wriothesley,

> The eight daie of Februarie everie parish church within the citie of London and the suburbes of the same kept a solemne dirige by note, with a herse and tow tapers, and a knell, with all the bells ringinge, and on the morrowe a masse of requiem for the soule of King Henrye the Eight, which also was this daie observed through all churches in Englande.[13]

These proxy funerals typically involve a bier, hearse and lighted tapers, as if the king's corpse were present, and a bellman may go about the parish to announce the news.

> 1547 *At the king's highnes' dirige and masse.* For the mendinge of the bere and herse ... 2d | For the colowringe of two wodden can[dle]sticks blacke ... 2d | For five tapers ... 10d | For ringinge ... 6d | For brede and ale for the ringers then ... 4d ob. | For two papers of the king's armes to set on the king's herse ... 3d (Worcester)

> 1547 To the ringers for Kinge Henry the Eight ... 12d | To the belman the same time ... 2d (St Martin, Leicester)[14]

Six days later the actual corpse is on the move.

The 14th daie of Februarie the corps of King Henrie the Eight was solemnly with great honor conveyed in a chariot, with his image lying on it, toward Windsor, and rested that night at Sion, where was a rich herse made of waxe of nine stories high; the morrow, being the fiftenth daie, it was conveyed to Windsor, where at the townes end the Deane of Windsor, with all his quire in rich copes, with Eton College, met the corps, and so [it] was conveyed to the college* in the kinges palace at Windsor, where it was set under a rich herse of waxe of 13 stories high, and was buried the morrow after masse in the quire where his late wife Queene Jane lieth.[15]

This time parishes near the route play a particular part in proceedings.

> 1547 To the ringers and holders of torches when our late soveraign lorde King Henry the Eight went to burial ... 2s (St Martin in the Fields)

> 1547 To the poor men that did bere the copes and other necessaries to Knightsbridge, when that King Henry the Eighth was brought to his burial to Winsor, and to the man that did ring the bells ... 3s (St Margaret, Westminster)[16]

---

* St George's Chapel, home of the college of St George.

Edward VI,
after a portrait
thought to
have been
painted by
William Scrots
circa 1547

B: Under Edward VI

1. Laws and orders

More thoroughgoing reform occurs under the government nominally presided over by the young Edward VI. Injunctions issued on 31st July 1547 echo and extend those of 1538. The clergy are instructed

> that such images as they know ... to be or to have been abused with pilgrimage or offering of any thing ... they ... shall ... forthwith take down, or cause to be taken down, and destroy the same; and shall suffer from henceforth no torches nor candles, tapers or images of wax to be set afore any image or picture, but only two lights upon the high altar, before the sacrament, which for the signification that Christ is the very true light of the world, they shall suffer to remain still ...

This signals the end of the lights placed on the rood loft and about the Easter sepulchre. Processions are also to be suppressed.

> To avoid all contention and strife, which heretofore hath risen ... by reason of fond courtesy, and challenging of places in procession, and also that [those gathered] may the more quietly hear that which is said or sung to their edifying, they shall not from henceforth, in any parish church at any time, use any procession about the church or churchyard, or other place ...

The use of bells is to be reduced.

> In the time of the litany, of the mass, of the sermon, and when the priest readeth the scripture to the parishioners ... all ringing and knolling of bells shall be utterly forborne ... except one bell in convenient time to be rung or knolled before the sermon.

In addition the clergy are to 'instruct and teach ... that no man' should engage in other old customs such as

> casting holy water upon his bed, upon images, and other dead things, or bearing about him holy bread ... or making of crosses of wood upon Palm-Sunday, in time of reading of the passion ... or blessing with the holy candle, to the intent thereby to be discharged of the burden of sin, or to drive away devils ...

Finally, shrines and associated items are to be destroyed.

> They shall take away, utterly extinct and destroy all shrines, covering of shrines, all tables, candlesticks, trindles or rolls of wax, pictures, paintings, and all other monuments of feigned miracles, pilgrimages, idolatry and superstition: so that there remain no memory of the same in walls, glass windows, or elsewhere within their churches or houses.[1]

To ensure compliance there follows a general visitation, starting in September and extending into the following year. According to the Grey Friars Chronicle,

> The 5th day after in September beganne the kinges visitacion at Powles ... and the 9th day of the same month the said visitacion was at Sent Brides, and after that in divers other parishe churches; and so all images pulled downe thorow all Englonde at that time, and all churches new white-limed, with the commandmentes written on the walles.

At St Paul's some of the work is carried out at night, apparently to avoid trouble, but in the dark things go awry.

> The 17th day of [November] at nighte was pulled downe the rode in Powles with Mary and John, with all the images in the churche, and two of the men that labord at it was slaine and divers other sore hurte.[2]

According to Charles Wriothesley, only one person dies 'in the falling downe of the great crosse in the rode loft', and the accident is seized upon by 'the papish priestes' who say it 'was the will of God for the pulling downe of the said idols'.

Wriothesley also describes a sermon preached at St Paul's Cross by the Bishop of St David's ten days later.

> He shewed a picture of the resurrection of our Lord made with vices,* which put out his legges ... and blessed with his hand, and turned his heade; and there stoode afore the pulpit the image of our ladie which they of Poules had lapped in serecloth, which was hid in a corner of Poules church, and found by the visitors in their visitation. And in his sermon he declared the great abomination of idolatrie in images, with other fained ceremonies contrarie to scripture, to the extolling of Godes glorie, and to the great comfort of the awdience. After the sermon the boyes broke the idols in pieces.[3]

---

* Mechanical contrivances or devices by which something is worked.

The action of the boys is echoed far away at Durham, where one of the king's commissioners 'did treade and breake in peices with his feet' a 'rich shrine in St Nicholas church called Corpus Christi shrine ... with many other ornaments'.[4]

Meanwhile an Act passed in November orders that the people should again receive the sacrament in both kinds, bread and wine, as they did in the early Church, a change which has the effect of reducing the sense of distinction between clergy and people.[5]

In December a new Act is passed for dissolving chantries. Ostensibly they are targeted because they encourage 'superstition and errors', above all belief in purgatory, and the proceeds are to be directed to 'good and godlie uses'. However, like the earlier dissolution of the monasteries, it is a more or less blatant seizure of vast assets by the crown. From the following Easter 'all manors, landes, tenements, rents, tithes, pencions, porcions, and other hereditaments' belonging to 'all manner of colleges, free chapels and chauntries' and 'appointed to the finding of any preist ... shall ... be in the verie actual and real possession ... of the king our soveraigne lorde and his heirs and successors for ever, without any office or other inquisicion therof to be had or founde'. In the same way the crown is to have all lands and other endowments left by people in their wills to fund 'any anniversarye or obite or ... any light or lampe in any churche or chapel'.

The Act also picks other ripe fruit in the form of guilds and fraternities. Those of a religious nature are abolished and their assets pass to the crown. Lay guilds are allowed to survive but forfeit any assets used to fund intercessions for the dead.

The purging of images, paraphernalia and people,
from the 1570 edition of John Foxe's Book of Martyrs

The Act makes some exceptions, displaced priests are to receive a pension, and some of the seized assets may be assigned to provide extra priests in large towns and parishes if the king's commissioners think it 'necessarye ... for the ministering of the sacraments'. In conjunction with earlier measures, however, the effect in many parish churches is profound: the small army of auxiliary priests, the background hum of their activity at side altars as the dead are remembered, the support of guilds and fraternities, individual endowments bestowed in faith over generations, all are gone.[6]

In January and February 1548 other old customs are effectively discontinued including creeping to the cross on Good Friday and the use of ashes, palms and Candlemas candles. The Easter sepulchre is still not expressly forbidden, but no lights may be set beside or inside it, and it is included among other forbidden customs in articles of inquiry issued by Thomas Cranmer, Archbishop of Canterbury, for his own diocese.[7]

Meanwhile, as the general visitation progresses, the resistance shown in the hiding of the image of the Virgin Mary at St Paul's is repeated across the country. Those of a conservative bent naturally claim that cherished images have not been 'abused' by pilgrimage and offerings and so do not need to be removed. To close this loophole the council issues an order to Cranmer dated 21st February 1548.

> In many ... places much strife and contention hath risen ... some men being so superstitious, or rather wilful, as they would ... retain all such images still, although they have been most manifestly abused; and in some places also the images, which by the ... injunctions were taken down, be now restored and set up again; and almost in every place is contention for images, whether they have been abused or not. And whiles these men go about on both sides ... contending whether this or that image hath been offered unto, kissed, censed, or otherwise abused ... we have thought good to signify unto you, that his highness' pleasure ... is that ... you shall ... give order that all the images remaining in any church or chapel ... be removed and taken away ...[8]

The following year sees the introduction of a new liturgy in the form of the Book of Common Prayer. It avoids taking a clear-cut position on the eucharist, referring inclusively to 'The Supper of the Lord and holy Communion, commonly called the Mass', but removes many old feast days and ceremonies and renders services entirely in English. Its use is enforced by an Act of Uniformity and prompts a popular rising in the west. The rebels' demands are robustly conservative.[9]

> We will have the mass in Latin as was before and celebrated by the priest ...
>
> We will have the sacrament hang over the high altar and there to be worshipped as it was wont to be ...
>
> We will have holy bread and holy water made every Sunday, palms and ashes at the times appointed and accustomed, images to be set up again in every church, and all other ancient old ceremonies used heretofore by our mother the holy church. ...

We will have our old service of matins, mass, evensong, and procession in Latin, not in English, as it was before. ...

We will have every preacher in his sermon and every priest at his mass pray specially by name for the souls in purgatory as our forefathers did.[10]

Their protest proves in vain and by the end of 1549 parish worship and the appearance of churches have been radically altered across the country.

Over the following three years the various changes are reinforced. In January 1550 an Act for the abolishinge and putting awaye of diverse Bookes and Images orders that a range of Latin service books, including antiphoners, missals and processionals, are to be 'clerelye and utterlye abolished, extinguished and forbidden for ever'. In addition 'any images of stone, timber, alabaster, or earthe, graven, carved or painted' are to be defaced and destroyed by the end of June.[11]

Another contentious subject is highlighted by John Hooper, preaching before the king and privy council on 5th March.

There should among Christians be no altars ... It were well then, that it might please the magistrates to turn the altars into tables ... to take away the false persuasion of the people they have of sacrifices to be done upon altars; for as long as the altars remain, both the ignorant people, and the ignorant and evil-persuaded priest, will always dream of sacrifice.[12]

Within months a new Bishop of London, Nicholas Ridley, orders the removal of altars from all churches within his diocese, to be replaced by 'the Lord's board after the form of a table ... for that the form of a table may more move and turn the simple from the old superstitious opinions, and to the right use of the Lord's supper'. Accordingly, 'all the aulters in every parishe through London were taken away, and a table made in the quire for the receivinge of the communion', and in November the privy council orders that 'all the aulters in everie churche' across the country 'be taken downe, and in the liewe of them a tabell set up'.[13]

In 1552 a new and more Protestant prayer book is introduced, enforced by another Act of Uniformity and further undermining the old sense of hierarchy and mystery. The priest celebrating communion is no longer to wear 'a vestment or cope' but a simple surplice and he is to stand not 'afore the midst of the altar' but 'at the north side of the table', thereby distancing the ceremony from traditional mass.[14]

In the same year the king's commissioners are sent out again to survey church goods, 'because we be informed that in many places great quantity of ... plate, jewels, bells, and ornaments be embezzled by certain private men'.[15]

1552 To Mr Curat and Nicholas Poole, for making the book of the church goods, to be presented to the king's commissioners, and for the pains they took about it, &c. ... 10s (St Margaret, Westminster)

1553 In expences at Abingdon when the churche goods were caryed to King Edwardes comissioners ... 20d (Stanford, Berks)[16]

2. The impact in parish churches

The effect of most of the reign's changes can be traced in detail in churchwardens' accounts. The attitudes of those carrying out or recording them are more or less never indicated, but we may perhaps detect regret at the loss of the old services in the following.

> 1548 Paid to the preist & clarkes & childerne that sowng the last of owr lady mas ... 4d (St Nicholas, Bristol)[1]

On the other hand the following suggests Protestant enthusiasm for the changes.

> 1547 Expended for cleansing the church from popery ... £1 13s 4d (Rye, Sussex)[2]

In practical terms the new prayer books and other **books in English** need to be provided.

> 1549 To Sir Richard a Deane for riding to Windsor for the service in Englishe ... 4s | For paper and inke for pricking the songs in Englishe ... 7d (St Lawrence, Reading)

> 1549 To Persy clarke for the altringe of the servis hought of Latine in to English by the consent of the vikar Mr Carow ... 2s | For a quire of whit paper for him ... 3d | To Persy clarke at the seconde time ... for ye transposing vons againe of the servis hought of Latine in to English ... 3s 4d (Bishop's Stortford)

> 1552 For the new booke of the comen prayer ... 4s (Smarden, Kent)[3]

Meanwhile Latin ones need to be sold or surrendered.

> 1549 In expences when we went to cary owr churche bookes of Latten to Worcester ... 12d (South Littleton, Worcs)[4]

Some clergy are reluctant in making the change and others find the new English translations harder to read than the familiar Latin. A parishioner at Deal complains that whenever the parson reads anything in English he 'putteth on his spectacles, and maketh such jerking and hemming that the people cannot understand him, yet when he readeth the Latin service in the quire he doeth it without his spectacles and readeth it so distinctly and plainly that every man may hear'. Another parishioner complains that the parson discourages him and others from reading the scriptures in English, saying 'You oughteth not to read it, it doth pass your capacity, it is fit for such men as be learned'.[5]

Shrines and side **altars** are removed, along with or in advance of the main altar.

> 1548 To 5 laborers for 3 dayes at 6d at the pulling downe of the awlters ... 7s 6d | For 2 baskets at the breking downe of the awlters ... 7d (St Stephen, Walbrook)

> 1548-1550 For taking downe of the alters and paving where the seid alters stode ... 3s 4d (Worcester)

1551 For rasing & defacing of the alters & plucking of them downe & reparing the walles agene & for a table & a frame & form in the quire ... 45s 9d (St Botolph, Aldersgate)[6]

As the last entry shows, a replacement for the main altar needs to be provided, and forms or benches are sometimes added.

1551 Paid Robert Starkye for making the communion table ... 11s (Banwell, Somerset)

1552 For the communion table & 4 formes, with the carryeing ye same ... 23s 4d (Brightlingsea, Essex)[7]

In 1551 the vicar of Blean in Kent is presented for having set up a table resembling an altar. He is ordered to 'breke down the bords' in front of his parishioners 'and declare that he hath done evil in suffering it'.[8]

The reduced use of **lights** in churches is evident mainly in the decline of relevant expenditure. In contrast the erasure, painting over and removal of **images**, including carved figures and those in windows, leaves a clear trail.

1547 To darken the images faces ... 2d (Worksop, Notts)

Defaced panels, Barton Turf, Norfolk

1547 For taking downe of the image of Seint Georg ... 4d | 1548 For taking downe of the horse of the image of Seint Georg & of 2 standinges more ... 8d (Stratton, Cornwall)

1548 For taking down our lady in ye chaunsell ... 4d (Yatton, Somerset)

1548 For one days work of the church wardens in taking down the tabernacles with ye images ... 12d | To Duffyn for washing out the images for 3 days & a halfe ... 21d | To Duffyn, James Dysley & Richard Parker for white liming ... ye church ... 47s | To Henry Borage for making clean the church after the white liming ... 12d (Baldock, Herts)

1548 To a mason for cuttinge downe the stones that ye images stood upon ... 16d (St Michael, Cornhill)[9]

1548 To John Harman for defacing of 2 windows ... 2s 6d (St Michael, Lewes, Sussex)

1549 For le taking down the image and the tabernacles, and burning the same ... 3s 4d (Ashburton, Devon)

1549 To a pore man for carrying owt of ye images out of the churche ... 2d (St Andrew, Canterbury)

1550 For washing out of ye dome [doom painting] in ye rode loft ... 16d (Wing, Bucks)[10]

The most prominent casualty is the central rood, with its carved figure of Christ upon the cross, flanked by figures of the Virgin Mary and St John the Evangelist.

1548 To workemen for taking downe Mary and John in the rood loft ... 16d (St Michael, Cornhill)

1548 To Thomas [Season] and others for takinge downe of the roode and the images ... 6s 8d | For nailes to hange up clothes* when the images was pulled downe ... 4d (Ludlow)

c. 1550 For drinke at the pullinge down the rode ... 4d (Great Dunmow, Essex)[11]

In one Cornish parish the rood is reinstated briefly during the Prayer Book rebellion.

1549 For taking downe of the rode & the pagentes in the rodeloft & setting up the rode agen ... 10d (Stratton)[12]

Rood lofts are not yet forbidden, but their adornments are removed and access may be stopped up.

1548 To William Marteyne for a dayes worke makinge the rode loft plaine ... 6d (Ludlow)

---

* Cloths, perhaps to catch dust and debris.

1548 To the brikleyer for making up the dore where the roode lofte stode [etc] ... 6s 8d (St Matthew, Friday Street)[13]

In some places the loft itself is removed anyway.

1548 For making clean of the church after the rodloft was taken downe ... 4d (St Nicholas, Bristol)[14]

The prominent position of the ones that survive makes them ideal for displaying the **texts** which are now introduced in many churches as part of the new focus on scripture, intelligibility and learning by heart.

1547 For 35 ells of clothe for the fronte of the rode lofte where[on] the Commandments be written ... 23s 4d (St Margaret, Westminster)

1547 For cariage of timber for scaffoldes for the rode loft when it was painted ... 14d | For ropes to binde the scaffoldes ... 16d | For painting of the rode loft with scriptures ... £4 (St Mary at Hill)[15]

Texts are also added elsewhere in the church.

1547 For 2 wainscotte boards for the high alter ... 1s | For the wrighting of the scriptures upon the same boards ... 5s | 1550 To a carpenter for a day's working, for to set up the skaffold for him that did write the 6 chapter of St John's gospel in the quire ... 8d | To him that did paint and write the 6 chapter ... £2 (St Margaret, Westminster)

1549 To ye paintare ... for writinge of oure cherche the spase of 19 days, for him and his man ... 44s 4d | For hiringe of one to reade unto him the spase of 15 days at 3d ye day ... 3s 9d | For 6 bushels of coals for ye painte ... 12d (Burnham, Bucks)[16]

The final stamp of change, added in some places, is the **royal arms**, signalling that the Church is now subservient to the state. In some cases little or no distinction is made between the arms and holy writ.

1548 The saide churche was painted with textes & sentences of the scripture & a great peace of canvas set upon a frame & painted with the kinges armes & scriptures above on the rode lofte ... (St Mary Abchurch, information provided to the king's commissioners)

1551 For pulling downe of the rowde lofte and setting up of the scriptures that is to saye the creacion of the worlde, the coming of our saviour Christe, the beatitudes, the ten commaundements, the 12 articles of our belief, and the Lordes prayer, the judgment of the world, the kinges majesties armes ... £3 12s 6d (Wandsworth)[17]

As these entries suggest, it is common for the arms to be placed upon the rood loft or above the chancel arch, filling the visual void left by the removal of the rood figures. The fact that the arms feature animals as heraldic supporters provokes dismay among traditionalists. 'Downe with the sacramente, downe with the masse,

Tudor arms (in this case probably of Henry VIII)
featuring a dragon and a greyhound, Rushbrooke, Suffolk

downe with the aultars, downe with the armes of Christe, and up with a lion and a dog,' one later complains to Cranmer. 'Is it the word of God,' asks another, 'that ... beside the armes of the realme setteth up a dogge and a dragon in the place of the blessed virgine Mary mother of God, and St John the evangelist, which were wont to stand on either side of the signe of Christ crucified?'[18]

3. The sale of church goods

Parish accounts record income from the sale of a wide variety of items now forbidden or no longer required, providing in the process glimpses of the paraphernalia found in pre-Reformation churches.

i. Altar stones

Some of these are redeployed as paving within churches. Others are sold to individuals, often for sepulchral use.

> 1550 [Received from Richard Couper for] ye awlter stone for to make a grave stone to laye on his fathers grave ... 5s (Harwich, Essex)[1]

Some are put to profane use as hearth-stones and in sinks and troughs. In Lincolnshire in the 1560s it is reported that two altar stones from Kelby are 'laid in high waies and serveth as bridges for sheepe and cattall to go on', while at Habrough one is laid in the church porch and two others serve as stepping stones for the churchyard stile. At Canewdon, Essex, an altar stone is later recovered from the floor of the vicarage pigsty.[2]

ii. Images and tabernacles

1547 Of Robert Everard for all the images, being defaced ... 18d (St Lawrence, Reading)

1547 To Wm. Calow the younger the tabernacle of Thomas Bekete ... 4s 8d (Holbeach, Lincs)

1548 Of Thomas Hony for the image of Saint George that stode in the chapelle ... 18d | Of Walter Rosse for the dragon that the image of Saint George stode upon ... 7d | Of Robert Mollyngre and David ap Richard for the lofte that Saint George stode on ... 6s (Ludlow)

1549 Of the vicar for owld imagis ... 12d | Of Barthelmew Wormell for an image case ... 4d (Melton Mowbray, Leics)

1549 Of Mr Rede for 2 freres [friars] of wood painted which were spoiled, cut and defaced by us the churche wardens, to him solde for ... 1s 4d (All Hallows, Bread Street)[3]

iii. Cloths and image clothes

1547 A napkin of silke, a roode clothe, other old clothes that covered ye images in Lent & ye vaile ... 6s 6d (Rainham, Essex)

1549 Of Wm. Gibson for our ladyes coate and her sonnes of gold [etc] ... 14s (All Hallows, Bread Street)

1549 Solde to John Nichols 4 coates that were for the image of our ladye ... 8s 4d (St Stephen, Coleman Street)[4]

iv. Easter sepulchre

1547 To Richard Raynford the sepulcre light waying 3 score and 75 li. ... 21s 10d ob. (St Martin, Leicester)

1547 Received of Mr Mounslo for a sepulker ... £3 3s 4d | Of Mr Beche for 2 curtens whiche hong about the sepulker ... 9s (St Matthew, Friday Street)

1551 Sold to Harry Wallis ... a sepulchre cloth of red and green Bruges satin with fringe of silk ... 7s 4d (St Margaret, New Fish Street)[5]

v. Rood loft

1547 Solde to Simon Burton the 25 daye of Decembre 62 li. of waxe of the roode light and the sepulcre light at 4d the pounde ... 20s 8d (St Katharine Cree, Leadenhall Street)

1548 To John Stockmede the roode lofte [weighing] 3 tonnes with the organes ... £18 (St Peter, Cornhill)

c. 1550 The refuse woode of the roode lofte ... 12d (St Botolph, Aldgate)[6]

vi. Metal

Various changes in the period, including the reduced use of lights and bells, result in a surplus of metal.

> 1547 To William Southwood the golde that cam of divers images ... 20s (St Lawrence Jewry)

> 1549 Receved for 109 li. of bell mettell and brasse ... 34s 4d (Worfield, Shropshire)

> *c.* 1550 2 hand bells and the candelstiks sold to the tinker of Horndon ... 30s 4d (Great Warley, Essex)[7]

Valuable items may be carried to London.

> 1549 To Simon Sinckler for his cost in ridinge to London when we sold the great crosse by ye space of 3 days findinge himself and his horse ... 3s | For his labor and pains therein ... 2s | Received for the great crosse sold at London weyinge 83 ounces 8 dw.* ... £22 4s (Thame)[8]

While organs survive in a number of parishes, many are removed or silenced, reformers seeing their music as a distraction from the word of God.[9]

> 1547 For the old orgayens with the pipes of tinne ... 4s (St Andrew, Canterbury)

> 1548 Solde to John Cutlar the pipes of the olde organs... 10s 4d (All Hallows Staining)

Perhaps the latter ended up as cutlery.†[10]

Inscriptions and images on graves and monuments suffer the same fate as other items considered superstitious.

> 1547 Oliver Tatam, churchwarden, took up as much old copper off the tombs and grave stones in the church as came to one hundred weight, for which he took 36s to the use of the church. (St Andrew, Holborn, note by Thomas Bentley)

> 1553 Of John Saunders for 300 lacking 9 li. of metal that was taken up of the graves and of olde candlestickes ... 46s 2d (St Mary, Reading)[11]

vii. Vestments &c.

> 1549 Solde to Humfrey Baskerfeld a cope of red velvet inbrodered with dogges ... 5s 4d (St Michael Bassishaw)

---

* Pennyweight, equivalent to a twentieth of an ounce, *d* standing for *denarius*, the name of a Roman coin used to indicate an English penny. The usual abbreviation is 'dwt'.
† Two years later the same man bought '2 paire of candelstikes with other copper, lede and iron' for 30 shillings.

Spaces left by brasses 'most impiously stolen away', Stoke by Nayland, Suffolk.
From John Weever's *Ancient Funerall Monuments*, 1631.

1549 To Thomas Bryan grocer two copes, one with hawkes and thother with shippes, [etc] ... 39s 6d | To Mr Gaywood an image of the resurrection and a vestiment of blewe starres ... 20s 10d (St Mildred, Bread Street)

1550 Sold to John Abell ... an old vestment eaten with rattes ... 3s 4d (St Michael, Wood Street)[12]

Items relating to the now forbidden custom of the boy bishop are also sold.

1548 Sent Nicholas' cote and woode [hood] greatly eaten with moth ... 3s 4d (Long Melford)

1550 To James Altham ... a coarse mitre of needlework which served for the bishop at St Nicholas tide ... 1s 8d | To William Baker, pewterer, three small copes for children of cloth of bawdekin of several colours ... 4s (St Martin Outwich)

1551 Sold ye rede cote & qwood [hood] that Seint Nicholas did wear ...
6s | Ye vestment & cape that Seint Nicholas did wear ... 11s (St Mary
the Great, Cambridge)[13]

The Long Melford and Cambridge entries above are probably just using 'St
Nicholas' as a shorthand form for the boy bishop, although possibly they indicate
the appearance of someone portraying the saint himself. The red coat and hood
are of course suggestive of a later incarnation of the same.

Others items used in plays and processions may suffer the same fate.

1547 To John Thorpe for Herod's coate ... 18d | To Wm. Calow the
younger all thapostels coats and other rags ... 8s 4d | To Antony Heydon
for the coats of the 3 kings of Cologne* ... 5s 4d | To Humphrey
Hornesey the canopye that was born over the sacrament ... 20d | To
Henry Elman for 7 baner clothes ... 9s 4d (Holbeach, Lincs)

c. 1550 4 old stremers sold to Thomas Magotts wife ... 10d (Great Warley,
Essex)[14]

viii. Miscellaneous

Old **service books** are now redundant.

1547-49 Of Master Foye for the Laten bokes ... 20s (St Alphage, London
Wall)

1550 Solde to a boke binder in Powles churche yarde whose name we know
not nor cannot lerne all the olde bokes belonging to our churche ... 8s
(St Michael Bassishaw)[15]

Crosses taken down and disposed of may include the main churchyard one.

1547 Solde to John Haywarde the crosse stones in the churche yarde ...
13s 4d | To Thomas Spenser the stones that laye under the crosse ... 12d
(St Katharine Cree, Leadenhall Street)

1548 To Master Clopton the broken crosse in the churche yard with all
the stones therewith ... 2s 4d | To John Dowty a planke and halfe, the
crosse ... 8d (Long Melford)[16]

There is less call for **lights** of various kinds.

1548 Solde to divers in the parishe 8 torches ... at a peny the pounde ...
13s 7d | Solde to Wiliam Strete the torche case ... 12d (St Katharine
Cree, Leadenhall Street)

1550 Two angels of gilt wood holding candlesticks ... 10s (St Peter,
Cheapside)[17]

* The Magi, reputedly interred in Cologne Cathedral.

A particularly full clearout is made at St Dionis Backchurch, London, in 1550, raising over £125. The following are a few of the sales of vestments and cloths, with a range of local craftsmen and traders among the purchasers.

> *To Gresythen ye taylor in Bowe Lane.* 1 cope of red badkin with greate broken lions in the border and the flowers gold ... 24s
>
> *To Robard ye purse maker.* 1 hole sute of vestments of crimson velvet with branched woven gold ... £12
>
> *To David Vaughan bedmaker.* 1 cope for a childe called Sainte Nicolas cope ... 14s | 1 vestment inbrodred called the players cote ... 4s | 2 alter clothes and ye curtens of counterfet cloth of gold with 2 riche panes of Mary and John in them ... 33s 4d | 1 vestment of rotten red velvet with roses in ye crosse ... 12d
>
> *To Harry the painter.* 20 yardes of painted clothes ... 3s 4d.

Other disposals include:

> *Sold in Lad Lane.* 200 quarter and halfe of marbelers metal that was upon the graves and upon ye tombs ... £3 3s 4d
>
> *To John Dymock.* Ye beame of ye rode lofte [and] ye rode beame ... 13s 4d
>
> *To George Eaton.* 46 fote of old glasse ... 3s 10d
>
> *To Richard Kele stasioner.* Ye old Latten books ... 40s
>
> *To a Portingale* [Portuguese]. 1 paier of small organes with the appurtenances ... 29s
>
> *To Thomas Unckell.* 1 cheste that did [be]longe to the morowmas alter ... 3s
>
> *To John Waterskot goldsmith.* 4 ounces 3 quarters silver that cam of a vestment that was burnte ... 20s 8d.

Regarding the last item, costs at this time include:

> Paide to Kettell the goldsmith for melting of silver that cam of a vestment that was burnt ... 12d[18]

A large number of items find their way into private houses, as Peter Heylyn notes in his history of the Reformation, written a century or so after the event.

> Many private men's parlours were hung with altar-cloths, their tables and beds covered with copes, instead of carpets and coverlids; and many made carousing cups of the sacred chalices ... It was a sorry house, and not worth the naming, which had not somewhat of this furniture in it, though it were only a fair large cushion made of a cope, or altar-cloth, to adorn their windows, or make their chairs appear to have somewhat in them of a chair of state. Yet how contemptible were these trappings, in comparison of those vast sums of money, which were made of jewels, plate, and cloth of tissue, either conveyed beyond the seas, or sold at home, and good lands purchased with the money ...[19]

Queen Mary,
after a portrait by
Anthonis Mor,
circa 1554

C: Queen Mary: Reversing the Reformation

1. Laws and orders

The tide turns dramatically with the accession of the Catholic Mary Tudor in July 1553. Even before any orders are issued, old practices resume in some places. According to Charles Wriothesley, on St Bartholomew's day, 24th August,

> the olde service in the Latin tongue with the masse was begun and sunge in Paules in the Shroudes, now St Faithes parishe. And likewise it was begun in 4 or 5 other parishes within the Citie of London, not by commandement but of the peoples devotion. ... | Againste the feaste of All Saintes the sacrament of the bodie and blood of Christe was hanged up againe in Paules churche over the highe alter under a riche canopie of cloth of golde, after the olde custome ...[1]

The first major statutory change also comes in the autumn with an Act of repeal. It renders void most of the religious laws passed under Edward VI and orders that from 20th December 'all suche divine service and administration of sacramentes, as were most commonly used' in the last year of the reign of Henry VIII are to be used 'throughe the whole realme of Englande ... and ... no other kinde nor order of divine service'. According to the diary of Henry Machyn, a proclamation issued to the same effect adds that every parish is to set up an altar and to have, among other things, a cross and staff, holy bread and holy water, and palm and ashes.[2]

Then, on 4th March 1554, Mary issues injunctions which make clear her wish to reinstate 'the laudable and honest ceremonies which were wont to be used', including 'all such holy days and fasting days ... as was observed in the latter time of King Henry VIII', along with 'all manner of processions ... after the old order of the church, in the Latin tongue'. Two weeks later, as Wriothesley records,

[On] Palme Sunday the old service after the use of Sarum in Latin was begun againe and kept in Paules and other parishes within the Citie of London, with also bearinge of palmes, and creepinge to the crosse on Good Fridaye, with the sepulcher lights and the resurrection on Easter daye. | Also the scriptures written on rood-lofts and about the churches in London, with the armes of England, was washed out againste the feast of Easter in moste parte of all the parishe churches of the diocese of London.[3]

In the summer Mary marries Philip of Spain, allying England with a major Catholic power. This prompts a rapprochement with the papacy, which sends Cardinal Pole to England to complete the process of reconciliation. At the end of the year the undoing of the Reformation is more or less completed by a second repeal Act which restores papal supremacy and renders void many of the relevant laws passed under Henry VIII, returning the country's official religion broadly to its position in 1530.* Prayers for the pope (Julius III) are now said in English churches again, and when he dies in the following year bells are rung for him across England.[4]

1554 A boke of collects to be saide for Julius tercius of that name pope ... 2d (Stanford, Berks)

1555 For ringinge of the bell at dirige and masse for the pope ... 23d (St Martin, Oxford)[5]

The darker side of the new regime is seen in the revival of heresy laws and the burning of nearly 300 Protestants, including Thomas Cranmer, who as Archbishop of Canterbury had compiled the Book of Common Prayer.

Meanwhile ordinary parishioners need to take care over their behaviour in church. In *Actes and Monuments*, his partisan chronicle of Protestant suffering, John Foxe tells of one Drayner of Smarden in Kent who,

being chosen justice, to shew himselfe diligent in seeking ye trouble of his neighbors, made in ye rodeloft nine holes, that he might looke about the church in masse time. In which place alway at the sacring therof, he would stand to see who looked not, or held not up his hands therto: which persons so not doing, he would trouble & punish very sore, wherby he purchased a name there, and is called to this day Justice nine holes ...

Later, when Protestantism has been restored, Drayner apparently denies having had any interest in 'who adored ye sacrament, or who not,' saying he used his rood loft vantage point 'rather to looke upon faire wenches' than anything else.[6]

The determination to achieve conformity is nonetheless real. A visitation in Kent in 1557 orders the vicar of Benenden not to 'minister the sacramente at Easter unto suche as will not crepe to the crosse' or to 'burie any that do refuse to be

---

* At least as far as it related directly to parishes. Monasteries and chantries were another matter, the large scale distribution of their assets into private hands making a return to the status quo ante impracticable.

confessed or to receive the sacramente', and several other ministers are similarly instructed. For not receiving the sacrament at Easter Elizabeth Poste of Ulcombe is ordered that

> she should openlie in the parish churche upon Sondaie nexte declare that in the sacramente of the alter there is the verie bodie and bloode of Christe reallie, and also that she should confesse that all the sacramentes, sacramentalles and all the ceremonies nowe used in the churche be good and godlie, and afterwardes to be penitentlie confessed to the curate, and then reverentlie to receave the blessed sacramente of the alter.[7]

2. Parishes return to the old ways

i. Recovery

One result of the wholesale reversal of religious policy is that parishes have to re-equip with a range of items disposed of only a few years earlier. In a few places the old items can be retrieved from storage, or at least hopeful search for them can be made.

> 1553 For fetching of ye table that is at ye alter from ye vicarage barne & for to do the drinke [for those] that set it ... 6d (Cratfield, Suffolk)

> 1553 In expences going abroad to seke for saints and other of ye churche stuffe that was lacking ... 6d (Stanford, Berks)

> 1553 In reward to Mr Sturtons at the receiving of 2 tabernacles, and for expense goinge about to seek for them in divers parishes ... 2s 5d (St Mary Woolnoth)

> 1554 For making serch for the chales ... 2s 4d (St Margaret, Leicester)[1]

Given the cross channel trade in forbidden paraphernalia during the preceding reign, the following may also refer to such an item.[2]

> 1557 To Steven Harte for bringinge over the roode out of France ... 20d (Lydd, Kent)[3]

Often attempts to recover old items encounter problems. The Kent visitation of 1557 is told at Newington that 'the vicar toke away the alter stones', while at Brabourne 'Sir Robert Haynes now vicar of Marden tok away ther latten candlestickes'. At Thornham a widow, Johanna Wood, admits having the canopy cloth but says her dead husband bought it, and she promises its return only if 'the churchewardens do repaye unto her againe the money that it coste'. At Rolvenden one Frencham, who 'boughte the organs of the commisioners', is more compliant. After being commanded 'that he sell not awaye the organs which nowe he hathe home in his house', and to appear 'to shew a cause' why he should not be compelled to restore them, he quietly yields them up.[4]

In most cases, however, the parish must start again.

ii. Altars &c.

Installing a stone altar is heavy work.

> 1554 Paid 4 men for to helpe up with the alter stones ... 4d | For a thousand of bricke for the two side alters ... 8s | For wax candles at ye consecration of ye alter ... 5d (St Mary Woolnoth)

> 1554 Paid Organ the mason for 10 days ½ about the altar and the steppes ... and for laborars to tend apon him ... 20s 5d | For the lone of 2 rollars to help in the altar stones ... 8d | For takin down the chanssell dore and pottinge uppe agenn to bring the altar stones in ... 4d (St Werburgh, Bristol)[5]

Once in place it needs to be covered, and any other recent innovations in the chancel may need to be reversed.

> 1554 For bringeinge in & settinge up the greate awlterstone ... 6s 8d | For here [hair] clothes for the hye awlter of 5 yardes longe at 7d the yarde and for makinge ... 3s 3d | For an awlter cloth of 4 elles of whited Normandye ... 4s 8d | For takinge downe the newe pewes that stoode in the chauncell, the backes towarde the awlter ... 1s 2d (St Michael, Cornhill)[6]

In addition the reserved sacrament needs to be suspended above the altar again.

> 1553 To Gregory Rowse for making of a pully for ye sacrament ... 12d (Cratfield, Suffolk)

> 1553 To Barrow for making of ye ierne that ye pyx hangethe on ... 6d (St Michael, Lewes, Sussex)[7]

Many parishes take a short cut to providing a stone altar, the 1557 Kent visitation finding a number using gravestones instead. At Sutton Valence they are ordered

> to take off the tombe from the highe alter and to laye the same in the olde place and to take uppe the alter stone that lieth in the ile of the churche and to laye it upon the alter and to cause the same to be newe consecrated and also to make inquisition of the residewe of the alter stones.

It turns out that the main stone 'lieth in the chimney of Master Harper'. Similarly 'the highe alter stone' of Hartlip has been taken to Norwood where it 'lieth in Master Nortons chimney'. Meanwhile at Smarden 'it is commanded that the alter stone be taken up that lieth in the highe waye and to be brought againe to the churche'.[8]

At Mere in Wiltshire they restore another important stone item.

> 1556 For two lode of stones with the cariage for the newe makinge of the crosse in the churchyarde ... 4s | To the masons for theire labor for the newe making of the same crosse ... 17s 6d[9]

iii. Images

More work and cost arises in recreating the arrangement in rood lofts, with a central rood flanked by Mary and St John being the minimum required. In the first case below it seems that the main item arrives by sea.

> *c.* 1554 Bringing the rood from London to the Strand, and thence to the church ... 3s 4d | Two iron candlesticks that stand before the rood ... 1s 8d (Rye, Sussex)

> 1555 To the carvar of Asshefforthe [Ashford] for the rood, Mary & John & for caringe of them home ... 27s 8d | To Pelland for iron to fasten the crosse in the rood lofte ... 4d | For bread & drinck to them that did helpe to have up & downe the ladders to set up the rood ... 9d (Smarden)

> 1556 To Peter the joiner for makinge the roode, Marye and John ... £8 10s | To a carpenter for the beame that the roode stondes on ... 17s | For carrige of the beame from St Giles and to get it in on rowlors ... 10d (St Michael, Cornhill)

> 1556 To the men of Winssowre [Windsor] for the making of the rode with Mary and John ... £5 | For our charges riding to Winsore to see ye rode ... 20d | To ye carpentars for making of the steyars and the dore [to the rood loft] and setting up of the rode with Mary and John, for 3 days worke ... 6s | For a seasoned borde to make ye dore of ... 12d (Wandsworth)[10]

Injunctions for Gloucester diocese issued in 1556 require provision of 'a decent rood of five foot in length at the least, with Mary and John, and the patron or head saint of the church, proportionate to the same, not painted upon cloth or boards, but cut out in timber or stone'.[11]

At Leverton, Lincolnshire, they opt for a cheap temporary solution but soon find themselves having to commission proper carved figures.

> 1556 For three yards canvas for a clothe to paint thereon the rood with Marye & John ... 20d | To John Knight for paintinge the same ... 3s 4d | 1557 Paid in going to Lincoln for to covenaunde [covenant, agree] the making of the rood, Marye & John, in expenses ... 4d | For bringing the saide rood, Marye & John from Lincolne 10d & for bringing from Boston 4d. | For charges in answering to a citacion for because the saide rood, Marye & John were not set up, in expenses ... 4s[12]

Similarly the Kent visitation reports that at Boughton Monchelsea 'the Marie & John and the patron of the church be not carved but painted'. At Queenborough 'they have no roode, Marye nor John but of painted clothe', but in their defence 'they say they never had other', and so are given some time to put things right.[13]

Fortunately many images in windows have only been painted over, in part to avoid the cost of replacing the glass, and the visitation orders this darkening to be

Tympanum in chancel arch, Ludham, Norfolk, probably commissioned in haste after the return of Catholicism, with the rood and attendant figures painted rather than carved

reversed. At Westwell they are 'to make cleane the images faces that be blotted in the glasse windowes', while at Barham they are 'to make the faces of the pictures in the glasse windowes white or els to take them cleane away and set in newe glasse'.[14]

iv. Paraphernalia

In order for churches to resume their old lives a number of other items are required, many of them associated with the performance of mass.

> *c.* 1553 For a masse booke ... 5s | For a manual and a dirige book ... 4s 6d | For a holy water vat and a paire of sensors ... 4s | For frankincense ... 5s | For 2 holy water sprinkells ... 2d | For a candelstick of 11 pound for the awlter ... 2s 8d | For a crosse of coper ... 6s 8d | For a sakring bell ... 4d (Louth)[15]

And across the country the old ceremonies resume.

> 1553-54 Received at the obit of Christopher Jennison ... 3s 4d | [Paid] for watching the sepulture ... 8d | For the pascal and Judas ... 12d | For 3 banner clothes ... 1s 4d (St Margaret, Leicester)

> 1556 For carryenge of the cross and canapeys, and to the clerke on Corpus Christi daye ... 6d (St Michael, Lichfield, Staffs)[16]

v. Texts removed

To complete the reversion the texts painstakingly added around churches only a few years earlier now suffer the fate that befell medieval images of saints at that time.

1553 To a plasterer for washing owte and defacing of such Scriptures as in the time of King Edward the VIth were written aboute the chirche and walls ... 3s 4d (St Benet, Gracechurch Street)

1554 For striking oute of the scriptur upon the rode loft ... 6d (Ashburton, Devon)

1557 For making of 3 serplys [surplices] of the cloth that hung before the rode-loft written with the Commandments ... 2s (St Margaret, Westminster)[17]

D: Under Queen Elizabeth

1. Orders and destruction

Despite a phantom pregnancy which sees bells rung across London in expectation, Mary dies childless on 17th November 1558, and Catholic England dies with her.[1]

The first law passed under her successor Elizabeth, in January 1559, is a Supremacy Act abolishing 'all usurped and forreine power and authoritie, spiritual and temporal' and repealing many of the other legislative changes made under Mary. It is followed by an Act of Uniformity which reinstates the Prayer Book of 1552, with minor alterations, and orders that 'suche ornamentes of the churche ... shall be reteined and be in use as was in the Churche of Englande ... in the seconde yere of the reigne of King Edwarde the Sixthe'. It also introduces a fine of a shilling for not attending church on Sundays and other holy days, the proceeds to go 'to the use of the poore' of the parish.[2]

In the summer royal injunctions are issued which in many respects echo those issued under Edward VI twelve years earlier. The bible in English is to be set up again and processions are banned, although this time an exception is made for perambulations of the parish bounds. Importantly for parish churches, the clergy are ordered to

take away ... and destroy all shrines, coverings of shrines, all tables, candlesticks, trindals, and rolls of wax, pictures, paintings, and all other monuments of feigned miracles, pilgrimages, idolatry and superstition, so that there remain no memory of the same in walls, glass windows, or elsewhere within their churches and houses ...

Altars are again to give way to communion tables, although to restrain Protestant enthusiasm the taking down of those still in place is to be done 'by oversight of the curate of the church and the churchwardens, or one of them at the least, wherein no riotous or disordered manner [is to] be used'. The 'holy table' is to be kept 'in the place where the altar stood', against the east wall. However, during the time of communion it is to be 'placed in good sort within the chancel' so that 'the minister may be more conveniently heard' by the communicants and to make the process of taking communion easier.[3]

The injunctions and related articles of inquiry form the basis for another visitation of the whole country. Many of those carrying it out are Protestants newly returned from exile during Mary's reign and are determined to root out all traces of the old religion. From the account by Sir John Hayward in his annals it seems their enthusiasm is widely shared.

> The orders which the commissioners set were both imbraced and executed with greate fervency of the common people, especially in beating images downe, breakinge and burning images which had been erected in the churches ... Yea, in many places, walls were rased, windowes were dashed downe, because some images (little regarding what) were painted on them. And not only images, but rood-loftes, relickes, sepulchres, bookes, banners, copes, vestments, altar-cloathes were, in diverse places, committed to the fire, and that with such shouting, and applause of the vulgar sort, as if it had beene the sacking of some hostile city.[4]

Charles Wriothesley describes events in London.

> Saterdaye the 12 of August the aulter in Paules, with the roode, and Marye and John in the rood-loft, were taken downe ... | This month also, on the even of St Bartlemewe, the daye and the morrowe after, were burned in Paules church-yarde, Cheap[sid]e, and divers other places of London, all the roodes and images that stoode in the parishe churches. In some places the copes, vestments, aulter clothes, bookes, banners, sepulchers, and other ornaments of the churches were burned, which cost above £2,000 renuinge againe in Queen Maries time.[5]

Meanwhile in Exeter, according to antiquary John Hooker, the visitors

> lodged in the dean's house, and during their stay, defaced and pulled down and burnt all images and monuments of idolatry, which all were brought into the churchyard of St Peter's. And they who in Queen Mary's days were accounted to be most forward in erecting and maintaining them, were now made the instruments to make the fire to burn them.[6]

Excesses lead to a royal proclamation in September 1560 'against defacers of monuments in churches'. It aims to prevent vandalism of those monuments which are designed simply to commemorate individuals 'and not to nourish any kind of superstition', but in many cases it comes too late.[7]

A few months later, in January 1561, the queen instructs the commissioners for causes ecclesiastical 'to order, that the tables of the Commandments may be comlye set or hung up in the east end of the chauncell'. Some parishes have already reinstated such texts and others soon fall into line.[8]

> 1560 To the painter for writing of the Scriptures in the church ... £1 11s 8d |
>   To Mr Davison, for taking it out of the bible, and for his pain to read it to the painter ... 1s 8d (Rye, Sussex)

1561 For the setting up of the 10 Commandements ... 12d (Molland, Devon)[9]

A further order in October balances conservatism and change. Fonts are to stay in their accustomed places and chancel steps need not be removed, but rood lofts must now be reduced, the old justification of preventing 'strife' being deployed again.

> For the avoiding of much strife and contention that hath heretofore risen among the queen's subjects in divers parts of the realm ... it is thus decreed ... that the rood-lofts ... shall be so altered that the upper part of the same ... be quite taken down unto the upper parts of the vaults, and beam running in length over the said vaults, by putting some convenient crest upon the said beam towards the church ...[10]

More generally, as seen in the accounts by Hayward and Wriothesley, the main result of Elizabeth's religious settlement in parish churches is destruction. As under Edward VI, **altars** are a prominent casualty.

1558 For pulling down of the aulters and carying away the rable thereof ... 3s 4d (Barnstaple, Devon)

1562 To a gallon of sack to the men that did helpe owte with the altar stones ... 1s 8d (Christ Church, Bristol)[11]

Images too are destroyed wholesale

1558 For defacing the images and whiting the places where the aulters were ... 2s | For burning the images ... 4d | To John Hosier for wood &c. that the images were burnt with ... 12d | To William Gryble for dressing of the places where the images were ... 1s 4d (Barnstaple)

1559 For taking down the angels ... 8d (St Margaret, Leicester)

1559 For taking down of the images ... 2s 2d | For their labor that carried the images to be burnt, and the drinking ... 10d (Ashburton, Devon)

1562 To Prime for ye scrapeing owt of the paintinges all ye lengthe of ye quire ... 16d (Long Melford)[12]

although some survive for quite a time.

1570 Unto Ireland for cuttinge downe the images hedes in the churche ... 20d | Unto Robert Jonson for whit liminge of the churche ... 40s | Unto him more for takinge downe the angels winge and removinge of his lether ... 12d (St Martin, Leicester)

1582 For pullinge down the idols ... 6d (Holy Trinity, Coventry)[13]

Images in windows are expressly mentioned in the injunctions of 1559, and in some places they suffer accordingly.

1559 To John Harode for blotting owt of the images of the glasse windoosse ... 4d (Heybridge, Essex)

1560 To Drane the glasiar for defacing of the glass windows according
[to] the quenes instrucions ... 6d | For glasing the same agene & all
other places amended ... £4 6s 8d (Chelmsford, Essex)[14]

In other places removal is considerably delayed.

1583 Hacker puttinge out the picture of the father in ye east windowe at
Mr Subdeanes commandement ... 4d (St Thomas, Salisbury)[15]

The tardiness is explained by William Harrison in his 'Description of Britaine'
(1577).

All images, shrines, tabernacles, roodloftes, and monumentes of idolatry are
removed, taken downe, and defaced; onely the storyes in glasse windowes
excepted, which for want of sufficient store of new stuffe, and by reason of
extreame charge that should grow thorow the alteration of the same into
white panes thorow out the realme, are not altogether abolished in most
places at once, but by little and little suffered to decaye, that white glasse
may be provided and set up in their roomes.[16]

In most churches the greatest labour and upheaval again relate to the **rood loft**
and its images. Typically the images come down first, in some cases having only
just been installed.

1558 To Edward Molle and his man for a daies worke for setting uppe the
images of St Marie and St John on the rood loft ... 5d | 1559 To Molle
for taking downe the images ... 7d | To Cotes and But for breking the
images ... 4d (Bungay)

1559 For taking downe ye rood, ye Mary and the John ... 16d | For bringing
downe of ye imagis to Rome lond* and other thinges to be burnt ... 12d
(St Mary at Hill)

1559 To John Rial for his 3 days work to take down the rood, Mary and
John ... 2s 8d | For cleaving and sawing of the rood, Mary and John ...
1s (St Margaret, Westminster)

1559-61 For takinge downe of the rode ... 6d | For the defacinge of the
images of the 12 apostles whiche were painted in the face of the rode
lofte ... 12d (Mere, Wilts)[17]

At Great Dunmow, Essex, the accounts record simply, 'Spent at the burning
of the rood ... 2s'.[18]

The loft may be taken down at the same time, but often it survives for a year
or two longer.

1561 Drink at pulling down the rud loft ... 4d (Woodbury, Devon)

---

* Romeland, a piece of waste ground beside the Thames at Billingsgate, owned by the
parish. In 1547 the churchwardens received 7s 'of a Spanyerd for lying his ship ther'.

> 1561 To Edward Molle and his man for taking down the perke [rood loft] ... 2s 8d | 1562 To a mason for stopping ye holes wher ye beame laye ... 12d | For making 4 sleeved surpl[ic]es of the clothe that was before the roodloft ... 2s (Bungay)

> 1561 For the pluckinge downe of the rowde lofte ... 4s | 1563 For stopping uppe the rode lofte dore ... 10d (St Petrock, Exeter)[19]

Some parishes need pushing to carry out the removal, perhaps because of the loft's usefulness, perhaps from attachment to the old ways, or perhaps simply because, given the disruption and cost involved, they would rather wait a while in case the country's religious position should be reversed once more.

> 1561 To the somner for bringing the order for the roode lofte ... 8d | To the carpenter and others for taking down the roode lofte [etc] ... 15s 8d (St Helen, Abingdon, Berks)

> 1563 Paid for the excomm[un]icat[ion] of my men because the rood-loft was not taken down ... 3s 5d (South Tawton, Devon)

> 1563 Spend by Mathew Travas in going to Chester [to see] wether the roode lofte could have ben licensed [and let] stand for the ease of the paroche ... 2s | For taking ... the roode lofte downe ... 4d (Prescot, Lancs)[20]

A visitation in Sussex in 1569 notes that in some places 'the rood lofts do yet stand though they were commanded to be taken down, and the timber of them that be taken down lieth still in many churches ready to be set up again'. At Lindfield money is spent 'in takinge downe the roodelofte' as late as 1583.[21]

In other places, too, they drag the process out. At Ashburton, Devon, the loft is 'pulled' or 'taken' down three times, or rather in three stages: first in 1563, eight men being being fetched for the purpose; second in 1576; and finally in 1579, when, after '2 dayes labour' the timbers are sawn and carried away.[22]

2. The fate of church goods

Such timbers are prominent among the items sold off by parishes after this second wave of destruction.

> 1558 Recevid of Thomas Clarke for the rowdelofte ... 23s 4d | Of Web the clarke for the broken peces of the rowdelofte ... 2s (St Peter, Cheapside)

> 1562 Of Pamers of Sudberye for gilte of the rode lofte and for the carved timber of ye same ... 26s | Of William Dashe for timber that ye rode stode upon ... 2s 11d (Long Melford)[1]

Vestments, cloths and banners are also widely sold for their material.

> 1564 Baner cloths and other stuff ... 6s 8d | St Hugh's cote, and others ... 6s 8d | 3 vestments and 1 cope ... £6 13s 4d (St Margaret, Leicester)[2]

Alternatively the offending part may be removed.

1568 To one William a singing man for the image of our ladie which was taken [out] of the blewe velvet alter clothe by the commaundement of the archdeacon ... 6s (St Mary the Great, Cambridge)

1569 For the taking out of the signe of the crosse out of an alter clothe, to Higges wife ... 2d (Ludlow)[3]

A range of other items are also sold, from handbells to angels.

1559 Of John Morlye for Latten bokes ... 6d (St Michael, Lewes, Sussex)

1561 For the leade of the holie water stoupe ... 3s 4d | Of Goodwin for 2 peces of ye crosse ... 20d (Bungay)

1562 Of Richard Marion for a hand bell solde unto him for [use as] the marquete bell ... 5s (Chelmsford, Essex)

1570 For the chalis ... 37s | For cherubims ... 20d | 1572 Of Master Marrys for wooden angels ... 4d (Stratton, Cornwall)[4]

As the above disposals suggest, the 'cleansing' of churches of paraphernalia associated with the old ways occurs unevenly and in some places only after much delay.

The process is well illustrated in returns provided to royal commissioners in 1566 by Lincolnshire parishes in which they list items used in Mary's reign but now considered superstitious or unnecessary. The questions put to parishes have not survived, but from the replies it seems clear that they were expected to confirm that each item had either been destroyed or put to profane use, showing the importance attached by the authorities to 'desacralising' formerly religious items so as to undermine whatever power they had previously possessed in the eyes of parishioners.[5]

The following are a few of the return entries, arranged by item type.

Altars

Our altar stones – broken and paved in our churche anno quinto [fifth year] Elizabethe. (Ashby de la Launde)

2 alter stones – one Mr Sheffield hath made a sinck of in his kitchine and thother maketh a bridge in the towne. (Croxby)

One alter stone sold to William Thixton and he caused it to be laide on his grave when he departed. (Owmby)

Bells

One sacring bell – William Eland had and hung it by his horse eare a longe time but nowe it is broken. (Burton Coggles)

Our handbell was gone out of our church (as our vicar saith) by a mad woman a yeare ago. (Market Rasen)

One sacringe belle which honge at a May pole toppe and what is become thereof we know not. (Waddingham)

Books

All the mass bookes and all bookes of papistrie were torne in peces in anno primo Elizabeth and sold to pedlers to lap spice in. (Aswardby)

A messe boke, a graile, a portess [portable breviary] and a manuell cut in peces before my lord of Lincoln 4 yeres sens when he was there preaching. (Branston)

Our mass booke with all the rest of the same belonginge to the popishe sinfull service was taken awaie by one South, the quenes majesties pursevant [pursuivant, messenger], anno primo Elizabeth, who (as he said) had authoritie to take ye same and what he did with it we knowe not ... (Market Rasen)

Cloths

To Robert Bellamee 2 corporax sold this yere wherof his wife made of one a stomacher for her wench and of thother being ript she will make a purse. | The covering of the pix sold to John Storr, and his wife occupieth it in wiping her eyes. (Branston)

Two banner clothes which [our] vicare had and he hath made curtaines for a windoe of them. | One cannapie which our said vicare had and he hath made a testor of a bed thereof. (Haconby)

All the banner clothes and crosse clothes were cut in peces by Sir Robert Towne our parsonne and made playing cotes for children of them. (Waddingham)

Images

Our images of the rood, Mary and John, with all other images – burned anno 3 Elizabethe. (Ashby de la Launde)

Rood, Marie & John were burned the last yere, to make a plummer fier which mended ye churche leades. (Croxby)

The rood, Marye and John and all other idoles and pictours, mass bookes, legend bookes and all other papisticall bookes and sermonyes [? ceremonies] was openlye burned at the crosse called the market crosse in the [first year of the queen's reign]. (Grantham)

Rood lofts

A rood loft – sold to Richard Langlandes of the said parishe since ... 1565 ... and is by the said Longlandes broken in peces who hathe now made a bridge for his sheep to go over into his pasture. (Boothby Pagnell)

The rood loft taken downe and the bordes thereof were nailed up at thest [the east] end of the churche to kepe oute raine and winde and the beames or postes thereof we have reserved to mend a common house in our towne. (Springthorpe)

The rood loft taken downe ... and seates made in the churche of the same for people to sit in. (Swayfield)

Paraphernalia

One crismatorie sold to a tinker but it was first broken in peces. (Aswardby)

2 pixes are defaced and given awaie ... this yeare unto a child to plaie with all. (Broughton)

One holy water vat of stone which our said vicare hath made a swines troughe of. (Haconby)

Easter sepulchres

One sepulcre – sold to Johnne Orsōn and he hath made a presse thereof to laie clothes therein. (Denton)

Sepulcre was broke & sold to ... William Storre and Robert Cappe who have made a henne penne of it. (Dorrington)

A sepulker – given to a poore woman five year ago who brent it. (Dowsby)

A sepulker – defaced whearof we made a bear to carie the dead corps and other thinges. (Stallingborough)

Vestments

Two vestmentes were cut in peces yesterdaie and sold to Thomas Waite and George Holmes and they have put them to prophane use. (Aswardby)

2 albes and two linen sheetes – cut in peces and given to three poor women. (Burton Coggles)

Two vestmentes – the one hath Thomas Wrighte of Horblinge and hath cut it in peces and made bedde hanginges therof and thother was given to Richard Colsonne a scoller and he hath made a players cote therof in anno primo Elizabeth. (Horbling)[6]

Those writing up the returns appear compliant in the disposal process, and even enthusiastic about it, but, as Eamon Duffy has pointed out, this is belied by the fact that in many cases they retained forbidden items for some years after they should have disposed of them.[7]

3. Hiding treasures

In some parishes such reluctance leads to cherished items being hidden away. In 1563 a visitation finds that at Briston, Norfolk, 'they have pictures and other superstitious things hidden in the rood-loft'. In 1567 five vicars of Ripon minster are accused of having taken 'the keyes of the church from one John Daie the sacristan there, and that night all the images and other trumperie were conveighed forthe of the said churche and bestowed by the said vicars where it is not known'. In 1569 the visitation in Sussex already mentioned finds that there are 'yet ... in many places ... images hidden up, and other popish ornaments ready to set up the mass again within 24 hours' warning'. In 1574 the vicar of Preston, Lancashire, informs his bishop that 'I digged of late in mine owne grownes [grounds] and found a grate number of alabaster images', perhaps buried by his predecessor, 'which I destroyed'.[1]

A few years later a more varied cache is discovered in Northamptonshire.

The 5 daye of October in ye yere of our lorde 1581 in ye towne howse of Scaldwell were founde sartaine images, & other monumentes of poperye, that is to say, ye picture of Christ called ye rood, ye picture of Saint Peter, bothe of woode undefaced, the picture of ye Trinitye & ye picture of Saint Mudwyn [Modwen] with her cowe standing by her, bothe of alabaster undefaced, & a table or tabarnacle of wood which in ye time of popery did stande upon ye aulter, with a great number of images appertaining to ye same, all of alabaster undefaced. In ye same howse was a coffer made of wood in ye which was 7 candlesticks of laten, the chrismatory, with ye oile & chrisme as it was used in ye time of popery, a pece of ye canapy that ye sacrament did hang under, the censers whole as they were used in ye church, one sanctus bell, & one hande bell, a wooden clappe, and a box of wood to fetch candlelight to ye church in ye time of popery, and sartaine socketes of laten, which were used either upon the sepulcher or else upon ye rood lofte.[2]

In some places those responsible for hiding images and other forbidden items are punished by being forced to burn them in public.

Among various cases in Yorkshire, in 1565 Edward Wreakes of Boroughbridge confesses to having kept books and vestments in a chest in his house. He is committed to York Castle and at his subsequent trial is ordered to

take the bookes and carye the same to the Pavement within the citie of Yorke and there to make a fier and burne them aboute one of the clocke tomorrow at afternoone declaring that he hathe offended in keeping the same ... and ... he shall carry away the vestments shewed in this court upon Satterday next to the said Pavement and there rip and sell the same and employ the money to the churche of Borrowbrige.[3]

Three years later John Lawson of Rothwell has to take an offending book to church and deliver it up so that the 'superstitious' parts can be 'cut forth'. After communion 'he shall prepare a fire to be maid at the church dore and there before all the people as they come forth of the church shall burne all the leaves cut forth of the booke'.[4]

A much larger discovery occurs at Aysgarth *circa* 1565. According to one of the Bishop of Chester's officers, on visiting the church he

did finde in a chest within the queare ... one pix with the canapie which was wont to be hung over the same, a crismatory, and a litle box for oile, a corporax with a case for the same, a super altare with certein other Latten books ... and in a valte or a holow place in the rode lofte [he] did finde two great images holie undefaced of Mary and John.

From the evidence of other witnesses it emerges that 'certein little images' were also found in the rood loft and that the Mary and John had previously been hidden in a lime kiln in the churchyard.

After some delay nine men are judged responsible for the concealment. Their punishment is that on Sunday 20th April 1567 they are to 'bringe or cause to be broughte all the same images to the church stile' on the west side of the churchyard. They are then to appear in church 'bare headed, bare foted and bare legged' with a sheet over their other apparel. After kneeling in the choir they are to 'stande besides the pulpit with their faces towards the people' and confess that they have

> concealed and kepte hid certaine idoles and images undefaced and likewise certaine olde papisticall bookes in the Latin tonge ... to the high offence of Almighty God, the breache of the most godly lawes and wholsome ordinances of this realme, the greate danger of our owne soules, and the deceaving and snaring of the soules of the simple, for the whiche we are now most hartely sorry.

Once the service is over they are to put on their ordinary clothes again and 'go to the same church stile and there burne all the images before so many of the parishioners as shalbe there assembled'.[5]

In a similar case at Askrigg four years later the curate and churchwardens are required to 'make declaration of their falte and cary the images to the fier and put the fier with their owne hands to them till the images be consumed'.[6]

Some concealments are more successful.

At Wakefield twenty-five images are hidden away in a chapel roof and only discovered in the 1750s.

At Flawford, Nottinghamshire, three alabaster images, one of the Virgin and Child, are uncovered in 1779 by workmen taking up the chancel floor.

At West Farleigh, Kent, a crucifix is found six foot below ground on Boxing Day 1832 by the parish clerk while digging a grave.

At Buckenham, Norfolk, a crucifix and an alabaster tablet carved with the martyrdom of a saint are wrapped in sedge and buried two feet below the chancel, where they remain until unearthed in 1840.

And at Epworth, Lincolnshire, the heads of a number of alabaster carvings (some of which are shown *right*) are found in a paddock near the church in 1843.[7]

Quite when these and other acts of concealment occurred is unknown, but it is likely that most were prompted by the three waves of Protestant vandalism presided over in the mid 16th century by Henry VIII, Edward VI and Elizabeth.

Other hidden items are presumably still lying in the dark, undiscovered.

Partially decapitated statue of St Margaret of Antioch found in the reveal of a window at Fingringhoe, Essex, in 1968. Whether it was concealed piously in hope of better days, or simply discarded and used to bulk out building material, is uncertain.

14th-century alabaster combining the Nativity with the Epiphany, Long Melford, Suffolk. The first magus or king proffers an urn containing gold, having already presented a golden apple; the second clutches a box containing myrrh; and the beardless third bears a jar of frankincense. On the left is the apocryphal Salome, holding forth the hand withered as punishment for her doubting of the Virgin Birth, while on the right Joseph catches up on some sleep. The tablet was probably among items which passed into the care of the local squire, Mr Clopton, in about 1548. At some point it was buried under the chancel, where it remained until recovered by workmen late in the 18th century.

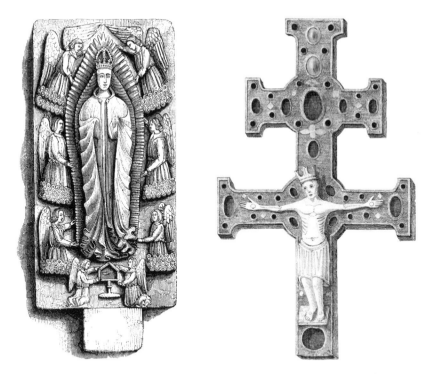

ABOVE LEFT Stone carving of the Assumption of the Virgin Mary, buried face down near the south porch at Sandford, Oxfordshire, and rediscovered in 1723.

ABOVE RIGHT & BELOW Crucifix and tablet unearthed at Buckenham, Norfolk, 1840.

Part 2: Civil War and Puritans in Power

The second great interruption to parish life begins with the outbreak of the Civil War in 1642 and lasts until the Restoration of the monarchy eighteen years later.

1. Church strife

Following the Reformation the Church of England is marked by ongoing tension between its Catholic and puritan wings, the former tending to favour hierarchy, ceremony and ritual, and the use of images and music as an aid to worship, the latter wishing to focus on scripture and preaching, to pare away decoration and ceremony, and to replace rank and hierarchy with a levelled world. This tension is part of the larger ongoing cultural struggle between conservatives/royalists/Cavaliers on the one hand and puritans/parliamentarians/Roundheads on the other, and as such it increases in the years leading up to the civil war. In particular it is exacerbated by the tenure of William Laud as Archbishop of Canterbury. Appointed in 1633, he seeks to restore the status of Church and clergy, to restrict puritan practice, and to impose a relatively ceremonious form of worship which his opponents see as 'English popery'.[1]

The most heated controversy involves the arrangement of the communion table or altar. Following the Reformation many altars/tables come to be placed as preferred by puritans, in the nave or at the west end of the chancel rather than at its east end, and oriented west-east as a table that can be approached by all, emphasising a sense of communion among equals.

> 1626   For the matte to kneele on
> round the communion table
> and for nailes to naile it downe
> ... 2s (Waltham Abbey, Essex)[2]

Laud and his followers, on the other hand, favour the pre-Reformation arrangement, with the altar (rather than table) set at the east end of the chancel and oriented north-south, emphasising the role of the priest and the sacrificial aspect of the eucharist. They also favour rails to protect the altar and having the chancel raised above the nave and separated from it by steps.

LORDS SUPPER.

Arrangements favoured by puritans and widely used until the Laudian reforms.
ABOVE From *A Booke of Christian Prayers*, 1578.
FACING PAGE From *A Course of Catechising*, 2nd edition, 1674.

1635 To John Carver for railing in the high altar ... £3 5s (North Walsham, Norfolk)

1636 To Boorows the joiner for the raile about the communion tabell ... £3 18s | To the mason & his man for 4 days worke about the raising & paving the chansell [etc] ... 10s 8d (St Clement, Ipswich)³

The spread of this 'Laudian' arrangement during the 1630s naturally provokes resistance from puritans.⁴

2. Ejection of scandalous ministers

In many parishes the rising conflict leads to the position of 'conservative' or cere-monialist clergy coming under threat. Puritan parishioners make their complaints not to the Church authorities – which they tend to oppose – but to parliament, and in December 1640 the House of Commons sets up a Committee for Scandalous Ministers to consider all the petitions submitted.* At first few ministers are ejected from their livings, but following the outbreak of civil war the purge gets into its stride. In late 1642 a new Committee for Plundered Ministers is set up to find livings for puritan ministers ousted from royalist areas, and in July 1643 it is given additional powers 'to consider of the informations against scandalous ministers' and 'to put out such as are scandalous'. Over the following years some 2,500 are removed, representing nearly 30 per cent of livings. In London, where puritanism and parliament are strong, the sequestration rate is as high as 86 per cent.¹

* While some of the allegations considered relate to conduct that is 'scandalous' in the modern sense, the word is here used to indicate ministers considered unfit for office by dint of heresy or unbecoming conduct. According to the *OED*, the earliest meaning of 'scandal' was 'discredit to religion occasioned by the conduct of a religious person'.

One early casualty is Nicholas Andrewes, vicar of Godalming, whose parishioners submit a list of fourteen articles against him in 1640. Among other things they allege that

1. He is a man much affected to his ease and pleasure [and] an enemy to preachinge ...
4. He is a haunter and frequenter of tiplinge in innes and tavernes, and useth gameinge both at cards and tables as well upon the Lords dayes as others ...
5. When he hath beene desired by some of his parishioners to church their wives at their houses, by reason of their weakenes and impotencie, he hath refused it ...
7. He is a greate presser and superstitious observer of innovated ceremonies ... as namely by his lowe and frequent cringeinge unto the font and comunion table, his preachinge of damnacon unto such as were covered in the sermon time,* and personatingt† them in the pulpett ... and by bowinge to the communion table in the time of the administracon of the sacrament ...
10. He is of a verie proude, presumptuous, imperious and tyrannicall caryage and disposition, encrochinge upon the rights and priviledgs of the parishioners, and takeinge upon him to alter and change diverse of their good and orderly customes and usages ...
11. He is popishly affected and keepeth in his house at the vicarage ... diverse crucifixes (whereof some are of greate price), one hanginge in his bedchamber, and another curious one is kepte in a boxe with foldinge windowes in his studie, and diverse Romishe pictures which he keepeth secretly behinde the hangings in his said house.
12. He and Mr Wayferar, parson of Compton, in the said countie of Surry, rode to Southampton to eate fishe and to make merrie togeather, and there (diverse times) drank healthes to the pope calling him that honest olde man.[2]

In such times the consequences are serious. Andrewes's benefices are sequestered in 1643, after which he is 'hurried from jail to jail, some time imprison'd on shipboard, and died under this barbarous treatment and confinement'.[3]

The charges against Andrewes are fairly typical, combining as they do accusations of personal misconduct, complaints about the conduct of services, and private dislikes and grievances. In many cases overtly political charges are added to the mix. For example, the first article submitted in 1643 against Mr Mapletoft, parson of

---

* 'No man shall cover his head ... in the time of divine service, except he have some infirmity; in which case let him wear a night-cap or coif.' (Canons of 1604, no. 18).
† *Personate*. Mention by name, describe satirically, mimic or impersonate.

Downham, Cambridgeshire, is that 'he usually preaches against the parliament and calls them a company of wicked rebels', while William Heywood, of St Giles in the Fields, London, has his living sequestered 'for being a most notorious rotten-hearted popish ceremonie-monger … and a most pestilent and intolerable malignant against the parliament'.[4]

Allegations of personal misconduct typically involve drink (as with Andrewes) and lust, and there are also cases of colourful language. Edward Jenkinson, parson of Panfield, Essex, 'hath compared the godly, reverend ministers living about him to *salt-bitches, which dogs runne after*, and to *roasted dogs, which draw away other mens pigeons*, because his people went to heare them preach, when they had no sermon at home'. Meanwhile Ambrose Westrop, of Great Totham in the same county, engages in 'most obscene medling and dilating on the secrets of women in the pulpit, abusively and familiarly comparing women to sowes, to make the people laugh, calling such women *whores* who refused to heare him thus speake in the pulpit, together with abundance of such-like most filthy trash'.[5]

The use of such personal and political accusations to reinforce religious ones, and so turn moderate opinion against the accused, is evident throughout *The First Century of Scandalous, Malignant Priests*, a catalogue of offenders published in 1643 by John White, chairman of the Committee for Plundered Ministers. In his epistle to the reader he condemns conservative clerics on all three counts: they are 'whoremongers and adulterers' and 'men swallowed up with wine and strong drinke'; they are 'ill affected to the peace and safety of the kingdome'; and they wish to 'have the people … impoisoned with the destructive errors of popery'. Further to prejudice the reader against such 'priests of Baal' he begins his catalogue with the case most likely to outrage contemporary opinion.[6]

> The benefice of John Wilson, vicar of Arlington in the county of Sussex, is sequestred, for that he in most beastly manner, divers times attempted to commit buggery with Nathaniel Browne, Samuel Andrewes and Robert Williams his parishioners, and by perswasions and violence, laboured to draw them to that abominable sinne … and [he] hath also attempted to commit buggery with a mare, and at baptizing of a bastard child, blasphemously said, openly in the church, that *Our Saviour as he was in the flesh, was a bastard* … and hath in his sermons much commended images in churches, as good for edification, and that men should pray with beades, and hath openly said, that the parliament were rebels … and that *Whatsoever the king commands, we are all bound to obey, whether it be good or evil*, and hath openly affirmed, that *Buggery is no sinne*, and is a usual frequenter of ale-houses and a great drinker.[7]

Ministers who refuse to bow down before the new orthodoxies face intimidation and worse, as Dr Daniel Featley, rector of Acton and Lambeth, discovers. In November 1642 his tithe barn at Acton, containing corn worth over £200, is burnt down by soldiers, who also break the altar rails and smash the windows in the church. A few months later, on 19th February 1643, worse happens at Lambeth, according to the royalist newsbook, *Mercurius Rusticus*.

> Even in the midst of divine service, at the reading of the *Te deum laudamus*,* foure or five souldiers rushed into the church with pistols, and drawn swords, affrighted the whole congregation out, wounded one of the inhabitants (whereof he soone after died), shot another dead, as he hung by the hands on the church-yard wall ...
>
> It was gathered by many circumstances ... that their principal aim ... was to have murthered the doctor, which tis probable they had effected, had not some honest inhabitants premonished the doctor, who was at the same time on his way toward the church, intending to have preached.
>
> About the same time many of these murtherers were heard expressing their rancour against the doctor thus: Some said they would chop the rogue as small as herbs to the pot ... Others said they would squeeze the pope out of his belly, with such like scurrilous and malicious language.[8]

A month later Featley appears before the Committee for Plundered Minsters to face seven charges submitted by a group of disgruntled parishioners. They include:

1. He ... preacheth for bowing at the name of Jesus, and doth bow at the name of Jesus himselfe ...
2. Whereas the communion table did stand in the middle of the chancel, [it] is new removed and is set up at the east end of the chancel, and three ways compassed about with railes, the said table standing divers steps high, and he boweth towards the east end of the chancel ... and [he] refuseth to give the sacrament to such as will not come up and kneele at the railes.
3. He preacheth for organs, shewing how necessary they are to be in churches ...
4. [He] said, that all those that pull downe the railes from the communion table, or speake against them, and oppose the ceremonies of the church, are of the seed of the serpent, and enemies to God.
6. When the doctor was demanded what moneys he would give or lend to the king or parliament, he used delayes in giving an answer, and at last would do nothing ...[9]

Featley, a noted theologian, defends himself robustly but is on the wrong side of the times and suffers accordingly. In September 1643 he loses his livings and is placed in prison where his health declines, and less than two years later he is dead. His last words are, 'The poor Church of God is torn in pieces.'[10]

---

* 'You, God, we praise'. In the Book of Common Prayer an English version of this ancient Latin hymn is read or sung after the first lesson at morning prayer.

3. Removal of 'superstitious' items from churches

Suspect ministers are not the only things to be purged. On 1st September 1641 the House of Commons orders

> that the churchwardens of every parish church ... do forthwith remove the communion-table from the east end of the church ... into some other convenient place; and that they take away the rails, and level the chancels as heretofore they were before the late innovations. | That all crucifixes, scandalous pictures of any one or more persons of the Trinity, and all images of the Virgin Mary, shall be taken away and abolished; and that all tapers, candlesticks, and basons, be removed from the communion-table.[1]

Puritan Nehemiah Wallington describes the result in his London parish.

> On the beginning of October, 1641, at [St] Leonard's, Eastcheap, being our church, the idol in the wall was cut down, and the superstitious pictures in the glass was broken in pieces, and the superstitious things and prayers for the dead in brass were picked up, and broken, and the picture of the Virgin Mary on the branches of candlesticks was broken. And some of those pieces of broken glass I have, to keep for a remembrance to show to the generation to come what God hath done for us, to give us such a reformation that our forefathers never saw the like ...[2]

In August 1643 there follows a more comprehensive Ordinance for the utter demolishing, removing and taking away of all Monuments of Superstition or Idolatry. It widens the range of proscribed items, ordering that

> all altars and tables of stone shall before the first day of November ... be utterly taken away and demolished ... And that all crucifixes, crosses, and all images and pictures of any one or more persons of the Trinity, of the Virgin Mary, and all other images and pictures of saints, or superstitious inscriptions in ... churches or ... churchyards ... shall ... be taken away and defaced ...[3]

In May 1644 a further ordinance extends things again. All chancel steps are now to be removed, not only those added recently. In addition it orders that

> all representations ... of any angel ... shall be taken away, defaced, and utterly demolished ... and that no copes, surplisses, superstitious vestments, roods ... or holy-water fonts shall be ... any more used ... And that all organs, and the frames or cases wherein they stand ... shall be taken away, and utterly defaced ... And that all copes, surplisses, superstitious vestments, roods, and fonts aforesaid, be likewise utterly defaced ...[4]

As a result parishes set to work, including in Daniel Featley's old church.

> 1643 To John Pickerskill for taking downe the railes that were about the comunion table ... 1s | 1644 To Edward Marshall for 2 dayes worke in leveling ye chancel ... 4s | To the carpenters for worke in taking downe the screenes betweene the church and ye chancel ... 13s (Lambeth)[5]

Crosses are among the items now to be removed.

1644 Paid an officer which brought an order to demolish the cross and other superstitious things about or in the church ... 1s (St Mary Woolchurch)[6]

In some cases the materials are sold, and for healthy sums.

1643 Paid for taking down the cross upon the belfry ... 1s 6d | Received of Mr North [for] 200 of lead taken of the cross on the belfry ... 18s 8d (St Helen, Bishopsgate)[7]

Fonts, which passed largely unscathed through the Reformation, are now replaced by simple basins.

1643-46 Received for the lead of the font ... 3s | Paid for the pewter bason for to baptize in ... 2s 8d (Wilmslow, Cheshire)[8]

In comparison with the situation a century earlier, churches now have relatively few images, but those there are must be removed along with any inscriptions considered superstitious, for example the Latin words *orate pro anima* (or *animabus*), pray for the soul (or souls), found on many tombs and monuments.

1642 To Ducket for takeing downe images at the font ... 1s (St Peter Mancroft, Norwich)

1642 To Wm. Glenne for new glasing the church-windowes when ye scandelous picktures were pulled downe by Acte of parliament ... 3s 6d (Woodford Halse, Northants)

1643 To the painter for washing the twelve apostles off the organ-loft ... 4s 6d (St Giles in the Fields)

Defaced font, Walberswick, Suffolk

1643 Paid Robert Miles free stonemason for scaffolding and use of boards and poles with his and other masons and labourers wages in taking away the superstitious images of the Virgin Mary and the angels attending her and framing them into another decent shape ... £9 | Paid the carvers for worke done by them in the like kinde in altering of images ... £3 8s 6d | Paid the carver for taking up and laying down with brass pins the monuments and defacing the superstitious inscriptions and cutting others in their stead that are not offensive ... £4 9s 6d | Paid Robert Miles for filling up the places where the superstitious images of brass were taken up and not fit to be put downe againe ... £1 4s 6d | Paid for the care and reliefe of a workeman that was hurt with a fall from one of the scaffolds ... £4 15s | Allowed for 77 lb. of old brass taken out of superstitious monuments ... 41s 9d (St Mary Woolchurch)[9]

At Chelmsford the church accounts offer only a simple record

1642 Taking downe pictures and setting up new glass in ye windows ... £5

but *Mercurius Rusticus* tells a fuller story.

There was standing in the chancel a goodly faire window at the east end, untouched from the first foundation of the church, in which was painted the history of Christ from his conception to his ascension: and ... in the vacant places there were the eschochions and armes of the ancient nobility and gentry, who had contributed to the building and beautifying that faire structure. In obedience to the order [of September 1641] the church-wardens tooke downe the pictures of the blessed Virgin, and of Christ on the crosse, and supplied the places with white glasse. But the sectaries ... did rest very ill satisfied with this partial imperfect reformation [and] on the fifth of November in the evening, all the sectaries assemble together, and in a riotous manner with long poles and stones beat downe and deface the whole window.[10]

While organs are only added to the list of prohibited items in 1644, in some parishes puritan enthusiasm runs ahead of the law.

1642 Spent of ourselves and 5 more that did helpe to remove the organes and take them in sunder ... 8d | 1643-46 Received for organe pipes ... 8s | Received for the organe case, railes and the cover for the old font ... 12s (Wilmslow)[11]

Roundhead soldiers purging a church,
from *A Sight of ye Transactions of these latter Yeares*, 1646

4. Iconoclasm in the east: William Dowsing

In most places the changes required by parliament are carried out peacefully by the parishes themselves. In parts of East Anglia, however, there is a systematic campaign of destruction led by a middle-aged Suffolk farmer called William Dowsing. In December 1643 he is commissioned by the Earl of Manchester, parliamentary commander for the Eastern counties, to remove superstitious monuments from churches, and over the following ten months he and a number of deputies carry out the task with fanatical zeal.[1]

Dowsing wrote a terse journal cataloguing the destruction, starting with the churches and college chapels of Cambridge in late December 1643 and moving on to the rest of the county in the new year. The following entries are fairly typical.

> At *Peter's parish*, December 30 1643. We brake downe 10 popish pictures, we tooke off 3 popish inscriptions of prayers to be made for theire soules & burnt the railes, digged up the steps, & they are to be levelled by Wedensday.
>
> *Brinkley*, February 20. I tooke downe 2 superstitious inscriptions in brass, *Orate pro animabus* [etc]. I brake 10 superstitious pictures, one of Christopher carying Christ on his shoulders, & gave order for taking downe 2 more in the chancel, & to level the chancel.[2]

At intervals he and his deputies are also busy in Suffolk.

> *Clare*, Jan. the 6th. We brake down 1000 pictures superstitious. I brake down 200, 3 of God the Father, and 3 of Christ, and the holy lamb, and 3 of the holy ghost like a dove with wings; and the 12 apostles were carved in wood on the top of the roof, which we gave order to take down; and 20 cherubims to be taken down; and the sun and moon in the east window, by the king's arms, to be taken down.
>
> *Sudbury, Peter's parish*, Jan. the 9th. We brake down a picture of God the Father, 2 crucifixes, and pictures of Christ, about an hundred in all, and gave orders to take down a cross off the steeple, and diverse angels, 20 at least, on the roof of the church.
>
> *Sudbury, Gregory parish*, Jan. the 9th. We brake down 10 mighty great angels in glass, in all 80.
>
> *Walberswick*, April 8th. Brake down 40 superstitious pictures, and [gave orders] to take off 5 crosses on the steeple and porch; and we had 8 superstitious inscriptions on the grave stones.
>
> *Blythburgh*, April the 9th. There was 20 superstitious pictures, one on the outside of the church; 2 crosses, one on the porch, and another on the steeple; and 20 cherubims to be taken down in the church and chancel, and I brake down 3 *orate pro animabus*, and gave order to take down above 200 more pictures within 8 days.[3]

The 'cherubims' at Blythburgh presumably are or include the roof angels, but fortunately for posterity the roof remains largely intact: perhaps the order was ignored, or perhaps the position of the angels rendered their removal impracticable.

Roof angels at Blythburgh, serenely beyond the reach of the iconoclasts

There is a tradition that Dowsing and his men shot at the roof to try to bring the angels down, or at least to damage them. However, during restoration work in 1974 the lead shot peppering the roof was found to be of a type which only came into use in the 18th century, and a 1761 entry in the church accounts includes payment for 'powder and shot to shoot jackdaws'.

Meanwhile at Walberswick the visit is recorded in the accounts. They show the parish, in common with others, having to pay for the vandalising of its church.

> 1644 April 8th. Paid to Master Dowson that came with the troopers to our church, about the taking down of images & brasses off the stones ... 6s | Paid that day to others for taking up the brasses of gravestones before the officer Dowson came ... 1s

It seems likely that this shows the parish assisting the iconoclasts, the 'brasses of gravestones' being the inscriptions mentioned in the journal.[4]

Some parishes, on the other hand, are certainly uncooperative. Ufford is first visited in January when a good deal is destroyed and instructions are left for the taking down of further 'superstitious pictures' and levelling the chancel. In May Dowsing sends a man to check on progress but he finds no sign of it and the wardens refuse to give him the key to the church. The result is a second full visit on 31st August when, as an indignant Dowsing notes,

> we were kept out of the church above 2 hours ... and now neither the churchwardens, nor William Brown, nor the constable James Tokelove, and William Gardener, the sexton, would not let us have the key in 2 hours time. ... And Samuel Canham, of the same town, said, 'I sent men to rifle the church', and William Brown, old churchwarden, said, 'I went about to pull down the church, and had carried away part of the church.'

Eventually the visitors gain access and set to work.

> In the chancel we brake down an angel ... and 12 cherubims on the roof ... and we brake down the organ cases, and gave them to the poor.

Dowsing adds a brief description of the church's most celebrated treasure: 'There is a glorious cover over the font, like a pope's triple crown, with a pelican on the top, picking its breast, all gilt over with gold.' It is tempting to see this as a sign that even Dowsing's iconoclasm has an aesthetic chink, but, as M. R. James pointed out, he is using 'glorious' critically to indicate something vainglorious, 'not handsome but pretentious'.[5]

5. Iconoclasm across the country

In other parts of the country damage is inflicted more haphazardly on those churches which happen to fall in the path of Roundhead soldiers.

In the summer of 1642 at Acton, Middlesex, soldiers 'defaced whatsoever was decent' in the church and 'tore the bible and Book of Common-Prayer, sticking the leaves of them upon the walls with their excrements'. In 1643 at Yaxley, near Peterborough, 'some of Captain Beaumont's souldiers coming thither, they break open the church doors, piss in the font, and then baptize a horse and a mare, using the solemn words of baptism, and signing them with the sign of the cross'.[1]

Similar sacrilege occurs at Lostwithiel, Cornwall, in 1644.

When the Earl of Essex was there with his army, one of his souldiers brought a horse into the church, led him up to the font, and made another hold him, whilst he sprinkled water on his head, and said, *I signe thee with the signe of the cross, in token thou shalt not be ashamed to fight against the Round-heads at London*, with a deale more of such blasphemous stuff; blowing up that church with gunpowder at their departure.[2]

More varied damage is reported at Sudeley, Gloucestershire, where soldiers arrive in January 1643. According to *Mercurius Rusticus*,

for each part of the church they find a peculiar way to profane it: the lower part of it they make their stable, the chancel their slaughter-house. Unto the pulpit ... they fasten pegs to hang the carcasses of slaughtered sheep. The communion-table, according to their own language, they make their dresser or chopping-board to cut out their meat; into the vault, wherein lay the bodies of the Chandoses, an ancient and honourable family, they cast the guts and garbage, mingling the loathsome intrails of beasts with those bones and ashes which did there rest in hope of a joyful resurrection. The nave or body of the church was all covered with the dung and blood of beasts, and ... they defile each part and corner both of church and chancel with their owne excrements; and going away left nothing behinde them in the church (besides walls and seats) but a stinking memory that part of the parliament army, raised for the defence of religion, had been there.[3]

Cathedrals offer more extensive scope for desecration. At Canterbury soldiers pull down statues with ropes while at Exeter they strike off their heads. At Lichfield soldiers stable their horses in the nave and 'every day hunted a cat with hounds throughout the church, delighting themselves in the echo from the goodly

Vandalism in action. LEFT From *The Times Displayed in Six Sestyads*, 1646.
RIGHT At Canterbury Cathedral, from the title page of *Mercurius Rusticus*, 1646.

vaulted roof'. They also bring in a calf, 'wrapt in linen, carried it to the font, sprinkled it with water, and gave it a name in scorn and derision ... of baptism'. At Peterborough they make a bonfire of the altar rails and carry the organs to the market place where they play upon the pipes and dance 'lascivious jigs'. At Winchester soldiers 'enter the church with colours flying, their drums beating ... and ... some of their troops of horse also accompanied them in their march, and rode up through the body of the church, and quire, until they came to the altar'. After destroying whatever they can lay their hands on, including various tombs, 'those windows which they could not reach with their swords, muskets, or rests, they brake to pieces, by throwing at them the bones of kings, queens, bishops, confessors and saints'.[4]

Meanwhile soldiers are quartered in Westminster Abbey in July 1643 and make themselves at home.

> They put on some of the singing mens surplesses, and in contempt of that canonical habit, ran up and down the church: he that wore the surpless was the hare, the rest were the hounds. ... They set forms about the communion table, there they eat, and there they drink ale, and [take] tobacco ... They did the easements of nature, and laid their excrements about the altar, and in most places of the church. ... Nay, which is the height of all impiety, they familiarly kept their whores in the church, and ... lay with them on the very altar itself, and did in that place commit such things as are unfit to be done by Christians.[5]

6. Soldiers in churches

Many churches suffer more casually as a result of the arrival of soldiers in the area. Perhaps the most dramatic instance occurs at Great Torrington, Devon, on 16th February 1646, after parliamentary troops under Sir Thomas Fairfax prevail over royalist ones. Fairfax's secretary, John Rushworth, describes what happens in a letter written next day.

> Many prisoners were taken and put into the church, but many more threw away their arms and escaped in the darkness. No sooner were we possessed of the town than the enemy's magazine, about eighty barrels of powder, which were in the church, blew up, whether fired by accident or on purpose we cannot yet learn. Many of the prisoners were killed, many houses defaced, and the whole town shaken. Some of our men in the churchyard were killed, and two great pieces of lead fell within half a horse's length of the General. One whole barrel of powder was blown out into the street without taking fire.[1]

Other churches, too, are used for holding prisoners, although without such explosive results.

1648 For taking down the windows and removing the things out of the church when the Colchester prisoners lay there ... 4s | For nailing up the church door when the prisoners were there ... 6d | Paid a tax for bread and cheese for the prisoners ... 9d | To a man for making clean the church after the prisoners were gone ... 7s 6d (St Peter, St Albans, Herts)[2]

The need to clean up after enforced occupation is typical.

1644-45 For mending seats in the church which the soldiers broke downe ... 3s 2d | To Francis Thackham for halfe a load of wood burned in the church by the soldiers ... 6s 6d | To Daniel Browne for making cleane the church twice, & for pitch & frankincense ... 5s | 1645-46 To Daniel Browne for watching in the church when the soldiers were here, & making it cleane when they were gone ... 2s 6d (St Lawrence, Reading)

1645 For taking downe the wall for the carryinge of straw into the church for the souldiers ... 6d | For making cleane the church when the souldiers went away ... 5s (Burford, Oxon)

1648 To Thomas Warman for clensing the church and for sweeting it and washing the seats after the soldiers ... 13s 4d | To him for mending the chimes and wires that the soldiers broke ... 3s (Bishop's Stortford)[3]

Items may be removed, either in petty theft or as a result of puritan zeal.

1645 What was received at the communions on April 13 and May 11, being about 30s, was taken out of the poor men's box by the soldiers at the taking of Leicester. (St Martin, Leicester)

1647 May 1st. The surplis and Books of Common Prayer were taken away by the soldiers. (Witney, Oxon)

1647-48 Paid Charles Deyman for preserving of the chalice from the troopers ... 13s 4d (Hartland, Devon)[4]

The church's lead is a natural target with a view to military use.

1645-46 Paid to souldiers for redeminge the churche leade ... 2s 6d | To redeeme the tower leade ... £1 8s (Newbury, Berks)[5]

And of course there are extra bodies to bury, as churchwardens' accounts record.

1643 For a shroud for a souldier that died at the Crosse Inne ... 3s | For another shroud for a souldier that died under Penylesse Bench ... 3s | For making of 10 graves in the churchyard for soldiers ... 3s 4d | 1645 To Goodman Carpenter for burying of poor souldiers at the Jewes Mount ... 10s (St Martin, Oxford)

1643-44 Paid for digging twenty-one graves, 7s, and for carrying six men and digging their graves, 8s. | Received for Henry Roe, a soldier's knell, 1s, and for Joachim Van Herne, a soldier's knell, 2s. (Basingstoke, Hants)[6]

7. Parish registers

The deaths of combatants also appear in many registers of the period.

> 1643 A souldier that came downe press'd with ye Earle of Essex, by his vocation a silke weaver of King strete in Westm[in]ster, in his returne from Gloc. [Gloucester] was consumed of vermine, died, & was buried September 29th. (Brimpsfield, Glos)

> 1644 Nov. 4th. A Scots man, a souldier, dying at Cornforth, the souldiers themselves buried him, without any minister, or any prayer said over him. (Bishop Middleham, co. Durham)

> 1645 The 14th day of August there were two soldiers killed, ye one at Alkmanton pistolled with two bullets in at ye backe and out at ye belly, his name as it said was George Harris, borne in Buckinghamshire in a towne called Grimslow. | At the same time was buried William Savage a soldier slaine at Hungrey Bentley. He was killed with a sword wherewith he had many thrusts. (Longford, Derbyshire)[1]

Those who desert pay a heavy price.

> 1642 Philip Greensmith a soldier was executed upon a tree at the green of Coton for deserting his colours, March 31st. The tree died by degrees. (Lullington, Derbyshire)[2]

There are also occasional civilian deaths.

> 1645 John Malley was attacked & had his house broken in sundry places by souldiers the first of November in the night & because [they] could not get in & he would not yield they shot him with a slugge into the heade & so died & was buried the 2nd day of November. (Longford)[3]

Perhaps the most notable burial entry of the period is a simple one.

> 1644-45 Jan. 11th. William Laud, Archbishop of Canterberry, beheaded. (All Hallows Barking)[4]

He had been executed on Tower Hill the day before, having been imprisoned in the Tower in 1641 and subjected to a show trial in 1644.

Parish registers themselves suffer as a result of the upheavals, with many gaps appearing. Memoranda are sometimes added in explanation.

> 1643 Here the register is defective till 1653. The times were such. (St Bridget, Chester)

> 1644-45 [Baptisms] Theare is maney that is unregestered by reason of Prince Ruperts coming into Lankieshire & this booke being hid for feare of the enimie taking it. | [Burials] From May 20 till February 2 this boke hath be neclected by reason of wars. (Croston, Lancs)[5]

8. Taking sides

Some parishes contribute actively to the conflict, whether by choice or otherwise.

1642 Oct. 15th. For the carpenters works of the floore over the stairs, where the powder and bullets and match lieth ... £1 15s | Nov. 3rd. Given to the officers of the Tower of London and labourers that delivered the powder, bullet and matche ... 14s | For the building and making of courts of guard and sluces* for the safetye of this towne, and for posts and chains in St James Street and King Street .... | 1645 To the beadles to drink while they watched the chains ... 1s (St Margaret, Westminster)

1642 Given to the clarke for goinge about the parish to give notice to the parishioners for bringing in old saddles [etc] ... 1s 6d | To the sexton and another for carriadge of meate when it was sent to the army at Brainford [Brentford] ... 1s (St Anne & St Agnes, Aldersgate)

1643 For bread and drinke for the people that went to dig in the trenches ... 6s 6d (St Katharine Cree, Leadenhall Street)

1644 For biskett and cheese which was sent to the souldiers in their marche to Gloucester ... 14s 9d (St Mary Woolchurch)[1]

The accounts of Stockton, Norfolk, chart the progress of one reluctant combatant.

1643 To John Bird at the christening of his childe ... 1s 2d | To John Bird for his presse mony ... 1s | For keeping of the said Bird after he was prest, foure dayes, & for two men to looke to him all that while ... 11s | To Thomas Goslen, John Bellard & Richard Revet also, for looking to the said Bird to keep him in awe ... 2s 6d | When we carried the said John Bird to Brooke ... 4s | 1645 Given to John Bird souldier when he returned home maimed from Naseby fight ... 2s[2]

Parishes also provide charity to some of those wounded or displaced by the conflict.

1643 Laid out to a company of folkes that came out of Shrop Sher and had bene plundred by the kings forses as they said and had lost all and did desier to be relevd ... 6d (Toft Monks, Norfolk)

1644 Given to Thomas Robins a poore man that was wounded at Edgehill ... 6d (St Ethelburga, Bishopsgate)

1646 Paid a poore souldier who had lost his eyes ... 6d | To two poore women whose husbands were slaine in the parliaments service ... 2s (St Bartholomew Exchange)[3]

---

* *Sluice* perhaps in the now obsolete sense of 'drawbridge'.

At Waltham Abbey they are even-handed.

> 1644-45 Given Ellen Goodwin & Marie Handin whose husbands were
> killed by the rebbles ... 2s | Given to John Cynes & his wife that were
> plundered in Devonshire by the king's forces ... 2s[4]

Notable victories and defeats, and the arrival of royalist and parliamentarian
leaders, are marked by ringing the church bells. In the early years royalists have
cause to celebrate.

> 1643 For ringinge at the cominge in of Prince Rupert, March the 11th ...
> 2s 6d | For ringinge the 25th of March for joy of the victory by Prince
> Rupert over the enemy at the seige of Newark, by special commaund
> of the mayor and governor ... 3s 4d (St Mary on the Hill, Chester)

> 1643-44 To Bushnell for watchinge on the tower ... 6d | For ringinge
> when the king was in towne ... 5s (Newbury, Berks)

> 1644 For faggots for a bonfire upon the routing of the Earl of Essex in
> the west, by the governor and mayors commands ... 3s 10d (St Peter
> in the East, Oxford)[5]

In some cases the relative amounts spent perhaps suggest the sympathies of
those involved.

> 1643-44 For ringing when the king came last to towne ... 10s | For ringing
> a peale when the Earle of Essex came to towne ... 2s 6d (St Lawrence,
> Reading)[6]

As the war goes on, however, the ringing is increasingly for one side only.

> 1646-47 Ringing when Sir Thomas Fairfax came through the towne with
> his greate gunnes ... 5s 6d | Ringers upon the publique day of thankes-
> giving for the delivering the castles and fortes into the handes of the
> parliament ... 8s (St Edmund, Salisbury)[7]

9. Innovations, from the Covenant to beheading the king

Away from the battlefield the parish faces a series of innovations. One is the
requirement for everyone over the age of 18 to take the Solemn League and
Covenant, a copy of which is sent to every church. It includes undertakings to
'assist the forces raised and continued by both Houses of Parliament, against the
forces raised by the king' and not to assist the latter in any way. The manner in
which it is to be taken is set out in an order dated 5th February 1644.

> The minister to read the whole Covenant distinctly and audibly in the pulpit,
> and during the time of the reading thereof, the whole congregation to be
> uncovered, and at the end of this reading thereof, all to take it standing,
> lifting up their right hands bare, and then afterwards to subscribe it severally,
> by writing their names (or their marks, to which their names are to be added)

i 6 a Solemn 4 3

LEAGVE AND COVENANT,
for Reformation, and defence of
Religion, the Honour and happinesse
of the king, and the Peace and safety of the
three kingdoms of
ENGLAND, SCOTLAND, and IRELAND.

We Noblemen, Barons, knights, Gentlemen, Citizens, Burgesses Ministers of the Gospel, and Commons of all sorts in the kingdoms of England, Scotland, and Ireland, by the Providence of God living under one king, and being of one reformed Religion, having before our eyes the Glory of God and the advancement of the kingdome of our Lord and Saviour Iesus Christ, the Honour and happinesse of the kings Maiesty and his posterity, and the true publique Liberty, Safety, and Peace of the kingdoms, wherein every ones private Condition is included, and calling to minde the treacherous and bloody Plots, Conspiracies, Attempts, and Practices of the Enemies of God, against the true Religion, and professors thereof in all places, especially in these three kingdoms ever since the Reformation of Religion, and how much their rage, power and presumption are of late, and at this time increased and exercised, whereof the deplorable state of the Church and kingdom of Ireland, the distressed estate of the Church and kingdom of England, and the dangerous estate of the Church and kingdom of Scotland, are present and publique Testimonies: We have now at last (after other meanes of Supplication, Remonstrance Protestations, and Sufferings) for the preservation of our selves and our Religion, from utter Ruine and Destruction, according to the commendable practice of these Kingdoms in former times, and the Example of Gods people in other Nations, After mature deliberation, resolved and determined to enter into a mutuall and solemn Legue and Covenant, Wherein we all subscribe and each one of us for himself, with our hands lifted up to the most high God, do sweare;

march · 22 · 1643

Preamble to the League and Covenant, bearing the old style date 1643
and showing congregations 'lifting up their right hands bare'

in a parchment roll, or a book, wherinto the Covenant is to be inserted, purposely provided for that end, and kept as a record in the parish.

Those who refuse are to be asked again on the next Sunday, and if they still refuse their names are to be submitted to the House of Commons, which will decide how to deal with them.[1]

1644 For a sheete of parchment and for wrighting the covenant in it ...
2s 6d (Weybread, Suffolk)

1644 Paid the scrivener for writing the names of those which would not take the League and Covenant 2s, and going to Westminster to deliver it and back, and spent 4s. (St Mary Woolchurch)[2]

Other changes are also unsettling to those of a conservative disposition. In 1644 an Ordinance for the better observation of the Lords-Day forbids sports, dancing, church ales and 'ringing of bells for pleasure or pastime' on that day. It also bans the Maypole, 'a heathenish vanity, generally abused to superstition and wickedness'. In the following year the Book of Common Prayer, which has formed the basis of services for nearly a century, is abolished, to be replaced by a Directory of Public Worship, and in 1646 the Church hierarchy is decapitated by the abolition of bishops and archbishops.[3]

A little over two years later it is the king himself who loses his head, the execution being recorded in boldly royalist terms in the register of Selattyn, Shropshire.

1648-49 January. Charles the first, King of Great Britain, France, & Ireland, defender of the faith, suffered martyrdom upon a scaffold before the gate of his royal palace of Whitehall in Westminster the thirtieth day. The memory of the just is blessed.[4]

Of the further changes made under the Commonwealth that affect parishes directly, the most important arise from the 1653 Act touching Marriages, which secularises procedure in several ways. It gives responsibility for conducting marriages to justices of the peace; offers those intending to marry the option of having the banns read in the market place on market days rather than in the church on Sundays; and places registers under the care of a new official rather confusingly called the 'parish register', who is to be elected by the parishioners.[5]

1657 Nov. 16th. Married John Vinall & Mary Suzen of West Firle before Harbert Morley esquire. | 1659 Oct. 4th were married Richard Swane & Dorothy Wolfe of Glynde, their bannes of matrimony having been thrice published in Lewes market by Richard Savage, register there. (Glynde, Sussex)[6]

In addition the purge of clergy is extended by an ordinance of 1654 for the ejection of 'scandalous, ignorant and insufficient ministers and schoolmasters'. The grounds on which they can be forced out now include countenancing 'any Whitson-ales, wakes, Morris-dances, May-poles, stage-plays, or such like licentious practices' or 'writing, preaching, or otherwise publishing their disaffection to the present government'.[7]

Bishops falling, from *A Decade of Grievances*, 1641. 'The tottering prelates, with their trumpery all, | Shall moulder downe, like elder from the wall.'

10. Royal arms: fall and return

In most churches the royal arms survive until the king's execution, although in a few they suffer in advance of the event.

> 1647 For puting out the kings armes ... 1s (Loose, Kent)

> 1647 Paid Hopes for defacing the K. armes ... 3s 6d (Holy Trinity, Coventry)[1]

In 1650 an order is made for taking down the king's image and arms throughout the country, and the arms are soon replaced by those of the state.[2]

> 1650 Charges for searching [for] the king's pickture and armes ... 1s (Houghton-le-Spring, co. Durham)

> 1650 For lime paches [? patches] and workmens wages for the deabolishing of the kinges armes according as an order from the parliament did injoine it to be done ... 2s (Wilmslow, Cheshire)

> 1650 To the glazier for mending the church windowes & for takeing out all monarchiall armes ... 17s 9d | To my lord mayors clerke for writing a ticket to certifie [to] my lord mayor the pulling downe and demolishing of the late kings armes in our church ... 1s 6d | Painting the Commonwealths armes ... £4 10s (St Alphage, London Wall)[3]

The accident recorded in the following burial register entry at Faversham, Kent, perhaps affords scope for royalists to point a moral.

> 1650 March 23rd. John Cooke, sexton. By taking down the prince's arms in the church fell from the lather [ladder] and after died.[4]

The state's arms are in turn taken down at the Restoration, with individual craftsmen sometimes replacing their own work.

> 1650 To Robert Smedley for painting of the Commonwealths arms in the chancel ... 21s | 1660 To Thomas Kaye and his sonne for one days work in making scaffold for the erecting of his majesties arms over the chancel door ... 2s 3d | To Robert Smedley for setting up his majesties arms in the chancel [etc] ... £5 (St Mary, Beverley, Yorks)

> 1651 Paid John Dixon and John Wren for defacinge the kings arms and setting up the states arms with nailes, hooks and rearing of ladders ... £1 2s 4d | 1660 Paid John Dixon for makeing the kings arms ... £2 12s 6d (Abbey Church, Shrewsbury)

> 1660 To Mr Isborne for painting the king's armes ... £4 | For ringinge when the king's armes were set up ... 5s 6d (St Peter Mancroft, Norwich)[5]

On 9th April 1661 Pepys attends a sale by candle. 'Among other things sold, there was all the state's armes, which Sir W. Batten bought, entending to set up some of the images in his gardens and the rest to burn on the coronacion night.'[6]

11. Restoration

Restoration of the old order is widely marked by bell-ringing and other celebration.

> 1660 April 16th. For a bonfire and ringing upon ye kings majesties returne into England ... 4s 6d (St Peter in the East, Oxford)

> 1660 For ringing all night, when the king came to London [29th May] ... 12s (Holy Trinity, Coventry)

> 1660 For candles that night that they did ringe for the king's coming into London ... 1d (Wilmslow, Cheshire)

> 1660 Spent the day the king was proclaimed upon the ringers and drummers ... 13s (Wrington, Somerset)

> 1661 For ringing on the coronation [23rd April] ... £1 | To the town waits for playing ... £2 10s | Delivered to them in bread and wine ... 5s 2d | To several porters which brought in the blew cloths into the vestrie, that the king walked upon at his coronation ... 17s 6d | For a hogshead of French wine which ran at the coronation ... £8 | To Henry Richards for making of a scaffold in the engine-house, to set the hogshead of wine upon ... 5s (St Margaret, Westminster)[1]

It is also recorded with feeling in many parish registers.

> 1660 Charles the Second, at our bonefire in this parish, was proclaimed king &c. ye 29 of May, by me, with soleme prayers, praises, alms, and other triumphs. Then also I was restored to my rectory here. *Sit nomen Domini benedictum* [The Lord's name be praised] &c. (Burgh St Peter, Norfolk)[2]

The writer of this entry, Henry Watt, is one of the fortunate royalist clergy who survive to recover their livings under an Act for the Confirming and Restoreing of Ministers, passed in 1660, which also sees nearly 700 puritan ministers ejected.[3]

Another early change is noted by Pepys on 17th June of the same year: 'This day the organs did begin to play at White-hall before the king.'[4]

A slightly modified prayer book takes a little longer, but is introduced in conjunction with an Act of Uniformity in 1662 and remains the official prayer book of the Church of England to the present day.

> 1663 For the common prayer booke and the gettinge of him ... 8s 8d (Locking, Somerset)[5]

Meanwhile fonts are reinstated or replaced and used once again.

> 1660 May 4th. Jane, daughter of Thomas and Vrey Browne, and the first child was baptised in the font since it was Anabaptistacaly abused. (St Dunstan, Canterbury)

> 1662 For making the font and other charges ... £8 5s 6d | To eight porters for carrying of the font to the church ... 3s (St Andrew, Plymouth)[6]

The process of recovery is sometimes recorded.

1661 Feb. 4th. Agreed, that the font of stone formerly belonging to the church shall be set up in the antient place, and that the other now standing near the desk be taken down. | 1662 Paid widow Smith for the font stone, being the price her husband paid for it ... 7s (St Martin, Leicester)

1661 August the 1st. The font of All Saints was set up this day by Cuthbert Maxwell of this town, mason, who had saved it about twenty years before from the barbarous hands of the Scots armie, who did indeavour to breake it. (All Saints, Newcastle)

1662 Paid for getting of the font stone out of Mr Bickerton's garden ... 1s | Spent upon those men that fetcht it, & the servants who showed them to it ... 1s | Paid for drawing of the font stone to the church from Mr Bickerton's ... 1s | Paid unto Ralph Downam for the setting up of the font stone ... 12s (St John the Baptist, Chester)[7]

As for the vexed question of the position of the communion table, on 6th April 1662 John Evelyn notes with satisfaction in his diary that, 'being of the vestry [of St Nicholas, Deptford], in the afternoon we ordered that the communion table should be set (as usual) altar-wise, with a decent rail in front, as before the rebellion'. While this is the new norm, puritan ways persist for some time in many places. Parochial visitations in Essex in the 1680s, for example, find many churches still adhering to the old arrangement and issue instructions accordingly.[8]

1685 The table must be placed altarwise under ye east window in ye chancel, and a comunion rail to be provided and set before ye comunion table, and the seates that are in ye chancel must be removed. (Thundersley, Essex)[9]

Altar rails, Woodbury, Devon

Part 3: Plague and Fire

Plague

Parishes are also disrupted, and in even more deadly fashion, by the periodic arrival of plague.

1. Outbreak

A relatively early mention of plague in parish accounts occurs at All Saints, Oxford. Several of the victims are attached to Lincoln College, including a boy servant of the rector and a bible clerk.

> 1507 For waching-candels* for the poore childe ... 1½d | For his shroud and making his pit ... 8d | For ringing and the mese-penne† ... 5d | To a woman that kepe him 2 nights and 2 days ... 8d | For treacle‡ ... ½d | For Henry that rede the bibell, for singing [requiem mass] and his pit ... 6d | To the woman that kepe him, and his shroud ... 6d | To two women [who] clend Henry's chamber ... 2d (All Saints, Oxford)[1]

A major outbreak of another infectious disease, sweating sickness, in 1551 gives rise to various familiar names.

> 1551 June. The swatt, called *New acquyntance*, alias *Stoupe knave and know thy master* began the 24th of this monthe. (Loughborough, Leics, note in register)[2]

According to Thomas Hancock, minister of Poole in Dorset, it 'posted from towne to towne throughe England and was named *Stope gallant*, for it spared none, for they were dancing in the courte at 9 a'clocke that were dead [bef]or eleven a'clocke'. In the same vein a note in the margin of the register of Uffculme, Devon, refers to it as 'the hote sickness, called *Stup-gallant*'.[3]

Sometimes, as at Loughborough, the register notes ominously the arrival of contagion.

> 1592 Sep. 12th. —, ye first of ye plague, out of ye Red Lion taverne. (St Michael, Cornhill, burial)

> 1597 Here began the sicknes, 21 May, 1597. [Entries for 93 burials follow, including those of the vicar and parish clerk.] (Stranton, co. Durham)[4]

Those believed to have brought the sickness into the parish may be identified.

---

* *Watching candles*, placed around the corpse before burial.
† *Mass-penny*. Offering made for having a mass said, especially for one who has died.
‡ In the now largely obsolete sense of a medicinal compound, originally a kind of salve. Venice treacle, among others, was often recommended against plague.

1578 August 10th. Lore, the wife of Jo. Smith. | This Lore Smith was ye instrument the Lord used to bring the infecon of the plague into this towne. She was the first that died of that infectious sicknes, and the most of these that followed died of the same, until the cold winter time came, when the Lord in mercie stayed the same. The woman was commonlie noted to be a notable harlot. (Coggeshall, Essex)

1606 December. Henry Renoulds was buried the 16 day. [In margin:] Henry Renoulds came from London where he dwelt, sicke of the plague and being received by William Browne, died in his house. The said William soon after fell sicke of the plague and died, so did his sonne, his daughter, and his servant; only his wife and her maide escaped with soars. The plague brought by this means to Peterburgh continued there till September following. (St John the Baptist, Peterborough)

1665 Jeremy Read, of Gillingham in Kent, bringer of the plague, of which died about 30 persons out of Sunderland in 3 months – buried 5 July. (Bishopwearmouth, co. Durham)[5]

A more forgiving record shows the impact on an individual household.

1647 N.B. My daughter Sarah Lenthall was buried ye eleventh day of August. She came from London to Wickham and on ye Saturday only to see us and so to returne ye morrow in ye afternoone to Wickham againe, but then fell sick and on Wednesday morning following being ye 11th of August about an houre before sun rise died of ye sickness, and so in ye evening we buried her in ye meade called ye Kitchenmeade by ye hedgeside as you go downe into it on your left hand, a little below ye pond at ye entrance into ye meade. She was aged 14 yeares, eleven months and seventeene dayes — had she lived to Bartholomew day she had bin full 15 yeares of age. | Susanna Lenthall my wife departed this life Thursday evening about 8 a clock ye 26 of August. She died of ye sickness comfortably and in peace and was buried August ye 27 by her daughter Sarah. | John Gardiner a child that lived in my house died of ye sickness and was buried August ye 29th. | Adrian Lenthall my sonne a hopefull yong man and were one and twenty yeares of age departed this life of ye sickness, Thursday morning a little before day breake and was buried at ye head of his sister Sarah's grave ye same day, being ye 2d of September. | My cosen John Pickering a lad about 13 yeares of age, dying of ye sickness, was buried the 25 of September 1647. | Robert Lenthall, rector. (Great Hampden, Bucks)[6]

During outbreaks the registers of populous parishes include page after page of simple lists of names, often with 'Plague' or 'P' appended to indicate the cause of death in each case. At Loughborough in 1611 'A plague, a plague, a plague' is written across the tops of several pages.[7]

A note in another register paints a dramatic picture of what may be involved.

> 1665 The plague takes them very strangely, strikes them black one side &
> then they run mad, some drown themselves, others would kill themselves,
> they die within few hours, some run up & down the streets in their shirts
> to the great horrour of those in the city. (St Mary on the Hill, Chester)[8]

Perhaps the most striking entry occurs at Malpas, Cheshire, where the burials
of nine members of the Dawson household are recorded.

> 1625 Richarde Dawson, being sicke of the plague, and perceiveing he must
> die at that time, arose out of his bed, and made his grave, and caused his
> nefew, John Dawson, to cast strawe into the grave, which was not farre
> from the howse, and went and laid him down in the said grave, and
> caused clothes to be laid upon, and so departed out of this world; this he
> did because he was a stronge man, and heavier than his said nefew and
> another wench were able to burye. He died about the 23th of August ...[9]

2. Prevention

i. Appealing to God

Plague is seen as God's just punishment for the sins of mankind. During an outbreak
in 1597 William Eddye, vicar of Cranbrook, Kent, notes among various significant
points that it 'began in the house of one Brightlinge, out of which much thieving
was committed, and that it ended in the house of one Henry Grymocke, who was
a pot companion and his wife noted for much incontinency which both died
excommunicated'. Moreover, 'the infection was got almost into all the inns and
victualling houses of the town, places then of great misorder, so that God did seem
to punish that himself which others did neglect and not regard'.[1]

The correct response to the arrival of plague is therefore to fast and pray and
amend one's life in the hope that He will relent. Accordingly, during severe outbreaks
the government issues prayers to be said in churches.

> 1563 For ye booke of prayers for the plague ... 6d (Stoke Charity, Hants)

> 1592 For 2 bookes of prayer to be read in the time of plague ... 4d (St
> Ethelburga, Bishopsgate)

> 1625 2 bookes of the newe prayers to God for staye of the plague ... 2s
> (Winterslow, Wilts)[2]

Fasts are observed to the same end.

> 1602 For two bookes for the fast for Wednesdays and Fridays for the
> present time of sickness ... 8d (St Ethelburga, Bishopsgate)

> 1603 To John Simson for ye lending of black cotton at ye fast ... 2d
> (Worksop, Notts)[3]

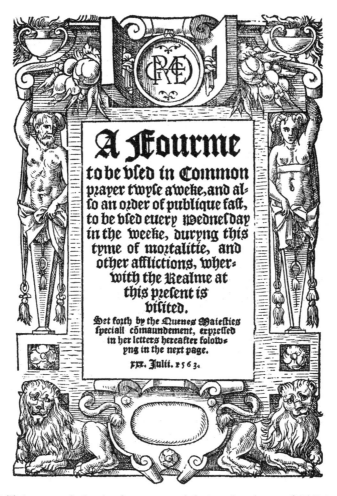

ABOVE Title page of a book of prayers used during the plague of 1563 in parishes including Stoke Charity. BELOW A well-attended sermon at St Paul's Cross, 1625.

The responses of parishioners naturally vary. 'This was most grievous unto me of all,' notes William Eddye at Cranbrook, 'that this judgment of God did not draw the people unto repentance the more, but that many by it seemed to be more hardened in their sin.' On the other hand

> 1576 For bread and wine at the comunion ministred by Mr Price about the feaste of St Michael, at wiche time a great nombre of every parishe in the town did receve in the time of plague ... 3s 8d (St Mary, Shrewsbury)[4]

ii. Tackling perceived sources of infection

As it is believed that God acts through the material world, another option is to address the perceived physical causes of plague, infected air being widely suspected. In directions 'for this time of pestilential contagion' in 1603, Francis Hering advises,

> Let the aire be purged and corrected, especially in evenings which are somewhat cold, and in places low and neare the river (as Thames streete and the allies thereabout) by making fires of oaken or ash wood, with some few bundels of juniper cast into them. | Let men in their private houses amend the aire by laying in their windowes sweete herbes, as marjoram, time, rosemarie ... Likewise by burning juniper, rosemarie, time, bay-leaves, cloves, cinamon, or using other compound perfumes. The poorer sort may burne wormewood, rue, time.[5]

A similar approach is still in place sixty year later. According to directions issued by the College of Physicians in 1665,

> Fires made in the streets often, and good fires kept in and about the houses of such as are visited, and their neighbours, may correct the infectious air; as also frequent discharging of guns. | Also fumes of these following materials: rosin, pitch, tarre, turpentine, frankincense, myrrhe, amber; the woods of juniper, cypress, cedar; the leaves of bays, rosemary ... | Brimstone burnt plentifully in any room or place, though ill to be endured for the present, may effectually correct the air for the future. ... | Such as are to go abroad shall do well to carry rue, angelica, masterwort, myrrhe, [etc].[6]

Parishes in London are therefore ordered to burn fires in the streets to help prevent contagion.

> 1603 For pitch and faggotts that were burnt in ye streete by my lord mayors command ... £1 15s (St Benet, Gracechurch Street)

> 1626 For earthen pannes, charcolles, stove, pich, francomsense and incence to burne in the streats accordinge to my lord mayor his order ... £1 8s 4d (St Christopher le Stocks)[7]

On 6th September 1665 Samuel Pepys sees 'fires burning in the street ... by the lord mayors order', and then, on a boat journey, 'all the way fires on each side of the Thames'.[8]

Various items are also burnt inside churches, frankincense being particularly popular.

1563 For francinsense to aire the church ... 1d (St Mary Woolnoth)

1603 For pitch, rosen and frankincense to perfume ye church after Tom his goinge out of the steeple ... 8d | For makinge a cabin for Tom ... 21d* | 1605 For 5 pounds of pitch to perfume the church after the buriall of Widowe Tropp, for she died of the sicknesse ... 8d (St Mary on the Hill, Chester)

1666 For three chafing dishes,† resin, franckincense and tobacco sticks to burn in the church in the time of the visitation ... 1s 6½d (Basingstoke, Hants)[9]

In the following case particular care is taken, apparently because one of those who work in the church has been infected.

1638 To John Carre's wife for washinge the carpet and cerplis when Thomas Adkins first fell sick of the plagee ... 1s | To John Carre's wife in the same case for airinge the church bookes ... 6d | For pitch, tarre and roszen to perfume and aire the church at the sickness time ... 2s (St Giles, Northampton)[10]

It is also believed that dogs carry infection, with the result that orders are issued for their destruction. For example in 1608 the Lord Mayor of London instructs 'that no hogges, dogges, or cattes, or tame pigeons, or conies be suffered to be kept within any parte of the citie ... and that the dogges be killed by the dog killers, appointed for that purpose'. The result is canine carnage.[11]

1563 To John Welch for the killing and carrying away of dogs during the plague, and for putting of them into the ground, and covering of the same ... 3s 2d | 1592 To the dog-killer for killing dogs the first time of infection ... 16s | More to the dog-killer for killing more dogs ... 10s 10d | 1625 To the dog-killer for killing of 24 dozen of dogs ... £1 8s (St Margaret, Westminster)

1593 [Vestry] September. It was ... agreed that Daniell Stocken of West-minster should kill the dogges of this parishe, and to allowe unto him for killinge of every dogges 2d. | [Accounts] Paid ye 16th day unto ye dogge killer for killinge of dogges ... 3s 4d (St Martin in the Fields)

1644 To a souldier for killing dogs in the streets in the time of infection, by warrant from Mr Mayor ... 2s (St Martin, Oxford)[12]

---

* It seems likely he had the plague. Cabins were built beside the river and in quarries outside the city walls to provide isolated accommodation for the infected, and the parish made 'collections for the cabins'.
† Vessels to hold burning charcoal or other fuel.

Humans, particularly strangers, are also feared.

1603   To Walter Parker and Hickson for keepinge the townsfolke of
       Tythe and Asswell out of our market being suspected for the plague ...
       6d (Melton Mowbray, Leics)

1626   To the visited maid that lay at the Burie ... 3s | For a passport to
       send her awaie ... 4d (Waltham Abbey, Essex)

1636   Paid a warder to keepe out strangers at church in the chiefest time
       of the plague ... 3s (Mortlake, Surrey)

1772   For a warant to warne those persons that wached by ye water side to
       keep out ye ships that come beyond sea where ye plague was ... 10s 1½d
       (Widdecombe, Devon)[13]

3. Orders for plague time

According to orders issued in 1578 by Queen Elizabeth, in towns

the houses of such persons out of the which there shall die any of the
plague ... or where it shall be understood that any person remaineth sicke
of the plague, [are] to be closed up on all parts during the time of restraint,
viz. sixe weekes after the sicknesse be ceased in the same house ...

It is accepted that in more rural areas the inhabitants may need to leave their
houses 'for the serving of their cattel, and manuring of their ground', but they are

to be neverthelesse restrained from resorting into companie of others ...
during the said time of restraint, and to weare some marke in their uppermost garments, or beare white rods in their hands at such time as they
shall go abroade ...

Should there be any doubt as to compliance,

then shall there be appointed two or three watchmen by turnes ... to attend
and watch the house, and to apprehend any person that shall come out of
the house contrary to order, and [those so offending] shall be a competent
time imprisoned in ye stocks in the highway next to the house infected:
and furthermore, some special marke shall be made and fixed to the doores
of every of the infected houses ...

'Certaine persons' are to be appointed

to provide and deliver all necessaries of victuals ... to keepe such as are of
good wealth being restrained at their owne proper charges, and the poore
at the common charges: and the said persons so appointed [are] to be
ordered, not to resort to any publique assemblie during the time of such their
attendance, as also to weare some marke on their upper garment, or to beare
a white rod in their hande, to the ende others may avoide their companie.

Every parish is also to have people, commonly called 'searchers',

> to view the bodies of all such as shall die, before they be suffered to be buried, and to certifie the minister of the church and churchwarden ... of what probable disease the said persons died: and the saide viewers [are] to have weekly some allowance ... and the choice of them to be made by direction of the curate of the church, with three or foure substantial men of the parish.

In addition, there is to be established

> some place apart in each parish for the burial of such persons as shall die of the plague ... They [are to] be buried after sunne setting, and yet never-thelesse by daylight, so as the curate be present for the observation of the rites and ceremonies prescribed by the lawe, foreseeing as much as conveniently he may, to be distant from the danger of infection of the person dead, or of the companie that shall bring the corse to the grave.[1]

These national orders are repeated more or less verbatim in subsequent outbreaks, for example in 1593, 1603 and 1625.

Separate orders are issued for London by the lord mayor which vary in some respects from the national ones and tend to be more detailed. Those issued in 1608, for example, include more specific instructions regarding the manner of identifying affected dwellings.

> Every house visited [is to] be marked with a red crosse of a foote long, in the middle of the doore, evident to be seene, and with these usual printed wordes: that is to say, *Lord have mercy upon us*, to be set close over the same crosse, there to continue until lawful opening of the same house.

> Rods are also to be red (a change made back in 1583) and are to be carried by more of those involved.

> The searchers, chirurgions [surgeons], keepers and buriers are not to passe the streetes without holding a redde rodde or wand of three foote in length, in their hands, open and evident to be seene ...

Examiners are to be appointed 'to enquire and learne ... what houses in every parish be visited ... and if they find any persons sicke of the infection, to give order to the constable, that the house be shut up'. It is then to be attended by a day and a night watchman, and should either of them need to be absent on other business he is 'to locke up the house, and take the key with him'.[2]

As for burial, it can now take place 'either before sunne rising or after sunne setting with the privity of the churchwardens, or constable, and not otherwise, and ... no neighbours, nor friends, [are to] be suffered to accompany the coarse to church ... nor the same coarse be suffered to be brought within the church'.[3]

However, a mayoral order of 1625, repeated in 1665, clearly envisages burial inside churches, stipulating as it does

> that no corps dying of infection shall be buried or remaine in any church in time of common prayer, sermon, or lecture. And that no children be suffered at time of buriall of any corps in any church, churchyard, or burying place, to come neare the corps, coffin or grave. And that all the graves shall be at the least six foot deepe.[4]

4. Dealing with the infected

Implementation of these and other rules results in various extra costs for parishes, particularly in London, where infection tends to be most extensive and there are detailed mayoral orders to be followed.

Rods may be provided for the infected to carry when they go abroad.

> 1584 For redde wands for them that have the plague ... 1d (St Peter, Cheapside)[1]

Their homes need to be marked.

> 1582 To William Barnard for making of *O Lord have mercy upon us* to set upon the doores ... 6d (Bishop's Stortford)[2]

In London an order of 1563 stipulates a blue cross upon the door, with writing below to indicate that the infection is within and that the house is to be avoided.[3]

> 1563 To the painter of Tothil Street, for painting of certain blue crosses, to be fixed upon sundry houses infected ... 6d (St Margaret, Westminster)[4]

Later, as seen above, red crosses on doors become standard.

> 1593 For setting two red crosses upon Anthony Sound his dore ... 4d (St Mary Woolnoth)

> 1605 For settinge 5 red crosses on the doores of viseted howses at 4d a pece ... 1s 8d (St Alphage, London Wall)[5]

On 7th June 1665 Pepys sees red crosses for the first time on 'two or three houses' in Drury Lane, accompanied by the usual legend, 'Lord have mercy upon us'.[6]

Men to keep an eye on the houses are also required.

> 1639 To Bummer the beadle for watching a house all night in Gardiner's-Lane, which was shut up and supposed to be visited ... 8d (St Margaret, Westminster)[7]

If the occupants are restive, or the watchman has to be elsewhere, houses need to be secured.

> 1642 For two padlocks and hasps, for visited houses ... 2s 6d (St Giles in the Fields)[8]

Balancing such severity, food and other relief are distributed to those shut away, at the public charge in the case of the poor.

> 1578 Payed to the poore people of Newton Popleforde when they were shute up for the plague ... 26s 8d (Woodbury, Devon)

> 1603 To Hoyden for carieing water to ye visited howses ... 6d (St Martin in the Fields)

> 1637 Paid a nurse to buy necessaries for the visited house, 3 persons ... 5s (All Hallows Barking)[9]

Various items considered effective against the disease may also be provided.

> 1644 For sacke, sallet oile & gunpowder for the sick folkes at ye visited houses ... 3s (Battersea)

> 1665 For tobacco for ye visited ... 1s 4d (Bletchley, Bucks)[10]

In some parishes the total expenditure is considerable.

> 1647 Disbursements for the use of the poore visited with the plague in this parish ... £165 10s (St Margaret, Westminster)

> 1665 Paid and distributed to the reliefe of the poore infected that were shut up &c. and for the coles which made the fires by order of the lord mayor &c. ... £52 12s 7d (St Alphage, London Wall)[11]

Tending to those affected is usually done by the poor, mainly women, who are prepared to incur the risks involved in return for relatively high pay.

> 1563 To Joane Oke and Joane Roo for keping of sick folks in the sickness time ... 2s (Woodbury)

> 1625 To Commynge for his charges going to London to get two women to come up to keep the sicke, the people being all sicke ... 2s 6d (Putney, Surrey)

> 1641 To widow Baggit for looking to the visited people at Lambeth Marsh ... £2 2s (Lambeth)[12]

Where incidence of plague is heavy a common pest-house may be constructed in order to secure a number of victims in one place.

> 1639 To Mr Smith woodmonger for boards for the pesthouse and other timber ... £3 | 1640 To the bricklayer for mending the pesthouse ... 5s 1d | To the smith for a locke and key and for hinges for the pesthouse ... 2s (Lambeth)

> 1642 Received out of the black chest* at several times for the building of the new pest howses ... £200 | Total of the charge for building of the pest howses ... £257 7s 9d (St Margaret, Westminster)[13]

* See p139.

Those infected then need to be taken there.

> 1626 To Mr William Williamson cunstabell for sendinge of visited persons to the pest house out of the house of the goodwife Madox in the Castell alleye ... £11 3s 4d | Spent that night for attendance to helpe them awaye and to see them conveyed ... 2s 6d (St Christopher le Stocks)

> 1643 Paid & given Mr Lyn, the beadle, for a piece of good service for the parishe, in conveying away of a visited household out of ye parishe to London Pest House, forth of Mr Higgons's house at Bloomsbury ... 1s 6d (St Giles in the Fields)[14]

In later outbreaks sedan chairs are sometimes used, presumably not for their elegance but because they make it possible to carry someone without coming into physical contact with them.

> 1665 Paid for 3 sent to the pest house and sedan to carry one ... 6s (St Mary Woolchurch)

> 1665 July 16th. At a vestrey held the said day, it was agreed ... that there be a sedan made & provided by the churchwardens for the removing of the sick to the pest-house. (Hackney, Middlesex)[15]

Once arrived, sufferers need to be looked to and maintained.

> 1604 Paid to Chettam, keeper of the pest house, for diverse poore of the parish sent thither sicke of the plague, for their diete, phisick, &c. ... £9 10s (St Michael, Cornhill)

> 1640 To Cooke and his familie from the 7th of September to the 5 of Octo- ber being shut up in the pest house, and to his warder ... £3 (Lambeth)[16]

5. Dealing with the dead

Every corpse in the parish must be checked for symptoms of plague, another task generally undertaken by poor women.

> 1573 Sep. 27th. It was ordered and agreed ... that there shoulde be two women appointed within the said parishe for to serche and see all suche as shall die and decease within the said parishe, and to give notice to the churchwardens or constable ... of what dezease the persons so deceasing do die of. [Payment to be] 4d a pece [i.e. per corpse]. (St Bartholomew Exchange, vestry)

> 1607 Paid unto the searchers of deade bodies for the whole yeare ... 10s (St Mary Woolchurch)

> 1626 For the searchinge of the goodwife Madox child after it was dead ... 8d (St Christopher le Stocks)[1]

Rods or wands need to be provided for those involved.

1605 For red wandes for the serchers of viseted howses to carry in ther handes ... 2d (St Alphage, London Wall)[2]

On 30th October 1665 Pepys meets 'the searchers with their rods in their hands'.[3] However, reports provided by searchers are often considered unreliable and mayoral orders set out that surgeons are to inspect as well, 'to the end there may be a true report made'.[4]

1636 Paied the surgeon of the pest howse for viewing the body of John Allen after our searchers had beene there, for better satisfaction ... 6s 3d (St Anne & St Agnes, Aldersgate)

1665 To Mr Upton master of the pest house for coming twice into Bearbinder Lane to view the bodies of two dead boys ... 10s (St Mary Woolchurch)[5]

Once a corpse has been checked it needs to be removed. Biers, coffins and barrows are often designated or constructed for the purpose.

1593 For mendinge the beer whereon visited folkes were carried & nailes to ye same ... 8d (St Martin, Leicester)

c. 1598 For a new beare to cary the infected people that died and paintinge of it black ... 6s 2d (St Margaret, King's Lynn, Norfolk)

1625 For a coffin to cary the dead of the plague to burieing ... 12s (Chelmsford, Essex)

1644 For three whole deale boards and a halfe that was used to carry the ancient folkes to church that died of the plague ... 3s 6d | For three slit deale boards for carrying children dying of the same disease to church ... 3s 9d | For a hand barough that was made to carry the dead folkes to church upon ... 2s (Battersea)[6]

Those carrying and attending to corpses need to be paid.

1603 To the 4 bearers of the dead ... 4s (St Martin in the Fields)

1640 To the bearers that came from London and a deale board to beare the corps to church ... 11s 4d (Fulham, Middlesex)[7]

Sometimes no one can be found to do the job. At Cranbrook, where 190 plague deaths are recorded between April 1597 and April 1598, the vicar adds a note in the register.

Also this year others of the plague who were buried neere to theire several dwellings because they could get none to carry them unto the church ... The certaine day of their buriall we could not learne.[8]

When bearers can be found they may take advantage of people's desperation.

1625   August 7th. At a vestry ... it was ordered & decreed ... that whereas certaine dwelling about Stepney take upon them to be common bearers of such as die of the pestilence and other diseases, and ... do exact cruelly of men for the bearing of the dead to the ground, such summes of mony as are no wayes sufferable. It is therefore ordered that the said bearers may yet continue theire said bearing as formerlie provided that they content themselves with such satisfacion and payment as in this order is expressed. (Stepney, Middlesex)

A Corpes Bearer

From a series of London Cries published in 1655

The charges are to be 4d for those who cannot pay for themselves, 6d for those who can, and 8d for those using the church cloth. In addition, so that 'they may be knowne to be common bearers of those who die of the plague, they shall go without cloakes and cary red wands in theire hands', the wands to be provided by the sexton.[9]

During outbreaks gravediggers are also hard at work.

1603   For the graves of 451 poor folks ... £1 17s 7d (St Margaret, Westminster)

1605   To Miles Rose sexten for buryenge of Edmonde Bowle & of his householde and children who died of the infecion of the plague, & for ringing of the bell for divers sick persons of the plague at sondrie times ... 3s 4d (St Matthew, Ipswich)

1625   Unto Ned Andrews for burieing 6 of the plague ... 4s (Chelmsford)[10]

At St Peter, Cornhill, four daughters of the sexton Walter Younge – Martha, Temperance, Elizabeth and Mary – are buried between 12th July and 1st August 1665, all dead of the plague. The register does not record who dug their graves.[11] Other cases too are close to home.

1591   Paid to Mr Parson when the seckness was [in the] parsonage to kepe his house for feare of the infection ... 16d | To Edward Blachford for making of the parsons grave ... 5d (Dartington, Devon)[12]

Both bearing and burial are supposed to take place after sunset, resulting in additional trouble and cost.

1637   For linckes to carry before them that were buried in the night ... 2s 6d (St Anne & St Agnes, Aldersgate)

1642   For links and candles for the night bearers ... 10s | 1643 Paid the sexton for making 10 graves, and for links ... 5s 6d (St Giles in the Fields)[13]

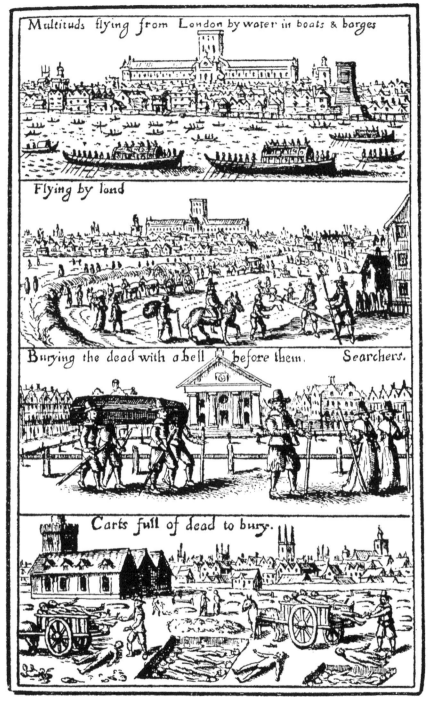

Plague scenes, 1665, from a contemporary print. In the third, wands are carried and a handbell is rung before the corpse as it is borne through Covent Garden.

Sometimes it is found necessary to ignore this requirement. 'The people die so,' notes Pepys in August 1665, 'that now it seems they are fain to carry the dead to be buried by daylight, the nights not sufficing to do it in'. A few weeks later he notes the disregarding of another rule – that friends and neighbours should not attend the corpse – being surprised as he travels along the Thames 'to see in broad daylight two or three burialls upon the Bankeside, one at the very heels of another – doubtless all of the plague – and yet at least 40 or 50 people going along with every one of them'.[14]

As seen earlier, even during outbreaks burial inside churches continues.

> 1638 Oct. 10th. Marie Furing, in the chansell on the north side under Mr Bulls pue, of the plague. (St Pancras, Soper Lane, Cheapside)[15]

If it was your pew you might be a little uneasy. However, such burials continue both because parishes need the income and to honour the natural wishes of dead parishioners and their surviving relatives.

Some precautions are taken

> 1603 March 18th. Agreed, that no servante shalbe buried in the churche, if he do die of plague, without consent of the parson and church wardens. (St Stephen, Walbrook, vestry)

> 1665 For hearbs for the church & digging the graves deeper ... 6s 6d (St John Zachary)[16]

and those who act laxly may be punished. In 1606 the sexton of St Giles, Cripplegate, who allows an infected corpse to remain unburied in the church overnight, is set in the stocks for four hours with a notice upon his head recording his offence.[17]

In addition, as already seen at Cranbrook, a good number of burials occur away from church.

> 1644 March 14th. John Reed, the son of Robert Reed, being suspected to have died of the plague, was buried besides his own dwelling. (St Helen, Auckland, co. Durham)

> 1665 Sep. 4th. Elizabeth Knatt, widow, buried at the pesthouse. | Sep. 10th. Jeremy Knatt, buried in the fields neere the pesthouse. (Wandsworth)

> 1666 August 25th. William Marchall of Eshinge [Eashing], in garden, of distemper. | August 30th. Elizabeth Norris, in ye garden. | Sep. 1st. Mrs Katharine Fortrie, in hur garden. (Godalming, Surrey)[18]

Should outsiders try to offload their dead, the response may be robust.

> 1666 For pouder shott delivered ye watchmen to keepe Moulsham from coming to bury theire infected dead in ye churchyard ... 1s 8d (Chelmsford)[19]

6. Miscellaneous effects

Outbreaks of plague also throw up a range of incidental problems.

> 1564 Memorandum. Owinge of Wilkes for a cowe grasse and a calfe in the churche yarde ... 4d. Whereof the wardens pray to be discharged, for that they have not received the same, nor knew not how to remedy the same, for that he is dedde of the plage. (St Michael, Lichfield, Staffs)

> 1578 Nov. 5th. Mr John Hodgesonne, woolewinder, late churchwarden, of the plague, who died before he had given up his accounte. (St Olave, Hart Street, burial)

> 1645 Mr Stephen Thorington, buried Oct. 13, at which time the plague of pestilence was here; and in twelve months there died 52 persons, whose names are not inserted, the old clerk being dead who had the notes. (St Peter, Dorchester, Dorset)[1]

At Lambeth Richard Hind, one of the churchwardens for 1641-42, dies during the year and 'his accompts could not be found'.[2]

Services may be suspended or held elsewhere.

> 1610 Sep. 16th. John son of Nicholas Chatfield was baptized at Linfield because the plague was then in Ardingleigh, and at that time ther were no praiers at the church for two Sundayes. (Ardingly, Sussex)

> 1645 Isabel, the daughter of Phillip Bainbridge of Stanton, was baptised 25 May because they would not go to Barnard Castle with it, for ye plague. (Whorlton, co. Durham)[3]

Other gatherings may be cancelled or forbidden.

> 1578 This present yere ... ther was no May ale made, for that Waters howshold was visited with sickness & suspected with the plague. (Wing, Bucks)

> 1666 Paid for the warrant to dismisse the faire because the plague was much at Maidstone and some other places in this county ... 1s (Smarden, Kent)[4]

At Holt, Norfolk, in 1593 the rector 'weareth not the surples by reason of ye sickness which was latelie in the towne ... ye surples beinge in the custodie of the churchewardens, whose houses were visited and both died'. At West Dean, near Chichester, in 1625 the wardens report that 'our church porch is in mending, but by reason of the infeccion being so nere the church the workmen lefte it unfinished'.[5]

Another problem is the unnerving effect of all the bells being rung for the dead. On 30th July 1665 Pepys remarks that 'it was a sad noise to hear our bell to toll and ring so often today, either for deaths or burials'. The problem is noted by Francis Hering in an earlier outbreak, that of 1603.

Some physitians thinke it not convenient, that the bells should be rong for those that die of the sicknesse, because much ringing striketh great terror into the hearts of those that are sound, and may hurt those that are by nature fearfull. I am of mind ... that the bells should not be so long time rong or tolled as they are, whereby a continuall dolefull noise soundeth in the eares of men day and night.[6]

Thomas Dekker writes of corpses being buried in the same year 'without the dead mans musick (his *Bell*)'. In *The Silent Woman*, first performed in 1609, Ben Jonson has the character Morose so troubled by the 'perpetuitie of ringing' in plague time that he devises 'a roome, with double walls, and treble seelings, the windowes close shut, and calk'd, and there he lives by candlelight'.[7]

Similarly disconcerting is the impact upon the appearance of churchyards of the burial of so many dead in a short time. In January 1666 Pepys ventures to St Olave, Hart Street, for the first time since leaving London during the outbreak of the previous year, 'and it frighted me indeed ... more than I thought it could have done, to see so [many] graves lie so high upon the churchyard'. He decides not to visit again for a good while.[8]

7. Thanksgiving

Eventually the horror passes and those who have survived can gather to give thanks to God.

> 1563 For 4 books of prayer and thanksgivinge for withdrawinge the sickness ... 4d (St Peter, Cheapside)

> 1593 Oct. 29th. About this time the plague of pestilence, by the great mercy and goodness of almighty God, stayed past all expectacion of man, for it ceased upon a sodaine at what time it was dispersed in every corner of this whole parishe, there was not two houses together free from it, and yet the Lord had the angel stay as in David's time, his name be blessed for it. Edward Bennett, minister. (All Saints, Derby, note in register)

> 1625 For bread and wine at the communion at the public thanksgiving for the ceasing of the plague ... 3s 3d (St Peter in the East, Oxford)[1]

Thanks may also be given to individuals who have helped the parish through.

> 1606 For a double gilte boule which was given to Mr Wattes our minister for his extraordinary paines taking amongst us in the parrishe at two several times when the sickness was amongst us ... £4 5s 6d (St Mary the Great, Cambridge)[2]

FACING PAGE Churches ablaze in the Fire of London, from a ballad printed in 1680

The Great Fire

In London the last great outbreak of plague in 1665 is soon followed by a fire that devastates many parishes and their churches. Pepys records that, after a long drought, everything proved combustible, 'even the very stones of churches', and he watches as the steeple of St Laurence Pountney catches fire 'in the very top' and burns until it collapses. His fellow diarist John Evelyn describes 'the fall of towers, houses, and churches,' and in particular the stones of St Paul's Cathedral flying 'like grenados, the melting lead running down the streets in a stream'.[1]

The destruction is also recorded in the vestry minute book of St Bartholomew Exchange, in matter of fact terms.

> The second of September 1666 a sore and lamentable fire happend in Pudding Lane which burnt downe almost all the City within the walls. About 80 churches were burnt whereof the parish of St Bartholomewes behinde the Exchange was one, and that whole parish was then burnt exceptinge three houses ...[2]

As the fire takes hold an immediate imperative is to carry the church goods to safety.

> 1666　For carrying the cloath and plate away when the fire was and bringing it back ... 2s 6d (St Giles without Cripplegate)

> 1666　For removing the vestments, plate, bookes and cushings in the time of the Fire to several places in the country and bringing them into London againe and then removing them to several places to secure them, and carriage about the same ... £5 6s (St Mary Woolchurch)[3]

As the latter entry suggests, once the worst is over there is a need to protect what has survived.

1665-66 Paid for a watchman in ye sickness time and to several persons at several times for watching in and aboute the church since the fire ... £3 15s 6d | For a lanthorne to watch with ... 1s 8d | For two padlocks for the church dore ... 4s | Paid Mr Bates ... for his care and paines in preserving the church goods ... £3 (St Christopher le Stocks)

1666 To several watchmen to secure what was left unburnt about the church ... £9 18s (St Mary Woolchurch)[4]

Ruined materials can then be gathered and sold.

1666-67 Jan. 8th. It was agreed that the lead and bell metal lying loose in the church, and subject to imbezellement, shalbe secured in casks, that the dust wherein any bell metal is shalbe refined and the weight taken, and that all the iron and brass shalbe sold. (St Michael, Cornhill, vestry)

1666-67 Feb. 11th. At a vestry or meetinge held ... at the dwellinge house of Mrs Mary Beckner widow situate in Copt-hall Alley ... it was ... order'd that ... the said churchwardens shall and may sell all such lead & bell-metle as belongeth to the said parish church, now saved since the late & dreadfull fire, together with the iron also. | [Accounts] Received for lead, bell-metle, and iron ... £178 2s (St Bartholomew Exchange)[5]

Looted items may be recovered, or at least search may be made.

1666 To Girles for discovering some stolen lead ... 2s | Paid the porters for carrying ye thieves to Bridewell ... 2s (St Christopher le Stocks)

1666 Paid upon the inquiry and search after one of the bells ... £2 15s (St Bartholomew Exchange)[6]

As in times of plague, the usual rites of passage may be disrupted.

1666 Kasia ye daughter of Morgan Dandy was borne 2 September 1666 (being ye day ye dreadfull Fire began in London) & baptized in ye country. (St Mary le Bow)

1666-67 Jan. 10th. Mr Francis Tryon, merchant, was buried in the ruines of the chauncell. (St Dionis Backchurch)[7]

Collections are made in churches across the country for those affected.

1666 Oct. 10th. Collected then at ye church & at ye houses in Battersea towards ye relief of ye city of London upon ye account of ye fire ... £12 8s 9d (Battersea)

1666 Oct. 11th. Collected towards the reliefe of the poore inhabitants of London who have lately suffered by the lamentable fire ... £11 5s 9½d (Tavistock, Devon)[8]

More ad hoc relief may be found in nearby towns and villages.

1666 To monee given to several that were in distress after the fier and that Mr Cop did recommend ... 14s (Leyton, Essex)[9]

Afterwards there is a determination to rebuild, and in time churches rise again in new forms, a bricks and mortar resurrection, helped by one architect in particular.

1672 Paid when Dr Renn [and] Mr Hooke with some parishioners dined together ... £4 12s | Spent at going about raising the second £500 for building the church ... 1s 6d (St Mary, Aldermanbury)

1673 Oct. 1st. In coach hire and water going to Doctor Renn with a present ... 2s 2d | 1677 Spent this year in attending Sir Christopher Wrenn about ye several artificers in order to finishing the church ... £2 10s 6d (St Bartholomew Exchange)

1682 Mr Newman the carver ... £57 13s | Upon a man for giving his judgment on the carver's work ... 8s | Mr Kempster the stone-cutter ... £5 10s | Mr Kempster for speedily paving and finishing the east end of the church ... £5 7s 6d | Lord mayor's officer for summoning the aldermen to our church ... 5s | Two bottles of sherry and pipes at the opening of the church ... 3s 4d | Wax links to enlighten my lord mayor home ... 4s 6d (St James Garlickhythe)[10]

St Mary le Bow, Cheapside, as rebuilt by Wren, looking east

Note on the text

Much of the text consists of extracts from churchwardens' accounts (CWA) and other old records. The aim has been to retain as much as possible of the original character of this material, including its informality, while reducing obstacles to ready comprehension for the modern reader. To this end the following adjustments have been made silently.

The use of capitals has been greatly reduced. • Abbreviations have usually (but not always) been spelt out. • Double letters that appear redundant to the modern eye (e.g. att, bee, uppon) have usually been removed. • Where *e* in older spellings appears redundant it has been removed when it might slow up the reader (e.g. 'doe' becomes 'do') but otherwise retained. • Where appropriate *y* has been converted to whichever letter (almost always a vowel) tallies with or comes closest to modern usage. • A few simple transpositions have been made e.g. 'Jhon' becomes 'John'. • Spelling has generally been standardised within entries to the form closest to modern use. • Spaces have usually been closed or opened up e.g. 'a nother' becomes 'another', 'apaire' becomes 'a paire'. • Miscellaneous other adjustments have been made to spellings to ease comprehension but these have been limited to changing one letter in any word. • Punctuation has occasionally been adjusted, mainly involving the addition or omission of commas. • A few dates have been omitted where the information has been provided in the preceding narrative. Other dates have been moved to the starts of entries and their formats standardised to 'March 9th' etc.

Any changes beyond those listed above are indicated in the Source notes below. 'Adjusted' in the notes indicates that more general licence has been taken. In a few cases this includes the omission or addition of a word or two.

In all other cases, as is customary, omissions from the text are indicated by ellipses and any words added are in square brackets.

Apostrophes are often omitted in the source material and have not been added unless needed in order to avoid confusion.

CWA almost always straddle calendar years, running for example from Easter 1656 to Easter 1657. Such dates have been simplified to the first year (1656). Where the accounts cover a longer period (e.g. 1656-1658) the span is given.

If an entry refers to a historical event of known date then that date is used.

Where it is evident that a register or CWA entry relates to a date which falls in different old and new style years (i.e. between 1st January and 24th March prior to 1752) both years are given.

More generally CWA dates should be regarded as having a degree of imprecision: accounts were often written up some time after the cost or event in question occurred, and printed editions (including the present one) often muddy things further by simplifying dates.

Parish information is provided along the lines set out in the Glossary (page xiii) with the following exceptions. *Dedication omitted after first instance*: St Mary, Bungay, Suffolk • St Mary, Manchester • St Michael in Bedwardine, Worcester. *County omitted after first instance*: Battersea, Surrey • Bishop's Stortford, Hertfordshire • Bungay,

Suffolk • Lambeth, Surrey • Long Melford, Suffolk • Louth, Lincolnshire • Ludlow, Shropshire • Thame, Oxfordshire • Wandsworth, Surrey. In addition the county is omitted if already provided within the same section.

Counties are taken from Arthur Meredyth Burke's *Key to the Ancient Parish Registers of England and Wales* (1908) and in a few cases may differ from those obtaining today.

Two other things are perhaps worth noting.

- Almost all the material quoted comes from printed volumes, and the handling of the original records by the editors in each case varied a good deal: some pains-takingly transcribed and reproduced the material as found; some modernised spellings; some paraphrased a bit without recording the fact.
- Early records are usually in Latin so any material quoted which dates from before about 1500 has probably been translated, whether by the editor of any printed edition or anew, and this is not indicated case by case.

The approach outlined above has no doubt been applied inconsistently in places, and will disappoint (and perhaps dismay) purists, but it is hoped that it goes some way towards making potentially off-putting material approachable for the general reader.

Acknowledgements

I am grateful to the following for permission to quote from material of which they own the copyright: Devon Archives (Cullompton churchwardens' accounts); the Kent Archaeological Society (*Kentish Visitations … 1511-12* ed. K. L. Wood-Legh); the Lancashire and Cheshire Record Society (*Churchwardens' Accounts of Prescot* ed. F. A. Bailey); and the Royal Historical Society (*Journal of William Schellinks' Travels in England* ed. Maurice Exwood and H. L. Lehmann).

I am also grateful to various institutions which have made illustrations available, including the Library of Congress and the Folger Shakespeare Library, Washington; the J. Paul Getty Museum, Los Angeles; the Metropolitan Museum of Art, New York; Rijksmuseum, Amsterdam; the Lewis Walpole Library, Farmington, Connecticut; and the Yale Center for British Art, New Haven, Connecticut. The most significant debt is to the Geograph project and its contributors, above all Michael Garlick, many of whose outstanding photographs enrich these pages.

As an amateur effort the present book is greatly indebted to others by pioneers and experts in the field: notable examples include those by J. Charles Cox, Eamon Duffy, H. J. Feasey, Ronald Hutton, Nicholas Orme, N. J. G. Pounds and Daniel Rock listed in the bibliography. It also rests heavily on the untrumpeted labours of those who have transcribed and published churchwardens' accounts and other records over the years. Among those whose work has been drawn upon most heavily are Charles Drew, Edwin Freshfield, Henry Littlehales, William Mc Murray, John Nichols, William Henry Overall, Henry James Fowle Swayne and H. B. Walters.

In addition I am grateful for valuable help received from staff at the British Library and the London Library.

Gratitude of another order entirely is due to my parents, and this book, for all its shortcomings, is dedicated to them: to my father and to the memory of my mother, who died while it was at the printer's.

Source notes

Details of sources not given in full in these notes can be found in the Bibliography under parish, author or title (whether of a series or monograph). Titles are only italicised here if they do not appear there. For parish references it will usually be quickest to check in the Bibliography first under parish and, should the source not be listed there, then under author or title.

Parishes are listed here in concise form, usually simply by place name. In the case of London parishes, and others for which the dedication is needed for purposes of identification, acronyms are typically used. For example, St Mary the Great, Cambridge, is listed as Cambridge SMG.

The following parishes which appear often are referred to in a more abbreviated form without the place name being included in full. Unless indicated they are in London.

BS	St Michael, Bishop's Stortford, Herts	SLP	St Laurence Pountney
SAH	St Andrew Hubbard	SMC	St Michael, Cornhill
SASA	St Anne and St Agnes, Aldersgate	SMF	St Martin in the Fields
SBE	St Bartholomew Exchange	SMH	St Mary at Hill
SCLS	St Christopher le Stocks	SMW	St Margaret, Westminster
SES	St Edmund, Salisbury, Wilts	SP Cheap	St Peter, Cheapside
SGWC	St Giles without Cripplegate	WM	Wimborne Minster, Dorset
SJZ	St John Zachary		

In addition, in the case of the following parishes which appear often the source volume is not indicated in the notes because it is the same for all the material quoted. Details can be found in the Bibliography under the parish name in each case.

Battersea | Bishop's Stortford | Long Melford | Lydd | St Anne and St Agnes, Aldersgate
St Edmund, Salisbury | St John Zachary | St Laurence Pountney
St Mary at Hill | Walthamstow | Wimborne Minster

Some other short forms used:

adjusted Licence beyond that set out in the Note on the text has been taken with quoted material
CWA Churchwardens' accounts
orig. Indicates original spelling or other detail
q, qs Indicates the source of one or more quotations in the text
Reg. Parish register or registers
reseq The sequence within quoted material has been altered.

Any spelling changes beyond those carried out silently (as set out in the Note on the text) are indicated in brackets.

Definitions and etymological information used in footnotes and elsewhere have been drawn largely from the *Oxford English Dictionary* (OED). This is only recorded in a few cases, typically where direct quotation is made.

Introduction and Glossary
1 Yeovil: Collectanea Topog. iii 136 / Rye: Holloway 482 / Chester HT: Chester & NW AAHSJ xxxviii 155 / South Molton: DART xxxvi 247. 2 BS 24 / SES: 152, 157 / Kilmington: Cornish 63, 68 / SBE CWA 94b, 117a / Leicester St Mary: Leicestershire AAST vi 359. 3 Regarding towns etc with more than one old church, typically the county is omitted for those which it seems likely the general reader will be able to place easily (e.g. Reading) but included for some which may be less familiar (e.g. Auckland, co. Durham). W. M. Burke's *Key to the Ancient Parish Registers* (1908) has been used as a guide to which places contain more than one old parish but some cases have no doubt been overlooked, not least because Burke only lists parishes still extant in 1908.

Churchyard
1 **Entrance**. 1 Reydon: Cox, Bench-ends 8 n. 2 Yatton: Hobhouse 145 / Redenhall: Candler 89. 3 Pittington: Durham CWA 43. 4 Bungay: EA 1S i 425. 5 Woodbury: DART xxiv 320 /

Warburton: Purvis, Docs 177 / Aston, Idols 797-799. **6** Richard Travers Smith, *St Basil the Great*, 1879, pp121-122 (citing *De Spiritu Sancto*, cap. xxvii 66; q) / Aquinas xi 74 (pt 2.2, question 84, article 3). **7** CE i 365 / John of Damascus, *Exposition of the Orthodox Faith* (De fide orthodoxa), trans. S. D. F. Salmond, Oxford, 1899, p81 / Lancelot Andrewes, *A Learned Discourse of Ceremonies*, 1653, p64. **8** Aquinas xi 74 (pt 2.2, question 84, article 3). **9** CE iii 508a / Owen 77-79, 85-86 / Maskell i 242-243 n. / Burn EL i 333-335 / Pounds 257, 428 / SMH xcv-xcvi (citing register of Robert Hallam, Bishop of Salisbury 1408-1417).
2 Place of burial. 1 William Barlow, Bishop of Lincoln, consecrating Fulmer church and yard, 1 Nov 1610, in *English Orders for Consecrating Churches in the Seventeenth Century* ed. J. Wickham Legg, Henry Bradshaw Soc., 1911, p10 / CE iii 73a (Durand q) / Durand 1859 p707 (book 7, chapter 35, sections 39 and 40) / Rock ii 381 n. 48 / Daniell 147-149 / Geoffrey Rowell, *The Liturgy of Christian Burial*, 1977, p66. **2** Mirk F 294. **3** North Cray: Wills, West Kent B 15-16 / East Langdon: Wills, East Kent 184 / Dinn 245-247 / Badham 234-235. **4** Bury St Edmunds SM: Wills, Bury 92. **5** Articles ... Ely, 1662, p7 (no. 17) / Pounds 425-427 / Cressy BMD 470. **6** Taunton: Report on ... Extramural Sepulture 37. **7** Chester SM: Earwaker 123. **8** Selborne: White 270. **9** Dinn 246. Report on ... Extramural Sepulture pp16, 18 gives examples of such pits in London. **10** Rye: Holloway 484 / Warwick: Notices 31.
3 Animals. 1 Mersham: Vis. Warham 157 / Alne: Purvis, Condition 19 / Tydd SG: Vis. Palmer iv pt 8 p377 / Articles ... Norwich, 1638, sigs. A3r (no. 4), C3r (no. 25). **2** Worfield: Shropshire ANHST 4S ii 42 / South Molton: DART xxxvi 247. **3** Whitstable: Vis. Hussey xxvii 226 / Ardeley: Vis. Hale 118 / Pounds 419-420. **4** SMF: Kitto 125 / Kingston UT: Surrey AC viii 84 / SM Bourne: Stevens 229. **5** SBE CWA 14a, 30a.
4 Yews. 1 Wandsworth: Surrey AC xviii 138 / Chedder: HMC 3rd report app. 330b / Littleham: Webb 127. **2** Strood: Plomer 129. **3** Ashburton: CWA 37-38 (orig. £12 to bowyer; Cox gives as 12s, which seems more likely) / Cox, Fittings 36-37 / Lydd 350 / Woodbury: DART xxiv 314 (1775) / Brand ii 257 / Friar 500-501. **4** Cratfield: Raven 117 / SMW: NI 30. **5** Gibson, Codex, 1713, i 233-234 (q) / SR i 221 (where undated) / Wilkins ii 140b-141a (Synod of Exeter, 1287, cap. xiv). **6** Johnson ii 401 (1343) / East Shefford: Vis. Waltham 121 (1391). **7** Lancing: Vis. Sussex i 93, 94 (reseq).
5 Processions. 1 Ruckinge: Vis. Woodruff 53 (1502) / Barham: Vis. Warham 186 (1511). **2** Grantham: Clark 126-128. This was only part of the sentence, and if the weather proved bad the procession and disciplining were to take place inside the church.
6 Churchyard games. 1 Northampton SP: Serjeantson 1904 p120. **2** Cox, Fittings 43. **3** Friar 121 / Kilmington: REED Devon 208 (from the lack of comment the editor seems to have assumed the players were involved in drama) / Wrington: Bath Nat. Hist. Field Club Proc. ii 449 / Somerton: Muncey 127-128 / Babcary: James Woodforde, *The Diary of a Country Parson* ed. John Beresford, vol 1, 1926, p37.
7 Jangle of commerce. 1 SR i 98a (13 Edward I, statute of Winchester, 1285) / Davis 82-83 (no. 88). **2** SAH: British Mag. xxxi 245 / SES 37, 50. **3** Beverley: Poulson ii 747. **4** SK Cree: Malcolm iii 309-310. **5** SMW: NI 64 (orig. 1660).

Church
1 Roof. 1 Stockton: NORA i 173. **2** Lindfield: Sussex AC xix 42. **3** Prescot: CWA 51 (reseq) / Bristol St James: Bristol P&P ii 39b. **4** Cumberland etc AAST xlix 161. **5** Stanford: Antiquary xvii 210b / Redenhall: Candler 68. **6** 'Weather Vanes and Weather Cocks', *Country Life*, 19 March 1932, lxxxi / Glenn Knoblock & David Wemmer, *Weathervanes of New England*, Jefferson, N. Carolina, 2018, p21 / Durand 1843 p199. The information relating to early popes is widely repeated but authoritative sources for the details have proved elusive. **7** Norwich SPM: Norfolk Antiq. Misc. ii 331 / Coventry HT: Sharp 109-110 / Plymouth: Rowe 231. **8** Louth: Dudding 181. **9** Stow i 326. **10** Canterbury HCW: OPB ii 47 / Fulham: Fèret i 163.
2 Porch. 1 Wall 12-15 / Pounds 387-388. Some churches do of course have more than one porch. **2** Great Yarmouth: Palmer 1856 p144 / Ludlow: Shropshire ANHST 2S i 271. **3** Netheravon: Vis. Chandler 30 (no. 58) / SES 190-191 (10 March 1629, presumably old style) / Wenhaston: Clare 23. **4** Gateshead: Ambrose Barnes 387 / Northill: Elliott 58 / Newcastle AS: Sopwith 129. **5** Hope: Cox, Derbyshire ii 259 n. / Plymouth: Rowe 81 (1830s) / Cartmel & Hawkshead:

Stockdale 83. Recollection of James Stockdale from his 'early days' after 'a long life'. He was writing in 1870. **6** Mitcham: Cox PR 73 / SP Cheap: London & Middx AST 1S iii 364 / Aston Abbots: Records of Bucks x 30. **7** Wandsworth: Surrey AC xix 170 / Norwich SPM: Norfolk Antiq. Misc. ii 357. **8** Aubrey, Remaines 26. **9** High Halstow: Wills, West Kent B 35 / Chislehurst: Wills, West Kent B 12. **10** SMF: Kitto 480 (entry in accounts). **11** Canterbury SM Northgate: Letters and Papers of Henry VIII xviii pt 2 p300 (*c.* 1543) / Wall 21.

3 Alms box etc. 1 Frere & Kennedy ii 127 / Davis 80 (no. 84). **2** Paglesham: Essex AST 1S iv 232 / SBE CWA 94b. **3** Reading SM: Garry 142. **4** Pounds 248, 396 / Cox, Fittings 288. For some examples of flagstones being installed see Durham CWA pp97 (Pittington, 1634), 147-148 (SO, Durham, 1607), 281-282 (Houghton-le-Spring, 1604). **5** SAH: British Mag. xxxii 32 / BS 37. **6** Wall 210, 216 / Pounds 334 / Gibson, Codex, 1713, i 435 (q). **7** SAH: British Mag. xxxii 394. **8** Hawkhurst: Cox CWA 152.

4 Nave etc. 1 Edward L. Cutts, *A Dictionary of the Church of England*, 2nd edition, 1889, p421. **2** SMH 229. **3** SMC: Overall 57. **4** Worfield: Shropshire ANHST 3S iii 110 / Blatherwycke: Wills, Northants 277. **5** St Olave Silver St: WR 554-555 (1547 inventory) / Canterbury St Andrew: Cotton pt 1 p8 (1485 inventory) / Sandwich SC: Wills, East Kent 281 (1507). **6** Thame: Berks etc AJ viii 73; xiii 50. **7** Cox, Fittings pp144-147 lists three ways in which lofts were supported: i. screen plus parallel beam; ii. vaults or groinings projecting westward from upper part of screen; iii. two parallel screens (the least common method). **8** Yatton: Hobhouse 95-98 (reseq). **9** Bond, Screens 111 / Cambridge SMG: Sandars & Venables 65 (q). **10** Bond, Screens 115. **11** Chester SM: Earwaker 218. **12** Thame: Lee 69. **13** SS Walbrook: London & Middx AST 1S v 341-342 / SP Cheap: JBAA xxiv 257. **14** Hopkins 153-157. 'The term *pair* really signified a *set*, or a sufficient number to serve a specific purpose' (p154). **15** Lydd 343. A similar payment occurs at All Saints, Bristol, in 1472 (Records ii 68). **16** Long Melford 71 (quoting Roger Martyn) / Vallance 70. **17** Thame: Berks etc AJ xvi 88 / Leicester St Martin: North 75. **18** SMW: Cox CWA 179 / Thame: Lee 51. **19** WR 265 (St Edmund, 1548 sale); 414-415 (St Mary Abchurch, 1541 inventory, 1547 sale); 617 (St Thomas Apostle, 1547 sale). **20** SMH 361. **21** Bridgwater: Arthur Herbert Powell, *The Ancient Borough of Bridgwater in the County of Somerset*, Bridgwater, 1907, p132 n. **22** SS Walbrook: London & Middx AST 1S v 341. **23** SM Woolnoth: WR 470-471 (1552 inventory).

5 Other images. 1 There are of course different ways of doing this. Rosewell p33 lists nine categories for murals alone. **2** ODCC 282b / CE iii 729a. **3** Fn. ODCC 1145a (Purgatory, re 1274 Council). **4** SES xv / Thompson, Growth 24, 40-43, 109-11 (Ludlow) / Pounds 392-293 / Gasquet 59-60. Burgess, Right Ordering p xx has a plan showing various altars set in easterly positions at All Saints, Bristol. **5** Wisbech, Guild HT: Palmer, Gilds 379 (reseq). The guild was founded in 1379 to build a chapel in honour of the Holy Trinity, so 1380 seems a reasonable estimated date for these costs. **6** Wisbech, Guild SJB: Palmer, Gilds 378. While the costs are not dated they are said to be attached to the guild certificate of 1389. **7** Saffron Walden: Braybrooke 224 / SAH: British Mag. xxxii 146; xxxiii 569 / BS 39. **8** Reading SL: Kerry 69 / Smarden: Memorials 244 / SP Cheap: JBAA xxiv 261. **9** Reading SL: Kerry 45 (date given as 1534) / Coates 221 (for coat entry only; date given as 1536, and has three calves' skins but same cost). **10** Walberswick: Lewis 67 / WM 91. **11** Long Melford 81 / SS Coleman St: WR 602 (1549 sale). In some cases such clothes may have been used for the rood group image of Mary. **12** Peterborough SJB: Mellows 84 / Wymondham: NORA ix 266. **13** PK f36v. **14** 'Answers to ... the rebels, Devon, anno 1549' in John Strype, *Memorials of ... Thomas Cranmer*, vol 2, Oxford, 1848, p542 / William Perkins, *A Reformed Catholike*, Cambridge, 1598, p177 ('not meete'). **15** Cobham: Wills, West Kent A 261 / Bromley: Wills, West Kent A 257 / Morebath: Binney 24. **16** Bramley, Hants: Williams 30, 32. **17** High Halstow: Wills, West Kent B 34 / Allhallows, Hoo: Wills, West Kent A 273 / Long Buckby: Wills, Northants 289. **18** Allhallows, Hoo: Wills, West Kent A 273 / Beckenham: Wills, West Kent A 255. **19** Aston, Iconoclasts 33. **20** Exeter St Petrock: DART xiv 431 / SAH: British Mag. xxxii 153 / Sutterton: AJ xxxix 62.

6 Texts etc. 1 Fn. Cardwell, Annals i 262 (1561 letter) / Davis 79-80 (no. 82). **2** Kingston UT: Surrey AC viii 102 / Stoke Charity: Williams 95 / Chelmsford: Essex AST 1S ii 212 / Weybread: EA 1S ii 4 / Saffron Walden: Essex AST 2S xxiii 337 / Towcester: Northants

NQ iii 26. **3** Ludlow: Shropshire ANHST 2S i 265 / SBE CWA 130b. **4** SMW: NI 72.
5 SM Friday St: JBAA xxv 362 / Canterbury St Andrew: Cotton pt iv 29 / Thatcham: Barfield
ii 107 / Peakirk: Northants NQ ii 24. **6** Boughton M: Vis. Harpsfield ii 199. **7** SP Cheap:
JBAA xxiv 157. **8** SM Abchurch: WR 414-415. **9** Articles ... Ely, 1662, p7 (no. 17). **10** Selborne
& Faringdon: White, *Selborne* 264-265. **11** Ashford-in-the-Water: Reliquary i 10-11.
Garlands are also discussed in *Country Life*, 8 Nov 1902, xlv-xlvi and 18 Feb 1944, p298. A
longer account is Rosie Morris, 'The "innocent and touching custom" of maidens' garlands:
A field report', *Folklore*, vol 114, Dec 2003, pp355-387. She notes the continuation of the
custom into recent times, a garland being made at Ashford-in-the-Water in 1995.

7 Consecration crosses. **1** Becon, Reliques ff256r-257r (q). His account appears to be taken
from Durand (book 1, chapter 1, section 1, p41 in 1859 edition). **2** CE iv 280-282 / Maskell
i 208-209 n.14 / John Wordsworth, *On the Rite of Consecration of Churches*, 1899, pp11-12 (q).
3 Durand 1843 pp125-126. **4** John Henry Middleton, 'On consecration crosses', Archaeologia
xlviii 446-464 / Dewick 1-34. External crosses appear to be largely peculiar to England.

8 Pews. **1** Pounds 468-470. **2** Cox, Bench-ends 17-18 / Margaret Aston, 'Segregation in church',
in *Women in the Church* ed. W. J. Sheils & Diana Wood, Oxford, 1990, pp 237-294 (in
particular pp238, 274). **3** SMC: Overall 16 / Worcester: Amphlett 129. **4** St Alphage LW:
Hall 31. **5** WM 132 / West Walton: Susan Dwyer Amussen, *An Ordered Society: Gender
and Class in Early Modern England*, Oxford, 1988, pp137-138 (quoting letter from Clement
Corbett, July 1633). **6** Blofield: EA 2S v 147. **7** SAH: British Mag. xxxi 398 / SMW: NI 31.
8 Cox, Bench-ends 20. Churches where the pew was near the font include St Edmund and
St Thomas, Salisbury (Swayne xxii) and St Andrew, Plymouth (Rowe p225). **9** Heales i 134-135.
Writing in 1872, Heales indicates that separate seating for unmarried women then continued
in many country churches. **10** SAH: British Mag. xxxiii 577 / Leicester St Martin: North
140 / Cambridge SMG: Foster 397. **11** Great Dunmow: Hale 1841 p44 / Oxford St Ebbe:
Vis. Peyton xxxii (citing Archd. papers, Oxon, c. 118, f95; no date given but 1617 is the date
of a related entry on f96) / Nettlebed: Vis. Peyton xxxii (citing Archd. papers, Oxon, c. 160,
f218; 1663). **12** SES 190 (16 Jan 1629, probably old style). **13** SBE CWA 59b / Hackney:
Simpson iii 142. **14** SMW: NI 29 / SBE CWA 65a. **15** SMC: Overall 164 / SCLS:
Accomptes 76a, 78a / SES 213 / Norwich SPM: Norfolk Antiq. Misc. ii 339. **16** Reading
SM: Garry 56 / Lancaster: Roper iii 612. **17** Pounds 476. At All Saints, Bristol, a payment
for two seats is recorded in 1409 and another payment occurs in an undated account apparently
c. 1407 (Records i 49, 51). **18** Somerton: Somersetshire ANHSP xxxix pt 2 pp68-69.
19 SES 60, 62 / SM Friday St: JBAA xxv 362. **20** SES 223-224. **21** Salisbury ST: Swayne
288, 335. **22** Durham SN: Durham CWA 231, 244. **23** Northampton HS: Cox & Serjeantson
206 / Ulverston: Bardsley 125 / Bradford: *Bradford Observer* 13 Feb 1851 p1f. **24** SMC:
Overall 31, 35 / SES 188 / Leyton: Kennedy 152. **25** Pepys ii 238 / Leicester St Martin:
North 217 (1708). **26** Lambeth: Drew i 74 / SM Friday St: JBAA xxv 362 / Reading SM:
Garry 137. **27** SES 60-139 / Salisbury ST: Swayne 273-303. **28** Heales i 183-184 / Cox,
Bench-ends 38 / Addleshaw & Etchells 95-96. **29** *The Poems of Richard Corbet* ed. Octavius
Gilchrist, 4th edition, 1807, xlvii (citing Harl. Ms. 750; q). *Documents illustrating the History
of St Paul's Cathedral* ed. W. Sparrow Simpson, Camden Soc., 1880, pp134-139 gives date
and an alternative text. **30** Wren 301. **31** Thame: Vis. Peyton 186. **32** Selborne: White 265.
33 Wilkins ii 140a (Synod of Exeter, cap. 12) / Terrington: Purvis, Docs 90 / Congleton:
Marsh 302 (citing Cheshire Record Office, EDC5, 1576.44) / Oxford St Ebbe: Vis. Brinkworth
ii 171 (wheupon, theime). **34** Eltham: Archaeologia xxxiv 64 (1596). **35** Richmond:
Richard Crisp, *Richmond and its Inhabitants from the Olden Time*, 1866, pp138-144. **36** Chester
HT: Chester & NW AAHSJ xxxviii 159. **37** J. M. Neale, *The History of Pews*, Cambridge,
1841, p3 / Pounds 478. **38** Canterbury St Andrew: Cotton pt i 35 / Eltham: Hasted i 205a /
Salisbury ST: Swayne 286 (thest > the east). **39** SLP 125a / Cambridge SMG: Foster 369.
40 SMF: Kitto 255 / SM Friday St: JBAA xxv 362. **41** SMW: NI 10 / AH Staining: British
Mag. iii 417. **42** Barrow: Antiquary ii 96a (1713).

9 Pulpit etc. **1** Pounds 479. **2** St Ethelburga: Cobb 9 / Mortlake: Anderson 50. **3** Hawkshead:
Henry Swainson Cowper, *Hawkshead ... its History* [etc], 1899, p422. **4** Leicester St Martin:
North 115 / SP Cheap: JBAA xxiv 257. **5** SBE CWA 6a (1598), 104a (1635) / Youlgreave:

Cox, Derbyshire ii 337-338 (1621) / Durham SO: Durham CWA 188 (1634) / Durham SN: Durham CWA 232 (1672) / Wandsworth: Surrey AC xviii 145 (1599) / Chester-le-Street: Blunt 85 (1620). **6** Earliest CWA reference found is at Wandsworth in 1560 (Surrey AC xvii 143). Cox & Harvey pp156-157 and Cox, Fittings p184 say there was an hour glass at Lambeth as early as 1522 but this may arise from a misunderstanding of Thomas Allen's *History of Lambeth*, 1827, p66. **7** SK Cree: Malcolm iii 309 / BS 60 / Hartland: HMC 5th report app. 572a / Reading SM: Garry 91. **8** SGWC: Baddeley 65 / Newcastle AS: Ambrose Barnes 460. **9** Dyer, Gleanings 204 / *Maidstone and Kentish Journal* 18 Nov 1867 p3b (Savoy). **10** Ipswich SC: EA 2S iv 6 / Norwich SB: EA 1S iv 51. **11** Chester HT: xxxviii 142 / Duffield: Derbyshire ANHSJ xxxix 31. **12** Whitby: *Country Life* 5 Mar 1904 p350. **13** Coventry HT: Sharp 102 / Redenhall: Candler 85.

10 Mass. 1 Schroeder 238-239, 259 (4th Lateran Council, canons 1, 21) / CE v 578b-579a / ODCC 322b-323a. Fn. Aquinas xvii 287 (pt 3, question 76) / Johnson ii 273-275 (1281) / Lyndwood 9a. Orme p284 notes that lay access to the chancel to receive communion seems to have increased after the 13th century. **2** Lay Folks Mass Book 37-39 (adjusted). **3** Duffy, Altars 112-116. **4** Becon, Prayers 270, 279 (from *The Displaying of the Popish Mass*, written in the 1550s) / Mirk I 10 / Duffy, Altars 100.

11 Chancel before Reformation. 1 Dewick 34 / Pounds 442-443 / Becon, Reliques ff257r-258r (adjusted). **2** Owen 73-74. **3** Lambeth: Drew i 33 / SB Gracechurch St: WR 189. **4** Dearmer 7 / Barton 27-32. **5** Milton: Wills, West Kent A 280. **6** Cox & Harvey 39-45 / Schroeder 259 (4th Lateran Council, canon 20) / Johnson ii 76 (council of 1195, renewal, one of many similar orders). **7** SAH: British Mag. xxxii 37 / Prescot CWA 10. **8** Thompson, Growth 122 / Bond, Chancel 26-27 / Arch. Cant. xxxvii 30-31 (Leland L. Duncan on Cranbrook church) / Barton 30-31. **9** P. S. Barnwell, 'Low side windows: ventilating a 170-year old controversy', *Ecclesiology Today*, issue 36, June 2006, pp49-76 / Blomefield vi 484 (Paston). **10** George Williams, *The Holy City*, 2nd edition, vol 2, 1849, p81 / Justin E. A. Kroesen, *The Sepulchrum Domini through the Ages*, Sterling, Virginia, 2000, p69 / Arculfus 6 / CE i 699. **11** Fn. V. Sekules, 'Easter Sepulchre', Grove Art online / Christopher Herbert, 'English Easter Sepulchres: The History of an Idea', unpublished thesis, Leicester University, 2015, *passim*. **12** SMH 63 / Cambridge SMG: Foster 81. **13** All Hallows UTS: WR 96. **14** Brooks 76-77 / Feasey 141. **15** Shrewsbury SM: Owen & Blakeway ii 346. **16** Glynde: Wills, Sussex ii 210. **17** Matthew 27:62-66 (watch), 28:2 (angel). **18** SMH 301. **19** Bristol SMR: George Pryce, *Memorials of the Canynges Family and their Times*, Bristol, 1854, pp268-269 (adjusted; reseq; parts omitted). Brooks p83 suggests that the elaborate description may relate to a resurrection play rather than to a regular sepulchre.

12 Chancel after Reformation. 1 Ketley 76, 265 (fn. re mass), 283 (fn. re frequency) / Pounds 226 (wine). **2** Exeter St Petrock: DART xxiv 274. **3** Addleshaw & Etchells 108-147 / Pounds 456-457, 462, 482 / Bond, Chancel 121-136. **4** Chester HT: Chester & NW AAHSJ xxxviii 128. Bond, Chancel p19 and Orme p96 differ as to chancel floor levels. **5** Cox & Harvey 18 (1636 q) / Cardwell, Annals ii 202 / Articles ... Norwich, 1638, sig. A4v (no. 11). **6** Tadlow: *The Works of ... William Laud*, vol 5 pt 2, Oxford, 1853, p367. By this time Matthew Wren had become Bishop of Ely and Tadlow fell within his diocese. Later, facing impeachment by the House of Commons, and seeking to defend his approach to rails, he alluded to the incident, adding the detail that the dog 'leap[t] upon the communion-table' in order to take the bread. He also argued that rails 'do preserve the Lord's table from sundry other ... abuses, not only of boys rioting, leaning, stepping, leaping, or throwing hats upon it, but also of sitting and standing upon it; yea, servants have heretofore been seen to hold young children upon it till they defiled it' (Wren pp76-77). **7** Stockton: NORA i 176. **8** Hawkhurst: Cox CWA 104 / Bungay: EA 1S iii 199. Without giving a date, *Proceedings of the Society of Antiquaries of London*, vol 4, 1859, p156 says the Bungay screen was 'removed by two over-zealous churchwardens, who were removed from office for their pains, and a new screen made at the cost of the parish'. **9** Harrison f77r / Frere & Kennedy iii 109 (1561) / Vallance 86.

13 Vestry. 1 Salisbury SM: Baker 34. **2** AH Staining: Povah 367. **3** Lydd 376 / Fulham: Fèret i 169 (firesholve) / Chipping: Smith 79. **4** Tooting: Morden 174. **5** SBE CWA 65b / SCLS: Accomptes 118b. **6** Bury St Edmunds SM: Tymms 153.

14 **Organs etc**. 1 Hopkins 428 / Williamson 219. 2 Boxford: Dict. of Organs 38 / SC Danes: Freeman 636b. 3 Grove Music Online, 'Organ', section on construction by Barbara Owen and Peter Williams. 4 Canterbury St Andrew: Cotton pt ii 34 (delived). 5 Addleshaw & Etchells 98. 6 SES xxix, xxx, 75, 77 (Water > Walter), 78, 113. Reseq. The costs relating to letters, curtains and seat are from undated accounts. In her introduction Amy Straton assumes they relate to the 1567 installation, an assumption followed here. 7 Sandwich SM: Dict. of Organs 29 / SM Outwich: NI 273 / SMH 361 / BS 43 / SB Gracechurch St: Freeman 636a / Somerton: Somersetshire ANHSP xxxix pt 2 p69. 8 Andover: Williams 5 / AH Staining: Povah 365 / Ludlow: Wright 121. 9 SAH: British Mag. xxxi 397 / Cambridge SMG: Foster 18 / SMH 375. 10 Leicester St Martin: North 224. 11 SMH 328, 343, 349 / SES 89 / Mere: Wilts ANHM xxxv 27 / SGWC: Baddeley 118 / Hackney: Simpson iii 273. 12 SMH 349 / Cambridge SMG: Foster 85 / Ludlow: Wright 10. 13 Cox, Fittings p240 says a bassoon was bought for Bunbury church, Cheshire, as early as 1712. 14 Youlgreave: Cox, Derbyshire ii 340 / East Budleigh: DART xxvi 362 / Edenbridge: Arch. Cant. xxi 123 / Helpston: Sweeting, Notes 92.

15 **Clocks**. 1 Ludlow: Wright 39 / Wandsworth: Surrey AC xv 115. 2 The following account is indebted to Beeson, in particular pp13-24, 99-100. 3 Wills, Bury 28 (Baret) / Beeson 99 ('the mechanism'). 4 Ludlow: Shropshire ANHST 2S iv 138 / Bury St Edmunds SM: Tymms 153 / Derby AS: W. H. St John Hope, 'An account of the clock and chimes of the parish church of All Saints, Derby', Derbyshire ANHSJ ii 92-100 (q 99). 5 Reading SL: Kerry 97. 6 Reading SM: Garry 114-117 (reseq). 7 Leicester St Martin: North 24 / SES 110 / Wandsworth: Surrey AC xviii 140 / Yarnton: Stapleton 243 / Soham: Fenland NQ i 372.

Bells

1 **Sanctus and sacring**. 1 SMH 101 / Cambridge SMG: Foster 35. 2 Henley: Inventories, Oxon 94. 3 Thame: Berks etc AJ xi 117. 4 Thurston, Bells 389-401 / CE ii 422a; xiii 433b / Edmund Buckle, 'Sanctus bell', *Notes and Queries for Somerset and Dorset*, vol 3, Sherborne, 1893, pp74-75 / Walters, Bells 123-135 / Inventories, Lancs i 21 (Eccles), 46 (Bury); ii 57 (Warrington), 131 (Brindle). Some commentaries conflate the sanctus and sacring bells, but while practice varied, and in some places one bell was no doubt used for both purposes, they are fundamentally distinct. 5 Wilkins ii 52a (1281), 132b (1287) / Thurston, Bells 394 (1287), 396 (1281). Regarding ringing 'on one side' (1281), the original Latin is *pulsetur campana in uno latere*. 'To *toll* a bell ... is to make him strike onely of one side' (John Minsheu, *The Guide into the Tongues*, 1617, p493a).

2 **Belfry**. 1 Pounds 490. 2 Reading SL: Kerry 87. 3 Minchinhampton: Archaeologia xxxv 432 / SES 170-171. 4 Quainton: Records of Bucks xii 31-32 / Duffield: Derbyshire ANHSJ xxxix 29 / Lancaster: Roper iii 629 / Northampton SG: Serjeantson 246.

3 **Casting etc**. 1 Ludlow: Shropshire ANHST 2S iv 123. 2 Castle Cary: Somersetshire ANHSP xxxvi pt 2 p65. 3 Kirkby Malzeard: Ellacombe 479-480 (reseq). 4 Ludlow: Shropshire ANHST 2S ii 127-130 (reseq). The 'gable' was paid for by weight and was possibly a cable. 5 Wood L&T i 211-212; ii 332. 6 SMH 274 / SES 153. 7 Peterborough SJB: Mellows 144 / Hartland: HMC 5th report app. 573b / Barton: North, Bells Lincoln etc 301-302. 8 Woodbury: Ellacombe 172 / Prescot: CWA 47 / Cranbrook: Stahlschmidt, Kent 238. 9 Houghton: Durham CWA 339. 10 Woodbury: Ellacombe 173 / Newcastle AS: Sopwith 127 / Woking: Stahlschmidt, Surrey 212-213 (wear > were). 11 Gillingham: Rochester Records 78 (Gillingham with Upberry). 12 Lambeth: Drew i 88 / SMC: Overall 179 / Chester SM: Earwaker 25. 13 SES 233. 14 Cullompton: Raven 227 (q) / Ellacombe 60 (makes no mention of suicide).

4 **Hallowing**. 1 Chambers DW appendix xix-xx. From the pontifical of Anianus, Bishop of Bangor, 1268. 2 Great Yarmouth: John L'Estrange, *The Church Bells of Norfolk*, Norwich, 1874, p17 n.8 (reseq). 3 Selborne: White 269.

5 **Supernatural powers**. 1 Golden Legend f22v col. a (in section 'The Letanyes the more and the lesse'; adjusted). Writing in the same period, Durand (1843 pp87-88) speaks in very similar terms regarding bells and storms. 2 Yeovil: Collectanea Topog. iii 136, 140 / Sandwich SM: Cox CWA 212 (1464); Stahlschmidt, Kent 394 (1507) / Spalding: North, Bells Lincoln etc 657. 3 Stow vol 1 pp vii, 196 (q). 4 Dawlish: A. J. Davy, 'Ringing bells during a thunderstorm',

Devon Notes and Queries, vol 1, Exeter, 1901, pp18-20 (q 18). **5** Hering 1625 sig. A4v. **6** Walters, Bells 261.

6 Used to mark time. 1 Luke 1:28 / CE i 486-488. **2** Lydd 340. **3** Cropredy: D. Royce, *Historical Notices of the Parish of Cropredy, Oxon*, Transactions of the North Oxfordshire Archaeological Society for ... 1879, Oxford, 1880, p43. **4** Blakesley: Wills, Northants 277 / Walberswick: Lewis 63, 65. **5** SES 90 / WM 124.

7 Curfew bell. 1 Edward Freeman, *The History of the Norman Conquest of England*, vol 3, 1869, p185 / Walters, Bells 146-149. **2** SM le Bow: Northampton Records i 252-253 (*Liber Custumarum*, compiled *c.* 1460; passage quoted appears to relate to an ordinance dated 1391) / Stow i 256. **3** Louth: Dudding 13-14 (1500; be > by). **4** Cropredy, West Rasen, etc: Edwards 223-227. **5** Wokingham: Edwards 202-204. The wording is not entirely clear and it is possible only the evening bell was rung for half an hour. **6** SM at Cliffe: Edwards 225 / Dyer, Social Life 192-193 (q). **7** Barton: Edwards 223-224 / Andrews, Curiosities 93-94.

8 Further uses. 1 Louth: Notices 51 / Eastbourne: Sussex AC xiv 132. **2** Barrow: Antiquary ii 96a (1713) / Driffield: Tyack 235. **3** St Alphage LW: Carter 74 / Cambridge SMG: Foster 421. **4** SES 212. **5** John Taylor, *Jack a Lent*, 1620, sig. B2. **6** Oxford SMV: Hearne viii 50 (27 Feb 1722-23) / Wellingborough: Northants NQ ii 51 (quoting *Wellingborough News*, 12 Mar 1886) / Maidstone: Wright i 13-15. **7** Warwick: Notices 30. **8** *The Works of Joseph Hall*, new edition, vol 11, Oxford, 1839, p126.

9 Passing bell. 1 SES 39 / Walsingham: NORA i 121 / SM Woolchurch: Walters, Bells 154. **2** Grose 66-67. **3** Durand 1843 p95 / Gerschow 7 (1602) / Articles ... Chichester, 1638, sig. B (Of visitation of the sick, no. 6). **4** Brand ii 203, incorrectly giving the Tower as the place of death. She died Katherine Seymour, Countess of Hertford. Her keeper at Yoxford was Sir Owen Hopton. / Abel Redevivus 490 (Rainolds). **5** Articles ... Worcester, 1662, p9. **6** Davis 65. A similar order had been issued in 1566 (Advertisements issued by Archbishop Parker, in Gee & Hardy p471). **7** Bourne 7-8. **8** Melton Mowbray & King's Cliffe: North, Bells Northants 131. Melton: quoting John Nichols. King's Cliffe: recollections of a Mrs Law who died in 1874, 'aged about 94 years'.

10 Post-mortem ringing. 1 Northampton SM: Wills, Northants 380. **2** Hooper 197 (Answer to the Bishop of Winchester's Book). **3** Gee & Hardy 471 (Advertisements issued by Archbishop Parker) / Davis 65 (no. 67). **4** EA 2S v 269 (contribution by H.A.W., parish not indicated). **5** Tyack 195-197 / North, Bells Lincoln etc 174-186. **6** Leverton: Thompson, Boston etc 574 / Marsham: Walters, Bells 159. **7** Durand 1843 pp95-96.

11 Funerals etc. 1 Durand 1843 p96 / Gee & Hardy 471 (1566) / Ellacombe 246. **2** *Chambers Etymological Dictionary of the English Language*, 1904, p278b (knell). **3** SMH 310-311 / SMC: Overall 223 / SMF: Kitto 315. **4** Wills, Lincoln ii 89. **5** Henry Thomas Ellacombe, *The Bells of the Cathedral Church of S. Peter, Exon*, Exeter, 1874, p7. **6** SES 239. **7** Peterborough SJB: Mellows 6. **8** Cranbrook: Stahlschmidt, Kent 240. **9** SMH 246 / SAH: British Mag. xxxiv 533 / Warwick: Notices 31.

12 Occasional ringing. 1 Ludlow: Shropshire ANHST 2S ii 140; iv 153-154 / SES 216, 233 (fn. re pulleys, 1656) / Salisbury ST: Swayne 340 / Bristol SP: Bristol P&P ii 135a. **2** WM 123 / Lambourn: Footman 120. **3** One relatively early example is the ringing at Andover in 1472 for the Duke of Clarence of Malmsey butt fame (Williams p5). See also main text p176 for duties at Bristol, 1462. **4** Lambeth: Drew i 108; ii 169, 195 / BS 71 / AH Staining: British Mag. iv 148 / Deptford: Hasted i 35a / Chelsea: Thomas Faulkner, *An Historical and Topographical Description of Chelsea and its Environs*, 1810, p133. **5** SES 152. **6** Wandsworth: Surrey AC xviii 150. **7** Lydd 373 / Leicester St Martin: North 173 / Burford: Monk 195. **8** Kensington: Thomas Faulkner, *History and Antiquities of Kensington*, 1820, p282. **9** SMH 198 / SMW: NI 13 / Coventry SM: Sharp 68 / Twickenham: Cobbett 189. **10** Machyn 310.

13 Marking history. 1 SMH 266 / Yatton: Hobhouse 164. **2** SB Bishopsgate: Malcolm i 327 (orig. 1585). **3** SB Aldgate: Atkinson 112 (orig. 1586) / Minehead: Cox CWA 219 (orig. 1586). **4** Salisbury ST: Swayne 297. **5** Plymouth: Rowe 233. **6** SMW: NI 28. **7** Prestbury: Morris 220 (orig. 1688). **8** SMW: NI 18 / Wilmslow: East Cheshire i 115 / Salisbury SM: Baker 43. **9** Ashover: *Country Life* 7 Jun 1902 p711a. **10** Lambourn: Footman 124 (orig. 1694) / Weybread: EA 1S ii 36 (orig. 1694). **11** Starston: Some Account 54 (orig. 1819).

12 Chester-le-Street: Blunt 68 (citing unspecified 'parish books').

14 Maintenance. 1 SES 39, 109, 112 / Leverington: Fenland NQ vii 188 / Redenhall: Candler 144 (makyy > making). **2** Stanford: Antiquary xvii 171b. **3** Rainham: Arch. Cant. xv 334a / Lambeth: Drew i 28 / Strood: Plomer 87 / Durham SO: Durham CWA 146 / Shrewsbury SM: Owen & Blakeway ii 368. **4** Peterborough SJB: Mellows 105. **5** *The Oxford Dictionary of Idioms* ed. Jennifer Speake lists bell clappers and an item of milling equipment as the two possible sources of 'like the clappers' (p67 of 2000 paperback edition). **6** Cranbrook: Stahlschmidt, Kent 239 / SES 160. **7** Strood: Plomer 137, 145 / Birchington: Stahlschmidt, Kent 177-178. **8** Eltham: Hasted i 206a / SMW: NI 19. **9** SES 90 / Bramley, Hants: Williams 47 / BS 59 / Ludlow: Shropshire ANHST 2S i 260 / Manchester: CWA 14. **10** Ludlow: Wright 30 / Lambeth: Drew i 77; Stahlschmidt, Surrey 172 (amount) / Kendal: Cumberland etc AAST ix 280. **11** Mere: Wilts ANHM xxxv 84. **12** Barham: Vis. Harpsfield i 78 (1557, noted with a view to its being recovered for the church) / WM 127 (1663).

15 Bell-ringers and rules. 1 Barnstaple: Chanter 84. **2** Canterbury SD: CWA 42, 64 / SMH 327 / Cullompton: CWA 370. **3** SES 242 (vestry book) / Kendal: Cumberland etc AAST xvi 212 / Tydd SM: North, Bells Lincoln etc 721 (the problem had been resolved by 1882). **4** Hastings: Sussex AC xxiii 197. John Potter Briscoe, *Curiosities of the Belfry*, 1883, includes a fairly comprehensive collection of ringing rules. **5** Burnley: NQ 3S viii 17b-18a. **6** Pitminster: NQ 5S iv 62. **7** Ellacombe 258.

16 Abuse and accidents. 1 Mere: Wilts ANHM xxxv 68 / BS 66 / Wenhaston: Clare 22. **2** Banbury: Vis. Peyton 205. **3** Prescot: CWA 153 / Kendal: Cumberland etc AAST ix 281. **4** Barrow: Antiquary ii 96a (1713). **5** Stoke Albany: Haigh 68. **6** Twickenham: Cobbett 112. **7** Manchester: CWA 15 (1682, 'pr' > 'for' x 3), 29 (1679). **8** Holbeach: Lincs NQ iv 69-70. **9** Oxford St Michael: *Oxford City Documents, Financial and Judicial, 1268-1665* ed. J. E. Thorold Rogers, Oxford, 1891, pp158-159; *Records of Medieval Oxford* ed. H. E. Salter, Oxford, 1912, p9b. **10** King's Lynn: B[enjamin] Mackerell, *The History and Antiquities of ... King's-Lynn in the County of Norfolk*, 1738, p233. **11** Culworth: North, Bells Northants 241. **12** Bungay: EA 1S iii 28. Quote is from contributor's summary, not a contemporary record. **13** Stamford: North, Bells Lincoln etc 669. **14** Chapel-en-le-Frith: Reliquary vi 67.

17 Delight. 1 Bramley, Hants: Williams 61. Similarly at St Edmund, Salisbury, in 1652 they receive a shilling from 'some strangers for ringinge for pleasuer' (Swayne p226). **2** *A Journey into England by Paul Hentzner, in the year* [*1598*], trans. Horace Walpole, 1757, p89. **3** Gerschow 7.

Paraphernalia

1 Vestments. 1 The phrase appears quite often in old accounts – at St Mary at Hill, for example, they hire out 'the churche stuffe' in 1479-81 (p94). It usually denotes vestments, cloths, etc, but is here applied more loosely. **2** Thame: Berks etc AJ x 88 / Walberswick: Lewis 55 / Saxilby: AASRP xix 388. **3** SES 39 / Cambridge SMG: Foster 56. **4** Norwich SPM: NORA xiv 154 (date), 197-198, 200, 204, 205. **5** SMH 26 (1431) / Reading SL: Kerry 105 (1517) / Thame: Berks etc AJ xii 15 (1448) / Canterbury SD: CWA 28 (1500; they are of course rochets) / AH Bread St: WR 86 (1552). **6** Warwick: Notices 20 / SMH 100 / SAH: British Mag. xxxii 145. **7** SMW: NI 30 / SBE CWA 99b. **8** Becon, Prayers 259-260 (from *The Displaying of the Popish Mass*).

2 Bread, wine etc. 1 SMC: Overall 29 / SB Gracechurch St: WR 189. **2** Fordwich: C. Eveleigh Woodruff, *A History of ... Fordwich*, Canterbury, 1895, p153 / Macclesfield: Wills, Lancs etc ii 166. **3** Rock i 110-113 / Cox CWA 58, 96-97. **4** Louth: Notices 49 / Leicester St Martin: North 34. **5** Yatton: Hobhouse 122 / Stanford: Antiquary xvii 118b. **6** Battersea 359, 373. **7** SMH 351 / Worcester: Amphlett 129 / Hartland: HMC 5th report app. 573b / SCLS: Accomptes 105b / Weybridge: Surrey AC xxi 146 / St Mabyn: London Society xliv 641b / Hawkhurst: Arch. Cant. v 78. **8** Smarden: Memorials 273 (presentment, 1608) / St Neot: AJ xlviii 73. **9** Salisbury ST: Swayne 288. **10** Manchester: CWA 23 / Cox CWA 94.

3 Other ceremonial items. 1 Peterborough SJB: Mellows 150. **2** Ashburton: CWA 36. **3** Prescot: CWA 15 / Chester SM: Earwaker 226. **4** Norwich SPM: NORA xiv 209 (inventory, *c.* 1500). **5** Aquinas xvii 457 (pt 3, question 83, article 5). **6** Cratfield: Raven 43. **7** Cox & Harvey 51-53.

Each of the types also has other uses but those listed are the main ones. **8** Worcester: Amphlett 30. **9** SMH 101, 343 / Bungay: EA 1S ii 277. **10** SP Cheap: JBAA xxiv 159 / SES 6 / Canterbury SD: CWA 26. **11** SAH: British Mag. xxxiii 565.

4 Books. **1** OED (missal etc) / AJ lxx 241-242 / Wordsworth & Littlehales, *passim*. / Rock iv 245-247. The use of some of the terms varies and changes over time. **2** Tavistock: Worth 6 / Cambridge HT: Cox CWA 111 / Wandsworth: Surrey AC xv 114. **3** Reading SL: Kerry 116-117 (edited and reseq). **4** SMC: Overall 40 / Louth: Dudding 92. **5** Hartland: HMC 5th report app. 573a. **6** BS 56 / Hartshorne: Derbyshire ANHSJ vii 41 / Ash: J. R. Planché, *A Corner of Kent, or, Some Account of the Parish of Ash-next-Sandwich*, 1864, p165. **7** Dartington: British Mag. vi 379. **8** Leverton: Archaeologia xli 339 / SMH 243, 256. **9** Cambridge SMG: Foster 281. **10** SMH 226 / Great Hallingbury: Essex AST 2S xxiii 110 / Bungay: EA 1S iii 198. **11** Cardwell, Annals i 9. **12** Great Hallingbury: Essex AST 2S xxiii 110 / Devizes: Cox CWA 121 / Fulham: Fèret i 186. **13** Mere: Wilts ANHM xxxv 34 / Hartland: HMC 5th report app. 572b / Salisbury ST: Swayne 303. **14** SMH 187 / SB Gracechurch St: Malcolm i 316. **15** Duffield: Derbyshire ANHSJ xxxix 35. **16** SD Backchurch: London & Middx AST 1S iv 205 / Battersea 238 / Leicester St Martin: North 212 / Chester-le-Street: Blunt 104. **17** Halesworth: Cratfield ed. Raven 121.

5 Lights. **1** Yatton: Hobhouse 84 / Bassingbourne: Cox CWA 165. **2** Prescot: CWA 24 / Chester HT: Chester & NW AAHSJ xxxviii 112. **3** Bristol SE: Bristol GAST xv 158 / Prescot: CWA 11 / SLP 122b / Lambeth: Drew i 71. **4** CE i 347b; iii 247 / Cox CWA 160-161. **5** Reading SL: Kerry 51. **6** SMC: Overall 123, 179 / Bath SM: Somersetshire ANHSP xxvi 122 / Prescot: CWA 40 / SP Cheap: JBAA xxiv 261. **7** OED (cotton candle, etc). 'White candles' not found in OED but they are mentioned by Rock (vol 2 p391 n.66). **8** SMH 277 / Ludlow: Wright 29 / Cambridge SMG: Foster 150 / St Alphage LW: Hall 41. **9** Ockley: Bax 52. **10** Rotherfield: Sussex AC xli 36 / Lewes St Andrew: Sussex AC xlv 46. **11** Walgrave: Wills, Northants 422 / Lydd 359. **12** Bristol AS: Bristol P&P i 202b / Walberswick: Lewis 7 / Bungay: EA 1S ii 151 / Thame: Lee 74 / SM Aldermanbury: Carter 1913 p107. **13** Cambridge SMG: Foster 29 / Bungay: EA 1S ii 277 / SBE CWA 74b. **14** SMH 251. **15** SAH: British Mag. xxxi 402; xxxii 33. **16** SMH 296 / St Alphage LW: Carter 88. **17** Reading SL: Kerry 53 / Lambeth: Drew i 25. **18** SMH 358 / Ludlow: Shropshire ANHST 2S ii 121. **19** SMC: Overall 84, 157 / Lambeth: Drew i 74. **20** SBE CWA 38a / SASA 337a. **21** SBE CWA 109b / SASA 341a. **22** Ludlow: Shropshire ANHST 2S iv 135 / BS 165. **23** Canterbury SD: CWA 46. **24** Canterbury St Andrew: Cotton pt iii 10 / St Alphage LW: Carter 67.

6 Chests. **1** SMH 255, 278, 306 / Rye: Holloway 478 / Tavistock: Worth 18 / SBE CWA 94b, 200b. **2** SMW: NI 25. **3** Leicester St Martin: North 163. **4** Burke 7 n. (adjusted). **5** Morebath: Binney 104. **6** Tate, Parish Chest 45. **7** Rodmarton: Burn PR 68.

7 Miscellaneous. **1** Cambridge SMG: Foster 315 / Hammersmith: Faulkner 206. **2** SM Outwich: London & Middx AST 2S vi 88 / Bungay: EA 1S iii 198 / Wandsworth: Surrey AC xx 173 / Rotherham: John Guest, *Historic Notices of Rotherham*, Worksop, 1879, p195. **3** Manchester: CWA 31 / Walthamstow ii 50 / Liskeard: Allen 153. **4** Wakefield: *Old Church Life* ed. William Andrews, 1900, p226. **5** Ulverston: Bardsley 110. **6** Bromley: William Hone, *The Table Book*, 1827, p465. **7** SS Walbrook: London & Middx AST 1S v 339 (date), 340. **8** Dry Drayton: Vis. Bradshaw 342.

8 For secular activities. **1** SMW: NI 18 / Chedder: HMC 3rd report app. 330a. **2** Woodbury: DART xxvi 353 / Chelmsford: Essex AST 1S ii 225. **3** SM Woolchurch: B&H li / Wandsworth: Surrey AC xx 189 / Norwich SPM: Norfolk Antiq. Misc. ii 335 / SCLS: Account Book 20b. **4** Salisbury ST: Swayne 325 / SASA 343a-b / Manchester: CWA 24. **5** Lambeth: Drew ii 138 / Ludlow: Shropshire ANHST 2S ii 106; iv 146. **6** SCLS: Archaeologia xlv 119. **7** SBE CWA 185b / Manchester: CWA 4. **8** Cox CWA 319. **9** WM 96 / SGWC: Baddeley 152 / SCLS: Accomptes 115a. **10** SB Aldersgate: Cox CWA 320 (1632). **11** SBE CWA 145a / SGWC: Baddeley 154 / SMW: NI 65 / St Ethelburga: Cobb 29. **12** Maidstone: Gilbert 213 / Norwich SPM: Norfolk Antiq. Misc. ii 337 / Ludlow: Shropshire ANHST 2S v 99 / Leyton: Kennedy 394. **13** Salisbury SM: Baker 83. **14** Wenhaston: Clare 23. **15** SR iii 425-426 (24 Henry VIII cap. 10); iv 498-499 (8 Elizabeth cap. 15). **16** Wandsworth: Surrey AC xvii 169 / Forncett: EA 1S ii 356.

9 Payments for vermin. 1 Shrewsbury, Abbey Church: Shropshire ANHST 1S i 59 / Prescot: CWA 92 / Thatcham: Barfield ii 114b / Beverley: Poulson ii 745 / North Lydbury: Shropshire Parish Docs. 218. **2** Chiddingly: Sussex AC xiv 247 / SM Bourne: Stevens 244 / Youlgreave: Reliquary iv 191 / Barnstaple: Chanter 90. **3** Moggerhanger: Elliott 56 / Kempston: Elliott 50 / Northill: Elliott 61. **4** SMF: Kitto 273 / Manchester: CWA 16 / Battersea 250. **5** Woodbury: Brushfield, Vermin 296 / Milton Bryan: Elliott 55 / Forncett: EA 1S ii 365. **6** Frithelstock: Brushfield, Vermin 307 / Milton Bryan: Elliott 56. **7** Countisbury: DART xxxviii 220 / Ravensden: Elliott 67. **8** Milton Bryan: Elliott 55.

Upkeep
1 Building repairs etc. 1 SMH 332 / Baldock: St Albans & Herts AAST 1928 pp136-137 / Chedder: HMC 3rd report app. 330b. **2** Worfield: Shropshire ANHST 4S ii 31-32 (reseq) / SES 181. **3** BS 24 / Peterborough SJB: Mellows 75 / SMC: Overall 135 / SBE CWA 45b / Reading SM: Garry 134 / Ludlow: Shropshire ANHST 2S iv 130. **4** Thame: Berks etc AJ x 87, 89. **5** Lydd 340-341 (reseq) / Crondall: Williams 121 / Cambridge SMG: Foster 248 (reseq) / Salisbury ST: Swayne 348. **6** Yatton: Hobhouse 138 / Ludlow: Shropshire ANHST 2S iv 131 / Durham SO: Durham CWA 194. **7** Leverton: Archaeologia xli 349. **8** Ludlow: Shropshire ANHST 2S iv 156 / Warwick: Notices 63 / Durham SO: Durham CWA 212. **9** SAH: British Mag. xxxi 402-403 / SMH 220 / Oxford SPE: Tyssen 299. **10** SMF: Kitto 405 (reseq) / Worfield: Shropshire ANHST 3S x 79; 4S ii 32-33 (reseq) / Northwold: NORA xxviii pt 4 p286. **11** Thame: Berks etc AJ viii 76 / SES 152 ('a' omitted before 11) / Chester HT: Chester & NW AAHSJ xxxviii 148. **12** Peterborough SJB: Mellows 107 / Louth: Dudding 220. **13** Eastington: Glos NQ iii 249. **14** SBE CWA 95a, 100a-b. **15** SBE CWA 13b. **16** Leicester St Martin: North 101 (Ynge > Younge) / Northwold: NORA xxviii pt 4 p287. **17** Ludlow: Wright 43 / Loughborough: Reliquary xiii 202 / Manchester: CWA 5. **18** Kingston UT: Surrey AC viii 80. **19** SMC: Overall 72 / Coventry HT: Sharp 109 / Ludlow: Shropshire ANHST 2S iv 120. **20** Reading SG: Nash 64 / Eltham: Hasted i 206a / Ludlow: Shropshire ANHST 2S ii 131-132 (reseq) / Kendal: Cumberland etc AAST ix 274 / Manchester: CWA 31. **21** Kendal: Cumberland etc AAST ix 274. **22** Hearne xi 338 (12 May 1734). **23** Ludlow: Shropshire ANHST 2S i 252-254 (reseq). **24** Hartland: HMC 5th report app. 573a / SJZ 378a / Mere: Wilts ANHM xxxv 275 / BS 73. **25** BS 50 / Ludlow: Wright 159. **26** SMW: NI 70. **27** SH Bishopsgate: J. E. Cox 224. **28** Norwich SPM: Norfolk Antiq. Misc. ii 329 / SASA 366a.
2 General upkeep. 1 Kilmington: Cornish 47 / Newbury: Money 529 / Oxford St Martin: Fletcher 47 / Derby SW: Derbyshire ANHSJ xxxix 223 / SASA 368b. **2** Ludlow: Wright 34 / SM Woolnoth: B&H xxv / Kendal: Cumberland etc AAST ix 281. **3** SMW: NI 4, 245 / SM Friday St: JBAA xxv 362 / SM Woolnoth: B&H xxvii. **4** SMH 235 / Ludlow: Shropshire ANHST 2S iv 141 / High Wycombe: Records of Bucks viii 57. **5** SASA 372a / St Olave Hart St: Povah 232 / Chester-le-Street: Blunt 108 / Salisbury SM: Baker 52.
3 Cleaning etc. 1 Cambridge SMG: Foster 351. **2** Lambeth: Drew ii 224 / SBE CWA 40a / Leominster: George Fyler Townsend, *The Town and Borough of Leominster*, Leominster, 1863, p237 (chapter on church contributed by Edward A. Freeman). **3** SAH: British Mag. xxxii 37, 148 / Canterbury SD: CWA 12 / Ludlow: Wright 7 / SBE CWA 144b / Salisbury ST: Swayne 338 / Smarden: Memorials 253. **4** SMW: NI 10 / Peterborough SJB: Mellows 149 / Redenhall: Candler 70. Fn. Morebath: Binney 111. **5** Battersea 241. **6** Walberswick: Lewis 15 / Norwich SPM: Norfolk Antiq. Misc. ii 339 / Cambridge SMG: Foster 397. **7** Salisbury ST: Swayne 300. **8** Yatton: Hobhouse 125 / Peterborough SJB: Mellows 85, 149 / Bramley, Hants: Williams 43 / Ockley: Bax 47. **9** SMF: Kitto 190 / Chester HT: Chester & NW AAHSJ xxxviii 144. **10** SAH: British Mag. xxxii 156 / Lichfield: Harwood 523 / WM 110 / SASA 337b / Ludlow: Shropshire ANHST 2S iv 160 / Kendal: Cumberland etc AAST ix 278 / Manchester: CWA 15. **11** SASA 347a / Fulham: Fèret i 277. **12** Peterborough SJB: Mellows 173. **13** Bristol SE: Bristol GAST xv 158 / SBE CWA 65a, 117a; fn. OED (scavenger) / Wilson, Plague 26-27. **14** Ipswich SC: EA 2S iii 290 / Ludlow: Shropshire ANHST 2S ii 110. **15** SJZ 388a, 399a. **16** SMH 240, 373 / SM Woolnoth: B&H lxiv. **17** SMH 378. **18** Cambridge SMG: Foster 208. **19** SMC: Overall 24 /

Kirkham: Dyer, Gleanings 332 / Wilmslow: East Cheshire i 114. **20** SMC: Overall 13 / Battersea 251. **21** Kendal: Cumberland etc AAST ix 283 / Derby SW: Derbyshire ANHSJ xl 235 / Brentford: Faulkner 1845 p148. **22** WM 92 / Reading SL: Kerry 93 / Almondbury: Hulbert 103.

4 Fumigation etc. 1 'St Margaret, Fenchurch Street' [? SM Pattens]: H. Westall, *The Case for Incense*, 1899, p162 (reseq) / Norwich St Margaret: East Counties Collectanea 11 / Norwich SPM: Norfolk Antiq. Misc. ii 346. **2** Ludlow: Wright 60 / SES 109-110 / SMC: Overall 180. **3** Pittington: Durham CWA 28 / BS 69. **4** Oxford SPE: Tyssen 301.

5 Birds etc. 1 Cambridge SMG: Foster 81 / Louth: Notices 50 / Worksop: White 331. **2** Kingston UT: Surrey AC viii 100 (year not entirely clear from wording and possibly 1569). **3** Worfield: Shropshire ANHST 3S ix 124-125 / Coventry SM: Sharp 70. **4** Leicester St Martin: North 115 / Lambeth: Drew i 123 / Coventry SM: Sharp 70 / Chester SJB: Lectures 161. **5** Worksop: White 337 / Redenhall: Candler 90. **6** Coventry SM: Sharp 70 / Cranfield: Elliott 37. **7** Peterborough Cathedral: Sweeting, Notes 53 / Leicester St Martin: North 107. **8** Leicester St Martin: North 103, 108 / Sapcote: *Leicestershire and Rutland Notes and Queries*, vol 1, 1891, p310. **9** Shrewsbury SM: Owen & Blakeway ii 359 / Cambridge SMG: Foster 455. **10** Stockton: NORA i 191 / High Wycombe: Records of Bucks viii 58. **11** Sandwich SM: Boys 365 (yer on > theron; oyer > other). **12** Wilmslow: East Cheshire i 116. **13** Sandwich SM: Boys 363 (no date indicated) / Redenhall: Candler 92 (1743). **14** Long Melford 116. **15** South Littleton: Midland Antiquary i 106. **16** Southwark SS: W. Taylor, *Annals of St Mary Overy: An Historical and Descriptive Account of St Saviour's Church and Parish*, 1833, p127 (1562). The passage quoted may be Taylor's summary. **17** SMC: Overall 40 / SMH 322, 379 / Wenhaston: Clare 21 / Maidstone: Gilbert 216 / Hardingstone: Northants NQ iv 203.

Routine & People
Routine
1 The outline attempted here is based largely on Bowers and on Wordsworth & Littlehales pp15-20. Barnwell, 'The Use of the Church', p48 notes the important caveat that, because of varying local customs and resources, 'it remains impossible to establish with certainty what actually happened in a parish church, even on Sundays and major feasts'. **2** Maskell vol 3 xxix-xxxi / Orme 220 / Barnwell 49. Bowers p136 suggests that by the later Middle Ages the lesser hours were observed by the clergy 'in private in the parsonage study or anywhere convenient'. **3** Gasquet 144 / Bowers 137. **4** SMC: Overall 208. **5** SMC: Overall 207 (1504) / Doncaster: Page i 175 (1546, certificate of St Nicholas chantry). **6** Bowers 135-136 / J. Wickham Legg in *Essays on Ceremonial by various authors* ed. Vernon Staley, 1904, p68 / OED (high mass, low mass). **7** Wakefield: Page ii 311 (1546 certificate) / Mirk I 10. Fn. Johnson ii 84, 440. **8** York SD: Page i 61 (reseq). **9** The Synod of Exeter (1287) instructs priests to move their parishioners to attend church 'on feast days, and specially on the Lord's days, to hear the divine office', and in 1401 Archbishop Arundel orders them to exhort people to attend 'at least parish mass' on those days. Wilkins ii 145 (1287); iii 266 (1401) / Edward Vansittart Neale, *Feasts and Fasts*, 1845, pp283-286 / Maskell vol 3 xxx-xxxiv / Orme 231-233. **10** The sequence given is based largely on the ones provided by Wordsworth & Littlehales (pp18, 20) for Masham and Doncaster. **11** Legg includes this list of duties in The Clerk's Book and largely treats it as relating to clerks. **12** Coventry HT: Sharp 122-124. The extracts have been condensed, resequenced and otherwise adjusted and spelling has been partly modernised. Further extracts relating to miscellaneous chores are given later in this chapter and a few others relating to annual festivals (e.g. Easter, All Souls' Day) in the Year chapter. **13** Henry Barclay Swete, *Church Services and Service-books before the Reformation*, 1896, pp172-174 / Duffy, Altars 124 / Orme 236.

People
1 Clergy. 1 SMH liv-lv, 130, 340. **2** ODCC 1380-1381. Useful brief accounts of tithes can be found in Tate, Parish Chest pp134-143 and Pounds pp43-66, 208-214. **3** Herne: J. R. Buchanan, *Memorials of Herne, Kent*, 1887, pp57-58. **4** Pounds 214-216. **5** Pounds 176-177 / Lindley 281. **6** High Wycombe: Clark 166. **7** South Kirkby: Page i 165. **8** Coventry HT: Sharp 122-124. Adjusted as with the extracts used above under Routine. Legg li-liii

discusses the distribution of holy water. **9** Davis 50, 52 (nos. 50, 52). **10** Worfield: Shropshire ANHST 4S ii 41 / Weybread: EA 1S ii 37. **11** Battersea 262 / SM Woolchurch: B&H liv. **12** SMW: NI 11 / Tavistock: Worth 33 / SBE CWA 152b. **13** Pounds 158-159 / Orme 57-60 / SR iv 67 (2 & 3 Edward VI cap. 21, An Acte to take awaye all punitive lawes againste Marriage of Priestes) / Bishop Barnes 17-18.

2 Singers. 1 SMC: Overall 22 / SMH 256 / SMF: Kitto 91. **2** SMH 197, 322 / SM Woolnoth: B&H xxiii. **3** SMH 305, 322, 327, 350 (for fn.) / SES 103 / Salisbury ST: Swayne 293. **4** SMH xxi-xxii, 275, 316. **5** Hayes: Antiquary xviii 65b.

3 Parish clerk. 1 Davis 85 (no. 91) / Preston: Smith 276 (1754 payment to Henry Barns, 'alias Amen'). Legg's introduction to The Clerk's Book, xvii-lxii, is a detailed account of clerks and their duties. **2** SD Backchurch: Chester 189 / Steeple Ashton: Wilts NQ vi 427 / Waltham Abbey: Winters 111 / Billington: Elliott 27. **3** Louth: A. E. B. Owen 136. **4** East Ham: Vis. Hale 238. **5** Buxted: Sussex AC iv 255. **6** Totteridge: Burn PR 129. **7** SLP 121a-b. **8** Davis 85-86 (no. 91). **9** Myddle: Gough 22.

4 Sexton. 1 Bingley: *Curious Epitaphs* ed. William Andrews, 1899, p130 / Chester SJB: Lectures 149 (quoting 'record' of service of Carter, who was sexton from 1752). **2** Faversham: Arch. Cant. xx 206-208 (q; ilis > aisles) / Legg, appendix 5, p79 (skomering). **3** Loughborough: Reliquary xiv 128 (condensed and adjusted). The contributor suggests that 'from the handwriting and expressions used' the list may date from the reign of Edward VI, but it is perhaps earlier. **4** Hackney: Simpson iii 85-86 (the interpolation is perhaps Simpson's) / Northampton HS: Cox & Serjeantson 175. **5** SASA 426-427. At St Laurence Pountney six women in a row held the post from 1757, the sixth being elected in 1812 (Wilson p172). **6** SMH 290 / Houghton-le-Spring: Durham CWA 314. **7** Plymouth: Rowe 242 / Stepney: Hill & Frere 39-40, 191 / Leicester St Martin: North 196. In fairness to the Plymouth sexton, it seems he later repented and returned the money. **8** Crowland: Fenland NQ iv 225-227, including letter from Robert Hardy of Mountfield Court Lodge, Sussex, dated 26 Oct 1782. **9** Peterborough SJB: Mellows 150, 170, 172, 176. **10** ODNB (Robert Scarlett) / Northants NQ i 249-251 (q; scarbabe).

5 Dogwhipping etc. 1 SMW: Smith, Catalogue 43 / Cambridge SMG: Foster 376 / Smarden: Memorials 252 / Battersea 250 / Leicester St Martin: North 228. **2** Barnsley: Andrews, Curiosities 177 / Ulverston: Bardsley 100. **3** Salisbury SM: Baker 45. **4** Chislet: Edwards 222. **5** Ludlow: Wright 102, 134. The whipper at Cullompton, Devon, was also equipped with a bell: CWA p379 (1726). **6** Bray: Cox CWA 309 / Burnsall: Stavert 11 / North Lydbury: Shropshire Parish Docs. 216. **7** Mullion: Cox CWA 308 / Youlgreave: Cox, Fittings 295. **8** Antony: *The Voyce of the Lord in the Temple, or, A most strange and wonderfull relation of Gods great power ... in sending ... a fiery ball into the church of Anthony in Cornwall*, 1640, p10. **9** Bath Abbey: [Philip Thicknesse], *The New Prose Bath Guide, for the year 1778*, p90. **10** Northorpe: Lincs NQ i 88 (contribution of Edward Peacock). **11** AH Staining: British Mag. iii 654 / Chester HT: Chester & NW AAHSJ xxxviii 155 / Plymouth: Rowe 240, 241 / Cullompton: CWA 376 / Almondbury: Hulbert 106 / SGWC: Baddeley 159. **12** Swayne p325 refers to a 1647 vestry order at St Thomas, Salisbury, which seeks to prevent children sitting at the front of the gallery 'to the annoyance of those that sit under'. **13** Battersea 253. **14** SMW: NI 30 / Fulham: Fèret i 278 n. **15** Almondbury: Hulbert 103 / Prestwich: NQ 5S iv 71. **16** Sutton-on-the-Hill: Cox, Derbyshire iii 332 (1754, vestry).

6 Beadle etc. 1 Basingstoke: Baigent 526 (vestry). **2** Handsworth: NQ 5S iii 415a (letter from George Worley). **3** Durham SN: Durham CWA 245 / Fulham: Fèret ii 2 / Shoreditch: *The Account of Jeremiah Long, senior Churchwarden, from November the 24th, 1846, to June the 17th, 1847*, [1847], p91. **4** Leyton: Kennedy 383 / Mortlake: Anderson 68 (1787; quotation may be partly summarised by Anderson). **5** Derby SW: Derbyshire ANHSJ xl 226-227. **6** Tooting: Morden 93.

7 Churchwardens. 1 Davis 84-85, 97-100 (nos. 90, 109-113). Tate, Parish Chest pp95-98 summarises the varied tasks that fall to churchwardens. **2** Davis 83 (no. 89) / Webb 22 / SM Lothbury: Vestry Book xvii. **3** Exeter St Petrock: DART xiv 409. For a detailed account see Katherine French, 'Women churchwardens in late medieval England', in The Parish in Late Medieval England, pp302-321. **4** Fn. Woodbury: DART xxvi 338. Pounds p185 cites a couple of other possible exceptions to the unpaid rule. **5** SMF: Kitto 183 / Cambridge SMG: Foster 286 / Cratfield: Raven 168. **6** Salisbury ST: Swayne 311. **7** SAH: British Mag. xxxv 281 / SMF: Kitto 537. **8** Westminster SJ: JHC xxiv 240b-241b. Two sequences in a row are headed 1723. Extracts are from the second sequence and so perhaps relate to 1724. **9** Kendal: Cumberland etc AAST xvi 171. **10** Cambridge SMG: Foster 163, 370-371 / SBE CWA 51a, 83a, 119b (1641, an even higher fine, £30, paid by a Mr Farington) / SJZ 386a (1639). **11** Sutton: Vis. Sussex i 73 / Tortington: Vis. Sussex i 101.

8 The vestry. 1 Webb 36-37. Cox CWA pp12-14 and Pounds pp192-193 are useful brief accounts of the vestry system. **2** SM Lothbury: Vestry Book 29b-30a / Fulham: Fèret i 275 / Tooting: Morden 58 / Minchinhampton: Webb 53. **3** Norwich SPM: Webb 35 n.3 (citing vestry minutes, April 1797). **4** SCLS: Accomptes 113b / Leicester St Mary: Leicestershire AAST vi 235 / Salisbury ST: Swayne 343 / Otterton: DART xxvi 394. **5** Morebath: Duffy, Morebath 29-31 (also four and five) / Pittington & Houghton: Durham CWA 52, 277. **6** Kumin 252 (59 out of 109) / SB Aldgate: Gibson, Codex, 1761, ii 1476. **7** SA Holborn: Griffith 67-73 (information presented to the star chamber in 1635; qs 68, 71). **8** Defoe 9 (repairs), 10 (rogues). **9** SMF: Kitto 585-586 / Cox CWA 14 / JHC xxiv 201a-202a (candles 1736-40; wine 1727; glazing 1730; present and dinner 1726). **10** Lambeth: Drew iii 207 / Hastings: Sussex AC xxiii 99. **11** Stoke Damerel: Webb 93 / Bethnal Green: Webb 89 n.1. **12** Walter C. Ryde, *The Local Government Act, 1894, with full explanatory notes*, 1894, *passim.*, including pp22, 79, 82.

Year

Preamble. 1 Dates are largely drawn from Edward Alexander Fry, *Almanacks for Students of History*, 1915, table 15 and pp80-81. **2** Hutton ME and SS *passim.* / Pounds 259 / Duffy, Altars 46.

New Year's Day. 1 Ecclesfield: Andrews, Curiosities 195. **2** Sutton-in-Ashfield: Vis. Notts xxxi 138.

Epiphany. 1 Great Yarmouth: Blomefield xi 366 (1465 and 1506); Palmer 1856 p117 (1512). **2** Great Yarmouth: L. G. Bolingbroke, 'Pre-Elizabethan plays and players in Norfolk', NORA xi 332-351 (q 334-335). His account appears to derive (perhaps via Palmer 1872 vol 1 p350) from Fosbroke pp47b-48a. Fosbroke in turn drew (in his case with acknowledgement) on the entry for 'Stellae Festum' in Charles du Cange's *Glossarium* of medieval and late Latin writers first published in 1678 (vol 6, Paris, 1846, p367c). It appears that the only contemporary evidence for the ceremony at Yarmouth lies in the brief CWA entries quoted. See also Hutton ME pp15-16.

Plough Monday. 1 Hutton ME 75. **2** Tilney: Stallard 153, 154 / Leverton: Archaeologia xli 368. **3** North Muskham: E. C. Cawte, 'It's an ancient custom, but how ancient?', in *Aspects of British Calendar Customs* ed. Theresa Buckland & Juliette Wood, Folklore Soc., Sheffield, 1993, p51. **4** John Bale, *Yet a Course at the Romyshe Foxe*, 1543, f28r (censing) / *Select Works of John Bale* ed. Henry Christmas, Parker Soc., Cambridge, 1849, p528 (conjuring) / Hutton ME 16. **5** Anne Baker, *Glossary of Northamptonshire Words and Phrases*, vol 2, 1854, pp123-124. 'Trick or treat' style consequences are also described in GM (Dec) 1762 p568b. **6** Kingston upon Hull: Chambers, Mediaeval Stage ii 370-371 (accounts of Trinity House, a guild of master mariners and pilots; q; reseq) / Andrews, Curiosities 19-20.

Candlemas. 1 Yatton: Hobhouse 100 / SM Pattens: AJ xlii 325. **2** Warren ii 289. **3** Beverley: Smith, Gilds 149-150 (1389 ordinance). **4** Mirk F 59-60 / Duffy, Altars 15-16 / Hutton SS 141-142.

Shrove Tuesday. 1 *Homilies of the Anglo-Saxon Church* ed. Benjamin Thorpe, vol 1, 1844, pp164-165. **2** *The Journal of William Schellinks' Travels in England 1661-1663*, translated and edited by Maurice Exwood & H. L. Lehmann, Camden Soc., 1993, p73. **3** Records of Bucks viii 80. **4** Matthew 26:34, 69-75 / *Poetical Works of ... Sir Charles Sedley baronet*, 1707, p64. Hutton, SS p153 says 'it made sense to kill off poultry if eggs were forbidden in Lent', but this does not explain the particular choice of cockerels for slaughter. **5** Badsey: Barnard 15 / Harrow: Lysons ii 588. **6** East Bergholt: Suffolk AIP xiii 395 (visitation book of Archdeacon of Suffolk). **7** Hayes: Antiquary xviii 65b (quoting Rev. C. Manning). **8** Wakefield: W. S. Banks, *Walks in Yorkshire: Wakefield and its Neighbourhood*, 1871, p84 /

High Wycombe: Records of Bucks viii 80. **9** Sussex AC xxxiii 239. **10** Knotting: CSP Domestic 1637 p508.

Ash Wednesday. **1** Matthew 4:2 / Mark 1:13 / Luke 4:2. **2** Coventry HT: Sharp 123 (1462; adjusted). **3** Dorcastor sig. B iii-iiii. The author's stated intent (sig. A ii) is to set out the 'supersticious trumpery' of the unreformed Church. See also Warren vol 1 pp143-151. **4** Rock iv 71-72 / Thurston, Lent 89-93 / Orme 262. **5** Feasey 1-49 / Hope & Atchley 59 (timing). **6** Great Yarmouth: Palmer 1856 p119 / WM 96. **7** Faversham: Arch. Cant. xviii 111 / SMM Old Fish St: WR 480. **8** Becon, Early Works 111. **9** SS Coleman St: Archaeologia l [50] 43, 44 (*Covyngs*) / SCLS: Archaeologia xlv 117. **10** Bungay: EA 1S ii 277. **11** Hope & Atchley 59 ('The Lenten veil was hung ... at first on the Saturday after Ash Wednesday, but in the 14th century on the Monday after the first Sunday in Lent') / Feasey 2, 14-17 (p14: 'from the first Monday after Ash Wednesday ... or the first evensong on the first Sunday in Lent') / Hutton ME 20-21. **12** Thame: Lee 33 / Long Melford 85 (1529 inventory). **13** PK f49v. **14** SR iv 65 (An Acte for abstinence from Fleshe, 2 & 3 Edward VI, cap. 19). **15** SR iv 422-428 (An Acte ... for the maintenance of the Navye, 5 Elizabeth cap. 5; qs 424-425; Mighell > Michael) / SBE CWA 102a. **16** Wedmore: *Wedmore Parish Registers: Baptisms 1561-1812* ed. S.H.A.H., Wells, 1890, p97. **17** St Alphage LW: Hall 25 / Henley: Cox CWA 252. **18** Waters 78 / Tate, Parish Chest 156.

Palm Sunday. **1** Sources for this section include: Warren i 217-229 / Feasey 53-83 / Tyrer 45-68 / Rock iv 264-268 / Hutton ME 20-21. **2** Feasey 62 / Hutton ME 20-21. **3** Lydd 389. **4** Dorcastor sig. B v ('The halowing of Palmes') / Duffy, Altars 24. **5** SMH 364 / Peterborough SJB: Mellows 150 (cost covers two years). **6** SMH 364. **7** Warren i 220 / Becon, Early Works 112-116 (Potation for Lent) / Tyrer 57-58 / Davison 2. **8** Matthew 21:1-9 (q) / Tyrer 57 / Warren i 222-223 / Erler 63-64. **9** Warren i 222 n.2 / Tyrer 58-59 / Sarum Processional ed. Henderson vi, 50 / Erler 72 / Feasey 75. Henderson notes that the boy prophet is first found in the Processional of 1508. **10** Long Melford 72. Martyn recalls the boy as singing 'Behold, thy king cometh unto thee,' which the Sarum Missal (Warren i 222) says is to be sung by the three clerks. **11** Erler 64-65. **12** St Alphage LW: Hall 17 / Reading SL: Kerry 25 (1559, rubbish), 238. The Loreman references could of course be to different people of the same name. **13** REED Ecc. London 363. **14** SS Walbrook: Cox CWA 255 / SMH 354. **15** SMH 327, 373 / SM Woolnoth: B&H xvii, xix. **16** Davison 12 / Feasey 63, 65-66 ('the second station in parish churches appears to have been generally made in the cemetery or churchyard, at the cross') / Warren i 224. **17** Long Melford 72 (Martyn) / Dialogue or Familiar Talke sig. D. iii verso ('Then cakes'). **18** Becon, Early Works 114-115. **19** Canterbury St Andrew: Cotton pt ii 39 / Lewes St Andrew: Sussex AC xlv 49. **20** In the CWA seen the angel does not feature alongside any prophet(s), perhaps suggesting it was an alternative. **21** AH Staining: Povah 365. **22** PK f50r. **23** Warren i 225 / Becon, Early Works 115 / Duffy, Altars 25 / Feasey 67, 79. **24** Brampton: Cambs & Hunts AST iv pt 3 pp82-83 (Cardinal Pole's visitation). **25** Canterbury SD: CWA 33. **26** Warren i 228 / Feasey 64, 79-80 / Duffy, Altars 25-26. **27** SP Cheap: JBAA xxiv 263 / Reading SL: Coates 217.

Wednesday in Holy Week. **1** Warren i 235 / Chambers DW 94. **2** Feasey 84-94 / Tyrer 81-84. Formally it is the night office of the Thursday, Friday and Saturday of Holy Week but it became customary to perform it on the preceding evenings in anticipation. **3** Stanford: Antiquary xvii 120a. **4** Mirk F 117-118 (adjusted). Fn. 1 (tre): Dartmouth: Watkin 329 / Skillington & New Sleaford: PF 138. Fn. 2 (hearse): Bramley, Hants: Williams 31. **5** Feasey 87, 91 (Sarum Breviary 24 candles; Canterbury and York 25; Roman use 15) / Chambers DW 95 / CE vii 162b-163a. **6** Mirk F 118 (adjusted). **7** Thurston, Lent 270-271. **8** PK ff50v-51r. Feasey p90 notes similar disturbances at Florence and Seville and the custom appears to have been more commonly recorded on the Continent than in England.

Maundy Thursday. **1** OED (Maundy, Sheer Thursday) / Mirk F 125 (adjusted). **2** Warren i 236-241 / Feasey 101 / Tyrer 86-89 / Thurston, Lent 309-314. **3** Feasey 102-104 / Tyrer 96-105 / Thurston, Lent 315-325. **4** Duffy, Altars 28 / Feasey 107-110. **5** Dartmouth: Watkin 322. Main text p319 has a reference to washing at High Halstow, Kent, and Sharp p124 notes the relevant duties of the deacons of Holy Trinity, Coventry. **6** Mirk F 126 (adjusted). **7** Warren i 242 / Feasey 102, 105-107 / Tyrer 105-108.

Good Friday. 1 Tyrer 117. **2** Rites of Durham 11-12 (adjusted). **3** Feasey 123. **4** SM Pattens: Sacristy i 262 / Cambridge SMG: Foster 138. **5** William Kethe, *A Sermon made at Blandford Forum*, 1571, ff18v–19r (bacon) / John Old, *A Short Description of Antichrist*, 1555, f8r (apples) / Feasey 125. **6** SMW: NI 8 / Ludlow: Wright 78. **7** Rites of Durham 12 / Dennington: *Handbook for Essex, Suffolk, Norfolk, and Cambridgeshire*, pub. John Murray, 1870, pp153b-154a / Earl's Colne: Essex AST 2S xxi 243 (1500). **8** SCLS: Archaeologia xlv 117 / SN Cole Abbey: WR 532. **9** SMH 234 / Chester SM: Earwaker 212. **10** SMH 343. **11** SD in the East: WR 251 (1550 inventory) / Poole: John Sydenham, *The History of the Town and County of Poole*, Poole, 1839, p313 (1545 inventory: 'A tewell to cover the crosse & the pelow in ye sepulcor ye Good Friday'). A pillow is also used at Woodbury, Devon (DART xxiv 350, 1546 inventory). **12** Hagworthingham: Lincs NQ i 7 / Lewes St Andrew: Sussex AC xlv 45 / Stratton: Archaeologia xlvi 211 / Oxford St Martin: Fletcher 37. **13** Tyrer 141 / Feasey 158-159 ('The Sarum rubrical direction was that one wax taper at least was to burn before the sepulchre ... At Hereford a lighted candle was to be placed within the sepulchre with the cross, and the door closed'). **14** Ludlow: Wright 78. **15** Walberswick: Lewis 16, 33. **16** Sibertswold: Wills, East Kent 307 / Chelsfield: Wills, West Kent A 248 / Luddington: Wills, Northants 360 / Bradden: Wills, Northants 282-283. **17** SD Backchurch: London & Middx AST 1S iv 208. **18** Becon, Actes f. ccccvi [406] r. **19** Feasey 168 (Orleans) / Warren i 263 (pyx). **20** PK f51v. **21** SAH: British Mag. xxxii 280 / Canterbury St Andrew: Cotton pt iii 26 / Worcester: Amphlett 12. **22** Coventry HT: Sharp 123-124 (1462).

Easter Eve. 1 Feasey 187 / Luke 23:44-45 / Rock iv 107-108. **2** Warren i 265 / Coventry HT: Sharp 123-124 (1462; adjusted). **3** Warren i 267-269. **4** Feasey 192-193. **5** Machyn 169 (21 March 1558). **6** SLP 121a / Lydd 416. **7** WR 51. **8** Reading SL: Kerry 51 / SLP 121a. **9** Feasey 221. **10** SP Cornhill: WR 580 / Bletchingley: Surrey AC xxix 28. **11** Walberswick: Lewis 5 / Lambeth: Drew i 15. **12** Confusingly the term Judas has several, not always evidently distinct meanings in relation to church lights.

i. A support for the paschal candle, as indicated in the main text, whether a simple base, a socket candlestick, a pricket, or an inner column around which the wax is cast. '1519. Memorandum, that the Judas of the pascall, that is to sey the timbre that the wax of the pascall is dreven upon, weyeth 7 lb. di.' (St Mary at Hill) [SMH 308].

ii. A stand for the candles extinguished during the Tenebrae service. '*c*. 1500. Lumber timber. Item, a thing called Judas with prikketts for candells upon tenable days.' (St Peter Mancroft, Norwich, inventory) [NORA xiv 227]. Adding to the scope for confusion, another versatile term, 'hearse', is also used for a stand serving this purpose.

iii. A stand or holder for other church lights including processional ones. '1488. Ther bith 6 Judas staves for torches peinted, having iche a castell gilded to set inne torchetts to bere with the sacrement on Corpus Cristi daye and other times.' (St Christopher le Stocks, inventory) [Archaeologia xlv 119] | '1503-1505. Paid a carpenter for 3 new Judases in the rood loft & nailes to the same ... 5d | 1514-1516. Paid to Dennes smithe for the platinge of 4 Judas for torchis agenst Corpus Christi daye ... 2s' (All Hallows Staining) [British Mag. ii 244] | '1533. Paid to the goodman Gaats for painting of the Judas or stook of the roode light ... 4s 4d' (St Peter, Cheapside) [JBAA xxiv 256].

iv. Candles or other lights affixed to one of the above types of stand. '1527. For Tenebre candelles & Judas candelles ... 11d | 1531-33. For 2 lb. of Judas candelles ... 12d' (St Andrew Hubbard) [British Mag. xxxiv 187, 302] | '1534. [Paid to the chandler] for our sepulchre light, our paschall & Judas candells called teneber candells [etc] ... 10s 10d' (All Hallows Staining) [British Mag. iv 244] | '1558. For timber & the making of the crosse that bereth the Tenebre light other wyze cawled the Judas light ... 18d' (Stanford, Berks) [Antiquary xvii 120b].

In addition, according to Durand, in some churches during the Tenebrae service 'the candles are put out with a wax hand, which signifies the hand of Judas' which betrayed Christ (*Rationale* book 6, chapter 72, section 24; p515 in 1859 edition), although whether such snuffers were used in parish churches in England is not evident from the CWA seen.

The varied uses of the term at St Michael, Oxford, are listed by H. E. Salter in his edition of the church's accounts (pp xvi-xvii). Some entries at All Hallows Staining are gathered in the *British Magazine* vol 2 pp243-245 and other examples, chiefly relating to processions in Coventry, in vol 4 pp19-22 of the same publication. **13** Lambeth: Drew i 23. **14** Rites of Durham 10-11 (q), 202-203. Fn. Thurston, Lent 438 (q) / Feasey 238. **15** Warren i 270, 272. **16** Durand 1859 p545 (book 6, chapter 80, section 9) / Feasey 208-209 / CE xi 515b-516b. **17** Warren i 272-274 (qs) / Feasey 231 / Mirk F 151-152. **18** Warren i 282-284. **19** SAH: British Mag. xxxiv 19 (q), 21, 29 / Thurston, Lent 438 n. / Feasey 237 / Rock iv 111-114. **20** PK f52r.

Easter Day. **1** OED (Easter). **2** Rites of Durham 12-13. **3** Warren i 289-290. **4** Bee hive ff200v-201r. **5** Reading SL: Kerry 237 / Kingston UT: Surrey AC viii 86 / Rye: Holloway 482 / SMF: Kitto 165. **6** Lambarde 459. **7** Matthew 28:1-10 / Mark 16:1-9 / Luke 24:1-10 / John 20:1-18 / Fosbroke 55a-b (citing du Cange, v. Sepulchri Officium (the office of the sepulchre); qs). Bond, Chancel pp228-230, and Rock, vol 4 pp116-117, describe a similar enactment, and PK f52v gives 'where the Maries three do meete' as an example of the 'pageants' played out 'in some place[s]' on this day. Brooks, p71, says that in England performance of the *visitatio* 'seems to have been rather of a local nature'. **8** Taunton: Wills, Somerset ii 53. **9** Hooper 45-46 (from *A Declaration of Christ and his Office*). **10** Foxe 1469a. **11** Mirk F 129-130 (adjusted). **12** Micklethwaite 53. See also the will of Alice Bray in the main text p228. Duffy, Altars p31 says it was removed 'before mass on the Friday in Easter week'.

Hocktide. **1** Leland v 298. **2** Reading SL: Kerry 239 / SES 50 / Cambridge SMG: Foster 34 / Portsmouth: Williams 203. **3** BS 26, 40 / SMH 230 / SES 102. **4** Oxford SPE: Anthony Wood, *The Antient and Present State of the City of Oxford* ed. J. Peshall, 1773, p83.

St George's Day. **1** Grace 18 / REED Norwich xxvii. **2** NORA iii 337-338. **3** Grace 17 (gunpowder, 1429), 67 (order, 1471) / Muskett 3 n. (oranges). **4** Muskett 3-6 (adjusted). **5** Grace 16-18, 25 / REED Norwich xxvii-xxviii, 47 / Muskett 16 (q, 'there shall be'; date adjusted by reference to REED p47) / Chambers, Mediaeval Stage i 222-224 / Hutton SS 214-217. **6** Bristol SW: Bristol P&P ii 223b / Eastchurch: Stahlschmidt, Kent 262.

May Day. **1** Stubbes sig. M2 (adjusted). **2** Douce 598-599. **3** Hutton SS chapter 25, 'Morris and Marian' (pp262-276), is a detailed discussion of the origins of Morris dancing and of the role of Robin Hood in popular celebrations. **4** Kingston UT: Lysons i 227-229. Footnote suggestion of gilt leather is from Lysons. **5** St Columb: Cox CWA 280 / Great Marlow: NI 135. **6** Hutton SS 271. **7** Stratton: Archaeologia xlvi 233. **8** Hugh Latimer, *Seven Sermons before Edward VI, on each Friday in Lent, 1549* ed. Edward Arber, 1869, pp173-174. **9** SMW: Cox CWA 285 (1499); NI 8 (1518) / Great Dunmow: Essex AST 1S ii 235. **10** Lowick: Cox CWA 286. **11** Stubbes sig. M3v-M4r. Fn. Machyn 201. **12** SA Undershaft: Stow i 143-144. Haigh pp65-66 gives examples of some later disputes. **13** Machyn 20 (26 May 1552). **14** Cerne Abbas: Wright ii 219. **15** Firth & Rait i 421 (An Ordinance for the better observation of the Lord's-Day, 8 April 1644) / *The Cities Loyalty Display'd ... with a true relation of that high and stately cedar erected in the Strand*, 1661, pp4-5. **16** Oxford SPE: Tyssen 295-296. **17** Oxford AS: Wood L&T i 314 (q), 317. **18** Rostherne: *The Life of Adam Martindale, written by himself* ed. Richard Parkinson, Chetham Soc., 1845, pp156-157. The incident seems to have occurred in 1661.

Rogation Days. **1** PK f53r. **2** Owst 215 (citing Lincoln Cathedral Library ms. A. 6. 2 f136; adjusted). **3** Owst 201 (quoting sermon headed '*Dies Rogacionibus*' in the same manuscript). Owst suggests it may be by John Mirk whose sermon in the Festial (p150) for the Rogation days describes the use of banners and bells in notably similar terms. **4** Golden Legend f22v (adjusted). **5** Durand 1859 p604 (book 6, chapter 102, section 9). Durand's account is largely derived from that of Jean Beleth written over a century earlier, *circa* 1160. **6** Sarum Processional 103-104, 121-122 / Wordsworth, Ceremonies 92-93 / *Monasticon Anglicanum* ed. John Caley et al., vol 6 pt 3, 1846, p1367b (Windsor) / Orme 290-292. It is of course possible that stuffed Rogationtide dragons were prevalent in England in early periods for which no or few CWA survive, but it seems unlikely. **7** Bassingbourne: Cox CWA 263 / BS 43. **8** Frere & Kennedy iii 15. **9** Grindal, Remains 240-241. **10** Frere & Kennedy iii 264 (1571). **11** Stanford: Antiquary xvii 169a. **12** John Strype, *The Life and Acts of Matthew Parker*, Oxford, 1821, vol 1 p303 (1564) / Frere & Kennedy iii 378 (Winchester, 1575). **13** St Ethelburga: Cobb 10 / Chester SM: Morris 188. **14** SGWC: Baddeley 151. **15** Pepys ii 106 (23 May 1661). **16** Sir John

Hawkins, *A General History of ... Music*, vol 2, 1776, p112 n. **17** SBE CWA 6a / SM Woolchurch: B&H lv. **18** Chelsea: Lysons ii 146 / King's Lynn AS: Hillen ii 476 / Turnworth: Waters 82-83. **19** Purton: Mrs T. Story Maskelyne, 'Perambulation of Purton, 1733', Wilts ANHM xl 119-128. **20** Epping: C. B. Sworder, 'A perambulation of Epping parish, 1762', *Essex Review*, vol 36, Colchester, 1927, pp135-140. **21** Windsor: Tighe & Davis ii 560. **22** Salisbury SM: Baker 55 (1826; reseq). **23** Scopwick: GM (Feb) 1833 pp116-117 (letter from George Oliver). **24** SMW: NI 62 / SBE CWA 168b. **25** Leadam 164-168. The outcome of the case is not stated. **26** SASA 369b / Leicester St Martin: North 226. **27** Herbert 157-158. **28** SMW: NI 15, 24 / Leyton: Kennedy 140-141 (reseq) / Deptford: Hasted i 34b / Liskeard: Allen 152. **29** Deptford: Hasted i 35. **30** Leyton: Kennedy 139. **31** Windsor: Tighe & Davis ii 560. **32** SGWC: Baddeley 161. **33** Great Waltham: Essex AST 2S xix 9 (also spelt Oughting). **34** Yapton: Vis. Sussex i 16. **35** Cuckfield: Sussex AC lxi 40-52 (qs 41, 51).

Ascension Day. **1** Rock iv 292-293. **2** Reading SG: Nash 34 / SMC: Overall 124. **3** CE i 767 / PK f53r (q). **4** Bee hive f201r. **5** H. Haines, *A Guide to the Cathedral Church of Gloucester*, [1867], p68 n.1, citing 'Furney's mss.' **6** Mirk F 151-152 / Warren i 274.

Whitsunday. **1** Acts 2:1-4. **2** OED (Whitsunday) / Hutton SS 277. **3** SM Friday St: JBAA xxv 361. **4** Bee hive f201r. **5** PK f53v. **6** Louth: Dudding 7, 192 / Chester SM: Earwaker 218. **7** Lambarde 459. **8** *The Ecclesiologist*, vol 17, 1856, p199 (1552) / *Liber Albus* ed. Henry Thomas Riley, 1859, p29. **9** Strood: Plomer 104. **10** Leicester St Margaret: Nichols, Leicester i pt 2 p562 n.1. **11** Leicester St Mary: Nichols, Leicester i pt 2 pp314 n.2, 310b, 311a (down > done) / Leicester St Martin: North 70, 78. **12** Leicester St Martin: North 86, 93. **13** Marston: Weaver & Clark 26 / SES 128 / Congleton: Morris 172-173. **14** Reading SL: Kerry 228 (fn. bower suggestion is from Kerry) / Melton Mowbray: Kelly 64 / Salisbury ST: Swayne 299. **15** Reading SM: Garry 34 / Minchinhampton: Archaeologia xxxv 432. **16** Cratfield: Raven 21 / Wing: Archaeologia xxxvi 226 / Long Melford 105 / Great Marlow: NI 135. **17** *The Antiquarian Repertory*, vol 3, 1780, pp23-24 has an undated agreement to this purpose between various Derbyshire villages. **18** Walberswick: Lewis 33. **19** At least as far as is recorded in the CWA. Mere: Wilts ANHM xxxv 30 / Ware 72. **20** Reading SL: Kerry 240 / Stratton: Archaeologia xlvi 213. **21** Seale: Surrey AC ii 34-35. **22** Brentford: Faulkner 1845 pp81, 84 / Chiswick: Lysons ii 221. **23** St Ives: John Hobson Matthews, *A History of the Parishes of Saint Ives, Lelant, Towednack and Zennor, in the County of Cornwall*, 1892, pp145, 154 (q) / Mere: Wilts ANHM xxxv 36-38. **24** Stubbes sig. M4v-M5r. **25** Richard Carew, *The Survey of Cornwall*, 1602, ff68v-69r. **26** William Prynne, *Canterburie's Doome*, 1646, p151 (possibly a misprint for p143). **27** Kington St Michael: Aubrey, Wiltshire 10.

Trinity Sunday. **1** ODCC 1394b / CE xv 47.

Corpus Christi. **1** SAH: British Mag. xxxi 534 / Ludlow: Wright 30. **2** SM Pattens: AJ xlii 329 (inventory, 1511) / SP Cornhill: WR 579-580 (inventory, 1546; their to). **3** Yeovil: Collectanea Topog. iii 140. **4** Smith, Gilds 232-233 (ordinance, 1389). **5** Bristol SN: Bristol P&P ii 163b. **6** SMH 131 (1487), 264 (1507), 305 (1519, q, prest), 322 (1523), 326 (1524). **7** SAH: British Mag. xxxii 395 / AH Staining: Povah 362. **8** Ashburton: CWA 10, 17, 20-21, 25, 35. **9** Bungay: Eastern Counties Collectanea 272.

Midsummer. **1** PK f54v. **2** SAH: British Mag. xxxii 393 / BS 30. **3** Wootton: Vis. Brinkworth i 43-44. **4** Stow i 101. **5** Long Melford 73. **6** Bourne 210-211.

Lammas. **1** SP Cheap: JBAA xxiv 262.

Assumption of Virgin Mary. **1** SMH 332 / SLP 122b.

[Harvest.] **1** Pounds 333 / Rustington: Vis. Sussex i 49 / Bourne 229 (1725).

Michaelmas. **1** Cressy, Bonfires 29.

All Hallows & All Souls. **1** Walter Farquhar Hook, *A Church Dictionary*, 14th edition, 1887, p24b (All Souls). **2** Bungay: EA 1S i 424. **3** Lydd 355 / Tilney: Stallard 157 / Stanford: Antiquary xvii 119b. **4** St Alphage LW: Carter 64 / North Elmham: Legge 49 / Bristol SJB: Bristol P&P ii 152a. **5** Coventry HT: Sharp 123 (1462) / Hagworthingham: Lincs NQ i 9. **6** SES 368 (nyzth > night). **7** Bungay: EA 1S i 375 / Wing: Archaeologia xxxvi 226. **8** Lydd 365. **9** Frere & Kennedy ii 304 (no. 62). **10** Frere & Kennedy iii 209 (no. 9). **11** Kirkby Overblow: Purvis, Docs 174 (where other examples are also listed) / Melton Mowbray:

Leicestershire AAST iii 192-193. **12** Zurich Letters 2S p361 (Perceval Wiburn) / Wanstrow: Haigh 67 / Ripon: Memorials iii 348. **13** Weaverham: Purvis, Docs 65 (1578).

Gunpowder Treason. 1 SR iv 1067-68 (3 James I cap. 1, 1605-06). **2** Durham SO: Durham CWA 144 / WM 116. **3** Ipswich SC: EA 2S iv 7 / Tavistock: Worth 49 / Cranborne: *Notes and Queries for Somerset and Dorset*, vol 3, Sherborne, 1893, p155.

Accession day of Queen Elizabeth. 1 Hutton SS 387-390. **2** BS 58 / Worfield: Shropshire ANHST 3S x 66 / Great Wigston: NI 148 / SS Walbrook: London & Middx AST 1S v 373.

Advent Sunday. 1 ODCC 19b.

St Nicholas. 1 Gregorie 113-120 (adjusted). **2** Gregorie 95-96. **3** Aubrey, Remaines 171. **4** REED Ecc. London 14-15 (St Paul's) / *Liber quotidianus contrarotulatoris garderobae, anno regni Regis Edwardi primi ... A.D. MCXCIX & MCCC*, 1787, p25 (wardrobe accounts of Edward I, Heton). **5** Chambers, Mediaeval Stage i 352-359 (including York criteria); ii 287-289 (1396 supper etc, Latin text) / Camden Miscellany vol 7 xi-xv (1396 supper q; reseq). John de Cave's visits were made 'between Christmas and Candlemas' (Chambers vol 1 p357), beyond the usual period of the boy bishop's tenure. **6** Bristol SN: St Paul's EST v 112 / Robert Ricart, *The Maire of Bristowe is Kalendar* ed. Lucy Toulmin Smith, Camden Soc., 1872, pp80-81. **7** SM Pattens: AJ xlii 319 / Sandwich SM: Boys 376 / Norwich SPM: NORA xiv 200. **8** Louth: Dudding 9, 83, 91 / Lambeth: Drew i 56-57 / Lewes St Andrew: Sussex AC xlv 45 / AH Staining: British Mag. iii 158 (bishoppe). **9** Wilkins iii 860b. **10** Machyn 121 (adjusted). **11** Foxe 2082a (towne > Tower).

Christmas Day. 1 Aquinas xvii 437 (pt 3, question 83, article 2) / SMW: Cox CWA 167 / Wandsworth: Surrey AC xv 95. **2** Banwell: Knight 444 / Rye: Holloway 484. **3** Micklethwaite p44 n.6 makes the comparison. **4** Reading SL: Kerry 52 / Bristol SN: Bristol P&P ii 163b. **5** Thame: Berks etc AJ x 57 / Bristol SMR: Bristol P&P ii 210a / Chester HT: Chester & NW AAHSJ xxxviii 144. Chester entries are also in REED Chester p230 where 8d is given as the cost of the cord. **6** Chester SM: Earwaker 218, 245, 247. **7** Thame: Berks etc AJ xvi 88 / Ludlow: Wright 1 / SM Woolnoth: B&H xxiv. **8** Coventry HT: Sharp 124 (second deacon's duties, 1462). **9** Stow i 97. **10** Pepys i 321. **11** Thame: Berks etc AJ ix 56 / Allhallows Hoo: Rochester Records 25. **12** Eltham: Arch. Cant. xlvii 88 / SES 129. **13** Lambeth: Drew i 74 / Manchester: CWA 6. **14** Graffham: Vis. Sussex i 126. **15** Dewsbury: J. Eyre Poppleton in *Yorkshire Archaeological Journal*, vol 17, Leeds, 1903, p439. He adds that the custom 'is said to have fallen into disuse for some years prior to the getting of the new bells in 1828', suggesting it was not a modern innovation. **16** St Alphage LW: Carter 75. **17** SAH: British Mag. xxxiii 570 / Canterbury St Andrew: Cotton pt 2 p60 / Rye: Holloway 484. **18** Hutton ME 14. **19** Bristol AS: NQ 2S xii 500b (21 Dec 1861) (Vyche). Records ed. Burgess ii 304 for 'Byche'. **20** Ludlow: Wright 76. **21** Myddle: Gough 20. Gough says the custom prevailed in the time of Will Hunt, the first clerk he remembered. **22** Bourne 141. **23** Wordsworth, Medieval Services 126-127 (similar payments occur in later years) / PK f45r. **24** Peterborough SJB: Mellows 33 / Ashburton: CWA 23. **25** Reading SL: Kerry 52. **26** Luke 2:9-14, from *The Byble in Englyshe*, 1539, Newe Testament f23v.

Baptism & Churching

Baptism

1 The Ceremony. 1 Gibson, Codex, 1713, i 437 (q) / Gasquet 188. **2** Cressy BMD 100-101, 149-150 / Orme 302-303. **3** Orme 306-309. **4** Rationale of Ceremonial li-liii n.2 (date), 6-12 / Sarum Manual 8-16. The account given here does not include every stage of the ceremony. **5** PK f31r. **6** SM Pattens: Sacristy i 262a. **7** Cardwell, Common Prayer 325-337 (in particular pp328, 334, 336) / Cressy BMD 163 / OED (chrisom) / ODCC 285b / Douce 299-300 / Cox PR 59 / Sophie Oosterwijk, 'Chrysoms ... a question of terminology?', *Church Monuments* vol 15, 2000, pp44–64. Oosterwijk's main argument concerns the depiction of infants on monuments but in the process she draws attention to various uncertainties regarding the use of chrisom cloths. **8** Halstead: Essex AST 2S v 61. **9** Wall 53 / Whiting 38 / Muncey 142-143 / Nicholas Groves, 'Myth-busting: The "Devil's Doors" Revisited', on medievalart.co.uk. **10** Charlotte Latham, 'Some West Sussex superstitions lingering in 1868', in *The Folk-Lore Record*, pt 1, 1878, pp11-12. **11** Grose 51.

2 Steps taken. 1 Drinkstone: EA 2S v 327-328 / Thornton: Reg. 24. **2** Bobbingworth: Cox PR 57. **3** Mirk I 3-4 (adjusted) / Johnson ii 134-135 (1236). **4** GM (Dec) 1785 ii 939. **5** Thatcham: Barfield ii 81a. **6** Ardingly: Loder 3. **7** Staplehurst: Arch. Cant. ix 201 (Joha. > John) / Duffy, Morebath 13-14 (source of partial birth suggestion). Fn. Chislet: *The Register of ... St Mary, Chislet, in ... Kent, from ... 1538 to 1707* ed. Robert Hovenden, 1887, p40a / Ardingly: Loder 103 (1597). **8** Bishop Barnes 18. **9** Francis Procter, *A History of the Book of Common Prayer*, 5th edition, 1861, p379 / Cressy BMD 121-122. **10** Bishopwearmouth: Sharpe 75.
3 Some register entries. 1 Newick: Sussex AC iv 256 / Laxfield: EA 1S ii 256. **2** Canterbury SP: OPB vol 2, additional section p18. **3** Forcett: Sharpe 128 / Wadhurst: Sussex AC iv 279 / Winchcombe: J. Edward Vaux, *Church Folklore*, 1894, p76.

Churching
1 Leviticus 12:2-8. See also the main text's account of Candlemas (p204). **2** Warren ii 164-165. **3** Canterbury SD: CWA xii, 28, 29 / SP Cornhill: WR 580. **4** Wilmslow: East Cheshire i 109. **5** Cardwell, Common Prayer 387-388 (q) / Cressy BMD 205, 210-211. **6** Salisbury ST: Wilts NQ v 513; vi 391 (adjusted), 457. **7** Salisbury ST: Wilts NQ vi 108, 209, 268. **8** Pittington: Durham CWA 43 / Chipping: Smith 78. **9** Barking: Vis. Hale 216. **10** South Benfleet: Vis. Hale 225. **11** Wolverhampton: CSP Domestic 1637-1638, p382.

Marriage
1 Restrictions. 1 Twickenham: Waters 33. Fn. Warren ii 143-144. **2** Cox PR 79-81 / Cressy BMD 298-305. **3** Johnson ii 340 (Archbishop Reynold's Latin constitutions, 1322) / Davis 61 / James T. Hammick, *The Marriage Law of England*, 2nd edition, 1887, p341 (49 & 50 Victoria cap. 14, An Act for extending the hours within which marriages may be lawfully solemnized). **4** Sherborne: Glos NQ i 260. **5** Davis 93 (no. 100) / Cressy BMD 312. **6** Firth & Rait ii 718 (An Act touching marriages and the registring thereof). **7** SR iii 792 (32 Henry VIII cap. 38, 1540, 'without') / Davis 93 (no. 99) / Blunt, Church Law 138-144 / Burn EL ii 439-450 / Cressy BMD 313. The 1540 Act was repealed under Mary but this element was reinstated by 1 Elizabeth cap. 1 section 3, 1558-59 (SR iv 351).
2 Banns. 1 Johnson ii 340 (1322) / Clay 217 (1559 prayer book) / Davis 61 (no. 62). **2** Maidstone: Burn PR 168. **3** Great Warley: Vis. Hale 186. **4** Wye: Vis. Warham 189, 191. Surnames vary in originals: Agnes Hawke then Halke, Richard Hawks then Halke. It seems likely they were related but this is not indicated. **5** West Walton: Fenland NQ ii 153. **6** Firth & Rait ii 715. **7** Boston: Thompson, Boston etc, 756 (314 to 131) / Cressy BMD 306.
3 Usual ceremony. 1 Warren ii 144-161 (qs) / Sarum Manual 17-26. There are minor differences between the Missal and Manual and between various editions of each. **2** Ketley 127-134, 302-310. Cressy BMD pp338-339 summarises the post-Reformation changes.
4 Smock marriages etc. 1 Leicester St Martin: John Throsby, *The History and Antiquities of the Ancient Town of Leicester*, Leicester, 1791, pp263-264 / Bury St Edmunds SJ: EA 2S iii 247. **2** Firth & Rait ii 715-716. **3** Castle Hedingham: EA 1S ii 33 / Wartling: Sussex AC iv 287. **4** Cox PR 85. **5** Much Wenlock: *Extracts from the Register of Sir Thomas Butler, Vicar of Much Wenlock, in Shropshire* ed. Charles Henry Hartshorne, Tenby, 1861, p13 / Masham: John Fisher, *The History and Antiquities of Masham and Mashamshire*, 1865, p408. **6** Saddleworth: Cox PR 86. Other examples include *Manchester Mercury* 12 March 1771 p4d and *Chester Courant* 24 June 1800 p3d. **7** Whitehaven: *Annual Register ... for the year 1766*, 4th edition, 1785, Chronicle p106.
5 Some register entries etc. 1 Newcastle SA: Sharpe 91 / Walpole: EA 1S iii 169. As printed it is not clear whether the Walpole entry relates to the parish of St Andrew or that of St Peter. **2** Stixwold: *Illustrated London News* 7 Feb 1857 p106b. **3** Sheldon & Bakewell: *Derby Mercury* 12 Jan 1753 p4c & 26 Jan 1753 p4c. It seems likely that 'the Rev. Gentleman' is a generic rather than a surname reference. Fn. Dyer, Social Life 144 (register entry).

Death, Burial and Beyond
1 Visitation of sick. 1 Johnson ii 85, 264. According to canons of 1200, 'a candle and cross' should be carried before the sacrament 'unless the sick man dwell at too great a distance'. **2** SAH: British Mag. xxxii 38 / Leverton: Archaeologia xli 347, 356 / Bristol SN: St Paul's

EST v 113 n.1 / North Elmham: Legge 36. **3** Gasquet 203-204. **4** Mere: Wilts ANHM xxxv 64 / Bywell: Archaeologia Aeliana xiii 150.

2 Extreme unction. **1** *Sixteen Revelations of Divine Love, shewed to ... Mother Juliana, an anchorete of Norwich* ed. R. F. S. Cressy, 1670, p7 (q) / Sarum Manual 44 / Duffy, Altars 314. **2** Louth: Dudding 220. **3** Sarum Manual 111-112 (adjusted). Mirk I pp63-65 gives a longer version. **4** Sarum Manual 112 (adjusted). **5** *The Boke of the Craft of Dying*, a translation from a Latin tract *De arte moriendi*, in *Yorkshire Writers: Richard Rolle of Hampole and his followers* ed. C. Horstman, vol 2, 1896, p420 (adjusted). **6** Mirk I 56 / Duffy, Altars 313 / Durand 1843 p179 (q) / Rock ii 368. **7** Ketley 139, 316-317 / BCP 1662 pp303-315.

3 Burial before the Reformation. **1** General sources for this section: Sarum Manual 56-85 / Rock ii 377-388, 404-405 / Litten 148-151. The account given largely follows Rock. **2** Hallow: AASRP xi 322 / Ludlow: Wright 68. **3** Rock ii 383 n.51 ('This Commendatio Animarum, to be found in the Salisbury Manual ... immediately after ... matins and lauds for the dead ... used to be sung over the corpse, just before mass, and while the priest was in the churchyard marking the grave') / Sarum Manual 74-75. Litten p150 says the priest went to mark out the grave during matins and lauds. **4** Wills, Bury 17 (q) / Wordsworth, Medieval Services 88 / Lepine 31. **5** Mirk F 294-295 (adjusted). Fn. *Ordo officiorum ecclesiae Senensis ab Oderico*, Bologna, 1766, p504. **6** Eastbourne: Wills, Sussex ii 114. **7** Johnson ii 394 (q) / Duffy, Altars 369. **8** Helpston: Wills, Northants 340 / Aldingbourne: Wills, Sussex i 7-8. **9** York AS: Wills, York Clergy ii 13.

4 Campaign for salvation. **1** ODCC 1145 / CE viii 549-553; xii 575-580. **2** *The Sermons and Life of ... Hugh Latimer* ed. John Watkins, vol 1, 1858, p48 (sermon before convocation of clergy, 9 June 1536). **3** Nether Seale: Wills, Derbyshire 56-58 (will does not say where Vernon lived or was buried but he left clothes to cover any debt to the church of 'Schele' and money to be distributed there) / Ixworth: Suffolk AIP i 108. **4** Daniell 56. **5** Aldingbourne: Wills, Sussex i 8.

5 Seeking salvation. **1** Southease: Wills, Sussex iv 152. **2** Warren ii 64-65. **3** Kingston, Sussex: Wills, Sussex iii 60. **4** Glynde: Wills, Sussex ii 210. **5** Warren ii 198-199 / Duffy, Altars 293-294. **6** Wilmington: Wills, Sussex iv 356. **7** OED (Scala Caeli) / AJ lxx 247-248 / NQ 1S i 402b, 455b / Duffy, Altars 375-376. **8** Newton: Wills, Northants 246. Date added from Josiah C. Wedgwood, *History of Parliament: Biographies of the Members of the Commons House 1439-1509*, 1936, p618. **9** Upton: NORA i 261 (orig. '31 messes', probably in error) / Naseby: Wills, Northants 369 (Jhu > Jesu). **10** Wills, Furnivall 4, 6 (West) / Rodmell: Wills, Somerset i 80 / Sheffield: Wills, North Country 144-145. **11** Trent: Wills, Somerset i 59. **12** Faversham: Wills, East Kent 129 / Weldon: Wills, Northants 428 ('Richard Bawe of Cleyndon'; Cleyndon not identified but perhaps Glendon) / Hamsey: Wills, Sussex ii 255. **13** Lepine 26. **14** Farleigh Hungerford: Wills, Test. Vet. i 181 / Lewes SJB: Wills, Sussex iii 111 / Layer Marney: Essex AST 1S iv 156. **15** Badham 192 / Wills, Furnivall 116-117 (Tewkesbury) / Thomas Martin, *The History of the Town of Thetford*, 1779, appendix 8 p40. **16** Naseby: Wills, Northants 369 / Old: Wills, Northants 437 / Firle: Wills, Sussex ii 168-169 / Beddingham: Wills, Sussex i 107. **17** Paston Letters iii 462-463. **18** Bury St Edmunds: Wills, Bury 92 (adjusted). **19** Danbury: Essex AST 1S v 297-307 (q 300) / Walsingham: NORA i 257 / Gravesend: Wills, West Kent A 253. **20** Denton: Wills, Northants 312 / Lilford: Wills, Northants 357. **21** Patrixbourne: Wills, East Kent 245 / Erith: Wills, West Kent B 24. **22** Steyning: Wills, Sussex iv 164. **23** Fletching: Wills, Sussex ii 184 (1523-24). **24** High Halstow: Wills, West Kent B 34-35 / Cuckfield: Wills, Sussex ii 56-57 / Bosham: Wills, Sussex i 173 (profight). **25** Bury St Edmunds: Wills, Bury 28 / Boxgrove: Wills, Sussex i 186. **26** Kettering: Wills, Northants 353. **27** Boston: Wills, Lincoln ii 189-191. **28** High Halstow: Wills, West Kent B 34. **29** Ashburton: CWA 16-17 / Bungay: EA 1S ii 149 / Abingdon: NI 140. **30** Great Berkhamsted: Wills, Bury 85-86 / Withycombe: Wills, Somerset iii 14.

6 Guilds. **1** Stratford, Guild HC: Smith, Gilds 215, 217 (reseq) / Lincoln, Guild St Michael: Smith, Gilds 178 / Ludlow, Guild Palmers: Smith, Gilds 194, 195 n. (date). **2** Wiggenhall, Guilds HT & SP: Smith, Gilds 110, 117 (both adjusted). The Guild of the Assumption makes a similar commitment (p113). **3** Stratford, Guild HC: Smith, Gilds 215 / Wiggenhall, Guild SP: Smith, Gilds 117 (adjusted). **4** Stamford, Guild St Katherine: Smith, Gilds 190-191 (adjusted; towr > town). **5** King's Lynn, Guild St George: Smith, Gilds 75 / Wiggenhall, Guild

Assumption: Smith, Gilds 113 / Lincoln, Guild Resurrection: Smith, Gilds 176. **6** Stamford, Guild St Katherine: Smith, Gilds 190 (adjusted). **7** Wymondham, Guild All Saints: NORA ix 264, 268 / SES, Guild Jesus Mass: Swayne 270. **8** H. F. Westlake, *The Parish Gilds of Medieval England*, 1919, p44. **9** Wymondham, Guild HT: NORA ix 253. **10** Bardwell, Guild St Peter: Suffolk AIP xi 143. **11** Stratford, Guild HC: Smith, Gilds 215.

7 After the Reformation. 1 PK ff27v-28r. **2** Litten 126. **3** Cressy BMD pp398-402 notes the persistence of old burial customs into the later 16th century. **4** Tate, Funerals 216-221. **5** BCP 1662 pp315-322 / Litten 156, 161. **6** *M. Misson's Memoirs and Observations in his Travels over England ...*, trans. Mr Ozell, 1719, pp88-93.

8 Some parts of the process in more detail

i. Covering. 1 Eastbourne: Wills, Sussex ii 114 / Clayton: Wills, Sussex ii 24. **2** Pulham: EA 1S iv 278 / Leverton: Archaeologia xli 370 / St Alphage LW: Carter 80. **3** Litten 57, 61 / Mirk F 294 (q, adjusted). **4** Oxford SMV: *A History of the Church of S. Mary the Virgin, Oxford* by the present vicar [E. S. Ffoulkes], 1892, p237 / Wilmslow: East Cheshire i 115. **5** SM Pattens: AJ xlii 323 / SM Woolnoth: WR 468 / SMH 53. **6** SMF: Kitto 302, 390 / St Ethelburga: Cobb 6. Fn. Shelford: John T. Godfrey, *Notes on the Churches of Nottinghamshire, Hundred of Bingham*, 1907, p430. **7** AH the Less: WR 107 / SD Backchurch: WR 237 / Wenhaston: Clare 23. **8** WM 116. **9** Gillingham: Rochester Records 79.

ii. In woollen. 1 Manchester: CWA 24. **2** Helmdon: Cox PR 122. **3** Derby SW: Derbyshire ANHSJ xl 233 / Swainswick: Peach 151 / Canterbury HCW: OPB ii 28. **4** SR v 598 (18 & 19 Charles II cap. 4, 1666), 885-886 (30 Charles II cap. 3, qs). **5** Hammersmith: Faulkner 1839 p201 / Battersea 266. **6** Pounds 424 (citing 54 George III cap. 108).

iii. Coffins. 1 St Alphage LW: Carter 79. **2** Reading SG: Nash 25 / Norwich St Mary Coslany: Eastern Counties Collectanea 283. **3** Louth: Dudding 217. **4** SAH: British Mag. xxxv 399. **5** St Alphage LW: Hall 21-22 / SBE: Vestry Books 6a. **6** SP Paul's Wharf: Littledale iv 208. **7** Harding pp59-60 notes in relation to London churchyards that coffined burial was 'unusual' before at least the late 16th century but that by the mid 17th century most burials were probably coffined. **8** Mortlake: Anderson 56 / Battersea 245. **9** SM Colechurch: Harding 142 (citing Guildhall Library ms. 66 f14). **10** SP Cornhill: Gower i 137-138. **11** Canterbury HCW: OPB i 52 / Houghton-le-Spring: Durham CWA 342. **12** Hearne viii 205 (30 April 1724) / Thurne: NORA v 212 (Ferrer then Ferror).

iv. Carrying. 1 Louth: Dudding 91 / Lambeth: Drew iii 266. **2** Long Melford 110. **3** Salisbury ST: Swayne 291 / Canterbury St Andrew: Cotton pt iv 58. **4** Gateshead: Ambrose Barnes 326 / Durham SO: Durham CWA 191. **5** SES 226 (q), 244 (1692, similar fees). **6** Louth: Notices 49 (bryngyhyng) / SMW: Catalogue 85 / Battersea 247 (Taylor: 'Probably this was a case of pestilence').

v. Hearse. 1 OED (hearse, 'similar in form to the ancient harrow') / CE vii 162b (prickets). **2** The following draws largely on the OED and Edward Peacock's list of the word's meanings in PF pp127-129 n. In a separate essay (Peacock, Hearse pp215-216) he makes the suggestion about the adoption of 'hearse' for light-holding structures used at burials. **3** Wills, Test. Vet. i 127. **4** William Dugdale, *The Antiquities of Warwickshire*, 1656, p354a. **5** *Vetusta Monumenta*, vol 4, 1815, plate 18, p3 (q) / Pendrill 272. **6** Leland v 307-323 ('The entierment of ... Princes Mary the first of that name, late Queene of England'; qs 318). **7** *Desiderata Curiosa, or, A Collection of diverse, scarce and curious Pieces* ed. Francis Peck, vol 2, 1779, p253. **8** Litten pp10-12 notes the decline, but see main text p341 for two notable 17th-century examples. **9** Rippingale: PF 127 / Bishop Barnes 24 (1577). **10** OED (hearse, sense 8, first instance 1650) / Wood L&T ii 245 (1672). **11** a) Some CWA entries may of course relate to Tenebrae hearses rather than to funeral ones. b) Some secondary accounts (e.g. Cox CWA p170) appear to assume that it was standard practice to place both lights and cloth on a single hearse structure at the same time. However, medieval depictions usually show the lights at a slight distance from the cloth, either by being free-standing or by being held in a surrounding frame. **12** Lydd 362 / Stanford: Antiquary xvii 118b / Cambridge SMG: Foster 222. **13** Dearmer plate xxvi shows a hearse with crosses at each corner and at the head and foot. **14** Frindsbury: Wills, West Kent B 27. **15** Canterbury St Andrew: Cotton pt i 27 / Louth: Dudding 220-221 (Mathe) / Eltham: Arch. Cant. xlvii 82. **16** Chelsfield: Wills, West

Kent B 11 / Milton: Wills, West Kent A 249 / Milton: Wills, West Kent B 54. **17** Lambeth: Drew i 53 / SAH: WR 148. **18** High Wycombe: Records of Bucks viii 113 (Jhc > Jesus Christ) / SS Coleman St: Archaeologia l [50] 48 / Greenwich: Arch. Cant. viii 160, 163. **19** Kingston upon Hull: Wills, York v 172 / AH the Great: WR 94. **20** Bristol AS: Hope & Atchley 118 (gift noted in vestry book, 'between 1470 and 1485'). **21** Battersea 244. Taylor breaks the quotation into three by interpolating glosses and it may not be continuous in the original. **22** Rock iii 74-75 n.82 / Litten 127-128. According to Rock, the 'frame or smaller kind of hearse seemed almost requisite for giving a seemly look to the pall spread over it. From often being cut out after this shape, so as to fit such a sort of frame, the pall itself got to be named the hearse-cloth'. **23** SM Abchurch: WR 408. **24** Unless of course the churches in question also possessed different sizes of hearse. **25** AH Staining: WR 121 / SM Martyr: WR 348 (while the second entry does not mention size it seems likely that the cloth in question was smaller than the 'cloth for men & women').

vi. Blacks. 1 SMW: NI 21 / St Alphage LW: Carter 79. **2** Leyton: Kennedy 159 (accounts), 395 (vestry order).

vii. Lights. 1 Duffy, Altars 361 (power of blessed candles). **2** SAH: British Mag. xxxi 247 / SMW: NI 3, 6 (reseq) / SMF: Kitto 87, 97 / Wandsworth: Surrey AC xvii 137.

viii. Choosing where to be buried. 1 Wills, Test. Vet. i 77. **2** Bruton: Wills, Somerset iii 49. **3** Wills, Halifax i 24. It seems likely that 'Sandall' is Kirk Sandall, Yorkshire. **4** SMH 19 / Greenwich: Wills, West Kent A 270 / AH Hoo: Wills, West Kent A 273 / Plumstead: Wills, West Kent B 60 / Chiddingly: Wills, Sussex ii 2 / West Malling: Wills, West Kent A 278. **5** Farningham: Wills, West Kent B 26 / Canterbury St Alphage: Wills, East Kent 42. **6** Gravesend SM: Wills, West Kent B 28 / Irchester: Wills, Northants 347. **7** SN at Wade: Wills, East Kent 274 / Dartford: Wills, West Kent B 20 / Lewisham: Wills, West Kent B 49. **8** East Hanningfield: Essex AST 2S vi 310.

ix. Charges. 1 Southwark: Duties cols. a, b / St Alphage LW: Hall 28. **2** SMH 248 / BS 56 / Reading SM: Garry 61 / Cardington: Shropshire ANHST 1S iv 319. **3** Louth: Dudding 189, 212 (charges in 1517, 1521) / Battersea 245 / AH Staining: British Mag. iii 158 (reseq). **4** Chelmsford: Essex AST 1S ii 224 (sexton's fees). **5** SBE CWA 88b. **6** SAH: British Mag. xxxiii 564. **7** Kendal: Cumberland etc AAST ix p278-279 (1683). **8** Burnley: *The Registers of the Parish Church of Burnley in the County of Lancaster ... 1562 to 1653* ed. William Farrer, Rochdale, 1899, p291. **9** Battersea 276. **10** SMW: NI 4 / Bramley, Hants: Williams 68. **11** SAH: British Mag. xxxiv 533 / Burford: Monk 190 (whether the fees were to be paid by executors or parish is not indicated). **12** Swainswick: Peach 140. Original has different surname (Ashley) for the grave-maker in the second entry but this has been omitted as it seems clear it was the same man. **13** Tottenham: Robinson 126 / Manchester: CWA 25. **14** St Alphage LW: Hall 28 / SGWC: Baddeley 197. **15** Southwark: Duties col. b / SGWC: Baddeley 197.

x. Burying promptly. 1 SMF: Kitto 282 / Hackness: Reg. 102. **2** Rainham, Essex: Vis. Hale 248. **3** SS Coleman St: Archaeologia l [50] 49 (q) / Cressy BMD 466. **4** Southwark: Duties col. c. **5** Cambridge SE: Vis. Palmer iv pt 8 p319; also pp348 (1639, St Mary the Less), 363 (1638, Littleport), 405 (1662, Dry Drayton, 'are not'). **6** SGWC: Baddeley 196 / SH Bishopsgate: J. E. Cox 143 / Woolwich: Hasted i 167b. **7** Wood L&T iii 503. **8** SASA 368b.

xi. Overcrowding. 1 SO Hart St: Reg. 147 (An > Ann) / SN Acons: Brigg 135. **2** SJZ 398b. **3** SLP 172-173. **4** SM Aldermanbury: Carter 1913 p129. **5** Report on ... Extramural Sepulture 11 (SA Holborn), 20 (SA by the Wardrobe), 30 (SM Poultry). Some other examples are on pp16, 18, 27. **6** SB Aldgate: *The Times* 8 Sep 1838 p7b-c. **7** Catharine Arnold, *Necropolis: London and its Dead*, 2006, pp120, 171.

xii. Tools. 1 BS 50 / SMC: Overall 158 / St Alphage LW: Hall 42. **2** Salisbury ST: Swayne 288 (reseq) / Warwick: Cox CWA 170 / Manchester: CWA 31 / Hardingstone: Northants NQ iv 203.

9 Mortuary etc. 1 Johnson ii 317. **2** Cox PR 125 / Tate, Parish Chest 69. **3** Halifax: Wills, Halifax i 2 / Maxey: Wills, Northants 260. **4** Great Wakering: Essex AST 2S i 167 / Mundon: Essex AST 2S i 168 / East Hanningfield: Essex AST 2S ii 368. **5** Cooling: Wills, West Kent B 14 (orig. Cowling). **6** SJ in Roseland: Baildon 23-24 (no. 20). **7** Oxford AS: Clark 7 (from phrasing this is presumably Clark's translation from Latin original). **8** SR iii 288-289

(21 Henry VIII cap. 6). **9** Ripe: Sussex AC iv 287. **10** Tate, Parish Chest 70. **11** Basingstoke: Baigent 513-514 (reseq) / Lambeth: Drew iii 132, 140 / Godalming: Surrey AC iv 211.

10 Burial of excommunicated etc. 1 Davis 66. **2** Eltham: Hasted i 212a. **3** Sutton on the Hill: Cox, Derbyshire iii 332 / Longford: Cox, Derbyshire iii 195. **4** Pounds 428. **5** Chesterfield: Cox PR 105 / Weedon Bec: Burn PR 117 / Mellis: Suffolk AIP i 80. **6** Salehurst: Sussex AC xxv 157 / Albrighton: *Shropshire Parish Registers, Lichfield Diocese*, vol 3, Shropshire Parish Register Soc., 1901, pp35-36 / Newcastle SN: Sharpe 101. **7** Warleggan: Waters 69. **8** Hackness: Reg. 73. **9** Saffron Walden: Braybrooke 196 / SD Backchurch: Reg. 270. **10** York SM le B: Collins i 52 / North Elmham: Cox PR 108. **11** Lydd 361 / Dulwich: Lysons i 107.

11 Burial of suicides etc. 1 SJZ 84-85 / SASA 91-92. **2** Drypool: Reliquary x 55 / Helpston: Sweeting, Notes 91 / Wolsingham: Sharpe 33. **3** Oxford SMM: Wood L&T ii 280-281 (Roseenstan). **4** Blunt, Annotated BCP 513-515. **5** SP Cornhill: Gower ii 107 / Waltham Abbey: Winters 75 / Yaxley: Sweeting, Notes 185. **6** Canterbury SG: Canterbury Records 216. **7** SM le Bow: Stow i 254-255 / SO Hart St: Povah 184 / St Giles in Fields: Parton 269. **8** Pleasley: Cox PR 114. **9** SB Aldgate: Atkinson 116 (adjusted). **10** *The National Register* 5 Jan 1812 p12b. **11** *The Times* 27 June 1823 p4c / *Morning Post* 2 July 1823 p3e / *Morning Advertiser* 3 July 1823 p2d. **12** *Statutes of the United Kingdom of Great Britain and Ireland, 4 George IV, 1823*, 1823, p320 (4 George IV cap. 52). **13** York SM le B: Collins i 25 / Chester SM: Earwaker 119. **14** Stamford AS: North, Bells Lincoln etc 668.

12 Delaying burial. 1 Salisbury SM: Baker 46 / Battersea 251 / Chester SJB: Lectures 212. **2** Widdecombe: Dymond 53 (reseq). **3** Tate, Funerals 218 (q) / Burn EL i 258-260. **4** Alstonfield: Cox PR 126 / Sparsholt: Cox PR 126. **5** John Macky, *A Journey through England*, 2nd edition, 1722, pp213-214 / *The Letters of Horace Walpole* ed. Mrs Paget Toynbee, vol 6, Oxford, 1904, p45 (letter to Horace Mann, 9 April 1764) / Arthur Penrhyn Stanley, *Historical Memorials of Westminster Abbey*, 3rd edition, 1869, p203 n. (1811). **6** *Journal and Letters of the late Samuel Curwen* ed. George Atkinson Ward, New York, 1842, pp406-407 (entry dated 19 June 1784).

13 Particular practices. 1 Eltham: Hasted i 212b / SM Bourne: Stevens 240. **2** Cuckfield: Renshaw 157 / Coggeshall: Beaumont 250-251. **3** Cox PR 116-117 / Harding 196, 227-228 / Litten 161-163. **4** SMF: Kitto 294 / SB Bishopsgate: Malcolm i 346 / Reading SM: Coates 125.

14 Three grand funerals. 1 Blomefield vi 482-485 (adjusted, resequenced, some headings added). It is not always entirely clear from the account as printed which costs relate to which location. **2** Stoke Newington: *Antiquities in Middlesex and Surrey*, being the second volume of the *Bibliotheca Topographica Britannica*, pub. J. Nichols, 1790, appendix to Stoke Newington section, pp1-4 (adjusted). The 'expences' as printed refer to burial on 17 Jan but according to Nichols the burial register has 12 Jan. **3** SA Holborn: Waters 52-55 (adjusted, resequenced, headings added).

15 A modest end. 1 Oundle: Wills, Northants 385-386 / Greenwich: Wills, West Kent B 31.

The Parish and Those in Need

General notes. a) It is often hard to distinguish costs and payments relating to the parish's own poor from those relating to outsiders, and some of the examples given in the respective sections in this chapter may inadvertently be in the wrong place. b) Some entries in this chapter are from separate accounts kept by overseers of the parish poor, but this accounting distinction is not indicated in the text.

The Parish Poor

1 Legal responsibility. 1 Tate, Parish Chest 190-196 / Kumin 248. **2** Lambeth: Drew iii 84 / SBE CWA 108b / SR iv 962-965 (43 Eliz. cap. 2; qs 962). Elements of the Act had appeared in earlier legislation. For example, An Acte for the setting of the Poore on Worke (18 Eliz. cap. 3, 1575-76, in SR vol 4 pp610-613) ordered the setting up of stocks of wool, hemp, etc. **3** Chester HT: Chester & NW AAHSJ xxxviii 145.

2 Badges. 1 Houghton-le-Spring: Durham CWA 279 / SJZ 380a. **2** SR iv 281 (An Acte for the Reliefe of the Poore, 2 & 3 Philip & Mary cap. 5, section 10) / SR vii 282 (An Act for supplying some defects in the laws for the Relief of the Poor, 8 & 9 William III cap. 30, section 2). **3** St Giles in Fields: Parton 314 / Cowden: Sussex AC xx 115 / Swainswick: Peach 167.

3 Forms of charity. 1 SMC: Overall 109 / Strood: Plomer 9 / Metfield: Suffolk AIP xxiii pt 2 p141. **2** St Giles in Fields: Parton 311 / St Mabyn: London Society xliv 644b / Camberwell: Blanch 118 / Leyton: Kennedy 147. **3** St Ethelburga: Cobb 33 / Walthamstow i 22 / Marholm: Sweeting, Notes 209. **4** Leicester St Martin: North 46 / Coventry HT: Sharp 121 / St Giles in Fields: Parton 303 / Canterbury HCW: OPB i 83. **5** Northampton SG: Serjeantson 1911 p238 / SGWC: Baddeley 149 / High Wycombe: Records of Bucks viii 68. **6** Brightlingsea: Essex AST 2S i 15 / SBE CWA 126a, 234b / Camberwell: Blanch 116, 117. **7** SASA 371a / Puxton: Knight 227. **8** SBE CWA 158a / Oxford SPE: Tyssen 293 / Canterbury HCW: OPB i 132 / Smarden: Memorials 261 / SGWC: Baddeley 151 / Otterton: DART xxxi 228 / SASA 370a. **9** Thatcham: Barfield ii 103a / SLP 128a / Kingston, Sussex: Sussex AC xxix 158. **10** SMC: Overall 110 / Thatcham: Barfield ii 106. **11** SBE CWA 77b / SGWC: Baddeley 159. **12** Redenhall: Candler 118 / Derby SW: Derbyshire ANHSJ xl 236 / Icklesham: Sussex AC xxxii 115. **13** SMC: Overall 157, 159 / St Alphage LW: Carter 90. **14** SM Lothbury: Vestry Book 17b, 18a (in March 1587 it is reported that she has finally vacated the vestry) / Cranbrook: Stahlschmidt, Kent 233 / King's Sutton: Vis. Peyton 290. **15** Cowden: Sussex AC xx 114. **16** SBE CWA 150a / Derby SW: Derbyshire ANHSJ xli 48 / Walthamstow i 24.

4 Encouraging work. 1 Cambridge SMG: Foster 280, 308 / Lambeth: Drew iii 5. **2** Northampton SG: Serjeantson 1911 p238 / High Wycombe: Records of Bucks viii 67. **3** Derby SW: Derbyshire ANHSJ xli 48 / Smarden: Memorials 259 / Icklesham: Sussex AC xxxii 114. **4** Battersea 240 / St Ethelburga: Cobb 31 / SJZ 404b. **5** Redenhall: Candler 113 / Youlgreave: Cox, Derbyshire ii 342 / East Budleigh: DART xxxi 239 / Burford: Monk 101. **6** Cowden: Sussex AC xx 99 / Leyton: Kennedy 138, 157 / East Budleigh: DART xxxi 239 / SASA 370b. **7** Lambeth: Drew iii 183 / Smarden: Memorials 261 / SBE CWA 227b (orig. marchet), 228a. **8** SASA 366a, 367b, 369a, 371a. **9** Deptford: Hasted i 35b / Walthamstow i 23 / SJZ 408b.

5 Encouraging marriage. 1 SM Bourne: Stevens 254 / East Malling: Rochester Records 30 / High Wycombe: Records of Bucks viii 68. **2** Great Staughton: Andrews, Curiosities 194. **3** Yarnton: Stapleton 279. **4** SM Lothbury: Vestry Book 25b.

6 In sickness. 1 Lapworth: Hudson 206 / St Alphage LW: Hall 42 / Walthamstow ii 51 (scal'd). **2** St Giles in Fields: Parton 304 / Redenhall: Candler 115 / St Ethelburga: Cobb 31. **3** North Petherton: Somersetshire ANHSP xi pt 2 pp170-171. **4** Minchinhampton: Archaeologia xxxv 450. **5** Derby SW: Derbyshire ANHSJ xli 46 / SASA 367a. **6** SASA 367a, 369b. **7** Redenhall: Candler 119 / St Alphage LW: Carter 93. **8** SJZ 400b. **9** Redenhall: Candler 115-116 / Edenbridge: Arch. Cant. xxi 122. **10** Morebath: Binney 46 / St Mabyn: London Society xliv 645a / Marholm: Sweeting, Notes 209. **11** Battersea 240 / Bramley, Yorks: Andrews, Curiosities 184. **12** Lambeth: Drew iii 43 / Walthamstow i 23 / SASA 369a.

7 Mental illness. 1 SBE CWA 150a / Deptford: Hasted i 35a / Ealing: Edith Jackson, *Annals of Ealing*, 1898, p37 / Youlgreave: Cox, Derbyshire ii 342 (Ellin Leey in first instance) / Leyton: Kennedy 155. **2** SCLS: Account Book 20b-21b / SJZ 409a / SASA 372a.

8 Death and its costs. 1 Derby SW: Derbyshire ANHSJ xli 45 (reseq) / Walthamstow i 23. **2** Stockton: NORA i 175 (reseq) / AH Staining: British Mag. iv 148 / Weston super Mare: Knight 99. **3** Pulham: EA 1S iv 279-280 (reseq). **4** SM Lothbury: Vestry Book 105b. In similar vein at East Bergholt, Suffolk, it is decided in 1719 to take an inventory of the goods of any applicant before providing them with parish relief (NQ 2S ii 122b).

9 Children. 1 Lambeth: Drew iii 73-74. **2** St Giles in Fields: Parton 313 / Cowden: Sussex AC xx 118 (reseq). **3** SCLS: Account Book 11a / Mainstone: Shropshire Parish Docs. 222.

Outsiders

1 Laws. 1 SR ii 58 (12 Richard II cap. 7, 1388) / SR iii 328-329 (22 Henry VIII cap. 12, 1530-31) / Tate, Parish Chest 190. **2** Kingston UT: Surrey AC ii 92 / SR iv 590-593 (14 Eliz. cap. 5, 1572). **3** SR iv 899-902 (39 Eliz. cap. 4, 1597-98). **4** SR iv 1024-1025 (1 James I cap. 7, 1603-04).

2 Charity to strangers. 1 Melton Mowbray: Leicestershire AAST iii 201 / Chester-le-Street: Blunt 78 / SJZ 404b. **2** Strood: Plomer 3 / Worcester: Amphlett 51 / Kilmington: Cornish

27 / Chedder: HMC 3rd report app. 329b / Oxford St Martin: Fletcher 32. **3** SBE CWA 225a / Canterbury HCW: OPB i 123 / Hargrave: Northants NQ iv 143 / SGWC: Baddeley 149.

3 The stories. 1 Chester-le-Street: Blunt 101 / Worle: Knight 245. **2** Deptford: Hasted i 35b. **3** Leverton: Archaeologia xli 369 / Newbury: Money 529 / SLP 127b (fn. AH Staining: British Mag. iii 655) / East Budleigh: DART xxxi 277 / Starston: Some Account 50. **4** Thatcham: Barfield ii 108b / East Budleigh: DART xxxi 277. **5** SK Cree: Malcolm iii 312 / Chedder: HMC 3rd report app. 331a. **6** Stockton: NORA i 181-182 / Chedder: HMC 3rd report app. 330b. **7** SASA 355a / East Budleigh: DART xxxi 277. **8** Leverton: Archaeologia xli 369 / Pittington: Durham CWA 76 / St Ethelburga: Cobb 23. **9** Hartland: HMC 5th report app. 573b / Stroud: Paul Hawkins Fisher, *Notes and Recollections of Stroud, Gloucestershire*, 1871, p357. **10** AH Barking: Maskell 122 / Quainton: Records of Bucks xii 36 / Leek: Reliquary iii 216. **11** Mortlake: Anderson 56 / SES 240. **12** Church Pulverbatch: Shropshire Parish Docs. 124 / Uffington: Shropshire ANHST 2S xii 363 / Sandridge: St Albans & Herts AAST NS i pt 4 p293.

4 Whipping. 1 SBE CWA 14a / SM Woolchurch: B&H lii / Chudleigh: Jones 24. **2** Eltham: Archaeologia xxxiv 62 / Melton Mowbray: Cox CWA 338. **3** Stokesley: *The Registers of the Parish Church of Stokesley, co. York, 1571-1750* ed. John Hawell, Yorkshire Parish Register Soc., Leeds, 1901, p54 / Godalming: Malden 274 / Brentford: Faulkner 1845 p88.

5 Encouraging departure. 1 Lambeth: Drew iii 41 / Ockley: Bax 53. **2** Bromley SL: Dunstan 146 / Towcester: Northants NQ iii 26. **3** Shrewsbury, Abbey Church: Shropshire ANHST 1S i 68 / Twickenham: Cobbett 195 / Chester SJB: Lectures 123 / Leyton: Kennedy 151. **4** Ludlow: Shropshire ANHST 2S iv 156 / SCLS: Account Book 41b / SASA 364b, 367a. **5** SMC: Overall 185 / Cratfield: Raven 122 / SS Walbrook: London & Middx AST 1S v 374 / Walthamstow i 21.

6 Death and burial. 1 St Alphage LW: Hall 38 / Leyton: Kennedy 152, 154. **2** Oxford SC: Wood L&T ii 473-474. **3** Deptford: Hasted i 35a. **4** Lambeth: Drew ii 149 / Milton Abbot: DART xi 217 / Canterbury HCW: OPB i 96 / SGWC: Baddeley 148. **5** SMH 78, 128-129 / Ludlow: Wright 65. Assumptions made: a) those paying are parishioners; b) the deceased were not their personal friends. These seem reasonable but may be wrong. **6** Merrington: Sharpe 20 / Framlingham: EA 2S v 112. **7** Redenhall: EA 1S iv 151 / Laxfield: EA 1S ii 257 / SD Backchurch: Reg. 309.

7 Baptisms. 1 Birchington: Canterbury Records 15. **2** Wimbledon: Dyer, Social Life 123-124. It is not clear where the baptism took place.

8 Gypsies. 1 SR iii 327 (22 Henry VIII cap. 10, 1530-31). **2** SR iv 242-243 (1st & 2nd Philip & Mary cap. 4, 1554). **3** SR iv 448-449 (5 Eliz. cap. 20, 1562-63) / Cox CWA 339. Fn. Bury St Edmunds SM: Tymms, St Mary p144. **4** Loughborough: Reliquary xiii 196 / Camberwell: Blanch 176 / Leyton: Kennedy 152. **5** Durham SN: Sharpe 49.

Foundlings

1 Children found. 1 SB Paul's Wharf: Littledale i 14. **2** SM Aldermary: *The Parish Registers of St Mary Aldermary, London ... from 1558 to 1754* ed. Joseph Lemuel Chester, Harleian Soc., 1880, p98 / Penn: Waters 39. **3** Stepney: Hill & Frere 6-7. **4** SM Colechurch: Milbourn 62 / SM Woolnoth: B&H 81 / SM Bread St: *The Registers of St Mildred, Bread Street, and of St Margaret Moses, Friday Street, London* ed. W. Bruce Bannerman, Harleian Soc., 1912, p8 / Thornton: Reg. 30. **5** SM Woolnoth: B&H 24 / SCLS: Reg. i 18b. **6** Auckland: Sharpe 23 / Northmoor: Berks etc AJ xvi 73. **7** SM Friday St: London & Middx AST 1S iii 333-334, 363. **8** Ongar: *The Parish Registers of Ongar, Essex*, printed for Frederick Arthur Crisp, 1886, p102 / SASA 353a. **9** SCLS: Reg. ii 65b. **10** SR iv 1234-1235 (21 James I cap. 27, An Acte to prevent the murthering of bastard children). **11** Oxford SPE: Tyssen 301.

2 Attempts to avoid responsibility. 1 SBE CWA 181a. **2** SBE CWA 133b, 150a / SM Woolchurch: B&H lvi. **3** SM Aldermanbury: Carter 1913 p69.

3 Baptism. 1 SO Hart St: Reg. 15. **2** Johnson ii 77 (q), 85-86 (reiterated 1200). **3** SN Acons: Brigg 17-18.

4 Naming. 1 SA Budge Row: *The Parish Registers of St Antholin, Budge Row, London ... and of St John Baptist on Wallbrook, London* ed. Joseph Lemuel Chester & George J. Armytage,

Harleian Soc., 1883, p33 / SM Poultry: Milbourn 28 / SD Backchurch: Reg. 116 / AH Bread St: Reg. 41. **2** SBE CWA 89b-90a / SBE: Vestry Books 111b-112a. **3** SS Walbrook: Reg. i 8 / AH Bread St: Reg. 15 / SASA 321 / SM Woolnoth: B&H 79. **4** SJ Clerkenwell: Reg. ii 11 / Oxford St Martin: Fletcher 133 / Romford: NQ 3S iii 84b. **5** SJZ 402b-403a. **6** SH Bishopsgate: J. E. Cox 93 / SS Walbrook: London & Middx AST 1S v 379 / SBE CWA 222a / SB Bishopsgate: *The Registers of St Botolph, Bishopsgate, London* ed. A. W. Cornelius Hallen, vol 2, 1893, p433a. **7** SJ Clerkenwell: Reg. iv 136. **8** SM Woolchurch: B&H 330, 331, 332, 339. **9** AH Bread St: Reg. 11 / St Gregory: Burn PR 78 / Chipping: Smith 119. **10** Wolstanton: Tate, Parish Chest 62.

5 Seeking the parents. **1** SS Walbrook: London & Middx AST 1S v 372, 379 / Canterbury HCW: OPB i 43 / Bristol SJ: Bristol P&P ii 40a. **2** Myddle: Gough 166. Gough gives no date for the incident. He was born in 1635 and wrote the history *c.* 1700. **3** Cardington: Shropshire ANHST 1S iv 321 / Newcastle AS: Sopwith 130. **4** SASA 363b. **5** SCLS: Accomptes 81b / SJZ 389b. **6** SCLS: Reg. ii 26b / SM Woolnoth: B&H 83.

6 Care. **1** Lambeth: Drew iii 41 / Cardington: Shropshire ANHST 1S iv 321. **2** SASA 336a, 338a / SJZ 400a. **3** SBE CWA 95b, 99a. **4** SMC: Overall 183 / Worcester: Amphlett 155, 159.

Pregnant women
1 Encouraging departure. **1** SCLS: Accomptes 81b / Bromley SL: Dunstan 144 / Leyton: Kennedy 150. **2** Norwich SPM: Norfolk Antiq. Misc. ii 357 / SCLS: Accomptes 88a / Battersea 262 / Deptford: Hasted i 34a / St Alphage LW: Carter 93. **3** AH Barking: Maskell 121 / SASA 341b-342a. **4** SCLS: Account Book 9b. **5** SS Walbrook: London & Middx AST 1S v 380 / SASA 354b, 367b, 372b.

2 Support. **1** SMC: Overall 169 / SP Cheap: JBAA xxiv 265 / St Alphage LW: Carter 81 / SBE CWA 108a / SJZ 406a / High Wycombe: Records of Bucks viii 64. **2** SBE CWA 173b / SD in West: *An Historical Account of the Constitution of the Vestry of the Parish of St Dunstan's in the West, London*, 1714, p19.

Bastards
1 Chesham: *A transcript of the first volume, 1538-1636, of the Parish Register of Chesham, in the County of Buckingham* ed. J. W. Garrett-Pegge, 1904, p16 / Durham SN: Sharpe 48 / SMC: Reg. 94 / Petersham: Surrey AC ii 94 / Rampton: Cambs & Hunts AST vol 1 pt 2 p274. **2** Newcastle AS: Sharpe 106 / Stoke Poges: *The Register of the Parish of Stoke Poges, in the County of Buckingham, 1653-1753* ed. Lionel Reynolds, 1912, p134 / Richmond: *The Parish Registers of Richmond, Surrey* ed. J. Challenor C. Smith, vol 1, 1903, p129. **3** Waldron: Waters 38 / Cratfield: Raven 144. **4** Barking: Essex AST 1S ii 129 / Toft Monks: EA 2S iii 10. **5** Chelsea: Burn PR 85 / SN Acons: Brigg 7 / Stepney: Burn PR 85. **6** Aston: Cox PR 73 / Chelsea: Burn PR 85 / SM le Bow: Bannerman 1914 p58. **7** Castle Combe: Wilts ANHM xxii 17. **8** Walthamstow ii 52. **9** Lambeth: Drew iii 213 / Littleham: Webb 121 / Walthamstow i 22. **10** SR iv 610 (18 Eliz. cap. 3, An Acte for the setting of the Poore on Worke, 1575-76). **11** York SM le B: Collins i 31 / Stepney: Burn PR 85 / Cuckfield: Renshaw 81. **12** Cropredy: Vis. Peyton xxv (citing Archdeacon's papers, Oxon, c. 156, f25). **13** Walthamstow i 22 / Lapworth: Hudson 211. **14** SM Aldermanbury: Carter 1913 p125 / Tooting: Morden 76. **15** St Alphage LW: Carter 93. **16** SH Bishopsgate: J. E. Cox 179-180. **17** Bungay: EA 1S iii 200 / Seale: Surrey AC ii 42 / Walthamstow i 21.

Disorder
1 Bringing problems to light. **1** Gibson 1717 vi (q). Other general sources for this section include Gibson 1711 and Gibson, Codex, 1713, vol 2 pp996-1008. **2** Davis 82 (no. 86) / Hoskin xi-xiv. Gibson 1711 pp7-12 sets out some details of the process. **3** Gibson, Codex, 1713, ii 998, 1008 / Burn EL iv 18 / Ian Forrest, 'The transformation of visitation in thirteenth-century England', *Past and Present*, no. 221, Nov. 2013, pp3-38. **4** Ware 11 ('Twice a year as a rule the archdeacon ... held a visitation or kept a general court (the two terms being synonymous)') / Davis 108 (no. 125) / Pounds 299-300. **5** Dartington: British Mag. vi 267 / Leverington: Fenland NQ vii 300. **6** Davis 97-105 (nos. 109-119; q 99) / Gibson 1717 p88 (Articles of enquiry, 1713). **7** Chardstock: Vis. Chandler 112 (no. 315) / SM

Woolchurch: Vis. Hale 98 / Tollesbury: Vis. Pressey xix 4 / Brewham: Haigh 155-156.
8 Vis. Brinkworth vol 1 x-xvi. **9** Tydd SG: Vis. Palmer iv pt 8 p377. **10** Pounds 294.
2 Misbehaviour in church. 1 Davis 98 (no. 111). **2** West Thorney: Vis. Sussex i 120-121 /
Ferring: Haigh 90 / Dodford: Haigh 88 / Shelley: Vis. Pressey xix 20. **3** Burnham: Vis. Hale
171 / Downham: Vis. Hale 212 / Grays Thurrock: Vis. Hale 234 (1607). **4** Aldborough:
Purvis, Docs 94 / Harby: Vis. Notts xxx 56 / Wivelsfield: Vis. Renshaw 62 / Steeple: Vis.
Hale 261-262. **5** Oxford SP-le-Bailey: Vis. Brinkworth ii 171 / Little Baddow: Vis. Hale
258 / St Olave Silver St: Vis. Hale 263-264 (1639-40). **6** Hawkhurst: Vis. Woodruff 27 /
Theydon Garnon: Essex AST 2S vii 175 / Worcester: Amphlett 60 / Slaugham: Vis.
Renshaw 53 (1600-01). **7** Wivelsfield: Vis. Renshaw 64 (1637-38) / Vis. Peyton xxxiii n.2
(citing Southwell Act Books, 6 Feb 1587; no parish indicated). **8** SD in West: Pepys
viii 389 (18 Aug 1667). **9** Iden: Vis. Renshaw 54 (1603-04) / Reculver: Vis. Hussey xxv
48-49. **10** Leigh: Vis. Hale 252 / Wisbech: Vis. Palmer iv pt 8 p380 / Fryerning: Vis. Hale
260. **11** Chelmsford: Essex AST 1S ii 213 / Scotter: Burn PR 176 n. **12** SM Aldermanbury:
Carter 1913 p114.
3 At weddings and funerals. 1 West Ham: Vis. Hale 225-226 / Grays Thurrock: Vis. Hale
229 / Arlington: Vis. Renshaw 64. **2** Whitstable: Vis. Hussey xxvii 226. **3** King's Sutton: Vis.
Peyton 292 (1617), 298 (1619). **4** Flintham: Vis. Notts xxx 52 (1608-09).
4 Involving animals etc. 1 White Notley: Vis. Hale 124 / Brancepeth: Bishop Barnes 122 /
Beddingham: Vis. Renshaw 53 (1600-01) / Hawton: Vis. Notts xxx 54. **2** West Pennard:
Haigh 176 / Buckland SM: Haigh 176 (1621). **3** Culmer 18. **4** Wolsingham: Durham
Depositions 231-232. **5** Langdon Hills: Vis. Hale 172-173 (1579; theie > they). **6** Buxted:
Sussex AC iv 251-253. **7** Winchelsea: Vis. Renshaw 54 (1603-04).
5 In the churchyard. 1 Boughton: Vis. Notts xxx 42 (1585) / Childwall: Vis. Warrington 184 /
North Stoke: Vis. Brinkworth i 43. **2** Goring: Vis. Brinkworth i 43 / Manchester: Vis.
Manchester 67. **3** Great Baddow: Vis. Hale 218 / Warsop: Vis. Notts xxx 44 (1612-13).
4 Boxgrove: Vis. Sussex i 27 (q). Fn. *Sussex Cricket in the Eighteenth Century* ed. Timothy
J. McCann, Sussex Record Soc., Lewes, 2004, xxxiii. **5** SR iv 133-134 (An Acte againste
fightinge and quarelinge in Churches and Churcheyardes, 5 Edward VI cap. 4, 1551-52).
Durham Depositions contains numerous cases from the later 16th century e.g. pp73-76,
258-263, 286-292, 295-300, 305-307. **6** King's Sutton: Vis. Peyton 287 / Margate:
Vis. Hussey xxvi 28-29. **7** St Gregory: Burn PR 124. **8** Rye: Holloway 81-82, 519.
6 Absence from church etc. 1 SR iv 355-358 (An Acte for the Uniformitie of Common
Prayoure and Divine Service, 1 Eliz. cap. 2, 1558-59). On attendance before the Reformation
see Routine p169 and the related source note. **2** Ramsgate: Vis. Hussey xxvi 32 / Davis 84-85
(no. 90). **3** SR v 1 (An Acte for punishing of divers abuses committed on the Lords day,
1 Charles I cap. 1). **4** SR v 25 (An Act for the further reformacion of sondry abuses committed
on the Lords day, 3 Charles I cap. 2, 1627). **5** SR v 848 (An Act for the better observation
of the Lords day, 29 Charles II cap. 7). **6** Margate: Vis. Hussey xxvi 19 / Lullington: Vis.
Renshaw 56 / Smarden: Memorials 274 / Laughton: Vis. Renshaw 60. **7** Up Marden:
Vis. Sussex i 78 / Sutton: Vis. Palmer iv pt 8 p365 / Ely HT: Vis. Palmer iv pt 8 p361.
8 East Mersea: Vis. Pressey xix 21. **9** Hartshorne: Derbyshire ANHSJ vii 55. **10** Smarden:
Memorials 273 / Benenden: Haslewood 220-221 / Chichester SO: Vis. Sussex i 114 /
Twickenham: Cobbett 201. **11** Colchester SG: Vis. Hale 125. **12** Islip: Vis. Brinkworth
i 5 / Attenborough: Vis. Notts xxx 44 / Mansfield: Vis. Notts xxx 44 / Farndon: Vis. Notts
xxxi 144 / Everton: Vis. Notts xxxi 144 / Slaugham: Vis. Renshaw 62. **13** Tuxford: Vis.
Notts xxx 42. **14** Banbury: Vis. Peyton 206 (1611-12) / Mansfield Woodhouse: Vis. Notts
xxxi 143 / Lambourn: Footman 120 / Wisbech SP: Vis. Palmer iv pt 8 p381 / Lullington:
Vis. Sussex ii 26. **15** SMW: NI 64. The sum is so high it is perhaps a misprint e.g. for 18d.
16 Clifton: Vis. Notts xxx 44 / Birchington: Vis. Hussey xxv 16. **17** South Benfleet: Vis.
Hale 217 (1597-98) / Yapton: Vis. Sussex i 66. Fn. Frere & Kennedy iii 22 (1559) / Davis
59 (1604, no. 59). **18** Whitstable: Vis. Hussey xxvii 227. **19** Camberwell: Blanch 116,
117 / SASA 368a-b. **20** Manchester: Vis. Manchester 66 / St Giles in Fields: Parton 271.
21 Colchester SG: Vis. Hale 125. **22** Slaugham: Vis. Renshaw 61 (1628-29). **23** Herne:
Vis. Hussey xxv 27. **24** Chislet: Vis. Hussey xxv 25.

7 **Fornication**. **1** Banbury: Vis. Peyton 213 (includes interpolations by Peyton) / Graffham: Vis. Sussex i 8, 31. **2** Kennington: Vis. Warham 203-204 (reseq). **3** Kennington: Vis. Warham 204 / Smarden: Memorials 272. **4** Grantchester: Vis. Palmer vi pt 1 p22 / Birchington: Vis. Hussey xxv 18. **5** King's Sutton: Vis. Peyton 299 (1619).

8 **Magic and witchcraft**. **1** Leverington: *Proceedings of the Cambridge Antiquarian Society*, vol 39, Cambridge, 1940, p74 / Margate: Vis. Hussey xxvi 19 / Bilsthorpe: Vis. Notts xxx 51 (1594-95) / Purleigh: Vis. Hale 219. **2** Thatcham: Barfield ii 99a. **3** Gateshead: Ambrose Barnes 354 (reseq). **4** Monks Eleigh: EA 1S i 48. **5** Wingrave: GM (Feb) 1759 p93a (Wingrove). **6** James I, *Daemonologie*, 1603, p80 (misprinted as p64; reseq) / William Connor Sydney, *England and the English in the 18th Century*, vol 1, 1891, p283 (instance of bible test at Oakley, Bedfordshire, 1735).

9 **Abusing churchwardens and ministers**. **1** Felpham: Vis. Sussex i 33 / Rudgwick: Vis. Sussex i 124. **2** West Ham: Vis. Hale 197-198. **3** Benenden: Haslewood 220-222 (*c.* 1608). **4** Elsdon: Durham Acts 184-185 (1637-38). **5** Towersey: Vis. Peyton 194. **6** Stondon Massey: Vis. Hale 239. **7** SJ in Roseland: Baildon 23-25 (no. 20). **8** Aldborough: Purvis, Docs 168-169 (1596). **9** Deighton: Purvis, Docs 92. **10** King's Sutton: Vis. Peyton 286 (wear > were). **11** Gamlingay: EA 2S vi 5.

10 **Religious punishments**. **1** Pounds 295-297. **2** Ely Penances 266-267 (Newton), 270 (Ely HT), 272 (Babraham). **3** Durham SN: Durham Depositions 107-108 (adjusted). **4** Appleby: Vis. Leicester 636-637. **5** Gateshead: Ambrose Barnes 401 / Manchester: CWA 15 (pr > for) / Chester SJB: Lectures 127, 137. **6** Headcorn: Smarden, Memorials 275-276 (1592). **7** Stapleford: Ely Penances 274-275. **8** Croydon: Collectanea Topog. iv 93. **9** West Ham: Vis. Hale 210 / Great Whelnetham: *Great Whelnetham Parish Registers, 1561 to 1850* ed. S.H.A.H., Bury St Edmunds, 1910, p207. **10** Leyton: Vis. Pressey xix 17 / Buttsbury: Vis. Pressey xix 17 (1662). **11** NQ 6S vol 6 p166 quotes a report from *Western Morning News*, 2 Aug 1882. **12** Cheltenham: *Cheltenham Examiner* 20 Oct 1847 p2c. **13** Burn EL ii 243 / ODCC 490. **14** Luccombe: Cox PR 110-111 (letter dated 23 May 1628). **15** Haigh 162-163 / Vis. Peyton lxvii n.2 (citing Archdeacon's papers, Bucks, c. 230, f60; no parish indicated; q). **16** Vis. Warrington 187 (Leigh), 188 (Ormskirk), 190 (Winwick), 192 (Wigan).

11 **Fines**. **1** Battersea 363. **2** SMW: Catalogue 85 / St Giles in Fields: Parton 271 / SBE CWA 232b. **3** Windsor: Tighe & Davis ii 115 / St Giles in Fields: Parton 270 / Waltham Abbey: Winters 110. **4** St Giles in Fields: Parton 270. **5** SR iv 1142 (4 James I cap. 5, 1606-07) / Bakewell: Reliquary v 75. **6** SR iv 1229-1230 (21 James I cap. 20, 1623-24) / Firth & Rait ii 393-394 (An Act for the better preventing of prophane Swearing and Cursing) / SR vi 591-592 (6 & 7 William & Mary cap. 11, An Act for the more effectuall suppressing prophane Cursing and Swearing). **7** St Giles in Fields: Parton 270. **8** St Alphage LW: Carter 91. **9** AH Staining: British Mag. iv 148. **10** Lambeth: Drew iii 7 / SBE CWA 88a. **11** Tollesbury: Cox PR 220-221.

12 **Civil crime and punishment**. **1** Dartington: British Mag. vi 377 / St Ethelburga: Cobb 27 / Leyton: Kennedy 155, 156, 390 (vestry) / Battersea 253. **2** Youlgreave: Cox, Derbyshire ii 337 / Bristol SJ: Bristol P&P ii 40a / Walthamstow ii 51. **3** SBE CWA 71b / Deptford: Hasted i 34b / SCLS: Account Book 30b. **4** St Alphage LW: Carter 82 / Newcastle AS: Sopwith 129 / Edenbridge: Arch. Cant. xxi 122. **5** Chedder: HMC 3rd report app. 330a / Bywell: Archaeologia Aeliana xiii 163 / Hutton: Knight 374. **6** Mortlake: Anderson 60 / Hammersmith: Faulkner 1839 p207. **7** Waters p75 notes that a man was ducked at Rugby in 1786 for beating his wife. **8** Chudleigh: Jones 24 / Lambeth: Drew iii 274 / Bakewell: Derbyshire ANHSJ lxii 97. **9** Kingston UT: Surrey AC ii 91.

13 **Complaints against ministers**. **1** Davis 74 (no. 75). **2** Vis. Warham 76 (Swalecliffe), 180 (Littlebourne), 185 (Patrixbourne: Claryngbole; advoutry), 242 (Linsted: ensample). **3** Rufforth: Purvis, Docs 167-168. **4** Monkton Moor: Ripon, Memorials iii 345 (visitation book of Archbishop Young). **5** Gainford: Bishop Barnes 131 / Great Warley: Vis. Hale 213 / Broughton: Vis. Peyton xvii n.5 (citing 'Bucks, c. 230'). **6** Little Wakering: Vis. Hale 214-215 (q, adjusted), 224. Mercer was still at Little Wakering in 1601 when he was presented for administering the communion while excommunicated. **7** Eardisley: *English Historical Review*, vol 45, 1930, p447. **8** Barnard Castle: Bishop Barnes 138-141 (reseq; adjusted).

14 Dilapidation. 1 Vis. Bradshaw 297-328 including p307 (Great Abington), p318 (Long Stow), p328 (Meldreth), pp327-328 (Oakington), pp311-312 (Sawston), p320 (Toft). **2** Huddersfield: Purvis, Docs 181 / Up Marden: Vis. Sussex i 96-97. **3** Little Laver: Hale 1841 pp6-7 (wharby) / Staines: Hale 1841 p58. **4** SES 227-228 (apparently from vestry book). **5** Wye: Arch. Cant. xxi 196-197 (letter from George Oxenden to Archbishop Sancroft, 6 April 1686). **6** Acrise: Vis. Woodruff 51 / Trumpington: Vis. Palmer v pt 5 p262 / Seaham: Bishop Barnes 118 / Reculver: Vis. Hussey xxv 46 / Northampton AS: Northampton Records ii 392-393 / Pitsea: Vis. Pressey xxi 113. **7** Chilham: Vis. Warham 176 / Luddenham: Vis. Parker 299 / Leigh: Vis. Pressey xx 242. **8** York SJB: *The Fabric Rolls of York Minster* ed. James Raine, Surtees Soc., 1859, p248; Dymond 469 n.21 / Sheppey: Vis. Warham 256 / Haltwhistle: Durham Acts 6 / Chester SP: Chester & NW AAHSJ iii 370 (vestry order) / Northampton AS: Serjeantson 1901 p301. **9** Sturton: Vis. Notts xxxi 129 / SLP 174a, 175a / Durham SO: Durham Depositions 296 (undated, but cases before and after are 1575). **10** Colchester SB: Essex AST 2S xi 38 / Northampton AS: Northampton Records ii 393 / SBE CWA 14a. **11** Canterbury St Andrew: Cotton pt iv 49-50 (reseq). **12** Locking: Knight 393. **13** SP Cheap: JBAA xxiv 252 / Burford: Monk 188.
15 Thefts. 1 SMW: NI 10 / Reading SL: Coates 222. **2** SMH 83 / Camberwell: Blanch 121. **3** Worksop: White 332 / Lambeth: Drew i 93 / St Giles in Fields: Parton 271. **4** North Wingfield: Dyer, Social Life 244. **5** Deptford: *The Sun* 22 Oct 1801 p3c / *Ipswich Journal* 7 Nov 1801 p2d. The particular parish is unclear: these early reports say St Paul, but later ones (e.g. *London Courier* 9 Nov 1801 p4c and GM 1801 p1143) say St Nicholas. **6** Morebath: Binney 64 (adjusted). **7** Lambeth: Drew iii 41. **8** Duffy, Altars 487. **9** East Ham: Essex AST 2S ii 242, 243 (adjusted) / Little Ilford: Essex AST 2S ii 240. **10** Lydd 388 / Lambeth: Denne 383. The Lambeth notice appeared in the *London Gazette*, 25 July 1710 p2b. **11** Fulham: Fèret i 182.
16 Bodysnatching. 1 Oxford SPE: Hearne viii 156-157 (diary entry, 11 Jan 1724; shrewd > shroud). **2** St George, Bloomsbury: *Morning Chronicle* 9 Dec 1777 p4c-d (qs) / *Public Ledger* 13 Dec 1777 p3b. **3** Report ... on Anatomy 17, 71 (question nos. 35, 791, 792). **4** Bailey 77-78 and illustration fp78 / Pannal: Friar 53-54. **5** Report ... on Anatomy 70 (no. 766), 72 (no. 799), 120-121 (nos. 1447, 1449, Clerkenwell). **6** Fulham: Fèret i 283 / Battersea 247. **7** Fulham: Fèret i 282, 283.

History Intrudes
The Reformation
A: Under Henry VIII
1 SR iii 465 (25 Henry VIII cap. 21, 1533-34) / SR iii 492 (26 Henry VIII cap. 1, 1534) / Frere & Kennedy ii 1-11 (1536). **2** SMW: NI 11 / SM Woolnoth: B&H xvii. **3** Frere & Kennedy ii 34-43 (1538). **4** Wriothesley i 83 / J. C. Dickinson, *The Shrine of Our Lady of Walsingham*, Cambridge, 1956, p65. **5** Frere & Kennedy ii 42 (injunctions) / Wilkins iii 848b (proclamation). **6** Bungay: EA 1S i 424. **7** SES 84 / Cambridge SMG: Foster 96. **8** Frere & Kennedy ii 53-60 (qs 57, 59-60). **9** Wilkins iii 860a. **10** North Elmham: Legge 15, 20. **11** Canterbury St Andrew & Canterbury St Mary Northgate: Letters and Papers ... Henry VIII xviii pt 2 p300. **12** Wing: Archaeologia xxxvi 227 / North Elmham: Legge 13 / Oxford St Martin: Fletcher 37. **13** SR iii 988-993 (37 Henry VIII cap. 4, chantries) / *Acta Regia*, vol 3, 1727, pp348-349 (will) / Wriothesley i 181. **14** Worcester: Amphlett 17-18 (reseq) / Leicester St Martin: North 23. **15** Wriothesley i 181-182. **16** SMF: Kitto 123 / SMW: NI 12.
B: Under Edward VI
1 Laws and orders. 1 Cardwell, Annals i 4-23 (qs 7, 14-17). **2** Cardwell, Annals i 41-51 / Duffy, Altars 453 / Chronicle of the Grey Friars 54-55 (q). **3** Wriothesley ii 1 (adjusted). He dates the accident to the night of 16th rather than 17th Nov and the sermon to 27th Nov. **4** Durham SN: Rites of Durham 69 (q), 108. **5** SR iv 2-3 (1 Edward VI cap. 1, 1547). **6** SR iv 24-33 (1 Edward VI cap. 14, 1547; qs 24-27) / Lindley 289-290 / Duffy, Altars 454-455. **7** *Miscellaneous Writings and Letters of Thomas Cranmer* ed. John Edmund Cox, Parker Soc., Cambridge, 1846, p417 (letter, 27 Jan 1548) / TRP i 416-417 (no. 299, proclamation,

6 Feb 1548) / Frere & Kennedy ii 183 (articles of inquiry, 1548), 184 n. (referring to order of council, 18 Jan 1548) / Duffy, Altars 457. **8** Gilbert Burnet, *The History of the Reformation of the Church of England* ed. Nicholas Pocock, vol 5, Oxford, 1865, pp191-192. **9** Ketley 16 (q) / Diarmaid MacCulloch, *Tudor Church Militant: Edward VI and the Protestant Reformation*, 2001, p89 / SR iv 37-39 (2 & 3 Edward VI cap. 1, 1548). **10** *Troubles connected with the Prayer Book of 1549* ed. Nicholas Pocock, Camden Soc., 1884, pp145-177 ('The articles of us the commoners of Devonsheir and Cornwall'; qs 153, 154, 165, 169, 173). **11** SR iv 110-111 (3 & 4 Edward VI cap. 10; alleblaster) / Duffy, Altars 469 (January date). The Act had been preceded by a proclamation of 25 Dec 1549 ordering bishops to destroy old service books (TRP i 485-486 (no. 353)). **12** Hooper 488 (fourth sermon upon Jonas). **13** Frere & Kennedy ii 241-245 (injunctions for London diocese, 1550; q 242-243) / Wriothesley ii 41 ('all ... communion') / *Acts of the Privy Council of England*, NS vol 3, ed. John Roche Dasent, 1891, pp168-169 ('all ... up') / Cardwell, Annals i 89-90. **14** SR iv 130-131 (5 & 6 Edward VI cap. 1) / Ketley 76-77 (1549 qs), 217 (surplice), 265 (north side) / Duffy, Altars 473-475. **15** Cardwell, Annals i 99-102 (instructions for commissioners in Northampton; q 101). **16** SMW: NI 14 / Stanford: Antiquary xvii 118a.
2 **Impact in parish churches**. **1** Bristol SN: St Paul's EST v 112 n.8. **2** Rye: Holloway 492. **3** Reading SL: Coates 223 / BS 51 ('parsy clarke', so clarke could be a surname) / Smarden: Memorials 242. **4** South Littleton: Midland Antiquary i 104 (wocetr). **5** Deal: Arch. Cant. xxxi 99, 101 (1548, consistory court book). **6** SS Walbrook: London & Middx AST 1S v 366 (reseq) / Worcester: Amphlett 25 / SB Aldersgate: WR 202. **7** Banwell: Knight 431 / Brightlingsea: Essex AST 2S i 15. **8** Blean: Arch. Cant. xxxi 104 (consistory court). **9** Worksop: White 330 / Stratton: Archaeologia xlvi 220 / Yatton: Hobhouse 160 / Baldock: St Albans & Herts AAST 1928 p139 (Ryd > Richard) / SMC: Overall 66. **10** Lewes St Michael: Sussex AC xlv 53 / Ashburton: CWA 31 / Canterbury St Andrew: Cotton pt iii 43 / Wing: Archaeologia xxxvi 231. **11** SMC: Overall 66 / Ludlow: Wright 33-34 / Great Dunmow: Essex AST 1S ii 236 (date given simply as 'temp. Edward VI'). **12** Stratton: Archaeologia xlvi 221. **13** Ludlow: Wright 35 / SM Friday St: JBAA xxv 362. **14** Bristol SN: Bristol P&P ii 163b. **15** SMW: NI 12 / SMH 387. **16** SMW: NI 12-13 / Burnham: Records of Bucks v 117. **17** SM Abchurch: WR 416 / Wandsworth: Inventories, Surrey 132. **18** Foxe 1876b (Dr Martin, 1556, 'Downe') / Thomas Harding, *A Confutation of a booke intituled An Apologie of the Church of England*, 1565, f225r ('Is it').
3 **Sale of church goods**. **1** Harwich: Essex AST 2S xxiv 37-38. **2** Kelby: PF 110 (1566 inventory) / Habrough: PF 93 (1566 inventory) / Canewdon: Essex AST 2S xxiv 37. **3** Reading SL: Kerry 68 / Holbeach: Marrat ii 105 / Ludlow: Wright 36-37 (reseq) / Melton Mowbray: Leicestershire AAST iii 183 / AH Bread St: WR 88. **4** Rainham, Essex: Essex AST 2S ii 173 / AH Bread St: WR 91 / SS Coleman St: WR 602. **5** Leicester St Martin: North 26 / SM Friday St: JBAA xxv 364-365 / SM New Fish St: WR 365. **6** SK Cree: WR 322 / SP Cornhill: WR 581 / SB Aldgate: WR 208 (listed under 1551 but apparently an error for 1550). **7** SL Jewry: WR 328 / Worfield: Shropshire ANHST 3S ix 113 / Great Warley: Essex AST 2S ii 180 (1552 inventory, 'sold since the ... firste yere' of Edward VI). **8** Thame: Lee 68 (reseq). **9** Frere & Kennedy ii 235 n. **10** Canterbury St Andrew: Cotton pt iii 39 / AH Staining: WR 122-123. **11** SA Holborn: Bentley xv / Reading SM: Garry 1. **12** SM Bassishaw: WR 490 / SM Bread St: WR 521-522 / SM Wood St: WR 517. **13** Long Melford 94 / SM Outwich: WR 394-395 / Cambridge SMG: Foster 118-119. **14** Holbeach: Marrat ii 105-106 (reseq) / Great Warley: Essex AST 2S ii 180 (1552 inventory, 'sold since the ... firste yere' of Edward VI). **15** St Alphage LW: Carter 69 / SM Bassishaw: WR 491. **16** SK Cree: WR 322 / Long Melford 93-94 (reseq). **17** SK Cree: WR 323 / SP Cheap: WR 569. **18** SD Backchurch: London & Middx AST 1S iv 206-208 (Vogan, Vagam, Waghan > Vaughan; vesmet; Unckyll), 210. Reseq. and otherwise adjusted. **19** Peter Heylyn, *Ecclesia Restaurata, or, The History of the Reformation of the Church of England*, 2nd edition, 1670, p134.
C: Queen Mary
1 **Laws and orders**. **1** Wriothesley ii 101, 104. **2** SR iv 202 (1 Mary statute 2 cap. 2) / Machyn 50 / John Strype, *Ecclesiastical Memorials ... under King Henry VIII* [etc], vol 3 pt 1, Oxford,

1822, p79. **3** Frere & Kennedy ii 322-329 (injunctions; qs 327-328) / Wriothesley ii 113-114.
4 SR iv 246-254 (1 & 2 Philip & Mary cap. 8) / Gee & Hardy 385. **5** Stanford: Antiquary
xvii 119a / Oxford St Martin: Fletcher 40. **6** Smarden: Foxe 2112-2113. **7** Vis. Harpsfield
ii 180 (Benenden), 183, 185, 207 (Ulcombe).
2 Parishes return to the old ways. 1 Cratfield: Raven 83 / Stanford: Antiquary xvii 118a / SM
Woolnoth: B&H xx / Leicester St Margaret: Nichols, Leicester i pt 2 p560a. **2** CSP Foreign
series 1547-1553 p55 has a letter dated 10 Sep 1550 from Sir John Mason, ambassador to
France, informing the privy council that 'three or four ships have lately arrived from England
laden with images, which have been sold at Paris, Rouen, and other places'. **3** Lydd 421.
4 Vis. Harpsfield i 22 (Brabourne), 131-132 (Rolvenden); ii 221 (Thornham), 249 (Newington).
5 SM Woolnoth: B&H xx (reseq) / Bristol SW: Bristol P&P ii 221a. **6** SMC: Overall 111,
113 (reseq). **7** Cratfield: Raven 83 / Lewes St Michael: Sussex AC xlv 55. **8** Vis. Harpsfield
i 125 (Smarden); ii 203-204 (Sutton Valence), 246 (Hartlip). Other examples in vol 2 include
Benenden (p180), Chart (p201), Lenham (p227) and Otham (p210). **9** Mere: Wilts ANHM
xxxv 25. **10** Rye: Holloway 497-498 (Holloway's preamble says Rye church 'soon felt the
influence' of the new regime but he leaves this and other entries undated) / Smarden: Arch.
Cant. ix 231 / SMC: Overall 131 / Wandsworth: Surrey AC xv 121-122 (reseq; adjusted).
11 Frere & Kennedy ii 406 (no. 33). **12** Leverton: Archaeologia xli 361-362. **13** Vis.
Harpsfield ii 200 (Boughton Monchelsea), 273 (Queenborough). **14** Vis. Harpsfield i 77
(Barham), 115 (Westwell). **15** Louth: Notices 50-51 (reseq). **16** Leicester St Margaret:
Nichols, Leicester i pt 2 p560a (listed as 1553 but adjusted as first Easter in Mary's reign
fell in 1554) / Lichfield: Harwood 523. **17** SB Gracechurch St: Malcolm i 314 / Ashburton:
CWA 34 / SMW: NI 15.
D: Under Queen Elizabeth
1 Orders and destruction. 1 SMC: Overall 123 / Lambeth: Drew i 73. **2** SR iv 350-355 (1 Eliz.
cap. 1; q 352) / Gee & Hardy 442 / SR iv 355-358 (1 Eliz. cap. 2; qs 358, 357). **3** Cardwell,
Annals i 178-209 (qs 187 perambulations, 189 shrines etc, 201-202 altars). The wording
concerning altars is perhaps intentionally ambivalent. On the one hand it 'seemeth no matter
of great moment' whether there is an altar or not and their universal removal is not explicitly
ordered. On the other hand, on three counts removal is at least implied and at most effectively
required. First, the reference to their orderly removal says it is to be done 'for observation
of one uniformity through the whole realm' and 'for the better imitation of the law in that
behalf', considerations which point to universal removal. Second, the instruction that 'the
holy table' be placed 'where the altar stood' suggests that there is no longer to be an altar.
Third, the fact that the table is to be portable (being ordinarily kept 'where the altar stood'
but 'placed in good sort within the chancel' at communion time) effectively rules out
traditional altars of stone. **4** Cardwell, Annals i 210-216 (articles of inquiry) / Duffy, Altars
568-569 / Hayward 28. **5** Wriothesley ii 146. **6** George Oliver & J. P. Jones, *Ecclesiastical
Antiquities of Devon*, Exeter, 1828, p48 n. (citing Hooker's 'ms. history'). **7** Cardwell, Annals
i 257-260 (q 257). **8** Cardwell, Annals i 262 (22 Jan 1561). **9** Rye: Holloway 501 / Molland:
DART xxxv 216. **10** Frere & Kennedy iii 108-110 (q 108). **11** Barnstaple: Chanter 77 /
Bristol CC: Bristol P&P ii 176b. **12** Barnstaple: Chanter 77-78 (reseq) / Leicester St Margaret:
Nichols, Leicester i pt 2 p560b / Ashburton: CWA 38 / Long Melford 110 (Pryme, but
in other entries Prime). **13** Leicester St Martin: North 119 / Coventry HT: Sharp 120.
14 Heybridge: Essex AST 2S xxii 36 / Chelmsford: Essex AST 1S ii 218. **15** Salisbury ST:
Swayne 294. Aston, Idols p638 quotes several reports of 'supersticious images' in the windows
at Tenterden, Kent, in the 1580s. **16** Harrison ff76r-77v. **17** Bungay: EA 1S ii 277, 278 /
SMH xlii (for fn.), 412 / SMW: NI 15 / Mere: Wilts ANHM xxxv 31. **18** Great Dunmow:
Essex AST 1S ii 236 (editor dates simply 'temp. Elizabeth'). **19** Woodbury: DART xxiii
289 / Bungay: EA 1S iii 19-20 / Exeter St Petrock: DART xiv 459-460. At St Petrock
doubt is cast on the extent of the removal by a further entry in 1576 'for mending certain
holes in the rodeloft' (p466). **20** Abingdon: NI 142 / South Tawton: Bristol GAST xxiii 91 /
Prescot: CWA 53. **21** Birt 427-429 (1569 visitation of Chichester diocese) / Lindfield:
Sussex AC xix 40. **22** Ashburton: CWA 40, 47, 50.

2 Fate of church goods. 1 SP Cheap: JBAA xxiv 256 / Long Melford 109. **2** Leicester St Margaret: Nichols, Leicester i pt 2 p560b. **3** Cambridge SMG: Foster 164 / Ludlow: Wright 137. **4** Lewes St Michael: Sussex AC xlv 56 / Bungay: EA 1S iii 19 (reseq) / Chelmsford: Essex AST 1S ii 212 / Stratton: Archaeologia xlvi 229. **5** Duffy, Altars 585-586. **6** PF: Ashby de la Launde 29, 30; Aswardby 33; Boothby Pagnell 54; Branston 56, 57; Broughton 55; Burton Coggles 50; Croxby 64, 65; Denton 67; Dowsby 72; Dorrington (orig. Durrington) 73; Grantham 87-88; Haconby 94; Horbling 107; Market Rasen 124; Owmby 121; Springthorpe 143; Stallingborough 144; Swayfield 147; Waddingham 157. Adjusted. **7** Duffy, Altars 576.
3 Hiding treasures. 1 Briston: NORA i 240 / Ripon: Memorials iii 344 / Birt 428 (Chichester diocese) / Preston: Smith 43 / Aston, Idols 236-253 (for a general account of the subject). **2** Scaldwell: Northants NQ i 258-259. **3** Boroughbridge: Purvis, Docs 148. **4** Rothwell: Purvis, Docs 149. **5** Aysgarth: Purvis, Docs 144-146, 225-227. **6** Askrigg: Purvis, Docs 152 (1571). **7** Wakefield: GM (Dec) 1756 pp559-560 / Flawford: [Robert] *Thoroton's History of Nottinghamshire ... with large additions by John Throsby*, vol 1, 1797, pp130-131. The images are now in Nottingham City Museum. / West Farleigh: Arch Cant xl 49. It was buried some twenty yards north-east of the church. / Buckenham: NORA i 243-244 / Epworth: *Willis's Current Notes ... during the year 1853*, 1854, pp61-62.

Civil War and Puritans in Power

1 Church strife. 1 Viscount Falkland, *A Speech made to the House of Commons concerning Episcopacy*, 1641, p7 ('some have evidently labourd to bring in an English, though not a Roman, popery'). **2** Waltham Abbey: Winters 90. **3** North Walsham: EA 1S iii 271 / Ipswich SC: EA 2S iv 4. **4** Addleshaw & Etchells 108-147 / Aston, Idols 295-306.
2 Ejection. 1 JHC iii 183 (27 July 1643, q) / Green 508, 515, 522-523 / McCall 4-6. **2** Godalming: Surrey AC ii 210-223 ('He' silently added at start of each charge). Fn. Davis 21. **3** White, Century 8-9 (no. 21) / Walker 187b (q) / Matthews 348-349. **4** Downham: EA 2S vi 122-123 (depositions dated 22 March 1643) / St Giles in Fields: Just Correction 5-6. **5** Panfield: White, Century 15 (no. 32) / Great Totham: Just Correction 11. **6** White, Century sig. A2v, A3v. **7** Arlington: White, Century 1-2 (no. 1). **8** Acton & Lambeth: Mercurius A 166-168 (no. xviii). **9** Lambeth: Featley 1, 4, 8, 11, 14, 18. **10** Mercurius A 171-172 (no. xviii) / ODNB (Daniel Featley, q).
3 Removal of 'superstitious' items. 1 JHC ii 279a. **2** SL Eastcheap: Nehemiah Wallington, *Historical Notices of Events occurring chiefly in the reign of Charles I* ed. R. Webb, vol 1, 1869, p259. **3** Firth & Rait i 265-266 (26 Aug 1643). **4** Firth & Rait i 425-426 (9 May 1644). **5** Lambeth: Drew iii 171, 185. **6** SM Woolchurch: B&H liii. **7** SH Bishopsgate: J. E. Cox 225. **8** Wilmslow: East Cheshire i 111. **9** Norwich SPM: Norfolk Antiq. Misc. ii 333 / Woodford Halse: Northants NQ i 43 / St Giles in Fields: Parton 202 / SM Woolchurch: B&H liii. **10** Chelmsford: Essex AST 1S ii 213 (accounts) / Mercurius A 22-23 (no. iii). **11** Wilmslow: East Cheshire i 110-111.
4 Iconoclasm in the east. 1 Dowsing ed. White 6-7 (commission dated 19 Dec 1643). **2** Dowsing ed. Moule 7 (Cambridge SP), 8 (Brinkley). Adjusted. **3** Dowsing ed. White 15 (Sudbury SP, Sudbury SG), 15-16 (Clare), 27 (Walberswick), 27-28 (Blythburgh). Reseq. into chronological order and adjusted. **4** Walberswick: Dowsing ed. White 50 (q; officers of Dowson > officer Dowson, adjusted by reference to Dowsing ed. Cooper p379). While the opposite could be true – the brasses being removed and concealed ahead of the visit – the apparently respectful references to Dowson and the fact that the cost is recorded tend to suggest assistance. **5** Ufford: Dowsing ed. White 18 (first visit on 27 Jan), 29 / M. R. James, *Suffolk and Norfolk*, 1930, p98.
5 Iconoclasm across the country. 1 Acton: Dugdale, Troubles 557 / Yaxley: Simon Gunton, *The History of the Church of Peterburgh* [Peterborough Cathedral], 1686, p335. Acton church may in part have been targeted because of its rector, Daniel Featley – see main text pp497-498. **2** Lostwithiel: Dugdale, Troubles 560. **3** Sudeley: Mercurius A 58 (no. vi). **4** Culmer 23-24 (Canterbury) / Mercurius B 159 (no. iv, Exeter) / Dugdale, Troubles 559-560 (Lichfield) / Mercurius B 214-215 (no. v, Peterborough) / Mercurius B 145-152 (no. iii, Winchester; qs 146, 149). The various accounts are of course partisan and some are perhaps over-coloured as a result. **5** Mercurius B 154-155 (no. iv, Westminster Abbey).

6 Soldiers in churches. 1 Great Torrington: HMC 6th report app. 100b. **2** St Albans: Alfred Kingston, *Hertfordshire during the Great Civil War*, 1894, p87a n. **3** Reading SL: Kerry 95 (reseq) / Burford: Monk 191 (reseq) / BS 75. **4** Leicester St Martin: North 199 / Witney: W. J. Monk, *History of Witney*, Witney, 1894, p160 / Hartland: HMC 5th report app. 574a. **5** Newbury: Money 534 (reseq). **6** Oxford St Martin: Fletcher 46 (reseq), 47 / Basingstoke: Baigent 516 (reseq).

7 Parish registers. 1 Brimpsfield: Glos NQ i 404 / Bishop Middleham: Sharpe 32 / Longford: Cox, Derbyshire iii 195. **2** Lullington: Cox, Derbyshire iii 391. **3** Longford: Cox, Derbyshire iii 195. **4** AH Barking: Maskell 82. **5** Chester St Bridget: Cox PR 197 / Croston: *The Registers of … Croston in the County of Lancaster* ed. Henry Fishwick, Wigan, 1900, pp85, 229.

8 Taking sides. 1 SMW: NI 49, 50, 52 / SASA 338b / SK Cree: Malcolm iii 313 / SM Woolchurch: B&H liv. **2** Stockton: NORA i 184 (reseq), 187. **3** Toft Monks: EA 2S iii 24 / St Ethelburga: Cobb 17 / SBE CWA 129b, 130a. **4** Waltham Abbey: Winters 108. **5** Chester SM: Morris 197 / Newbury: Money 532-533 / Oxford SPE: Tyssen 296. **6** Reading SL: Kerry 95. **7** SES 216.

9 Innovations. 1 Firth & Rait i 175-176 (9 June 1643, The Covenant to be taken by the whole kingdom), 376-378 (5 Feb 1644). **2** Weybread: EA 1S ii 6 (orig. 1643) / SM Woolchurch: B&H liv. **3** Firth & Rait i 420-421 (8 April 1644, Lords-Day), 582 (4 Jan 1645, Ordinance for taking away the Book of Common Prayer), 755-757 (26 Aug 1645, Directory of Public Worship), 879 (9 Oct 1646, Ordinance for the abolishing of archbishops and bishops). **4** Selattyn: *The Register of Selattyn, Shropshire* ed. Mrs Bulkeley-Owen, 1906, p133. **5** Firth & Rait ii 715-718 (24 Aug 1653, An Act touching Marriages and the registring thereof). **6** Glynde: *The Parish Register of Glynde, Sussex, 1558-1812* ed. L. F. Salzman, Sussex Record Soc., 1924, pp40, 41. **7** Firth & Rait ii 968-990 (28 Aug 1654, q 977).

10 Royal arms: fall and return. 1 Loose: Stahlschmidt, Kent 338 / Coventry HT: Sharp 122. **2** CSP Domestic series 1649-1650 p481 has the following under 15th Jan 1650: 'The order of the House concerning the taking down of the king's image and arms, in all places throughout this nation, to be sent for, and offered to Council to-morrow.' The order itself has proved elusive. **3** Houghton-le-Spring: Durham CWA 305 / Wilmslow: East Cheshire i 111 / St Alphage LW: Hall 37 (reseq). **4** Faversham: Canterbury Records 81. **5** Beverley: Poulson ii 745-747 / Shrewsbury, Abbey Church: Shropshire ANHST 1S i 73, 74 / Norwich SPM: Norfolk Antiq. Misc. ii 342, 351 (reseq). **6** Pepys ii 69.

11 Restoration. 1 Oxford SPE: Tyssen 295 / Coventry HT: Sharp 116 / Wilmslow: East Cheshire i 114 / Wrington: Scarth 451 / SMW: NI 65-66 (reseq). **2** Burgh SP: EA 1S i 268. **3** SR v 242-246 (12 Charles II cap. 17) / McCall 8. **4** Pepys i 176. **5** Locking: Knight 394. **6** Canterbury SD: Reg. 24 / Plymouth: Rowe 229. **7** Leicester St Martin: North 206 / Newcastle AS: Sharpe 106 / Chester SJB: Chester & NW AAHSJ iii 63. **8** Evelyn i 362. **9** Thundersley: Vis. Pressey xxi 116 (plact > placed).

Plague and Fire
Plague
1 Outbreak. 1 Oxford AS: Clark 27 (adjusted). **2** Loughborough: Reliquary xiii 195. **3** *Narratives of the Days of the Reformation* ed. John Gough Nichols, Camden Soc., 1859, p82 (Hancock; hytt > it) / Uffculme: GM (Dec) 1808 p1057. **4** SMC: Reg. 204 / Stranton: Sharpe 6. **5** Coggeshall: Beaumont 37 / Peterborough SJB: Burn PR 131 / Bishopwearmouth: Sharpe 74. **6** Great Hampden: Cox PR 176. **7** Loughborough: Reliquary xiii 197. **8** Chester SM: Dyer, Social Life 90. **9** Malpas: Daniel Lysons & Samuel Lysons, *Magna Britannia, being a concise Topographical Account of the several Counties of Great Britain*, vol 2, 1810, pp845-846.

2 Prevention. 1 Cranbrook: Canterbury Records 59-60. **2** Stoke Charity: Williams 89 / St Ethelburga: Cobb 10 / Winterslow: Wilts ANHM xxxvi 40. **3** St Ethelburga: Cobb 12 / Worksop: White 335. **4** Cranbrook: Canterbury Records 60 / Shrewsbury SM: Owen & Blakeway ii 353. **5** Hering 1603 p5. **6** *Certain Necessary Directions, as well for the cure of the plague, as for preventing the infection … set down by the Colledge of Physicians*, 1665, pp7-9. **7** SB Gracechurch St: Malcolm i 316 / SCLS: Accomptes 60b. **8** Pepys vi 213. **9** SM Woolnoth: B&H xxiii / Chester SM: Morris 186 / Basingstoke: Baigent 522. **10** Northampton SG:

Serjeantson 1911 p53. **11** Plague orders, London: Orders ... agreed, 1608, unpaginated, 3rd page. Repeated verbatim in Orders and Directions, 1665, p3. **12** SMW: NI 17, 23, 35 / SMF: Kitto 453 / Oxford St Martin: Fletcher 47. **13** Melton Mowbray: Cox CWA 318 / Waltham Abbey: Winters 89 / Mortlake: Anderson 56 / Widdecombe: Dymond 53.

3 Orders for plague time. **1** *Orders, thought meete by her Majestie, and her privie Councell, to be executed ... in such ... places, as are ... infected with the Plague*, [1578], unpaginated, sections 5 ('the houses'), 7 ('to provide'), 4 ('to view'), 10 ('some place'). **2** Wilson, Plague 14, 179 (1583) / Plague orders, London: Orders ... agreed, 1608, unpaginated. **3** Plague orders, London: Orders ... thought fit, 1608, unpaginated. **4** Plague orders, London: Orders to be used, 1625 (q) / Orders conceived, 1665, in A Collection of ... scarce Pieces, p7.

4 Dealing with the infected. **1** SP Cheap: JBAA xxiv 265. **2** BS 62. **3** Machyn 310 / William Maitland, *The History and Survey of London*, vol 1, 1756, p255b. **4** SMW: NI 17. **5** SM Woolnoth: B&H xxv / St Alphage LW: Hall 26. **6** Pepys vi 120. **7** SMW: NI 46. **8** St Giles in Fields: Parton 262. **9** Woodbury: DART xxvi 377 / SMF: Kitto 578 / AH Barking: Maskell 125. **10** Battersea 252 / Bletchley: Records of Bucks viii 246. **11** SMW: NI 54 / St Alphage LW: Hall 38. **12** Woodbury: DART xxvi 377 / Putney: Lysons i 418 / Lambeth: Drew iii 169. **13** Lambeth: Drew iii 153, 162 / SMW: NI 49, 50. **14** SCLS: Accomptes 60b / St Giles in Fields: Parton 263. **15** SM Woolchurch: B&H lvi / Hackney: Simpson iii 66-67. **16** SMC: Overall 193 / Lambeth: Drew iii 162.

5 Dealing with the dead. **1** SBE: Vestry Books 3a (q; their > there); Wilson, Plague 65 (usual fees) / SM Woolchurch: B&H lii / SCLS: Accomptes 60b. **2** St Alphage LW: Hall 26. **3** Pepys vi 283 (entry dated 31 Oct 1665). **4** Plague orders, London: Orders heretofore conceived, 1625, unpaginated (q on 2nd page) / Orders conceived, 1665, in A Collection of ... scarce Pieces, p4. **5** SASA 336a / SM Woolchurch: B&H lvi. **6** Leicester St Martin: North 137 / King's Lynn St Margaret: Hillen i 298 / Chelmsford: Essex AST 1S ii 224 / Battersea 253. **7** SMF: Kitto 578 / Fulham: Fèret iii 227. **8** Cranbrook: Canterbury Records 60. **9** Stepney: Hill & Frere 107-108. **10** SMW: NI 27 / Ipswich SM: EA 2S iv 155 / Chelmsford: Essex AST 1S ii 224. **11** SP Cornhill: Gower i 216-217. **12** Dartington: British Mag. vi 378. **13** SASA 336a-b / St Giles in Fields: Parton 262-263. **14** Pepys vi 189 (12 Aug 1665), 213-214 (6 Sep 1665). **15** St Pancras Cheapside: Bannerman 1914 p301. **16** SS Walbrook: London & Middx AST 1S v 382 / SJZ 392a. **17** SGWC: Wilson, Plague 41. **18** Auckland: Sharpe 23 / Wandsworth: *The Registers of the Parish of Wandsworth in the County of Surrey, 1603-1787* ed. John Traviss Squire, Lymington, 1889, p335 / Godalming: Reg. 294. **19** Chelmsford: Essex AST 1S ii 214.

6 Miscellaneous effects. **1** Lichfield: Harwood 526 / SO Hart St: Reg. 115 / Dorchester: Burn PR 50. **2** Lambeth: Drew iii 162. **3** Ardingly: Loder 17 / Whorlton: Sharpe 84. **4** Wing: Archaeologia xxxvi 239 / Smarden: Memorials 261. **5** Holt: NORA xxviii pt 2 p82 (visitation record) / West Dean near Chichester: Vis. Sussex i 105. **6** Pepys vi 175 / Hering 1603 p13. In the 1625 edition, quoted in main text (p101), Hering nonetheless advocates the frequent ringing of bells to purify the air. Perhaps he changed his mind, or perhaps the two types of ringing were sufficiently distinct that the air-purifying type did not strike 'great terror into the hearts'. **7** Wilson, Plague 177-178 (Dekker and Jonson qs; former is from *The Seven Deadly Sinnes*, 1606). **8** SO Hart St: Pepys vii 30 (30 Jan 1666).

7 Thanksgiving. **1** SP Cheap: JBAA xxiv 267 / Derby AS: Cox, Derbyshire iv 99 / Oxford SPE: Tyssen 296. **2** Cambridge SMG: Foster 294.

The Great Fire

1 Pepys vii 269 (2 Sep 1666) / Evelyn ii 11 (3 & 4 Sep 1666). **2** SBE: Vestry Books 102a (in 2nd pagination sequence). **3** SGWC: Baddeley 25 / SM Woolchurch: B&H lvi. **4** SCLS: Account Book 10b-11b / SM Woolchurch: B&H lvi. **5** SMC: Overall xiv / SBE: Vestry Books 102a-b (2nd pagination sequence) & SBE CWA 190b. **6** SCLS: Account Book 11b (reseq) / SBE CWA 191a. **7** SM le Bow: Bannerman 1914 p29 / SD Backchurch: Reg. 237. **8** Battersea 229 / Tavistock: Worth 55. **9** Leyton: Kennedy 139. **10** SM Aldermanbury: Carter 1913 p115 / SBE CWA 198a, 206a / SJ Garlickhythe: London & Middx AST 1S iii 398 (reseq).

Illustration and caption sources

Entries in this listing are typically arranged as follows:

1. Page location of the image within this book. For pages with several illustrations **a**, **b**, **c** et cetera indicate the particular image, the references working from left to right and then from top to bottom. 2. Brief description. 3. Any manuscript and/or printed source. 4. Any source collection or other copyright holder. 5. Any sources of captions and/or further information.

Most of the books from which images have been taken are listed in the Bibliography although a few (generally those not drawn on for the text and from which only one image is derived) are detailed here. Other images appear courtesy of a range of institutions, some of those listed often being abbreviated as follows:

Folger   Folger Shakespeare Library, Washington
Geo   Geograph Britain and Ireland project (geograph.org.uk)
Getty   The J. Paul Getty Museum, Los Angeles
LOC   Library of Congress
LWL   Lewis Walpole Library, Yale University
Met.   Metropolitan Museum of Art, New York
YCBA   Yale Center for British Art

Other abbreviations used:

BM   British Museum
C: source of caption information.
eng.   engraving / engraved
fp   facing page
frontis.   frontispiece
JL   photograph by editor
MG   photograph by Michael Garlick, a contributor to Geograph
n.d.   lacks publication date
pl.   plate
pub.   published

In many cases details of original images have been used and this is not indicated separately in each entry.

All images from PS (Pontifical Services) vol 4 were printed in Venice in 1520.

Images from the Folger Shakespeare Library are used under a Creative Commons Attribution-ShareAlike 4.0 International licence, those from Geograph under an Attribution-ShareAlike 2.0 Generic licence, and those from Walters Art Museum, Baltimore, Maryland, under a CC Zero: No Rights Reserved licence.

> Every effort has been made to identify copyright holders, to obtain any necessary permissions to reproduce text and illustrations, and to include appropriate acknowledgements. The publishers would nonetheless be grateful to be notified should any error or oversight have occurred.

Jacket

For images which also appear within the book the relevant page number is given here and details can be found in the main list below under the page in question.

Front flap Yew tree: p9. *Front panel* Ground plan: p20. Priest: p174. Bell: p579. Baptism: From a window originally in a house in Leicester, *c.* 1500. Nichols, Leicester vol 1 pt 2 pl. 37 (fp514). Maypole: p245. Sexton: p187. Dog: p79. Bones: p354. Betrothal: From 'A pleasant new Ballad of Tobias', 1640. RB ii 624. *Spine* Bell: Reliquary vol 8 pl. 12 (fp138), rope added. Ringer: p121. *Back panel* Censing angel: p259. Hell mouth: p28. Gravedigger: p182. Curate: p174. Iconoclast: p505. *Back flap* Crow: p148. Devil: p302. Hog: p7.

Frontis. Principalities. See below under p25.

Title page Bell. See below under p579.

viii Initial letters. **a.** St Martin in Fields. Kitto fp242. **b.** St Michael, Cornhill. Overall fp132.

fp1 Lich-gates. **a.** Ditcheat. Geo, Neil Owen. **b.** Down St Mary. Geo, Derek Harper.

2 Churchyard cross, Tong. Geo, Philip Halling. Figure in background edited out.

3 **a & b.** Churchyard consecration. PS vol 4 figs. 44 (p47), 47 (p49).

4 Dead arising. *Booke of Christian Prayers*, 1578, f61r. Folger.

5 Chesterfield church, [? 1819]. LWL.

6 Hythe crypt. **a.** From an old postcard. LOC. **b.** Skull. Geo, Pam Fray.

7 Hog by Timothy Burrell. Sussex AC iii 139.

8 Archers, Ugborough. Bond & Camm ii 247.

9 **a & b.** Yews, Clayton and Wilmington. JL.

11 Procession. 'South Netherlandish'. Met.

13 **a.** Bushey churchyard. YCBA. **b.** St Margaret, Westminster, by Benjamin Cole, detail of a view including Westminster Abbey, n.d. YCBA.

14 **a.** Spire, Piddinghoe. **b.** Shingles, Southease. **c.** Weathercock, Ripe. All JL. The Piddinghoe fish is sometimes identified as a sea trout, and Kipling thought it was a dolphin. However, an article in the *Hastings and St Leonards Observer*, 29 Sep 2016, quotes an undated earlier report from the *Sussex County Herald*, which newspaper had tracked down a Mr Blaber who fashioned the fish in 1882. Blaber had then been working for Wightman & Parrish, ironmongers in nearby Lewes, and went with his foreman to a fishmonger in the town where he 'took the necessary measurements from a real salmon'.

17 Porch, Aylsham. Geo, MG.

19 Niches. **a.** Wenhaston. Geo, MG. **b.** Arlington. JL.

20 Ground plan. Based on a plan by Walter Godfrey of Beddingham church, Sussex. By kind permission of the churchwardens.

21 Almsboxes. **a.** Watton. NORA iii fp394. **b.** St Peter, Walpole. Geo, MG. **c.** 'Old Walsingham', by John Sell Cotman, *c.* 1810. YCBA.

22 Font, Hook Norton. Geo, MG.

23 **a.** Angel finial, Ewelme. Howard & Crossley 333. **b.** Font, East Winch. Weever 849. Folger.

24 Nave roof, Cawston. Geo, MG.

25 **a.** Rood screen, Barton Turf. **b.** Cherubim (detail). **c.** Principalities (detail). All Geo, MG.

26 **a.** Rood figure, Cartmel Fell. Vallance, plates 3, 4 and 5. **b.** Head and foot, South Cerney. Vallance, plates 1 and 2. C: Vallance 12; Richard Marks, 'From Langford to South Cerney: The rood in Anglo-Norman England,' JBAA vol 165 pp172-210. Now in BM.

28 **a.** Wenhaston Doom. **b.** Hell mouth (detail). **c.** Chancel arch, Raunds. Central light fitting edited out. All Geo, MG.

29 Rood loft, St Margaret's. Geo, Philip Pankhurst.

31 **a, b & c.** Rood stairs, Denton. All JL.

32 Rood loft, Llanelieu. Vallance pl. 33.

33 **a.** Loft niche, Eastbourne. JL. **b.** Loft doorway, Harlaxton. Acabashi, via Wikimedia, under a CC Attribution-ShareAlike 3.0 Unported licence.

34 **a.** Entombment, Easby. Geo, MG. **b.** Stained glass, Ticehurst. Geo, Julian P. Guffogg.

35 **a.** Misericord, Wintringham. **b.** Mythical beasts, Hailes. **c.** Chancel arch, Coombes. All Geo, MG.

36 **a.** Misericord, Beverley. **b.** St Catherine, Kingerby. Both Geo, MG.

37 St Christopher. Getty.

39 Parclose, Winthorpe. Howard & Crossley 221.

42 Bees and cow by Timothy Burrell. Sussex AC iii 132, 148.

45 **a.** Creed etc, Burnham Overy. Geo, MG. **b.** Texts and arms, Ellingham. Geo, bell.

46 Royal arms. **a.** Preston. Geo, John Salmon. **b.** Croscombe. Geo, MG.

47 Garland on coffin. RB i 186.

48 Garlands. **a.** Matlock. Reliquary vol 1 pl. 2 (fp8); C: 10. **b.** Abbotts Ann. *Country Life* 18 Feb 1944 p298.

49 Alphabet cross. Maskell i 210.

50 **a.** Consecration cross, Thompson. Geo, MG. **b.** Bishop on ladder. Muncey, frontis.; C: 67.

51 **a, b** & **c.** Consecration. PS vol 4 figs. 13 (p15), 23 (p25), 36 (p39).

53 Pews, Cawston. Geo, MG.

56 Seat, Tintinhull. *Country Life* 28 Dec 1945 p1147.

58 **a.** Milbanke pew, Croft on Tees. **b.** Bolton pew, Wensley. Both Geo, MG.

61 **a.** Poppy head, Combs. Geo, MG. **b.** Bench end, Crowcombe. Geo, Chris Andrews. **c.** Dog carving, South Elmham. Geo, John Salmon. **d.** Hassock. *Country Life* 18 Mar 1949 p619.

63 Hour glasses. **a.** Chelmondiston. Geo, Adrian S. Pye. **b.** Compton Bassett. Cox, Fittings 189.

64 **a.** Sounding board, Lenham. Geo, MG. **b.** Pulpit, Chesterfield. Geo, Julian P. Guffogg.

65 Hogarth, 'The Sleeping Congregation'. LWL.

66 Eagle lectern, Wiggenhall. Crossley pl. 201 (fp101).

68 **a.** Communion in both kinds. From Coronation Book of Charles V, King of France, *c.* 1370, BM Cotton Ms. Tiberius B VIII/2 f72r. Chambers DW fp392. **b.** Communion in one kind. From BM Royal Ms. 6 E VI/2 f337v, *c.* 1370. Gasquet fp222. **c.** Elevation. From the Trivulzio Book of Hours. LOC.

69 Elevation. Foxe, 1570, title page. Folger.

70 Enclosing relics. BM Lansdowne Ms. 451. PS vol 2 fig. 33 (pl. 11).

71 Anointing altar. PS vol 4 fig. 38 (p41).

72 **a.** Dove pyx. Met. **b.** Pyx, Exning. Suffolk AIP vol 1 fp157; C: 157. Now in BM.

73 **a.** Patron saint, Wilmington. JL. **b.** Low side window, Branscombe. Geo, Philip Pankhurst. **c.** Sedilia, Alfriston. JL.

75 Easter sepulchres. **a.** Selmeston. **b.** Alfriston. Both JL.

76 & 77 Easter sepulchres and details. **a.** Patrington. Geo, MG. **b.** Holcombe Burnell. Wikimedia, public domain, creator unnamed.

79 **a.** Dog, from Sudbury arms. *Book of Public Arms: A Cyclopedia* ed. Arthur Charles Fox-Davies & M. E. B. Crookes, 1894, pl. 65. **b.** Communion. From title page of *The Whole Duty of receiving worthily the Blessed Sacrament*, 5th edition, 1717. Chambers DW fp404.

81 **a** & **b.** Positive and portative organs. Francis W. Galpin, *Old English Instruments of Music*, 1910, pp221, 222.

84 **a.** Organ pipes, Framlingham. **b.** Musician, Barton le Street. Both Geo, MG.

86 **a.** Jack, Blythburgh. JL. C: GM (Sep) 1808 p776 (letter mentioning 1682 date). **b.** Jack, Southwold. Geo, MG. **c.** Clock, Raunds. Geo, MG.

87 Clock, Cullompton. Geo, MG. C: Beeson 105 / Rye: Holloway 480 / Reading SL: Kerry 97.

89 Clock, Rye. JL. C: Beeson 115.

90 Binsey. YCBA.

91 **a.** Ringing sanctus bell. From BM Royal Ms. 10 E IV (Decretals of Gregory IX, *c.* 1300-1340), f257r. Walters, Bells 127. **b.** Sacring bell, Salhouse. NORA i 242.

92 Belfry, Stevington, by Mrs Delves Broughton. *Country Life* 4 June 1904 p806.

93 **a, b** & **c.** Ringing chamber, Felmersham; Stairs, Felmersham; Steps, Flitton. All by Mrs Delves Broughton. *Country Life* 6 June 1903 p741.

94 **a** & **b.** Bell-founder's window, York Minster. Raven, Bells, frontis. and fp74; C: 72-74.

97 Bell moving, Broad Clyst. *Country Life* 30 Oct 1937 p456. C: Ellacombe 100.

99 **a** & **b.** Bell hallowing. PS vol 4 figs. 60 (p65), 62 (p67).

100 St Michael, Cornhill, tower. Overall fp199.

103 Bench end, Aspall. Geo, MG.

105 Praying woman and man. From 'The Sinners Supplication', 1630. RB ii 498.

106 Angel grasps soul, from a Book of Hours. Master of Sir John Fastolf. Getty.

115 Bell. Bell mark, Duffield, 1763. Reliquary vol 16 pl. 11 (fp113).

116 Boy with tankard. From 'Mondayes Worke', 1632. RB ii 151. Image reversed.

117 Ringer, Stoke Dry. Geo, MG.

118 **a & b.** Ringers, Fressingfield and Halesworth. Both *Country Life* 4 May 1945 p782.

121 Bell-ringers. After woodcut in 'The True Trial of Understanding', 1750, p22. Ashton, Chap-books 313.

122 **a.** Amice and alb. Chambers DW fpp32, 34. **b.** Chasuble detail. V&A Cat. pl. 24. **c.** Chasuble back. V&A Cat. pl. 23. **d.** Orphrey detail. V&A Cat. pl. 14.

123 Stole. Early 14th century. Chambers DW fp47.

125 **a.** Cope. V&A Cat. pl. 20. **b.** Detail, Great Bircham. Cox, Fittings 292; C: 296. **c.** 'Jesse' cope detail. V&A Cat. pl. 11.

127 **a.** Houseling cloth. From BM Royal Ms. 2 B VII f259v. Chambers DW fp343. **b.** Chalice, Rendham. Geo, MG. **c.** Communion cup, Mobberley. Cox, Fittings 261. **d.** Hallowing chalice etc. PS vol 4 fig. 49 (p53).

129 **a.** Clerk. From BM Royal Ms. 10 E IV f108v. Gasquet 113. **b.** Censer, Easby. Geo, MG.

130 Hallowing a cross. PS vol 4 fig. 53 (p57).

137 Candles. From the Getty Apocalypse. Getty.

140 Register, Dunwich. Cox PR 14.

141 **a.** Chest, Dersingham, by John Sell Cotman, 1815. YCBA. **b.** Chest, Harty. Cox, Fittings 15. **c.** Decorated initial, St Michael, Cornhill. Overall fp126.

142 Broom by Timothy Burrell. Sussex AC iii 150.

143 **a.** Umbrella. LWL. **b.** Watch-box, Ivychurch. Geo, Marathon.

144 Armour, Brington. Cox, Fittings 171.

147 **a.** Fire hooks, Raunds. Cox CWA fp320. **b.** Fire engine eng. W. H. Toms. YCBA.

148 **a.** Crow. From arms of John Croker. London & Middx AST 1S vol 2 appendix, 'Evening meetings' p5. **b.** Hedgehog, by Antonio Tempesta, *c.* 1650. Rijksmuseum.

149 **a.** Crow net. From *A Booke of Engines and Traps*, 1590, p87. Cox CWA 296. **b.** Fox, Ripon. Geo, MG.

153 Gargoyle, Cannington. Geo, MG.

157 Window, Lambeth, by Thomas Allen. Allen fp62. C: Drew ii 241 (1607); Denne 381, 383 (1703); Allen 62. There are various versions of the pedlar story e.g. *The London Encyclopedia* (3rd edition, 2008, p59, 'Belvedere Road') relates one in which the dog discovers buried treasure.

158 Lock, East Brent, Somerset. *Proceedings of the Clifton Antiquarian Club*, vol 1, Bristol, 1888, pl. 11 (fp90).

161 Drinking man. Book of Hours, Cambrai, f150v. LOC.

165 **a.** Chough. London & Middx AST 1S ii 246. **b.** Owl, Combs. Geo, MG. **c.** Bolt. Douce 102.

167 Ratcatcher. Wilson 37.

168 Congregation. Heures [Use of Rome], Philippe Pigouchet, Paris, 1497, f84v. LOC.

172 Rectors. **a.** Harlington, by Daniel Lysons. YCBA. **b.** Whichford. Bloxam 253.

173 Reapers. Enamel, 1795. YCBA.

174 **a.** Priest, Wimborne Minster. 'Incised slab formerly in Brembre's chantry.' Mayo 58. **b.** Curate. LWL. C: *Catalogue of ... Satires ... in the British Museum*, vol 6, 1938, p748, no. 7777.

175 **a & b.** Ordinations. From BM Add Ms. 14805. PS vol 2 figs. 62 (pl. 20), 51 (pl. 18).

179 Singers, North Tuddenham. Geo, MG.

182 Gravedigger, South Mimms. YCBA.

184 Hester Hammerton. James Caulfield, *Portraits, Memoirs, and Characters of Remarkable Persons*, vol 3, 1820, fp268. C: Caulfield iii 268-272 / *London Evening Post* 5 March 1730 p1a / W. D. Biden, *The History and Antiquities of ... Kingston-upon-Thames*, Kingston, 1852, pp36-37 / Lysons i 243. Accounts differ as to various details: two or three fatalities; Hester or Esther; brother or brother-in-law buried with her; trapped for three hours or seven.

186 Spade and pickaxe. See under p331 for full image.

187 'Old Scarlet'. Eng. pub. J. Caulfield, 1793.

189 Dogs, Huntingfield. **a.** Stained glass. Geo, Evelyn Simak. **b.** On roof. Geo, MG.

192 Beadle. Eng. Abraham Raimbach, pub. 1834. YCBA.

193 **a** & **b.** Tankards by Timothy Burrell. Sussex AC iii 155, 165.

199 **a** & **b.** Vestry satires, 1795 and 1806. Both LWL.

200 Magi. Met.

202 Magi, Bishopsteignton. Geo, MG.

203 'A Stiff Pull [Suffolk]' by Peter Henry Emerson, 1888. Getty.

205 'Villagers on their way to church'. Getty.

206 Confession etc. Folio 24v (printed 18 in error) in 1505 edition on Early English Books Online. Kingsford fig. 12 (p25). Kingsford gives date of 1503 and title as *The Arte or Crafte to Live Well* (the running header in the 1505 edition).

207 Victory procession. From Romance of Alexander, Ms. Bodl. 264 pt 1 f89r, Bodleian Library. Strutt 394. The victory may well have been in a cock-fight rather than throwing at cocks.

209 **a** & **b.** Public penitents. PS vol 4 figs. 70 (p75), 75 (p81).

210 Lent cloths. From BM Add. Ms. 25698 f9r. J. Charles Wall, *An Old English Parish*, 1907, fp86.

213 **a, b** & **c.** Annunciation, East Tuddenham. All Geo, MG.

214 Tympanum, Aston Eyre. Geo, MG.

215 Doorways. **a.** Littlebury. *An Inventory of the Historical Monuments in Essex*, Royal Commission on Historical Monuments (England), vol 1, 1916, fp192. **b.** East Dean. JL.

216 **a.** Procession. Rock i 391. **b.** Bench end, Trull. Geo, MG. **c.** Sarum woodcut. Wordsworth, Ceremonies 67.

219 **a.** Turret, Long Melford. Vallance pl. 238. **b.** Prophets, Holme. Geo, J. Hannan-Briggs.

221 & 222 Tenebrae candlestick. By kind permission of La Suite Subastas, Barcelona. Lot 14 in sale of 25 June 2020, listed as 'Gothic. 15th century.'

223 Last Supper. From Gospels of St Augustine, Corpus Christi College, Cambridge, Ms. 286 f125r. Chambers DW fp240.

224 **a.** Penitents led. **b.** Blessing of oil. **c.** Feet washing. PS vol 4 figs. 84 (p91), 93 (p101), 77 (p83).

225 Pietà, East Harling. Geo, MG.

226 Creeping to cross. PS vol 4 fig. 97 (p105).

227 Easter sepulchre, Cowthorpe. Howard & Crossley 143.

231 Paschal candle. Chambers DW fp6.

236 Christ emerges, All Saints, Pavement, York. Geo, J. Hannan-Briggs.

237 Christ emerges. Walters Art Museum.

240 St George. Getty.

243 **a.** Hobby horse etc. Douce fp598. Apparent source is a painting of the Thames at Richmond now in the Fitzwilliam Museum, Cambridge. **b.** Robin Hood. From 'Robin Hood, Will. Scadlock, and Little John, or a narrative of their victory obtained against the Prince of Aragon and the two Giants'. RB ii 432.

245 Maypole. From 'The May-Day Country Mirth'. RB vii 79; C: 81 (date).

247 **a** & **b.** Maypoles, embroidery and printed textile. Both Met.

249 Rogation. Heures [Use of Rome], Philippe Pigouchet, Paris, 1497, f4r. LOC.

256 Ascension woodcut. Wordsworth, Ceremonies 93.

257 **a** & **b.** Ascension and Pentecost windows, East Harling. Both Geo, MG.

259 Censing angel, Salle. Geo, MG.

263 Cotswold games. From *Annalia Dubrensia*, 1636, second frontis. Folger.

264 Trinity. From Prayer Book of Charles the Bold. Getty.

265 Processions. **a.** Spinola Hours. Getty. **b.** Foxe, 1570, title page detail. Folger.

268 Assumption. Walters Art Museum. Image combines the Assumption of the Virgin Mary with her coronation.

269 Harvest scenes. **a.** On cotton. Met. Catalogued as 'Piece'. **b.** From 'A Lanthorne for Landlords'. RB i 547.

271 Mass for All Souls. Met.
275 Salisbury monument. C. A. Stothard, *The Monumental Effigies of Great Britain*, 1817.
278 Nativity, East Harling. Geo, MG.
280 Congregation by Adelaide Claxton, n.d. YCBA.
283 **a.** Shepherds. Met. **b.** Nativity. From William Austin, *Devotionis Augustinianae flamma, or Certaine devout, godly and learned Meditations*, 1635, title page detail. Folger.
285 Baptism. f37r. Kingsford 15. See note above regarding Confession image on p206.
286 Baptism, Tattershall. Geo, J. Hannan-Briggs.
287 Baptism. *Booke of Christian Prayers*, 1578, f41r. Folger.
293 Bride. From S[amuel] R[owlands], *The Bride*, 1617, title page.
295 Medieval wedding. From BM Royal Ms. 6 E VI/2 f375r. Gasquet fp216.
299 Rake's marriage. LWL. Image reversed to undo change that occurred at engraving stage.
300 Carrying sacrament. Kingsford fig. 25 (p47).
301 Bedside scenes. **a.** From a pontifical, Corpus Christi College, Cambridge, Ms. 079 f269r. PS vol 2 fig. 27 (pl. 9). **b.** From BM Royal Ms. 6 E VII/1 f70r. Pendrill fp135.
302 Devil. From Last Judgement above chancel arch in Chapel of the Trinity, Stratford upon Avon, copied by Thomas Fisher, [? 1804]. Folger.
303 **a.** Anointing. From *The Art of Good Living*, 1503, sig. l i verso. Gasquet 202. **b.** 17th-century deathbed. From 'An Hundred Godly Lessons', 1682. RB i 428. 'In my county (West Gloucestershire) they throw open the windows at the moment of death' (C. B. in NQ 1S vol 1 p350a).
304 Burial. Getty.
313 **a.** Beadsman and woman, perhaps a monk and a nun, Strelley. Geo, John Sutton. **b** & **c.** Windows, All Saints, North Street, York. Both Geo. **b.** J. Hannan-Briggs. **c.** Julian P. Guffogg.
314 **a.** Feeding the poor, Tattershall. Geo, J. Hannan-Briggs.
314 **b** & **c** and 315 **a, b, c** & **d.** Works of mercy. *Booke of Christian Prayers*, 1608, ff72v-75r. Folger.
316 'Pilgrim', Youlgreave. Geo, MG.
319 Last Judgement, detail. Getty.
326 Mourners. From 'The Mournful Subjects'. RB ii 211.
327 Shrouds. **a.** Chesterfield. Geo, Julian P. Guffogg. **b.** Fenny Bentley. Geo, Neil Theasby. **c.** Yoxford. John Sell Cotman, *Engravings of Sepulchral Brasses in Suffolk*, 1838, pl. 17 (fp12).
328 Burial, cross on shroud. Getty.
331 Affidavit, Gamlingay. YCBA.
334 **a.** Detail from 'The funeral of poor Mary Hackabout'. LWL. **b.** Bier, East Ruston. Geo, John Salmon.
335 Coffins carried. **a.** Weever. Folger. **b.** *Designs by Mr R. Bentley for six poems by Mr T. Gray*, 1753, p36. Eng. Charles Grignion. LWL.
336 Enclosure hearses. **a.** 'From a 15th century Book of Hours of Sarum Use, but written in France'. Dearmer pl. 16 (p79); C: 78. **b.** From a Book of Hours. Getty.
337 **a.** Bier, South Wootton. Funk & Wagnall's *New Standard Dictionary of the English Language*, New York, 1929, p271. **b.** Hearse, St Mary, Warwick. *Description of the Beauchamp Chapel, adjoining to the Church of St Mary, at Warwick*, 1803, pl. 4 (fp8).
338 Hearses. **a.** With beadsmen. From Fitzwilliam Museum Ms. 57, created in two runs, *c.* 1450 and *c.* 1490; it is possible this image is of the earlier date. W. H. St John Hope, *English Altars from Illuminated Manuscripts*, Alcuin Club, 1899, pl. 12 fig. 2. **b.** With beggar. By William Vrelant, from the Arenberg Hours. Getty. Gasquet p205 has an illustration of a similar structure which is there described as a hearse.
339 Islip hearse. Thomas Sharp, *A Dissertation on the Pageants or Dramatic Mysteries anciently performed at Coventry*, Coventry, 1825, pl. 10 (fp191).
340 Tombs. **a.** Arundel. Frederick H. Crossley, *English Church Monuments, A.D. 1150-1550*, 1921, p173. **b.** West Tanfield. Geo, MG.

341 **a** & **b.** Albemarle hearse and 'chariot'. *The Order and Ceremonies used for ... the solemn Interment of ... George, Duke of Albemarle ... 1670*, collected by Francis Sandford, 1671. Folger. Even at this date Sandford uses 'hearse' for the static structure and 'chariot' for the mobile one. John Nichols, *The Progresses ... of King James the First*, vol 4, 1828, fp1049 has an illustration of the hearse designed by Inigo Jones for the king's funeral in 1625.

343 Palls. **a.** Pendrill fp271. **b.** George Unwin, *The Gilds and Companies of London*, 1908, fp214.

349 Vaults, Battersea. Taylor fp280.

350 Gravedigging, Ecton. From a view of the church by J. Shipley, eng. W. H. Toms. LWL.

354 **a.** Skull headpiece. *The Antiquarian Repertory*, new edition, vol 2, 1808, fp14. **b.** Coffin ropes. Trivulzio Book of Hours, image 68. LOC.

357 Reconciling a church. BM Lansdowne Ms. 451. PS vol 2 fig. 34 (pl. 11).

363 Williams on cart. *Kirby's Wonderful and Eccentric Museum*, vol 5, 1820, fp113.

366-367 Tomb figures, St Mary, Warwick. *Description of the Beauchamp Chapel, adjoining to the Church of St Mary, at Warwick*, 1803, plates 2 and 6 (fpp4, 12).

371 Funeral invitation. John Ashton, *Social Life in the reign of Queen Anne*, vol 1, 1882, p49.

375 **a** & **b.** Smock and stocking by Timothy Burrell. Sussex AC iii 137, 150.

377 Spinning wheel. From 'Ragged, and Torne, and True', 1628. RB ii 411.

385 Beggars. **a.** From 'A new ballad, shewing the great misery sustained by a Poore Man in Essex, his Wife and Children'. RB ii 226. **b.** From 'The Blind Begger's Daughter of Bednal-Green'. RB i 42.

387 Travellers. From 'The Dutchesse of Suffolke's Calamity'. RB i 288.

388 Beggar on crutches. Ashton, Humour 386.

396 Foundlings by Hogarth. YCBA.

401 Crier. From 'The Country Crier' by W. Davison, *c.* 1815, after a print pub. 1793. LWL.

411 Court, St Nicholas, King's Lynn. Geo, J. Hannan-Briggs.

412 **a.** Visitation. From BM Royal Ms. 6 E VI/1 f132v. Gasquet fp216. **b.** Summoner. *Drawings of the 23 Tellers of the 24 Canterbury Tales*, copied by W. H. Hooper, pt 1, 1871.

414 Vomiting. From *Booke of Christian Prayers*, 1608, f41r. Folger.

416 Cuckold. From 'The Scolding Wives Vindication', 1689. RB vii 204.

418 Playing in churchyard, by Hogarth. LWL.

421 Windmill. From 'True Blue the Plough-Man', *c.* 1685. RB vol 6 pt 3 p520.

422 Mower. YCBA.

423 Huntsman. From 'The Fox-Chace, or, The Huntsmens Harmony', 1690. RB i 362.

425 **a.** Piper. From 'Mr Playstowes Epithalamium', 1615. RB ii 401. **b.** Drinker. Listed as from 'The Batchelor's Feast', [? 1636]. RB i 49. **c.** Drummer. After title page of *Kemps Nine Daies Wonder*, 1600. RB i 475.

427 Harvest fondle. Book of Hours, Cambrai, f10r. LOC.

428 Adam and Eve, Osbournby. Geo, Julian P. Guffogg.

430 Witch test. Wellcome Collection, under a CC Attribution 4.0 International licence.

438 Drunkards. After eng. on title page of *A Brown Dozen of Drunkards*. Ashton, Humour 286.

441 **a.** Kensington church. Printed for Henry Overton, n.d. LWL. **b.** Pillory, Wallingford, by L. Jewitt. Reliquary vol 1 pl. 19 (fp218).

442 Chairs. **a.** Sandwich. Reliquary i 156. **b.** Scarborough. *Journal of the Architectural, Archaeological, and Historic Society for ... Chester*, vol 2, Chester, 1864, fp203. **c.** In action. James Orchard Halliwell, *Notices of Fugitive Tracts, and Chap-books*, Percy Soc., 1849, p58. Versions of the image appear widely but the original source has proved elusive.

444 Detail from 'The funeral of poor Mary Hackabout'. LWL.

449 Horse by Timothy Burrell. Sussex AC iii 151.

453 Bodysnatchers. *The Book of Remarkable Trials and Notorious Characters* ed. Captain L. Benson, [1872], fp230.

454 Mortsafes, Warden. Geo, Andrew Curtis.

455 Battersea church by James Roberts the elder, after Jean B. C. Chatelain. YCBA.

456 Burnet title page. Folger.

459 Madonna, Winchester. Crossley, Craftsmanship pl. 63 (fp36). C: Philip Lindley et al., 'The Great Screen of Winchester Cathedral I', *Burlington Magazine*, vol 131, no. 1038 (Sep 1989), pp604-617.

461 Edward VI. Eng. Simon van de Passe. Pub. 1618. Rijksmuseum.

463 Purging. Foxe, 1570, p1483. Folger.

467 Defaced panels, Barton Turf. Geo, MG.

470 Royal arms, Rushbrooke. Geo, John Salmon. C: Cautley 18.

473 Brasses, Stoke by Nayland. Weever 773. Folger.

476 Queen Mary. Eng. George Vertue. Pub. 1732. YCBA.

481 Tympanum, Ludham. Geo, MG.

491 Carvings, Epworth. *Willis's Current Notes ... during the year 1853*, 1854, pp61-62.

492 **a.** St Margaret of Antioch, Fingringhoe. Geo, John Salmon. C: Aston, Idols p221 / James Bettley & Nikolaus Pevsner, *Essex*, 2007, p362. **b.** Magi, Long Melford. Geo, MG. C: Archaeologia xii 93 (paper read in 1794 by Craven Ord who says the carving was dug up 'a few years ago') / GM (Sep) 1830 pp204-205 (letter from R. Almack) / Parker 139-140 / Julius Baum, 'Fourteenth century alabaster reliefs of the Epiphany', *Art Bulletin*, vol 15, no. 4, Dec 1933, pp384-387.

493 **a.** Assumption, Sandford. *A Guide to the Architectural Antiquities in the Neighbourhood of Oxford*, pub. John Henry Parker, Oxford, 1846, p356. C: Charles Tracy, 'A forgotten Assumption of the Virgin: the reredos at St Andrew, Sandford-on-Thames', *Apollo*, vol 158, no. 499, Sep 2003, pp15-22. **b** & **c.** Crucifix & tablet, Buckenham. NORA vol 1 fpp243, 300; C: 243-44.

494 Lords Supper. John Harvey Treat, *Notes on the Rubrics of the Communion Office*, New York, 1882, p169. C: Addleshaw & Etchells pl. 6 (fp112).

495 Communion, 1578, f41v. Folger.

500 Font, Walberswick. Geo, MG.

501 Soldiers in church. John Vicars, *A Sight of ye Transactions*, 1646, p7. Folger.

503 Angels, Blythburgh. JL. C: Dowsing ed. Cooper 432-433 n.174.

505 **a.** Vandal. *The Times Displayed*, frontis. C: *Catalogue of* [Satires] *in the British Museum*, vol 1, 1870, p362 no. 656 (where figure is described as 'breaking the Tables of the Law'). **b.** Canterbury Cathedral. Mercurius A, title page. Folger.

511 League and Covenant. Cox PR fp198.

512 Bishops falling. *Decade of Grievances*, title page.

515 Altar rails, Woodbury. John Stabb, *Some Old Devon Churches*, vol 2, 1911, pl. 160.

519 **a.** Fourme, 1563. Folger. C: Clay 459. **b.** Sermon. From T[homas] B[rewer], *The Weeping Lady*, 1625, title page. Wilson 171.

523 Lord have mercy. 'Reconstructed from a sketch in state papers, domestic, Elizabeth, vol. 98, doc. 38.' Wilson 63.

528 Bearer. 'From a series of London Cries sold by R. Pricke, 1655.' Wilson 47.

529 Plague scenes. 'From a contemporary print in the Pepysian Library.' Wilson 149.

533 Fire. From *The Catholick Gamesters*, 1680. Folger.

535 St Mary le Bow. Pub. John Bowles, between 1720 and 1750. YCBA.

579 Bell mark of Abraham Rudhall of Gloucester (*d.* 1735). Walters, Bells 306; C: 228-229.

626 Churchyard visitor, Greenwich, by Thomas Rowlandson. YCBA.

Bibliography

Works cited once only are in most cases detailed solely in the Source notes. The following lists cover works cited more often along with a few of the other works consulted.

Where all references to a work relate to one parish it is generally listed under the name of that parish. Parishes in London are listed under the name of their dedication, those elsewhere under place name, followed by dedication if required in order to distinguish between parishes. Parish acronyms used in the Source notes are included in a few cases where they are not run of the mill e.g. Cambridge SMG, Canterbury HCW.

Place of publication is London unless otherwise indicated.

AE Accounts extracts. HS Harleian Society. NS New series. 1S 1st series; 2S 2nd series; etc.

i. Journals and series

The dates given are those of publication which quite often lag those of the proceedings recorded. Place of publication is included only for the first volume cited in each case and is omitted if London or not known.

AASRP *Associated Architectural Societies' Reports and Papers*. Vol 11, Lincoln, 1871; vol 19, 1887; vol 28 pt 1, 1905, and pt 2, 1906

AJ *The Archaeological Journal*. Vol 39, 1882; vol 42, 1885; vol 45, 1888; vol 48, 1891; vol 58, 1901; vol 65, 1908; vol 70, 1913

The Antiquary, A magazine devoted to the study of the past. Vol 2, 1880; vol 17, 1888; vol 18, 1888

Arch. Cant. *Archaeologia Cantiana*, being Transactions of the Kent Archaeological Soc. Vol 5, 1863; vol 8, 1872; vol 9, 1874; vol 15, 1883; vol 18, 1889; vol 20, 1893; vol 21, 1895; vol 25, 1902; vol 26, 1904; vol 27, 1905; vol 29, 1911; vol 31, 1915; vol 37, 1925; vol 40, 1928; vol 47, 1935

Archaeologia, or Miscellaneous Tracts relating to Antiquity, published by the Society of Antiquaries of London. Vol 12, 1796; vol 34, 1852; vol 35, 1853; vol 36 pt 2, 1855; vol 41, 1867; vol 42, 1869; vol 45, 1877; vol 46 pt 1, 1880; vol 48, 1885; vol 50, 1887

Berks etc AJ *The Berks, Bucks and Oxon Archaeological Journal*. Vol 8, 1902; vol 9, 1903; vol 10, 1904; vol 11, 1905; vol 12, 1906; vol 13, 1907; vol 16, 1910

Bristol GAST *Transactions of the Bristol and Gloucestershire Archaeological Soc*. Vol 15, 'for 1890-91', Bristol; vol 23, 'for 1900'

The British Magazine, and Monthly Register. Vol 2, 1832; vol 3, 1833; vol 4, 1833; vol 6, 1834; vol 31, 1847; vol 32, 1847; vol 33, 1848; vol 34, 1848; vol 35, 1849; vol 36, 1849

Cambs & Hunts AST *Transactions of the Cambridgeshire and Huntingdonshire Archaeological Soc*. Vol 1 pt 2, Ely, 1904; vol 4 pt 3, 1919; vol 4 pt 8, 1929; vol 5 pt 1, 1930; vol 5 pt 5, 1935; vol 6 pt 1, 1938

Chester & NW AAHSJ *Journal of the Chester and North Wales Architectural, Archaeological and Historic Soc*. The society's name has varied over time. Vol 3, Chester, 1890; vol 38, 1951

Cumberland etc AAST *Transactions of the Cumberland and Westmorland Antiquarian and Archaeological Soc*. Vol 9, Kendal, 1888; vol 16, 1900; vol 49, 1949

DART *Reports and Transactions of the Devonshire Association for the Advancement of Science, Literature, and Art*. Vol 11, Plymouth, 1879; vol 14, 1882; vol 23, 1891; vol 24, 1892; vol 26, 1894; vol 29, 1897; vol 31, 1899; vol 35, 1903; vol 36, 1904; vol 38, 1906

Derbyshire ANHSJ *Journal of the Derbyshire Archaeological and Natural History Soc*. Vol 2, 1880; vol 7, 1885; vol 39, 1917; vol 40, 1918; vol 41, 1919; vol 45, 1923; vol 62, 1941

EA *The East Anglian*, or, Notes and Queries on subjects connected with Suffolk, Cambridge, Essex, and Norfolk. 1S vol 1, 1864; vol 2, 1866; vol 3, 1869; vol 4, 1870. NS [2S] vol 3, 1890; vol 4, 1892; vol 5, 1894; vol 6, 1896.

Essex AST *Transactions of the Essex Archaeological Soc*. 1S vol 2, Colchester, 1863; vol 4, 1869; vol 5, 1870. NS [2S] vol 1, 1878; vol 2, 1884; vol 5, 1894; vol 6, 1898; vol 7, 1900; vol 11, 1909; vol 19, 1927; vol 20, 1930; vol 21, 1933; vol 22, 1936; vol 23, 1942; vol 24, 1951.

Fenland NQ *Fenland Notes and Queries*. Vol 1, Peterborough, 1891; vol 2, 1894; vol 4, 1900; vol 7, 1909

Glos NQ *Gloucestershire Notes and Queries*. Vol 1, 1881; vol 3, 1887
GM *The Gentleman's Magazine and Historical Chronicle*. 1756; 1759; 1762; 1785; 1808; 1830; 1833
JBAA *The Journal of the British Archaeological Association*. Vol 3, 1848; vol 24, 1868; vol 25, 1869; vol 164, 2011; vol 165, 2012
JEH *Journal of Ecclesiastical History*. Vol 46, Cambridge, 1995; vol 50, 1999; vol 53, 2002; vol 61, 2010
Leicestershire AAST *Transactions of the Leicestershire Architectural and Archaeological Soc*. Vol 3, Leicester, 1874; vol 6, 1888
Lincs NQ *Lincolnshire Notes and Queries*. Vol 1, Horncastle, 1889; vol 4, 1896
London & Middx AST *Transactions of the London and Middlesex Archaeological Soc*. 1S vol 2, 1864; vol 3, 1870; vol 4, 1875; vol 5, 1881. NS [2S] vol 6, 1933.
NORA *Norfolk Archaeology*, or Miscellaneous Tracts relating to the Antiquities of the County of Norfolk. Vol 1, Norwich, 1847; vol 3, 1852; vol 5, 1859; vol 9, 1884; vol 11, 1892; vol 14, 1901; vol 28 pt 2, 1943; vol 28 pt 4, 1945
Northants NQ *Northamptonshire Notes and Queries*. Vol 1, Northampton, 1886; vol 2, 1888; vol 3, 1890; vol 4, 1892
NQ *Notes and Queries*, a Medium of Inter-communication for Literary Men ... etc. 1S vol 1, 1849. 2S vol 2, 1856; vol 12, 1861. 3S vol 3, 1863; vol 8, 1865. 5S vol 3, 1875; vol 4, 1875. 6S vol 6, 1882.
Records of Bucks *Records of Buckinghamshire*, published by the Architectural and Archaeological Soc. for the County of Buckingham. Vol 5, Aylesbury, 1878; vol 8, 1903; vol 10, 1910; vol 12, 1927
The Reliquary, A depository for precious relics, legendary, biographical, and historical. Vol 1, 1861; vol 3, 1863; vol 4, 1864; vol 5, 1865; vol 6, 1866; vol 8, 1868; vol 10, 1870; vol 13, 1873; vol 14, 1874; vol 16, 1876
St Albans & Herts AAST *St Albans and Hertfordshire Architectural and Archaeological Soc. Transactions*. NS vol 1 pt 4, St Albans, 1903; 'Transactions 1928', 1929
St Paul's EST *Transactions of the St Paul's Ecclesiological Soc*. Vol 3, 1895; vol 5, 1905
Shropshire ANHST *Transactions of the Shropshire Archaeological and Natural History Soc*. 1S vol 1, Shrewsbury, 1878; vol 4, 1881. 2S vol 1, 1889; vol 2, 1890; vol 4, 1892; vol 5, 1893; vol 12, 1900. 3S vol 3, 1903; vol 9, 1909; vol 10, 1910. 4S vol 2, 1912.
Somersetshire ANHSP *Proceedings of the Somersetshire Archaeological and Natural History Soc*. Vol 11 pt 2, Taunton, 1863; vol 26, 1881; vol 36 pt 2, 1891; vol 39 pt 2, 1893
Suffolk AIP *Proceedings of the Bury and West Suffolk Archaeological Institute*. Vol 1, Bury St Edmunds, 1853; vol 11, 1901; vol 13, 1909; vol 23 pt 2, 1938
Surrey AC *Surrey Archaeological Collections*, published by the Surrey Archaeological Soc. Vol 2, 1864; vol 4, 1869; vol 8, 1883; vol 15, 1900; vol 17, 1902; vol 18, 1903; vol 19, 1906; vol 20, 1907; vol 21, 1908; vol 29, 1916
Sussex AC *Sussex Archaeological Collections*, published by the Sussex Archaeological Soc. Vol 4, 1851; vol 14, 1862; vol 19, 1867; vol 20, 1868; vol 23, 1871; vol 25, 1873; vol 29, 1879; vol 32, 1882; vol 33, 1883; vol 41, 1898; vol 45, 1902; vol 49, 1906; vol 61, 1920
Wilts ANHM *The Wiltshire Archaeological and Natural History Magazine*. Vol 22, Devizes, 1885; vol 35, 1908; vol 36, 1910; vol 40, 1919
Wilts NQ *Wiltshire Notes and Queries*. Vol 5, Devizes, 1908; vol 6, 1911

ii. Other sources

Abel Redevivus, or, The Dead yet Speaking: The lives and deaths of the moderne divines, written by severall able and learned men, 1651
Addleshaw, G. W. O. & Etchells, Frederick, *The Architectural Setting of Anglican Worship*, 1948
All Hallows, Bread Street W. Bruce Bannerman (ed.), *The Registers of All Hallows, Bread Street, and of St John the Evangelist, Friday Street*, London, HS, 1913
All Hallows Barking Joseph Maskell, *Collections in illustration of the Parochial History and Antiquities of the Ancient Parish of Allhallows Barking, in the City of London*, 1864

Almondbury Charles Augustus Hulbert, *Annals of the Church and Parish of Almondbury, Yorkshire*, 1882

Ambrose Barnes *Memoirs of the Life of Mr Ambrose Barnes … sometime alderman of Newcastle upon Tyne* ed. W. H. D. Longstaffe, Surtees Soc., 1867

Andrews, Williams, *Curiosities of the Church*, 1890

Aquinas, Thomas, *Summa Theologica*, literally translated by Fathers of the English Dominican Province, 22 vols, 1915-1927

Arculfus *The Pilgrimage of Arculfus in the Holy Land, about the year A.D. 670*, translated by James Rose Macpherson, 1889

Ardingly Gerald W. E. Loder (ed.), *The Parish Registers of Ardingly, Sussex, 1558-1812*, Sussex Record Soc., 1913

Articles of Enquiry and Direction for the Diocese of Norwich, 1638

Articles of Enquiry (with some Directions intermingled) for the Diocese of Ely, 1662

Articles of Visitation and Enquiry … within the Diocese of Worcester, 1662

Articles to be inquired of throughout the Diocesse of Chichester, 1638

Ashburton *The Parish of Ashburton … as it appears from extracts from the Churchwardens' Accounts, A.D. 1479-1580*, 1870

Ashton, John, *Chap-books of the Eighteenth Century*, 1882

Ashton, John, *Humour, Wit, and Satire of the Seventeenth Century*, 1883

Aston Abbots William Bradbrook, 'Aston Abbots: Parish register' and 'Aston Abbots: Parish account book', Records of Bucks vol 10 pp29-34, 34-50

Aston, Margaret, *Broken Idols of the Reformation*, Cambridge, 2016

Aston, Margaret, *England's Iconoclasts: Laws against images*, Oxford, 1988

Aubrey, John, *Remaines of Gentilisme and Judaisme, 1686-87* ed. James Britten, Folklore Soc., 1881

Aubrey, Wiltshire *Wiltshire: The Topographical Collections of John Aubrey* ed. J. E. Jackson, Devizes, 1862. Preface to 'An essay towards the description of the north division of Wiltshire'.

B&H > Brooke & Hallen

Badham, Sally, *Seeking Salvation: Commemorating the Dead in the late-medieval English Parish*, Donington, Lincolnshire, 2015

Badsey E. A. B. Barnard (ed.), *Churchwardens' Accounts of the Parish of Badsey, with Aldington, in Worcestershire from 1525 to 1571*, 1913

Baildon, William Paley (ed.), *Select Cases in Chancery, A.D. 1364 to 1471*, Selden Soc., 1896

Bailey, James Blake (ed.), *The Diary of a Resurrectionist 1811-1812*, 1896

Bakewell 1. W. R. Bell, 'An account of the oldest parish registers of Bakewell, Derbyshire', *Reliquary* vol 5 pp73-79. | 2. Hilda M. Hulme, 'Derbyshire dialect in the seventeenth century, from the Bakewell parish accounts', Derbyshire ANHSJ vol 62 pp88-103.

Baldock F. E. Croydon, 'The Edwardine Reformation in a Hertfordshire parish', St Albans & Herts AAST 1928 pp135-144

Bannerman, W. Bruce (ed.), *The Registers of St Mary le Bowe, Cheapside, All Hallows, Honey Lane, and of St Pancras, Soper Lane, London*, pt 1: Baptisms and Burials, HS, 1914

Bardwell, Guild of St Peter F. E. Warren, 'A pre-Reformation village gild', Suffolk AIP vol 11 pp134-147

Barnes > Ambrose Barnes & Bishop Barnes

Barnstaple J. R. Chanter, *Memorials, descriptive and historical, of the Church of St Peter, Barnstaple*, Barnstaple, 1882

Barnwell, P. S., 'The Use of the Church: Blisworth, Northamptonshire, on the eve of the Reformation', *Ecclesiology Today*, issue 35, Sep 2005, pp43-62

Barrow on Humber Thomas North, 'A Lincolnshire parish clerk in the olden time', *Antiquary* vol 2 pp95-97

Barton, Allan B., 'The ornaments of the altar and the ministers in late-medieval England', in *Mass and Parish in Late Medieval England: The Use of York* ed. P. S. Barnwell et al., Reading, 2005, pp27-40

Basingstoke Francis Joseph Baigent & James Elwin Millard, *A History of the Ancient Town and Manor of Basingstoke*, 1889

Bath, St Michael Accounts, Somersetshire ANHSP vol 26, appendix (pp101-138 of accounts, earlier parts having appeared in vols 23-25)

Battersea John George Taylor, *Our Lady of Batersey: The Story of Battersea Church and Parish told from original sources*, 1925

BCP 1662 > Book of Common Prayer

Becon *The Early Works of Thomas Becon* ed. John Ayre, Parker Soc., Cambridge, 1843. Includes 'A potation for Lent', first published in 1542.

Becon, Thomas, *Actes of Christ and of Antichrist*, in *Worckes of Thomas Becon* pt 3, 1564

Becon, Thomas, *Prayers and other Pieces* ed. John Ayre, Parker Soc., Cambridge, 1844

Becon, Thomas, *The Reliques of Rome*, 1563

The Bee hive of the Romishe Churche, translated by George Gilpin, 1579, from the original work of 1569 by Philipp van Marnix

Beeson, C. F. C., *English Church Clocks, 1280-1850*, 1971

Benenden Francis Haslewood, *The Parish of Benenden, Kent*, Ipswich, 1889

Beverley, St Mary George Poulson, *Beverlac, or, The Antiquities and History of the Town of Beverley, in the County of York*, vol 2, 1829

Birt, Henry Norbert, *The Elizabethan Religious Settlement: A study of contemporary documents*, 1907

Bishop Barnes *The Injunctions and other Ecclesiastical Proceedings of Richard Barnes, Bishop of Durham, from 1575 to 1587* ed. James Raine, Surtees Soc., 1850

Bishop's Stortford [BS] J. L. Glasscock, jun. (ed.), *The Records of St Michael's Parish Church, Bishop's Stortford*, 1882

Bletchingley AE 1546-1552 ed. Theodore Craib, Surrey AC vol 29 pp25-33

Blomefield, Francis, continued by Charles Parkin, *An Essay towards a Topographical History of the County of Norfolk*, vol 6, 1807; vol 11, 1810

Bloxam, Matthew Holbeche, *Companion to the Principles of Gothic Ecclesiastical Architecture*, 1882

Blunt, John Henry, *The Annotated Book of Common Prayer*, 1876

Blunt, John Henry, *The Book of Church Law* rev. Walter G. F. Phillimore, 2nd edition, 1876

Bond, Francis, *The Chancel of English Churches*, 1916

Bond, Francis, *Screens and Galleries in English Churches*, 1908

Bond, Frederick Bligh & Camm, Bede, *Roodscreens and Roodlofts*, 2 vols, 1909

The Book of Common Prayer from the original manuscript attached to the Act of Uniformity of 1662, 1892

A Booke of Christian Prayers, 1578; also 1608 edition

Bourne, Henry, *Antiquitates Vulgares, or, The Antiquities of the Common People*, Newcastle, 1725

Bowers, Roger, 'Liturgy and music in the role of the chantry priest', JBAA vol 164 pp130-156

Brand, John, *Observations on the Popular Antiquities of Great Britain* ed. Sir Henry Ellis, vol 2, 1849

Brentford Thomas Faulkner, *The History and Antiquities of Brentford, Ealing and Chiswick*, 1845

Bristol P&P J. F. Nicholls & John Taylor, *Bristol Past and Present*, 2 vols, Bristol, 1881

Bristol, All Saints 1. Clive Burgess (ed.), *The Pre-Reformation Records of All Saints', Bristol*, 3 vols, Bristol Record Soc., 1995, 2000, 2004. | 2. Clive Burgess, *'The Right Ordering of Souls': The Parish of All Saints' Bristol on the Eve of the Reformation*, Woodbridge, Suffolk, 2018.

Bristol, St Ewen Sir John Maclean, 'Notes on the accounts of the procurators, or churchwardens, of the parish of St Ewen's, Bristol', Bristol GAST vol 15 pp139-182, 254-296

Bristol, St Nicholas E. G. Cuthbert F. Atchley, 'Medieval parish clerks in Bristol', St Paul's EST vol 5 pp107-116

Bromley St Leonard James Dunstan, *The History of the Parish of Bromley St Leonard, Middlesex*, 1862

Brooke, J. M. S. & Hallen, A. W. C., *The transcript of the Registers of the united Parishes of S. Mary Woolnoth and S. Mary Woolchurch Haw, in the City of London ... together with some interesting extracts from the churchwardens' accounts*, 1886 [B&H]

Brooks, Neil C., *The Sepulchre of Christ in Art and Liturgy*, Urbana, Illinois, 1921

Brushfield, T. N., 'On the destruction of "vermin" in rural parishes', DART vol 29 pp291-349

Bungay, St Mary AE, EA 1S vol 1 pp375-377, 423-425; vol 2 pp147-151, 275-278; vol 3 pp19-21, 198-200

Burford W. J. Monk, *History of Burford*, 1891

Burke, Arthur Meredyth, *Key to the Ancient Parish Registers of England and Wales*, 1908

Burn EL Richard Burn, *Ecclesiastical Law*, 6th edition, ed. Simon Fraser, 4 vols, 1797

Burn PR John Southerden Burn, *Registrum Ecclesiae Parochialis: The History of Parish Registers in England*, 2nd edition, 1862

Burnsall W. J. Stavert (ed.), *The Churchwardens' Accounts of the Parish of Burnsall-in-Craven, 1704-1769*, Skipton, 1899

Burrell 'Extracts from the journal and account-book of Timothy Burrell [of Cuckfield], 1683-1714', Sussex AC vol 3 pp117-172

Bury St Edmunds, St Mary Samuel Tymms, *An Architectural and Historical Account of the Church of St Mary, Bury St Edmund's*, Bury St Edmunds, 1854

Buxted Register extracts, Sussex AC vol 4 pp251-p255

Bywell A. Johnson, 'Bywell', *Archaeologia Aeliana, or, Miscellaneous Tracts relating to Antiquities*, Society of Antiquaries of Newcastle-upon-Tyne, NS vol 13, Newcastle, 1889, pp89-166

Calendar of State Papers. Domestic series: 1637 ed. John Bruce, 1868; 1637-1638 ed. John Bruce, 1869; 1649-1650 ed. Mary Anne Everett Green, 1875. Foreign series: 1547-1553 ed. William B. Turnbull, 1861. [CSP]

Camberwell William Harnett Blanch, *Ye Parish of Camerwell: A brief account of the parish of Camberwell, its history and antiquities*, 1875

Cambridge, St Mary the Great [SMG] 1. J. E. Foster (ed.), *Churchwardens' Accounts of St Mary the Great Cambridge from 1504 to 1635*, Cambridge, 1905. | 2. Samuel Sandars, *Historical and Architectural Notes on Great Saint Mary's Church, Cambridge*, with *The Annals of the Church by the Rev. Canon Venables*, Cambridge, 1869.

The Camden Miscellany, vol 7, 1875. Includes 'Two sermons preached by the Boy Bishop ... edited by John Gough Nichols ... with an introduction giving an account of the festival of the Boy Bishop in England by Edward F. Rimbault'.

Canterbury Records C. Eveleigh Woodruff (ed.), *An Inventory of the Parish Registers and other Records in the Diocese of Canterbury*, Canterbury, 1922

Canterbury, Holy Cross Westgate [HCW] J. Meadows Cowper, *Our Parish Books, and what they tell us: Holy Cross, Westgate, Canterbury*, 2 vols, Canterbury, 1885 [OPB]

Canterbury, St Andrew Charles Cotton (ed.), *Churchwardens' Accounts of the Parish of St Andrew, Canterbury*, 1916. In five parts, each with its own pagination. Pt 1: 1485-1509. Pt 2: 1509-1523. Pt 3: 1524-1553. Pt 4: 1553-1596. Pt 5: 1597-1625.

Canterbury, St Dunstan 1. J. M. Cowper (ed.), *Accounts of the Churchwardens of St Dunstan's, Canterbury, A.D. 1484-1580*, 1885. | 2. J. Meadows Cowper (ed.), *The Register Booke of ... Saint Dunstan's, Canterbury, 1559-1800*, Canterbury, 1887.

Canterbury, St Peter Additional section, 'The churchwardens' accounts of St Peter's, Canterbury', with new pagination but no title page found, at end of vol 2 of J. Meadows Cowper, *Our Parish Books*, 1885: see above under Canterbury, Holy Cross Westgate.

Cardington AE, Shropshire ANHST 1S vol 4 pp317-325

Cardwell, Edward, *Documentary Annals of the Reformed Church of England ... from the year 1546 to the year 1716*, 2 vols, Oxford, 1839

Cardwell, Edward, *The Two Books of Common Prayer set forth ... in the reign of King Edward the Sixth*, 3rd edition, Oxford, 1852

Castle Cary AE 1628 to 1699, Somersetshire ANHSP vol 36 pt 2 pp60-69

The Catholic Encyclopedia ed. Charles G. Herbermann et al., 15 vols, New York, 1907-1912 [CE]

Cautley, H. Munro, *Royal Arms and Commandments in our Churches*, Ipswich, 1934

CE > Catholic Encylopedia

Chambers DW John David Chambers, *Divine Worship in England in the Thirteenth and Fourteenth Centuries contrasted with and adapted to that in the Nineteenth*, 1877

Chambers, E. K., *The Mediaeval Stage*, 2 vols, 1903

Chedder Henry Thomas Riley (ed.), 'The churchwardens', moorwardens', and constables' accounts for the parish of Chedder, in Somerset, A.D. 1612-74', HMC 3rd report, appendix pp329-331

Chelmsford AE 1557 to 1668 ed. Archdeacon Mildmay, Essex AST 1S vol 2 pp211-228

Chester, Holy Trinity AE 1532 to 1633 ed. J. R. Beresford, Chester & NW AAHSJ vol 38 pp95-172

Chester, St John the Baptist 1. AE ed. S. Cooper Scott, Chester & NW AAHSJ vol 3 pp48-70. | 2. S. Cooper Scott, *Lectures on the History of S. John Baptist Church and Parish, in the City of Chester*, Chester, 1892.

Chester, St Mary on the Hill J. P. Earwaker, *The History of the Church and Parish of St Mary-on-the-Hill, Chester* ... ed. Rupert H. Morris, 1898

Chester, St Peter Isaac England Ewen, 'Gleanings from an old city church, being a short history of St Peter's, Chester', Chester & NW AAHSJ vol 3 pp365-390

Chester-le-Street Rev. Canon Blunt, *A Thousand Years of the Church in Chester-le-Street*, 1884

Chiddingly Mark Antony Lower, 'Parochial history of Chiddingly', Sussex AC vol 14 pp207-252

Chipping Tom C. Smith, *History of the Parish of Chipping, in the County of Lancaster*, Preston, 1894

Chronicle of the Grey Friars of London ed. John Gough Nichols, Camden Soc., 1852

Chudleigh Mary Jones, *The History of Chudleigh, Devon*, 2nd edition, Exeter, 1875

Clark, Andrew (ed.), *Lincoln Diocese Documents, 1450-1544*, Early English Text Soc., 1914

Clay, William Keatinge (ed.), *Liturgies and Occasional Forms of Prayer set forth in the reign of Queen Elizabeth*, Parker Soc., Cambridge, 1847

Coates, Charles, *The History and Antiquities of Reading*, 1802

Coggeshall George Frederick Beaumont, *A History of Coggeshall, in Essex*, 1890

Collectanea Topographica et Genealogica, pub. John Bowyer Nichols and Son, vol 3, 1836; vol 4, 1837; vol 5, 1838

Cowden Edward Turner, 'Ancient parochial account book of Cowden', Sussex AC vol 20 pp91-119

Cox CWA J. Charles Cox, *Churchwardens' Accounts from the Fourteenth Century to the close of the Seventeenth Century*, 1913

Cox Derbyshire J. Charles Cox, *Notes on the Churches of Derbyshire*, 4 vols, Chesterfield, 1875, 1877, 1877, 1879

Cox Northants J. Charles Cox, 'The parish churches of Northamptonshire, illustrated by wills, *temp.* Henry VIII', AJ vol 58 pp113-132

Cox PR J. Charles Cox, *The Parish Registers of England*, 1910

Cox, J. Charles, *Bench-ends in English Churches*, 1916

Cox, J. Charles, *English Church Fittings, Furniture, and Accessories*, 1923

Cox, J. Charles, *Pulpits, Lecterns, and Organs in English Churches*, 1915

Cox & Harvey J. Charles Cox & Alfred Harvey, *English Church Furniture*, 2nd edition, 1908

Cratfield John James Raven (ed.), *Cratfield: A transcript of the Accounts of the Parish, from A.D. 1490 to A.D. 1642*, with Notes by the late Rev. William Holland, 1895

Cressy BMD David Cressy, *Birth, Marriage, and Death: Ritual, religion, and the life-cycle in Tudor and Stuart England*, Oxford, 1999

Cressy, David, *Bonfires and Bells: National memory and the Protestant calendar in Elizabethan and Stuart England*, 1989

Crossley, Frederick H., *English Church Craftsmanship*, 1941

CSP > Calendar of State Papers

Cuckfield 1. W. C. Renshaw (ed.), *The Parish Registers of Cuckfield, Sussex, 1598-1699*, Sussex Record Soc., 1911. | 2. Miss M. H. Cooper, 'A perambulation of Cuckfield, 1629', Sussex AC vol 61 pp40-52.

Cullompton, St Andrew Ms. churchwardens' accounts, Devon Archives, 2404A/PW/2, with pencilled page numbers

Culmer, Richard, *Cathedrall Newes from Canterbury, shewing the Canterburian cathedrall to bee in an abbey-like corrupt and rotten condition* ..., 1644

Daniell, Christopher, *Death and Burial in Medieval England, 1066-1550*, 1997

Dartmouth Hugh R. Watkin, *Dartmouth*, vol 1, Pre-Reformation, Devonshire Association, 1935

Davis, C. H. (ed.), *The English Church Canons of 1604*, 1869

Davison, Nigel, 'So which way round did they go? The Palm Sunday procession at Salisbury', *Music and Letters*, vol 61, Jan 1980, pp1-14

Dearmer, Percy, *Fifty Pictures of Gothic Altars*, 1922. Originally published 1910.

Defoe, Daniel [as Andrew Moreton], *Parochial Tyranny, or, The House-keeper's Complaint against ... Select Vestries, &c.*, 1727

Derby, St Werburgh Thomas L. Tudor, 'Notes on an old churchwardens' account book (1598-1718) concerning the church and parish of St Werburgh in Derby', Derbyshire ANHSJ vol 39 pp192-223; vol 40 pp214-237; vol 41 pp38-51

Dewick, E. S., 'Consecration crosses and the ritual connected with them', AJ vol 65 pp1-34

A Dialogue or Familiar Talke betwene Two Neighbours, 'from Roane [Rouen], by Michael Wodde', 1554

Dictionary of Organs and Organists ed. Frederick W. Thornsby, 2nd edition, 1921. Includes, pp7-72, Records of British organ builders, 940 to 1660, by Andrew Freeman.

Dinn, Robert, '"Monuments answerable to mens worth": Burial patterns, social status and gender in late medieval Bury St Edmunds', JEH vol 46 pp237-255

Ditchfield, P. H., *The Parish Clerk*, New York, 1907

Dorcastor, Nicholas, *The Doctrine of the Masse Booke*, 'from Wyttonburge' [i.e. ? London], 1554

Douce, Francis, *Illustrations of Shakspeare, and of Ancient Manners*, new edition, 1839

Dowsing ed. Cooper *The Journal of William Dowsing* ed. Trevor Cooper, Woodbridge, Suffolk, 2001

Dowsing ed. Moule *The Cambridge Journal of William Dowsing 1643* ed. A. C. Moule, 1926

Dowsing ed. White *The Journal of William Dowsing, of Stratford, parliamentary visitor ...* ed. C. H. Evelyn White, Ipswich, 1885

Duffield J. Charles Cox, 'The registers and churchwardens' accounts of the parish of Duffield', Derbyshire ANHSJ vol 39 pp1-49

Duffy, Eamon, *The Stripping of the Altars: Traditional religion in England c. 1400 – c. 1580*, 1992

Dugdale, William, *A Short View of the late Troubles in England*, Oxford, 1681

Durand 1843 *The Symbolism of Churches and Church Ornaments*: A translation of the first book of the *Rationale divinorum officiorum* written by William Durandus, ed. John Mason Neale & Benjamin Webb, Leeds, 1843

Durand 1859 Gulielmo Durando, *Rationale divinorum officiorum*, Naples, 1859

Durham Acts W. H. D. Longstaffe (ed.), *The Acts of the High Commission Court within the Diocese of Durham*, Surtees Soc., 1858

Durham CWA James Barmby (ed.), *Churchwardens' Accounts of Pittington and other Parishes in the Diocese of Durham from A.D. 1580 to 1700*, Surtees Soc., 1888

Durham Depositions James Raine (ed.), *Depositions and other Ecclesiastical Proceedings from the Courts of Durham, extending from 1311 to the reign of Elizabeth*, Surtees Soc., [c. 1846]

Dyer, T. F. Thiselton, *Church-lore Gleanings*, 1892

Dyer, T. F. Thiselton, *Old English Social Life as told by the Parish Registers*, 1898

Dymond, David, 'God's disputed acre', JEH vol 50 pp464-497

East Budleigh 1. AE ed. T. N. Brushfield, DART vol 26 pp335-400. | 2. T. N. Brushfield, 'Aids to the poor in a rural parish', DART vol 31 pp199-284.

Eastbourne George F. Chambers, 'Contributions towards a history of East-bourne', Sussex AC vol 14 pp119-137

The Eastern Counties Collectanea ed. John L'Estrange, Norwich, 1872-73

Eastington AE, Glos NQ vol 3 pp246-254

Edenbridge AE ed. Granville Leveson-Gower, Arch. Cant. vol 21 pp118-125

Edwards, H., *A Collection of Old English Customs, and Curious Bequests and Charities*, 1842

Ellacombe, H. T., *The Church Bells of Devon ...* to which is added a supplement on various matters relating to the bells of the Church, Exeter, 1872

Elliott, J. Steele, *Bedfordshire 'Vermin' Payments concerning the destruction of 'vermin' by parish officials* ..., Luton, 1936

Eltham 1. AE ed. G. R. Corner, *Archaeologia* vol 34 pp51-65. | 2. AE 1554-1561 ed. Aymer Vallance, Arch. Cant. vol 47 pp71-102.

Ely Penances Hubert Hall, 'Some Elizabethan penances in the diocese of Ely', *Transactions of the Royal Historical Soc.*, vol 1, 1907, pp263-277

Erler, Mary, 'Palm Sunday prophets and processions and eucharistic controversy', *Renaissance Quarterly*, vol 48, New York, 1995, pp58-81

Evelyn *Diary and Correspondence of John Evelyn* ed. William Bray, new edition, vols 1 and 2, 1857

Exeter, St Petrock Robert Dymond, 'The history of the parish of St Petrock, Exeter, as shown by its churchwardens' accounts and other records', DART vol 14 pp402-492

Fairholt, F. W., 'Pulpit hour-glasses', JBAA vol 3 pp301-310

Faversham 1. F. F. Giraud, 'Goods and ornaments at Faversham church in A.D. 1512', Arch. Cant. vol 18 pp103-113. | 2. F. F. Giraud, 'On the parish clerks and sexton of Faversham, A.D. 1506-1593', Arch. Cant. vol 20 pp203-210.

Feasey, Henry John, *Ancient English Holy Week Ceremonial*, 1897

Featley, Daniel, *The Gentle Lash, or the Vindication of Dr Featley, a knowne champion of the Protestant religion*, 1644

Firth, C. H. & Rait, R. S. (eds.), *Acts and Ordinances of the Interregnum, 1642-1660*, 3 vols, 1911

Forncett St Peter AE, EA 1S vol 2 pp356-358, 364-366

Fosbroke, Thomas Dudley, *British Monachism, or Manners and Customs of the Monks and Nuns of England*, 3rd edition, 1843

Foxe, John, *Actes and Monuments ... in the Church ... with the bloudy times, horrible troubles, and great persecutions against the true martyrs of Christ*, newly revised, 1583. Also 1570 edition for illustrations.

Freeman, Andrew, 'Father Howe, an old-time maker of organs', *Musical Times*, vol 62, no. 943, 1 Sep 1921, pp633-641

French, Katherine L., *The People of the Parish: Community life in a late medieval English diocese*, Philadelphia, Pennsylvania, 2001

Frere, W. H. & Kennedy, W. P. M. (eds.), *Visitation Articles and Injunctions of the period of the Reformation*, 3 vols, 1910. Vol 1 ed. Frere only; vol 2 covers 1536-1558; vol 3 covers 1559-1575.

Friar, Stephen, *A Companion to the English Parish Church*, Stroud, Glos, 1996

Fulham, All Saints Charles James Fèret, *Fulham Old and New*, 3 vols, 1900

Gasquet, Abbot [Francis], *Parish Life in Medieval England*, 1906

Gee, Henry & Hardy, William John (eds.), *Documents illustrative of English Church History*, 1896

Gerschow, Frederic, 'Diary of the journey of Philip Julius, Duke of Stettin-Pomerania, through England in the year 1602' ed. Gottfried von Bülow, *Transactions of the Royal Historical Soc.*, vol 6, 1892, pp1-67

Gibson, Edmund, Archdeacon of Surrey, *Articles and Directions, in order to a parochial visitation*, 1711

Gibson, Edmund, Bishop of Lincoln, *Of Visitations Parochial and General ... To which are added some other tracts* ..., 1717

Gibson, Edmund, *Codex Juris Ecclesiastici Anglicani, or, The Statutes, Constitutions, Canons, Rubricks and Articles of the Church of England, methodically digested*, 2 vols, 1st edition, 1713; 2nd edition, Oxford, 1761

Godalming 1. J. Evans, 'The vicar of Godalming and his parishioners in 1640', Surrey AC vol 2 pp210-223. | 2. Alfred Heales, 'Godalming church', Surrey AC vol 4 pp194-213. | 3. Henry C. Malden (ed.), *The Parish Registers of Godalming, Surrey*, pt 1, 1904.

Golden Legend *Legenda aurea sanctorum*, translated and published by William Caxton, 1487. Compiled *c.* 1270 by Jacob de Voragine.

Grace, Mary (ed.), *Records of the Gild of St George in Norwich, 1389-1547*, Norfolk Record Soc., [Norwich], 1937

Great Dunmow AE ed. Lewis A. Majendie, Essex AST 1S vol 2 pp229-237
Great Hallingbury AE 1526-1634 ed. J. F. Williams, Essex AST 2S vol 23 pp98-115
Great Yarmouth, St Nicholas 1. Charles John Palmer, *The History of Great Yarmouth*, 1856. |
    2. Charles John Palmer, *The Perlustration of Great Yarmouth*, vol 1, Great Yarmouth, 1872.
Green, I. M., 'The persecution of "scandalous" and "malignant" clergy during the English Civil
    War', *English Historical Review*, vol 94, 1979, pp507-531
Gregorie, John, 'Episcopus puerorum, in die Innocentium, or, A discoverie of an ancient custom
    in the church of Sarum, making an Anniversarie Bishop among the choristers', in *Gregorii
    Posthuma, or, Certain Learned Tracts written by John Gregorie*, 1649, pp95-123
Grindal *The Remains of Edmund Grindal* ed. William Nicholson, Parker Soc., Cambridge,
    1843
Grose, Francis, *A Provincial Glossary*, 1787

Hackness Charles Johnstone & Emily J. Hart (eds.), *The Register of the Parish of Hackness
    co. York, 1577-1783*, Leeds, 1906
Hackney, St John R. Simpson (ed.), *Memorials of St John at Hackney*, pt 3, Guildford, 1882
Hagworthingham 'Hagworthingham church book', Lincs NQ vol 1 pp5-13
Haigh, Christopher, *The Plain Man's Pathways to Heaven: Kinds of Christianity in post-Reformation
    England, 1570-1640*, Oxford, 2007
Hale 1841 William Hale Hale, *Precedents in Causes of Office against Churchwardens and Others*,
    extracted from the Act books of the consistory court of London, and the archidiaconal courts
    of St Alban's, Essex, Middlesex, and Lewes, 1841
Hale See also under Vis. Hale
Hammersmith Thomas Faulkner, *The History and Antiquities of the Parish of Hammersmith*, 1839
Harding, Vanessa, *The Dead and the Living in Paris and London, 1500-1670*, Cambridge, 2002
Hardingstone AE ed. J. T., Northants NQ vol 4 pp201-208
Hargrave AE ed. R. S. Baker, Northants NQ vol 4 pp143-147
Harrison, William, 'Description of Britaine', in Raphael Holinshed (et al.), *The Firste volume
    of the Chronicles of England, Scotlande, and Irelande*, 1577
Hartland Henry Thomas Riley, 'The parish documents of Hartland, N. Devon', HMC 5th
    report, appendix pp571-575
Hartshorne Thomas North, 'Parish records of Hartshorn', Derbyshire ANHSJ vol 7 pp40-62
Hasted's History of Kent, corrected, enlarged, and continued ... ed. Henry H. Drake, pt 1, The
    Hundred of Blackheath, 1886
Hastings, All Saints Thomas Ross, 'Hastings documents' and 'Wall paintings in All Saints'
    Church, Hastings', Sussex AC vol 23 pp85-118, 192-199
Hawkhurst W. J. Lightfoot, 'Notes from the records of Hawkhurst Church', Arch. Cant. vol 5
    pp55-86
Hayes J. H. Thomas, 'Parish registers in the Uxbridge deanery', *Antiquary* vol 18 pp62-67
Hayward, Sir John, *Annals of the First Four Years of the reign of Queen Elizabeth* ed. John Bruce,
    Camden Soc., 1840
Heales, Alfred, 'Easter sepulchres: their object, nature, and history', *Archaeologia* vol 42 pp263-308
Heales, Alfred, *The History and Law of Church Seats, or Pews*, 2 vols, 1872
Hearne *Remarks and Collections of Thomas Hearne* ed. C. E. Doble et al., 11 vols, Oxford Historical
    Soc., 1885-1921
Herbert, George, *A Priest to the Temple, or, The Countrey Parson, his character, and rule of holy
    life*, 1652
Hering, Francis, *Certaine Rules, Directions or Advertisments for this time of Pestilentiall Contagion*,
    1603; new edition, 1625
Heybridge AE ed. W. J. Pressey, Essex AST 2S vol 22 pp28-36
High Wycombe 1. R. S. Downs, 'The parish church of High Wycombe', Records of Bucks
    vol 8 pp55-87. | 2. W. H. St John Hope, 'Inventories of the parish church of All Saints,
    and of the chapel of the Blessed Virgin Mary, Wycombe', Records of Bucks vol 8 pp103-145.
Hillen, Henry J., *History of the Borough of King's Lynn*, 2 vols, Norwich, [1907]

HMC Historical Manuscripts Commission. 3rd report, 1872 (Chedder); 5th report, 1876 (Hartland); 6th report, 1877 (Great Torrington)

Hobhouse, Bishop (ed.), *Church-wardens' Accounts of Croscombe, Pilton, Yatton, Tintinhull, Morebath, and St Michael's, Bath*, Somerset Record Soc., 1890

Holbeach W. Marrat, *The History of Lincolnshire*, vol 2, Boston, 1814

Hooper, John *Early Writings of John Hooper, D.D., Lord Bishop of Gloucester and Worcester, Martyr, 1555* ed. Samuel Carr, Parker Soc., Cambridge, 1843

Hope, William St John & Atchley, E. G. Cuthbert F., *English Liturgical Colours*, 1918

Hopkins, Edward J., 'The English medieval church organ', AJ vol 45 pp120-157, 423-440

Hoskin, Philippa M., *A Decent, Regular and Orderly State? Parochial visitations of the archdeaconries of York and the East Riding, 1720-1730*, York, 2010

Howard, F. E. & Crossley, F. H., *English Church Woodwork: A study in craftsmanship during the medieval period, A.D. 1250-1550*, 1917

Hutton ME Ronald Hutton, *The Rise and Fall of Merry England: The ritual year 1400-1700*, 1994; paperback edition 1996

Hutton SS Ronald Hutton, *The Stations of the Sun: A history of the ritual year in Britain*, 1996; paperback edition 1997

Hutton, Ronald, 'The local impact of the Tudor Reformations', in *The English Reformation Revised* ed. Christopher Haigh, Cambridge, 1987, pp114-138

Icklesham Theodore T. Churton, 'Icklesham church', Sussex AC vol 32 pp105-122

Inventories, Lancs John Eglington Bailey (ed.), *Inventories of Goods in the Churches and Chapels of Lancashire, taken in the year A.D. 1552*, Chetham Soc., 2 vols, 1879, 1888

Inventories, Oxon Rose Graham (ed.), *The Chantry Certificates and the Edwardian Inventories of Church Goods*, Oxfordshire Record Soc., Oxford, 1919

Inventories, Surrey John Robert Daniel-Tyssen (ed.), *Inventories of the Goods and Ornaments in the Churches of Surrey, in the reign of King Edward the Sixth*, 1869. Reprinted from Surrey AC.

Ipswich, St Clement AE, EA 2S vol 3 pp289-291; vol 4 pp4-7

JHC > Journals of the House of Commons

Johnson, John (ed.), *A Collection of the Laws and Canons of the Church of England*, new edition, vol 2, Oxford, 1851. First published 1720.

Journals of the House of Commons, vol 2 (1640-1642), 1803; vol 3 (1642-1644), 1803; vol 24 (1741-1745), 1803 [JHC]

A Just Correction and Inlargement of a Scandalous Bill of the Mortality of the Malignant Clergie of London, and other parts of the Kingdome, which have been justly sequestred from their pastorall-charges ... by J. V, 1646

Kelly, William, *Notices Illustrative of the Drama, and other Popular Amusements, chiefly in the sixteenth and seventeenth centuries ...* extracted from the chamberlains' accounts and other manuscripts of the borough of Leicester, 1865

Kendal 1. AE ed. George Rushforth, Cumberland etc AAST vol 9 pp269-283. | 2. J. F. Curwen, 'The parish church of Kendal', Cumberland etc AAST vol 16 pp157-220.

Ketley, Joseph (ed.), *The Two Liturgies, A.D. 1549 and A.D. 1552*, with other documents set forth by authority in the reign of King Edward VI, Parker Soc., Cambridge, 1844

Kilmington Robert Cornish (ed.), *Kilmington Church Wardens' Accounts [1555-1608]*, Exeter, 1901

Kingsford, H. S., *Illustrations of the Occasional Offices of the Church in the Middle Ages from contemporary sources*, Alcuin Club, 1921

Kingston upon Thames Alfred Heales, 'Early history of the church of Kingston-upon-Thames ...', Surrey AC vol 8 pp13-156

Kingston, Sussex AE, Sussex AC vol 29 pp155-160

Knight, Francis A., *The Sea-board of Mendip*, 1902

Kümin, Beat A., *The Shaping of a Community: The rise and reformation of the English parish, c. 1400-1560*, Aldershot, 1996

Lambarde, William, *Dictionarium Angliae topographicum et historicum: An alphabetical description of the chief places in England and Wales*, 1730

Lambeth 1. Charles Drew (ed.), *Lambeth Churchwardens' Accounts 1504-1645 and Vestry Book 1610*, 3 vols, Surrey Record Soc., 1941, 1941, 1943. | 2. Samuel Denne, *Historical Particulars of Lambeth Parish and Lambeth Palace...*, printed by John Nichols, 1795. Part of 'Miscellaneous Antiquities in continuation of the Bibliotheca topographica Britannica'. | 3. Thomas Allen, *The History and Antiquities of the Parish of Lambeth and the Archiepiscopal Palace*, 1827.

Lambourn John Footman, *History of the Parish Church of Saint Michael and All Angels, Chipping Lambourn*, 1894

Lancaster *Materials for the History of the Church of Lancaster* ed. William Oliver Roper, vol 3, Chetham Soc., 1906

Lapworth Robert Hudson, *Memorials of a Warwickshire Parish, being papers mainly descriptive of ... the parish of Lapworth*, 1904

The Lay Folks Mass Book ed. Thomas Frederick Simmons, Early English Text Soc., 1879

Leadam, I. S. (ed.), *Select Cases before the King's Council in the Star Chamber commonly called the Court of Star Chamber, A.D. 1477-1509*, Selden Soc., 1903

Leek AE and register extracts ed. John Sleigh, *Reliquary* vol 3 pp211-217

Legg, J. Wickham (ed.), *The Clerk's Book of 1549*, Henry Bradshaw Soc., 1903

Leicester, St Martin Thomas North (ed.), *The Accounts of the Churchwardens of S. Martin's, Leicester, 1489-1844*, Leicester, 1884

Leicester, St Mary AE 1652-1729 ed. Colonel Bellairs, Leicestershire AAST vol 6 pp229-268, 353-394

Leland, John Joannis Lelandi, *De rebus Britannicis collectanea* ed. Thomas Hearne, 2nd edition, vol 5, 1770

Lepine, David, '"Higher solemn ceremonies": The funerary practice of the late medieval English higher clergy', JEH vol 61 pp18-39

Letters and Papers, Foreign and Domestic, of the reign of Henry VIII ed. James Gairdner & R. H. Brodie, vol 18 pt 2, 1902

Leverington AE, Fenland NQ vol 7 pp184-190, 203-207, 247-251, 271-275, 297-302, 329-334

Leverton AE ed. Edward Peacock, *Archaeologia* vol 41 pp333-370

Lewes, Sussex, St Andrew & St Michael H. Michell Whitley, 'The churchwardens' accounts of St Andrew's and St Michael's, Lewes, from 1522 to 1601', Sussex AC vol 45 pp40-61

Leyton John Kennedy, *A History of the Parish of Leyton, Essex*, Leyton, 1894

Lichfield, St Michael Thomas Harwood, *The History and Antiquities of the Church and City of Lichfield*, Gloucester, 1806

Lindfield Mark Antony Lower, 'On some old parochial documents relating to Lindfield', Sussex AC vol 19 pp36-52

Lindley, Philip, '"Pickpurse" Purgatory, the dissolution of the chantries and the suppression of intercession for the dead', JBAA vol 164 pp277-304

Liskeard John Allen, *History of the Borough of Liskeard and its Vicinity*, 1856

Litten, Julian, *The English Way of Death: The common funeral since 1450*, 1991

Littledale, Willoughby A. (ed.), *The Registers of St Benet and St Peter, Paul's Wharf, London*, vol 1, Christenings, 1909; vol 4, Burials, 1912

Littleham William Webb, *Memorials of Exmouth*, Exmouth, 1872

Long Melford Sir William Parker, *The History of Long Melford*, 1873

Loughborough 1. Register extracts and AE ed. W. G. Dimock Fletcher, *Reliquary* vol 13 pp194-201, 201-202. | 2. W. G. Dimock Fletcher, 'Bellman's duties at Loughborough', *Reliquary* vol 14 p128.

Louth 1. *Notitiae Ludae, or Notices of Louth*, Louth, 1834. | 2. Reginald C. Dudding (ed.), *The First Churchwardens' Book of Louth, 1500-1524*, Oxford, 1941. | 3. A. E. B. Owen, 'The Louth parish clerks in 1500', *Reports of the Lincolnshire Architectural and Archaeological Soc.*, NS vol 10 pt 2, Lincoln, 1964, pp134-137.

Ludlow 1. Thomas Wright (ed.), *Churchwardens' Accounts of the Town of Ludlow, in Shropshire, from 1540 to the end of the reign of Queen Elizabeth*, Camden Soc., 1869. | 2. Accounts ed.

Llewellyn Jones, Shropshire ANHST 2S vol 1 pp235-284 (1575 to 1607); vol 2 pp105-140 (1607 to 1629); vol 4 pp119-174 (1629 to 1691); vol 5 pp87-112 (1691 to 1749).

Lydd *Records of Lydd*, translated and transcribed by Arthur Hussey and M. M. Hardy, edited by Arthur Finn, Ashford, 1911

Lyndwood, William, *Provinciale, seu constitutiones Angliae*, Oxford, 1679

Lysons, Daniel, *The Environs of London*, 4 vols, 1792, 1795, 1795, 1796

Machyn *The Diary of Henry Machyn, Citizen and Merchant-taylor of London, from A.D. 1550 to A.D. 1563* ed. John Gough Nichols, Camden Soc., 1848

Maidstone Walter B. Gilbert, *Memorials of the Collegiate and Parish Church of All Saints, in ... Maidstone*, Maidstone, 1866

Malcolm, James Peller, *Londinium redivivum, or An Ancient History and Modern Description of London*, vols 1 to 3, 1802, 1805, 1805. Publication dates from prefaces.

Manchester AE 1664-1710 ed. Ernest Broxap, Chetham Miscellanies, NS vol 4, Chetham Soc., Manchester, 1921

Marsh, Christopher, 'Sacred space in England, 1560-1640: The view from the pew', JEH vol 53 pp286-311

Marston F. W. Weaver & G. N. Clark (eds.), *Churchwardens' Accounts of Marston, Spelsbury, Pyrton*, Oxfordshire Record Soc., Oxford, 1925. Marston pp9-34.

Maskell, William, *Monumenta ritualia Ecclesiae Anglicanae: The Occasional Offices of the Church of England according to the old Use of Salisbury* [etc], 3 vols, 2nd edition, Oxford, 1882

Matthews, A. G., *Walker Revised, being a revision of John Walker's Sufferings of the Clergy during the Grand Rebellion, 1642-60*, Oxford, 1948

Mc Murray, William (ed.) *The Records of Two City Parishes: A collection of documents illustrative of the history of SS. Anne and Agnes, Aldersgate, and St John Zachary*, London, 1925

McCall, Fiona, *Baal's Priests: The Loyalist Clergy and the English Revolution*, Abingdon, Oxon, 2016. First published 2013.

Melton Mowbray AE ed. Thomas North, Leicestershire AAST vol 3 pp180-206

Mercurius A [parishes] *Mercurius Rusticus, or, The Countries Complaint of the Barbarous Out-rages committed by the Sectaries of this late Flourishing Kingdome*, 1646

Mercurius B [cathedrals] *Mercurius Rusticus, or, The Countries Complaint of the Sacrileges, Prophanations, and Plunderings, committed by the Schismatiques, on the Cathedral Churches of this Kingdom*, 1685

Mere AE ed. T. H. Baker, Wilts ANHM vol 35 pp23-92, 210-282

Metfield AE ed. Norah M. Bower, Suffolk AIP vol 23 pt 2 pp128-147

Micklethwaite, J. T., *The Ornaments of the Rubric*, Alcuin Club, 1897

Milbourn, Thomas, *The History of the Church of St Mildred the Virgin, Poultry, in the City of London, with some particulars of the church of St Mary Colechurch (destroyed in the Great Fire, A.D. 1666)*, 1872

Milton Abbot Accounts for 1588 ed. W. Pengelly, DART vol 11 pp213-255

Minchinhampton AE ed. John Bruce, *Archaeologia* vol 35 pp409-452

Mirk F *Mirk's Festial: A Collection of Homilies by Johannes Mirkus (John Mirk)* ed. Theodor Erbe, Early English Text Soc., 1905

Mirk I *Instructions for Parish Priests by John Myrc* ed. Edward Peacock, Early English Text Soc., 1868

Molland AE ed. Sir John B. Phear, DART vol 35 pp198-238

Morebath 1. J. Erskine Binney (ed.), *The Accounts of the Wardens of the Parish of Morebath, Devon, 1520-1573*, Exeter, 1904. | 2. Eamon Duffy, *The Voices of Morebath: Reformation and Rebellion in an English Village*, 2001.

Morris, Rupert H., *Chester*, 1895. Part of 'Diocesan Histories' series.

Mortlake John Eustace Anderson, *A History of the Parish of Mortlake, in the County of Surrey*, [*c.* 1886]

Muncey, R.W., *A History of the Consecration of Churches and Churchyards*, Cambridge, 1930

Muskett, Charles (publisher), *Notices and Illustrations of the Costume, Processions, Pageantry, &c. formerly displayed by the Corporation of Norwich*, Norwich, 1850

Myddle *Antiquities and Memoirs of the Parish of Myddle, County of Salop, written by Richard Gough, A.D. 1700*, Shrewsbury, 1875

Newbury Walter Money, *The History of the Ancient Town and Borough of Newbury, in the County of Berks*, 1887

Newcastle, All Saints T. Sopwith, *A Historical and Descriptive Account of All Saints' Church in Newcastle upon Tyne*, Newcastle, 1826

NI John Nichols (ed.), *Illustrations of the Manners and Expences of Antient Times in England ... deduced from the accompts of churchwardens, and other authentic documents ...*, 1797

Nichols, John, *The History and Antiquities of the County of Leicester*, vol 1 pt 1, 1795; pt 2, 1815

North Elmham Augustus George Legge (ed.), *Ancient Churchwardens' Accounts in the Parish of North Elmham, from A.D. 1539 to A.D. 1577*, Norwich, 1891

North, Thomas, *The Church Bells of the County and City of Lincoln*, Leicester, 1882

North, Thomas, *The Church Bells of Northamptonshire*, Leicester, 1878

Northampton Records *The Records of the Borough of Northampton* ed. Christopher A. Markham (vol 1) and J. Charles Cox (vol 2), 1898

Northampton, All Saints R. M. Serjeantson, *A History of the Church of All Saints, Northampton*, Northampton, 1901

Northampton, Holy Sepulchre J. Charles Cox & R. M. Serjeantson, *A History of the Church of the Holy Sepulchre, Northampton*, Northampton, 1897

Northampton, St Giles R. M. Serjeantson, *A History of the Church of St Giles, Northampton*, Northampton, 1911

Northampton, St Peter R. M. Serjeantson, *A History of the Church of St Peter Northampton, together with the Chapels of Kingsthorpe and Upton*, Northampton, 1904

Northwold AE 1626-1795 ed. Percy Millican, NORA vol 28 pt 4 pp285-295

Norwich, St Peter Mancroft [SPM] 1. 'St Peter Mancroft, Norwich: Its parish history in the sixteenth and seventeenth centuries', *The Norfolk Antiquarian Miscellany* ed. Walter Rye, vol 2 pt 2, Norwich, 1883, pp321-358. | 2. W. H. St John Hope, 'Inventories of the parish church of St Peter Mancroft, Norwich', NORA vol 14 pp153-240.

Ockley Alfred Ridley Bax, *The Church Registers and Parish Account Books of Ockley, co. Surrey*, 1890

ODCC / ODNB / OED See under Oxford

Orme, Nicholas, *Going to Church in Medieval England*, 2021

Owen, James, *The History of the Consecration of Altars, Temples and Churches*, 1706

Owst, G. R., *Preaching in Medieval England*, Cambridge, 1926

The Oxford Dictionary of the Christian Church, 2nd edition ed. F. L. Cross & E. A. Livingstone, Oxford, 1983 [ODCC]

Oxford Dictionary of National Biography, online edition [ODNB]

Oxford English Dictionary, online edition [OED]

Oxford, St Martin Carteret J. H. Fletcher, *A History of the Church and Parish of St Martin (Carfax) Oxford*, 1896

Oxford, St Michael H. E. Salter, *The Churchwardens' Accounts of St Michael's Church, Oxford*, Oxfordshire Archaeological Soc., Shipston-on-Stour, Worcestershire, 1933

Oxford, St Peter in the East [SPE] AE ed. A.D. Tyssen, *Proceedings of the Oxford Architectural and Historical Soc.*, NS vol 1, Oxford, 1860-64, pp286-301

Page, William (ed.), *The Certificates of the Commissioners appointed to Survey the Chantries, Guilds, Hospitals, etc., in the County of York*, 2 vols, Surtees Soc., 1894, 1895

Palmer, W. M., 'The village gilds of Cambridgeshire', Cambs & Hunts AST vol 1 pt 2 pp330-402

The Parish in Late Medieval England: Proceedings of the 2002 Harlaxton Symposium ed. Clive Burgess & Eamon Duffy, Donington, Lincolnshire, 2006

The Paston Letters, 1422-1509 A.D. ed. James Gairdner, vol 2, 1874; vol 3, 1875

Peacock, Edward (ed.), *English Church Furniture, Ornaments and Decorations, at the period of the Reformation*, as exhibited in a list of the goods destroyed in certain Lincolnshire churches, A.D. 1566, 1866 [PF]

Peacock, Edward, 'Hearse: How a word has changed its meaning', in *Curious Church Gleanings* ed. William Andrews, 1896, pp209-223

Pendrill, Charles, *Old Parish Life in London*, 1937

Pepys *The Diary of Samuel Pepys* ed. Robert Latham & William Matthews, 11 vols, 1970-1983

Peterborough, St John the Baptist W. T. Mellows (ed.), *Peterborough Local Administration: Parochial government before the Reformation*, Kettering, 1939. Includes accounts 1467-1573.

PF > Peacock 1866

PK > Popish Kingdome

Plague orders, London 1. Orders conceived and agreed ... by the Lord Mayor and Aldermen of the Citie of London, [1608]. | 2. Orders conceived and thought fit ... by the Lord Maior of the City of London, 1608. | 3. Orders heretofore conceived ... by the Lord Mayor and Aldermen of the Citie of London, [1625]. | 4. Orders to be used ... within the Citie and Liberties of London, 1625. | 5. The Orders and Directions of ... the Lord Mayor ... during ... Plague, [1665]. | 6. Orders conceived and published by the Lord Maior and Aldermen of the City of London, concerning the infection of the Plague, 1665, reprinted in *A Collection of very valuable and scarce Pieces relating to the last Plague in the year 1665*, 2nd edition, 1721, pp1-12.

Plymouth, St Andrew J. Brooking Rowe, 'The parish and vicars of St Andrew, Plymouth', and 'The church of St Andrew, Plymouth', *Annual Report and Transactions of the Plymouth Institution* [etc], vol 5 pts 1 & 2, Plymouth, 1874-75, pp71-104, 205-249.

Pontifical Services, printed for the Alcuin Club. Vols 1 & 2 'illustrated from miniatures of the XVth and XVIth centuries' ed. Walter Howard Frere, 1901. Vols 3 & 4 'illustrated from woodcuts of the XVIth century': vol 3 ed. F. C. Eeles, 1907; vol 4 ed. Athelstan Riley, 1908. [PS]

The Popish Kingdome or reigne of Antichrist, written in Latin verse by Thomas Naogeorgus and Englyshed by Barnabe Googe, 1570; reprint ed. Robert Charles Hope, 1880 [PK]

Pounds, N. J. G., *A History of the English Parish*, Cambridge, 2004. First published 2000.

Povah, Alfred, *The Annals of the Parishes of St Olave Hart Street and Allhallows Staining, in the City of London*, 1894

Prescot F. A. Bailey (ed.), *The Churchwardens' Accounts of Prescot, Lancashire, 1523-1607*, Lancashire and Cheshire Record Soc., Preston, 1953

Preston Tom C., Smith, *Records of the Parish Church of Preston in Amounderness*, 1892

PS > Pontifical Services

Pulham, St Mary Magdalen AE ed. George Rayson, EA 1S vol 4 pp277-280

Purvis, J. S., *The Condition of Yorkshire Church Fabrics 1300-1800*, 1958

Purvis, J. S., *Tudor Parish Documents of the Diocese of York*, Cambridge, 1948

Quainton AE, Records of Bucks vol 12 pp29-46

Rainham, Kent AE ed. John Walter, Arch. Cant. vol 15 pp333-337

The Rationale of Ceremonial, 1540-1543 ed. Cyril S. Cobb, Alcuin Club, 1910

Raven, J. J., *The Bells of England*, 1906

RB > Roxburghe Ballads

Reading, St Giles W. L. Nash (ed.), *The Church-wardens' Account Book for the Parish of St Giles, Reading*, pt 1 (1518-46), 1881

Reading, St Lawrence Charles Kerry, *A History of the Municipal Church of St Lawrence, Reading*, Reading, 1883

Reading, St Mary Francis N. A. Garry & A. G. Garry (eds.), *The Churchwardens' Accounts of the Parish of St Mary's, Reading, Berks, 1550-1662*, Reading, 1893

Redenhall Charles Candler, *Notes on the Parish of Redenhall with Harleston in ... Norfolk*, 1896

REED Records of Early English Drama series, pub. University of Toronto Press. *Chester* ed. Lawrence M. Clopper, 1979. | *Devon* ed. John M. Wasson, 1986. | *Ecclesiastical London* ed. Mary C. Erler, 2008. | *Norwich 1540-1642* ed. David Galloway, 1984.

Report from the Select Committee on Anatomy, ordered by the House of Commons to be printed, 22 July 1828

Report on a General Scheme for Extramural Sepulture, presented to both Houses of Parliament, 1850

Ripon J. T. Fowler (ed.), *Memorials of the Church of SS. Peter and Wilfrid, Ripon*, vol 3, Surtees Soc., 1888

Rites of Durham, being a description ... of all the ancient monuments, rites, & customs belonging or being within the monastical church of Durham before the suppression, written 1593, ed. J. T. Fowler, Surtees Soc., 1903. The author is now thought to be a late 16th century Durham antiquary called William Claxton.

Rochester Records *The Parish Registers and Records in the Diocese of Rochester: A summary* ... with an introduction by W. E. Buckland, Kent Archaeological Soc., 1912

Rock, Daniel, *The Church of Our Fathers, as seen in St Osmund's Rite for the Cathedral of Salisbury*, new edition ed. G. W. Hart & W. H. Frere, 4 vols, 1905

Rosewell, Roger, *Medieval Wall Paintings in English and Welsh Churches*, Woodbridge, Suffolk, 2008

Rotherfield AE ed. Rev. Canon Goodwyn, Sussex AC vol 41 pp25-48

The Roxburghe Ballads, printed for the Ballad Society, Hertford, vol 1, 1871; vol 2, 1874; vol 6 pt 3, 1888; vol 7, 1893 [RB]

Rye, St Mary William Holloway, *The History and Antiquities of the Ancient Town and Port of Rye, in the County of Sussex*, 1847

Saffron Walden Richard Lord Braybrooke, *The History of Audley End, to which are appended notices of ... Saffron Walden*, 1836

St Alphage, London Wall 1. G. B. Hall (ed.), *Records of St Alphage, London Wall*, [1882]. | 2. Pierson Cathrick Carter, *History of the Church and Parish of St Alphage, London Wall*, 1925.

St Andrew Hubbard [SAH] John C. Crosthwaite (ed.), 'Ancient churchwardens' accounts of a City parish', *British Mag.* vol 31 pp241-250, 394-404, 526-537 (1454-1476); vol 32 pp30-40, 144-157, 272-282, 390-399 (1476-1495); vol 33 pp564-579, 664-677 (1495-1509); vol 34 pp15-33, 171-187, 292-307, 395-409, 524-533, 674-681 (1509-1550); vol 35 pp50-57, 178-186, 273-284, 396-405, 520-529, 635-642 (1552-1574); vol 36 pp158-163, 338-341, 550-555 (1574-1582)

St Andrew, Holborn 1. Edward Griffith, *Cases of Supposed Exemption from Poor Rates* ... with a preliminary sketch of the ancient history of the parish of St Andrew, Holborn, 1831. See also following. | 2. 'Some monuments of antiquities ... collected ... by Thomas Bentley ... in the year of our lord 1584', appendix to Griffith, 1831.

St Anne and St Agnes, Aldersgate [SASA] > Mc Murray

St Bartholomew Exchange [SBE] 1. Edwin Freshfield (ed.), *The Account Books of the Parish of St Bartholomew Exchange in the City of London, 1596-1698*, 1895 [SBE CA]. | 2. Edwin Freshfield (ed.), *The Vestry Minute Books of the Parish of St Bartholomew Exchange in the City of London 1567-1676*, 1890.

St Botolph, Aldgate A. G. B. Atkinson, *St Botolph Aldgate: The story of a City parish*, 1898

St Christopher le Stocks [SCLS] 1. Edwin Freshfield (ed.), *Accomptes of the Churchwardens of the Paryshe of St Christofer's in London, 1575 to 1662*, 1885. | 2. Edwin Freshfield (ed.), *The Account Book of the Parish of St Christopher le Stocks in the City of London, 1662-1685*, 1895. | 3. Edwin Freshfield (ed.), *The Register Book of the Parish of St Christopher le Stocks, in the City of London*, 3 vols, 1882. | 4. Edwin Freshfield, 'On the parish books of St Margaret-Lothbury, St Christopher-le-Stocks, and St Bartholomew-by-the-Exchange, in the City of London', *Archaeologia* vol 45 pp57-123.

St Dionis Backchurch 1. William Durrant Cooper, 'St Dionis Backchurch', London & Middx AST 1S vol 4 pp201-223. | 2. Joseph Lemuel Chester (ed.), *The Reiester* [sic] *Booke of Saynte De'nis Backchurch Parishe*, HS, 1878.

St Ethelburga the Virgin W. F. Cobb (ed.), *The Church of Saint Ethelburga the Virgin within Bishopsgate: The churchwardens and their accounts*, 1905

St Giles in the Fields John Parton, *Some Account of the Hospital and Parish of St Giles in the Fields, Middlesex*, 1822
St Giles without Cripplegate [SGWC] John James Baddeley, *An Account of the Church and Parish of St Giles, without Cripplegate, in the City of London*, 1888
St Helen, Bishopsgate John Edmund Cox, *The Annals of St Helen's, Bishopsgate, London*, 1876
St James, Clerkenwell Robert Hovenden (ed.), *A True Register of ... the Parishe of St James, Clarkenwell ...*, vol 2, Christenings, 1701 to 1754, HS, 1885; vol 4, Burials, 1551 to 1665, HS, 1891
St John Zachary [SJZ] > Mc Murray
St Laurence Pountney [SLP] H. B. Wilson, *A History of the Parish of St Laurence Pountney, London*, 1831
St Mabyn AE ed. John Isabell, *London Society*: An illustrated magazine, vol 44, 1883, pp641-648
St Margaret, Lothbury Edwin Freshfield (ed.), *The Vestry Minute Book of the Parish of St Margaret Lothbury in the City of London 1571-1677*, 1887
St Margaret, Westminster [SMW] John Edward Smith (ed.), *A Catalogue of Westminster Records*, 1900
St Margaret Pattens 1. AE, *The Sacristy*: A quarterly review, vol 1, 1871, pp258-262. | 2. W. H. St John Hope, 'Ancient inventories ... of St Margaret Pattens in the City of London', AJ vol 42 pp312-330.
St Martin in the Fields [SMF] John V. Kitto (ed.), *St Martin-in-the-Fields: The Accounts of the Churchwardens, 1525-1603*, 1901
St Martin Outwich C. W. F. Goss, 'The parish and church of St Martin Outwich, Threadneedle Street', London & Middx AST 2S vol 6 pp1-91
St Mary Aldermanbury Pierson Cathrick Carter, *The History of the Church and Parish of St Mary the Virgin, Aldermanbury*, 1913
St Mary at Hill [SMH] Henry Littlehales (ed.), *The Medieval Records of a London City Church (St Mary at Hill) A.D. 1420-1559*, Early English Text Soc., 1905
St Mary Bourne Joseph Stevens, *A Parochial History of St Mary Bourne*, 1888
St Matthew, Friday Street 1. AE 1547-1603 ed. W. S. Simpson, JBAA vol 25 pp356-381. | 2. W. Sparrow Simpson, 'Notes on the history and antiquities of the united parishes of S. Matthew Friday Street and S. Peter Cheap, in the City of London', London & Middx AST 1S vol 3 pp332-391.
St Michael, Cornhill [SMC] 1. William Henry Overall (ed.), *The Accounts of the Churchwardens of the Parish of St Michael, Cornhill, in the City of London, from 1456 to 1608*, [1868 or later]. | 2. Joseph Lemuel Chester (ed.), *The Parish Registers of St Michael, Cornhill, London ... from 1546 to 1754*, HS, 1882.
St Neot AE ed. General Sir J. H. Lefroy, AJ vol 48 pp65-76
St Nicholas Acons William Brigg (ed.), *The Register Book of the Parish of St Nicholas Acons, London, 1539-1812*, Leeds, 1890
St Olave, Hart Street W. Bruce Bannerman (ed.), *The Registers of St Olave, Hart Street, London, 1563-1700*, HS, 1916
St Peter, Cheapside [SP Cheap] W. Sparrow Simpson, 'Inventory of the vestments, plate, and books, belonging to the church of St Peter Cheap, in the City of London, 1431', and 'On the parish of St Peter Cheap, in the City of London, from 1392 to 1633', JBAA vol 24 pp150-160, 248-268
St Peter, Cornhill Granville W. G. Leveson Gower (ed.), *A Register of ... Saint Peeters upon Cornhill*, pt 1, HS, 1877; pt 2, HS, 1879
St Stephen, Coleman Street Edwin Freshfield, 'Some remarks upon the book of records of the parish of St Stephen, Coleman Street, in the City of London', *Archaeologia* vol 50 pp17-57
St Stephen, Walbrook 1. Thomas Milbourn, 'Church of St Stephen Walbrook', London & Middx AST 1S vol 5 pp327-402. | 2. W. Bruce Bannerman & Major W. Bruce Bannerman (eds.), *The Registers of St Stephen's, Walbrook, and of St Benet Sherehog, London*, pt 1, HS, 1919.
Salehurst, Sussex R. C. Hussey, 'Some entries in Salehurst parish books', Sussex AC vol 25 pp152-162

Salisbury, St Edmund [SES] > Swayne

Salisbury, St Martin T. H. Baker, *Notes on St Martin's Church and Parish*, Salisbury, 1906

Salisbury, St Thomas 1. See Swayne. | 2. Edmund R. Nevill, 'The Chrysom Book of St Thomas, New Sarum', Wilts NQ vol 5 pp462-468, 510-514, 561-566; vol 6 pp19-25, 57-60, 107-110, 208-211, 266-268, 302-305, 344-348, 391-395,455-459, 492-498, 547-550

Sandridge AE ed. H. R. Wilton Hall, St Albans & Herts AAST, NS vol 1 pt 4 pp289-297

Sandwich, St Mary William Boys, *Collections for an History of Sandwich in Kent*, Canterbury, 1792

Sarum Manual [Abbreviated version in] *Manuale et processionale ad usum insignis ecclesiae Eboracensis* [York Manual] ed. W. G. Henderson, Surtees Soc., 1875, appendix 1

Sarum Missal > Warren

Sarum Processional *Processionale ad usum insignis ac praeclarae ecclesiae Sarum* ed. W. G. Henderson, Leeds, 1882

Saxilby AE ed. A. Gibbons, AASRP vol 19 pp376-390

Schroeder, H. J., *Disciplinary Decrees of the General Councils*, 1937

Seale William Henry Hart, 'On the churchwardens' accounts, and other records, relating to the parishes of Seal and Elstead', Surrey AC vol 2 pp27-44

Sharp, Thomas, *Illustrative Papers on the History and Antiquities of the City of Coventry*, Birmingham, 1871

Sharpe [Cuthbert Sharpe (ed.)], *Chronicon mirabile, or Extracts from Parish Registers, principally in the North of England*, 1841

Shrewsbury, Abbey Church William Allport Leighton, 'Notes relating to the Abbey Church estate, Shrewsbury', Shropshire ANHST 1S vol 1 pp15-98

Shrewsbury, St Mary H. Owen & J. B. Blakeway, *A History of Shrewsbury*, vol 2, 1825

Shropshire Parish Documents [ed. E. C. Peele & R. S. Clease], Shrewsbury, [*c.* 1902]

Smarden 1. Francis Haslewood, *Memorials of Smarden, Kent*, Ipswich, 1886. | 2. Francis Haslewood, 'Notes from the records of Smarden church', Arch. Cant. vol 9 pp224-235.

Smith, Toulmin (ed.), *English Gilds: The original ordinances of more than one hundred early English gilds*, Early English Text Soc., 1870

Somerton AE 1641-1747 ed. Douglas L. Hayward, Somersetshire ANHSP vol 39 pt 2 pp67-86

South Littleton AE ed. Thomas P. Wadley, *The Midland Antiquary*, vol 1, 1882, pp103-113

Southwark, St Saviour (formerly St Mary Overy) *A Rate of Duties belonging to the Corporation of the Churchwardens of the Parish of St Saviour of Southwarke ...*, 1613

SR > Statutes of the Realm

Stahlschmidt, J. C. L., *The Church Bells of Kent*, 1887

Stahlschmidt, J. C. L., *Surrey Bells and London Bell-founders*, 1884

Stanford in the Vale AE 1552-1602 ed. Walter Haines, *Antiquary* vol 17 pp70-72, 117-120, 168-172, 209-213

Starston *Some Account of the Parish of Starston, Norfolk*, by the Rector [E. C. Hopper], Norwich, 1888

The Statutes of the Realm, 7 vols, 1810-1820 [SR]

Steeple Ashton AE ed. E. P. Knubley, Wilts NQ vol 6 pp364-376, 420-428, 468-473, 518-523, 567-570. Continues in vol 7.

Stepney G. W. Hill & W. H. Frere (eds.), *Memorials of Stepney Parish; that is to say the vestry minutes from 1579 to 1662*, Guildford, 1890-91

Stockdale, James, *Annales Caermoelenses, or Annals of Cartmel*, 1872

Stockton G. A. Carthew (ed.), 'Extracts from the town book of the parish of Stockton in Norfolk, containing the churchwardens' accounts, from 1625 to 1712', NORA vol 1 pp167-192

Stow, John, *A Survey of London*, reprinted from the text of 1603, 2 vols, Oxford, 1908

Stratton AE ed. Edward Peacock, *Archaeologia* vol 46 pt 1 pp195-236

Strood Henry R. Plomer (ed.), *The Churchwardens' Accounts of St Nicholas, Strood*, Kent Archaeological Soc., 1927

Strutt, Joseph, *The Sports and Pastimes of the People of England*, new edition ed. William Hone, 1830

Stubbes, Philip, *The Anatomie of Abuses*, 1583

Sutterton AE ed. Edward Peacock, AJ vol 39 pp53-63

Swainswick R. E. M. Peach, *The Annals of the Parish of Swainswick, near the City of Bath*, 1890

Swayne, Henry James Fowle (ed.), *Churchwardens' Accounts of S. Edmund and S. Thomas, Sarum, 1443-1702*, with an introduction by Amy M. Straton, Salisbury, 1896. Includes (pp248-272) accounts of the Fraternity of Jesus Mass, founded in the church of St Edmund.

Sweeting, W. D., *Historical and Architectural Notes on the Parish Churches in and around Peterborough*, 1868

Tate, Francis, 'Of the antiquity, variety, and ceremonies of funerals in England. By Mr Tate. 30 April 1600', in *A Collection of Curious Discourses written by eminent antiquaries* ed. Thomas Hearne, vol 1, 1771, pp215-221

Tate, W. E., *The Parish Chest: A study of the records of parochial administration in England*, 3rd edition, Cambridge, 1969

Tavistock R. N. Worth, *Calendar of the Tavistock Parish Records*, Plymouth, 1887

Thame, St Mary the Virgin 1. Frederick George Lee, *The History, Description, and Antiquities of the prebendal Church of the Blessed Virgin Mary of Thame*, 1883. | 2. Accounts from 1442 ed. W. Patterson Ellis, Berks etc AJ. Scattered in short sections through many vols, those cited being 8-13, 16.

Thatcham Samuel Barfield, *Thatcham, Berks, and its Manors*, vol 2, appendices, 1901

Thompson, A. Hamilton, *The Historical Growth of the English Parish Church*, 2nd edition, Cambridge, 1913

Thompson, Pishey, *The History and Antiquities of Boston, and the Villages of Skirbeck* [etc], 1856

Thornton C. C. Dawson-Smith (ed.), *The Register of the Parish of Thornton, in the County of Buckinghamshire, 1562-1812*, Exeter, 1903

Thurston, Herbert, 'The bells of the Mass', *The Month*, vol 123, 1914, pp389-401

Thurston, Herbert, *Lent and Holy Week*, 1914

Tilney A. D. Stallard (ed.), *The transcript of the Churchwardens' Accounts of the Parish of Tilney All Saints, Norfolk, 1443 to 1589*, 1922

Toft Monks Register extracts and AE ed. W. J. Ashby, EA 2S vol 3 pp7-10, 23-24

Tooting W. E. Morden, *The History of Tooting-Graveney, Surrey*, 1897

Tottenham William Robinson, *The History and Antiquities of the Parish of Tottenham High Cross, in the County of Middlesex*, Tottenham, 1818

Towcester AE, Northants NQ vol 3 pp24-26

TRP Paul L. Hughes & James F. Larkin (eds.), *Tudor Royal Proclamations*, vol 1, 1964

Twickenham R. S. Cobbett, *Memorials of Twickenham, parochial and topographical*, 1872

Tyack, George S., *A Book about Bells*, [1898]

Tyrer, John Walton, *Historical Survey of Holy Week, its services and ceremonial*, 1932

Uffington AE 1627-1693 ed. W. G. D. Fletcher, Shropshire ANHST 2S vol 12 pp357-369

Ulverston Charles W. Bardsley, *Chronicles of the Town and Church of Ulverston*, Ulverston, 1885

V&A Cat. *Catalogue of English Ecclesiastical Embroideries of the XIII to XVI centuries*, Victoria & Albert Museum, 1916

Vallance, Aymer, *English Church Screens*, 1936

Vis. Bradshaw Henry Bradshaw (ed.), 'Notes of the episcopal visitation of the Archdeaconry of Ely in 1685', in *Collected Papers of Henry Bradshaw*, Cambridge, 1889, pp297-332

Vis. Brinkworth E. R. Brinkworth (ed.), *The Archdeacon's Court: Liber actorum, 1584*, 2 vols, Oxfordshire Record Soc., 1942

Vis. Chandler T. C. B. Timmins (ed.), *The Register of John Chandler, Dean of Salisbury, 1404-17*, Wiltshire Record Soc., Devizes, 1984

Vis. Grindal W. J. Sheils (ed.), *Archbishop Grindal's Visitation, 1575, comperta et detecta book*, York, 1977

Vis. Hale William Hale Hale, *A Series of Precedents and Proceedings in Criminal Causes* [from] *1475 to 1640, extracted from Act-Books of ecclesiastical courts in the diocese of London*, 1847

Vis. Harpsfield L. E. Whatmore (ed.), *Archdeacon Harpsfield's Visitation, 1557*, Catholic Record Soc., vol 45 [vol 1], 1950; vol 46 [vol 2], 1951

Vis. Hussey Arthur Hussey (ed.), 'Visitations of the Archdeacon of Canterbury', Arch. Cant. vol 25 pp11-56; vol 26 pp17-50; vol 27 pp213-229

Vis. Leicester A. Percival Moore (ed.), 'Proceedings of the ecclesiastical courts in the archdeaconry of Leicester, 1516-1535', AASRP vol 28 pt 1 pp117-220; pt 2 pp593-662

Vis. Manchester William Fergusson Irvine, 'Church discipline in the 16th century, as shown by extracts from the Bishop of Chester's ms. visitation books for the deanery of Manchester', *Transactions of the Lancashire and Cheshire Antiquarian Soc.*, vol 13, Manchester, 1896, pp56-69

Vis. Notts R. F. B. Hodgkinson (ed.), 'Extracts from the Act books of the Archdeacons of Nottingham', *Transactions of the Thoroton Soc.*, vol 30, Nottingham, 1927, pp11-57; vol 31, 1928, pp108-153

Vis. Palmer W. M. Palmer (ed.), 'Episcopal visitation returns, Cambridgeshire, 1638-1662', Cambs & Hunts AST vol 4 pt 8 pp313-411, and vol 5 pt 1 pp1-38; 'Churchwarden's bills or returns for the deanery of Barton, Cambridgeshire for Michaelmas, 1554', ibid. vol 5 pt 5 pp257-265; 'The archdeaconry of Cambridge and Ely, 1599', ibid. vol 6 pt 1 pp1-28

Vis. Parker Claude Jenkins (ed.), 'An unpublished record of Archbishop Parker's visitation in 1573', Arch. Cant. vol 29 pp270-318

Vis. Peyton Sidney A. Peyton (ed.), *The Churchwardens' Presentments in the Oxfordshire Peculiars of Dorchester, Thame and Banbury*, Oxfordshire Record Soc., 1928

Vis. Pressey W. J. Pressey (ed.), 'The records of the archdeaconries of Essex and Colchester' and 'Visitations held in the archdeaconry of Essex in 1683', Essex AST 2S vol 19 pp1-21, 260-276; 'Visitations held in the archdeaconry of Essex in 1684', ibid. vol 20 pp216-242; ditto 'in 1685', ibid. vol 21 pp100-119, 306-326

Vis. Renshaw Walter C. Renshaw, 'Notes from the Act books of the archdeaconry court of Lewes', Sussex AC vol 49 p47-65

Vis. Sussex Hilda Johnstone (ed.), *Churchwardens' Presentments (17th Century)*, pt 1, Archdeaconry of Chichester, and pt 2, Archdeaconry of Lewes, Sussex Record Soc., 1948, 1949

Vis. Waltham T. C. B. Timmins (ed.), *The Register of John Waltham, Bishop of Salisbury, 1388-1395*, Canterbury and York Soc., Woodbridge, Suffolk, 1994

Vis. Warham K. L. Wood-Legh (ed.), *Kentish Visitations of Archbishop William Warham and his deputies, 1511-1512*, Kent Archaeological Soc., Maidstone, 1984

Vis. Warrington William Fergusson Irvine (ed.), 'Visitation of Warrington deanery by the Bishop of Chester, in the year 1592', *Transactions of the Historic Soc. of Lancashire and Cheshire*, vol 46 (NS vol 10), Liverpool, 1895, pp183-192

Vis. Woodruff C. Eveleigh Woodruff (ed.), 'An archidiaconal visitation of 1502', Arch. Cant. vol 47 pp13-54

Walberswick 1. R. W. M. Lewis (ed.), *Walberswick Churchwardens' Accounts A.D. 1450-1499*, 1947. | 2. AE in Thomas Gardner, *An Historical Account of Dunwich ... with remarks on some places contiguous thereto*, 1754, pp147-161.

Walker, John, *An attempt towards recovering an Account of the Numbers and Sufferings of the Clergy of the Church of England ... in the late times of the Grand Rebellion*, 1714

Wall, J. Charles, *Porches and Fonts*, 1912

Walters, H. B., *Church Bells of England*, 1912

Walters, H. B., *London Churches at the Reformation with an account of their Contents*, 1939 [WR]

Waltham Abbey W. Winters, *Our Parish Registers, being ... Records of the Parish of Waltham Holy Cross*, Waltham Abbey, Essex, 1885

Walthamstow Stephen J. Barns (ed.), *Walthamstow Vestry Minutes, Churchwardens' and Overseers' Accounts*, vol 1, 1710-1740, and vol 2, 1741-1771, Walthamstow Antiquarian Soc., 1925, 1926

Wandsworth Accounts ed. Cecil T. Davis, Surrey AC, vol 15 pp80-127 (1545 to 1558); vol 17 pp135-175 (1558 to 1573); vol 18 pp96-152 (1574 to 1603); vol 19 pp145-194 (1603 to 1620); vol 20 pp169-222 (1620 to 1630)

Ware, Sedley Lynch, *The Elizabethan Parish in its Ecclesiastical and Financial Aspects*, Baltimore, Maryland, 1908

Warren *The Sarum Missal in English* translated by Frederick E. Warren, 2 vols, 1911. From the folio printed edition of 1526.

Warwick, St Mary *Notices of the Church of St Mary and the Beauchamp Chapel, Warwick*, Warwick, 1845

Waters, Robert Edmond Chester, *Parish Registers in England, their history and contents*, new edition, 1883

Webb, Sidney & Webb, Beatrice, *English Local Government ... [pt 1] The Parish and the County*, 1906

Weever, John, *Ancient Funerall Monuments within the United Monarchie of Great Britaine, Ireland, and the I[s]lands adjacent*, 1631

Wenhaston J. B. Clare, *Wenhaston, Suffolk: Curious Parish Records*, Halesworth, Suffolk, 1894

West Farleigh Aymer Vallance, 'A crucifix from West Farleigh', Arch. Cant. vol 40 pp49-52

Weybread AE ed. John Calver, EA 1S vol 2 pp4-6, 34-37

Weybridge AE 1622 to 1701 ed. Eleanor Lloyd, Surrey AC vol 21 pp130-164

White, Gilbert, *The Natural History and Antiquities of Selborne*, 1900

White, John, *The First Century of Scandalous, Malignant Priests ... or, A narration of the causes for which the parliament hath ordered the sequestration of the benefices of severall ministers complained of before them ...*, 1643

Whiting, Robert, *The Reformation of the English Parish Church*, Cambridge, 2010

Widdecombe Robert Dymond (ed.), *'Things new and old' concerning the Parish of Widecombe-in-the-Moor and its Neighbourhood*, Torquay, 1876

Wilkins, David, *Concilia Magnae Britanniae et Hiberniae*, vols 2 & 3, 1737

Williams, John Foster (ed.), *The Early Churchwardens' Accounts of Hampshire*, 1913

Williamson, Magnus, 'Liturgical music in the late medieval English parish', in *The Parish in Late Medieval England*, pp177-242

Wills, Bury Samuel Tymms (ed.), *Wills and Inventories from the Registers of the Commissary of Bury St Edmund's and the Archdeacon of Sudbury*, Camden Soc., 1850

Wills, Derbyshire S. O. Addy, 'Wills at Somerset House relating to Derbyshire', Derbyshire ANHSJ vol 45 pp42-75

Wills, East Kent *Testamenta Cantiana: A series of extracts from fifteenth and sixteenth century wills relating to church building and topography. East Kent* ed. Arthur Hussey, 1907

Wills, Furnivall Frederick J. Furnivall (ed.), *The Fifty Earliest English Wills in the Court of Probate, London*, Early English Text Soc., 1882

Wills, Halifax J. W. Clay & E. W. Crossley (eds.), *Halifax Wills, being abstracts and translations of the wills registered at York from the parish of Halifax*, vol 1, [1904]

Wills, Lancs etc G. J. Piccope (ed.), *Lancashire and Cheshire Wills and Inventories from the Ecclesiastical Court, Chester*, vol 2, Chetham Soc., 1860

Wills, Lincoln C. W. Foster (ed.), *Lincoln Wills registered in the district probate registry at Lincoln*, vol 2, 1505-1530, Lincoln Record Soc., Horncastle, 1918

Wills, North Country John Clay (ed.), *North Country Wills, being abstracts of wills relating to the counties of York, Nottingham, Northumberland, Cumberland, and Westmorland, at Somerset House and Lambeth Palace, 1383 to 1558*, Surtees Soc., 1908

Wills, Northants R. M. Serjeantson & H. Isham Longden, 'The parish churches and religious houses of Northamptonshire: their dedications, altars, images, and lights', AJ vol 70 pp217-452

Wills, Somerset F. W. Weaver (ed.), *Somerset Medieval Wills*, 3 vols, Somerset Record Soc., 1901, 1903, 1905. Vol 1: 1383-1500; vol 2: 1501-1530; vol 3: 1531-1558.

Wills, Sussex Walter H. Godfrey (ed.), *Transcripts of Sussex Wills*, 4 vols, Sussex Record Soc., Lewes, 1935, 1936, 1938, 1940. Vol 1: Albourne to Chichester; vol 2: Chiddingly to Horsham; vol 3: Horsted Keynes to Pyecombe; vol 4: Racton to Yapton.

Wills, Test. Vet. Nicholas Harris Nicolas, *Testamenta Vetusta, being illustrations from wills, of manners, customs, etc.*, vol 1, 1826

Wills, West Kent A Leland L. Duncan, 'The parish churches of West Kent, their dedications, altars, images, and lights', St Paul's EST vol 3 pp241-298

Wills, West Kent B *Testamenta Cantiana: A series of extracts from fifteenth and sixteenth century wills ... West Kent* ed. Leland L. Duncan, 1906

Wills, York *Testamenta Eboracensia: A selection of wills from the registry at York*, vol 5, ed. James Raine, Surtees Soc., 1884

Wills, York Clergy Claire Cross, *York Clergy Wills 1520-1600*, vol 2, City clergy, York, 1989

Wilmslow Earwaker, J. P., *East Cheshire, Past and Present, or A History of the Hundred of Macclesfield*, vol 1, 1877

Wilson, F. P., *The Plague in Shakespeare's London*, Oxford, 1927

Wimborne Minster [WM] [J. C. Mayo], *A History of Wimborne Minster*, 1860

Windsor Robert Richard Tighe & James Edward Davis, *Annals of Windsor, being a History of the Castle and Town*, vol 2, 1858

Wing AE ed. Frederic Ouvry, *Archaeologia* vol 36 pt 2 pp219-241

Winterslow W. Symonds, 'Winterslow church reckonings, 1542-1661', Wilts ANHM vol 36 pp27-49

Wood L&T Andrew Clark (ed.), *The Life and Times of Anthony Wood, antiquary, of Oxford, 1632-1695, described by himself*, 5 vols, Oxford, 1891-1900

Woodford Halse AE ed. Sir Henry Dryden, Northants NQ vol 1 pp41-45

Worcester, St Michael John Amphlett (ed.), *The Churchwardens' Accounts of St Michael's in Bedwardine, Worcester, from 1539 to 1603*, Oxford, 1896

Wordsworth, Christopher (ed.), *Ceremonies and Processions of the Cathedral Church of Salisbury* [with] woodcuts from the Sarum *Processionale* of 1502, Cambridge, 1901

Wordsworth, Christopher, *Notes on Medieval Services in England*, 1898

Wordsworth, Christopher & Littlehales, Henry, *The Old Service-books of the English Church*, 1904

Worfield Accounts ed. H. B. Walters, Shropshire ANHST 3S vol 3 pp99-138 (1500-1511); vol 4 pp85-114 (1512-1523); vol 6 pp1-24 (1523-1532); vol 7 pp219-240 (1533-1548); vol 9 pp113-140 (1549-1572); vol 10 pp59-86 (1572-1603). 4S vol 2 pp25-54 (1603-1648).

Worksop Robert White, *Worksop, 'The Dukery', and Sherwood Forest*, Worksop, 1875

WR > Walters, Reformation

Wren, Christopher (ed.), *Parentalia, or, Memoirs of the Family of the Wrens*, 1750

Wright, A. R., *British Calendar Customs* ed. T. E. Jones, 3 vols, Folklore Soc., 1936, 1938, 1940

Wrington AE ed. Rev. Prebendary Scarth, *Proceedings of the Bath Natural History and Antiquarian Field Club*, vol 2, Bath, 1873, pp444-454

Wriothesley, Charles, *A Chronicle of England during the reigns of the Tudors, from A.D. 1489 to 1559* ed. William Douglas Hamilton, 2 vols, Camden Soc, 1875, 1877

Wymondham G. A. Carthew, 'Wymondham gilds', NORA vol 9 pp240-274

Yarnton Mrs Bryan Stapleton, *Three Oxfordshire Parishes: A History of Kidlington, Yarnton and Begbroke*, Oxford Historical Soc., 1893. Yarnton pp199-317.

Yeovil J. G. N. [John Gough Nichols], 'Account of the proctors of the church of Yeovil, co. Somerset, 36 Hen. VI, 1457-58', *Collectanea Topographica*, vol 3, pp134-141

York, St Michael le Belfrey Francis Collins (ed.), *The Registers of St Michael le Belfrey, York*, pt 1, 1565-1653, Leeds, 1899

The Zurich Letters (second series) comprising the correspondence of several English bishops and others with some of the Helvetian reformers, during the reign of Queen Elizabeth, ed. Hastings Robinson, Parker Soc., Cambridge, 1845

Parish index, with other place references

Dedications of churches are included where necessary in order to distinguish between two or more parishes in the given place and in a few other ad hoc instances. In case of any uncertainty, given the age of most of the material in this book it is generally safe to assume that it relates to the older or oldest church in the given city, town or village.

Counties are taken from Arthur Meredyth Burke's *Key to the Ancient Parish Registers of England and Wales* (1908) and in a few cases differ from those obtaining today.

Italic indicates that the page or page range includes relevant illustration.

General index

Some entries for subjects which appear very often through the text are selective, [etc] at the end of an entry indicating the main instances.

> indicates 'see under' or 'see also under'.

Italic indicates that the page or page range includes relevant illustration.